MONOGRAPH 40

Prehistory of Agriculture

New Experimental and Ethnographic Approaches

Edited by Patricia C. Anderson

The Institute of Archaeology
University of California, Los Angeles
1999

Edited by Rita Demsetz, Marilyn Gatto, and Brenda Johnson-Grau
Designed by Brenda Johnson-Grau
Production by Linda Tang, Michael Tang, and Amy Chen

Library of Congress Cataloging-in-Publication Data
Préhistoire de l'agriculture. English
    Prehistory of agriculture : new experimental and ethnographic
approaches / edited by Patricia C. Anderson.
       p.   cm. -- (Monograph ; 40)
    Includes bibliographical references.
    ISBN 0-917956-93-1
    1. Agriculture, Prehistoric. 2. Hunting and gathering societies.
3. Plants, Cultivated--Origin. 4. Plants remains (Archaeology)
5. Palynology. I. Anderson, Patricia C. II. Title. III. Series :
Monograph (University of California, Los Angeles. Institute of
Archaeology) ; 40.
    GN799.A4P7413   1999
    630' .9'01--dc21   98-31101
                            CIP

Cover illustration: Domestic einkorn (*T. monococcum*). *Drawing by G.C. Hillman*

Originally published in French as *Préhistoire de
L'Agriculture: Nouvelles Approches Expérimentales et
Ethnographiques.* Monographie du Centre de
Recherches Archéologiques, no. 6, by the Centre
National de La Recherche Scientifique.

To Jack R. Harlan

An inspiration to generations of researchers in a great variety of disciplines, he instilled understanding and love of traditional plants and techniques.

Contents

Foreword

DURING THE SUMMER OF 1993 WHILE IN PARIS, I managed to track down and purchase (for 290 francs) a copy of the Center for Archeological Research of the National Center for Scientific Research's 1992 publication *Préhistoire de L'Agriculture*, edited by Patricia C. Anderson. I have read and consulted this volume many times since, and it has become a much sought after reference item for the faculty and graduate students in my department at Washington University in St. Louis. Together with everyone else who cares about early agriculture anywhere, but especially in western Asia and Europe, we all find this book to be absolutely indispensable. The stellar cast of authors describes, discusses, and illustrates the crucial plants, their natural history, the processes essential to their domestication, the tools and technology applied to them by human collecting/gathering/hunting groups and early farmers, and much, much more. What distinguishes this volume from any in the recent stream of publications on agricultural origins is the close juxtaposition of detailed, substantive, botanical, archaeobotanical, and experimental research. The volume resulted from a scholarly roundtable conference held in June 1988 at the CNRS laboratory and field station in Jalès (province of Ardeche) in southern France. The conference, entitled "L'exploitation des plantes en préhistoire: documents et techniques," emphasized experimental studies as well as other approaches, and so the replicative work is robustly present—both photos and text—in the subsequent volume of revised papers and presentations. The Publications Unit of the Institute of Archaeology, University of California, Los Angeles, has performed a signal service by making this critical book available to a wider audience than had access to the original edition. Articles that appeared in French in the 1992 version have all been translated in this publication. Some of the authors have updated their contributions or added postscripts to include important developments in the recent years, making this volume even more valuable than the original edition.

Prehistory of Agriculture: New Experimental and Ethnographic Approaches is a major landmark in the progress of knowledge about the earliest domesticated plants; the nature of the earliest farming economies; and the technology created by ancient human groups for collecting, cultivating, storing, and processing these plants. The authors, editor, and publisher are to be congratulated for producing this edition of a book essential to all those interested in the archaeology, ethnography, history, botany, and paleoethnobotany of early agriculture.

PATTY JO WATSON
Washington University, St. Louis

Preface

In June 1988 I organized an international meeting, entitled "Exploitation of Plants in Prehistory: Data and Techniques," at a small research center at Jalès in southern France. In 1992, a volume recounting some of the material presented at the roundtable session was published by Centre National de la Recherche Scientifique (CNRS) in France. This new edition features updated chapters, with those originally in French now presented in English.

The reasons for organizing this meeting and for soliciting (and then publishing) contributions from such a wide variety of disciplines—as can be seen from the table of contents—warrant recollection. The question of origins of agriculture, then as now, is usually approached by debate of various theories, based upon non-data-driven and untestable assumptions. At the other extreme, morphology of plant remains, and of artifacts, sometimes is used alone to provide behavioral information. These chapters reflect my opinion that a full gamut of methods need to function together, using interdisciplinary scientific inquiry including experimentation and measurement, to study this issue. Documenting and demonstrating techniques used by our ancestors in prehistoric and traditional contexts—in this instance, plant gathering, cultivation, and processing—are the best means of discovering keys to the processes behind the great transitions in human history, such as that to agriculture, and the process of domestication. The need to understand appears all the more important today: the transition continues, as traditional agriculture and the special associated lifeways and crops progressively disappear.

The spirit of the meeting was largely derived from an interdisciplinary group of European-based researchers who obtained reference data from agricultural experiments involving plowing, planting, harvesting, grinding, and storage. This group had met every two years or so since the late 1970s to evaluate progress in what meeting organizers called "agroarchaeology"—that is, the marks and traces of agricultural processes. It was felt by this group, which I joined in 1982, that mere morphological study of tools and plant remains was at a standstill in answering questions about agricultural techniques. In order to interpret ancient remains, experimentation and understanding of all data sets involved were required. Early experiments on cultivating and harvesting cereals were headed by Semenov and Korobkova in Russia in the 1950s and 1960s, by Steensberg and Lerche in Denmark in the same period, and by Reynolds (who carried out the most complete and longstanding research at Butser Iron Age Farm) in England in the 1970s. These efforts, as well as those of Hillman and Davies in Turkey and Wales and Harlan in the United States, served as inspirations to our project. Other experimental research was done later by Firmin in France and Meurers-Balke and Luning in Germany—and since 1986, by myself and Willcox. In an experimental setting where it was possible to test data and approximate the situations imagined for the Levantine Neolithic, we raised, harvested, and threshed, using stone tools and wild cereals as well as primitive domesticates. The experiments continued at Jalès and now at the Center for Archeological Research at Valbonne, and I often have worked in the company of colleagues who contributed chapters to this book.

The meeting and this book are an approach to understanding how remains of stone tools and plants could be translated into understanding of human activities leading to domestication and farming. This required evaluation of progress and potential in analysis of the ancient remains, a close look at traditional or historic uses of plants, conduct of experiments, and studies of modern plants in their natural habitats. Most of the chapters show how new experiments and observations have greatly enhanced our ability to distinguish specific techniques and reconstruct whole instruments, teasing out new information from the often inexplicit remains left by the archaeological record.

The book extends beyond the original working group based in Western Europe to include researchers in the United States, Australia, Israel, and Russia and to include other disciplines applied to origins of agriculture in the 1980s such as genetic botany, analysis of phytoliths, micromorphology of soils, and analysis of starch grain. Now, a decade later, many of the chapters have been updated by their authors to include progress made in the interim. The updates reconsider the debate over the beginnings of agriculture (Keeley, Cauvin) or provide new data on the age of certain agricultural activities derived from plant remains (Willcox) and interpretation of microwear traces and residues from use on cereal harvesting and processing tools (Anderson, Fullagar et al., van Gijn, Korobkova, Skakun), new experiments in harvesting and processing (Grégoire, Anderson), and important new genetic evidence (Zohary).

The book is still current in representing an accurate overview of each of the significant lines of research toward a picture of the origins and development of agriculture. Each article shows how this picture can be composed of data from analysis of specific attributes, which are derived from ethnographic observation (Harlan, Fullagar et al., Ataman, Skakun), from analysis of microwear traces on ethnographic (traditional) tools (Fullagar et al., Ataman, Skakun) on prehistoric tools, interpreted through experiments (Anderson, Unger-Hamilton, Korobkova, Skakun, van Gijn), from ethnohistorical information (Harlan, Keeley, Sievert, Butler, Grégoire, Sigaut, Ataman, Skakun), and from modern relics of ancient plants used (Harlan, Zohary, Miller) or archeobotanical remains (Buxo, Hansen, Kislev, Marinval, Willcox, for macroremains; Rosen, Anderson, postscript, for phytoliths). Many researchers (Harlan, Diot, Hillman and Davies, Willcox, Anderson, Unger-Hamilton, Rosen, Grégoire, Meurers-Balke and Luning, van Gijn, Gebhardt) describe, for replicative agricultural and processing experiments based upon ancient records and observations, marker traces produced of the activities tested (for example, remains in the soil or traces on tools) and the reaction of the plant to the process (yield, maturation, shattering at harvest, and reduction by threshing or grinding). Most chapters focus on exploitation of cereals, a few on pulses and tubers in the Old World, particularly Southwest Asia, but data sets derived from ethnographic research in North America (Keeley),

Australia (Fullagar et al.), and worldwide (Harlan) were invaluable in approaching questions on nonagricultural plant use.

The theoretical questions debated here mainly concern whether protoagricultural practices in the nuclear area of the Near Eastern system and adjacent areas were common and for what various reasons and in what circumstances such practices occur worldwide. As harvesting and many sowing methods which do not give rise to domestication are apparently standard hunter-gatherer practices of management and probably were used even before the period focused upon in this book, should they be considered protoagricultural or agricultural practices? Where is the line between management and cultivation to be drawn? Is whatever cultivation pattern that actually gave rise to crop domestication in the Near East more representative of the evolution of human behavior than other tending and management processes not producing selection for plants dependent on humans for reproduction (Harlan, Hillman)? Or did the particular combination of practices, known individually for millennia, that is, the particular form of cultivation activity that actually led to domestication, do so by a coincidence of circumstances unrelated to agriculture itself (attributable to ideology [see Cauvin] or to the exchange or displacement of persons and resources [Anderson, Zohary, Hansen])? Is there a progressive evolution and a set of innovations which lead to agriculture or does the significant period of human invention related to agriculture occur only once domestic plants were cultivated?

Agriculture is beginning to appear a more recent occurrence than previously assumed (see Zohary). Working of land with tools is clearly attested to *only after* domestic agriculture is well underway, perhaps beginning with irrigation structures (Anderson, Skakun, Grégoire). On the other hand, many practices considered to be agricultural are used in hunter-gatherer societies (Harlan and Keeley). They may, however, not be protoagricultural in the sense of being on the evolutionary pathway leading to an agricultural kind of management.

On the other hand, agricultural tools used for processing of morphologically domestic cereal crops, thought to be fairly recent traditions, are being shown to be far more ancient. For example, several chapters show that the threshing sledge concerns the prehistory of crop agriculture as well as the realms of ethnography and the historic record (Skakun, Korobkova, Anderson's postscript, Ataman). The human capacity for innovation appears to be constantly underestimated. During the original meeting there were lively and rich debates and discussions of all these viewpoints, which are now reflected in these chapters. This book will, I hope, inspire the reader to join in the debate and in the exploration process.

The participants in the roundtable meeting and others

writing chapters for this volume are due thanks for their warm and vigorous exchange in the course of their contributions. The publication of this volume in English was achieved largely owing to the herculean efforts and persistence of Dr. Françoise Audouze, Director of Research in the National Center for Scientific Research and former Director of the Center for Archeological Research in Valbonne, and to the help of Frank Braemer, Director of the Center for Archeological Research. The work was largely aided by the patient editorial work of Marilyn Beaudry-Corbett and Brenda Johnson-Grau at the Publications Unit of the Institute of Archaeology, University of California, Los Angeles, and of Jacqueline Gaudey of the CRA, CNRS, in Valbonne, who translated much of the volume into English. I wish to thank them, and others who helped at some stage or another, most warmly for their support.

Finally, I was indeed proud to have Jack Harlan attend the meeting and write a chapter for this book. He was most instrumental in inspiring and guiding me in my own early research on harvesting of wild plants and origins of agriculture in the Middle East, where he had had extensive and unique experience. It is indeed with great sadness that I learn at this writing of his death in August 1998.

PATRICIA C. ANDERSON

Chapter 1

Harvesting of Wild-grass Seed and Implications for Domestication

Jack R. Harlan

FOR OVER 25 YEARS, I DIRECTED RESEARCH ON grass-seed production of species native to the southern great plains of the United States. At the time, in the southern plains there were some 810 million hectares of abandoned farmland that we planned to stabilize by planting to adapted grasses. In the northern plains, several introduced species were satisfactory, but in the south none were as well adapted as the native grasses.

Seed supply was the main limiting factor. An experimental seed-production facility and grass-seed laboratory were established, and the research provided accurate information on the potential for seed production of several grass species. Wild stands were also harvested throughout these years. Yields of 500 to 800 kg/ha were regularly obtained from some species, and in good seasons more than one ton. These yields are within the range of domesticated cereals under conditions of traditional agriculture with no inputs of plant nutrients.

As with domesticated cereals, irrigation did not help much in increasing yields but it could help salvage a crop could be salvaged in dry years. Perennial grasses produced well the year of seeding and the year following, but by the third season most species gave low yields. No combination of irrigation, plant nutrients, or renovation techniques was found that could restore production to young stand levels. Annual species tended to produce more and be more reliable, as would be expected.

Among the native species studied, the most productive were *Panicum virgatum*, *Eragrostis trichodes*, *Buchloë dactyloides*, *Agropyron smithii*, *Elymus canadensis*, and *E. virginicus*. Such chaffy-seeded grasses as *Bouteloua* and *Andropogon* produced poorly in pure grain equivalents,

but the American Indians harvested them anyway. Seed size was not significant. All species of *Eragrostis* have small seeds, but several species yield very well (Harlan, Ahring, and Kneebone 1956).

As to harvesting techniques, I have personally harvested wild-grass seeds by hand-stripping and with flint-bladed sickles, beater and basket, beater and boat (*Zizania*), steel sickles, scythe, mechanical stripper, mechanical blower, binder, and power mower/swather followed by pickup combine and grain combine. Although, it is difficult to measure potential yield precisely, I estimate that no method will recover more than half the potential production. Of the traditional gathering techniques, the beater and basket method produced the cleanest and most uniform material. In sickling, much of the fully ripe seed was lost and the harvested material included many immature grains. These would mature somewhat on the stalk if threshing were delayed a few days.

Having used both sickle and beater, I have long wondered why the sickle was ever preferred to the beater. Freshly knapped flint blades cut about as well as steel, but, like steel, become dull with use and need to be resharpened. The sheen on sickle blades, so common in Western Asia and Africa, does appear to be owing to polish from silica cells in grass stems (Harlan 1967).

Harvests of wild-grass seed are not necessarily measures used to avert starvation. These seeds may, on the contrary, provide an easily obtained staple for people living where appropriate species thrive. Whole grass seeds are generally nutritious but higher in fiber than the highly processed flours used in modern societies.

1

Ethnographic Observations

Literature on grass-seed harvesting in traditional food procurement systems is extensive but widely scattered. I have tried to assemble some of it (Harlan 1975, 1989); others have contributed also (Ebeling 1986; Jardin 1967; Yanovsky 1936). I will not repeat the descriptions here but will attempt to extract the main features. In studying the data, one is immediately struck by the preference for certain genera around the world. Table 1.1 lists some that have been widely harvested, according to ethnographic reports.

Several species of a genus may be involved. For example, six species of *Panicum* are reported as harvested in North America, with one domesticated in Mexico (Gentry 1942); seven are listed for Africa (Jardin 1967), four in Australia, and *P. miliaceum* and *P. miliare* were domesticated in Asia. Five species of *Sporobolus* were harvested in North America (Yanovsky 1936), three in Africa, and three in Australia. Several species of *Eragrostis* were harvested in North America, six in Africa, and others in Australia, and so forth. Precise identifications are often uncertain from ethnographic reports because most observers were not botanists and specimen vouchers were seldom obtained. This does not alter the general pattern. Of 600 or so genera in the grass family, a relatively small number attracted the attention of gatherers, and these tended to be exploited wherever they occurred.

In all, Yanovsky (1936) and Ebeling (1986) together indicate that about 50 species of grasses were harvested in North America; Jardin (1967) lists about 60 for Africa, and Irvine (1957), Golson (1971), and others suggest about 25 for Australia. The exact number cannot be determined because of problems of synonymy and identification. We know relatively little about harvests of grass seed in Europe, Asia, and South America.

The commercial harvesting of wild-grass seeds for food is well documented in Africa and Europe, and the practice persists to this day in North America, where the wild rice *Zizania aquatica* is considered a delicacy and commands gourmet prices. Mannagrass, *Glyceria fluitans,* is also a water grass, once enormously abundant in the marshes of central and eastern Europe. It was harvested in commercial quantities as late as 1925 (Szafer 1966) and exported from the port of Danzig to countries around the Baltic. Common crabgrass, *Digitaria sanguinalis,* was once harvested in great quantities in central Europe and sold in the markets (Körnicke 1885). The most extensive commercial harvesting of grass seed documented in historic times took place in Africa.

The body of literature on African grass-seed harvests is important but largely ignored by anthropologists. I have assembled most of it in a paper on the subject (Harlan 1989), but since that publication may not be generally available, I cite the most important works here. These are nearly all travel accounts by Europeans visiting central Africa in the nineteenth and early twentieth centuries, with only occasional

Table 1.1 Grass genera harvested on two or more continents

GENUS	CONTINENTS	SPECIES DOMESTICATED
Coix	Africa; Asia; Oceania	1
Dactyloctenium	Africa; Australia	
Digitaria	Africa; Asia; Australia; Europe	3
Echinochloa	Africa; Asia; North America (introduced)	1
Eleusine	Africa; Asia; Australia	1
Eragrostis	Africa; Australia; North America	
Eriochloa	Africa; Asia; Australia; North America	
Glyceria	Europe; North America	
Oryza	Africa; Asia; Australia; Oceania; South America	2
Panicum	Africa; Asia; Australia; Europe; North America	3
Paspalum	Africa, Asia; Australia	1
Setaria	Africa; North America	1
Sorghum	Africa; Asia; Australia; Oceania	1
Sporobolus	Africa; Australia; North America	
Stipa	Africa; Australia; North America	

descriptions of the practice. In the paper cited, I have given volume and page numbers. Some of the travelers had botanical training and some did not (Barth 1857; Brunache 1894; Caillié 1830; Chevalier 1900, 1932; Cortier 1908; Denham, Clapperton, and Oudney 1826; Duveyrier 1864; Heuglin 1869; Nachtigal 1881; Rohlfs 1872; Schweinfurth 1874). There are more recent observations, and the practice persists today (personal observations and Champault 1969; Gast 1968; Jardin 1967; Nicolaisen 1963; Pernés 1984, and Oka and Morishima, pers. comm.), but commercial exploitation of wild-grass seeds is much less widespread today than it was a century ago.

The composite picture that emerges from independent observations may be summarized as follows. *Aristida pungens* was enormously important to the northern Tuareg where it was harvested in such an abundance that it sold in the markets for one third the price of barley (Duveyrier 1864). *Panicum turgidum* was a staple for tribes of central and southern Sahara, the Ahaggar, Aïr, and Adrar des Iforas massifs, for example. *Cenchrus biflorus* was a staple of tribes in southern Sahara and the Sahel. Barth, for a part of his journey, provisioned himself and his horses on seeds of this grass for he could find no other grain (Barth 1857, 1:482). From Bornu near Lake Chad to Dafur in Sudan, a complex of grasses was harvested on a massive scale. The mixtures were generally called *kreb* or *kasha* and included several species of *Panicum, Eragrostis,* and *Digitaria* as well as *Dactyloctenium aegypticum, Brachiaria deflexa, Latipes senegalensis,* and, no doubt, others. The kreb complex was basic to the diet of the local people and was stored in warehouses by the ton and exported by camel caravan to the Ahaggar and other needy areas for sale. In the savanna from western Sudan to the Atlantic Ocean, the native annual wild rice, *Oryza barthii,* was harvested in enormous amounts and provided the base of nourishment for many tribes. It, too, was warehoused by the ton in Bornu and widely sold in the markets. I have seen it for sale in Mali, Burkina Fasso, Chad, and Niger, but not on the scale of former times.

Wild-grass seeds occasionally reach the market place elsewhere, but on a very small scale today. Wild rice (*Oryza sativa*) is still harvested in India, and some is sold, in part because some devout Hindus believe that the wild form is a more appropriate offering than cultivated rice. P. T. Ho (1969) documented extensive wild rice harvests in China over a millennium of history. Cultivated rice had been grown in China for several millennia, yet the wild harvests were worth the effort and were of great benefit to the poor.

Domesticated Cereals

The processes of domestication are evolutionary in nature and follow a pathway from truly wild plants to those fully domesticated. The changes are genetic and concern ecological adaptation to conditions of the cultivated field.

Wild plants survive or thrive in the absence of human disturbance: fully domesticated races are so modified genetically that they cannot survive without human care. Most cereals are in an intermediate state in which weedy races evolve that are also adapted to the disturbances of agriculture but retain or recover the wild systems of seed dispersal and reproduction.

We have examined the situation in sorghum in some detail and found that weed races may evolve in several ways. First, some of the wild races have weedy tendencies themselves and have become naturalized in Australia and tropical America where they are not native. Second, wild and cultivated races hybridize naturally and aggressive; weedy forms emerge. This can be verified by the fact that in Sudan, where the cultivated races have dense, compact inflorescences, the weedy races that infest the fields also have dense, compact inflorescences, while in the highlands of Ethiopia, where the cultivated races have loose, open inflorescences, the weedy races have loose, open inflorescences. This kind of mimicry is found in other cereals as well and is due in part to gene flow and in part to human selection in weeding. Third, there are two genes that suppress the formation of abscission layers that permit shattering at maturity. Since these genes are recessive in expression, hybrids between the two genotypes will restore shattering, and weedy forms are produced. Fourth, in the US, far removed from the African homeland, a secondary seed dispersal mechanism has evolved. The abscission layers remain suppressed. but the inflorescence branch that supports a spikelet pair becomes very thin and breaks at maturity. The spikelet pairs that fall have a short piece of branch attached. This newly evolved weed is called shattercane and is a serious pest in many sorghum-growing regions of the US (Harlan 1975, 1982).

In addition, there is a class of dubiously domesticated grasses or, perhaps, species that were once grown and then abandoned. *Setaria geniculata* for example is known archaeologically in Mexico—where an increase in seed size over time can be detected and there are morphological evidences of nonshattering habit (Callen 1967). S. *palidifusca* is abundant in many archaeological sites in sub-Saharan Africa. Sketchy writings of conquistadors suggest that *Bromus mango* may have been cultivated in the southern Andes, but there are no indications of more recent culture. *Distichlis palmeri)* was harvested in large quantities on the lower Colorado in Sonora and there is some indication that it may have been manipulated by the people. *Koeleria cristata* and *Phalaris carolinianum* have been nominated for at least being semidomesticated because they are found in quantity in archaeological sites where these species do not occur today, and more or less nonshattering types of *Phalaris* are found. These grasses were used in quantity by Indians of the Cumberland Plateau and the Ohio watershed. The status of crabgrass in central Europe could be debated. It was sown and harvested and a recognizable morphological race evolved; yet, this race shatters seeds and behaves ecologically like other weedy races of the species.

Relating Harvests of Wild-grass Seed to Cereal Domestication

The ethnographic information in published sources is very erratic and incomplete. There are few observations for Asia, Europe, and South America. There is a fair body of information on wild harvests in Africa, but essentially nothing is recorded of wild sorghum and pearl millet, the most important of the African domesticates. I have talked to people who have harvested both wild and weed sorghums but I find almost no published accounts. Wild pearl millet seems like a very unlikely source of food, yet the crop was domesticated, modified enormously by selection, and now supports millions of people in Africa and Asia.

Comparing the domesticates, listed in table 1.2, with commonly harvested wild species, listed in table 1.1, it is evident that harvesting may or may not lead to domestication. Some species have been collected for millennia without the evolution of domesticated races. Harvesting alone does nothing to alter the genetic composition of the population. There is always enough seed escaping the harvest to maintain the stand. Domestication begins when the people plant that which has been harvested. Then there are two populations, the wild and the sown. It is then that mutations for nonshattering, synchronous ripening, loss of dormancy, and larger seed size receive positive selection pressures and the species is on the way to domestication.

To study the dynamics of plant domestication, then, it is necessary to analyze populations genetically to understand what is being planted and the probable fate of the key genes involved. Unfortunately, few such studies have been conducted so far. The differences between wild and cultivated

Table 1.2 Domesticated cereals

LATIN NAME	COMMON NAME	PLOIDY	PROBABLE ORIGIN	WORLD PRODUCTION*
Triticum	Wheats			510.0
T. monococcum	Einkorn	2x	SW Asia	
T. dicoccum/turgidum	Emmer/durum	4x	SWAsia	
T. timopheevii	Timopheevii	4x	Caucasus	
T. aestivum	Bread wheat	6x	South Caspian	
Zea mays	Maize	2x	Mexico	490.2
Oryza	Rice			372.6**
O. sativa	Asian rice	2x	India-China	
O. glaberrima	African rice	2x	West Africa	
Hordeum vulgare	Barley	2x	SW Asia	178.0
Sorghum bicolor	Sorghum	2x	Chad-Sudan	77.5
Avena	Oats			45.6
A. strigosa	Sand oats	2x	Mediterranean	
A. ethiopica	Ethiopian oats	4x	Mediterranean/Ethiopia	
A. sativa	Common oats	6x	SW Asia/Europe	
Secale cereale	Rye	2x	SW Asia/Europe	29.6
Millets: not reported separately				31.6
Pennisetum glaucum	Pearl millet		Sahara	
Panicum miliaceum	Panic/proso		China	
P. miliare	Slender millet		South India	
P. sonorum			Mexico	
Setaria italica	Italian millet		China	
Eleusine coracana	Finger millet		Ethiopia/Uganda	
Echinochloa crus-galli	Japanese/Chinese millet		China/Japan	
Paspalum scrobiculatum	Kodo millet		South India	
Eragrostis tef	Tef		Bornu-Kordofan/Ethiopia	
Coix lachryma-jobi	Job's tears/Adlay		SE Asia	
Digitaria exilis	Fonio/acha		West Africa	
D. iburua	Black fonio		West Africa	
D. crusciata	Hill millet		North India	
Phalaris canariensis	Canary grass		Mediterranean	
Brachiaria deflexa	Guinea millet		Futa Djalon, Guinea	

*   Reported in million metric tons; FAO 1985

** Rice is reported by FAO as " paddy," which means that the hull is included; this must be removed before consumption and 20% of production should be deducted to compare with other
     cereals. The correction has been made in this table.

races are, we suggest, generally rather simply inherited and subject to strong selection pressures. Nonshattering in cereals, pulses, and other seed crops is considered one of the key differences between domesticated and spontaneous races. Genes for nonshattering, or at least for greater seed retention, probably occur in all large populations of wild grasses at a significant frequency. I once made very striking progress in seed retention in sand bluestem, *Andropogon hallii*, in a single generation by simply harvesting seed about one month after most of the seed crop had shattered and fallen to the ground. This species has never been domesticated and the populations could be considered truly wild. Nonshattering and semishattering genotypes were readily found when looked for in *Zizania aquatica* (Elliot and Perlinger 1977).

Oka and Morishima (1971) conducted a series of experiments with populations of rice derived from wild x cultivated hybrids. Three generations of harvesting and planting shifted the populations very strongly toward cultivated rice with marked decrease in shattering, loss of dormancy, and reduction in awning habit. The same populations allowed to be self-sown shifted toward wild characteristics with increase in shattering and, increase in seed dormancy and awning of the spikelets. It is true that the alternative genes were present in these populations because of their origin, but the experiments showed that selection pressures for or against the domesticated syndrome are strong and that the simple acts of harvesting and planting are enough to bring about striking changes (see also Oka 1968:101).

We also found, in our studies at the Crop Evolution Laboratory, that three generations of harvesting and planting wild *Eleusine* almost eliminated seed dormancy (Hilu and de Wet 1976) and that seed size can be increased by deep planting. Larger seeds can emerge from deeper planting than smaller seeds and the selection pressures are very strong. Harvesting and planting also selects for synchronous ripening. Once the process begins, human selection can add very powerful selection forces. Farmers in traditional agricultural systems often select the stock seed for the next planting at the onset of harvest. The next generation, then, depends entirely on what the cultivator selects. Domestication of most cereals is relatively simple and straightforward, although morphological changes may be spectacular in some cases, for example, maize and pearl millet (Harlan, de Wet, and Price 1973).

Some genes that occur in wild populations have very profound and striking morphological effects. Single genes would, if used as taxonomic key characters, move species from one genus to another or even from one tribe to another. These may occur in grasses that have never been subject to deliberate human manipulation, but the potential of radical genes must be taken into account in the processes of domestication. A few examples will serve as models.

A general evolutionary trend found in several branches of the grass family is the reduction of florets and spikelets to sterile, rudimentary structures. A general evolutionary trend in domestication is for these structures to recover fertility. In barley, for example, the genus *Hordeum* is characterized by an inflorescence that is a spike bearing three spikelets at each node, the central one sessile and female fertile, the lateral ones pedicellate and female sterile. These are said to be two-rowed, and the sterile lateral spikelets serve a function in the self-planting mechanism. Some cultivars are six-rowed, in that all three spikelets are female fertile. Two loci are involved in the expression of fertility of spikelets in barley, but a single recessive gene can convert two-row to six-row. In wheat, there are gene combinations that cause the sterile glumes at the base of the spikelet to produce grains (Frankel and Roskams 1975; Wright 1972). Sterile glumes at the base of the spikelet are characteristic of the entire grass family and these genotypes violate the family descriptions (Frankel, Shineberg, and Munday 1969). In panicoid grasses, florets of the spikelets are reduced to a single fertile terminal one, but a rudimentary scale-like structure is usually present below. This floret recovers fertility in some cultivars of *Sorghum, Zea,* and *Panicum.* Among the Andropogonae, spikelets are arranged in pairs, one female fertile, the other male fertile or sterile. Under domestication, fertility is restored in maize and some cultivars of sorghum. In a few cultivars of maize, for example, "Country Gentleman," both sterile spikelets and sterile florets are rendered female fertile and the ears appear to have lost the arrangement of kernels in rows (Harlan 1982; Harlan and de Wet 1974).

Pearl millet is even more extreme in the sense that additional spikelets have evolved from sterile inflorescence branches that have no rudimentary structures to recover fertility. The wild forms all have a single fertile spikelet per fascicle. Cultivars may have as many as nine, although three to five is more common. These spikelets evolved de novo without morphological precursors (Brunken, de Wet, and Harlan 1971).

These evolutionary reversals are usually controlled by a single gene or by two genes acting in concert. Mutations of this nature occur in nature and are sometimes fixed to form distinct taxa. *Dichanthium fecundum* of Australia, for example, is characterized by fertility of both members of the spikelet pairs. Taxonomically, this would take it out of the Andropogonae and put it in the Saccharininae, but it is actually a sibling species of *D. annulatum,* a common species from Indonesia to Senegal in West Africa. Our genetic studies have shown that a single gene controls fertility of the usually sterile spikelet (Borgaonkar and de Wet 1960). We also found fertile spikelet pairs in populations of the related *Bothriochloa ischaemum* in the Karakoram mountains of Pakistan.

The most remarkable feminizing gene so far reported from wild populations has recently been described in *Tripsacum daclyloides* (Dewald et al. 1987). This grass is sufficiently related to maize that numerous hybrids have been made, and this fertility-restoring gene may provide some clues to the origin of maize for which a complete solution still eludes us. The racemes of *Tripsacum* normally have several female spikelets below, each embedded in a rachis joint and covered by a hardened glume. These spikelets are in pairs as with Andropogonae, but one is reduced to a rudiment and each spikelet has two florets, one of which is reduced to a rudiment. Above the female portion of the raceme, male flowers are borne in pairs of two-flowered spikelets. The feminizing gene, found in two wild populations in Kansas, restores female fertility to the reduced florets and to the reduced spikelets so that each fruitcase can produce four seeds instead of one. Many of the male flowers become female, producing two seeds per spikelet, or four seeds for spikelet pair, and the rest of the male flowers become perfect with both styles and anthers. If one gene can do all that in *Tripsacum,* why could not a similar or the same gene transform teosinte, *Zea mexicana,* to maize, *Z. mays?*

The point of all this is that the genes are there in populations of wild grass. The harvesting of wild-grass seeds may lead nowhere as far as domestication is concerned, but as soon as planting begins the definitive genes can begin to make a contribution. It is as if grasses subject to human manipulation are waiting to be invited into the domestic fold.

Chapter 2 ❧

Use of Plant Foods among Hunter–Gatherers
A Cross-cultural Survey

Lawrence H. Keeley

OF THE MANY QUESTIONS THAT ARCHAEOLOGISTS have asked regarding the origins of agriculture, this chapter will be concerned with only three which relate to the origins of so-called protoagriculture among hunter-gatherer groups. These questions are these: what induced prehistoric hunter-gatherers to intensify their dietary exploitation of plant foods?; what induced prehistoric hunter-gatherers to shift their plant diet toward the seeds of annuals?; and what induced prehistoric hunter-gatherers to begin those practices which lead to plant domestication or are necessary components of agriculture (for example, sowing seeds, soil preparation, and irrigation)?

Studying these questions through archaeological data presents some difficulties. The estimation of the plant component of prehistoric diets is still in its infancy, although methodological advances in paleobotanical and bone chemistry studies are grounds for optimism. The nature of archaeological plant remains makes it very difficult to estimate the dietary importance of different species in prehistoric diets. Unlike bone, plant remains survive very poorly in most archaeological contexts. Also, many common types of plant remains such as seeds, unlike the bones and other hard parts of animals, represent failures of consumption and not the necessary by-products of successful consumption. Therefore, it is difficult to give any estimate of the number of seeds consumed at a site, given the number of seeds found. It is also extremely difficult to tell whether a morphologically wild seed came from a plant which had been sown or tended in any fashion by humans.

The above difficulties do not apply so severely (and, in a few rare cases, not at all) to ethnographic data. Either direct observation or informant's memories can give a reasonable idea of the general proportions of major foods in a group's diet, as well as detailed information on how it was obtained. In a few cases, exact measurements of diet parameters were taken by ethnographers (for example, Lee 1979:271). In this chapter, then, the ethnographic record on hunter-gatherers will be examined to see which independent variables are most closely correlated with the dependent variables relating to the dietary use of plants.

However, as always, the only reasonable role for ethnographic data in archaeological reasoning is as a source of models or hypotheses about past events and processes. Models and hypotheses derived from the study of ethnographic cases must then be tested against the archaeological record to verify their applicability.

One danger inherent in such ethnographic studies, because they represent static data, is that independent and dependent variables (that is, causes and effects) can be confused. In this instance, it is assumed that the dietary choices of hunter-gatherers cannot affect certain variables given by geography—such as latitude, climate, and primary productivity—and that these are clearly independent. Certain demographic characteristics of hunter-gatherers are also treated as independent variables here.

The "independence" of the population sizes, growth rates, and densities of hunter-gatherers is extremely controversial and this complex issue will not be dealt with here. Instead, it will only be assumed that it is significantly easier to modify human dietary choices than human sexual drive. A previous cross-cultural study of hunter-gatherers by the author (Keeley 1988) produced some evidence that population densities were an independent variable affecting certain fundamental economic variables and that hunter-gatherer densities were more determined by the incidence of catastrophic natural mortality than cultural controls. In short, it is here assumed that population densities are more independent of diet choice than diet choice is of population density.

Another danger associated with cross-cultural analyses is that because of inadequacies and biases in sampling, independent variables of major importance may be dismissed. For example, the primary determinant of height in humans is age, and these variables are strongly positively correlated. If a sample of only adults were used, quite different conclusions would be reached. Indeed, since most individuals experience a slight decrease in height as they age after reaching maturity, we might even reach the absurd conclusion that age was negatively correlated with age and predict that newborns should be taller than their parents.

In correlational analyses, such errors are known as *truncations of range.* An example in cross-cultural hunter-gatherer research was Schalk's (1982) conclusion that population density was negatively correlated with social complexity based upon a sample of Northwest Coast groups. My own (1988) analysis of a worldwide sample of hunter-gatherers showed that socioeconomic complexity was strongly and positively correlated with population density. By truncating the range of his sample to only groups of very similar population densities and way of life, as well as making other errors, Schalk reached a conclusion equivalent to suggesting that height declines with age. The use of the widest range of hunter-gatherer groups is preferred.

The aims of this study are to analyze coded data from a representative sample of hunter-gatherers to discover what climatological, demographic, and socioeconomic variables are most closely correlated with several dependent variables relating to hunter-gatherers' dietary use of plants. The specific dependent variables are the proportion of plant foods in the diet and the nature of the staple plant foods (that is, whether they are soft fruits, roots, nuts, or seeds). The statistical analysis will be followed by a discussion of the practice of sowing wild seeds and irrigation of wild plants by Great Basin groups.

Statistical Methods

The statistical methods used here are the common ones of linear correlation and regression. The standard Pearson's correlation coefficients between dietary and other variables were calculated. Two additional concepts require some explanation: explained variance and stepwise multiple regression. *Explained variance* (R^2), is the variation in a dependent variable "explained" or accounted for by variation in one or more other variables. R^2 is simply the square of the correlation coefficient between a dependent variable and any number of independent variables. *Stepwise multiple regression* analysis involves adding independent or predictor variables to a linear equation to increase the explained variation. For example, we may find that 70% ($R^2= 0.70$, $r= 0.837$) of the variance in variable Y is explained by variable X, but this means that 30% of the variance is unexplained or residual. We may dismiss this unexplained variance as random or we may ask if there are any other variables that can account for any of this residual variance. By trying several other independent variables in the prediction formula, we may discover that, of these remaining variables, the addition of Z to X yields the next highest reduction in unexplained variance such that predicting Y using both X and Z yields an R^2 of 0.82. This process continues until the addition of any further variables yields no significant reduction in the unexplained variance.

One way of conceiving how stepwise regression is done is to regard it as correlating the residuals from the predictions of an earlier step with any unused independent variables. A residual in regression analysis is the difference between the actual value of a dependent variable and the value predicted by the regression formula. For example, we know that the best predictor of height in humans under the age of 18 is age, but we may suspect that nutrition also contributes to height. We could observe whether those individuals who exceed the height expected for their age (that is, show a positive residual height) are better nourished than individuals who are small for their age (that is, show a negative residual height). (Two of the variables used in this study, GL and IR, are residuals of this type.) By correlating this residual or age-relative height with variables measuring nutritional status, we could demonstrate that while age is the primary determinant of height, nutrition is a very important secondary determinant. Thus, in a stepwise regression we would expect age to be added in the first step and nutrition in the second step.[1]

Selection of Sample

The sample of ethnographic hunter-gatherers used here was created for a previous study of the associations between hunter-gatherer environments, demography, and socioeconomic complexity (Keeley 1988). It consists of 94 hunter-gatherer groups from all over the world. Over half, however, are from North America because that continent possessed the largest number, greatest variety, and highest concentrations of hunter-gatherers at the time of European expansion. (For details on sample selection, see Keeley 1988.)

Variables

Most of the codes used in this study are described in detail in Keeley (1988).

Diet (H1, F1, and G1). These codes were, with a few exceptions, taken from Murdock (1967, 1981). They represent the decile contribution of terrestrial animals (H1), of aquatic animals (F1), and of plants (G1) to a group's diet. The figures given for diet here do not always conform to Murdock's because a different definition of H1 was employed. In this study, H1 includes small land fauna and animal products (for example, honey) while these are included under G1 by Murdock. It must be conceded that these codes represent, with few exceptions, merely crude estimates of the proportion of bulk contributed from these sources to the annual diet. It also appears that Murdock's figures tend to underestimate the role of plants in diet (for example, compare Murdock's [1981] codes for the Hadza and Coast Salish with Woodburn [1968:51] and Suttles [1968:61]).

Latitude-relative plant diet (GL). This is the residual of G1 from that predicted on the basis of latitude. The prediction formula is (-0.109LAT) - 8.03. A positive value indicates that the actual proportion of plants in a group's diet exceeds that expected on the basis of their latitude while a negative value indicates the contrary.

Plant staples index (I). This classification represents a scale which codes several economic aspects of plant foods— increasing concentration of nutrients, increasing processing costs—and distinguishes between the edible parts of perennials (fruits, roots, and nuts) and annuals (seeds):

0 = none
1 = foliage, fungi, and so forth
2 = soft fruits including berries
3 = roots and fruits
4 = roots and other storage organs (for example, agave hearts)
5 = nuts/seeds and roots
6 = nuts (that is, hard seeds of perennial species including mesquite)
7 = nuts and seeds
8 = seeds

Relative intensity index (IR). This is the residual of I from that expected on the basis of the proportion of plants in a group's diet (G1). The prediction formula is (0.86G1)+ 1.15. A high positive value means that a group is exploiting more concentrated and more "costly" plant staples than expected given the proportion of plants in their diet.

Latitude (LAT). This represents the center of a group's territory to the nearest whole degree.

Mean annual precipitation (LPR). This variable is the normal log of the mean annual precipitation (in inches) for a group's territory. It is also a very rough measure of the amount of surface water available in a group's territory.

Index of continentality (CONT). An index of continentality, used by climatologists (Trewartha and Horn 1980:311), is

included in these analyses as a measure of variability of climate. Continental climates are more variable not only from season to season but also over longer time periods (Trewartha and Horn 1980:212, 299, 349, 351, 352).

Primary productivity (PP and LNPP). This represents the amount of new biomass produced each year per 2. It was calculated with Rosenzwieg's (1968) formula, from actual evapotranspiration rates. The normal log of this quantity (LNPP) is used in all analyses.

Secondary productivity index (LNPP1). Not all primary productivity is equally edible. The primary productivity represented by new wood is lost to most consumers. As Kelly (1985) points out, however, the secondary biomass ratio (that is, the ratio of consumers to producers) is an indication of the edibility of the plant material of an environment. Thus, a secondary productivity index (PP1) is calculated here by multiplying primary productivity by secondary biomass ratios as given in Kelly (1985). The normal log of this index (LNPP1) is used here.

Population density (LNP). The normal log of density (persons/ square mile).

Population pressure (LNZ). Normal log of the ratio of secondary productivity to population density (PP1/ PM2). A high value here means low population pressure while a low or negative value means a high population pressure.

Storage dependence (STOR). See Keeley (1988) for full a explanation of codes:

0 = no storage of food
1 = storage of supplemental foods (condiments, treats, and so forth)
2 = storage of staples, principal food source for less than 2 months
3 = storage of staples but with "hungry" period in spring
4 = storage of staples sufficient to last poor season
5 = storage of staples in surplus

Sedentism (STAY). Total and longest stay (in months) in winter or dry season in camp or village. The groups and their codes are given in table 2.1.

Results of Statistical Study
Examination of the correlation coefficients in table 2.2 indicates the main determinants of hunter-gatherer diets.

General Determinants of Hunter-Gatherer Diets
The proportions of aquatic animals and plants in diets are determined primarily by latitude: F1 is highly positively correlated while G1 is strongly negatively correlated with

Table 2.1 Hunter-gatherer sample and codes

GROUP	H1	F1	G1	GL	I	IR	LAT	LPR	CONT	LNPP	LNPP1	LNP	LNZ	STOR	STAY
Labrador Esk.	4	6	0	-1.71	0	-1.15	58	4.95	45	5.63	0.67	-3.10	3.77	2	5.0
Chipewyan	6	4	0	-1.49	0	-1.15	60	3.70	60	5.12	-1.10	-4.61	3.51	2	2.0
Angmaksalik	2	8	0	-0.84	0	-1.15	66	5.17	12	5.81	0.85	-1.61	2.46	4	8.0
Copper Eskimo	4	6	0	-0.62	0	-1.15	68	2.81	63	5.40	0.44	-3.51	3.94	2	3.5
Polar Eskimo	4	6	0	-0.47	0	-1.15	78	2.32	47	4.28	-0.68	-4.27	3.59	2	4.0
Iglulik	5	5	0	-0.40	0	-1.15	70	2.81	49	4.81	-0.15	-4.27	4.12	2	3.0
Tareumiut	3	7	0	-0.29	0	-1.15	71	2.00	40	4.07	-0.89	-2.03	1.41	5	9.0
Yaghan	2	7	1	-1.04	1	-1.01	55	4.58	8	6.56	1.60	-2.12	3.72	0	3.0
Caribou Esk.	5	4	1	-0.16	1	-1.01	63	3.32	61	4.48	-0.48	-4.61	4.13	2	3.0
Naskapi	7	2	1	-0.71	2	-0.01	58	4.25	59	5.63	-0.59	-4.34	3.76	2	1.0
Kutchin	4	5	1	0.16	2	-0.01	66	3.00	65	4.72	-0.58	-3.00	2.42	2	3.5
Han	5	4	1	0.06	2	-0.01	65	3.70	62	5.63	-0.59	-3.17	2.58	2	4.0
Chugash	1	8	1	-0.49	2	-0.01	60	7.18	15	6.40	0.88	-0.78	1.65	5	9.0
Slave	5	4	1	-0.27	2	-0.01	62	4.00	62	5.79	-0.44	-3.32	2.89	2	.
Kaska	4	5	1	-0.49	2	-0.01	60	3.70	59	5.33	-0.88	-3.65	2.77	2	4.5
Nunivak	3	6	1	-0.49	2	-0.01	60	4.32	27	6.24	1.27	-0.15	1.42	5	9.0
Ingalik	4	5	1	-0.27	2	-0.01	62	4.32	42	6.05	0.24	-2.23	2.48	4	8.0
Nunamiut	7	2	1	0.38	2	-0.01	68	3.70	51	5.13	0.17	-3.10	3.27	2	3.0
Aleut	3	6	1	-1.04	2	-0.01	55	6.02	8	6.42	1.45	0.58	0.87	4	9.5
Yukaghir	5	4	1	0.06	2	-0.01	65	2.81	79	4.74	-0.22	-4.42	4.20	0	4.0
Tanaina	4	5	1	-0.38	2	-0.01	61	4.91	33	6.14	0.33	-1.90	2.22	5	7.0
Tlingit	3	6	1	-0.71	2	-0.01	58	6.64	16	6.68	0.46	0.00	0.46	5	9.0
Nootka	2	7	1	-1.69	3	0.99	49	5.88	18	6.85	0.64	0.53	0.11	5	6.0
Micmac	5	4	1	-2.13	3	0.99	45	6.65	39	6.65	0.84	-2.81	3.65	2	1.0
Twana	3	6	1	-1.91	3	0.99	47	6.61	16	6.58	0.36	-0.17	0.54	4	5.5
Haida	2	6	2	-0.14	2	-0.87	54	5.83	10	6.73	0.51	0.90	-0.39	5	6.5
Dogrib	3	5	2	0.84	2	0.87	63	3.46	64	5.12	-1.09	-3.82	2.73	2	3.0
Nabesna	6	2	2	0.84	2	-0.87	63	3.81	58	5.38	-0.83	-3.91	3.08	2	4.5
Attawapiskat	5	3	2	-0.25	2	-0.87	53	4.39	58	6.25	0.03	-3.29	3.33	2	2.0
Saulteaux	4	4	2	-0.47	2	-0.87	51	4.32	64	6.28	0.07	-4.14	4.20	2	4.0
Alsea	2	6	2	-1.23	3	0.13	44	6.04	3	6.83	0.61	0.63	-0.01	4	7.0
Tshimshin	2	6	2	-0.04	3	0.13	55	6.97	13	6.76	0.54	0.75	-0.21	5	6.5
Chilcotin	3	5	2	-0.36	3	0.13	52	4.09	37	5.87	-0.35	-1.11	0.76	3	5.0
Cowichan	3	5	2	-0.69	3	0.13	49	5.36	17	6.61	0.39	-0.11	0.50	5	7.5
Quinault	3	5	2	-0.91	3	0.13	47	7.01	16	6.77	0.55	0.42	0.14	5	8.0
Carrier	4	4	2	-0.15	3	0.13	54	4.17	43	5.86	-0.36	-1.63	1.27	3	.
Thompson	3	5	2	-0.58	3	0.13	50	3.81	42	6.20	1.37	-0.15	1.52	3	5.0
Gilyak	3	5	2	-0.14	4	1.13	54	4.16	54	6.18	-0.04	-0.69	0.66	4	7.5
Karankawa	3	4	3	-1.87	3	-0.73	29	4.81	39	7.45	3.68	-0.69	4.37	0	1.5
Wongaibon	3	4	3	-1.43	3	-0.73	33	5.55	38	6.05	1.09	-0.69	1.79	0	
Shuswap	3	4	3	0.53	4	0.27	51	3.46	44	6.11	0.81	-0.92	1.73	3	6.5
Puyallup	2	5	3	0.09	4	0.27	47	5.29	16	6.71	0.49	1.61	1.12	5	8.5
Sanpoil	2	5	3	0.20	4	0.27	48	3.70	41	6.02	1.06	0.00	1.06	3	5.5
Agaiduka	3	4	3	-0.23	4	0.27	44	3.17	49	5.20	0.23	-3.22	3.46	2	.
Tenino	2	5	3	-0.13	4	0.27	45	4.91	29	6.14	0.33	-0.71	1.04	3	6.0
Ojibwa	4	3	3	0.31	5	1.27	49	4.32	63	6.55	1.25	-2.53	3.78	2	2.5
Klamath	2	5	3	-0.34	5	1.27	43	3.91	32	5.77	1.35	-0.43	1.78	3	6.5
Seri	2	5	3	-1.87	6	2.27	29	3.46	28	5.36	0.40	-2.12	2.52	2	1.0
Andaman	2	4	4	-2.72	3	-1.59	12	7.11	12	8.27	2.74	0.81	1.93	1	3.0
Tasmanians	4	3	4	0.55	4	-0.59	42	5.49	14	6.82	1.30	-1.90	3.20	0	2.0
Kidutokoda	4	2	4	0.55	5	0.41	42	3.70	42	5.23	0.26	-3.51	3.77	2	2.0
Atsugewi	3	3	4	0.44	5	0.41	41	4.09	37	6.31	1.48	0.18	1.30	3	6.0
Aweikoma	6	0	4	-0.98	5	0.41	28	6.13	26	7.16	1.35	-2.30	3.66	1	1.0
Yurok	1	5	4	0.55	6	1.41	41	5.24	1	6.57	0.35	1.55	-1.19	5	10.5
Washo	3	3	4	0.22	6	1.41	39	3.58	40	5.46	0.50	-0.29	0.79	3	6.0
Shasta	3	3	4	0.55	6	1.41	42	3.70	38	6.29	1.78	0.64	1.13	3	6.5
Sinkyone	3	3	4	0.33	6	1.41	40	5.04	10	6.54	1.71	1.94	-0.23	4	6.5

continued

Table 2.1 Hunter–gatherer sample and codes, *continued*

GROUP	H1	F1	G1	GL	I	IR	LAT	LPR	CONT	LNPP	LNPP1	LNP	LNZ	STOR	STAY
Tolowa	2	4	4	0.55	6	1.41	42	6.27	3	6.69	1.39	1.28	0.11	5	8.5
Wintu	2	4	4	0.44	6	1.41	41	5.04	28	6.70	1.87	1.97	-0.10	5	7.0
Wiyot	1	5	4	0.33	6	1.41	40	5.25	1	6.56	1.27	2.40	-1.13	5	10.0
Hupa	1	5	4	0.44	6	1.41	41	5.55	27	6.68	1.38	1.65	-0.27	5	9.5
Coast Yuki	2	4	4	0.33	6	1.41	40	5.25	10	6.51	0.70	1.43	-0.73	4	6.5
Pomo (East)	3	3	4	0.22	6	1.41	39	4.75	24	6.51	1.69	2.81	-1.13	5	8.0
Chumash	1	5	4	-0.22	7	2.41	35	4.17	6	6.36	2.22	3.07	-0.85	5	11.0
Botocudo	4	1	5	-0.96	2	-3.45	19	6.32	16	7.52	1.71	-1.20	2.91	0	.
Semang	3	2	5	-2.49	2	-3.45	5	7.23	17	8.49	2.96	-0.92	3.83	0	0.5
Guayaki	4	1	5	-0.31	2	-3.45	25	5.86	28	7.80	2.28	-2.70	4.98	0	0.5
Murngin	3	2	5	-1.72	3	-2.45	12	5.93	24	7.87	2.06	-2.04	4.10	0	3.5
Gidjingali	3	2	5	-1.72	3	-2.45	12	5.93	20	7.97	3.14	0.69	2.45	0	3.5
Mt. Maidu	3	2	5	1.33	6	0.55	40	5.29	30	6.37	1.54	0.97	0.57	4	6.5
Wappo	3	2	5	1.11	6	0.55	38	5.00	21	6.55	1.72	1.46	0.27	4	.
Tubatulabal	3	2	5	0.89	6	0.55	36	3.32	37	5.97	1.01	-0.26	1.27	4	7.5
Monachi	3	2	5	1.00	6	0.55	37	4.58	35	5.97	0.67	1.62	-0.95	4	8.0
Yana	2	3	5	1.33	6	0.55	40	5.49	34	6.41	1.59	0.04	1.55	3	7.0
Mono	4	1	5	1.00	7	1.55	37	3.00	39	4.43	-0.53	0.00	-0.53	3	5.5
Kuyuidoka	2	3	5	1.33	7	1.55	40	3.17	44	4.91	0.49	-0.73	1.22	3	5.0
Kiliwa	2	3	5	0.35	7	1.55	31	3.00	41	4.96	-0.01	-0.14	0.13	3	5.0
Gosiute	4	1	5	1.33	8	2.55	40	3.58	40	5.15	0.19	-3.22	3.41	2	.
Lake Yokuts	2	3	5	0.89	8	2.55	36	3.17	37	5.28	2.04	1.96	0.08	5	8.0
Mbuti	3	1	6	-1.81	2	-4.31	2	6.13	37	7.92	2.40	-0.79	3.19	0	2.0
Wikmunkin	2	2	6	-0.50	3	-3.31	14	5.55	34	7.68	4.41	-0.69	5.11	0	2.5
Luiseno	2	2	6	1.57	6	-0.31	33	3.70	17	6.03	1.20	1.90	-0.70	5	10.0
Cahuilla	4	0	6	1.57	6	-0.31	33	3.46	38	6.19	1.23	0.92	0.31	4	10.5
Nomlaki	3	1	6	2.22	6	-0.31	39	4.52	35	6.21	2.01	0.61	1.40	4	.
Sierra Miwok	3	1	6	2.11	7	0.69	38	5.04	37	6.55	1.25	0.36	0.90	4	8.0
Yavapi	4	0	6	1.79	7	0.69	35	3.46	48	5.70	0.73	-2.24	2.98	2	4.0
Serrano	4	0	6	1.68	7	0.69	34	4.09	29	6.19	1.23	-0.25	1.47	4	.
Aranda	4	0	6	0.59	8	1.69	24	3.46	49	5.31	0.35	-2.53	2.87	0	.
Panamint	4	0	6	1.89	8	1.69	36	2.00	56	3.81	-1.16	-2.90	1.74	2	4.0
Kung	3	0	7	1.15	6	-2.03	20	3.17	64	6.13	1.17	-1.39	2.55	0	3.0
Walbiri	3	0	7	1.37	8	0.83	22	2.81	55	4.52	-0.44	-3.38	2.94	0	3.0
Dieri	3	0	7	2.02	8	0.83	28	2.32	45	4.45	-0.15	-3.00	2.84	0	.
Kaibab	3	0	7	2.89	8	0.83	36	3.70	65	5.76	0.80	-2.34	3.14	2	.
Hadza	2	0	8	0.41	3	-5.03	4	5.04	62	7.12	3.35	-0.92	4.27	0	1.5

Table 2.2 Significant correlations between dietary and other variables

	F1	G1	GL	I	IR	LAT	CONT	LPR	LNPP	LNPP1	LNP	LNZ	STOR	STAY
H1	-0.298	-0.306	n.s.	-0.329	n.s.	0.335	0.577	-0.288	-0.366	-0.450	-0.703	0.556	-0.360	-0.521
	0.0035*	0.0027		0.0012		0.0010	0.0001	0.0049	0.0003	0.0001	0.0001	0.0001	0.0004	0.0001**
F1		0.817	-0.516	-0.580	n.s.	0.638	-0.304	n.s.	n.s.	n.s.	n.s.	-0.225	0.463	0.366
		0.0001	0.0001	0.0001		0.0001	0.0029					0.0003	0.0001	0.0007**
G1				0.777	n.s.	-0.837	n.s.	n.s.	n.s.	0.457	0.348	n.s.	n.s.	n.s.
				0.0001		0.0001				0.0001	0.0006			
GL				0.652	0.365	n.s.	0.277	-0.508	-0.382	n.s.	n.s.	n.s.	n.s.	0.305
				0.0001	0.0003		0.0068	0.0001	0.0001					0.0053**
I						-0.503	n.s.	n.s.	n.s.	n.s.	0.444	-0.427	n.s.	0.289
						0.0001					0.0001	0.0001		0.0085**
IR						n.s.	n.s.	-0.278		0.328	0.275	-0.542	0.535	0.468
								0.0066		0.0014	0.0072	0.0001	0.0001	0.0001**

n.s. Not significant, p<0.01.

*   Error probabilities; N = 94 unless marked otherwise.

**   N=82.

latitude. This decline in plant use with latitude was first recognized by Lee (1968). Here we can see that, in fact, aquatic animals replace plants in diets as latitude increases since F1 and G1 are strongly negatively correlated. This trend can be understood when we consider that although all ecological productivity declines with latitude, including that of aquatic animals, plant food availability becomes much more seasonal as latitude increases. The availability of aquatic animals, on the other hand, especially of the larger ones, is not so seasonal.

The proportion of terrestrial animals in diets is determined primarily by human population density and indirectly by variables that are closely related to population density—continentality and sedentism (see Keeley 1988). As human density rises, causing the development of a storage economy and its sedentary consequences, the role of terrestrial animals in the diet declines. Terrestrial animals are more mobile, usually have longer generation spans, and show lower densities than plants. This means that their populations are more vulnerable to over-hunting and that the larger species can migrate away from or avoid heavily hunted areas and, when their densities are low, become more difficult to locate. As human densities rise and exploitation territories shrink, terrestrial animals become a much less reliable and more costly food source. The dietary mix of any hunter-gather group then is determined by two main factors: latitude and population density.

Determinants of Proportions of Plants in Diet

By squaring the correlation coefficient between G1 and LAT, we can determine that latitude accounts for 70% of the variation in G1, leaving 30% of the variation unexplained. What other factors, then, determine the dietary importance of plants?

Given the opposition between aquatic animals and plants in diets, the availability of aquatic foods will clearly be of prime importance in determining the role of plants. Where there are severe constraints on the availability of aquatic foods, the proportion of plants will be maximized for any given latitude. Such constraints will obviously be maximal in regions with few or no permanent bodies of water. In climatic terms these are regions with low precipitation and/or high evaporation, that is, noncoastal deserts or near deserts. The best estimate of aquatic animal availability would be an actual measure of the area of permanent water within a hunter-gatherer group's territory. Such measures are not used here because they are not readily available and would be difficult to calculate. Instead, we will use an indirect measure—mean annual precipitation. Indeed, we do find that GL (latitude-relative plant diet) is highly negatively correlated with LPR (table 2.2). Stepwise regression indicates that LPR should be the second variable added to the regression equation and that latitude and annual precipitation together account for about 79% of the variance in G1.

If H1 declines while population density and pressure increase, obviously, F1 and G1 must rise. If F1 cannot rise because permanent waters are limited, then G1 must rise. Therefore, it is not surprising that the tertiary determinant of G1 is LNZ (population pressure).[2]

Latitude, log-normal precipitation, and population pressure account for 82% of variability in G1. The prediction formula is:

$$G1 = (-0.122LAT) + (-0.558LPR) + (-0.231LNZ) + 11.553$$

Continuing the stepwise regression indicates that the addition of further variables does not significantly increase the explained variance. The remaining 18% of the variance may be due to the crudity of G1 as a measure, random error, or variables that were not included in this study.

To summarize the findings: hunter-gatherer dietary concentration on plant foods will reach a maximum in low-latitude dry regions with high population densities. For any given latitude, the proportion of plants in the diet will rise as precipitation declines (causing a decline in permanent surface waters) and/or relative population density (that is, population pressure) increases.

Determinants of Plant Staples

The main determinant of the type of plant staples (I) is the percentage of plant foods in the diet (table 2.3). Groups with high proportions of plants in the diet tend to exploit nuts and seeds, while groups with little dietary interest in plants tend to exploit fruits or roots. The percentage of plants in the diet explains about 60% of the variability in staple crops.

All of the most extreme negative exceptions to this rule (that is, despite high proportions of plants in the diet, reliance is mainly on fruits and roots) are all tropical groups: Hadza, Mbuti, Guayaki, Semang, Botocudo, Murngin, Gidjingali, and Andamanese. Except for the Hadza, they are all groups of the wet tropics. If Murdock's (probably underestimated, see above) figures for G1 (G1 = 6) were used for the Hadza, as was the case for the rest of the sample groups, rather than the much higher figures of Woodburn (1968:51), they would not be so exceptional.

The deviations of I from that expected on the basis of G1 (IR) are highly correlated with LNZ and STOR. As previous work (Keeley 1988) has argued, storage dependence is a consequence of population pressure, so the correlation here with STOR is through the correlation with LNZ. Indeed, the stepwise regression analysis indicates that LNZ is the second variable to be added. Thus, as population pressure on productivity increases, hunter-gatherers are driven toward plant staples of more concentrated nutrients and higher processing costs. Together, G1 and LNZ account for about 72% of the variability in I.

The last significant determinant of plant staples is precipitation (LPR). When it is added to the model, about

78% of the variance in I is accounted for by G1, LNZ, and LPR. The prediction formula is:

$$I = (0.804G1)+(-0.543LNZ)+(-0.451LPR)+4.38$$

In other words, as the proportion of plants in the diet increases (responding to the variables discussed above) and as population pressure increases and rainfall decreases, the use of nuts and seeds will increase.

Summary of Statistical Results

Firstly, for any given latitude outside of the Arctic and Subarctic. as aridity and population pressure increase, the dietary concentration on plants, especially those with higher processing costs such as nuts and seeds, will increase.

It is also notable, secondly, that there is no necessary connection between socioeconomic complexity (for example, storage dependence and sedentism) and intense reliance on plant food.

Thirdly, population pressure is merely a secondary or tertiary (although still significant) factor in the intensification of plant exploitation by hunter-gatherers. Latitude and precipitation are more important determinants.

Protoagricultural Practices among Hunter-Gatherers

Among ethnographic hunter-gatherers, the practices of planting, irrigating, or otherwise tending wild food plants are extremely rare.[3] However, such practices were known among a few Shoshonean groups in the Great Basin (HNAI 1986:93–94). The Owens Valley Paiute irrigated wild root crops. Several groups in the central Basin burned over areas and then sowed them with the seeds of wild food plants. All groups in the Basin were in a region of low precipitation (less than 16 inches per year) and low primary productivity and exploited the same general plant staples (pinyon nuts, rice grass, mentzelia, and so forth) using similar technologies. A study of the distribution of these practices in the Great Basin suggests the reason. The principal difference between groups that practiced sowing or irrigation and those that did not is the significantly higher population density of the former (table 2.4). Except for a marginal case, the Little Smoky group, all Shoshonean groups using such practices had densities in excess of 0.10 persons per square mile. (The population density figure for the Gosiute is for all Gosiute and is not representative of the much denser Deep Creek group, the only Gosiute to practice burning and sowing; see note to table 2.4) Since pinyon nuts are the principal staple in all of these groups and the nut crop was so highly variable (Thomas 1972:674, 684–690), the encouragement of these secondary staples was probably a form of insurance necessary only where population pressure on the pinyon crop was high. One can easily imagine that a trend of diminishing pinyon crops would drive these higher-density Paiute groups into a more intense use of seeds and of protoagricultural

Table 2.3 Proportions of plants in diet (G1) vs. plant staple

Plants in Diet	\ Plant Staple Index	FRUITS	FRUITS	ROOTS	ROOTS	NUTS	NUTS	SEEDS	SEEDS
	0	1	2	3	4	5	6	7	8
0	7	+	+						
1		2	13	3					
2			5	+4	1				
3				2	5	2	1		
4				1	1	+3	10	1	
5			3*	2*		+	5	3	2
6			1*	1*			3	+3	2
7							1	+	3
8				1**					+

+++ Expected values
* Groups from "wet" tropics
** Hadza

Table 2.4 Population densities and protoagricultural practices among the Shoshone of the Great Basin

GROUP	P/MI²	DENSITY PRACTICE
Reese River	1.10	Burning and sowing of wild seeds
Owens Valley	0.48*	Irrigation and planting (?) of roots and seeds
Ruby Valley	0.36	Sowing of wild seeds
Humboldt River (aver.)	0.29	Sowing of wild seeds
Huntington Valley	0.29	
Diamond Valley	0.26	Burning and sowing of wild seeds
Spring and Snake Valleys	0.16	Some agriculture
Railroad Valley	0.11	Burning and sowing of wild seeds
Deep Springs	0 09	
Antelope Valley	0.09	
Saline Valley	0.06	
Kawich Mountains	0.06	
Little Smoky	0.06	Occasional sowing
Lemhi	0.04	
Grouse Creek	0.04	
Las Vegas	0.04	
Gosiute (Deep Creek only**)	0.03	Burning and sowing
Death Valley	0.03	
Belted Mts.	0.03	
Beatty	0.02	

Sources: Steward 1938: HNAI 1986:93.

* Bettinger's (1982) more recent estimate doubles Steward's estimate, used here for consistency, for the Owens Valley.

** According to Steward (1938:134,138), only the Deep Creek Gosiute followed this practice and they had a much denser population than other Gosiute groups and "compared favorably with the more fertile localities in Nevada" (that is, the Ruby and Humboldt Valleys).

practices to encourage production.

From these Great Basin examples, several points are apparent: protoagricultural practices are associated with the highest regional population densities; these population densities were, nevertheless, low by comparison to the densities of other hunter-gatherers in less arid environments; and such practices were directed toward secondary, not primary, plant staples.

Discussion and Conclusions

First, the ethnographic data reviewed here strongly imply that social factors such as competitive feasts, the demands of so-called big men and chiefs, status competition, and so forth, show no relationship to the intensity of plant exploitation. The hunter-gatherer groups with the highest values for G1, GL, I, and IR are among the least socially complex groups in the sample. The most socially complex hunter-gatherers with the most intense social demands on food supplies, mostly California and Northwest Coast groups, show no particular inclination toward protoagricultural diets or techniques. It is just as well, then, that Bender (1978, 1985), the main proponent of the causative role of social factors in the origins of agriculture, dismisses positivism and the importance of empirical tests for hypotheses (Bender 1985:49–50). Certainly, her ideas fail the test of comparative ethnographic data.

The patterns in plant usage discovered in this study help explain why the earliest evidence for plant domestication is found in the dry subtropics: the Near East and northern Mesoamerica. The low latitudes of these regions mean that potential productivity (with sufficient water!) and plant species diversity are high. The restricted distribution of permanent bodies of water in the noncoastal areas of these regions, however, forces maximum concentration on plant foods. Relatively slight increases in population density in such environments cause plant exploitation to shift toward nuts and seeds, which have a higher processing cost than other forms of plant food, the seed crops having, of course, a greater agricultural potential. In such environments, even at densities low in comparison to other hunter-gatherers, food plants, especially seedbearing ones, are encouraged by such protoagricultural practices as sowing and irrigation.

This study also suggests why the worldwide climate changes of the terminal Pleistocene and Early Holocene played such an obvious role in the origins of agriculture. Outside the tropics and the Arctic, these changes were equivalent to a lowering of latitude for any fixed point on the earth's surface because they involved a poleward movement and expansion in latitudinal extent of the subtropical, temperate, and subtemperate climate zones. This would have the effect of increasing the role of plants in noncoastal hunter-gatherer diets in the middle latitudes. In any area that also experienced a decrease in surface water and/or a decline in precipitation the dietary importance of plants

would be brought to a maximum. Were populations increasing or already high when these climate shifts occurred, a shift toward nuts and seeds away from roots and fruits would be expected. When, due to increasing population, decreasing productivity, or both, population pressure reached a certain level, protoagricultural encouragement of seed crops would begin.

These arguments also offer an explanation of why sedentary villages with storage economies precede plant domestication in the Near East but follow it in Mesoamerica. While population pressure appears to be a primary factor in the development of sedentary storage economies (Keeley 1988), it is only a secondary factor in the development of protoagriculture. The population pressure threshold for protoagriculture is much lower than that for storage economies and only occurs when certain relatively narrow environmental conditions are met. Storage economies, on the other hand, occurred over a wide range of latitudes and precipitation regimes (note the distribution of storage codes 3, 4, and 5 in table 2.1). The suggestion, then, is that the density Rubicon for sedentary village life was reached in the Near East before the climatological conditions necessary for protoagriculture appeared in the early Holocene, while in the less densely and more recently settled New World, the densities were sufficient for protoagriculture when the post-glacial climate changes occurred but were still insufficient for the development of sedentary-storage economies. A more detailed discussion of this point and of the archaeological and paleoclimatic evidence relevant to agricultural origins in the Near East and New World will be the subject of a paper now in preparation (jointly with James L. Phillips). At any rate, ethnographic comparisons indicate that proto-agricultural origins and the development of hunter-gatherer social complexity are independent phenomena and not necessarily linked, even if climatic and human demographic factors play a role in each.

In conclusion, let us formulate tentative answers to the questions raised at the outset:

- The role of plants in the diet of prehistoric hunter-gatherers would increase if there was a decrease in effective "latitude," in aquatic resources (usually because of declining precipitation), or, secondarily, an increase in population pressure.

- The importance of seeds in the diet would increase as the dietary importance of plants and population pressure increased.

- Protoagricultural practices would begin when population pressure on the staple crop reached some definable point (approximately 0.10 p/mi^2 in the Great Basin) and would involve secondary staples or supplemental foods. These answers are really hypotheses that must be tested against the archaeological and paleoecological records from regions where the earliest agriculture arose. They imply diachronic relationships that the synchronic ethnographic record cannot document and represent, at best, estimates of probable cause.

Notes

1. All analyses were conducted using the SAS statistical package available through the Computer Center of the University of Illinois at Chicago.
2. STOR was equally qualified for inclusion at this step but because it is highly correlated with LNZ and because the author has argued elsewhere (Keeley 1988) that it is a consequence of population pressure, LNZ is included in preference.
3. The use of such practices in the raising of tobacco, however, was widespread in western North America (Jorgensen 1980: 123).

Postscript: October 1998

In this brief postscript, I will not even pretend to refer to the many pertinent worldwide publications concerning agricultural origins, theoretical or specific, since 1988. My fellow authors' postscripts, collectively, will surely provide such references for our readers. Instead I will take a more parochial, even egotistical view.

Above, I disdain Bender's illogical and admittedly untestable hypothesis that certain social demands (increased trade, class expropriations, and so forth) incited hunter-gatherers to become farmers. Two years later, in a justly influential paper, Brian Hayden (1990) transformed Bender's vague postmodernist notion into a realistic, rational, and, most important, testable hypothesis. From his clear formulation of the social-demand hypothesis, he logically derived several key empirical implications that could be directly tested in the ethnographic and archaeological record. Hayden argued that agriculture first appeared among or was accepted by societies living in rich environments (an ecological variable he never defined or measured) in which increased labor could readily produce surpluses. In such so-called rich regions, collective rituals, competitive feasts, and external exchanges organized by informal or institutional leaders (for example, so-called big men or incipient chiefly classes) could evoke more intensive hunting-gathering, including especially the cultivation and herding of certain plants and animals. The plants and animals that were the foci of these socially forced intensifications would all be ritual offerings or ceremonial gifts and/or exchange items. By Hayden's argument, domestication and agriculture could first appear or later spread only among socially complex hunter-gatherers living in a rich environment. Thus, by reference to a few social features having a similar environmental context, Hayden sought to simultaneously explain the development of complex intensive hunter-gatherers, the earliest origins of agriculture in several independent hearths, and the later diffusion of farming from these hearths. He illustrated key components of this hypothesis with facts drawn from a wide variety of archaeological and ethnographic cases. Given the realism, generality, rationality, parsimony, and testability of this hypothesis, it has rightly become very popular among prehistorians. Nevertheless, a key question remains: Is it empirically correct?

In a paper subsequent to this chapter (Keeley 1995), I attempted to test all the empirical expectations Hayden (1990:38–39) deduced from his scientific formulation of the social-demand hypothesis. With a few changes, I used the same ethnographic sample as above. But I introduced or retained codes for protoagricultural practices (that is, burning for and sowing of morphologically wild plants) and certain socially demanding features (ceremonial and complementary gift giving, wealthy or hereditary classes, sedentism, and reliance upon seasonally stored food). I also used data accumulated much earlier on agriculture and certain aspects of social complexity. A statistical analysis of such relevant worldwide ethnographic data completely contradicted all five of Hayden's social-demand expectations. I observed that the robust facts recovered by archaeology in the Near East and Mesoamerica for the last 40 years also falsify the social-demand hypothesis. Social complexity, as Hayden has defined it, appeared more than 2000 years earlier in the Near East but at least 2000 years later than plant domestication in Mesoamerica, the two most obviously independent and completely unrelated agricultural hearths. Thus, in one instance, the supposed cause preceded its supposed effect by a rather long time; in the other, the supposed cause followed long after its supposed effect. A vigorous and well-argued defense against my arguments and supporting data on these issues can be found in Hayden (1995). Regarding the origin of anything, including agriculture, it will always be logically and empirically impossible for any effect to precede its efficient cause or for any type of cause (that is, efficient, material, formal, or functional) to be uncorrelated with its supposed effects.

Bacon's dictum, "Truth emerges more from error than confusion," should be every archaeologist's watchwords. Because of Hayden's clear, logical, and testable formulation of the social-demand hypothesis and what I hope is my comparable formulation of the ecological/risk-reduction hypothesis, no one should be confused. Either one of us, even both of us, may prove to be empirically wrong, but the physical circumstantial evidence produced by archaeology can never be matched against interpretations that are imprecise or untestable.

Chapter 3

Residue Analysis of Ethnographic Plant-working and Other Tools from Northern Australia

Richard Fullagar, Betty Meehan, and Rhys Jones

DESPITE THE INTRODUCTION BY EUROPEANS of agriculture and pastoralism, aborigines in northern Australia during the past century have maintained many elements of a hunting and gathering economy. It is ironic that even the modern capitalist economy of the pastoral industry in northern Australia has depended in part upon aboriginal cooperation, employment, and technology (McGrath 1987). Whereas a hunting and gathering subsistence mode has survived in many aboriginal communities, especially in Arnhem Land, the actual material culture has undergone many changes.

Research presented here forms a small part of a project, the aim of which was to study the material culture of subsistence in Arnhem Land (Jones 1980; Meehan 1982) and to compare present and past technologies. This research involved detailed recording and collecting of aboriginal artifacts used in subsistence tasks. A use-wear and residue analysis of the ethnographic artifacts was conducted by Fullagar (1988) whose main purpose was to describe traces of use and manufacture relevant to interpreting similar traces on archaeological tools. In this chapter we discuss change in material culture and prospects for identifying plant processing by hunter-gatherers in the past. The focus is subsistence tools with an objective of explaining the replacement or loss of some items and the addition or survival of others.

Raw Materials and their Uses

Before Macassans and Europeans arrived on the coast of northern Australia in the seventeenth century, aborigines used a wide range of raw materials readily available in their environment to manufacture artifacts. All of them continue to be used today, but new items such as glass, metal, nylon, and plastic have been incorporated into manufacturing processes (table 3.1).

Stone

In the past, stone was used for many purposes (table 3.2), as anvils, ax heads, flakes, pounders (figure 3.1), scrapers, and spear heads. Anvils and pounders were used together to crush animal flesh and bone, roots, nuts, and fruits; to soften strips of bark in order to make string and rope; and to grind ochers which were then applied to artifacts and human bodies as decoration, or for ceremonial purposes. Ground edged axes were hefted with supple plant stems, bound with string made from the root bark of *Ficus* trees and cemented into place with wax collected from the hives of wild bees.

Table 3.1 Raw materials used by aborigines

PRESENT	PAST
Adhesive	Adhesive
Blood	Blood
Bone	Bone
Ocher	Ocher
Plant fiber	Plant fiber
Shell	Shell
Stone	Stone
Wood	Wood
Glass	
Metal	
Nylon	
Plastic	

Table 3.2 Material culture, past and present

	PAST											PRESENT											
	Body decoration	Ceremony	Fure	Food processing	Food procurement	Manufacturing	Music performance	Shelter	Surgery	Transportation	Warefare/fighting	Body decoration	Ceremony	Fure	Food processing	Food procurement	Manufacturing	Music performance	Shelter	Surgery	Transportation	Warefare/fighting	Sale
STONE																							
Anvils				x		x									x		x						
Ax heads					x	x											x						x
Flakes				x		x			x														
Pounders				x		x									x		x						
Scrapers						x																	
Spear heads		x			x						x		x									x	x
SHELL																							
Knife				x	x				x						x	x				x			
Containers				x	x											x	x						x
Dog collars				x																			x
Graters				x												x							x
Musical instrument							x											x					x
Necklaces	x											x											x
BONE																							
Knife				x											x								x
Nose ornament	x																						
Points			x	x												x	x						x
Spatula				x												x							x
Spear prong				x												x							x
WOOD																							
Canoes				x						x					x						x		x
Paddles				x						x					x						x		x
Digging sticks		x		x					x			x			x							x	x
Firesticks			x														x						x
Mortars				x												x							x
Nut retriever, shaft				x												x							
Nut retriever, point				x																			
Points				x	x											x	x						x
Pounders				x												x							
Spear heads		x		x							x	x			x								x
Spear shafts		x		x							x	x			x		x						x
Spearthrower		x		x							x	x			x		x						x
PLANT FIBERS																							
Bags		x		x	x						x		x		x	x						x	x
Baskets				x	x											x	x						x
Containers				x												x							x
Fish nets				x												x							x
Fish traps				x												x							x
Mats				x				x							x				x				x
Mosquito nets								x											x				x
Ornaments	x	x										x	x										x
Sieves				x												x							x
ADHESIVE																							
Axes				x		x																	x
Ornaments	x	x										x	x										x
Spears		x		x							x		x				x						x
Spearthrowers		x		x							x		x				x					x	x

continued

Table 3.2 Material culture, past and present, *continued*

	PAST											PRESENT											
	Body decoration	Ceremony	Fure	Food processing	Food procurement	Manufacturing	Music performance	Shelter	Surgery	Transportation	Warefare/fighting	Body decoration	Ceremony	Fure	Food processing	Food procurement	Manufacturing	Music performance	Shelter	Surgery	Transportation	Warefare/fighting	Sale
GLASS																							
Flakes															x		x			x			
Scrapers																	x						
METAL																							
Axes													x		x	x	x		x				
Binding, spears													x			x	x					x	x
Corrugated iron															x				x				
Files															x	x	x						
Hammer															x		x						
Knives															x		x						
Nut retriever, point																x							x
Razor blades												x	x							x			
Spear points													x										x
Tomahawks													x		x	x	x						
NYLON																							
Bags															x								
Fishing line															x	x							
Nets															x								
String												x			x	x							
PLASTIC																							
Bags															x	x							
Building material																			x				
Containers																x	x						
Covers															x	x			x		x		
Ropes															x	x			x		x		

Finished implements were used to butcher and process animal and plant foods and to cut timber and bark for constructing shelters and canoes. Stone flakes were used to cut meat and plant flesh and plant fiber and to scarify human bodies in accordance with tradition. With stone scrapers, people could prepare plant stems as spear shafts and manufacture a range of other objects, mundane and ceremonial. Spear heads, or *lawuks* as they are still called in several western Arnhem Land languages, were hefted onto light wooden shafts, using *Ficus* string and beeswax. They were used to hunt animals, as spears in warfare, and as part of ceremonial regalia.

In many parts of coastal Arnhem Land, suitable stone is unavailable, so stone tools were rarely used there. Today, stone spear heads are still sometimes made (Jones and White 1988). Men take them to secret Kunapipi ceremonies in much the same way some Englishmen might take their regalia to a gathering of Freemasons. Such spear points normally are well made artifacts, often quite old. The large number nowadays made for sale in the artifact market, some incorporating stone points collected from old archaeological surface sites, are not so carefully prepared. Ground edged ax heads are also collected by aboriginal people as surface finds and hafted according to tradition for sale to art and craft outlets. As far as is known, no craftsperson is still able to make a ground edged ax from a piece of raw material. Anvils and hammerstones remain important elements in subsistence technology, being used still to crush animal bones for marrow, plant foods, and root bark to make string (figure 3.2). Because stone is scarce in some areas of coastal Arnhem Land, anvils and hammerstones are highly prized, usually hidden at camp sites awaiting the return of the owner, and aggressively sought after if taken by someone else.

Shell

The intertidal zone of northern Arnhem Land is rich in molluscan species. Freshwater bodies contain one or two species of mussel and in woodland areas there are several species of land snail which are useful to human foragers. The coastline is strewn with prehistoric thin linear midden scatters and also large, discrete shell mounds—ample evidence that past inhabitants ate quantities of shellfish. In an environment so rich in molluscan species it is no surprise that some of the shells were used as tools. The problem for archaeologists is to

Figure 3.1 Frank Gurrmanamana crushing flesh of "red apple" with stone pounder

Figure 3.2 Nancy Bandeiyama preparing *Ficus* root bark for string. It is pounded with a stone and sucked for sweet juices.

Figure 3.3 Detail of Frank Gurrmanamana scraping a long pipe stem (*Scaevola taccada*, called *wanarranba* in the Burarra language) with a shell valve (*Mactra meritiriciformes*)

find direct evidence for this use (Schire 1982:38, 63, 95–96, 120–129). The valves of some bivalve species—for example, *Mactra meretriciformis,* which had thin, sharp edges—were used as knives to butcher animal flesh, cut plant material (figure 3.3), and incise cicatrices onto the bodies of men and women at the time of initiation or mortuary ceremonies (table 3.2). The large baler shell *Melo amphora* was used to excavate wells and to carry water. The trumpet shell *Syrinx aruanus* with a *Ficus* string handle attached to it was also used as a water carrier. The flesh from both of these large gastropods was eaten after they had been cooked in hot ashes. Ground ochers, used to finish artifacts and to adorn human bodies, were stored in the valves of mangrove species such as *Batissa violacea.*

Shells of the land snail *Xanthomelon durvillii* were strung onto *Ficus* string and covered with white paint. They were put around the necks of hunting dogs on moonlit evenings. The noise of the rattling shells and their white color allowed hunters to follow dogs' movement so the prey they cornered could be retrieved. Necklaces and rattles were made in a similar way but were decorated with red, yellow, white, and dot black patterns. Rattles for musical performances, smaller than necklaces, were held in the musician's hand.

Utensils for grating yam tubers (*Dioscorea bulbifera* var. *rotunda*) were manufactured from snail shells by removing a small circle from the outer shell whorl with a sharp piece of hard wood or a strong fingernail. These globular tubers were cut into quarters before being baked in an earth oven and then grated. The snail shell grater was held by the left hand on a digging stick embedded in the ground at an angle and the tuber quarters were passed repeatedly over the grating hole. The long slivers of yam flesh passed through the aperture of the shell onto paper bark. The grated flesh was rinsed several times in fresh water then left to stand overnight being eaten.

All of these items continue to be made and used by aboriginal people today (table 3.2). some according to their original function and others, especially necklaces, as items for the arts and craft trade.

Bone

Macropod bone and the spines of stingray were used in the past as tools and ornaments. "Knives," nose ornaments, points, spatulas, and spear prongs were some of the artifacts made from these materials. Scapulae of macropods were sharpened along one side so that cooked tubers of *D. bulbifera* could be sliced before being put in fresh water to make them edible. Sharpened macropod and bird bones were put through the septum of the nose during initiation and left there as ornaments. Both pointed and spatula-shaped implements were made from macropod fibulae. The spatulae were used to remove raw and cooked oyster flesh from valves. Points were also used for this purpose as well as to cut green fronds into thin strips to make pubic coverings, to pierce holes in bark and other plant materials, and as grooming objects (Trigger 1981; Meehan 1981). Macropod fibulae sharpened to a point and stingray barbs were used as the tips of composite fishing spears. These artifacts had one or several prongs and were used with a spearthrower to pierce fish.

Both the bone points and spatulae are occasionally made today. Sometimes they are used to procure oyster flesh; sometimes they are sold in craft shops. Bone "knives" remain important food processing items, especially in the interior of Arnhem Land. Coastal people tend to use snail shell graters instead.

Wood and Plant Fiber

Canoes, both dugout and those made from folded sheets of Eucalypt stringy bark, were used for transport across tidal rivers and on freshwater swamps (Jones and Meehan 1977). Fishing with multi-pronged spears and harpooning of turtles and dugong was done from these platforms.

Digging sticks of many different kinds of wood were made to prod for tubers and land snails or tortoises buried in the mud of freshwater environments. Two sticks were twirled to make fire by friction. Impressive mortars a meter in length made from dense wood were used to crush and pound fruit and nuts into edible consistency. In some parts of northern Australia nuts from *Pandanus spiralis* trees are an important food in the late dry season (Meehan, Gaffey, and Jones 1979). These delicious and energy-rich nuts are embedded in a thick fibrous drupe. They were transversely chopped. The implement used to free the nuts had a wooden handle and a point made from a piece of hardwood. Other wooden points were used to reduce plant fronds into thin strips suitable for incorporation into pubic coverings and to make holes in bark and other substances so they could be laced with cordage.

Hardwood batons or pounders were used on bush logs to de-husk edible flesh from the fruits of the toxic *Cycas angulata* plant. Many different kinds of spear heads were made from a variety of woods, as were spear shafts and spearthrowers.

The other main type of plant material in the manufacture of artifacts was fiber of many different types, used in weaving and cordage. Bags similar to European "string bags" were commonly used in subsistence activities, to carry and sieve food. Nets woven from string were used to catch fish, as were traps made of jungle vines, for example, *Flagellaria indica*. Circular mats woven from split *Pandanus* fronds were used to sit on, as a base for the preparation of food, and sometimes as a garment when modesty required. A host of ornaments—bracelets, belts, headbands—were created from plant fibers and worn by people in secular as well as ceremonial life. Many of the objects made from plant materials in the past continue to be manufactured today (table 3.2). Almost all are also made for sale, but many remain useful elements in aboriginal life.

Figure 3.4 Frank Gurrmanamana chops the drupes of *Pandanus spiralis* as children retrieve the nuts with a metal prong set in a wooden handle.

Figure 3.5 Plant residues on an ethnographic metal prong used for retrieving nuts from fruit of *Pandanus spiralis*. Width of field: 2.5 mm.

Adhesives

Wax from the hives of wild bees, gums of some trees such as *Terminalia*, and juice from tree orchids were used as adhesives in artifact manufacture. Beeswax made firm the bindings around stone ax heads and spear points and the launching pins of spearthrowers and were also used to attach feathers and other objects to ornaments. Orchid juice was used as a fixative for ochers being applied to bark and fiber objects.

Traditional adhesives continue to be used by aboriginal craftspeople today but European-made glues are also used to stabilize ocher designs on bark paintings and other artifacts.

Arrival of New Material

Since Macassans and Europeans began to visit northern

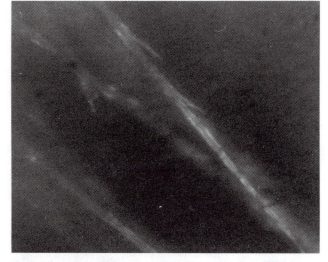

Figure 3.6 Feather barbules on a remnant of archaeological feather decoration set in resin with string attachment. The barbules can allow species identification. Width of field: 0.2 mm.

Table 3.3 Raw materials of artifacts examined

	ETHNOGRAPHIC ARTIFACTS	ARCHAEOLOGICAL ARTIFACTS
Glass	2	3
Bone	19	7
Tooth	1	1
Shell	7	8
Wood	7	37
Soft plant	1	1
Stone	1	72
Ocher	-	2
Feathers	-	1
Metal	8	2
TOTAL	46	134

colored wool are woven into bags of the same style as those made from *Ficus* string. People use nylon fishing lines with metal hooks and purchase nylon fishing nets to drag in tidal creeks. These replace the more fragile types manufactured in the past from *Phragmites* fiber.

Plastic containers, sheeting, and ropes are now common features of aboriginal life. Blue plastic fiber is used as sails for dugout canoes and to provide shade on exposed white beaches. Items and food are carried in plastic bags from local supermarkets and boats and canoes are secured with nylon rope.

New materials become available to aboriginal people all the time. One by one their qualities are assessed, then adopted, modified, or rejected. They replace materials used in the past or are used for new purposes. So far, however, despite the ready availability of new materials, people continue to use bush materials even though this means considerable expenditure of time and effort.

Residues on Artifacts

The residue analysis was undertaken in conjunction with a study of use-wear, manufacturing, and other traces. An aim of this analysis was to identify the kind of recognizable residues surviving on stone and a range of other raw materials used by the aborigines for many purposes. An important question addressed was: how well can residue analysis identify details of subsistence tasks? Or, what is the appropriate level or scale of analysis? Since the kind of microscope equipment used is an important limiting factor on the nature of the results, the equipment and techniques are described first.

All artifacts were examined under a low-power Nikon SMZ2 stereomicroscope, up to about 40 magnifications. Some traces on these artifacts were examined under a Leitz metallographic microscope with vertical incident illumination at magnifications of x120 and x300. A limitation of this analysis was that only brightfield illumination was available, not darkfield. This may have hindered the precise identification of some residues but not the recognition of their presence.

Hemastix urinalysis test strips were used to screen for blood residues (following Loy 1983, 1987). The solubility of some residues was tested in alcohol and water. Otherwise the main criteria for distinguishing residues depended upon recognition of distinctive structures such as plant cells and fibers, starch grains, mammal hairs, and collagen from skin, bone tissue, and feathers (figure 3.6).

An important aspect of this study was to examine residues on artifacts made from metal, wood, bone, glass, and shell as well as those on stone tools. This was important because little research has been conducted on metal or organic tools, as opposed to stone tools, and suitable flaking stone is known to be quite scarce in many parts of Arnhem Land.

Forty-six ethnographic artifacts and 134 archaeological

Australia, a host of new materials have become available to aboriginal manufacturers. The first was probably metal, followed closely by glass. After that a flood of items appeared such as cotton cloth or "calico" canvas and, more recently, nylon and plastic threads and fabrics.

Many glass implements such as flakes and scrapers have been found in the earliest levels of archaeological sites, some manufactured from the chunky bases of wine bottles (Allen 1969). Glass is still used today for cutting or scraping artifacts.

Metal has transformed the aboriginal toolkit. Metal axes and tomahawks have replaced their stone counterparts. Wire of different thickness and malleability is used to make prongs for fish spears and spatula-shaped ends of *Pandanus* nut retrievers (figures 3.4, 3.5) and to bind metal spear points onto wooden shafts. Corrugated iron is used to build shelters and as large plates on which to butcher kangaroos. Metal knives, hammers, and files are used, as well as other metal tools and cooking utensils.

Nylon string, often recycled from flotsam, and brightly

artifacts were examined microscopically (table 3.3). All archaeological artifacts examined are less than 2000 years old and most are probably less than a few hundred years old, suggesting that they are relevant to the period during and just before first contact with Europeans.

The tools examined for residues included the items in table 3.4. Residues were found to survive well on all ethnographic tools except metal digging sticks. Residues survived less well on archaeological tools and particularly poorly on metal, wood, and shell tools. The main difference between residues on ethnographic and archaeological tools was simply the quantity, which was considerably less on the archaeological ones. The archaeological tools came from both rock shelter and open sites. No wood was found in the open sites although bone, seeds, and other organic materials did survive (figure 3.7). Residues survived well on some stone tools from open sites.

Organic residues were found on several archaeological shells but, with the microscopes available, distinctive structures were visible on only one of them (figure 3.8). Blood residues were common on bone tools but there was some difficulty in interpreting the residues as the result of use or as remnants from manufacture out of the original carcasses. This problem may be resolved by identifying the blood to species level, as proposed by Loy (1987), and by detailed analysis of where the residues occur. For example, small bi-pointed spear prongs are completely worked by scraping and grinding. It is unlikely, therefore, that blood on the surface of these implements is from the original macropod carcasses during the stages of extraction and modification of the bone. These small prongs were also almost entirely smeared with wax or resin, which might affect reaction to blood screening tests and observations without darkfield illumination.

Discussion

The identification of residues in this study suggests that stone was used in a variety of tasks including the processing of both plant and animal materials. Although worked stones are rare as archaeological finds in many parts of Arnhem Land, residues on them seem to survive in better condition and are more easily identifiable than residues on bone or shell tools. The residues may thus give a false impression of the importance of stone relative to other raw materials. We would argue that one of the problems here is that too little is known about the mechanics and residue taphonomy of shell artifacts. There is a need for specialist studies of shell implements, particularly in those parts of Australia where stone is rare.

Ethnographic evidence is crucial in directing attention to shell artifacts which are common items of food debris, not normally examined for traces of use. Ethnography is also useful for assessing both the range of tasks that might be

Figure 3.7 Seeds set in resin on an archaeological shell tool. These grass seeds are related to the resin haft, not use. Width of field: 8 mm.

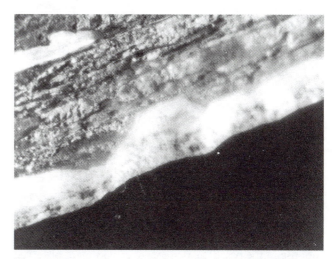

Figure 3.8 Use-wear and residues on an ethnographic shell tool used for scraping wood. Width of field: 8 mm.

identifiable and the management strategies for particular tools. For example, how were shell tools carried about and discarded? There is a need for ethnographic observations of life histories of individual artifacts, describing how they are made, what they come into contact with, where they are stored, and how they are used.

The replacement of bone by metal has been suggested by residue analysis which identified similar plant residues on archaeological bone and the ethnographic metal points. Study of cut marks on the wooden artifacts indicates that both metal and stone were used for woodworking in the recent past. Specialist points made from bone designed specifically for extracting nuts were probably replaced by specialist metal points of similar design. On the other hand, multi-purpose stone and shell tools were probably replaced by multi-purpose metal ones. Metal knives were not examined in this analysis.

Generally, the evidence suggests that residue analysis is particularly useful for reconstructing broad categories of

Table 3.4 Tools and residues identified in the microscopic analysis

	PLANT TISSUE	STARCH GRAINS	BLOOD	HAIR	COLLAGEN	HAFTING RESIN OR WAX	UNIDENTIFIED
STONE							
Flakes	x		x		x		x
Hammerstones			x				x
Pounding/grinding							x
Points	x						x
SHELL							
Scraper	x		x			x	x
Grater	x	x					x
BONE							
Grater	x	x	x				
Knife			x				
Point	x		x	x	x	x	x
Spatula	x		x				
Spear prong			x			x	x
WOOD							
Digging stick							x
Firestocks	x						
Nut retriever	x						
Point	x						
Spearhead							x
GLASS							
Flakes	x				x		x
METAL							
Digging sticks							x
Nut retriever	x						
Tomahawks							x

tool use in the past. The patterns of replacement observed ethnographically suggest that the contemporary material culture has maintained certain tool types, particularly specialized implements; only the raw material from which they are made has changed. In some cases, despite changes in manufacturing materials, names have remained the same. This has important implications for interpreting change in the archaeological record. Perhaps specialized single purpose tools are most sensitive to changes in raw material.

In some cases replacement seems to be purely functional, as with replacement of wooden digging sticks by more resilient metal rods. However, wooden sticks used for locating turtles were not replaced because metal would have pierced the carapace, which needs to be kept intact for cooking. Residue analysis would probably not be able to distinguish these varieties of digging sticks, although morphological criteria and size might suggest two functional types. In other cases, function may not be the most important factor in replacement. The butt of a metal ax, for example, is used interchangeably with a stone pestle in pounding some food roots; it all seems to depend on what is handy at the time. The mortar used in these grinding tasks is usually stone, for mostly functional reasons.

Some changes in material culture seem to involve only new raw materials providing an improved way of doing much the same thing. On the other hand, other introduced products such as guns, motorcars, and radios alter technology in a more significant way, by allowing access to a much wider range of goods and social contacts. The persistence of a distinctively aboriginal technology means that ethnography and residue analysis of material culture have great potential for reconstructing past subsistence patterns. This persistence is particularly apparent in plant processing, one of the few activities in which stone tools are still used.

Harris (1977) has argued that a cline exists from Melanesian horticulture across Torres Strait to the aboriginal hunting and gathering systems of north Queensland. Evidence for aboriginal management of plant foods in Australia ranges from swamp foods like bulrush (Gott 1982; Head 1987) and yams (Hallam 1986) to manipulation of the local environment by fire-stick farming (Jones 1969; 1980). These practices are ancient, perhaps extending back into the early Holocene and Pleistocene. The antiquity of seed grinding as indicated by grinding stones is probably a Holocene innovation (Smith

1988). Although the planting of crops was never practiced, it is likely that some intensification of plant food management occurred in the last three thousand to four thousand years (Beaton 1982; Beck et al. 1989; Lourandos 1985).

In Australia, therefore, the nature of the archaeological evidence for plant management is in stark contrast to that for the rest of the world. The indirect evidence from pollen, charcoal, phytoliths, and physical anthropology is sparse. So, too, is direct evidence from seeds. We argue that the evidence from residues on stone and shell tools is likely to provide some of the best evidence for plant exploitation and that ethnographic studies are crucial for adequate interpretation of the functions.

Postscript: October 1997

Reference to the antiquity of seed grinding in Australia requires revision. Recent discovery and analysis of a grinding-stone assemblage at Cuddie Springs suggest the culinary preparation of seeds and sporocarps about thirty thousand years ago (Fullagar and Field 1997). At this site in the arid margins of southeastern Australia, seed grinding becomes common as bones of extinct megafauna (including *Genyornis* sp. and *Diprotodon* sp.) become increasingly scarce. Of relevance here is the fact that it is precisely because of microwear and residue studies that such dietary details can be identified. Of particular importance are first, the role of ethnographic studies in structuring studies of plant food extraction and second, the analysis of starch grains and phytoliths on stone tools which provides some of the best evidence for plant exploitation.

_____

Acknowledgments. We would like to thank Neville White for providing us with some botanical identifications, Sally Brockwell for organizing the Kakadu archaeological material for us to examine, Jane Bible and Tania Konecny for providing the ethnographic material from storage at Rushcutter's Bay, and Sue Folwell and Jan Howarth for typing the manuscript. We would also like to thank Patricia Anderson for encouraging an Australian contribution to a volume on plant domestication.

Chapter 4

Root and Tuber Resources

Experimental Plant Processing and Resulting Microwear on Chipped Stone Tools

April K. Sievert

ROOT AND TUBER RESOURCES HAVE CONTRIBUTED to subsistence adaptations of foragers and horticulturalists in several areas of the world for a very long time (Yellen and Lee 1976; Roosevelt 1980; Coursey 1980). As Léon notes, tuber crops have, however, been viewed as crops secondary to the cereals (1977). Some early writers believed that dependence on root crops would not provide an adequate subsistence base on which to develop high populations and higher levels of cultural complexity (Darlington 1969). Roots and tubers are "often regarded as relics of primitive agriculture" (Léon 1977:20) and may have had a dampening effect on agricultural development (Darlington 1969).

Although domestication of cereals has been targeted by experimental archaeologists in Eurasia through botanical and technological experimentation, less is known about the potential role of tuber crops. Reasons for the lack of an interface between tuber cultivation and general studies of the rise of agriculture in Eurasia include the following:

- The world's major tuber and root crops are tropical or subtropical. Tuber domestication is evident in tropical areas: West Africa, Mesoamerica, South America, and Southeast Asia in particular. Cassava *(Manihot esculenta)* and yams *(Dioscorea)* are restricted to tropical climates. The sweet potato *(Ipomoea batatas)* and, to a lesser extent, the potato *(Solanum tuberosum)* and various hybrid forms have been adapted to temperate environmental regimes. Although temperate climates produce their own native tubers, roots, and rhizomes, the extent of their exploitation is debatable. The potato *(Solanum tuberosum)* is one tropical starchy tuber which has been widely accepted into the agricultural base of Eurasia.

- Doubts concerning the potential for starchy tubers to supply adequate nutrients and biases suggesting an uncomplicated level of technology involved in propagating tuberous resources have kept the study of tuber domestication and utilization to a minimum, especially in areas where tubers were clearly not a primary horticultural focus. While it is true that many tubers, roots, and rhizomes are not rich enough in protein adequately to fulfill nutritional needs for large populations, when coupled with other protein sources, root crops can easily supply the necessary carbohydrates (see table 4.1). The nutritive value of tubers as compared to grains has been addressed elsewhere (Cowgill 1971).

- Botanical remains of root crops are perhaps more ephemeral than remains from cereals. Usable portions of the plant, rhizomes and tubers, are subject to invasion and decay by fungi, bacteria, insects, and nematodes (Onwueme 1978, Coursey 1967). Some important tubers, such as *Dioscorea* spp., produce few seeds, a condition which is heightened by horticulture relying on vegetative propagation. Archaeological recovery of the botanical evidence for tuber utilization or horticulture has been, until recently, relatively low. Although it is possible to locate and identify starch grains and charred or desiccated root and tuber material in some archaeological contexts, these methods are still not widely applied (Hather 1994; Loy 1994; Ugent 1994). In some cases, evidence for the use of tubers derives from indirect evidence of ethnohistorical association coupled with technological correlates to root crop horticulture (Roosevelt 1980, Dole 1960, Davis 1975).

Nevertheless, there has been some speculation that intensive utilization of tubers played some role in the general intensification of plant use which may have preceded domestication of cereals in some areas. The Mesolithic has been characterized as a period supporting a general adaptation involving roots, nuts, and seeds (Zvelebil 1986). Climates of Europe during the Mesolithic may not have supported growth of large enough tubers to make the procurement of them profitable (Rowley-Conwy 1986:27).

Naturally, research on the development of tuber horticulture focuses on areas where important starchy tubers were domesticated: the Americas, West Africa, and Southeast Asia in particular. Léon (1977) offers a summary of worldwide tuber and root domestication and dispersals. There has been considerable concern about tuber (cassava primarily) utilization in South America and Mesoamerica (Roosevelt 1980, Bronson 1966, Davis 1975, DeBoer 1975, Cowgill 1971, Dole 1960). Likewise, there has been interest in cassava horticulture because of its implication in contributing to the subsistence base of the Maya. Bronson (1966) presented a case for dependency on tubers, especially cassava, as primary staple resources. Cowgill (1971) delineates the growing cycles and soil requirements of cassava and concludes that cassava would not grow well in the lowland Maya heartland of the Petén region in Guatemala, an opinion supported by Léon (1977:32). Marcus (1982) suggests that in later, postcontact Maya times, roots such as jicama were considered to be famine foods. It is clear, however, that tubers do become important food crops in tropical regions and in Andean South America. Processing implements have been cited as evidence for tuber horticulture in these areas (Davis 1975, Dole 1960) but DeBoer (1975:420) concludes that the presence of processing implements does not "cinch the case for manioc cultivation." DeBoer's work does summarize archaeological evidence for manioc cultivation in Mesoamerica. Roosevelt (1980) presents an excellent specific case study of a combined maize and cassava adaptation in South America by using ethnographic detail to interpret archaeological data. In South America, intensive cassava utilization is evident in the archaeological record as early as 4000 BP (based on the presence of large stone griddles used in baking manioc bread) and probably formed a key component in tropical trade networks (Lathrap 1973:174-176). Data from South America's west coast, where the extremely dry climate is ideal for preservation of organic materials, demonstrate that roots and tubers were in use by 1800 to 1500 BC (Ugent 1994; Ugent, Pozorski, and Pozorski 1981, 1982, 1984, 1986).

Tuber utilization is more problematic in areas where tubers are not known to have been domesticated. For

Table 4.1 Nutritional composition of selected tubers and roots*

	MOISTURE	FAT	CARBOHYDRATES	PROTEIN
Cassava (*Manihot*)	61	0.3	35	1.0–2.0
Yams (*Dioscoreae*)	60–80	0.1–0.3	25–29	1.0–2.8
Sweet potatoes (*Ipomoea*)	70	0.2	25–30	1.0–2.0
Potatoes (*Solanum*)	70–77	0.2	20–30	2.0

* by % of fresh weight; Sources: Salaman 1985: 122-123; Cowgill 1971; Onwueme 1978

example, if tubers figured at all in Mesolithic subsistence patterns, then we need to be aware of the types of procurement and processing procedures that typify tuber use. Root crops, by virtue of their life cycles and characteristics, do present a set of parameters for exploitation and cultivation, which should be identifiable to some degree in any area of the world. Examination of ethnographic reports regarding the use of tubers and roots, coupled with a general understanding of the botanical characteristics of tubers, can offer some suggestions as to what to look for in the archaeological record. Essentially then, we need to know much more about the utilization of tubers, roots, and rhizomes, especially as it applies to technology. My own research concerns Mesoamerican and South American technology, but this can be related to questions of root crop utilization in North America and Europe as well. In particular, the purpose of this chapter is to present findings concerning the use-wear traces which are formed on chipped stone implements used in processing tubers for storage and consumption.

Characteristics of root crops

There is considerable variability in the growth and reproductive cycles of tuber crops. In general, several factors characterize tuber crops, including photoperiodicity of tuber growth; high starch and, therefore, high caloric content of tubers; and toxicity. Tubers and roots represent storage organs for the plant and as such contain large quantities of starch and sugars. Although many types of root resources can be eaten, the ones which contain high starch contents are the most important as food staples (Roosevelt 1980: 137). Léon (1977:20) distinguishes between starchy tropical tubers—potatoes, yams, and taro—and those temperate varieties commonly considered to be vegetables, for example, parsnips, carrots, or beets. In this chapter, I focus primarily on cassava (*Manihot esculenta*), jicama (*Pachyrrizus erosus*), potatoes (*Solanum tuberosum*), and carrots (*Daucus carota*). Average ranges for nutrients for primary tuber and root crops are shown in table 4.1. Tubers can contribute calories and therefore energy to the diet. Protein content is variable in amount and kind and usually averages approximately 2% of fresh weight. In any case, tubers are structured such that starchy material and vascular organs are packed into a moist bundle and encased within an epidermis. This peel can be thin and flexible, as in the case of the potato, or thick and cork-like or bark-like, which characterizes yam and cassava.

Cassava, in particular has been widely studied archaeologically and presents an interesting case in point. There is only one species of cassava, *Manihot esculenta*. Commonly called manioc or yuca, this is a perennial dicotyledon producing a cluster of inflated roots which may range in size from 15 to 100 cm (Onwueme 1978:112). The plant does not exist in a wild state and was domesticated in northeast Brazil and probably also in Central America. Cassava grows well in warm, moist climates but is also, to some degree, drought tolerant. It requires over 1000 mm of rain annually. Cassava cannot tolerate water-saturated substrates, being highly susceptible to rot, a factor which necessitates adequate drainage. Tuber production is photoperiodic, requiring equal darkness and daylight hours for maximum growth. The optimal range is therefore between 15° north and 15° south latitudes (Onwueme 1978:110) with some growth potential between 15° and 30° north and south latitudes (Cock 1985:16).

Many tubers contain some sort of toxin to deter pests. Although some argue that tubers containing toxic substances require little extra preparation (DeBoer 1975: 420), others have demonstrated that significant additional preparation is required (Léon 1977, Dole 1960). In any case, special processing techniques can serve both in the removal of toxins and in the transformation of roots into a storable and palatable foodstuff. Cassava cultivars, in particular, contain some amount of cyanogenic glucosides, water-soluble compounds which convert through hydrolysis with the enzyme linamarase to hydrocyanic (prussic) acid (Onwueme 1978 , Cock 1985:26-27). So-called bitter varieties of cassava contain relatively higher contents of cyanogenic glucosides, which are present in the flesh of the tuber, the peel, and the plant itself. So-called sweet varieties also contain the toxic compounds, but in much smaller quantities and often only in the peel. Bitter cultivars have the advantage of a longer post-harvest storage life, whereas sweet varieties rot rapidly following harvest.

Even so, cassava tubers do not keep long after harvest and must be processed quickly and dried into a form which can then be stored (Cock 1985, Roosevelt 1980, Lathrap 1973:174). Bitter cassava cultivars deteriorate more slowly in the ground than do sweet cultivars (Onwueme 1978), so that the harvesting of bitter cassava may be done in a more leisurely fashion, with less time constriction. The amount of poison in the cassava depends not only on the genetic characteristics of particular cultivars but also on environmental conditions. Other tubers contain other types of toxic substances. Yam varieties, for example, contain alkaloids, tannins, and steroidal saponins (Coursey 1967:206). The presence of these toxins is especially high for wild yams and does present some risk when wild yams and tubers are exploited in famine situations (Coursey 1967:148). The consideration of toxicity is therefore an important one, even among foraging groups.

Ethnographic use of tubers and roots

Evidence in the ethnographic literature on the utilization of tubers or roots suggests that foragers in temperate regions do rely on tuber resources. Indigenous populations along the North American northwest coast, the Columbia Plateau, and the Great Basin, for example, use roots extensively (see table 4.2). Certain roots, including camas (*Quamasia quamash*) were considered to be exploited intensively and were highly valued for storage. Among foraging groups in temperate environments, tubers are often regarded as staple resources, but are always combined with other resources. They are often used in conjunction with important protein sources such as Pacific salmon. In these areas, no cultivation was practiced and populations along the Northwest Coast maintained a highly sedentary settlement system. Although many types of roots are utilized, camas is the most important as a staple. These roots are small, however, and in most cases would not require the use of stone implements in processing. I located only one case, that of the Klallam Indians of the Olympic Peninsula, where knives of any kind were used. Here, the roots were scraped with shell knives (Gunther 1927:210). Roots which are small, that is less than 10 cm in any dimension, are unlikely to be processed using stone tools. Small roots can be dried without processing as soon as they are harvested, cooked fresh, pounded into a paste, or made into a flour without using knives. Only in cases in which larger roots like cassava, yam, and possibly potato are used intensively would some sort of cutting implement be necessary. The most common use of stone tools in root-processing is in a process of grating large raw roots to form a flour or paste.

Tuber horticulture focuses on the larger fleshy roots and tubers found in tropical environments. Cassava is a widely used and important food crop in tropical lowland South America, Central America, and the Caribbean (see table 4.3). Here it is the primary source of starch and calories. Because cassava is not a nutritionally complete food, cassava horticulture is often combined with fishing or other foraging and horticultural activities (see Roosevelt 1980: 126–137). In Amazonian South America, especially, the technology for processing cassava has been studied (Dole 1960, Farabee 1924; Meggars 1971; Roosevelt 1980; Wilbert 1972; Roth 1924). Processing methods serve both to remove hydrocyanic acid and render the tubers storable. The process for producing manioc meal or flour includes harvesting, peeling, grating, pressing, pounding, and sifting. Methods of processing cassava carry the following implications for the use of chipped stone tools. The roots must be peeled prior to grating, a process that requires some form of cutting implement. Grating the tubers usually involves the use of a manufactured abrading utensil of some kind. This may assume a number of forms, including rough groundstone implements (Sturtevant 1969:180) and manufactured composite grating boards.

Table 4.2 Uses of tuber or root resources among North American foraging groups

CULTURE	ROOT PLANTS	USES	SOURCE
Klamath	Camas (*Quamasia quamash*), arrowroot	Staple spring food, stored	Stern 1965: 12, 26
Nisqually	Unspecified roots	Dug with sticks, boiled	Haegerlin and Gunther 1930: 20–21
Sanpoil	Camas	First spring plant food	Ray 1930: 98–100
Kutchin	Parsnip-like tuber	Important early winter food	Osgood 1936: 29
Bannock	Camas	Stored	Steward 1938: 202
Shoshoni	Camas	Dug and used for storage	Steward 1938: 209
Klallam	Fern roots	Skin scraped using shell knife; roasted, pounded, dried, and made into flour	Gunther 1927: 210
Wishram	Camas	Staple food—roasted, pounded	Spier and Spier 1930: 183
	Onions, wild potato of many types, carrot and carrot-like roots	Peels of some scraped off. Some small roots like "bitter wild potato" pounded, dried, and made into loaves	
Tanaina	Fern roots, parsnip-like root	Eaten and traded	Osgood 1937: 41
Quinault	Camas, fern roots, snakehead	Camas roasted, mashed, made into loaves, baked, and stored; roots from "lady fern" roasted and peeled; snakehead eaten raw or cooked	Olson 1936: 53
Hopi	Wild potato	Gathered in late autumn	Beaglehole 1937: 51
Ojibwa	Jerusalem artichoke (*Helianthus tuberosus*)	Eaten raw	Densmore 1974: 319
	Wild potato (*Sagittaria latifolia*)	Dried and boiled	
	Bulrush (*Scirpus validus*)		

In the Amazon basin, cassava graters are usually manufactured by embedding small stone chips into a wooden board (Davis 1975; Meggars 1971; Roosevelt 1980, Roth 1924). I examined 14 cassava graters from the collections at the Field Museum of Natural History in Chicago (figure 4.1a). In most cases the stone pieces were very small, less than 8 mm in any dimension. I saw only graters made of quartz, small bits of sheet metal, or pieces of tree bark, but there is ethnographic evidence for the use of flint or chert as well as bone and shell (Meggars 1971, Roosevelt 1980, DeBoer 1975).

Experimental program

In evaluating the modes of use which may involve chipped stone tools and tubers, ethnographic research forms a basis for the construction of a set of experiments dealing with various tuber and root-processing activities. Because the most common activities involving large tubers require peeling, reduction into smaller sized pieces, and possibly grating, I carried out experiments involving peeling, grating, and slicing unpeeled tubers and slicing peeled tubers. My analytical technique is high-power wear analysis (see Juel Jensen 1988a; and Yerkes and Kardulias 1993 for a comprehensive review of this technique).

Some experimentation using chipped stone implements on roots or tubers has been reported. Lewenstein (1987:123) used obsidian blades to peel and slice cassava. She reports light edge rounding and no surface alterations other than deep bilateral striations, and scalar or crescentic edge damage. Davis (1975) produced a manioc grater using obsidian chips embedded into a wooden board which was used for a period of four hours. Wear analysis was done at 30x magnification. He notes a pattern of microflaking and what appears to be edge rounding. This he compares to edge damage noted on obsidian flakes from archaeological contexts. Walker (1980) also replicated a grater board using chert flakes produced through bipolar reduction. His aim was to reproduce lithic artifacts found at a site on St. Kitts in the Caribbean. Walker found that wear patterns of blunting and some microflaking were visible but did not develop as quickly as wear traces from performing other motions, such as cutting or sawing. Lewenstein and Walker (1984) also studied grater teeth of obsidian and found a subtle pattern of edge microflaking on experimental grater teeth that matched wear on some obsidian microliths from Mexico.

Aldenderfer et al. (1989) report briefly on the development and characteristics of root-processing alterations formed on chert tools used to process cassava and jicama (*Pachyrrizus erosus*), a sweet tuber eaten as a fruit or vegetable. In this case, edge rounding as well as some polish formation are noted for one piece used on cassava, but the incidence of experimental pieces exhibiting unequivocal alteration is low (1 out of 7). The details of alteration and polish are submitted in detail as follows. A chert flake was used to whittle a cassava root which had been partially peeled but allowed to dry somewhat before further processing. In this case, alteration from processing developed after 30 minutes. This occurred in the form of a faint brightening and a flattening of topographic features. The traces extend well back away from the edges of the pieces. They are evident primarily along the edge and on the edges of flake scars and ridges away from the edge. This experimental piece was made from a Guatemalan chert having two distinct structural areas, a fine-grained gray area and a coarse-grained light area. Wear traces are visible mainly on the better quality portion of the edge, even

Table 4.3 Uses of roots among South American horticultural groups

CULTURE	ROOT PLANTS	USES AND PREPARATION	SOURCE
Jivaro	Cassava (*Manihot esculenta*)	Most important plant staple	Stirling 1938: 107–108
	Sweet cassava, sweet potato	Year-round staples	Meggars 1971: 58–60
Caribs	Cassava	Used graters, squeezers, sifters	Taylor 1938: 130–131; 137–140
Marcusis	Cassava	Used stone graters	Farabee 1924: 20
Waiwai	Cassava	Used stone grater boards; used graters for tools	Farabee 1924: 157
	Bitter cassava	Peeled, grated, pounded, and sifted	Meggars 1971: 89
Camayurá	Cassava	Grated, peeled, squeezed, and made flour from cassava; staple food year-round	Meggars 1971: 47
Kayapo	Sweet potato, sweet cassava	Make bread	Meggars 1971: 69
Siriono	Sweet cassava, sweet potato	Primarily foraging group, only minimally cultivated; roots not a staple	Meggars 1971: 79
Makiritare	Bitter cassava	Peeled, grated, pounded, sifted, and made into bread; used stone grater boards	Wilbert 1972: 130–131
Various	Bitter and sweet cassava	Discussion of technology used for squeezing cassava pulp across Amazon Basin region	Dole 1960

though the working edge spans both areas. The traces resemble alteration produced from cutting meat; however, there is no greasy luster present. The traces do not really spread, nor are they particularly smooth. This apparent polish is only moderately bright. Edge damage is minimal. Traces do not exhibit directionality. If grit were introduced into the substrate, as in the case of cutting unpeeled or unwashed tubers, some striations might be expected. One striation was present on this experimental piece.

I initiated a more comprehensive experiment aimed at reproducing the polish and alteration noted in the prior experiment and extending the range of uses modes and root type. A series of timed experiments were performed using cassava, jicama, carrots (*Daucus carota*), and potatoes (*Solanum tuberosum*).

Also, in replicating the experiments of Davis (1975), Walker (1980), and Lewenstein and Walker (1984), I manufactured a manioc grater using 46 microliths of chert and 10 of obsidian. The mean maximum dimension of the 56 flakes I used is 13.7 mm. This is somewhat larger than the grater pieces reported by DeBoer (1975:430) at 8 mm, with none exceeding 1 cm. I embedded these pieces into a pine board. This posed some logistic problems because I wanted to keep damage and alteration from factors other than utilization to a minimum. I made holes in the wood using a nail, following the techniques described in grater board construction outlined by Wilbert (1972:130–131). The microliths were then inserted. In order to force the pieces into the wood, I cushioned each flake with cotton, positioned the head of a nail on the flake, and then lightly struck the point of the nail with a hammer, applying indirect percussion to each microlith, forcing them into the wood. The cotton kept the stone chips from becoming crushed or damaged. The layout of flakes is shown in figure 4.1b. Following insertion of all chips, I painted the wooden surface around

the chips with an organic mucilage, serving to anchor the pieces. Ethnographic studies show that a resin, or a natural latex, is often used for this purpose (Wilbert 1972, Meggars 1971); Walker (1980) used pine pitch in his experiment. The microliths extruded from the wood a mean distance of 5.2 mm. This is greater than the distance stone chips extend from the ethnographic graters I examined (approximately 2 mm). I did not want to apply enough force to bury the pieces because I was trying not to damage them and I wanted to be able to remove them with minimal damage after the grating process was finished (figure 4.1c).

Peeled cassava roots were grated by pushing the root gently over the extruding stone flakes. Force was applied downward, in one direction only. Two obsidian microliths came out immediately, and therefore should show no sign of wear traces other than those resulting from insertion into the wood. Six came out after 25 minutes of grating, one after 40 minutes, one after 50 minutes, and one after 60 minutes. One piece came out at an unknown point during the process and could not be found later. The remaining microliths were used for 80 minutes. Therefore, I was able to produce a set of microliths that would ideally show the development of wear after different amounts of time. Following the grating exercise the board was left to dry out naturally, uncleaned. Bits of grated cassava adhered to the stone for a period of one week. Some of the mucilage coating was removed during grating.

The microliths were removed by first soaking the utensil in water for 5 hours to soften the wood and the mucilage. Any loosened pieces were removed. Microliths which were immovable were removed by taking a small nail and pounding it into the wood approximately 1 to 2 mm away from each flake, widening each hole and also providing leverage to force the microliths up out of the wood. Although I was careful not to touch the metal nail to the stone, in some cases the metal may have scraped the stone, usually below the line

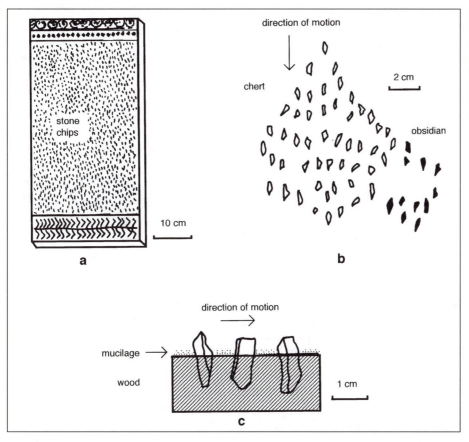

Figure 4.1*a*, decorated cassava grating board from Venezuela (Field Museum of Natural History catalog no. 243678); *b*, configuration of stone microliths on experimental cassava grating board; *c*, sample of microliths as embedded in experimental cassava grating board

of insertion into the wood. I therefore expect to find some traces of metal on the microlithic test pieces. Before removing the microliths, it was also necessary to mark lightly on the side of each piece with a pencil the level of insertion into the wood so it could be drawn. Therefore, some graphite tracings are expected. I also examined six microliths which were unused and unset as controls.

My expectation was that there might be traces of wear typical of woodworking on the edges which were in contact with the wooden board. I expected that for those pieces which moved in the wood, the highest concentrations of wear should be at the deepest point of insertion on the side pointing toward the cassava and on the side pointing away, on the margin. Traces of root-processing should be confined to the upper margin, above the line of insertion into the wood, and should be best developed on the edges pointing toward the top of the grater and on the tops of the microliths.

None of these expectations was met. Any alteration was extremely subtle and lacked directionality. Traces are not necessarily oriented to suggest direction of action. Many pieces appear to be unused. Results from the manioc-grating experiment were disappointing because few distinctive microtraces were identifiable on the microlithic stone tools used in the experiment. Except for some slight rounding on the flake used for 50 minutes, no microliths used for less than 80 minutes exhibited wear. Utilization for 80 minutes produced no well-developed polish but did produce some forms of polish-like alterations, albeit very subtle ones.

Alteration is primarily in the form of edge rounding and some faint brightening and smoothing along edges. In using the grater, only the tops of the microliths came into contact with the tubers. Sides of the pieces collected cassava which may have cushioned the pieces from direct motion and contact. No directionality was apparent on any of the cassava grater bits.

The result of microscopic wear analysis of grater microchips is summarized in table 4.4. The total umber of analyzable chips was 53 because one was lost and two were so highly lustrous as to obscure any actual wear traces. The degree of alteration is qualitative. Very slight and slight development implies a visible trace of use, but one that can not be ascribed to specific worked material. Fair represents the best developed microtraces noted for this particular experiment and, in the case of polish, implies a visible polish that conforms to the characteristics described for well-developed root-processing: flat, brighter topography with no directionality.

In addition, three chert flakes were damaged by metal abrasion or battering during insertion and removal. Traces of insertion into the wood were minimal. Of eight chips showing some sort of insertion trace, only two appear to have wood-typical polishes on ridges. Abrasion is present on two chips, at the margin of insertion into the wood, and four exhibit a weakly developed undistinguishable polish on edges or ridges. In no cases were the polishes either from use or insertion widely distributed on the pieces but occurred as

Table 4.4 Wear traces on microlithic tools from experimental cassava grating

DEGREE	EDGE DAMAGE				EDGE ROUNDING				WEAR POLISH		
	CHERT	OBSIDIAN	TOTAL		CHERT	OBSIDIAN	TOTAL		CHERT	OBSIDIAN	TOTAL
None	36	5	41		30	10	40		24	10	34
Very slight	2	0	2		6	0	6		10	0	10
Slight	5	5	10		6	0	6		8	0	8
Fair	0	0	0		1	0	1		1	0	1
TOTAL	43	10	53		43	10	53		43	10	53

N = 53

small patches on projections. Again, the problem is a short period of use. Ethnographically produced cassava graters require considerable time to manufacture and are used for many hours over many years, implying that ethnographic grater stones as well as prehistoric grater stones would present better developed wear traces.

Experiments done on jicama *(Pachyrrizus erosus)* were disappointing in that distinctive alteration was not produced experimentally. Jicama is a very moist root having a high sugar content and a texture resembling that of apples. Both obsidian and chert flakes were used for 10, 20, and 30 minutes on jicama. The chert used was collected from the Petén region of Guatemala, a Maya focal region. This particular chert presents a highly waxy luster and no identifiable alteration is visible. Given the rate at which polishes formed on pieces used on cassava and potatoes, these jicama tools were probably not used long enough for polishes to have developed. Minimal edge damage of a scalar or crescentic nature was the only alteration to the obsidian pieces.

Experiments were also done on potatoes *(Solanum tuberosum)*. Russet potatoes were cut/sliced for a total of 2 hours. They were not peeled prior to cutting. After one hour, traces resembling those found on the cassava tool described above (and in Aldenderfer et al. 1989) were identifiable. Well-developed traces were noted after 2 hours. The traces occur as a brighter line along both faces of the used edge of the piece (figure 4.2). Edge-rounding occurs. The traces are somewhat reminiscent of wear from mechanical weathering processes except that there is no abrasion, no striation, and no directionality present. As the polish developed, it became more extensively distributed but retained only moderate brightness. Areas of well-developed polish become smoother but are not glossy.

The texture of potatoes is like that of cassava in that the root is composed of a fleshy moist nodule of starch. There is little cellulose present in either type of root. In order to observe the characteristics of more fibrous, less starchy roots, an experiment was also carried out on carrots *(Daucus carota)*. Experiments were done using carrots for a total of one hour. The motion was a combination of cutting and chipping using chert flakes. After each 20 minutes of use, the pieces were examined. Alteration did develop during this time but was also quite subtle, resembling the traces produced

in the original experiment on cassava reported by Aldenderfer et al. (1989) and described in depth above. I expected that experiments on carrots, which are more fibrous and dense and less starchy than cassava or potatoes, might resemble traces produced customarily from working with soft woods or woody green plants. This was not the case. Traces on the tool used on carrots are not smooth, glossy, or spreading. Again, traces are very slow to develop, and after one hour the traces are clearly visible but not extensive. In none of these cases does the polish resemble that obtained by using chert on silicaceous plant material.

Microtraces on flint are slow to form when tuberous plant materials are processed. I agree with Lewenstein (1987:123) that processing roots with obsidian results in very little distinctive alteration. Use-wear consists of edge damage, in the form of crescentic microscarring. Lewenstein reports that no polishes were formed, which is to be expected given that she used obsidian rather than chert. I was able to produce microwear polishes on chert tools by working cassava, carrots, and potatoes. Although the alterations from working roots are very subtle, a polish does develop eventually. Several generalizations regarding these traces can be made:

- Traces resulting from processing tuberous roots are slow to form, but they do become visible eventually, especially after 2 hours or more of use. The stage at which polishes develop beyond a "generic weak stage" (Vaughan 1985:28) is reached much later for "subtle materials such as soft vegetable matter and fat or meat" (Juel Jensen 1988a:55). This is a well recognized consideration in distinguishing wear polishes (Juel Jensen 1986, Keeley 1980, Unrath et al. 1986). Starchy, moist roots certainly fall into a category of subtle plant materials. In one experiment, I allowed a peeled cassava root to dry out before whittling at it with a chert flake. In this case, polish developed clearly after 30 minutes of use, suggesting that possibly reduction in root moisture content increases the friction, accelerating the development of polishes past the threshold of distinctiveness. In any case, water still makes up the major part of root volume.

- Directionality is largely absent. This is a distinctive

feature in its own right. When striations are present, they are long and deep and are caused when grit from unwashed tubers is dragged along the surface of the stone. The polish itself does not exhibit directionality.

· Alteration consists of a brightening and smoothing out of natural topographic features of the stone. The topography of the polish itself is flat. It does not spread and has a matte surface except in areas of most intensive development, which do become smoother but never glossy.

· The microtraces, when they finally develop, are similar for all the roots with which I experimented, including fleshy tubers and more heavily vascularized roots.

· Poorly developed wear traces resemble natural or chemical weathering or erosion to some degree, except that there is no directionality or abrasive pattern noticeable.

· The polish is invasive and tapers off gradually to as much as a millimeter away from the edge of the experimental pieces.

The closest use-wear analogs to root-processing traces are those that arise from cutting meat, except that root-processing traces are entirely without a greasy luster. Further research should be directed at using tools for much longer periods of time, at least 2 to 4 hours, so that the traces from root-processing become more distinctive. This would ensure that polish formation passes the "weak" or "generic" polish phase.

Another consideration involves prolonging contact of the stone with the root substrate. Ethnographic graters I examined in the Field Museum of Natural History had never been cleaned of dried, grated cassava, and it would be unlikely for archaeological specimens to have been cleaned immediately after each use. The cassava used here had a very weakly acidic pH of 6, and I would expect little or no chemical change of polish over time given this particular root material. However, since some roots contain alkaloid poisons or other compounds, prolonged contact with the root residue could conceivably alter the use-wear after utilization. (See Plisson and Mauger 1988 for a comprehensive discussion of chemical alteration of wear polishes.) Alkaloid poisons or acids (prussic acid) could perhaps alter the microtraces that develop; however, this has never, to my knowledge, been empirically tested.

Conclusion

Perhaps the most telling aspect of polish produced from working starchy roots is its rather generic appearance. As such, the likelihood for attributing polishes or other use-wear traces on archaeological specimens to root-processing seems possible but remote as the wear traces will likely seem ambiguous.

DeBoer (1975:120) suggests that merely finding evidence

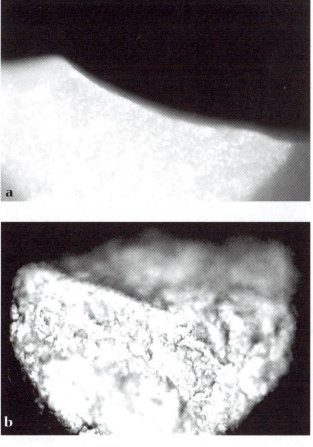

Figure 4.2 Wear traces from processing potatoes for 2 hours: *a*, polish appears as brighter area along edge (100x); *b*, polish appears as edge rounding and slight alteration of surface (200x)

of manioc or root-processing tools is not sufficient basis for assuming cultivation of root crops. I would qualify this assessment if the evidence for root-processing derives from identification of use-related polishes on stone tools. If microwear analysis does suggest root processing as an alternative function for chipped stone tools in an archaeological assemblage this might present a good case for intensive use of the tools. This, in turn, might be a good indicator that root crops were either very intensively used or perhaps even cultivated. This would be expecially true if root-processing tools occurred in a large proportion within an assemblage. In some cases, especially that of yams (*Dioscoreae* spp.), the roots are used in propagation. Unpeeled large roots are cut into pieces and re-rooted. This method of propagation, which is important in Africa and Southeast Asia, certainly implies the use of some sharp cutting implement. Prior to the use of metal implements, stone tools would be the obvious choice for such work, so that use-wear from root cutting might be expected.

The use-wear traces develop slowly, and therefore tools must be used for a considerable period of time before polishes develop. The maximum time of use in my experiment was 2 hours. It is reasonable to assume that people using stone tools for root-processing would work longer than this period of time, and that archaeological pieces would evince better development of microtraces. It may not be assumed that root-processing tools, once given up to this function, could not be reused for something entirely different or that there are not multipurpose household tools that are only occasionally used to process roots.

Attention to microtraces produced from processing roots will be most valuable in areas where roots are known to have been domesticated. In the South American centers for potato and cassava domestication, root-processing traces on stone tools should not be overlooked in archaeological asemblages. In other areas, especially temperate regions where wild roots are small, the overall likelihood of finding root-processing traces would be low. In other words, only a small proportion of plant processing use-wear would be attributable to root-processing. Also, since root-processing traces resemble meat-processing traces to a degree, this could add some uncertainty to identification of wear polishes and damage. Still, it may be useful for wear analysts to be aware that distinctive root-processing traces, however ambiguous and difficult to distinguish, do indeed exist. The potential for identifying root and tuber processing from stone tools will be much higher if residue analysis, which has the potential for locating starch grains, is done routinely as the first step.

Acknowledgments. I would like to thank the following people who aided in this research: Glen Cole at the Field Museum of Natural History, Chicago, for providing access to ethnographic manioc graters in their collections as well as James A. Brown, Mark Aldenderfer, Larry Kimball, and Patricia Anderson for their suggestions.

Chapter 5 ✍

Pulse Agronomy
Traditional Systems and Implications for Early Cultivation

Ann Butler

CURRENT OPINION HOLDS THAT GRAIN LEGUMES, or pulses, were domesticated in association with cereals during the earliest stages of agriculture in Southwest Asia and subsequently in Europe, Central Asia, and North Africa (Zohary 1989a). Recently the mechanisms and sequences of this domestication have been the subject of debate (Kislev 1988b, Ladizinsky 1987a, 1989a; Zohary 1989b, also see chapter 6). In spite of this acknowledgment of the significance of legumes since earliest times and the wealth of literature relating to the agronomic and crop-processing practices associated with pulses, little account seems to have been taken of these in published discussions on the beginnings of agriculture.

Hillman (1973a, 1981) and others have observed the need for more detailed studies of traditional farming practices still surviving today. The value of the analysis of crop processing in furthering our understanding of early crop residues from archaeological sites, and where both legumes and cereals were part of the crop assemblage recorded, has been demonstrated by Jones (1983, 1984) in a detailed study of cultivation in Greece.

This chapter attempts to redress the balance a little further toward the pulses by considering some of the activities employed in traditional systems of legume cultivation in the temperate Old World and discussing some implications.

Role of the Legume Crops
Legumes are cultivated to fulfill a number of economic needs. They are consumed by humans as a green vegetable or as a dried grain. In the green or dried states the whole plant is valuable fodder and can be grazed or fed as hay; the dried seed also may be feed for livestock. Legumes also offer a rich source of nutrients when used as a green manure (Osman et al. 1990). Under consideration here are legumes grown as pulse crops, harvested for the ripe seeds, primarily for human food in temperate areas of Asia and Europe, with some reference to North Africa.

Cultivated Species of Legumes in the Old World
The major species grown as pulses today, lentil, chickpea, broad bean, pea, and to a lesser extent, chickling pea, have been identified in archaeological deposits from early agricultural sites. Less familiar species of *Vicia, Lens,* and *Lathyrus* were also probably cultivated for human food in antiquity; indeed, in certain areas small scale cropping of some of these species still occurs, as exemplified by *Lathyrus ochrus* on Cyprus (Jones 1992), though mainly as a source of animal feed, both as grain and as hay (table 5.1). Today over 70% of pulse production worldwide has been estimated to be used in the form of dry seed for human consumption, rising to 90% in Southeast Asia (Malik et al. 1988).

Pea, lentil, broad bean, and chickpea share the same environment: the farming practices for each species are often quite similar (Buddenhagen and Richards 1988), though *Lathyrus sativus* and lentil are grown in dry areas and broad beans and pea in wetter regions (Summerfield and Roberts 1985).

A variety of cropping patterns has been developed in different regions. The system most readily observed and most familiar to those in Europe and West Asia is that of monocropping, the stages of which will be described briefly first, beginning with the preparation of the seedbed for planting and followed by notes on sowing, harvesting, and

Table 5.1 Species of the tribe Vicieae that have been cultivated

SPECIES	USE
Lathyrus annuus	Grain legume crop
Lathyrus aphaca	Fodder crop, India
Lathyrus cicera	Grain legume crop
Lathyrus clymenum	Grain legume crop, Greece
Lathyrus gorgoni	Animal fodder
Lathyrus hirsutus	Winter pasture, USA
Lathyrus latifolius	Cultigen,Turkey,W.Europe
Lathyrus ochrus	Grain crop, Greece and Turkey
Lathyrus odoratus	Essential oil extract horticulture
Lathyrus pratensis	Pasture
Lathyrus rotundifolius	Horticulture
Lathyrus sativus	Grain legume crop
Lathyrus sylvestris	Forage crop
Lathyrus tingitanus	Cultigen, Mediterranean, Morocco
Lathyrus tuberosus	Edible tubers, W.Asia
Lens culinaris	Grain legume crop
Lens nigricans	Grain legume crop
Pisum sativum elatius	Fodder crop
Pisum sativum sativum arvense	Fodder and grain crop
Pisum sativum satisum sativum	Grain legume crop
Vicia articulata	Grain legume crop, Turkey
Vicia benghalensis	Poultry feed, green manure
Vicia cracca	Cultigen, China and Japan
Vicia ervilia	Grain legume crop
Vicia faba	Grain legume crop
Vicia graminea	Cultigen, S.America
Vicia hirsuta	Fodder crop, India, Soviet States
Vicia johannis	Grain legume crop, Turkey
Vicia michauxii	Spring forage crop, Portugal
Vicia narbonensis	Grain legume crop and forage crop
Vicia pannonica	Grain legume crop, Turkey
Vicia sativa nigra	Green manure
Vicia sativa sativa	Fodder crop, Europe

Sources: Aykroyd and Doughty 1982, Davis 1970, Duke 1981, Jones 1992, Sarpaki and Jones 1990, Summerfield and Roberts 1985, Thulin 1983, Townsend and Guest 1974, Zhukovsky 1924

crop cleaning practices commonly employed in Southeast and West Asia and Southeast Europe. A number of alternatives to monocropping are next considered.

It must be stressed that throughout this introductory chapter many descriptions inevitably are generalizations: much regional variation has been omitted. Emphasis has been placed upon procedures that seem to differ from those commonly associated with cereal production.

Monocropping of Pulses
Preparation of the seedbed

Seedbed preparation consists of removing the remains of the crop of the previous season, weeding, and breaking up the soil surface to make ready for planting. The nature and scheduling of the previous crop, the availability of labor and equipment, the soil type, and the climate govern the treatments involved.

Commonly, cultivation of a legume crop will follow cereals or fallow in rotation. Following a cereal harvest, the stubble is usually grazed. Subsequently, the remaining weeds and stubble are plowed under. Similarly after a fallow period, the land is plowed. Differences are found in the extent of weed cover that tends to result from the two land uses: more weeds tend to grow after a cereal harvest, since the weed species will have shed their seed while the crop was standing prior to harvest and grazing and thus actually be encouraged to proliferate by the practice (Basler 1979).

The timing of the plowing is dependent upon the availability of soil moisture, perhaps the main constraint on legume growing (Papendick et al. 1988). In areas where autumn rains occur, the soil may be tilled shortly after the first rainfall. This tends to stimulate the germination of weeds, which are destroyed during tilling, before the seedlings become established, or they may be removed by hand before they set seed. In western and southern Turkey, for example, the ground for lentils is prepared by one or two plowings and weeding in the late summer, between August and September. The importance of weeding is greater in relation to legume crops than most others: characteristically legume species do not compete well, particularly at the seedling stage. Even for such cultigens as *Vicia faba*, which is robust and erect in habit, yield loss has been estimated at over 50% where weeding has been neglected (Kukula et al. 1985), while lentils can be reduced up to 75% (Muehlbauer et al. 1985). In regions where there is little or no autumn rainfall, the need is to conserve soil moisture. Seedbed preparation consists of up to three shallow plowings, or merely raking to remove the weed cover and break the soil crust. Evaporation may be reduced by leveling the furrows to decrease the surface area; planking (flattening of furrows by a piece of wood) is commonly employed in India (Lal 1985).

In regions where soil erosion is likely, such as in southern Iraq, it is minimized by coarse plowing to leave large clods in the fine silty soils (Charles 1988). In certain areas, it is the practice to reduce all tilling and retain the stubble of the previous harvest to prevent excess erosion from either water or wind (Harris and Pala 1987). Conservation tillage is a concept that is now being applied to many regions in the developing world (Papendick et al. 1988).

Stubble may be left standing in the fields over the winter prior to a spring sowing season such as is the practice in central Anatolia and the Iraqi Plateau, and here this may be burnt off as the initial tilling procedure. Stubble burning may reduce disease but has in fact been found to have little effect on weeds or subsequent seed yield of the crop (Harris and Pala 1987).

Sowing

The sowing time is the result of a compromise between provision of the maximum growing period for the crop and the possible effects of a number of variables: the availability of water, the likelihood of frost, the presence of weed competitors, parasites and predators, as well as temperature fluctuations and day length. Thus where conditions allow, autumn and winter are the preferred seasons for planting in the Old World, but different crop species are influenced differently by the various factors, and separate regimes may be used in the same areas for each species.

Typically, for lentils in the eastern Mediterranean region such as Greece, and coastal Turkey, southern Turkey and India, the sowing time is late October and early November (Jones 1983; Sakar et al. 1988; Lal 1985). In Syria and Jordan, the sowing period may be somewhat later, from December to January (El Matt 1979; Antoun and Quol 1979; Saxena 1979). Soil moisture is the main limiting factor in these areas, where winters are relatively mild. Experimental plantings of lentil have yielded up to 100% better yields in the autumn than in the spring (Sakar et al. 1988). However in the Central Plateau of Turkey, Iran, and Iraq, temperatures fall rapidly in the autumn, and frost damage curtails the establishment of early plant growth; thus lentils are not planted until early spring (Harris 1979).

Chickpeas, by contrast, are normally planted as a spring crop. The main constraint to early planting of this species is the susceptibility to attack by *Ascochyta* blight. Although frost damage is not normally considered a great risk, and despite the fact that delayed sowing carries the possibility of failure due to late rains, in the Mediterranean region and West Asia, the effects of blight are minimized and cropping maximized by planting in the spring (Murinda and Saxena 1985; Pala and Nordblom 1987). Today recently developed blight-resistant lines of chickpea are showing the increases in seed yield possible following winter planting (Reddy and Singh 1985).

Broad bean is another species that often is spring-sown. In Central Asia, in the highland areas, the relatively high water requirement of broad bean demands rainfed conditions found in spring; winter sowings have to be supported by irrigation. In eastern Europe and western Asia, broad bean grown as a pulse is not a major crop (Bond et al. 1985). Egypt is known to be an important center for broad bean growing, but here irrigation is almost invariably practiced.

Peas, being particularly sensitive to high temperature and drought stress, are normally grown in the cool season, where soil moisture is sufficient or there is autumn rainfall (Davies et al. 1985).

The method of sowing varies with the crop species and is dependent upon the size of the seed (Charles 1985). Small-seeded species, the lentils, vetches, *Lathyrus* species, and smaller varieties of pea and chickpea, are broadcast. In western Asia and most of the Indian subcontinent, broadcasting is followed by light plowing; however, this is known to produce irregular stands because of the unevenness of the soil cover. Broadcasting over shallow furrows or on ridges followed by leveling gives a more uniform result.

Sowing may be followed by light plowing or harrowing to cover the seed, but often, as is usual in Bangladesh, seeds may be sown without subsequent burying, in spite of heavy loss to birds (Malik et al. 1988). The usual planting depth varies from 10 cm in Syria (El Matt 1979) to 4 to 5 cm in cooler areas in the Near East (Saxena 1979).

Hand placement, where one or more seeds are placed by hand into prepared holes, on ridges, or along furrows, is the more usual method where seeds are large, as in the bigger pea and chickpea varieties and broad beans (Diekmann and Papazian 1985; Mayouf 1979). For lentil, too, drilled sowings are occasionally carried out in northern Syria and Jordan and give heavier yields than broadcast sowings (Saxena 1981; Snobar et al. 1988).

Fertilizers in the form of manure, or dung cakes, may be incorporated into the ground with the seeds but traditionally are not part of the soil treatment used in legume cultivation (Lahoud et al. 1979; Eser 1979). Where soil moisture is very limited, as in parts of India, seeds may be soaked before planting or planted at a depth where the soil is still damp, which requires plantings from over 10 to 25 cm deep (Papendick et al. 1988; Smithson et al. 1985). Traditionally most warm temperate pulse crops are rainfed (Papendick et al. 1988); irrigation is not a usual practice for legumes (Nassib et al. 1988), although some dry regions, such as the Central Anatolian Plateau, do have a long history of irrigation (Hillman 1990).

The sowing rate giving the optimal plant density and the best yield varies with the location and the species and variety of the cultigen. Figures quoted by Snobar et al. (1988) refer mainly to modern practices used to obtain the best results rather than to traditional sowings. However, these workers reported that farmers in Jordan plant from 50 to 200 kg of seeds per hectare in dryland areas and that the higher weights of seeds are used where the cultivar is larger seeded. Similar figures are found in Syria (El Matt 1979) and Ethiopia (Telaye 1979). Of interest is the conclusion that where the population density of the plants is increased above a certain level, the plants tend to be taller with fewer branches and fewer pods and therefore provide a lower seed yield (Murinda and Saxena 1985).

Broad bean, hand-placed into drills and ridges, is commonly planted at the rate of one or two seeds, 15 to 20 centimeters apart, in two rows per ridge in Egypt, for example, and at a slightly lower density in Cyprus (Snobar et al. 1988).

Harvesting

Hand harvesting of grain legumes is still practiced in much of West Asia, in certain areas of southern Europe, and in Ethiopia. The description given by Jones (1983, 1984) of pulse harvesting techniques on the Cycladic island of Amorgos is similar to those recorded in Turkey and Syria by

Hillman (1984a,b) and observed on Crete and Cyprus and in southeastern Turkey by the author. The legume plants are uprooted by hand or blunt sickle or are cut at low level by sickle or scythe. Weeds are left standing where possible. The cut crop is piled into small heaps regularly distributed across the field, weighed down by stones in windy regions, and left to dry. The drying period varies with the location and prevailing climatic conditions and may last from a few days (Jones 1983) to a few weeks (Lal 1985) or several months. Typically, at this stage the crop retains most or all of the straw and includes some weeds, particularly species that grow in intimate association with the crop, the climbing species, which are often legumes.

The time of harvest varies with the climate and growing period of the cultigen. In southern Turkey, for instance, May is the typical harvest month for lentils, with chickpea somewhat later. The stage at which the crop is cut is finely judged. Shattering of the pods can result in heavy losses of yield when the plants have reached complete maturity (Lal 1985). A compromise must be reached between ripeness (of the majority of the pods and their seeds) and greenness (of most of the plants). The moisture content needs to be about 30% (Haddad et al. 1988) and in lentils around 60% of the pods are golden brown (Erskine 1985) or the leaves are yellow (Lal 1985). In spite of such careful timing, up to a quarter of the yield may be lost through pod shatter.

Records have been made of the work involved in hand pulling pulses. In Syria, for lentil harvesting, between 12 and 20 days' work per hectare is usual (Khayrallah 1981; Diekmann and Papazian 1985). In Jordan, 10 days' work has been noted as sufficient (Haddad 1988). Today the expense of this labor is one of the biggest incentives toward mechanization (Hawtin and Potts 1988; Sakar et al. 1988).

Threshing
Threshing normally takes place near or immediately adjacent to the village on areas of relatively level ground trodden to a hard floor. However, where fields are remote, smaller local floors may be constructed. Today these sometimes have concreted surfaces.

Bundles of the dried crop are carried to the floors using animal transport where available, often ox, donkey, or mule. Movement of the dry material generally takes place at periods of the day when the strongest sun and highest temperatures are least likely, in order to reduce pod shatter and seed loss. The straw and pods are broken up by animal hooves or threshing sledges. Where the harvest is small, or under adverse conditions when processing has to take place under cover, sticks or flails may be employed (Hillman 1981).

Winnowing
Winnowing is carried out by means of a variety of equipment, ranging from hands, where the harvest is very small, to forks,

shovels, fans, or baskets (Jones 1983; Hillman 1981, 1984a). The time taken depends on the size of the harvest and the wind strength. Jones (1983) surprisingly recorded that still days were favored for winnowing because of the greater degree of control that could be exercised over the deposition of the fractions. Usually a steady gust-free breeze is considered optimal, as described by Hillman (1984b) on cereals.

Care is normally taken to retrieve all residues; the value of legume straw and pod by-products as animal feed is very high (Amirshahi 1979). Lentil straw is considered to be of particular value and is fed to the most prized animals (Erskine 1985; Khayrallah 1981). In Syria and Jordan, and other regions where the dry seasons limit the availability of other fodder, lentil residues may actually have more commercial value than the seeds themselves (Muelbauer et al. 1985).

Sieving and cleaning
Crop-sieving processes for pulses have been described in detail by Hillman (1981, 1984a). Large and heavy fractions, the straw nodes and pod fragments, are separated by coarse sieves of mesh sizes that may vary with the crop. For example, one coarse sieve recorded by the author in southern Turkey, with a mesh size of 4 to 5 mm, was routinely used for cleaning both the lentil and chickpea crop. The small weed seeds and other impurities that have separated with the crop may be removed by fine sieving. Hand sorting is a final stage usually carried out immediately prior to processing the grain for food, the cleanings commonly being used as chicken feed (Jones 1983, 1984).

It has been observed that implements connected with legume cultivation are usually the same as those used for cereals, that equipment specialized for processing pulses is not normally used. Plows, drilling tools, sickles, scythes, threshing sledges, winnowing forks and sieves, and animal transport and traction are common to both types of crop.

Similarly, the type of labor is the same: animals are usually driven by men, the operation of specialized equipment is by men; sowing, threshing, and winnowing with larger tools are male work. Females traditionally do the processing that may be carried out by hand, such as hand harvesting, weeding, and grain cleaning, together with the use of the least complicated implements such as sieves and sickles. Thus the techniques of seed agriculture used to be divided approximately evenly between the sexes. However, with the introduction of progressively more mechanization, it has been observed that men are now undertaking an increased proportion of the work (Rassam and Tully 1986).

Described above is the system of monocropping pulses, together with the crop-processing techniques that have been likened by Hillman (1981, 1984a, 1985) to those used for free-threshing cereals. However, other systems have been developed and are practiced today in a number of developing countries, and some of these are considered here that may have had a particular relevance in antiquity.

Multiple Cropping

Certain environments and soils will support more than one cropping per unit of land per season. Where water supplies are sufficient and the growing period prior to harvest is short, yield can be more than doubled in this way.

Legumes, with their soil enriching properties, are particularly suitable as components of these systems (Tiwari 1979). In Ethiopia, lentils are often planted as a second crop immediately after the wheat or barley harvest; *Lathyrus sativus* similarly may follow a summer chickpea crop (Westphal 1974).

In India, following the main summer harvest of maize, sorghum, or jute, the land may be used for lentil cultivation supported by the moisture retained in the soils from the earlier monsoon rains. In the northeast of the Indian subcontinent sometimes a third crop may be planted, although it is usual to apply some irrigation at this stage (Saxena 1981).

These practices represent a variation of the standard monocropping, and this intensification strategy has been considered by Thomas (1983) in his work on agriculture in the third millennium BC in northwest Pakistan.

Mixed Cropping

Mixed cropping systems, where more than one species are grown together in the same plot, are well known today throughout Asia, North Africa, and Europe. Often they are associated with tree crops or the production of annual species as animal fodder. It comes as something of a surprise to some of us in the West to find that there are many regions in the temperate Old World where grain crops for human consumption are grown as components of mixed systems and in which legumes play a major role.

The Indian subcontinent in particular displays a number of alternatives to monoculture involving pulses. Relay planting, known as *utera*, uses the broadcasting of legume seeds into a standing crop of rice in dry paddy. Sowing takes place ten days to three weeks prior to the rice harvest, the legume crop making use of the residual soil moisture from the monsoons, which resists evaporation because of the rice cover. This system is common in India and Nepal where lentil and *Lathyrus sativus* are deemed to be particularly suitable for growing in this way. In northern India, distinctions are made between species most suitable for planting when the rice crop is near to harvest, at which time chickpea is planted, and when the paddy crop is to be left standing for longer, at which time pea and *Lathyrus* are favored (Bharati 1986; Bhattarai et al. 1988; Saxena 1981; Tiwari 1979).

Somewhat similar is the practice of intersowing cereals with legumes in West Asia. In lower Iraq, for example, broad beans and barley are sown together and harvested separately. By careful cutting with a sickle, the barley may be harvested at the green stage up to three times successively before the beans have ripened. The beans are harvested by hand picking of individual pods. The stubble is subsequently grazed (Guest 1930).

In Ethiopia, broad beans and peas are commonly grown in association, and harvesting is timed to the stage when most of the leaves have dropped and the upper pods are yellow, which is when most of the pods are ripe and yet not all have dried, the beans and peas being harvested separately. The crop is cut with sickles and left in the fields to dry in stacks which may be covered with grass for as long as 4 to 6 weeks before being threshed with animal hooves or sticks and winnowed (Telaye 1979; Westphal 1974).

A more complex traditional system of mixed cropping of pulses involves the broadcast sowing of a number of different species in associations that resemble fodder cropping. Such mixed sowing is practiced widely on the Indian subcontinent. The individual species in these complex mixtures grow and ripen at different rates and times and require harvesting by hand picking as each matures. This entails the covering of the same plot a number of times which inevitably results in some loss of yield by treading. The grains are cleaned into separate populations for storage and use (Bharati 1985).

As examples of this system, in India, chickpea may be planted with wheat, barley, linseed, or mustard; broad bean may be intersown with castor, groundnut, or cotton (Tiwari 1979). In Nepal, mixtures of chickpea, lentil, pea, broad bean, and *Lathyrus sativus* are sown with rice, maize, linseed, or mustard in a variety of combinations (Bhattarai et al. 1988). Chickpea and lentil are commonly intercropped with mustard in Bangladesh (Papendick et al. 1988).

It has also been reported that broad bean, pea, and *Lathyrus* are grown mixed with barley in Afghanistan (Wassimi 1979).

The extent of success of mixed cropping of legumes with other species relates to the different growth requirements that each species withdraws from the soil and the degree of competition. Generally legumes compete poorly with species that have large leaf canopies. Yet species such as mustard can act as a supporting medium for plants that climb or sprawl and thus reduce the likelihood of lodging (Saxena 1981). Certain species in association, such as chickpea and mustard, make particularly effective use of the soil moisture, the deeper roots of the legume reaching water that the mustard does not utilize (Bhatterai et al. 1988; Tiwari 1979). The seeding ratios vary; an example of 50:50 by weight for cereals and legume mixtures has been reported by Mirchandani and Misra (1957).

The labor input required in mixed cropping is low for most stages except for harvesting itself, which is highly labor intensive. Traditionally hand harvesting is predominantly women's work (Rassam and Tulley 1986); thus, this method would be favored when the female workforce is large.

Considerations of the Cropping Systems

The range of cropping systems represents responses to different environmental conditions and differing attitudes of the farmers toward their various crops.

As mentioned above, in regions with autumn or winter rains, monocropping of pulses is usual. Where the winters are mild, autumn or winter sowings are practiced, as in the eastern Mediterranean and at the lower altitudes in Turkey and Syria. Where winters are more severe and carry risk of damage to crops from frost and snow, spring-sown monocropping is normal, as seen on the higher ground in central Turkey, Iraq, and Iran.

Where crops are supported on soil moisture retained from rainfall in the summer, mixed cropping for grain harvest is more usual, as seen in Afghanistan, the north of the Indian subcontinent, southern Iraq, and North Africa.

However, mixed cropping is readily observed across all these regions in the temperate Old World, when cultivation is for animal feed. Thus Jones (1983) described, on the Cycladic island of Amorgos, *Vicia sativa* and *Lathyrus sativus* grown separately for feed grain and together as a mixed crop for hay. Broad beans and cereals were commonly grown together as a fodder crop widely across Europe up to the early nineteenth century (Bond 1985). In north central Turkey *Vicia sativa* is sown as green fodder with autumn sown *Triticum durum* (Hillman 1990).

The difference that is most important between mixed cropping for human food and for feed lies in the harvesting and processing rather than the growing. Pulses, as has been described, are gathered, pulled, or cut as individual species when ripe, or nearly so. Crops for feed are commonly pulled or cut as hay in the green to dry stage, in a single operation for the mixed population. The hay is left to dry in the fields, similar to pulses under monocropping, before being transported in bundles for sale.

The possible role of producing animal feed in the development of early agriculture has been examined by Bohrer (1972). She remarks that *Lathyrus sativus* for example, when grown as fodder, can become a famine food by the addition of threshing to separate the grains from the straw residues, but she does not discuss the growing systems.

What does seem to require further thought is whether mixed cropping has played a major role in the development of pulse cultivation, and therefore whether mixed cropping represents more than a regional variation in cropping strategy. In other words, were pulses first cultivated in mixed systems? To start with, it is worthwhile to examine the attitude of the farmers toward pulse growing.

Legumes are seldom grown at their maximum productivity. In spite of their important role in nutrition, the aspect of pulses as crops that is most greatly exploited by the farmer seems to be their characteristic tolerance of relatively adverse growing conditions. Many agricultural systems reflect a priority of attention given to and demanded by cereals, with a minimum of expenditure of input into pulses. Thus, traditionally legumes are grown on marginal soils, often with limited availability of water, with little or no tillage and the addition of no manure. The growing season may be relegated to nonoptimal periods when the ground has been released from competing croppings and when labor and equipment can be diverted from other tasks (Papendick et al. 1988).

In traditional agriculture as practiced today, this attitude of the farmer is difficult to reconcile with the constantly reiterated statements about the significant position of legumes in the repertoire of food plants (Agostini and Khan 1988; Brady 1988; Kishk 1979; Malik et al. 1988; Marsi 1979). However, if such an attitude is itself part of a long tradition in agriculture, it might be a reflection of an adaptation in farming most in sympathy with the natural requirements of the species and a utilization of those species in the most versatile way. The species discussed above are all members of two closely related tribes, the Vicieae and the Cicerae. Characteristically, most members of these tribes are tendrillous and have a sprawling or climbing habit, often being supported on associated vegetation. They disseminate explosively and thus tend to establish diffuse populations. It can be seen therefore that mixed cropping systems can closely reproduce conditions obtaining in the wild. The nodulating root systems typical of the legumes support growth in ground where some other species find insufficient nutrient. Hypogeal germination allows for the development of seedlings under cool conditions with some degree of frost protection. Some species, notably *Lathyrus sativus* and lentil, have a marked tolerance of drought. Generally the members of the Vicieae and Cicerae compete poorly and grow best under conditions that act against strong growth of those plants that might otherwise dominate the habitat. Growing the pulse cultigen on marginal ground may be well tolerated, discriminating against other species and favoring the pulses.

Under the best climatic conditions, and on fertile soils, the harvest from pulse crops may not represent very good yields compared to those from cereals (Sanderson and Roy 1979). However, under poor conditions, pulses can really come into their own. In times of famine, in particular, they can provide a fail-safe source of grain. Together with the value of the seeds for human food, the straw and pod by-product as animal feed is of equal or greater worth. In times of food glut, the green plants can be plowed in and add to the nutrient status of the soil. Thus the pulse crops can be used by the farmer with great versatility under a number of different circumstances, often with a minimum of expense in terms of labor or land treatment.

Implications of Early Cropping Systems on the Initial Development of the Cultigens

The antiquity of mixed cropping is unknown, but it is of interest that most areas that apply such systems for pulses use landraces that have been defined as "traditional cultivars not subject to scientific selection: often a population or a mixture of related genotypes" (Polhill and van der Maesen 1985). These small-seeded varieties can respond with some success to the range of environmental conditions in their particular geographical region and usually show the least modification from the wild progenitors (Erskine 1985; Malik et al. 1988; Telaye 1979; Wassimi 1979).

An important characteristic of the legume taxa is their ability to exploit a wide range of environments (Adams and Pipoly 1980). Genetic diversity and phenotypic plasticity in the wild species are reflected in a great flexibility of response to the requirements of different habitats. The landraces retain much of this ability to adapt.

The cultigens of seed crops that we know today have developed in response to selection favoring the increased control by humans over the dissemination and germination of the plan, and increased seed yield. In the pulses, the most highly developed cultivars have markedly larger seeds, accompanying the generalized gigantism of many of the vegetative parts of the plant and tendencies towards an erect habit and determinate growth, as is most clearly demonstrated by broad bean (*Vicia faba*). The seeds of the landraces, by contrast, are often hard to separate from those of their wild progenitors by their gross morphology, a property that has particular relevance to those attempting to identify and interpret archaeological material.

It is commonly held that the cultivars grown for their seeds have lost their natural means of dissemination and also lost seed dormancy. In pulses within each population it is, however, common to find a range of states of dehiscence and dormancy, albeit reduced relative to that of the wild state.

The work of Ladizinsky (1985a, 1987a) on the genetics of seed dormancy in lentil has shown that the hard seedcoat conferring dormant properties on the seed is governed by a recessive genotype for two loci in *Lens orientalis*, the progenitor of the cultivated lentil, *Lens culinaris*. Similar genetic mechanisms act in the other species. The property of hardness of the seedcoat is conferred by such factors as biochemical constituents, the tannins (Hadas 1976; Marbach and Mayer 1975; Nozzolillo and de Bezada 1984; Vaillancourt et al. 1986), and morphological factors, such as the thickness of the seedcoat (Werker et al. 1979; Butler 1989), that may also be under environmental control (Argel and Humphries 1983; Evenari et al. 1966; Saxena and Hawtin 1981).

Further, dehiscence is not totally lost in cultivated legume species, as can be appreciated from the need for the careful handling of the ripe crop at harvest to prevent pod shattering described above and observed by Ladizinsky (1987a). Again, Ladizinsky (1979, 1985a, 1987a) has investigated the genetics of legume crop species. He has found that a single mutation and also possibly some modifying genes are responsible for preventing pod dehiscence in lentil, pea, and *Lathyrus sativus*, and that other cultivated *Vicia* species, *V. ervilia* and *V. sativa*, show varying amounts of pod shatter because of incomplete modification of seed dispersal, associated with their type of cultivation for hay rather than as pulse crops. Ladizinsky (1987a, 1989a) has concluded that pod indehiscence in pulses is less important than nonbrittle rachis in cereals.

It is apparent that legumes respond to a complex system of factors controlling both dehiscence and seed dormancy and that the loss of these functions in most of the cultivars is by no means complete. Thus perhaps it should be asked whether the selective pressures imposed by cultivation in the past have been of insufficient intensity to cause such a marked modification from the wild state as the total reduction of natural dissemination and dormancy.

Mixed cropping of legumes for their seed as practiced in the north of the Indian subcontinent would seem not to require synchrony of germination of a particular species in the sown mixture nor of ripening; thus, some dormancy would not be a disadvantage. Since harvesting generally is by hand picking as each component reaches the optimal state of maturity, similarly a degree of dehiscence would also be tolerable, and possibly even desirable, as can be the case with species cultivated as fodder crops (Bhalla and Slattery 1984).

Ladizinsky (1987a) has proposed that the pulses underwent modifications of their dormancy mechanism in the course of being gathered by pre-agrarian foragers before the first cultivation and thus differ from cereals. Zohary (1989b, see also chapter 6) conversely argues for the similarity between cereals and pulses as they both came into domestication, that they both must have lost the means of natural dissemination and dormancy by selection during early cultivation. Both workers in these publications seem to limit their considerations to the pulses growing under conditions imposed by monocropping.

Kislev has introduced the idea that pulses were the earliest domesticated plants in the Near East. He reasons that the legumes that are dispersed in small patches and ripen in the spring, a season in the Levant when resource stress is still very high, could have been under pressure from competing predation by animals as well as humans and that this pressure might have led to "experimentation in sowing pulses" (1988b). Kislev suggests that this was taking place before cereal cultivation.

Consideration of the cropping systems described above lends support to the idea of this earliest phase of pulse

Figure 5.1 Winnowing *Lathyrus sativus* in Tigray, Highland Ethiopia

Figure 5.2 A mixture of *Pisum sativum* and *Vicia faba* cultivated and harvested as a single crop in Shewa, Highland Ethiopia

cultivation, but I would suggest that it is possible that the broadcasting of seeds in mixed populations of different species was more than a transitory stage practiced at the earliest phase of cultivation and that it represents a widespread cropping strategy of risk spreading that would probably have existed hand-in-hand with the more intense cropping of a staple seed crop, such as the cereals.

Much is made in the literature of the complementary dietary status of legumes and pulses, particularly in terms of their respective amino acid contents. However, it has been noted by some authors that not all farming communities are aware of the particular food value of their crops (Malik et al. 1988). Thus it seems possible that legumes were first cultivated

for their properties of environmental tolerance and adaptation rather than as a source of particular nutrients.

Conclusions

Conventionally grain legumes and cereals tend to be viewed similarly as monocrops in discussions on early agriculture. Certainly, monocropping of both seed crops is an early tradition, particularly in the context of much of western Asia. However, in the broader geographical regions of the temperate Old World, a wide variety of mixed cropping systems is employed in the production of pulses for human food. These reflect an exploitation of legume crops more for their environmental tolerance and versatility of use than for maximum productivity of grain.

Mixed systems of legume cultivation are ubiquitous throughout Europe and Asia when used in the production of fodder and animal feed.

A portion of the seeds of most pulse cultivars tend to retain some of the character of dehiscence and dormancy of their wild relatives, which while disadvantageous in monocropping may be advantageous for mixed cropping.

These two observations lend support to the suggestion that mixed cropping may have been an important stage in the earliest cultivation of legumes for human food and possibly was practiced at a time when already established staples such as cereals were grown as monocrops.

The considerations of the different cropping systems for pulses discussed above represent initial thoughts on a new approach to pulses in early agriculture.

Much work needs to be done in recording methods of legume cropping for feed as well as food, in growing experiments involving mixed systems as well as monocropping, and in analysis of the effects of cultivating legume species under the different selective pressures that result. The work of Willcox (chapter 11) at Jalès will be an important contribution.

Postscript: 1998

Recently, further ethnographical studies of traditional grain agriculture in the Old World have been made by archaeobotanists, for example in Spain (Peña Chocarro 1995), Syria (Al-Mouayad Al Azem 1991), and Ethiopia (D'Andrea et al. 1997; Butler 1999).

Further observations on harvesting and crop processing

In Highland Ethiopia, ripe pulse crops such as *Lathyrus sativus* are carefully uprooted by hand to yield virtually weed-free harvests (McCann 1995: 62). For pulses and other grain crops, basketry sieves are used in the field as winnowing trays (figure 5.1) and are used in the home to separate the grains from contaminants such as small stones immediately prior to food preparation (Butler 1999).

Mixed cropping

In Highland Ethiopia, varieties of different crop taxa have been developed with synchronous rates of germination and seed maturation. Thus a mixed crop, such as pea with broad bean, which is broadcast sown in one episode, can be harvested together, and even may be processed, prepared for food, and consumed as one (Abate Tedla 1993; Butler observations made from 1993-1997; figure 5.2).

Acknowledgments. Travel to Turkey was funded by a grant from the University of London Central Research Fund. The fieldwork in central and southeast Turkey was supported by facilities supplied by the British Institute of Archaeology at Ankara. The 1996 and 1997 Ethiopian fieldwork was funded by the Social Sciences and Humanities Research Council of Canada. I am grateful to Susan Colledge and Tim Holden for reading the manuscript and for useful discussions together with Michael Charles, and to Gordon Hillman for his encouragement and advice. My thanks to Jennie Brigham for processing the manuscript and to Susan Colledge for her help with the references. The help of ICARDA in supplying much useful literature is acknowledged.

Chapter 6 ❧

Domestication of the Neolithic Near Eastern Crop Assemblage

Daniel Zohary

SOUTHWEST ASIA, EUROPE, AND THE NILE VALLEY are unique today as to the vast extent of their archaeobotanical exploration. In the last 40 years hundreds of Mesolithic and Neolithic sites have been excavated over these territories. Plant remains in many sites have been expertly identified, culturally associated, and radiocarbon-dated. The finds already identified the plants that gave rise to agriculture in this part of the Old World and pointed out (in general terms) where and when they had been taken into cultivation. (For recent reviews see the various chapters in van Zeist et al. [1991] and Zohary and Hopf [1993]).

Parallel progress has been achieved in determining the wild ancestry of Old World crops. The wild progenitors of most of these cultivated plants have now been satisfactorily identified, both by comparative morphology and by genetic analyses. Sound evidence on wild ancestry is already available for all eight members of the Neolithic Near Eastern crop assemblage (table 6.1). Furthermore, comparisons and crosses between the wild types and their cultivated counterparts revealed the evolutionary changes brought about by domestication. They also indicated how these plants could have acquired their adaptations to the new human-made environment. As a result of these achievements, Southwest Asia, Europe, and Egypt emerge as the first major geographic area in which the combined evidence from archaeology and the living plants allows a modern synthesis of crop plant evolution. The rich archaeobotanical documentation established the following facts:

- Three cereals, emmer wheat *Triticum turgidum* subsp. *diccocum*, barley *Hordeum vulgare,* and einkorn wheat *Triticum monococum* (and in this order of importance) were the main crops of the Pre-Pottery Neolithic B (PPNB) farming villages that appeared in the Near East

Table 6.1 Eight founder crops of Neolithic agriculture in the Near East and the wild progenitors from which these crops have been derived*

CROP	SPECIES NAME	WILD PROGENITOR	SPECIES NAME
Emmer wheat	*Triticum turgidum* subsp. *dicoccum*	Wild emmer	*Triticum dicoccoides*
Einkorn wheat	*Triticum monococcum*	Wild eikorn	*Triticum boeoticum*
Barley	*Hordeum vulgare*	Wild barley	*Hordeum spontaneum*
Lentil	*Lens culinaris*	Wild lentil	*Lens orientalis*
Pea	*Pisum sativum*	Wild pea	*Pisum humile*
Chickpea	*Cicer arietinum*	Wild chickpea	*Cicer reticulatum*
Bitter vetch	*Vicia ervilia*	Wild bitter vetch	*Vicia ervilia*
Flax	*Linum usitatissimum*	Wild flax	*Linum bienne*

* According to the rules of botanical nomenclature, once the wild progenitor of a cultivated plant is soundly identified, it should not be ranked as an independent species but considered as the wild race (subspecies) of the crop. This is because the wild type and the cultivated derivative are not yet reproductively fully isolated from one another and are usually interconnected genetically. As the progenitors of the eight Near Eastern founder crops are now satisfactorily identified. this rule should be applied to them. However, traditions die hard. Most archaeobotanists still refer to the wild progenitors by their traditional binomial names. To avoid confusion, they are referred to in this manner in this chapter also.

arc at the end of the eighth millennium bc and at the seventh millennium BC (uncalibrated ^{14}C time). Fortunately, in all three grasses the charred remains retrieved from the archaeological digs often retain diagnostic morphological signs indicating whether the excavated material represents wild or domestic forms. The telltale feature (Zohary 1969, Harlan et al. 1973, Hillman and Davies 1990a, Nesbitt and Samuel 1996) is whether the ears are brittle (in wild forms) or nonbrittle (in domestic forms). In wild emmer and wild einkorn the abscission scars are smooth, while in domestic forms they are distinctively rough. Fortunately in their spikelet forks, the upper scar is usually well preserved, making the forks (which are retrieved mainly by flotation) a key element for deciding whether one is confronted with wild or cultivated material. As argued by van Zeist and de Roller (1991–1992) the numerous spikelet forks (all with rough scars) retrieved from aceramic (7200 BC onwards) Çayönü provide convincing evidence that then and there wheat cultivation was practiced. In barley we have a parallel situation. In nonbrittle forms a small part of the adjacent internode frequently remains adhering to the triplet's upper node ("domesticated type" in the sense used in Kislev 1997). However, discrimination between wild and tame forms is complicated by the fact that also in wild barley the 1 to 2 basal triplets (at the bottom of the ear) do not shatter easily, and when entire ears are collected from the wild and threshed, a small fraction of basal triplets with such rachis breakage signs could "contaminate" the brittle remains of wild populations. Therefore a claim for domestication in barley (and also in wheats) should not be based on the presence of a small proportion of domesticated-type scars but on common occurrence of these elements. Gordon Hillman maintains that basal spikelets/triplets can be recognized morphologically in wild emmer, einkorn, and barley. Very likely, it will be possible to exclude such basal spikelets/triplets in future considerations. Another sign of domestication is the appearance of relatively plump seeds (van Zeist and Bakker-Heeres 1982). Compared with the scars, however, seed shape is a much less reliable indication for domestication.

• The domestication of wheats and barley apparently went hand in hand with the introduction into cultivation of additional plants. The majority of the archaeobotanically well explored Pre-Pottery Neolithic B sites in the Near East also yielded remains of lentil *Lens culinaris*, pea *Pisum sativum* and flax *Linum usitatissimum*. In several sites chickpea *Cicer arietinum* and bitter vetch *Vicia ervilia* are present as well (figure 6.1). Quantitatively all these five plants are less common than the cereals. Furthermore, their early remains usually lack diagnostic marks allowing discrimination between cultivated forms and material collected from the wild. As argued later, however, some direct clues and/or reasonable circumstantial evidence strongly suggest that lentil, pea, flax, chickpea, and bitter vetch were taken into cultivation together with the cereals or a short time later.

• The evidence for early domestication of additional Near Eastern plants is much less convincing. A find from PPNB Yiftah'el, Israel (Kislev 1985) hints that broad bean *Vicia faba* might also belong to the early Neolithic Near Eastern crop assemblage. Except for this single find of numerous charred seeds, there are no other rich records of broad bean from the seventh–sixth millennia bc, and the wild progenitor of this pulse has yet to be discovered. Therefore, more definitive conclusions about the time and place of *V. faba* domestication may be reached only when additional archaeological evidence is uncovered and/or when the wild ancestor of the crop is discovered. Grass pea *Lathyrus sativa* too could have been a Neolithic domesticant (see reviews by Kislev 1989a; Miller 1991; Zohary and Hopf 1993:115). Yet the bulk of Neolithic grass pea finds does not come from the Near East but from sixth and fifth millennia sites in Greece and Bulgaria.

• The plant remains retrieved from the Near Eastern PPNB sites reveal another important feature: As a rule, not a single crop but a combination of cereals, pulses, and flax seem to be the elements of food production in each of these early farming villages; from the middle of the seventh millennium onward sheep and goats were added as well. Moreover, the assemblage of the crops is basically the same all over the Near East "nuclear area" (see figure 6.1). In other words, a common "package" of crops and domestic animals characterizes the emergence of early Neolithic agriculture in the Near East arc.

• The subsequent expansion of Neolithic agriculture to Europe, central Asia, and the Nile Valley was based upon this Near Eastern crop assemblage. The crops that started food production in the Near East "nuclear area" also initiated agriculture all over these vast territories. (For a summary of the available documentation on their spread, consult the various regional papers in van Zeist et al. [1991] and Zohary and Hopf 1993: 230–233).

Now that the Neolithic Near Eastern crop assemblage is already fairly well defined and the wild progenitors satisfactorily identified, one is able to compare and contrast the wild and cultivated forms in various ways. This chapter

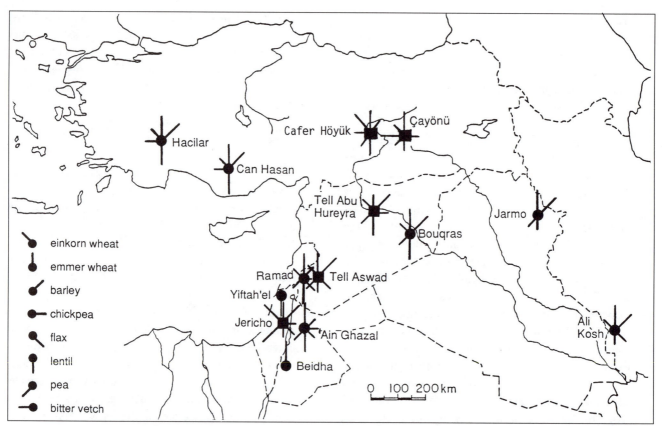

Figure 6.1 Crop assemblage in the early Neolithic farming villages in the Near East before 6000 BC (uncalibrated radiocarbon dates). Square signs represent the earliest sites, with deposits containing remains of domestic wheats (and probably also other founder crops) dated before 7000 BC. Round site signs represent somewhat later PPNB sites dated to the seventh millenium BC. A short whisker indicates that the crop is relatively rare and a long whisker that it is relatively common among the plant remains. *Adapted from Zohary and Hopf 1993: 37*

focuses on the time of domestication (that is, what are the earliest archaeobotanical signs for the cultivation of the Near East founder crops?), patterns of evolution under domestication (that is, how similar [or how different] are the evolutionary trends in the various crops, which belong botanically to three different families—grasses, legumes, the flax family?); and the mode of domestication (that is, was it monophyletic or polyphyletic?). In other words, was each of the founder crops taken into cultivation only once (or very few times) or, alternatively, has the wild progenitor been independently introduced into cultivation many times and in different places?

First Signs of Domestication
Emmer wheat

The earliest signs of emmer cultivation come from Tell Aswad, 25 km southeast of Damascus (van Zeist and Bakker-Heeres 1982). Here morphologically definable plump-seeded *dicoccum* remains appear in the lowest habitation level Ia (7800–7600 BC) and continue to occur in the two upper phases: Ib (7600–7300 BC) and II (6925–6600 BC). Significantly no narrow *dicoccoides*-like grains were retrieved from Tell Aswad. Moreover, the climate today in the rain-shadowed Damascus basin is far too dry for wild wheat. Very probably it was arid also 10,000

years ago. As van Zeist and Bakker-Heeres emphasized, the continuous presence of plump morphologically discernible *dicoccum* grains, the total absence (from the very start) of *dicoccoides*-like material, and the extreme dryness (less than 200 mm annual rainfall) suggest that emmer wheat was introduced into the Damascus basin—already as a domesticated cereal—not later than 7800–7600 BC. From 7500 BC onward, kernels corresponding morphologically to *dicoccum* start to appear also in Tell Abu Hureyra, Northeastern Syria (Hillman 1975; Hillman et al. 1989), and Jericho (Hopf 1983). Both spikelet forks and plump kernels were retrieved from the contemporaneous PPNB at Cafer Höyük (de Moulins 1994) and Çayönü (van Zeist and de Roller 1991-1992). Most convincing are the numerous forks retrieved (by flotation) from the latter site—all showing the telltale rough scar characteristic of nonbrittle cultivated emmer wheat. All these finds seem to indicate that at the middle of the eighth millennium BC emmer cultivation was well underway in the Levant. But as Nesbitt and Samuel (1996) have warned, the emmer remains retrieved from eighth millennium BC contexts are still few and their quality of preservation (and dating) is frequently far from ideal. Thus, because of soil salinity, glume forks did not persist in Tell Abu Hureyra (Gordon Hillman, pers. comm.).

The exact separation line between collection and cultivation is still hard to draw.

Barley

In an earlier published report of this study, the author concluded that the first definite signs of barley domestication appear in two Pre-Pottery Neolithic A sites, namely Netiv Hagdud and Gilgal, in the Jordan Valley. The basis for this conclusion was the Kislev et al. (1986) report on the presence of up to 10–11% nonbrittle barley triplets in samples obtained from Netiv Hagdud. However, in a much more comprehensive examination of the plant remains retrieved from this site, Kislev (1997) found that the frequency of the "domestication-type" barley remains was, in fact, much lower (only 4%). Such lower frequency of rachis breakage (mixed among a mass of brittle remains) does not necessarily signal domestication. It could also be the outcome of collection of *Hordeum spontaneum* from the wild—if entire ears (containing the much less brittle 1 or 2 basal triplets) were harvested. Therefore one has to conclude that there are not yet any convincing signs of domesticated barley in early eighth millennium BC contexts, and the date of barley domestication in the Near East has to be shifted forward. Reliable indications appear only in PPNB sites more or less at the end of the eighth millennium BC and onward. Other reports of nonbrittle remains in Near Eastern PPNB sites need quantitative reevaluation (particularly when only few nonbrittle elements were identified) and, following Gordon Hillman's suggestion, morphological reexamination to detect and exclude basal triplets. However, as Kislev (1997) stresses, the appearance of naked and/or six-rowed barley forms in Phase II East in Tell Aswad (van Zeist and Bakker-Heeres 1982) and in PPNB Tell Abu Hureyra (Hillman 1975; Hillman et al. 1989) is a sure sign that then and there barley was already under domestication.

Einkorn wheat

Also in einkorn wheat the oldest definite signs of cultivation come (to date) from the second half of the eighth millennium BC. More numerous remains appear in PPNB contexts dated to the end of the eighth millennium BC and the seventh millennium BC (see review by Nesbitt and Samuel 1996: Table 2). It is noteworthy that at Tell Aswad (van Zeist and Bakker-Heeres 1982) there are no signs of einkorn wheat in phase I, yet plump kernels corresponding morphologically to cultivated einkorn appear in this site in phase II (seventh millennium BC). A key find comes from PPNB (7300–6500 BC) Jericho (Hopf 1983). This site is located far away from the natural range of wild einkorn, thus indicating that einkorn was introduced into Jericho already as a domesticated cereal, and that in the more northern parts of the Near Eastern arc, einkorn cultivation must have started earlier. Einkorn spikelet forks (with diagnostic rough scars)

occur also in late eighth millennium BC Çayönü (van Zeist and de Roller 1991–1922).

Lentil, pea, and flax

In addition to wheats and barley, the majority of the early Neolithic sites in the Near East also contain charred seed of lentil, pea, and flax (figure 6.1 and reviews by Miller 1991; Zohary and Hopf 1993). Yet it is not easy to determine whether these remains represent cultivated forms or material collected from the wild. Usually the remains retrieved are few in number and lack diagnostic features needed to identify domestication. Increase in seed size is the most reliable trait. However, this change was slow and gradual. Large seeds, significantly different from the wild norms appear rather late and provide only a delayed confirmation. Assessment of the beginning of cultivation of lentil, pea, and flax depends more on circumstantial evidence than on direct morphological indications. Yet for all three plants, some clues are available.

Lentil seed dimensions in the seventh millennium BC contexts are not very different (2.5–3.0 mm) from those of the wild progenitor *Lens orientalis*. The proposition that lentil was taken into cultivation together with wheats and barley or very soon afterward (Zohary and Hopf 1973) relies on circumstantial evidence: its association with cultivation of cereals and the fact that when Near Eastern Neolithic agriculture spread to Europe (sixth millennium BC), lentil was part of it. This assumption received further support when an exceptionally large hoard of lentils was uncovered at 6800 BC PPNB Yifah'el, (Garfinkel et al. 1988). The sheer quantity of the find (around 1,400,000 seeds) suggests cultivation. It is hard to imagine that such a volume could be collected from wild plants, particularly in the neighborhood of the site where wild lentils are very sparse. The occasional occurrence of *Galium tricornutum* mericarps among the lentil seed in Yiftah'el is also suggestive. This *Galium* is a weed infesting traditional lentil cultivation. Since it does not grow together with lentil in wild environments, its presence also indicates cultivation.

Also for pea some direct evidence is available. It comes from examination of seed coat texture. In most charred remains this part of the seed does not survive, although occasionally segments of seed coats remain intact. They are indicative since wild peas have seed with a rough surface, while under domestication, smooth coats evolved. Significantly the remains from ca. 6500 BC Çayönü (van Zeist 1972) and 5850 to 5600 BC Çatal Hüyük (Helbaek 1964) already show the smooth coat texture characteristic of the domestic varieties. This is a clear sign of domestication.

Similar to lentil, the increase in seed size in flax provided only a delayed confirmation. The earliest signs of seed size increase come from 6250 to 5950 BC Tell Ramad, Syria (van Zeist and Bakker-Heeres 1982). In addition, support for early cultivation of flax comes from the PPNB cave in Nahal

Hemar near the Dead Sea. Here pieces of desiccated, exquisitely woven linen were discovered and radiocarbon dated to the second half of the seventh millennium BC (Schick 1988). It is hard to imagine that such sophisticated use was based on collection of the (rather rare) wild progenitor.

Chickpea and bitter vetch

The remains of these two pulses lack diagnostic marks for determining domestication. Moreover, the appearance of these two crops in early Neolithic Near Eastern sites is more sporadic than that of lentil or pea. In chickpea the seeds retrieved from 6500 BC Jericho (Hopf 1983) or from contemporary 'Ain Ghazal (Rollefson et al. 1985) could indicate cultivation, since both sites are situated far away from the distribution range of the wild progenitor (*Cicer reticulatum* is endemic to South-East Turkey). The same argument applies to bitter vetch. Charred seed of this pulse were recovered in several aceramic Neolithic sites in Southern Turkey (for review consult Zohary and Hopf 1993: 111). These sites lie within the distribution area of the wild progenitor, however, and there is no way to decide whether they came from wild or cultivated plants. Remains of bitter vetch occur also outside the range of wild bitter vetch—in several Neolithic farming villages in Greece and Bulgaria dated to the sixth and the early fifth millennia BC. These indicate that when agriculture spread to Greece, bitter vetch was part of the introduced crop assemblage. The beginning of its cultivation should have occurred earlier.

In summary, the archaeobotanical evidence shows that emmer wheat, barley, einkorn wheat, lentil, pea, and flax as well as chickpea and bitter vetch were the founder crops of Neolithic agriculture in the Near East. Both direct and circumstantial evidence indicate that all these grains crops were taken into cultivation more or less at the same time. In emmer (the most important crop in this package)—and to a lesser extent in einkorn—definite signs of cultivation already appear in the second half of the eighth millennium BC. All the other six founder plants were very probably under cultivation by 7000 BC. The fact that in the second half of the thirteenth millennium BC signs of emmer cultivation extend from southeast Turkey to the Jordan Valley (figure 6.1) indicates that cultivation of this cereal started significantly earlier.

Changes Under Domestication

When the wild progenitors and the cultivated derivatives of the eight Neolithic founder crops (table 6.1) are compared, the overall impression is not of wide differences but rather of close similarities (Zohary 1989b). All these grains crops seem to have been taken into cultivation in the same area (the Near Eastern "arc") and more or less at the same time. All were derived from annual, predominately self-pollinated wild progenitors. Consequently the genetic variation in both the wild ancestors and their cultivated counterparts is structured in the form of numerous true breeding lines. More important,

all eight crops—when compared with their wild ancestors—exhibit similar changes under domestication. The key characters showing such parallel evolution are the following.

Breakdown of the wild mode of seed dispersal

The most conspicuous change, it causes the retention of the ripe seeds on the mother plant. (The seeds "wait" for the harvester.) In wheats and barley (Zohary 1969; Harlan et al. 1973) the shift is from brittle to nonbrittle spikes. In pulses (Zohary 1989b) the change is from dehiscent to nondehiscent pods. In flax a splitting capsule changed into a nonsplitting one. Significantly, in emmer, einkorn, barley, lentil, and pea, and probably also in the three remaining founder crops, this shift is brought about by mutation in a single major gene or, more rarely, by mutations in two complementary genes.

Loss of the wild-type regulation of germination

Delayed and uneven germination is an essential survival strategy for most Mediterranean annual plants, including the wild ancestors of all eight near Eastern crops. In the wild they all use seed dormancy devices to spread germination over a span of time. Wild pulses show the most extreme delays. Under domestication all eight crops lost the wild-type dormancy devices and acquired full and immediate germination.

Increase in seed size

This too is a conspicuous development under domestication. The increase is most conspicuous in pulses and in flax. In cereals the gain was achieved mainly by evolving plumper seed.

Increase of yield potential

Under domestication, this was achieved by addition of extra fertile flowers, increasing the size or number of inflorescences, and so forth.

Changes in the plant habit

Development of relatively erect or more robust forms adapted to monoculture in the cultivated field also exhibiting uniform ripening of their seed or fruit.

As already argued by several workers (Darlington 1963; Zohary 1969, 1984; Harlan et al. 1973; Hammer 1984; Hillman and Davies 1990a), the evolution of these traits under domestication need not necessarily be the outcome of selection consciously carried out by the cultivator. Instead, the development of these traits (fully for 1, 2, and 5; partly for 3 and 4) can be best explained by assuming the operation of unconscious or automatic selection (for a review, see Heiser 1988). In other words, the development of these traits in the cultivated plants is, to a great extent, an automatic response to their introduction into the new system of tilling, sowing, and reaping. The similarities exhibited by all eight Near Eastern crops reflect their introduction into similar systems of cultivation.

Information is already available on the genetic nature of some of these changes under domestication. Best studied is the loss of the wild mode of seed dispersal. In all these Near Eastern crops the genetic basis for the breakdown of this wild-type adaptation is simple. It is brought about by mutation in a single gene or, more rarely, by two complementary mutations. With such genetic control, the shift to the retention of the seed on the mother plant could evolve quickly. How quickly depends on the rate of appearance of spontaneous mutations in these genes and the size of the initial cultivated populations. After the appearance of a given mutation, the establishment of mutant lines (by unconscious selection) could take place in only several decades of years (Hillman and Davies 1990a), because all these plants are predominantly self-pollinated. Because of this pollination system, selection could have been equally effective in both recessive and dominant mutations. In other words, the critical time element for the breakdown, at the start of cultivation, of the wild mode of seed dispersal was the time it took for the mutation to be induced.

Monophyletic vs. Polyphyletic Domestication

For each of the eight Near Eastern Neolithic crops (table 6.1) the question can be asked: Was its wild progenitor taken into cultivation only once? If so, the crop is a product of a single domestication event and monophyletic evolution. Alternatively, the wild progenitor could have been introduced into cultivation numerous times and in different places. If this is the case, one is faced with multiple events of domestication and with polyphyletic evolution of the crop.

Discriminating between these two types of origin can be of considerable help when one wishes to reconstruct the early history of cultivated plants. It has extra significance when applied to key crops known to have founded agriculture in a given region. If the mode of origin of such crops is elucidated, it can help to answer the basic question: how did agriculture begin in the Near East?

Theoretical considerations

As suggested by Zohary (1996) the following genetic tests and comparisons between crops and their closely related wild relatives can provide clues for discriminating between monophyletic and polyphyletic origins:

Founder effects. Founder effects, affecting genetic variation, are expected to occur when only a small sample of individuals are separated from their parental population to start a new population in a new place. Due to sampling, only a limited fraction of the total genetic variation present in the original population will enter the new one. Such effects are expected to have played a role also in domestication, because at any site of domestication only a small "slice" of the total genetic variation present in the wild progenitor will be introduced

into cultivation. Therefore, the richer is the genetic polymorphism in the wild progenitor and the poorer its representation in derivatives under domestication, the stronger is the suspicion that the crop concerned is a product of a single or very few events of domestication. Unambiguous are situations in which the wild background contains several distinct genetic variants, while under domestication we find only one of these types. Such uniformity among the cultivars, particularly if it repeats itself in different genes, strongly suggests monophyletic origin. Attractive are situations where the wild progenitor varies spatially and can be subdivided into distinct geographic races, each with its specific isozymes or DNA fingerprinting. In such cases the comparisons can pinpoint also the place of origin. In contrast, when the crop displays a large proportion of the genetic polymorphism which occurs in the wild, chances are that the wild ancestor was introduced into cultivation multiple times. Yet one should realize that such an interpretation is not always error-free. Secondary hybridization (after domestication) between the cultivars and their wild progenitor could also enrich the variability in the crop and blur the original founder effect patterns of variation.

Domestication traits. Clues for discriminating between single and multiple domestications can also be obtained by examining the genetic basis of domestication traits, that is, traits which are disadvantageous under wild conditions but which were automatically and promptly selected for once the wild plants were introduced into cultivation. Conspicuous changes of this kind are: (i) the establishment of nonbrittle ears (in the wheats and barley) and nondehiscent pods (in the pulses) and (ii) the loss of the wild-type germination inhibitions. As argued by Zohary (1996), the potential for the development of a given domestication trait is frequently found not in a single gene-locus but rather in several genes found in the crop's genome. Mutations in different genes can each bring about similar or "parallel" changes. Therefore, if in all cultivars in a given crop a domestication trait (such as nonbrittle ears) is found to be controlled by the same major gene (or the same combination of genes), the uniformity suggests a single origin. In contrast, when in different cultivars (or groups of cultivars) the domestication trait is governed by different (nonallelic) mutations, one should suspect multiple origins.

An obvious advantage of using domestication traits as indicators for discrimination between monophyletic and polyphyletic origins is that such traits evolved only under cultivation. They are absent in the wild progenitor. Therefore such analysis is free from "noises" of secondary hybridization (between the crop and its wild relatives), a problem that can plague founder effect assessments.

Species diversity. The rationale used in assessing founder effects can also be applied to species diversity. If the area of origin harbors not only the wild progenitor of a given crop but also several other closely related and equally attractive wild species, the question can be asked: how many of these wild species have derivatives under cultivation? Situations where the wild background contains several similar attractive candidates while in cultivation one finds the derivatives of only one of them suggest single or very few events of domestication. Of special significance are sibling species, that is, taxa that are morphologically almost indistinguishable from one another; yet, cytogenetic tests reveal that they are effectively reproductively isolated from one another by cross-incompatibility, hybrid inviability, or hybrid sterility barriers. For the present considerations, sibling species are even more reliable indicators than ordinary species. Because they are so similar morphologically, chances are that they would have been picked up for cultivation at random.

Available evidence

The following information is already available for assessing the mode of origin of the crops that started Neolithic agriculture in the Near East.

Founder effects revealed by chromosome polymorphism. Rich chromosomal polymorphism has been detected in the wild lentil *Lens orientalis*. Fifteen Near Eastern collections of this progenitor were tested cytogenetically (Ladizinsky et al. 1984) and found to represent six distinct chromosome races. Six accessions contained the "standard" karyotype. The other nine differed from this chromosome type (and frequently also from one another) by one or two reciprocal translocations. (For information on their geographic distribution see Zohary 1996: Fig. 9.2). In contrast, the cultivated lentil *L. culinaris* is chromosomally uniform; its karyotype was found to be identical with the "standard" chromosome arrangement in wild *orientalis*. As already argued by Zohary (1996), the chromosomal uniformity in the cultivars suggests that this Near Eastern pulse was domesticated only once or very few times.

Cytogenetic tests have also revealed (Ben-Ze'ev and Zohary 1973) that the wild progenitor of the cultivated pea, *Pisum humile*, is chromosomally polymorphic, although less than the highly variable wild lentil. Six collections of this wild pea have been tested, and they were found to fall into two chromosomal races. Chromosomes in two samples, one from the Golan in northern Israel and the other from central Turkey, were found to be identical to the "standard" karyotype characteristic of almost all pea cultivars. Four other accessions, obtained from southern and central Israel, differed from this karyotype by a single (and the same) reciprocal translocation. Compared to lentil, the data available on pea are much more fragmentary, yet they also point to a single origin.

Founder effects revealed by DNA polymorphism. Palmer and his associates (1985) found that the wild forms of *Pisum sativum* are polymorphic in their chloroplast DNA (cpDNA). Significantly, the cpDNA pattern characteristic of the cultivars was found in the same two accessions of wild *P. humile* which were found to contain (Ben-Ze'ev and Zohary 1973) the "standard" karyotype. Admittedly the number of the wild *humile* collections tested is insufficient. Yet the results hint again to a single origin.

Similarly Clegg et al. (1984) examined cpDNA variation in barley *Hordeum vulgare*, testing and comparing 11 accessions of wild barley *H. spontaneum* with 9 accessions of cultivated barley. They found that wild spontaneum plants comprised three chloroplast DNA lineages, while only one of these lineages was present in the cultivated material. These finds were later confirmed by the comprehensive tests made by Neale et al. (1988). A much larger sample of wild barley (245 accessions from 25 populations in Israel and 5 populations in Iran) was examined, together with a very representative collection (62 accessions) of cultivated barley (*vulgare, distichum, deficiens,* and *irregulare* forms). The three lineages (---), (--+), and (++-) first detected by Clegg et al. (1984) in wild H. spontaneum were represented in the wild samples tested by them. In fact, some of the wild barley populations contained two or even three chloroplast types. In contrast, with only two exceptions, all the cultivated material tested was uniform and belonged to the (---) chloroplast family. Such results suggest a single or very few events of domestication.

Recently Heun et al. (1997) analyzed DNA obtained from 68 representative lines of cultivated einkorn and 268 lines of wild einkorn. The latter originated both from the Near East "fertile crescent" (94 samples) and from other parts of the distribution area of this wild wheat (74 samples). Among the wild einkorn lines tested, a group of 11 lines which came from the Karakadağ range in southeast Turkey was distinctively separated from all other wild einkorn lines; and genetically most similar to the tested cultivated einkorn lines—indicating that they belong to the wild source from which the crop could have evolved. The scale of the tests and the resolution power of the amplified fragment length polymorphism DNA analysis make this work very reliable. The data obtained strongly support the assumption of monophyletic origin of cultivated einkorn wheat. They also pinpoint the Karakadağ mountain range as the place of origin of this crop.

Evidence from domestication traits: The shift from brittle to nonbrittle ears or from dehiscent to nondehiscent pods is the easiest to spot and the best studied domestication trait. In emmer wheat (Love and Craig 1924), einkorn wheat (Sharma and Waines 1980), barley (Takahashi 1964, 1972), pea (Zohary, unpublished data), and lentil (Ladizinsky 1985a), crosses between the wild progenitors and the crops have shown that in any tested cultivar the shift is controlled by a recessive mutation in a single major gene or (more rarely) by a joint effect of two complementary genes. In all these crops, breeders have also performed numerous crosses between cultivars. Except for barley, none of these within-crop crosses (which constitute tests for allelism) have been reported to produce shattering or dehiscent F1 hybrids or F2 segregants. Such results indicate that within each crop (emmer wheat, einkorn wheat, pea, and lentil) the same gene (or combination of two genes) is responsible for the breakdown of the wild-type adaptation. They therefore point to a monophyletic origin. Only in barley have crosses between some nonbrittle cultivars result in F1 hybrids exhibiting wild-type brittle ears—indicating the presence (under domestication) of recessive mutations in two independent, nonallelic, genes: bt1 and bt2 (Takahashi 1964, 1972).

A second common development under domestication is the loss of the wild-type inhibition of germination. This physiological trait lends itself to an easy examination in several of the Near Eastern pulses because in these crops it is associated with changes in seed-coat morphology (thicker, harder, impermeable testa in the wild forms; thinner, more permeable testa in the cultivars). A well studied case is the pea (Werker et al. 1979, Butler 1989). In some of these pulses also the genetic control of this trait has been worked out. Thus in lentil, crosses between cultivars and wild *orientalis* showed that the shift from thick to thin testa is governed by a single recessive mutation (Ladizinsky 1985a). Also in the pea and the chickpea this change seems to be controlled by a single major gene, or by a combination of two complementary genes. Breeders have already carried out numerous inter-varietal crosses in lentil, pea, and chickpea. Significantly, there are no reports on appearance of nonallelic interactions (wild-type seed coat) among the F1 or F2 hybrid derivatives in such crosses. This suggests a uniform genetic control of the breakdown (under domestication) of wild-type seed dormancy in each of these three pulses, and again supports a single origin.

Evidence from species diversity: Pea, lentil, chickpea, and wheats are each represented in the Near East not only by their wild progenitor but also by several additional closely related species that are very similar to the wild ancestor.

The genus *Pisum* contains not only *P. humile* and *P. elatius* (considered to be the wild stock from which the crop has been derived) but also wild *P. fulvum*. All these wild peas thrive in the Near East (Zohary 1996: 149). Also *P. fulvum* is an annual selfer, with sweet pods and tasty seeds. It is as productive and as attractive as the other two wild peas. Yet there are no signs that it has been taken into cultivation.

The genus *Lens* comprises four wild species: *L. orientalis*, *L. odemensis*, *L. ervoides*, and *L. nigricans*. All are annual selfers with more or less the same habit and similar lenticular seeds. Yet only one wild-type (*L. orientalis*) has been taken into cultivation, even though in the Mediterranean belt of the Levant and in southwest Turkey *L. ervoides* and *L.*

odemensis occur as well (see map in Zohary 1996: 150), and that the fourth wild lentil, *L. nigricans*, (which is distributed mainly over the central and western parts of the Mediterranean basin) also extends to western Turkey.

Five taxonomically closely related wild chickpeas, namely *Cicer reticulatum*, *C. echinospermum*, *C. judaicum*, *C. pinnatifidum*, and *C. bijugum*, are native to the Near East (see map in Zohary 1996: 151). Again all are selfers, and all have similar growth habit and taste. All have been placed (together with the crop) in series *Arietina* section *Monocicer* of the genus *Cicer* (van der Maesen 1972, 1987). Yet only *Cicer reticulatum* (which occurs only in southeast Turkey) has been taken into cultivation.

Evidence from sibling species: Perhaps the most indicative information comes from the wheats, *Triticum*, where we are faced by two pairs of sibling species.

Two wild tetraploid sibling wheats are native to the Near East: (i) Wild emmer wheat *Triticum dicoccoides* (genomic constitution: AABB) which is fully inter-fertile and genomically homologous with cultivated emmer, durum and other tetraploid wheat cultivars grouped in *T. turgidum*. (ii) Wild Timopheev's wheat *T. araraticum* (genomic constitution: AAGG) which is inter-sterile with the first wild-type (as well as with all *T. turgidum* cultivars). Wild Timopheev's wheat is inter-fertile and genomically homologous only with tetraploid *T. timopheevii*, a half-weed-half-cultivated wheat confined to a small area in the Republic of Georgia. It is almost impossible to distinguish morphologically between wild *dicoccoides* and wild *araraticum* wheats. However, extensive cytogenetic tests have already clarified the distribution of these two sibling species. Both occur sympatrically in the central and eastern parts of the near East "arc" (Zohary and Hopf 1993: Map 3). In addition, *dicoccoides* thrives alone in the south Levant, while *araraticum* extends to Transcaucasia. Significantly, in the extensive area in which these two wild wheats overlap, *araraticum* seems to be as common as (or even more common than) *dicoccoides*. Yet in spite of this extensive sympatry, only the AABB chromosome sets of wild *dicoccoides* are found in the thousands of the tetraploid *turgidum* wheat cultivars (as well as in the hexaploid AABBDD bread wheats). There are almost no cultivated derivatives with the *araraticum* AAGG genomic constitution. The only exception is the very local *T. timopheevii* native to the republic of Georgia, which is very probably not a primary cultigen but a more recent, secondary crop.

Also in the diploid wheats we are apparently faced—in the wild—with a pair of sibling species. As argued by Waines and Barnhart (1992) and Waines (1996), there is a growing body of evidence to suggest that in the Near East "arc" wild einkorn *T. boeoticum* (which is fully inter-fertile with cultivated einkorn *T. monococcum*) does not exist alone. It is frequently accompanied by a second diploid wild-type *T. urartu* which is morphologically very similar to wild einkorn, but inter-sterile both with the *boeoticum* wild forms and with the *monococcum* cultivars. The cytogenetic tests in the wild diploid wheats are not as extensive as in the wild tetraploid ones. Yet wheat geneticists (for example, Miller 1987a, Dvorak 1988, Waines and Barnhart 1992) already regard this inter-sterile wild *T. urartu* as a separate wild diploid wheat species and stress the fact that it has nothing to do with einkorn domestication.

In summary, both in tetraploid and diploid wheats, the presence of sibling species in the wild, compared to the uniformity under cultivation, suggests single rather than multiple domestications.

Conclusions

Barring two or three exceptions (Heun et al. 1997; Neale et al. 1988), genetic tests that are sufficiently comprehensive and specifically planned to throw light on the mode of origin of the Near Eastern crops have not yet been attempted. The evidence available consists mainly of facts extracted from experiments designed to answer totally different questions. Inevitably, these are just fragments of information, frequently in need of further confirmation and additional support from intentionally designed tests. But as argued by Zohary (1996), in spite of these limitations the gathered information already invites the following conclusions:

- The mode of domestications of cultivated plants need not remain an open question. Several kinds of tests can be proposed for obtaining critical evidence. If carried out on a sufficient scale such examinations could provide critical clues for discriminating between monophyletic and polyphyletic origins.

- Some of the available genetic evidence, such as cp DNA polymorphism in barley (Neale et al. 1988), chromosome polymorphism in lentil, sibling species in tetraploid wheats, or the information on allelism available for the genes determining nonshattering in wheats and barley (Zohary 1996), already appears indicative. Moreover, these pieces of information were recently beautifully augmented by the extensive DNA fingerprinting of wild and cultivated einkorn wheat (Heun et al. 1997) which not only suggests monophyletic origin but also pinpointed the location of einkorn domestication. Taken together with the taxonomic information on species divergence, the available information suggests that emmer wheat (the most important crop of southwestern Asian and European Neolithic agriculture), einkorn wheat, as well as pea and lentil (the main grain legumes) were probably each taken into cultivation only once, or at most very few times. Evidence pertaining to the mode of origin of chickpea, bitter vetch, and flax is more meager, yet what is available seems to be compatible with the notion of a single origin. Only in barley, where two different nonshattering genes t and bt2) have been discovered (Takahashi 1964, 1972), is there an indication that this important crop has been taken into cultivation more than once. Yet, even in this cereal, the cp DNA data (Neale et al. 1988) suggest that only very few events have occurred.

The available data, fragmentary as they are, appear to support the hypothesis that the development of grain agriculture in the Near East was triggered (in each crop) by a single domestication or, at most, by very few events. However, the data tell us very little about the way the Near Eastern Neolithic crop "package" was assembled. It remains an open question whether the eight founder crops were taken into cultivation together (in one place), or whether different crops were domesticated each in a different site. Yet once the first domesticated forms of wheats, barley, pulses, and flax appeared in the Near East, they probably spread over the "arc" in a manner similar to the way in which they later spread into Europe, Caucasia, central Asia and Egypt—not by independent introductions of the wild progenitors into cultivation in additional sites but rather by diffusion of the already existing domesticates over the Near East. As argued by Zohary (1996) and Diamond (1997), it is very likely that soon after the first nonshattering and ea gsinating cereals, pulses, and flax appeared, their superior performance under cultivation became decisive, and there was no need for repeated domestication of the wild progenitors (or addition of other grain species). Moreover, because this new system of crop cultivation expanded rapidly, there was little time for grain agriculture to develop independently elsewhere in southwest Asia or in the Mediterranean basin

Finally it should be noted that while monophyletic origin is indicated for the majority of the Old World Neolithic founder crops, it is an open question how common is this mode of origin in crop plant evolution. In most cultivated plants the genetic information necessary even for starting to choose between monophyletic and polyphyletic origins is still unavailable. In fact, only in two principal New World plants telltale data have already been gathered: They suggest that cultivated maize *Zea mays* had a monophyletic origin— or at least evolved from a geographically very restricted race of wild maize (Doebley 1990); while for the common bean *Phaseolus vulgare* indications are that it had a complex origin and was taken into cultivation both in Mesoamerica and in the Andes (Gepts and Debouck 1991). It also stands to reason that many secondary crops (which first evolved as weeds and only later entered food production) and many fruit crops were picked up not once but several times. Yet a solid assessment of the roles of monophyletic and polyphyletic origins in plants under domestication will have to wait until we acquire additional, critical data.

Chapter 7 ✐

Agriculture in the Near East in the Seventh Millennium BC

Mordechai E. Kislev

THE CONCEPT OF THE NEOLITHIC, OR agricultural, revolution introduced by Childe (1936:74; 1942:36) and Braidwood (1960:131) had profound impact on contemporary prehistorians and archaeologists. Some recent evidence however, seems to indicate that these broad terms may not adequately describe the historic process leading to domestication in the early Neolithic Near East. The lumping together of plant and animal domestication under a single headline blurs the independent evolutionary paths taken by various domesticated species. Still, *agricultural revolution* does accurately describe the nearly uniform spread from southwest Asia to southeast Europe of the ensemble of plants, including several species of wheat and barley, lentil, pea, bitter vetch, and flax and animals such as sheep, goat, cattle, and pig. Similarly, *Neolithic revolution* is applicable to the impact of plant and animal husbandry, as well as pottery, on the way of life, form of settlement, housing, vessels, tools, and food of the Europeans in the early Neolithic period.

On the other extreme stands Harlan with his courageous statements:

It has become apparent in the last two decades or so that a basic barrier to an understanding of the processes of plant domestication and agricultural origins is philosophic in nature and concerns human self-perception. The traditional view of all civilized peoples, as judged by their literature, oral traditions, mythologies, and religions, is that agriculture is an invention, an idea, a technique brought to humans by divine instruction....Recent studies have demolished all of these preconceptions....Studies of surviving

hunter-gatherers reveal a remarkable botanical knowledge of the plants they live with...agricultural systems evolved from a base of knowledge not ignorance. They could have originated at any time or place within reasonable ecological limits. (Harlan 1986:22)

However, for the Near East, it is suggested here that the term *evolution of agriculture* should be adopted, as each crop is likely to have evolved at different times and regions. Only later, following accumulation of a variety of domesticated species that occupied a whole array of niches, could the term *revolution* be applicable.

Pulses may provide the best example of diffuse beginnings of agriculture. It seems that the origin of chickling vetch (*Lathyrus sativus*) was not contemporaneous with the so-called agricultural revolution in the eighth millennium BC. We still cannot identify its progenitor, but the archaeobotanical evidence leads to the assumption that its domestication occurred somewhere in the Balkan peninsula, about 6000 BC (Kislev 1986; 1989a). A second pulse, which appears not to belong to the Neolithic ensemble of the Near East, is chickpea (*Cicer arietinum*). Neolithic remnants of this legume are very scanty and may, in fact, belong to wild species, or alternatively, constitute an admixture of minor importance in lentil or pea fields without being domesticated yet. Living specimens of its progenitor, *C. reticulatum*, can only be found in a relatively small region in southeast Anatolia, in the upper catchment area of the Euphrates and the Tigris, not too far from Cayonu (Ladizinsky 1975).

Indeed, most of the early Neolithic crops still grow wild in the Near East. For hunter-gatherers who could obtain their sustenance in the close vicinity of their villages, there is no good reason for them to have changed their way of life and begun to cultivate cereals and pulses. It is assumed that domestication could occur where people had close acquaintance with a plant, but not where it is available in quantity in the wild. A proper habitat for domestication may be a region where the crop can easily be grown, for example, in the fringe of its main area of distribution, but for some reason it actually did not grow there in abundance.

The most acute problem in studying the history of domestication from archaeobotanical evidence is that it is often extremely difficult to distinguish between a domesticated plant and its progenitor. In pulses, the best morphological trait for domestication is the retention of seeds in the mature pod. But it is practically hopeless to find direct evidence of that, at least by the present techniques, because pod remains are not uncovered from early sites. Unfortunately, in primitive cereals as well, such as emmer and einkorn wheats, it is still impossible to tell by the Neolithic remains whether a crop species was wild or domesticated. The ripe ear of wild wheat disarticulates spontaneously into separate spikelets, while the ear of domesticated hulled wheat disarticulates in the same manner during threshing.

Barley too produces some difficulties in determining the state of its domestication. Seven important elements have been used to distinguish between the wild and domesticated species: finds of twisted kernels; finds of internode fragments of six-rowed barley; finds of naked grains; grain shape and size; disarticulation of wild barley versus fragmentation of the rachis of domesticated type; nature of the rachis node disarticulation scar; and the histological structure of the abscission zone.

Finds of Twisted Kernels

These belong to side spikelets of six-rowed barley. The current view holds that the change from two- to six-rowed barley occurred in the domestic form (de Candolle 1886:370; Zohary 1969:55). Therefore, this character may be used to indicate a domesticated species. A few asymmetric naked grains have been observed at late aceramic Ramad, Ghoraife, and Aswad (van Zeist and Bakker-Heeres 1982:205).

Finds of Internode Fragments of Six-rowed Barley

These exhibit some morphological changes of the internode and its appendages, resulting from the appearance of two additional twisted kernels on both sides of the existing straight one. However, only one internode fragment from Ramad, Syria, dated to the late seventh millennium BC, has been identified to date as that of six-rowed barley (van Zeist and Bakker-Heeres 1982:178).

Finds of Naked Grains

Naked grains, where husks are not adhering to the grain when mature, may be evidence of domestication, as some two- and six-rowed strains are commonly grown today. The earliest archaeobotanical finds include about eighty naked kernels, out of a total of thirteen hundred barley kernels from the Damascus basin, dated to the seventh millennium BC (van Zeist and Bakker-Heeres 1982:205).

Grain Shape and Size

These characteristics have been used in the past, but are no longer considered very useful. " Modern grains of wild and domestic two-rowed barley are not difficult to separate, as the grain of wild barley are markedly thinner. However, in subfossil charred grains this distinction is often less clear, which is largely because of puffing and other deformations of the grain through charring. It should be mentioned that the size of the grains provides no clue in distinguishing between wild and domestic barley. Under favorable climatic and edaphic conditions *Hordeum spontaneum* (wild barley) may develop grains of considerable size (van Zeist et al. 1986:209).

Disarticulation of Wild Barley Versus Fragmentation of the Rachis of Domesticated Type

The clear diagnostic character distinguishing wild from domesticated barley is the ability of the ear to disarticulate at abscission zones along the rachis leading to separate spikelets (Bor and Guest 1968:244). All other characters are derivative. When ancient rachis segments show clear scars of disarticulation they definitely belong to the wild species; when these remnants exhibit more than one internode and are broken irregularly at random points along the internode, the signs of threshing, they are from the domesticated species. However, rachis fragments longer than a single internode are very rarely reported for the seventh and eighth millennia BC.

Nature of the Rachis Node Disarticulation Scar

Two types of scars can be distinguished among charred internodes. One exhibits an intact articulation scar due to natural ear disarticulation into individual spikelets and has been attributed to shattering, brittle-rachised wild barley (*H. spontaneum*). Not only is the node articulation scar undamaged, but the internode base is also generally intact. The second type shows a single internode or sometimes internode segment with an attached part of the next internode. It was identified as domesticated barley (*H. distichon*; van Zeist and Bakker-Heeres 1982: Figure 14, 8–10; Kislev et al. 1986:198). Hitherto detailed studies of archaeobotanical remnants were carried out without similar approaches to the modern, living populations. Recently, however, new observations have been carried out on a modern population of *H. spontaneum* in Jerusalem. It was demonstrated that after artificial disarticulation, namely breaking single spikelets one at a time by removing manually the upper part of the spikelet from the plane of the rachis, about 10% of the internodes retain a fragment of the upper internode attached to the articulation scar. Occasionally the lowest part of the rachis, a few internodes in length, remains intact, and the kernel alone is removed from the ear. This percentage increases when less fully ripe ears are artificially disarticulated. There are differences between the populations, but, in general, the lower third of the ear shows a more domesticated type of scar (Kislev 1989b). These results suggest that the small percentage of so-called domesticated barley in Netiv Hagdud, as well as in other early Neolithic sites, may be better interpreted as wild barley.

This is the place to describe, with a small example, the intellectual atmosphere existing at the 1988 roundtable meeting in Jalès. At the time of the first session it was difficult to accept the new idea that about 10% of domestic type may be normal in wild barley. It should be kept in mind that this domestic type was the only evidence for cereal domestication in the eighth millennium. If the old interpretation is not valid any more the participants had to change their concept on the age of agriculture. Therefore, it was decided to repeat, in the presence of the attendants, the checking of the nature of the rachis node disarticulation scar, in a sample of wild barley grown in the experimental plots at Jalès. The results of the mini experiment, which showed the same percentage, were exhibited during the final session of the meeting.

The histological structure of the abscission zone. Elaborate studies are reported on the related genera *Triticum* and *Aegilops*. It was found that the fragility of the wheat rachis is governed by several morphological and anatomical factors. Fragility is favored by increased amount of tissue in the breaking region, increased thickness of the abscission layer, small size of its cells, poor lignification of their walls, deep constriction at the rachis joint, and narrow base of the rachis internode (Srinivas 1969; Zimmermann 1934). Also in wild barley, the cells of the abscission zone are shorter than the adjacent ones (Frank 1964). Similarly, the scanning electron microscope has revealed that a charred segment of barley from Netiv Hagdud bearing a fragment of the upper internode exhibits the structure of wild barley (Kislev 1989b).

The data accumulated here reveals that we are not yet able to confirm whether most crops of the eighth millennium were domesticated or not. This conclusion is valid for all pulses whose wild progenitors are known, that is lentil, pea, bitter vetch, and chickpea, as well as for the primitive cereals einkorn and emmer wheats, except for two-rowed and wild barley. The results of about 10% of "domesticated" type among rachis nodes of barley in archaeobotanical studies fit with the characteristics of wild barley. Moreover, if one assumes that the 10% really represents domesticated barley, one needs to explain the delay of 1000 years in the establishment of the mutation in the fields. Only in the seventh millennium is there clear evidence of domestication. The finds of the naked wheat, *Triticum parvicoccum*, from Aswad II, Ghoraife, and Ramad from Syria as well as Can Hasan III from South Anatolia include a considerable number of rachis fragments, each including several internodes (van Zeist and Bakker-Heeres 1982: Figure 16; Hillman 1972: Table 1). These remnants unequivocally belong to domesticated species (table 7.1). Also, a considerable number of nonbrittle single internodes of barley occur in Ramad and perhaps in Aswad II. They may be considered as belonging to the domesticated species (van Zeist and Bakker-Heerees 1985: Table 18). However, it is difficult to explain why the early rachis fragments of domesticated barley consist of only single internodes, while those of *T. parvicoccum* contain several internodes.

It seems that aside from the morphological characters discussed above, there is no reliable or even indirect criterion for detecting a domesticated crop in the early Neolithic period. Very large quantities of archaeological remains of a crop may sometimes be a hint for domestication (Garfinkel et al. 1988), but the tens of thousands of wild barley triplets unearthed in Beidha (Helbaek 1966: 62) make the opposite point. After all, a hunter-gatherer may need rather similar amounts of food as a farmer. When an edible plant such as wild barley is available in unlimited amounts in the surroundings, it is not surprising to find large quantities in certain places in the site. The presence of kernels of certain weeds, such as *Lolium temulentum*, which have been changed morphologically under domestication, may be used as an indicator for the domestication of their host plants (Kislev 1980a:366). But, unfortunately, they have not yet been found in those early sites.

Table 7.1 shows that much more information is required before the beginning of agriculture can be accurately described. There are at the moment, for the whole Near East, about ten known sites per millennium that have produced cereal remains, or one per century on average. This means that there is a good chance that the conclusions drawn from table 7.1 may be considerably influenced by additional data. However, it is clear that in 6900 to 6600 BC *T. parvicoccum* begins to appear. This species is a free-threshing wheat, apparently tetraploid, that prevailed in the ancient Near East and Mediterranean regions (Kislev 1980b). It is sometimes called *T. durum/aestivum* or *T. turgidum* (van Zeist and Bakker-Heeres 1982:198; Zohary and Hopf 1988:44). In the same site (Ramad, SW Syria) and at the same time there is apparently sufficient evidence that domesticated barley also begins to appear (van Zeist and Bakker-Heeres 1982: Table 18). However, *T. parvicoccum* was preceded by emmer (*T. dicoccum*), which is a primitive, domesticated hulled wheat (for review see Kislev 1984b:67; Zohary and Hopf 1988:37).

Table 7.1 Wild and domesticated cereal remains from the Middle East in the eighth and seventh millennia BC

	SITE	COUNTRY	DATE (BC)	SAMPLES	T.MONOCOCCUM		T. DICCOCUM		T. PARVICOCCUM		HORDEUM VULGARE	
					GRAINS	FORKS	GRAINS	FORKS	GRAINS	INTERNODES	GRAINS	INTERNODES
1.	Abu Hureyra (M.)	Syria	9000-8500	11	-	-	++	++	-	-	+	-
2.	Mureybit	Syria	8000-7600	20	1900	-	-	-	-	-	48	-
3.	Netiv Hagdud	Israel	7750	50	-	-	+	+	-	-	++	+++
4.	Aswad I	Syria	7800-7300	9	-	-	25	270	-	-	32	23
5.	Jericho (PPNA)	Israel	7600-7200	4	-	3	6	6	-	-	35	2
6.	Cayonu 1-3	Turkey	7500-7000	36	23	37	61	98	-	-	2	-
7.	Ali Kosh (B.M.)	Iran	7500-6750	21	1	10	300	1400	-	-	170	-
8.	Ganj Dareh	Iran	7500-6600	70	-	-	-	-	-	-	180	2
9.	Jericho (PPNB)	Israel	7200-6500	14	2200	30	3100	27	-	-	1300	5
10.	Beidha VI	Jordan	6750	1	-	-	++	++	-	-	+++++	+++++
11.	Hacilar (acer.)	Turkey	6750	1	+	42	+	24	-	-	+	2
12.	Jarmo	Iraq	6750	-	+	+	+	+	-	-	++	+
13.	Aswad II	Syria	6900-6600	21	17	-	1900	14000	150	1	400	310
14.	'Ain Ghazal	Jordan	7200-6200	35	-	-	++	+	-	-	+++	++
15.	Nahal Hemar	Israel	6900-6300	4	-	-	-	11	-	-	1	-
16.	Ghoraife	Syria	6800-6200	35	16	100	120	760	59	7	19	11
17.	Can Hasan III	Turkey	mid-8th m	4	10	8	20	+	100	+	48	+
18.	Ali Kosh (A.K.)	Iran	6750-6000	13	2	10	135	450	-	-	41	-
19.	Abu Hureyra (N.)	Syria	6500-6000	54	++	-	+++	-	-	-	+++	-
20.	El Kowm	Syria	6300-6100	2	-	-	14	-	16	-	5	-
21.	Bouqras	Syria	6400-5900	6	-	-	1	2	1363	-	96	2
22.	Ramad	Syria	6200-6000	47	200	1700	4400	37000	2000	920	850	580

Sources:
1. Hillman 1975
2. van Zeist 1970
3. Kislev et al. 1986, and N.D.
4. van Zeist and Bakker-Heeres 1985
5. Hopf 1983
6. van Zeist 1972
7. Helbaek 1969
8. van Zeist et al. 1986
9. Hopf 1983
10. Helbaek 1966
11. Helbaek 1970
12. Helbaek 1953
13. van Zeist and Bakker-Heeres 1985
14. McCreery 1985
15. Kislev 1988
16. van Zeist and Bakker-Heeres 1985
17. Hillman 1972
18. Helbaek 1969
19. Hillman 1975
20. van Zeist 1986
21. van Zeist and Waterbolk-van Rooyen 1983
22. van Zeist and Bakker-Heeres 1985.

Notes: Dates are sometimes rounded. All in uncalibrated radiocarbon years; Mesolithic Abu Hureyra is included although it is dated to the ninth millennium BC; figures in the columns of *T. monococcum* include *T. boeoticum*; figures in the columns of *T. dicoccum* include *T. dicoccoides*; figures in the columns of *T. parvicoccum* include *T. durum* and *T. aestivum*; figures in the columns of *H. vulgare* include *H. distichon, H. spontaneum*, and naked barley. A single fragment or half a grain is calculated as one grain. Two glume bases are calculated as one fork. When identifications of remnants were too general, for example, *T. monococcum/T. dicoccum*, the sum of grains (or fork) was divided equally between the two taxa, if no comment was given by the author. When forks only were not identified to the species, they were divided according to grain proportions. When grains and internodes were found intact, they were recorded as if found separated. The figures have been rounded off for simplicity. Number of the + signs expresses relative abundance or order of magnitude.

Unfortunately, we do not know for how long domesticated emmer had been cultivated before its transformation to *T. parvicoccum*, in other words, when the mutation that changed wild emmer to domesticated emmer was adopted by humans. Was it one hundred years before 6900 to 6600 or a millennium?

When our concepts of plant husbandry in the eighth millennium are no longer influenced by today's accepted model of agricultural revolution, it will be easier to analyze data objectively and identify the points that must be further investigated. It seems, from the evidence, that barley of the eighth millennium was entirely wild. The absence of evidence for wheat domestication, together with today's massive living stands of wild barley, wild einkorn, and sometimes also wild emmer in the Near East, leads one to conclude that these species were not cultivated as well. The location of the sites investigated within a day's distance from wild cereal stands, and the relatively low human population density, strengthens this suggestion. Indeed, hundreds of remnants of (wild or domesticated) emmer wheat were found at Aswad I (7800–7300 BC), about 50 and 70 km from the isohyets of 300 and 600 mm, where wild emmer can grow naturally (van Zeist and Bakker-Heeres 1982:168). The data may be proof for establishment of cultivation when thinking of farmers, but, assuming a hunter-gatherer society, the same data provides good evidence for gathering of wild cereals. Moreover, *T. monococcum* reported from some sites well beyond its natural area, for example, Jericho (Hopf 1983:609), may well be interpreted as belonging to the uppermost or the basal one-grained spikelets of the ear of *T. dicoccoides*, especially when their number are very small—three. On this occasion, it must be stressed that further excavations of sites or layers dated to 7000 to 6500 BC will be important for clarifying the beginnings of agriculture of domesticated barley and free-threshing wheat. These dates cannot be shifted ahead because the expansion of agriculture in Europe and Middle Asia would then be too fast. However, the dates can be pushed back if new findings will validate earlier domestication. In addition, earlier archaeobotanical remnants of einkorn or emmer, well beyond their natural area of distribution, can provide information about the beginning of spread of domesticated hulled wheats. Mehrgarh in Pakistan may provide an example (Costantini 1984:31).

Based on the hypothesis that domesticated cereals were not the staple food in the eighth millennium, I would like to put forward a model on the evolution of agriculture. Several species of pulses, as well as fig as a fruit tree, and perhaps flax for clothing as well, were cultivated locally and on a small scale during the eighth millennium or earlier (Kislev 1987:289; Kislev and Bar-Yosef 1988:178). Remnants of the diffused, local pattern of cultivated species may be found even today in remote places of the Near East, where single farmers or people in isolated regions still grow odd pulses like *Vicia narbonensis*, *Lathyrus ochrus*, and so forth, for consumption. People of the eighth millennium could grow any legume with larger seeds. The finding of large quantities of lentil and horsebean from Yiftah'el (6800 BC) may be an example of this, though it belongs to a somewhat later period (Kislev 1985a:319; Garfinkel et al. 1988). A second example is pea, bitter vetch, and other unidentified wild pulses from Cayonu I (7500–7200 BC; van Zeist 1972:10). Among the progenitors

of the most important modern pulses, *Lens orientalis*, *Pisum humile*, wild *Vicia ervilia*, and *V. sativa* should be mentioned as possible crops. They, and perhaps other species, could have been grown near some sites, each in its favorable habitat. A wild pulse could easily substitute for protein-rich meat, where animals could not be easily hunted. By automatic selection they could be transformed into domesticates. When such a pulse serves not as a staple but only as an additional food, and when it is consumed for a relatively short time, the various toxic contents have insufficient time to accumulate in the body in quantities that may be dangerous to human health. This situation has been documented in some detail in the case of *Lathyrus sativus* in India (Spencer et al. 1986:303).

A system of small-scale agriculture could have continued for generations until large-scale cereal cultivation was practiced. At that time, the meeting of these two types of agriculture would have had a mutual influence and produced the ensemble of the Neolithic agriculture at about 7000 to 6500 BC.

Acknowledgment. This contribution was written during my sabbatical in London. I would like to thank the staff of the Department of Human Environment, Institute of Archaeology, London, for their encouragement and help.

Chapter 8

Cerealia-type Pollen in the Near East as Indicators of Wild or Domestic Crops

Sytze Bottema

IN NORTHWEST EUROPEAN ARCHAEOLOGY Cerealia-type pollen is invariably and traditionally linked with farming. Detailed analysis of the various structures, shapes, and dimensions of the pollen grains made a more detailed identification possible. The appearance of Cerealia pollen drew attention because the producing plants were not indigenous in that part of the world. The behavior of Cerealia pollen in records of the Near East is of great interest for those who want to know more about the wild ancestors of wheat and barley and the domesticates that subsequently developed. If we want to be informed about the history of the various cereal species in the wild as well as in various stages of cultivation certain conditions have to be fulfilled. The pollen types must differ enough from each other to be distinguished during analytical work and they must be dispersed in such numbers that they make up a fair share of the pollen precipitation.

Most pollen diagrams prepared for pollen sites in the eastern Mediterranean and the Near East originate from elevations over 500 to 600 meters where sediments are constantly covered by water or where organic deposits do not dry up during the summer. At lower elevations marshes can be found occasionally, for instance on the Mediterranean and the Black Sea coasts. Palynological evidence from the lowland steppe and desert steppe is scarce and if present rarely informative about the past vegetation because of selective corrosion. Sediments from oxbow lakes formed by the Balikh and the Khabur in the Syrian Djezireh were mostly devoid of pollen. Obviously seasonal drought caused the disappearance of the pollen. A good pollen diagram has been obtained from the Bouara depression on the border of Syria

with Iraq, but this highly saline area is and was unsuitable for cereal farming.

In the last 25 years a considerable number of pollen diagrams have been prepared for the Near East (figure 8.1). Many of these sites are not situated within the so-called "Fertile Crescent." This area is where the extensive stands of wild cereals must have occurred and is the one that is of interest for our investigations. Sites such as the Ghab, Akgöl (Konya), Van Söğütlü, Zeribar, and Urmia (figure 8.1) come into consideration, but even they are mainly located at the edges of the distribution area for wild wheats as shown by Harlan and Zohary (1966) and Sakamoto (1982).

Archaeological and paleoethnobotanical evidence from the Near East mostly originates from outside the area studied palynologically. Prehistoric settlements are generally situated in the foothill region or the steppic lowlands. Unfortunately not much reliable pollen evidence is available from these areas. In this respect one could refer to the results of palynological investigations of accumulation layers in settlements. The Groningen palaeobotanical department of the Biologisch-Archaeologisch Instituut was among the first to start such investigations, for instance in 1965 in the excavation of Bouqras in Syria. After careful and thorough studies this approach was rejected (Bottema 1975). The nature of accumulation in prehistoric sites differs very much from that in lake sediments or peat bogs. Accumulation in a settlement can be very irregular in time and is to a large extent formed by building debris, mainly mud brick that could even contain secondary pollen. Still the absolute pollen content in such settlement samples is unexpectedly low. This points to a considerable loss of original pollen. Such pollen assemblages

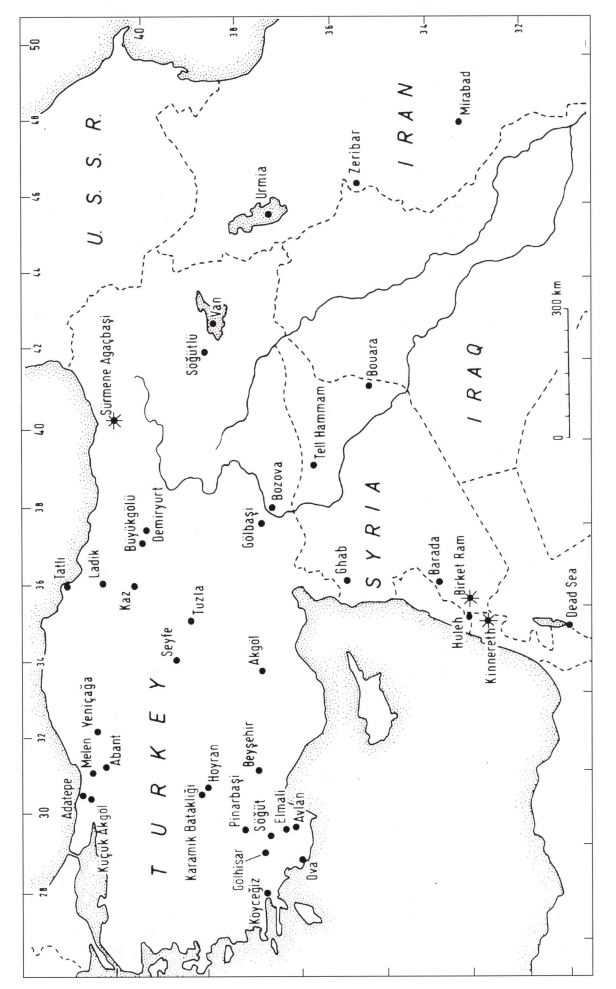

Figure 8.1 Map of the Near East showing the pollen sites studied by the Paleobotany department of the Biologisch–Archaeologisch Instituut (black dots) and others (asterisks)

hardly match the modern pollen precipitation or subfossil assemblages obtained from lakes or bogs. The pollen record obtained from samples taken from prehistoric sites in the Near East demonstrates a rather predictable high percentage of Liguliflorae and/or Tubuliflorae. Such values are hardly or not at all matched by those of extant vegetations demonstrating many Compositae. Other factors, such as selective preservation or nests of burrowing bees, also play a role. This led to the conclusion that palynological evidence on the role of wild cereal or domestic cereal species is preferably obtained from lake and marsh sediments.

In this chapter we will try to evaluate the use of the cereal pollen type as a tool to inform us about the role of food gathering and farming in prehistoric times. First, the identifiability of Cerealia pollen, its relative value in the pollen precipitation, its presence or absence in time, and the correlation of Cerealia-type pollen with other vegetational elements in subfossil assemblages will be discussed.

Identification, production, distribution, and representation of Cerealia pollen

An important characteristic for the identification of Cerealia pollen is the size of the pollen grain in combination with the size and shape of the annulus. In pollen analysis pollen grains ascribed to the Cerealia type have to be larger than 40 μ. For a discussion of this limit we refer to the extensive study by Beug (1961). The detailed study on identification of wild grass and cereal pollen by Andersen (1979) is not used in this study because the measurements taken by the author are maximum diameters. The smaller size in Andersen's study compared with the measurements in figure 8.2 must be explained by Andersen's adding the largest diameter M+ to M-, the diameter at a right angle to M+, and dividing this sum by 2. The term Cerealia type implies that palynologically speaking there remains the possibility that taxa other than Cerealia in the strict sense are included. In those areas, for instance northwestern Europe, where such types are thought to be produced almost exclusively by cereals, a subdivision on the basis of the grouping of the columellae is possible (Körber-Grohne 1957).

Beug measured the pollen of 84 species of Gramineae, including those of wild and cultivated cereals, and divided the various species according to size classes. The so-called wild grass type covers those species with a pollen grain smaller than 37 μ, the Cerealia-type is defined as larger than 37 μ. In practice 40 μ is used as the lower limit in defining Cerealia-type grains.

Beug measured Gramineae pollen grains embedded in glycerine, whereas the reference material and the subfossil samples of the Biologisch-Archaeologisch Instituut are embedded in silicone oil. Control measurements on pollen in silicone oil slides showed no important difference in size compared with Beug's measurements. It should be stressed

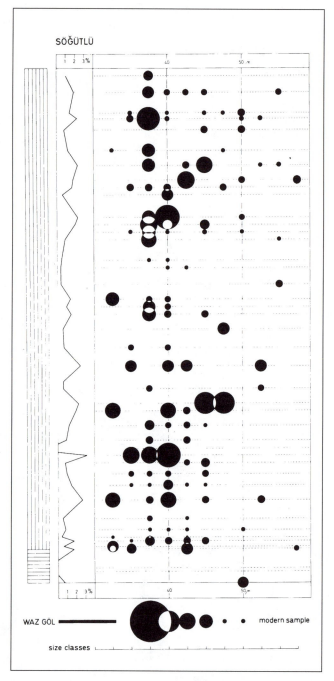

Figure 8.2 Schematic presentation of Gramineae pollen percentages of a series of size classes from 30 to 60 μ. The left column shows the lithology. Vertical hatching represents peat; horizontal hatching, clay. The transition of clay to peat is dated 7135 ± 180 BP (SI-736). The percentages are calculated on the basis of a pollen sum including arboreal types and upland herb types. Black circles indicate a range of 0.1 to 5% for the various dimensions. At the bottom a modern spectrum from Waz Göl in northern Syria is given for comparison.

that the wild grasses in Beug's study originated in Europe. Some of them can be found in the Near East; others are represented only by related species. We can be certain that the Cerealia type as defined by Beug also includes pollen of wild grasses in the Near East. This was also emphasized by van Zeist et al. (1975), who showed that pollen of *Aegilops kotschyi* is bigger than that of *Triticum aestivum*, the first type averaging approximately 55 μ. *Aegilops triuncialis* pollen from the reference collection of the Biologisch-Archaeologisch Instituut averages about 48 μ.

The specific Cerealia-type pollen size classes made by Beug are divided here into three groups : Group I (40–50 μ) includes, among others, *Hordeum vulgare*, *Triticum aegilopoïdes*, *Triticum dicoccoides*, *Triticum dicoccum*, and *Triticum monococcum* and many wild grasses. Group II (50–60 μ) includes *Triticum monococcum*, *Hordeum vulgare*, *Hordeum spontaneum*, *Triticum aegilopoïdes*, *Triticum dicoccoides*, *Secale cereale*, *Triticum dicoccum*, *Triticum durum*, *Triticum compactum*, *Triticum aestivum*, and *Triticum spelta* and various wild grasses. Group III (60–70 μ) includes *Triticum dicoccum*, *Triticum durum*, *Triticum compactum*, *Triticum aestivum*, *Triticum spelta*, and *Secale cereale*. No wild grasses fall within the limits of this group.

The representation of pollen of wild barley, wild einkorn, and wild emmer wheat in natural vegetations has been studied only partly up to now. Some information can be obtained from surface samples which have been taken in those parts of the Fertile Crescent where wild cereals may be present. This information will be discussed later.

Some information is available concerning the representation of pollen of domesticated emmer and bread wheat. Modern wheats are very much underrepresented in the pollen rain because the species are self-pollinating. Iversen (1973) postulated that primitive wheats are to some extent wind-pollinating and release more pollen into the air than, for instance, modern bread wheat. However, pollen of emmer wheat was absent or extremely rare in surface samples taken directly outside an emmer wheat field (Reynolds 1992).

Inside and close to fields of emmer wheat, bread wheat, and barley remarkably little pollen precipitates, as was shown by Firmin in his Vallée de l'Aisne project (1986). It was already indicated by Robinson and Hubbard (1977) that much pollen of hulled barley stays in the glumes.

The difference between Iversen's statement that the more primitive cereals are more wind-pollinating than their modern counterparts and the observation that hardly any cereal pollen is found in or outside test fields may be explained by the fertilization modes. Modern emmer wheat turns out to be 99% self-fertilizing. About 1% of the plants are cross-fertilizing. Three hours after self-fertilization cereals tend to release pollen into the air, according to Zohary, which could explain the presence of cereal-type pollen in the fossil record.

Cerealia Pollen and Other Pollen in Threshed Crops, Ripe Ears, and Flowering Ears

Robinson and Hubbard (1977) drew attention to unexpectedly high pollen contents of hand-threshed six-row hulled barley caryopses. They demonstrated that each cereal grain could have contained approximately 1500 cereal pollen and approximately 100 other pollen grains. They describe the way pollen may have remained or been trapped in spikelets or glumes. I therefore tested the pollen content of various cereal crops that were grown on my farm in Yde (Province of Drenthe) or produced by R. Neef on an experimental farm in Gittrup (West Germany).

The respective crops had been stored in different stages of threshing. Club wheat (*Triticum compactum*) was hand-threshed, winnowed, and stored as a clean sample. Einkorn (*Triticum monococcum*) and emmer wheat (*Triticum dicoccum*) had been threshed with an old-fashioned flailing-stick and the hulled grains were separated from the stems and stored. Naked two-row and six-row barley had been stored as sheaves or as ears that had been cut off from the stems. Pollen samples were prepared by boiling in 10% KOH, followed by acetolysis. Lumps of cereal pollen were hardly found. This may have been because of boiling with KOH (see also Robinson and Hubbard 1977). Sample size, number of pollen counted, and pollen types identified are listed in table 8.1. To calculate the absolute pollen content two Lycopodium tablets containing 1000 spores were added to each sample. The results are expressed as the number of cereal pollen per kilogram threshed material. This is done because harvest yields are generally given in kilograms per hectare. In the case of flowering ears the number of caryopses were counted and expressed in weight of dry, ripe material. The results of the two varieties of naked barley are in fact minimum numbers, as the glume bases and the chaff are included in the weight.

The results in table 8.1 show a high number of cereal pollen as well as of other pollen types per caryopsis. This agrees very well with the results given by Robinson and Hubbard. In the case of the hulled material this could be expected. Numbers of cereal pollen produced by einkorn, emmer wheat, naked six-row barley, and two harvests of naked two-row barley, one from the Netherlands and one from West Germany, are highly consistent, varying from 1.2×10^5 to 5.1×10^5 per kilogram. The relatively high value of pollen in the club-wheat sample is rather unexpected. Although the pollen measures only 1% of the previous series, it still contains 1600 pollen per kilogram, this in spite of the threshing process during which the caryopses were separated from the glumes and other vegetational parts by winnowing.

Flowering ears of *Hordeum vulgare* and *Triticum aestivum* contained 15 to 60 times more pollen than the threshed or harvested material. These numbers must be considered as minimum numbers as flowering was estimated when anthers were visible. As some anthers may have fallen off, pollen may have disappeared. Protective plastic bags fastened before flowering were not much of a success as they prevented evaporation. Thus the moisture content became so high that normal flowers hardly developed. As it was too late to develop another system, ears that showed flowers were collected. *Triticum aestivum* seed setting was already in an advanced stage although anthers were still present. Noncereal pollen was present in considerable amounts. The numbers of foreign types shown in table 8.1 are expressed in percentages of the Cerealia pollen. The results can be divided into two main groups. The ripe crops demonstrate a large number of noncereal types, some of which attain very high values. The flowering cereals demonstrate a low number of extraneous pollen types.

One might explain this difference by the time the crops are exposed in the field. Plants that ripened stayed in the field longer than those that were collected during the flowering stage. In theory contamination of the ripening ears occurred by a constant catch of pollen from nearby vegetations. It is, however, rather puzzling how the club wheat contained a high amount of *Betula* pollen, as the flowering of birch took place early in the season. Part of the contamination originates from wind-flowering species, for instance several tree species and grasses. Still the grass pollen percentages in the plots I, II, and III vary greatly (3.9, 41.0, and 2.3%, respectively) although the small plots bordered upon each other.

Part of the pollen found, such as *Pinus, Picea, Centaurea cyanus,* Ericaceae, *Filipendula, Linum, Sparganium*-type, or spore-producing *Sphagnum,* must come from regional sources as the species concerned were not growing in the garden nor in the vicinity of the plots. Many types are produced by insect-pollinated taxa such as *Matricaria*-type, Leguminosae, and *Oenothera lamarckiana* found nearby. Such pollen (and that of other insect-pollinated species) could have been brought in by insects. Two beehives stood at a distance of 15 meters from the experimental plots. The bees may have gathered pollen of *Oenothera* but they were never seen to visit the cereal stands. Nor were other insects observed on the crops, but it must be admitted that no special attention was paid to visiting insects.

The extra-local vegetation, consisting mainly of oak, lime, elm, and birch, was present in the cereal samples but not according to the proportions of these species in the tree stands. The inconsistency of the pollen assemblages indicates that the results are highly affected by coincidence. Still, one clear statement can be made. Crops brought into a settlement bring in enormous amounts of cereal pollen, especially at the spot where they are stored or processed, for instance by threshing. It is very likely that threshing and winnowing also release a significant amount of cereal pollen into the air.

After processing of cereal crop, pollen must have been deposited together with a great number of other pollen types in the settlement debris. The fact that especially the cereal pollen is very rarely found in high numbers in samples taken from the accumulation in prehistoric sites points to large-scale destruction. Cerealia-type pollen is only demonstrated in large quantities in samples from waterlogged deposits as is indicated by Robinson and Hubbard (1977). Pollen samples from water-logged sediments from the harbor of Carthage

(van Zeist and Bottema 1983) and dating from Punic, Roman, and Byzantine times contained up to approximately 23% Cerealia-type pollen. Triat-Laval (1985) demonstrated comparable results for the fifth century AD harbor of Marseille. In such cases these high percentages are probably not the result of local threshing activities but they may originate from transported cereals, as is indicated by the presence of a large number of pollen in a clean club-wheat sample (table 8.1). Nevertheless the effect of the town sewage systems of drainage towards the harbor, as was the case in Carthage, cannot be excluded without further investigation. The fact that cereal pollen, which could be expected in large numbers in prehistoric sites, is not found, is another reason to reject the palynological investigation of prehistoric sites if no waterlogged deposits are present. In the Near East such conditions can hardly be expected.

From what is stated above about distribution one might conclude that evidence concerning the presence of wild or domesticated cereals by means of palynological investigation of lake or marsh deposits is rather limited. Nevertheless Cerealia-type pollen has been identified in the pollen samples from cores taken in the Near East.

Cerealia-type Pollen Dimensions in Four Sites from Anatolia
During the analysis of four cores from Turkey, at Söğütlü, Tatli Gölü, Ladik Gölü, and Kaz Gölü, Cerealia-type pollen grains have been measured. As a comparison the modern Cerealia-type dimensions from Waz Göl in northern Syria are given.

The Söğütlü core (figure 8.1) is taken from the area in which *Triticum boeoticum* ssp. *thaoudar* can be expected to occur in the natural vegetation. The other three core localities are situated in northern Turkey, where wild cereals are not likely to be found.

For group III (60-70 µ) we have to consider *Triticum dicoccum, Triticum durum,* and possibly *Triticum aestivo/compactum.* Pollen of this size class are absent from all four pollen sites.

In group II (50-60 µ) *Triticum monococcum, Hordeum vulgare, Triticum aegilopoïdes, Triticum dicoccoides, Triticum dicoccum, Triticum durum, Triticum compactum, Triticum aestivo/compactum,* various *Avena* species and various wild grasses have to be considered. This group is represented with low numbers in Söğütlü after ca. 7000 BP, and in Tatli Gölü, Ladik Gölü, and Kaz Gölü this group is mainly absent.

The size class 40-50 µ (group I) includes the species mentioned in group II together with a large number of wild grass species. For the Söğütlü core this size class is present from ca. 7000 BP onward. From about 3500 BP up to modern times the size range for this group is concentrated between 40 and 45 µ. In the Ladik Gölü spectra, pollen of the size of group I are present from about the seventh millennium onward but some are found even before 12,000 BP. In Tatli Gölü this size

Table 8.1 Absolute number of cereal pollen per kg threshed material counted in samples from various plots

SAMPLE NUMBER	I	II	III	IV	V	VI	VII	VIII
Cerealia pollen counted	811	1032	1000	1000	506	1000	1368	1118
# of *Lycopodium* spores out of 1000	121	59	74	34	36	46	40	14
Calculated number of	1.6×10^3	1.4×10^5	1.2×10^5	2.0×10^5	2.2×10^5	5.1×10^5	6.5×10^6	7.3×10^6
Cerealia pollen per kg	ripe	ripe	ripe	ripe	ripe	ripe	flowering	flowering
Dry weight in grams	42	12.4	11.8	15	64	43	5.2	11.0

OTHER POLLEN FOUND (Calculated in percentages of Cerealia)

	I	II	III	IV	V	VI	VII	VIII
Aesculus	0.2	.	.	.	.	.	.	.
Alnus	0.9	0.1	0.1	.	2.4	1.4	.	.
Betula	10.4	.	.	0.1	4.6	0.2	.	.
Castanea	.	0.1	.	0.4	.	.	.	.
Corylus	0.4	.	.	.	0.8	.	.	.
Fagus	.	.	.	.	0.4	0.1	.	.
Hedera	0.1	.	.	.	.	.	.	.
Humulus	0.1	.	.	.	.	.	.	.
Picea	.	.	.	.	0.2	.	.	.
Pinus	1.0	.	0.2	.	0.4	.	.	.
Quercus	0.7	0.1	0.3	0.1	2.8	0.2	.	.
Salix	0.2	.	.	.	.	.	.	.
Sambucus	0.1	.	0.1	.	.	.	.	.
Tilia	0.1	.	0.5	.	1.6	0.5	.	.
Ulmus	0.1	.	.	.	0.6	.	.	.
Caryophyllaceae	.	.	.	.	0.4	0.1	.	.
Chenopodiaceae	0.4	1.8	0.5	27.2	6.6	3.0	.	0.3
Artemisia vulgaris-type	.	0.1	.	.	0.6	0.1	.	3.0
Centaurea cyanus	.	.	.	0.3	0.4	.	.	.
Cirsium-type	0.1	.	.	.	.	.	.	.
Matricaria-type	0.4	0.2	0.4	1.2	2.0	11.4	.	0.1
Senecio-type	.	.	.	.	.	.	.	0.1
Other Liguliflorae	0.1	0.1	.	.	.	.	.	.
Other Tubuliflorae	0.1	0.1	.	.	.	.	.	.
Capsella-type	.	.	.	.	0.4	.	.	.
Other Cruciferae	.	0.1	0.5	.	.	.	.	.
Ericaceae-*Calluna*	0.2	0.1	0.1	.	3.6	.	.	.
Euphorbia	.	.	0.1	.	.	.	.	.
Zea mays	.	.	.	.	.	0.2	.	.
Gramineae $< 40\,\mu$	2.3	0.8	8.2	4.0	41.0	3.9	0.7	1.4
Mentha-type	.	.	.	.	0.8	.	.	.
Lotus-type	.	.	.	.	.	1.2	.	.
Vicia cf. *faba*	.	0.1	.	.	0.4	.	.	.
Other Leguminosae	.	.	2.3	.	9.9	4.5	.	.
Linum	.	.	.	.	0.4	.	.	.
Malva	.	.	.	.	0.2	.	.	.
Oenothera lamarckiana	.	.	.	.	1.0	.	.	.
Papaver	.	.	.	.	0.2	0.1	.	.
Plantago lanceolata	.	.	0.1	.	0.4	0.3	.	0.1
Plantago media	.	.	.	.	0.2	.	.	0.1
Fagopyrum esculentum	.	.	.	.	0.2	.	.	.
Polygonum aviculare-type	.	.	.	.	0.2	0.1	.	.
Polygonum persicaria-type	.	.	.	.	1.2	.	.	.
Rumex acetosa-type	.	.	0.1	0.1	0.4	0.1	.	.
Crataegus-type	.	.	.	.	0.1	0.2	.	.
Filipendula	.	.	.	.	2.4	2.4	.	.
Potentilla-type	.	.	.	.	0.6	0.1	.	.
Other Rosaceae	.	.	.	.	.	0.1	0.1	.
Verbascum-type	.	0.2	0.6	.	0.8	0.2	.	.
Solanum nigrum	0.1	0.2	.	.	0.2	.	.	.

continued

Table 8.1 Absolute number of cereal pollen per kg threshed material counted in samples from various plots, *continued*

SAMPLE NUMBER	I	II	III	IV	V	VI	VII	VIII
OTHER POLLEN FOUND (Calculated in percentages of Cerealia), *continued*								
Galium-type	.	0.1	0.1	.	0.2	.	.	.
Sparganium-type	.	.	.	.	0.8	.	.	.
Aquilegia-type	.	.	.	.	.	0.1	.	.
Delphinium-type	.	.	.	.	.	0.1	.	.
Ranunculus acer-type	.	.	0.1	.	.	0.1	.	.
Malabaila-type	.	.	0.2	.	.	.	.	.
Other Umbelliferae	.	.	0.1	.	0.6	0.5	.	0.1
Urtica	.	0.3	0.9	0.1	0.6	1.7	0.2	1.8
SPORES								
Sphagnum	0.1	.	.	.	1.2	.	.	.
GREEN ALGAE								
Pediastrum kawraiskyi	.	.	0.1	.	.	.	.	.

I = *Triticum compactum*, Yde 1986; II = *Hordeum distichum* var. *nudum*, Yde 1986; III = *Hordeum vulgare* var. *nudum*, Yde 1986; IV = *Hordeum distichum* var. *nudum*, Gittrup 1986; V = *Triticum dicoccum*, Yde 1986; VI = *Triticum monoccum*, Yde 1986; VII = *Hordeum vulgare*, Yde 1987; VIII = *Triticum aestivum*, Gittrup 1987

is met with from about 6000 to 4000 BP and about 2800 to 1500 BP. Kaz Gölü shows some cereal-type pollen in this category at about 8000 BP. The dates mentioned above are inferred dates based upon few radiocarbon dates and assuming a constant sedimentation rate.

The results of the size analysis in the Söğütlü core will be discussed in more detail. The values of the pollen grains of different sizes from 30 to 60 μ are presented in figure 8.3 as percentages of the pollen sum. Measurements were done using an ocular micrometer at 400x magnification representing a scale corresponding with 2.5 μ intervals. The Söğütlü core represents a peat deposit down to approximately 1290 cm. From 1290 to 1380 cm clay is found. Part of the clay did not yield any pollen and those spectra shown in figure 8.3 that were analyzed are of poor quality. The fact that Cerealia-type pollen was mostly met with in the peat samples may be owing to preservation conditions, but the presence of such pollen grains could also be ascribed partly to wild grasses growing in the peat bog. The change in sedimentation at about 7000 BP must very likely be ascribed to a change in climate.

In the modern pollen precipitation in Waz Göl, situated in the upper reaches of the Balikh river in northern Syria, Cerealia-type pollen is present at a rate of about 6%. Of this percentage, most of the grains measure under 40 μ, a smaller number measure between 40 and 50 μ and none are over 60 μ. Cereal farming is found around Waz Göl, partly irrigated, partly as dry farming. The results of the Waz Göl analysis show that the Cerealia-type pollen found in Söğütlü may very well originate from cereal growing in that area.

Evidence of Cerealia Pollen in Subfossil and Modern Assemblages

The previous sections dealt with the identification of Cerealia-type pollen based upon the study of modern material.

Production, distribution, and representation were studied in controlled experiments. In this section the information available from the subfossil pollen record will be discussed. The Cerealia curves will be compared with curves of a selection of pollen types which are thought to represent vegetational groups of importance during prehistoric times.

Eight pollen diagrams from six sites have been selected. These are sites which lie within the distribution area of wild cereal species as indicated by Harlan and Zohary (1966). It should be stressed that wild barley, einkorn, and emmer wheat not necessarily are found together in all the sites which have been selected.

The information in the previous sections shows that the presence of Cerealia pollen has to be treated cautiously. The subfossil record of the selected sites shows that this pollen type is present during late Pleistocene and Holocene times. A time period representing the last 15,000 years has been chosen because it covers the time that farming developed as well as the postulated food-gathering that preceded it. Some diagrams represent only part of the last 15,000 years and it is indicated in figure 8.3 where portions of the record are available. In this schematic figure the relative Cerealia-pollen values have been expressed in percentages, calculated on the basis of a pollen sum that includes the arboreal pollen and the herb pollen types which are thought to be of regional origin. The time scale for the various pollen records is based upon radiocarbon dates and the sedimentation rate is calculated from such dates. In the case of the Van core that was originally varve-dated (Kempe and Degens 1978) the dating was corrected with the help of the nearby Söğütlü core. For a discussion on the dating problems of the Van core the reader is referred to Bottema (1986). The translation of the Cerealia-type percentages into quantitative vegetational record remains a problem as the absolute pollen influx is not known.

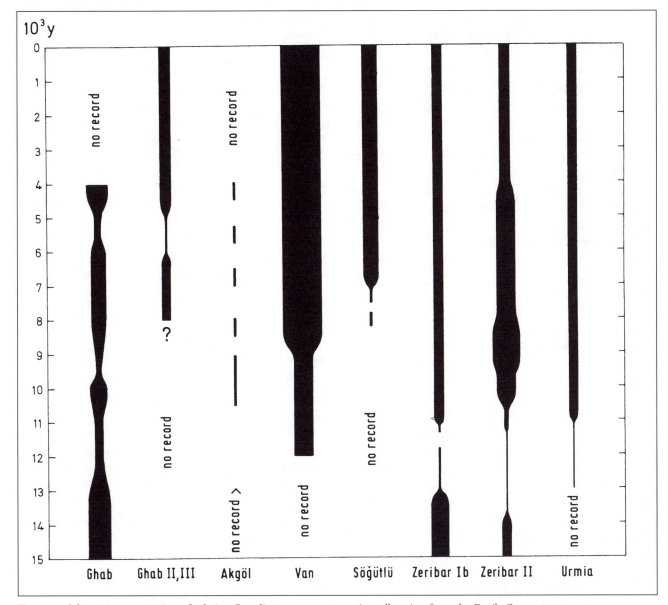

Figure 8.3 Schematic presentation of relative Cerealia-type percentages in pollen sites from the Fertile Crescent

The absolute pollen production from the vegetation may have changed during the period under discussion. There is evidence that the absolute pollen influx increased toward modern times, according to Tsukada (van Zeist and Bottema 1982). If this tendency is true, this may hold also for the Cerealia-type pollen.

The development of climate in the Near East as concluded from the pollen evidence very likely influenced the distribution area of the respective wild cereals. The cereal belt may have narrowed or shifted upward under drier conditions. Lower temperatures may have caused a downward shift. The postulated rise in precipitation that became more and more pronounced in the Fertile Crescent during Late Glacial and Holocene times (van Zeist and Bottema 1982) would have created suitable conditions for wild cereals at lower levels. Increasing moisture must also have extended the limits of dry farming up to about 5500 BP, after which time

modern conditions became established.

Three diagrams from two sites, the Ghab and Zeribar, demonstrate relatively important values up to 13,000 to 14,000 BP. After that time Cerealia-type values decrease considerably. This is also visible in the diagrams of Akgöl and Urmia, where the record starts about that time with low values. About 11,000 BP percentages increase again to reach values which are sometimes even higher than before 13,000 BP.

If the Cerealia type represents wild wheats and/or wild barley one could conclude that there was a decrease in numbers of plants from c. 14,000 to 11,000 BP. After 1,000 BP the proportion of these species soon reached optimal numbers, as concluded from the pollen percentages. This picture would suggest that the gathering of wild cereals was less favorable from ca. 14,000 to 11,000 BP. After 11,000 BP stands would have developed, offering better opportunity for food gathering. One exception has to be made. The climatic development of the Near East was reviewed by van Zeist and Bottema (1982). It was stressed that the climatic history of the Fertile Crescent as concluded from the pollen record was not synchronous. Increase in tree growth was very much in advance in northern Israel compared to eastern Anatolia and Iran. Favorable conditions were concluded from Tsukada's evidence on the Huleh record. Preliminary investigations on new material obtained from the Huleh marshes by Uri Baruch (Institute of Archaeology, The Hebrew University of Jerusalem) and Bottema led to the conclusion that extensive *Quercus ithaburensis* forest was present in that area dated 11,540±100 BP (GrN-14986). At the same time 4.6% Cerealia-type pollen was found that may have been produced by *Triticum dicoccoides* (measurements ranging from 40 to 49 μ). Conditions for this species must have been favorable in northern Israel, at least during the period that matched the Allerød of temperate Europe. Such conditions may have played an important role in connection with the Natufian culture. More to the north, in the Ghab valley in Syria, a delay in development was demonstrated by van Zeist and Woldring (1980). To test the validity of this speculative statement, information on charred remains from prehistoric settlements is necessary.

Harlan and Zohary(1966) provide information concerning the modern natural distribution of wild einkorn, emmer, and barley. Wild barley seems to be connected mostly with open oak forest; the two wheat species may occur in open oak forest but especially wild einkorn also forms pure stands. Although no detailed information on potential accompanying species—if there are any—is available, the subfossil record will be studied in this respect.

First the behavior of the general Gramineae curves will be compared to that of the Cerealia-type curve. The possibility remains that there is some overlap in identification. On the other hand, the changing climate indicated by the general vegetation development may have influenced the grass as well as the cereal species. From table 8.2 it can be seen that in some localities a positive correlation is present whereas in others no correlation or a negative correlation is found. In fact this leaves both questions unanswered.

In some of the pollen diagrams cited above the Cerealia type correlates clearly with some types, as is shown in table 8.3. This concerns the diagrams of Lake Urmia, Lake Zeribar, Van, and Söğütlü. A distinctly positive correlation was visible for *Quercus, Pistacia,* and to some extent for *Rheum* or *Plantago maritima*-type. A clearly negative correlation is visible for Chenopodiaceae, *Artemisia herba-alba*-type and in the Urmiǎ record for *Ferula*-type. The role of these pollen types is described in various publications on the vegetational history of the locations concerned (van Zeist and Bottema 1977; van Zeist and Woldring 1980; Bottema 1986). The reconstruction of the dominant vegetation type will be briefly discussed. The Chenopodiaceae and *Artemisia herba-alba*

Table 8.2 Correlation of curves of Cerealia type in various pollen diagrams with those of wild grass–type Gramineae

Ghab I, II, III	Positive correlation
Akgöl	Positive correlation
Van Gölü	No correlation
Söğütlü	Generally positive correlation
Zeribar Ib	No correlation or negative
Zeribar II	Positive correlation
Lake Urmia	Positive correlation

Table 8.3 Correlation of curves of Cerealia type in various pollen diagrams with those of other pollen types apart from Gramineae

Lake Urmia	Positive with *Pistacia, Quercus, Salix;* negative with Chenopodiaceae, *Artemisia herba-alba*-type, *Ferula*-type
Lake Zeribar Ib	Positive with *Pistacia, Quercus, Plantago,* and II *maritima*-type; partly *Rheum;* negative with Chenopodiaceae, *Artemisia herba-alba*-type
Van Gölü	Positive with *Pistacia, Quercus,* partly *Rheum;* negative with Chenopodiaceae, *Artemisia herba-alba*-type
Akgöl and Ghab	No clear correlation
Söğütlü	Positive with *Pistacla, Quercus;* negative with Tubiliflorae, Liguliflorae, *Centaurea solstitialis*-type

type dominated the pollen assemblages in the respective sites up to about 9000 BP. It is concluded that they represent a time period during which steppe vegetations dominated the area where the pollen cores were taken, namely eastern Turkey and northwestern Iran. Trees were completely absent apart from a few local pistachio trees or some *Salix* which may have occurred along streams or lakes.

At about 9000 BP a slight increase in tree pollen is found, indicating the occurrence of some *Quercus* and *Pistacia* trees. A forest-steppe developed that gradually closed up into an open oak forest, whereas at lower and drier elevations a forest-steppe with *Pistacia* was present. From about 7000 to 5000 BP modern conditions became established. During the expansion of tree species the role of the steppe vegetation in those parts diminished. *Artemisia* and Chenopodiaceae were gradually replaced by grasses which dominated the herb vegetation that was found in the steppe or open oak forest.

The vegetation development concluded from the pollen record must have been caused by a change in climate. From ca. 15,000 BP onward the global temperature gradually increased, as is demonstrated from ample evidence in other parts of the world. Temperature will not have been a limiting factor for tree growth during most of the period under discussion. The critical factor for many plant species, especially trees, was moisture. The species that produced the Cerealia pollen played a role before *Quercus* and *Pistacia* expanded, as can be seen in figure 8.2. The reason that the Cerealia-type values were lowest from ca. 13,000 to 11,000 BP must be explained by the fact that precipitation did not keep pace with the increasing temperature, resulting in greater dryness. For a detailed discussion on the climatic development of the Near East, the reader is referred to van Zeist and Bottema (1982).

That Cerealia-type producing grasses, possibly wild cereals, were of some importance before 13,000 BP may be explained by a lower moisture demand for these plants than is the case for trees.

At present the open oak forest, the Zagros oak forest, is found from about 800 to 1300 m. At lower elevations, receiving less precipitation, a steppe forest including *Pistacia* occurs. A steppe dominated by *Artemisia* and Chenopodiaceae prevails beneath the steppe forest. The distribution maps of wild barley, wild einkorn, and wild emmer drawn by Harlan and Zohary (1966) coincide to a large extent with that of the open oak forest. It is not surprising that the Cerealia-type values present in pollen records of the sites quoted in table 8.3 correlate positively with the values of *Quercus* and *Pistacia*.

It can be concluded that Cerealia-type producing plants profited largely from the same increase in precipitation that favored the expansion of the trees in the area. It still has to be proved that the Cerealia-type pollen found in the sediments was produced by wild cereal species, but it is a plausible explanation.

The situation in the Ghab and the Konya plain (Akgöl) differed from that of other sites (figure 8.3 and table 8.3). The marshes of the Ghab caught the pollen rain of the forested Jebel Alaouite in the west and the steppe in the east. Especially the forest communities on the Jebel Alaouite differ very much from those present at the other sites at the moment. The same was also true for prehistoric times. The Konya plain itself probably did not harbor wild cereals, which must have been confined to the slopes of the mountains bordering the plain. In the Akgöl pollen record Cerealia-type values are low and in many spectra the type is even absent. This must be explained by the distance of the site from the potential stands of wild cereals.

To translate subfossil pollen assemblages in terms of vegetation, van Zeist and his colleagues made a detailed study of the present-day pollen precipitation and its relation to the extant vegetation. We are relatively well informed on the representation of Cerealia-type pollen in the modern pollen precipitation of large parts of the Near East. Surface samples have been collected along transects from the Levantine coast up to the higher part of the Iranian Zagros and in various directions across the Anatolian plateau (Wright et al. 1967; van Zeist et al. 1968 [1970]; 1975; Bottema and

Barkoudah 1979). The aim of such studies was to arrive at a better understanding of the relation of the extant vegetation and the pollen production of such vegetation. However, one may question whether the ample evidence that was gathered does actually inform us about the relation between cereal-type pollen and the plant species that produced these types. On many occasions a relation could be demonstrated between high Cerealia-type pollen percentages and nearby cereal farming. That does not imply that low Cerealia-type percentages found elsewhere were related to wild cereals. The low values could of course have been produced by more distant farming. A close look at the plant species listed for the various surface sample sites reveals the absence of wild ancestors of domestic cereals. This may be largely due to the principal aim of the investigations, namely, the study of the behavior of arboreal pollen in relation to herb pollen that defined the choice of the sites. On the other hand lack of time often prevented a thorough description of the plant communities present. If sampling had not taken place under limited conditions, wild cereals would certainly have been noticed if present. Another disadvantage of this method of sampling results from the moment chosen for the descriptions of the vegetation. During other seasons the presence of certain species might have been demonstrated more easily; for some of the samples taken no description of the accompanying vegetation could be made whatsoever.

A closer study of the Cerealia-type grains found, for instance by means of phase contrast, is of no great help because of the relatively poor quality of pollen in surface samples due to corrosion. The conclusion is that although we are informed on the presence of Cerealia-type pollen in various kinds of locations, the problem of the species producing this type remains unsolved apart from situations where farming is obvious. To obtain information on the representation of wild cereal species in the modern pollen precipitation a more detailed analysis is required. Such investigations could be focused upon dense stands of wild einkorn as have been reported for the slopes of the Karaça Dag in southeastern Anatolia. At the same time an attempt could be made to study the subfossil record. Although no lakes are indicated on maps of the Karaça Dag, Dr. J.J. Roodenberg located 13 place names in that area that include the word *göl* (lake). Obviously small lakes must be present which may contain sediments that could inform us about the subfossil record of wild einkorn on the Karaça Dag.

Chapter 9 ✑

Pollen Analysis of Wild and Domestic Wheats Under Experimental Cultivation

Marie-Françoise Diot

WHEN STUDYING ARCHAEOLOGICAL SITES, pollen analysts are confronted with the problem of interpreting cereal ratios. By what percentages can crops be distinguished in pollen diagrams? This question is particularly interesting for regions where wild grain grew spontaneously and where humans introduced a gradual process of domestication, characterized by a series of ancient cereals and tied to genetic changes. Most often, the relevant answers refer to present data on modern cereals and use artificial or natural (moss) pollen traps.

We tested these results by analyzing not only modern cereals but also spontaneous and formerly domesticated ones in order to determine whether their pollen dispersal is identical. By analogy with pollen data available in archaeology, we also analyzed the atmospheric pollen dispersed then trapped into sediment.

This study of spontaneous and domesticated (ancient and modern) wheats was carried out within the framework of experimental cultivation at Jalès (Ardèche)[1] in Mediterranean climatic conditions. These conditions therefore resemble those that must have existed in the Near East some ten thousand years ago, at the beginning of agriculture. The research will be carried out over several years and is concerned with diverse domestic plants. The results below correspond to the beginning of this work, on six wheat species chosen according to their chromosome structure (see table 9.1).

The seed came from botanic gardens, gene banks, or experimental farms: Gatersleben, Germany, for 12B; Butser Farm, England, for 82B; and Plant Breeding Institute, Cambridge, for the rest. The same analyses were carried out on a field of modern wheat (*Triticum aestivum aestivum* L.,

Table 9.1 Chromosome structure (ploidy) of wheat species chosen for study

GROUP I DIPLOID (2n = 14 chromosomes)
Spontaneous (wild) einkorn wheat
　Triticum boeoticum aegilopoïdes (Link) Schiem (seed from plot 55B)
Domestic wheat
　Triticum monococcum L. var. *vulgare* Korn, einkorn (seed from plot 12B)

GROUP II TETRAPLOID (2n = 28 chromosomes)
　Triticum dicoccum Schrank, emmer (seed from plot 82B)

GROUP III HEXAPLOID (2n = 42 chromosomes)
　Triticum compactum Host (seed from plot 13B)
　Triticum spelta L., spelt (seed from plot 9B)
Modern wheat
　Triticum aestivum aestivum L., bread wheat, modern

talent variety) growing near the experimental crops. This research was designed to explore three areas: *identification* of the various wheat species by their pollen; *dispersal* of wheat pollen in comparison with the atmospheric sporopollen context; and *preservation* of this pollen in the soil, in and around the fields, and on the threshing floors.

Pollen Differentiation

First, it appeared necessary to distinguish wheat pollen and thus determine the percentage of each in the modern pollen rain around the fields at Jalès. Pollen from wild cereal species differs from that of domestic species in size only. It is conventionally accepted that the boundary between the two is at 40 micrometers (μm). Cereal domestication produced a gradual increase to about 60 μm. Species are characterized by more or less large classes whose boundaries overlap.

Size of the pollen was estimated by measuring maximum

diameter, following the methodology of H.J. Beug (1961). Ripe stamens were taken directly from unripe ears in the experimental plots and from a field of modern cereals. After dehydration and acetolysis, the pollen was mounted on slides using a glycerin-gelatin preparation; a total of 250 grains per species were counted. At 400x magnification, there is a 1.8 μm interval between two consecutive measurements.

The size classes are shown in the form of histograms in figure 9.1. Below the histograms are the measurements taken by Beug (1961) on a large number of herbarium specimens prepared in the same way. The different wheat pollens from the Jalès experimental plots are clearly distinctive, showing a gradual increase in size from einkorn pollen to modern wheat for the different species, according to their supposed order of appearance in archaeology.

We must, however, note the difficulty in attempting to determine the beginning of agriculture by measuring the maximum diameter of pollen. In our experience, the average diameter of einkorn (*Triticum monococcum*) pollen is close to 40 μm, hence lower than the mean values measured by Beug. It is very close to the size of the spontaneous (wild) wheat pollen sown in the Jalès experimental plots (*Triticum boeoticum aegilopoïdes*, plot 55B).[2]

Several observations seem to enable characterization of the kinds of wheat sown at Jalès through measurements of the maximum diameter of pollen. Emmer wheat (*Triticum dicoccum*, sample 82B), for example, falls into the lowest values, according to Beug. As for *Triticum compactum*, its size diversity is greater than that shown by Beug's numerous measurements; it is linked to to the heterogeneity of the wheat grain. This seed (plot 13B) may be derived from a mixed landrace. For modern wheat (*Triticum aestivum*), the two peaks at 56 and 61 μm seem to correlate with the two varieties sown together in the field, one bearded (*prinqual*) and the other not (*galla*).

These observations lead to the hypothesis that each class of maximum diameters for pollen is characteristic of one species or group of species in relation to its polyploidy. It would be interesting to make a series of measurements on genetically well-known wheats to check whether this hypothesis functions independently of environmental factors such as plant nutrition and climate.

Pollen on Wheat Stalks

Before studying the dispersal of wheat pollen into the atmosphere around the plots, let us examine what happens on the plant itself. Pollen is produced in stamens, which are contained in a net, then enclosed with the ovary in the flower by glumes and palea and lemma (husks). Upon maturity, fertilization takes place inside the flower (autogamy), then the stamen's net grows, making the stamen visible and allowing pollen to disperse into the atmosphere. Wind-driven crossfertilization (allogamy) varying between 1 and 9%

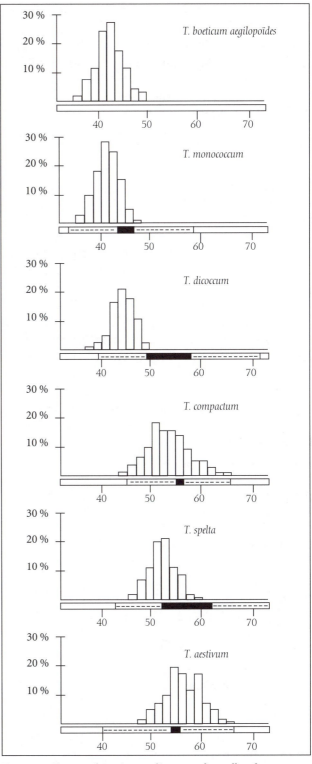

Figure 9.1 Classes of maximum diameters for pollen from wild and domestic wheats according to frequency (using 250 measurements). Below the histograms, maximum (broken lines) and mean (continuous lines) intervals are shown according to Beug (1981).

(Pesson and Louveaux 1984) was, however, shown by grain formation even after stamen ablation (Percival 1921). Fertilization can be influenced by climatic factors as well, when the ripe stamen leaves the flower owing to a rapid extension of the net before complete growth of glumes, lemma, and palea (Boyeldieu 1980).

Pollen is contained in large quantities in husks and may be released when the grain is threshed (Robinson and Hubbard 1977; Greig 1982). These quantities are estimated at 10^3 to 10^6 pollens per kilogram (Bottema 1988).

We did not count the absolute number of wheat pollen grains but their percentage compared with total pollen and spores, according to standard methodology in pollen analysis. We took samples of ears as well as samples of stalks and leaves from a plot of wild wheat and from a neighbouring field of a modern variety of wheat— therefore from the same general botanical environment. We rapidly washed the samples to gather pollen and spores.

The percentages of wheat pollen are high (table 9.2), between 56.3 and 98.1%. Nevertheless, the presence of other pollen is surprising, since the wheat stalks had come up only a few months earlier. Pollen from the surrounding vegetation corresponds to only twenty plants or so, including trees several kilometers away. Foreign pollen grains are more abundant on stalks and leaves than on ears, even though the wheat was planted very close together.

The quantity of wheat pollen found on stalks in plots appears to explain pollen concentration occurring when ears and straw (stalks and leaves) are stored or treated, as we see in the case of threshing floors. Although the pollen rain is probably the same in both fields, spontaneous wheats have a higher pollen ratio than domestic varieties. This difference is perhaps because of the greater atmospheric dispersal of pollen from wild wheats, which appears to contradict the natural law by which the largest pollen grains (of modern wheat) would be carried farther than smaller ones.

Pollen Preservation in Deposits

We attempted to determine whether pollen was preserved in and around the fields and on the threshing floors.

On threshing floors

Separation of grain and glumes releases pollen (van Zeist and Bottema 1983). Amounts of 20 to 35% of cereal pollen are interpreted as indicating threshing floors (Richard 1985). However, concentrations in threshing remains may vary from 1 to 100 (Behre 1981). In other structures (for example, latrines), ratios reach 35% and are interpreted as remains of cereal-based food (Greig 1981).

We explored this question using deposits from experimental threshing floors at Jalès where, in experiments, wild wheats were threshed by trampling or beating against a wall. For modern wheats, we took soil from a recent floor where threshing had been carried out using mechanical methods and abandoned only several years earlier. Wheat pollen represented 19.2 to 26.6% (table 9.3). Such results from the particular context at Jalès, in a Mediterranean-type

Table 9.2 Pollen ratio of wild and modern wheat in the plots prior to harvest (compared with the total amount of pollen and spores trapped)

	WILD WHEAT*	MODERN WHEAT**
Ears	98.1 %	76.2 %
Stalks and leaves	90.8 %	56.3 %

*Triticum boeoticum aegilopoïdes
**Triticum aestivum

Table 9.3 Pollen ratios for wild and modern wheats in deposits inside and around crops as well as on threshing floors (compared with overall pollen and spores counted)

	WILD WHEAT*	MODERN WHEAT**
Field	10.3 %	11.8 %
Border	2.9 %	3.1 %
At 10 μm	2.5 %	3.5 %
At 50 μm	1.4 %	
Threshing floor	26.6 %	19.2 %

* Triticum boeoticum aegilopoïdes
** Triticum aestivum

climate, fit well with the norms used in palyno-archaeology.

In and around the wheat fields

As we have seen, pollen remains on the plant itself and little disperses into the atmosphere. By studying natural traps (moss), Bastin (1964) observed less than 3% cereal pollen within 1000 meters of crops and a maximum of 5 to 12% on the field borders. Moreover, such ratios are not in related to the extent or proximity of crops (Heim 1970; Firmin 1986).

Our analyses dealt with the content of soil samples within fields of wild and domestic wheats, between plants and on field borders, as well as at 10 m and 50 m from plots. The samples, of the same geological and pedological nature, were taken at 1 cm depth. Although this superficial soil may result from mixing with an older deposit, this type of sampling seemed to us preferable to a horizontal pollen trap, given the context of experimentation for archaeology. The samples were prepared using the so-called classic method: hydrochloric acid (HCl) and hydrogen fluoride (HF), concentration in a liquor with a density of 2, and sieving between 5 and 200 μm. Microscopic observation first reveals the relatively poor condition of cereal pollen, which is often folded, complicating the measurement of maximum diameter. The results (table 9.3) show that within the field, hence at the level of the ears, the percentage of wheat pollen is 10.3 to 11.8, and therefore already relatively low. On the field border and at 10 m, it is close to 3%; at 50 m, it falls to 1.4%. These figures are of the same order as those obtained with natural or artificial traps and therefore unrelated to any factor involving preservation in soil deposits.

To summarize, cereal pollens disperse little outside the plant into the atmosphere, and samples taken from soil are as representative of this phenomenon as traps.

Conclusion

The pollen analyses carried out at Jalès demonstrate that it is possible, in the case of the wheat species tested here, to differentiate wheat species or groups of species by measuring the maximum diameter of pollen. It would be interesting to pursue this research in order to determine the relationship between pollen size and number of chromosomes.

Cereal pollen is preserved in high proportion compared with the general sporopollinic stock, on ears as well as on stalks and leaves. This may explain their abundance in places where ears and straw are used or stored. Their higher frequency for wild wheats is perhaps linked to a higher rate of wind dispersal than modern wheats.

The finding that the low dispersal of wheat pollen outside ears is shown by analyses of soil deposits as effectively as by analyses of traps is an advantage for archaeological research.

Acknowledgement. This chapter was translated from French by Jacqueline Gaudey, CRA, CNRS, France

Notes

1. Coordinated by P. Anderson.
2. See chapter 11 concerning this particular acquisition. Willcox and Anderson noted the even-ripening behavior of no. 55 in the field, which may indicate that it is a cross between wild and domestic einkorn.

Chapter 10 ✥

Domestication Rate in Wild Wheats and Barley Under Primitive Cultivation

Preliminary Results and Archaeological Implications of Field Measurements of Selection Coefficient

Gordon C. Hillman and M. Stuart Davies

IN THIS CHAPTER, WE ADHERE TO THE NARROW, classical definition of domestication, rather than the all-embracing application advocated by Rindos (1984:152–166; 1989). The term *domestication* here refers to that process that

a) occurs under cultivation in populations of wild-type crops sown originally from seed gathered from wild stands;

b) selectively advantages rare mutant plants lacking features (especially reproductive features) necessary for their survival in the wild; and

c) continues until these mutant types dominate the crop population and the original wild types are eliminated; that is, that process which renders crop populations dependent on human intervention for their survival, through the loss of wild-type adaptive features. Such a process involves genotypic changes (which are only tardily reversible) in entire populations, rather than fully reversible (plastic) changes in the phenotypes of individual plants of the sort that apparently distinguish wild and cultivated forms of Dioscorea yams in Africa and that have recently been reproduced experimentally by Chikwendu and Okezie (1989).

The shift from hunting and gathering to cultivation and pastoralism represents the single most dramatic (and ultimately the most catastrophic) set of changes that human society has experienced since the mastery of fire. The domestication of crop plants played a critical role in these events, if only at a late stage.

Domestication was recognized as an example of accelerated evolution by both Darwin (1859, 1868) and De Candolle (1886), but it was Vavilov (1917, 1926, 1951) and Engelbrecht (1917) who first postulated specific evolutionary pathways involved in the domestication of cereals such as the wild wheats and wild barley, and in the secondary domestication of cereals such as rye and oats. Since then, understanding of the possible processes involved has been further extended by the work of, for example, Darlington (1963, 1969, 1973), de Wet and Harlan 1975, Hammer (1984), Harlan (1965, 1975), Harlan and others (1973), Hawkes (1969, 1983, 1989A, b), Heiser, (1965, 1985, 1988, 1989), Johns (1989), Ladizinsky (1979, 1985B, 1987B, 1989), Pickersgill (1971, 1989), Pickersgill and others (1976, 1979), Riley (1965), Schiemann (1932), Schwanitz (1937), Wilson and Heiser (1979), and Zohary (1969, 1984, 1989ab, chapter 6). Research in this field continues apace, and the extent of still unresolved problems is reflected in the current debate between Ladizinsky (1987B, 1989ab)—proposing a model in which domestication of pulse crops such as lentils occurred prior to any cultivation and Zohary (1989b)—arguing that domestication of both pulses and cereals could have occurred only under cultivation.

For the wheats and barleys, the mechanism for domestication outlined in a seminal paper by Wilke et al. (1972) and extended by Harris (1976) foreshadows what our own studies suggest to have been the probable prehistoric pathway. Their hypothesis, however, overlooks certain factors necessary for domestication to have occurred at all, and, like most authors, they offer no estimate of the time required to achieve domestication under their proposed system of primitive cultivation. In the few published estimates, the time supposedly required to achieve unconscious domestication ranges from 1 to 1000 years. However, crop geneticists such as Harlan (1975), Ladizinsky (1987B) and Zohary (1969, 1984, 1989b, chapter 6)—with their unrivalled knowledge of the genetics and ecology of wild and domestic SW Asian cereals and pulses—have long recognised that the domestication of such crops could have been very rapid; thus Zohary (1969, chapter 6) suggests that "once the mutation occurred in the population taken into cultivation, mutant lines could have established themselves in a matter of a very few years." Indeed, in 1968, Zohary (in the unpublished discussion following presentation of his paper published in 1969) suggested a period of 20 years once the mutant was present, and Ladizinsky (1987B) similarly suggests that his proposed "domestication before cultivation" of lentils could have occurred in about 25 years (although some of his starting assumptions are puzzling). However, in no case known to us have estimates been based on measurements of those selection pressures responsible for domestication in the first place or on formal mathematical modelling. It was against this background that the present work was begun in 1972.

Assumptions

A dump-heap origin of domestic wheats and barley is improbable; after two decades botanizing in the wild-cereal heartlands of SW Asia, the first author has yet to see wild-type einkorn, emmer, or barley thriving in nitrogen-enriched ruderal habitats analogous to prehistoric middens—whether around human settlements, sheep/goat folds, or the heavily eroded and bedunged rest areas formed by domestic animals when grazing remote from their source settlement. The plants characterizing such habitats are generally dominated by genera toxic to livestock such as *Datura, Hyoscayamus*, and *Zygophyllum*, but not by wild cereals—even when they grow in abundance elsewhere in the same area (Hillman, unpublished field notes). (This is not to say that wild barley, for example, cannot grow in other habitats disturbed by humans, especially those analogous to naturally disturbed habitats such as mountain screes where wild barley often grows so prolifically.) Also, while some subtle effects of hunter-gatherer–mediated selection of the sort described by Rindos (1984: 154–158) are clearly not impossible, the pre-cultivation domestication scenario proposed for some pulses by Ladizinsky (1987b, 1989b)—and contested by Zohary (1989b) and previously dismissed in principle by Harlan et al. (1973)—cannot be extended to the cereals and seems improbable even for the pulses.

The first cereal crops must therefore have been sown by humans from seed gathered from wild stands and must have been essentially of the wild type. It was consequently in the course of cultivation that domestication (as defined above) occurred. In the case of einkorn wheat, for example, the domestic form (*Triticum monococcum* L. subsp.

Figure 10.1 Wild einkorn wheat (*Triticum monococcum* ssp. *boeoticum*): *a*, growing in oak (*Quercus cerris*) scrub on the lower S-facing slopes of the Munzur Mts. in eastern Turkey, 1971; *b*, growing in the ecotone between oak forest and steppe on the lower slopes of Karadağ in the Konya Basin of central Turkey, 1970. These were the two locations at which we undertook preliminary field measurements of the selection pressures generated by primitive methods of harvesting wild einkorn. When growing in these primary habitats, wild einkorn, like the other wild wheat–wild emmer—commonly forms vast, dense stands resembling unfenced fields and yielding just as much grain per hectare as some of their domesticated progeny reared under traditional cultivation. *Photographs courtesy of GCH*

monococcum) emerged from crops of its immediate ancestor—wild einkorn (*T. monococcum* L. subsp. *boeoticum* (Boiss.) A. and D. Löve) which still grows wild in the Near East—mainly in the ecotone between oak forest and steppe (figure 10.1). Throughout this chapter, cereals such as einkorn, emmer, and barley in their morphologically wild state but growing under cultivation are therefore called *cultivated, wild-type cereals*:

Wild einkorn (when cultivated, termed *cultivated, wild-type*)	*Triticum monococcum* subsp. *boeoticum* (also *T. urartu*)	Brittle rachis
Domestic einkorn	*Triticum monococcum* subsp. *monococcum*	Tough rachis (see below)

The term *wild cereals* is thus reserved for wild-type populations growing in wild habitats.[1]

Figure 10.2 Near-ripe ears of wild einkorn from which the upper spikelets have already been spontaneously shed. (The ears would originally have had 20 to 26 spikelets.) Hills above Asvan in eastern Turkey, 1971. *Photograph courtesy of GCH*

Aim of This Chapter

This chapter presents the preliminary results of an experimental approach to measuring domestication rate in crops of wild-type wheats and barley under primitive systems of husbandry. The results indicate that domestication will have occurred only if the wild-type crops were harvested in specific ways (and, in certain circumstances, may also have required shifting cultivation). The crop had to be harvested when at least partially ripe (and not while still green as evidenced archaeologically for some early cereals). Given these requirements, the crop could have become completely domesticated within two centuries, and maybe in as little as 20 to 30 years, without any form of conscious selection.

More specifically, the chapter considers the possible length of delays in the start of domestication owing to early crops of wild-type cereals lacking domestic-type mutants; examines the combination of primitive husbandry practices that would have been necessary for any selective advantage to have been unconsciously conferred on these mutants; considers the state of ripeness (at harvest) necessary for crops to be able to respond to these selective pressures; outlines field measurements of the selective intensities (selection coefficients) which arise when analogous husbandry practices are applied experimentally to living wild-type crops; summarizes the essential features of a mathematical model which incorporates these measurements of selection coefficients and other key variables and which describes the rate of increase in domestic-type mutants that would have occurred in early populations of wild-type cereal crops under specific combinations of primitive husbandry practices; considers why very early cultivators should have used that combination of husbandry methods which, we suggest, unconsciously brought about the domestication of these wild cereals; and concludes by considering whether these events are likely to have left recognizable traces in archaeological remains. There follows an appendix that assesses the usefulness of some of the criteria used by archaeobotanists in distinguishing wild and domestic remains of ancient cereals.

Differences Between Wild and Domestic Forms of Wheat and Barley

In cereals such as wheat, even the most primitive domesticated forms today differ from their wild progenitors in a number of polygenically determined grade characters such as awn robustness, glume rigidity, grain size, numbers of fertile florets, tillering tendency, uniformity of grain ripening, photosynthetic rate, and the abundance of barbs and hairs on the rachis and glumes (see, for example, Darlington 1963, 1969; de Wet 1977; Evans 1976; Hammer 1984; Harlan 1975; Harlan et al. 1973; Heiser 1988; Ladizinsky 1985b, 1987b, 1989a; Miller 1976; Percival 1921; Schiemann 1948; Schwanitz 1966; Sharma and Waines 1980; Zohary 1969, 1984, 1989a,b; chapter 6). All these authors note that the most critical adaptive differences, however, involve loss of wild-type seed dormancy and rachis fragility. Of these, only rachis fragility is readily apparent morphologically.

Differences in Rachis Fragility

In the wild wheats and barley, the mature rachis disarticulates between each of the fertile spikelets, thereby allowing them to be shed spontaneously. Disarticulation occurs from the top of the ear downwards (figure 10.3a). The arrow-like morphology of the spikelets with their smooth points, springy awns, long straight glumes, and backward-pointing barbs and hairs thereafter ensures that they quickly penetrate any surface litter and wedge themselves in cracks in the ground where at least a proportion of them remain relatively safe from birds, rodents and seed-eating ants. (In the Near East where wild wheats and barley are native, pressure from these predators is intense.) By contrast, in even the most primitive of the domesticated wheats and barleys, the rachis fails to disarticulate spontaneously, and the ear remains intact until the crop is harvested and threshed (figure 10.3b).[2]

If sown in the wild, these domestic plants are unable to reproduce themselves, as their spikelets are not efficiently disseminated and protected from predation. Indeed, even if their ears were eventually to disintegrate in the autumn rains, the fact that their spikelets lack the self-implantation features of the wild types ensures that they will fail to bury themselves; the rough break in the rachis impedes penetration of the ground litter, the glumes lack the recurved hairs and prominent barbs, and the awns are weak and readily deciduous and so fail in their task of pointing the spikelet downwards through leaf litter (figure 10.3b). Such spikelets quickly fall prey to birds, rodents, and ants, a fact that is evident from the extreme rarity in the Near East of feral domesticated cereals in anything other than modern habitats (such as the first half-metre of motorway verges) of a type unlikely to have existed in antiquity (*contra* the misleading

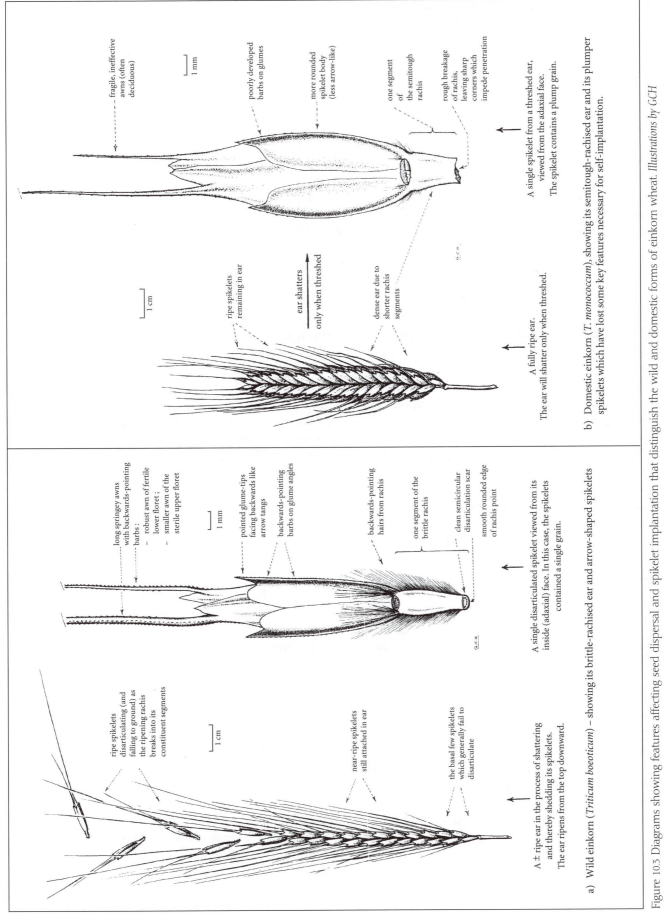

Figure 10.3 Diagrams showing features affecting seed dispersal and spikelet implantation that distinguish the wild and domestic forms of einkorn wheat. *Illustrations by GCH*

Top panel (right diagrams):

fragile, ineffective awns (often deciduous)

poorly developed barbs on glumes

more rounded spikelet body (less arrow-like)

1 mm

one segment of the semitough rachis

rough breakage of rachis, leaving sharp corners which impede penetration

A single spikelet from a threshed ear, viewed from the adaxial face. The spikelet contains a plump grain.

ripe spikelets remaining in ear

1 cm

ear shatters only when threshed

dense ear due to shorter rachis segments

A fully ripe ear. The ear will shatter only when threshed.

b) Domestic einkorn (*T. monococcum*), showing its semitough-rachised ear and its plumper spikelets which have lost some key features necessary for self-implantation.

Bottom panel (left diagrams):

long springey awns with backwards-pointing barbs:
– robust awn of fertile lower floret;
– smaller awn of the sterile upper floret

1 mm

pointed glume-tips facing backwards like arrow tangs

backwards-pointing barbs on glume angles

backwards-pointing hairs from rachis

one segment of the brittle rachis

clean semicircular disarticulation scar

smooth rounded edge of rachis point

A single disarticulated spikelet viewed from its inside (adaxial) face. In this case, the spikelets contained a single grain.

ripe spikelets disarticulating (and falling to ground) as the ripening rachis breaks into its constituent segments

1 cm

near-ripe spikelets still attached in ear

the basal few spikelets which generally fail to disarticulate

A ± ripe ear in the process of shattering and thereby shedding its spikelets. The ear ripens from the top downward.

a) Wild einkorn (*Triticum boeoticum*) – showing its brittle-rachised ear and arrow-shaped spikelets suggestions in Jarman 1972). This near-absence of feral cereals is the more significant in view of the widespread spillage of cereal grains and spikelets which regularly occurs along the waysides between between field and threshing yard. (For the amounts lost, see ICARDA 1980; BSTID et al. 1981). Outside cultivation, therefore, the domestic mutant is doomed.

Domestication Criterion

The measure of the degree of domestication in study populations was the ratio of plants with semitough rachises to plants with brittle rachises. The merits of using this criterion are as follows: rachis fragility plays a crucial role in the process of domestication, as the tougher forms of rachis are lethal in the wild but are favored under certain forms of cultivation; the different states of rachis toughness are potentially recognizable in archaeological remains (see below); and it is much easier to study in modern crop populations than characters such as seed dormancy.

Doubts regarding the usefulness of this criterion were voiced by Jarman (1972) but were mistaken: nobody who has harvested both wild einkorn in primary habitats and domestic einkorn under cultivation could fail to recognise the clear difference between the two forms in their degree of rachis fragility – except in basal rachis nodes (see appendix). This point is also strongly emphasised by Willcox (chapter 11) from the extensive field experiments at Jalès. As justification for her view, Jarman cites the infestation of crops with ostensibly self-sown domestic einkorn recorded by Schwanitz (1937). However, this weedy einkorn probably represented either contamination of seed stocks of the host crop by spikelets of normal (semitough) ears of weedy domestic einkorn which were harvested and threshed together with the host crop; self-sowing of relatively brittle-rachised forms which inevitably emerge in some weed populations of domestic einkorn—in response to the obvious selective advantage of spikelets being shed prior to the harvest of the host crop; a combination of both strategies (each based on a different rachis genotype) via disruptive selection of the sort observed by Hillman (1978: 168) in segetal populations of wild-type einkorn in Turkey. (See also Harlan 1975, 1982; Harlan, chapter 1; Harlan et al. 1973; and de Wet and Harlan 1975; who detail equivalent phenomena in, for example, millet, sorghum and sugarcane).

However, this should not lead us to imagine that using rachis fragility is without problems as a criterion for recognising domestication in archaeological remains. (Some of these problems are discussed below.) It should also be stressed that, in reality, domestication is a complex syndrome involving changes in many different characteristics, of which rachis fragility is but one.

Archaeological Evidence of Domestication
Rachis remains
Rachis remains of cereals such as wheat, barley, rye, and oats are quite commonly preserved on later archaeological sites. On most sites, they have resisted microbial decay only by virtue of having been charred by fire immediately before deposition. When preservation is good, these rachis remains can often provide clear evidence of whether the cereal was of the wild type with a fully brittle rachis (as in wild einkorn and emmer), of the domestic type with a semitough rachis (as in domestic einkorn and emmer), or of the domestic type with a fully tough rachis (as in bread or macaroni wheats). Distinguishing the first two can prove difficult, but generally, disarticulation in wild cereals leaves a clean, semicircular or reniform scar, while, in the semitough rachised domestic derivatives, the scar is linear, jagged, and irregular, with no clean abscission surface (figure 10.3; see also chapter 11). However, as stressed in the appendix to this chapter, there are at least two exceptions to this rule, and several other complicating factors. Uncertain identifications of problem specimens can nevertheless be checked by examining the histology of tissues in the abscission zone of the rachis node (Frank 1974, as cited by Kislev 1989B; Kislev 1989B).

Substitute criteria
Apart from the complicating factors discussed in the appendix, we also face the omnipresent problem that all forms of rachis remains are remarkably rare on those early archaeological sites dating from the beginnings of agriculture (that is, from the earliest phases of the Aceramic Neolithic). In consequence, archaeobotanists generally attempt to distinguish wild wheats and barleys from their domestic derivatives using secondary features such as grain shape. In the wheats, these grain features are often unsatisfactory, although in the barleys they can perform a useful role in distinguishing six-rowed and naked domesticates from the wild type.

Present Chronology of Remains of Domesticates
On the basis of these often problematic grain-based characteristics, the earliest appearance of seemingly fully domesticated cereals in western Eurasia is currently dated to ca. 7800 BC (radiocarbon years; ca. 8800 BC in calendar years) at Neolithic Aswad in southwestern Syria, and fractionally later at Jericho, Gilgal, and Netiv Hagdud in Palestine, the Neolithic occupation at Abu Hureyra in northern Syria, and slightly later again at Çayönü in southeastern Turkey. In each case, the cereals identified were emmer wheat and barley, except at Neolithic Abu Hureyra and Çayönü where einkorn was also found, together with rye at Abu Hureyra (Bar-Yosef and Kislev 1989; Helbaek 1969; Hillman 1975; Hillman Colledge and Harris, 1989; Hopf 1983; Kislev 1989B; Kislev et al. 1986; van Zeist 1972; van Zeist and Bakker-Heeres 1979). Of these sites, only Netiv Hagdud and Neolithic Abu Hureyra produced useful quantities of rachis remains.

Dating the Start of Cultivation (Rather than Domestication)
However, such finds do not necessarily date the beginnings

of cultivation; they merely date the completion of the ensuing process of domestication. If we are to date the beginnings of *cultivation*, we must take the earliest date for the emergence of ostensibly domesticated forms (currently ca. 8800 BC – calibrated) and add to it that block of time required to achieve full domestication once the crop was under cultivation. This we have termed the period of *predomestication cultivation*. However, not all forms of primitive husbandry advantage tougher-rachised forms (see below), and it is therefore possible that many of the earliest farmers would have applied practices of this ineffective type for an indefinite period of nondomestication cultivation before eventually adopting those techniques of predomestication cultivation which inexorably led to domestication.

This potentially long delay would have been preceded by an additional delay (that is, more nondomestication cultivation) because of the absence of semitough rachised mutants in the first crop populations (see chapter 6). However, this preliminary delay is likely to have been very short in most cases (see below).

To date the beginnings of even predomestication cultivation, we therefore need to know

a) how quickly semitough-rachised phenotypes could have appeared in early wild-type crops;

b) precisely which combination of husbandry methods would have effected domestication in a wild-type crop (including the state of maturity at which it had to be harvested);

c) whether other forms of husbandry would have been completely ineffective in this role;

d) whether the initial husbandry methods used by the first farmers were most likely to have been the ineffective ones, and, if so, how quickly they would have swapped over to the effective methods; and

e) how long the process would have taken once the effective methods were applied. All five questions are addressed below. (We return to the subject of the archaeological record towards the end of the chapter.)

Raw Materials of Domestication

The domestic forms of einkorn, emmer, and barley originated from semitough rachised recessive mutants produced in (and still being produced in) populations of brittle rachised wild forms. In these wild populations, the mutants are very rare because the net forward mutation rate of such genes is likely to be low (we have assumed a net forward mutation rate of 10 to 6 per plant generation); this mutation pressure is balanced by rapid elimination of the mutant phenotypes which have zero adaptive value in the wild; and this automatically eliminates half the mutant genes in the population because— although the mutant allele is recessive to the wild-type (brittle-rachis) allele and so is manifested only when homozygous— wild wheats and barley are inbreeders so that half the mutant alleles end up in the homozygous stock.

If we take einkorn as our example and if we assume (as do Sharma and Waines 1980: 215) that—of the two loci they identified controlling rachis fragility— only one was initially involved in domestication (see below), then large wild stands of this essentially inbreeding species will contain only one homozygous individual (producing semitough rachised ears) for every 2 to 4 million brittle-rachised individuals. The concentration of additional mutant alleles carried (unmanifested) in brittle-rachised heterozygotes will also be low; because einkorn is an inbreeder and because homozygous recessives are nonviable in the wild, half the recessive alleles are eliminated in each generation. The wild types will consequently be almost entirely homozygous with, nominally, only one or two heterozygotes per 2 to 4 million brittle-rachised types.

However, these estimates are no more than a convenient simplification. Not only was more than one locus eventually involved but modifier genes could also have altered patterns of dominance at these loci during the past eleven millennia (see below). Nevertheless, the estimates are adequate for the purpose of the provisional mathematical model presented here, particularly as we use a very broad range of values for each variable.

The Start of Cultivation

We must next consider what would have happened to these rare semitough-rachised mutants, when, sometime around the end of the Pleistocene, groups which had hitherto lived primarily by hunting and gathering took seed stocks from wild stands of brittle-rachised wheat or barley and sowed them on cleared land elsewhere. (Why they should have done this is not the subject of this chapter.)

In view of the very low frequencies of the mutants in wild populations, it is probable that no mutants were present in the initial stocks of seed gathered from wild stands (Zohary 1988). The vast majority (may be all) of the first crops would therefore have lacked the mutant and been entirely of the brittle-rachised type. Any selection for domesticates therefore had to wait until the mutants were thereafter generated spontaneously within the early crops themselves. Domestication can therefore be seen to have involved two distinct stages (Zohary 1988). The first (preliminary) phase involved cultivation of purely brittle-rachised populations totally lacking semitough-rachised mutants and will have continued until such time as the mutants were generated. The length of this phase depended on the size of the crop population, and in most cases is likely to have been very short. The second phase began with the appearance of the

Table 10.1 Size of early crop populations as basis for estimating the time required for the emergence of domestic mutants in the first wild-type einkorn crops

	GRAIN NEEDS*	AREAS SOWN**	
		ASSUMING YIELDS OF 500 KG PER HECTARE*****	ASSUMING YIELDS OF 1000 KG PER HECTARE******
Calculations based on 25% of economic grain equivalent consumed by present-day subsistence farmers of Near East***	700 kg	2.8 hectares	1.4 hectares
Calculations based on 25% of minimum caloric need of modern humans and laboratory measurements of calorie content of modern wheat grain****	330 kg	0.75 hectares	0.4 hectares

Note: The table suggests the hectarage of wild-type cereals likely to have been sown (by the first farmers) for each nuclear family of five, assuming that grain from cultivated cereals provided a modest 25% of their calorie requirements. The areas cultivated by extended families or entire farming communities would doubtless have been much larger.

* To provide 25% of total calorie requirements for a family of five per year
** To provide grain sufficient for 25% of calorie needs for a family of five
*** Clark and Haswell (1967) cite consumption of mean "economic grain equivalent" (that is, the economic equivalent of total dependance on grain) of 650 kg/adult/year. Such a figure allows for incomplete digestion/absorption of grain foods and for consumption in excess of theoretical minimum energy needs, but it is nevertheless well below the levels observed in recent Anatolian villages practicing traditional forms of subsistence (Hillman 1973).
**** Calorie needs of humans are here based on "standard nutritional unit" of 10^6 kcal/adult/year. The laboratory measurement of calorie yield of whole wheat flour used here = ca. 330 kcal/100 g (at 12% moisture). (Both figures are taken from Legge, in press.)
***** 500 kg/hectare accords with the lowest returns expected from wild or primitive domestic cereals (for example, see chapter 11; Hillman 1973; Russell 1988; Zohary 1969).
****** 1000 kg/hectare exceeds Zohary's (1969) top figures for wild emmer in primary habitats but is well below some of Willcox's (chapter 11) top figures for wild einkorn under primitive cultivation.

first mutant phenotypes (initially at very low frequencies), and its duration will have been largely independent of crop population size. This second phase would have followed one of two pathways: If husbandry methods were of a type which selectively advantaged the mutant phenotypes, then a period of predomestication cultivation would have automatically culminated in full domestication of the crop. If, however, the husbandry methods disadvantaged the mutants, then the crop would have remained in its wild state indefinitely (that is, nondomestication cultivation) until finally replaced by domesticated seed-stocks obtained from elsewhere.

Preliminary Phase: Delay in Domestication Because of Absence of Mutants in the First Crops

As noted above, the time required for semitough-rachised mutants to be generated spontaneously within the initial wild-type crop populations will have depended on the size of the crop populations; in large populations, it would have happened almost immediately; in small populations, it would have taken longer, and any possibility of domestication would then have been delayed for some years. In both cases, however, we are dealing only with probabilities, and there will have been exceptions.

How big an area of cereals were the first farmers likely to have sown and how long would the resulting predomestication delay have been? Regrettably, we still do not know the extent to which the first farmers depended on cultivated grain foods—and thence the areas they needed to sow. It is nevertheless clear from the range of possibilities considered below that the areas sown were likely to have been sufficiently large to ensure that the mutant became available within fewer than 20 years in most of the early crops of wheat and barley.

Table 10.1 offers estimates of the areas that might have been sown to provide a modest 25% of the total calorie needs of each nuclear family of five. (Although the figure of 25% was selected merely as a convenient example for the present calculations, it seems quite reasonable in the context of a new model for the initial adoption of einkorn cultivation in the northern Fertile Crescent [Hillman 1986]). There is sadly no agreed upon figure for the likely grain yields per unit area or for calorie yields from consumed grain, and we have therefore used two levels of each. On this basis, the areas under cultivation could have ranged from 0.3 to 3 hectares. (A hectare plot is 100 x 100 metres, or about 2.5 acres). If, however, cultivated grain foods provided only one-tenth of calorie needs, then the sown areas could have ranged from 0.1 to 1.2 hectares.

It is, however, generally considered that there is little point in going to the considerable trouble of cultivating staple sources of carbohydrate such as wheat and barley which are amenable to mass harvesting unless they meet a major part of total calorie needs. (This contrasts with the situation for other food crops such as the Old World pulses; see chapter 5.) The smaller areas suggested above are therefore rather improbable. Furthermore, all the above estimates assume separate cultivation by each family of five. Not only does this ignore the food needs of dependent members of the extended family, but, in reality, the collaborative subsistence strategies of most recent hunter-gatherers suggests that the earliest attempts at cultivating staples probably involved whole bands working jointly. The collective crops of entire bands would clearly have occupied areas much larger than those estimated in table 10.1.

Given a mutation rate of 10^{-6}, one homozygous mutant plant can be expected in every 2 to 4 million of the brittle-rachised wild type. At a modest sowing rate of about 200 spikelets per m^2, therefore, such a mutation could be expected to appear (in a single growing season) in a cultivated area of no larger than 1 to 2 hectares. (200 spikelets per m^2 is based on sowing rates for wheat under recent traditional husbandry; see Hillman 1973b). All the areas cited above (needed to provide just 25% of the calorie need of mere nuclear families) would have allowed mutants to be generated within just 5 years, and in inbreeders such as wheat and barley, the homozygous recessive would appear 1 year later. With the areas likely to have been collectively cultivated by whole bands, the mutants probably appeared in just 2 years.

Even if the areas sown were as small as one-tenth hectare (of roughly 30 x 30 m), the mutant form is likely to have appeared in 10 to 20 years. Potentially longer delays from cultivating yet smaller plots would probably have been cut short by the farmers obtaining domestic seed stocks from bands in whose crops the process of domestication started almost immediately. (The agronomic advantages of domesticates over wild-type crops would probably have been recognised by at least some of the earliest farmers, and the evidence for extensive social and trade networks amongst both recent and ancient hunter-gatherers suggests that few of the earliest farmers would have been cut off from seed stocks of domesticates for very long.)

For the majority of early cultivators, therefore, the constraints of crop population size and mutant availability are unlikely to have delayed the start of domestication to a degree which we can now detect archaeologically. [3]

Conscious or Unconscious Selection?

All the available evidence would suggest that, in the early stages of cultivation, selection favoring semitough-rachised mutants was entirely unconscious (that is, unintentional). Indeed, estimates of the frequency of homozygous recessives cited above suggest that farmers gathering their first seed stocks from wild stands will have been unaware of the existence of these tough-rachised mutant forms and that they would have remained oblivious of them for as long as the crop stayed in its essentially wild-type state. The reasons are as follows: The mutants forms were extremely rare (see above); in cereals such as wild einkorn, the ears ripen very unevenly (both within and between plants) such that mutant ears will have looked no different from the thousands of ears which had not yet shattered because they were still slightly unripe; any ears which remained intact in the field after all the others had shattered would have been rapidly predated by birds (they are much more readily predated if still attached to the top of a culm). The mutants could not therefore have been picked out by simply waiting until the end of the spikelet-shedding season.

There would therefore have been no real possibility of conscious selection during either nondomestication cultivation or the early stages of predomestication cultivation. Only once the frequency of semitough-rachised mutants had risen to a level at which they were obvious in the crop stand (perhaps around the 1 to 5% level) is conscious selection likely to have been applied (see figure 10.11).

Similar arguments also allow us to dismiss the thunderstorm theory, which proposes that, in wild stands of cereals or in early wild-type crops, passing thunderstorms would have shattered all the brittle ears, leaving only the rare, semitough-rachised ears as the source of seed for next year's crop. A fully domesticated crop would thus have been generated in just one year—with or without the farmers awareness on the part of. The uneven ripening of einkorn ears (coupled with rapid predation of isolated tough-rachised ears), however, renders such a scenario highly improbable.

Our conclusion that unconscious selection was involved in at least the early stages of domestication accords with conventional wisdom. Unconscious selection in early crops was first proposed by Darwin (1859, 1968). Its nature and possible consequences were subsequently explored by Vavilov (1926), and thereafter by Darlington (1963, 1969), Harlan (1975), Harlan et al. (1973), Ladizinsky (1987b, 1989a, b), Rindos (1984), and Zohary (1969, 1984, 1989b, chapter 6), and were recently reviewed by Heiser (1988).

Husbandry System Necessary for Domestication

Did this unconscious selection occur automatically at each and all the early settlements cultivating wild-type cereals? Our studies suggest not: the semitough-rachised homozygotes would have experienced a positive selective advantage only under specific conditions.

Assuming unconscious selection, evidence presented below suggests that semitough-rachised homozygotes would have been selectively advantaged in crops of wild-type wheat or barley only if particular harvesting methods were used (see Wilke et al. 1972); and the crops were harvested when partially ripe or near ripe.

In some cases, there would have been two additional pre-requisites, namely annual extensions or shifts in the areas under cultivation; and each year's seed stocks to be drawn from the harvests of the previous season's new plots.

In theory, these husbandry methods would not necessarily have been the most efficient nor the most familiar (from their hunter-gatherer backgrounds). Theoretically, therefore, the cereals of many of the earliest farmers could have continued in their wild-type, brittle-rachised state for a period until they were eventually replaced by domesticated forms brought in as seed stocks from other farming settlements where the effective (domestication-inducing) combination of husbandry techniques had been applied (Hillman 1978:167).

Figure 10.4 Harvesting trial plots of wild-type einkorn by beating at the Cleppa Park facilities of the Department of Plant Science, University College Cardiff (Wales) in 1979. On this occasion, GCH was using a butter-pat, but generally the bare hand was more effective. *Photograph courtesy of Isobel Ellis.*

Terms Used to Describe States of Ripeness

A fully ripe crop of a wild-type cereal is one in which the spikelets have all been shed, and harvesting then involves picking them up from the ground. The traditional methods considered below (beating, reaping, uprooting, and so forth) can thus be applied only to partially or near-ripe crops (in which disarticulation has begun but is still incomplete) or to completely unripe crops (in which no spikelets have yet starting disarticulating). Because wild einkorn ripens very unevenly, the terms *partially* and *near ripe* necessarily refer to the average state of the crop as a whole.[4]

Harvesting Methods and the Crop Maturity at Harvest

Our evidence indicates that, of the range of harvesting methods available, domestication would have occurred only if the crops were harvested while partially ripe (or near ripe) by means of sickle reaping or uprooting.

There are five main harvesting methods with which the earliest cereal cultivators are likely to have been familiar from their earlier experience as foragers. These methods will have included beating ripe spikelets into baskets—applied to partially or near-ripe stands in single or multiple passes (though never, of course, to completely unripe stands); reaping with sickles or other cutting implements—whether on near-ripe crops or on unripe ones; uprooting (likewise on near-ripe or unripe ears); plucking or hand-stripping; and harvesting by burning. The viability of each of these methods is attested by ethnographic studies of wild-grass seed foragers (whether hunter-gatherers or farmers supplementing their harvests of domestic grains), by archaeological evidence, by our own field experiments, by the field observations of scientists such as Harlan (1989 and chapter 1) and Zohary (chapter 6), and by experiments at archaeo-agricultural research establishments such as Butser Ancient Farm (see Reynolds 1981 and chapter 27) and the Jalès-based Institut de

Préhistoire Orientale (see chapters 11 and 12).

Harvesting by Beating the Ripe Spikelets into Baskets. Beating the ears such that all ripe spikelets are knocked into a basket can be very quick and efficient, and it involves the least stooping. Applied to partially or near-ripe wild wheats or barley, beating automatically harvests the spikelets from ripe brittle-rachised ears, but leaves behind any tough-rachised ears together with large numbers of unripe ears of the brittle type. (The latter—or a proportion of them—can be harvested a few days later in subsequent rounds of beating). Tough-rachised ears left behind after the harvest are stripped by birds, and even if their spikelets were to fall to the ground, their almost complete failure to penetrate ground litter and self-implant ensures their predation by rodents, birds, and ants. In consequence, they do not contribute to the ensuing generations of crops, even when the same patch is cultivated next season.

Some spikelets from brittle-rachised ears invariably fall to the ground during harvest. If the farmer relies on these to seed next year's crop, they will inevitably be of the wild type. Likewise, new plots sown from the harvested seed will be entirely of the wild type. Harvesting by beating thus selects strongly in favor of the wild type and against tough-rachised forms—regardless of what other husbandry practices accompany it.

Beating was the harvesting method we found to take the least effort and also produced the greatest yields per unit time whenever we harvested wild-type einkorn in dry weather (figure 10.4). Correspondingly, after trying many different methods on a wide range of grasses in four continents, Harlan (chapter 1) notes:

> of the traditional gathering techniques, the beater and basket method produced the cleanest and most uniform material.... Having used both sickle and beater, I had to wonder why the sickle was ever preferred to the beater…

It comes as no surprise, therefore, to find that beating was the method favored by most of those recent hunter-gatherers who were heavily dependent on wild-grass seed. In reviewing their harvesting methods, Bohrer was able to state that "sweeping, scooping and beating movements...characterize most accounts of wild-grass seed harvests in the world" (1972:145). For North America, Harris notes that "throughout the Great Basin grass seeds were harvested by beating with a wooden or basketry paddle to knock the ripe seeds into a basket" (1984:66). Most of the examples cited in the remarkable review by Maurizio (1927:33–53) again involve similar methods. (See also O'Connell et al. 1983 for a further Australian example). Even those farming and pastoral groups who supplemented their cultivated grain foods with wild-grass seed commonly harvested the seed by beating, even

Figure 10.5 Harvesting trial plots of wild–type einkorn with a flint–bladed sickle at University College, Cardiff in 1979: *a*, Fayum–type sickle, *b*, Carmel–type sickle . *Photograph courtesy of Isobel Ellis*

though they owned steel sickles (see, for example, Barth 1857 I:482, & III:29 [as cited by both Harlan 1989 and Bohrer 1972]; Harlan 1989; Maurizio 1927; Scudder 1971). It should be noted that these methods were also applied in harvesting the grain of wild *Elymus* spp. which, as fellow members of the tribe Triticeae, have ears not dissimilar to those of the wild wheats and barley (for example, Maurizio [1927] for Mongolia and northern Europe, and Stewart [1933, 1941] for North America).

Beating cannot, however, be applied to domesticated crops, and even if applied to wild-type crops, its advantage of high returns per unit of harvesting time is outweighed by the heavy harvesting losses per unit area. These disadvantages are considered in detail below.

Sickle reaping applied to partially ripe crops. This method (figures 10.5 and 10.6) can select strongly in favor of tough-rachised forms. However, in some cases this selection will occur only if the grain is sown on new plots of land each year using seed taken from last year's new plots.

When a sickle is applied to the culms of wild wheats and barley, some of the spikelets from the top (ripest) parts of the most mature ears promptly disarticulate and fall to the ground. No equivalent loss is experienced by the semitough-rachised ears, and their percentage representation in the harvested spikelets is therefore greater than it was in the parent field.

Crops sown from the harvested grain will reflect this increased proportion of tough-rachised forms, and this increase will continue, year on year, for as long as crops are always sown on new land from harvests taken from the previous year's new plot(s). Eventually, the crop will be composed entirely of tough-rachised forms, and at this point, domestication (in respect of the fixation of semitough rachis) is complete.

By contrast, those plots cultivated in previous years will maintain crops of exclusively wild types because they are self-sown by spikelets shed from brittle-rachised ears during the previous season's harvest. Clearly, then, seed taken from this old land and sown on virgin plots would reverse the process of domestication. (The effect of sowing additional harvested grain [containing mutants] on these old plots is considered below.)

Sickle reaping applied to unripe crops. Applied to completely unripe (green) stands, this method would have had no selective effect either way; potentially brittle rachises fail to disarticulate while still unripe (unless dried), and so both types get harvested in the same proportions in which they are represented in the field. Fields sown from the harvested spikelets will thence produce the same proportions of either type as in the previous year.[5]

However, if the crop is even fractionally ripe, there will be

Figure 10.6 Traditional sickle-reaping of wheat (in this case, an indigenous form of bread wheat) near Kaymakli in central Turkey in 1974. The sickles were of steel and were toothed. *Photograph courtesy of GCH*

Figure 10.7 Children harvesting barley by uprooting near Gölü Dag in central Turkey in 1974. Until very recently, barley was generally harvested by uprooting, whether with the bare hands or with the help of an uprooting hook (Tur.: kiliç; see Hillman 1984,1985). *Photograph courtesy of GCH*

some loss of spikelets from the tops of some brittle-rachised ears, and the semitough-rachised phenotype will thus be selectively favored. In view of the uneven ripening of einkorn, this effect will be avoided only in very unripe crops, and this is rare, because such crops produce shrivelled, unfilled (and therefore underweight) grain. In practice, therefore, unripe generally means partially ripe, and sickle reaping applied to such crops will still selectively advantage domesticates, albeit at lower intensities (see below).

Harvesting wild cereals and other grasses in a partially (or fully) unripe state offers the clear advantage of pre-empting most of the loss of spikelets from brittle-rachised ears which otherwise occurs during harvesting. This is especially so in species which ripen more evenly, such as wild emmer (*T. dicoccoides*), in which Unger-Hamilton (1989) found that potential loss of spikelets was almost completely pre empted by reaping it while it was green (see also Anderson-Gerfaud 1988; chapter 12; Anderson-Gerfaud et al. 1991; Willcox, chapter 11).

However, we know of only two cases of sickle reaping of

unripe wild grasses amongst recent hunter-gatherers; the first is the Kawaiisu harvest of *Oryzopsis* in Southern California (Zigman 1941:142, as cited by Bohrer 1972:147); the second is Allen's (1974:314) citation of an aboriginal people of S.W. Queensland (Australia) using flint knives to cut a wild millet—presumably in the partially unripe state in both cases, in order to avoid losses from shattering. In reviewing the Australian evidence for grass-seed harvesting, Harris (1984:65) also notes that Allen's example is the only case of blade harvesting known to him.

By contrast, when harvesting cereals as crops in their domesticated state, it is quite common to harvest them while still partially unripe. The sweet-flavoured, milk-ripe or dough-ripe grains of domestic wheats are used, for example, by farmers in Schwabia and Bavaria to make the highly esteemed *Grünkern*, by the Syrian Arabs and Palestinians to make *frikké*, and by the Turks to make *firig* (Hillman 1985:13–14). Indeed, Percival (1921:140) suggests that harvesting grain-crops when dough-ripe was fairly standard before the days of the combine harvester. Even when applied to these domesticated cereals, however, the advantages are the same: superior flavor and prevention of loss of grain during harvest and transport (see Percival 1921:140). These advantages presumably outweigh the disadvantage of the lower starch content per grain and lower gross yields.

Harvesting partially ripe wild-type crops by uprooting. This method (figure 10.7) shakes the ears in a manner similar to sickle reaping, and the resulting loss of spikelets from the ripe tops of near-ripe brittle-rachised ears selects for tough-rachised mutants exactly as described in "Sickle reaping applied to partially ripe crops" above. Once again, however, this selective effect can be guaranteed in all cases only if the seed stock is always taken from grain from last year's new plots and sown on new land each year.

With fully domesticated cereals, uprooting is still widely used in traditional agriculture, especially for barley (for example, Hillman 1985; Leser 1970) though not in areas with clay soils which dry out in summer. Archaeological evidence for uprooting of domesticates is also more widespread than hitherto supposed (Hillman 1981), although such finds often cannot determine whether the crops were ripe or unripe when harvested.

Uprooting completely unripe crops. Applied to completely unripe crops, this harvesting method, like sickle reaping (of completely unripe crops), has no selective effect either way (see "Sickle reaping applied to unripe crops" above) but offers the advance of sweeter grain and preempting grain loss during harvest. If the crop is even fractionally ripe, however, some positive selection for the semitough-rachised phenotype will occur, as above. Harvesting unripe wild grasses by uprooting has been recorded for a number of different aboriginal peoples of Australia; for example, Mitchell in 1835 (as cited by Allen 1974:313–4) observed it being applied on a massive scale in the Darling River valley.

Harvesting by hand-plucking or stripping. Hand-stripping was apparently used by a number of hunter-gatherer groups for harvesting the seed of paniculate grasses (see, for example, O'Connell et al. 1983). We have found that loose-handed stripping of the ripe, disarticulating spikelets (leaving behind the lower part of the ear) works like an inefficient form of beating—with similar selective effects (see "Sickle reaping applied to partially ripe crops" above). However, it is very slow compared with beating and seems unlikely to have been used on any scale for wild cereals in prehistory. (For a different view, see Anderson-Gerfaud 1988.)

For the domestic cereals, Sigaut (1984) argues that the stripping of whole ears has cultural affiliations which are distinct from those of plucking and that the two terms should be kept separate (see also Hillman 1985:6–7). However, applied to brittle-rachised cereals, the two methods work in the same way (see Anderson-Gerfaud 1988). Hand-plucking (in the Sigaut sense) has been applied experimentally to domesticated glume wheats with some success by Reynolds (1981), and hand-plucking/stripping was used by some Mongolian farmers to harvest domestic cereals (Rona Tas 1959:449, as cited by Bohrer 1972). On a larger scale, some farming groups in the Spanish province of Asturias (Sigaut 1978) and in the Georgian SSR (Bregadze 1982a:86–88) harvest their glume wheats by the bulk stripping of groups of ears with the aid of a "stripping clamp" (Spanish *mesorias*; Georgian *shamkvi, shankvi* or *shakvi),* consisting of a pair of sticks joined at one end with a thong. Again, however, this cumbersome method (as it would seem from Sigaut's film of its use in Asturias) would have been inappropriate for harvesting brittle-rachised cereals.[6]

Harvesting ripe or unripe crops with the aid of fire. The crop can simply be fired and the singed spikelets (or ears) thereafter gathered from the ground. However, there is no selective effect in either direction as the grain is killed by the parching, and the seed for subsequent crop generations has be harvested from separate plots by one of the other methods.

Firing offers the advantage of controlling weeds and of obviating the need for harvesting, threshing, primary winnnowing, and parching the spikelets before dehusking the grain (Hillman 1984b:141–3; 1985:11). Picking up the spikelets from the ground is very time-consuming, and, in our experience, it is difficult to get a fire to spread through a loose stand of cereals anyway.

Summary of harvesting methods. Of the range of harvesting methods that would have been available to the first farmers, the only ones which would have induced domestication were sickle reaping and uprooting applied when the crops were partially or near-ripe. Although these methods were relatively unpopular amongst recent hunter-gatherers exploiting wild-grass seed, there would have been good reasons for their use amongst some of the first farmers (see below).

Annual Shifts to Virgin Land Using Seed from Last Year's New Plots: Could Domestication Have Occurred Without Them? Existing evidence is equivocal but suggests that while this pair of conditions may sometimes have been supplementary prerequisites for domestication, in most cases domestication could probably have occurred without them.

Only a small proportion of the harvested spikelets are needed as seed for sowing next year's crop. As a result, only a small proportion of the harvested domestic-type mutants finally get sown. In crops regularly resown on old plots, the correspondingly reduced number of domestic mutants (present in the seed stock) could possibly get swamped by the self-sown wild-type spikelets shed spontaneously during the preceding harvest. On any reused plots where this swamping occurs, domestication clearly cannot proceed. Domestication at such settlements will then occur only if the farmer annually extends cultivation onto virgin land using seed stocks harvested from last year's new plots, as such a strategy automatically avoids the self-sown wild-type spikelets from the old plots ever contributing to subsequent crop generations.[7]

However, this swamping effect assumes that large numbers of the spontaneously shed wild-type spikelets survive ant, bird, and rodent predation between harvest and autumn sowing. If, conversely, the proportion of harvested spikelets sown on old plots by the farmer (say, 12%) is greater than the proportion of spontaneously shed spikelets which survive predation between harvest time and sowing (say, 10%), then domestication could still occur—assuming the method used to select the seed stocks from the harvested spikelets either maintains or increases the relative abundance of mutants in the seed (compared with their abundance in the bulk of harvested grain from which the seed stock is drawn). As quantified examples, a pair of possible scenarios (with opposite effects) are outlined in figure 10.8.

The determining factors are therefore the survival rate of the wild-type spikelets (from fully brittle ears) that fall to the ground during harvesting by sickle or uprooting; the proportion of the harvested grain set aside as seed stocks for sowing next year's crop (this will correspond to the yield ratio anticipated by the farmer ["yield ratio" = grain yield per unit of grain sown]); and the method used for selecting the grain for sowing.

Survival Rate of Spikelet
For wild stands, Zohary (1988) notes that

> from the time of harvesting to the time of the next planting, those seeds that evaded the reaper and got spread

[spontaneously] in the field...are exposed to strong predation by ants, rodents, and so forth. I estimate that, under Near Eastern conditions, at least 50 to 80% of these wild-type seeds will be eliminated.

On cultivated ground, Zohary (1989) suggests that the shed spikelets are less protected from predation, and as many as 90% of them might be lost.

Yield Ratio

Yield ratios observed (for example, by Hillman 1973B) in traditional, rain-fed wheat and barley cultivation in eastern Turkey fall in the range 1:6.5 to 1:9. In such cases, therefore, the farmers set aside 11 to 17% (roughly one-sixth to one-ninth) of their harvested grain for resowing. However, in the first two years of his experimental cultivation of wild einkorn, Willcox (chapter 11) obtained yield ratios ranging from 1:2 to 1:33. Differences of this order clearly argue against using any one value in the present calculations. Nevertheless, it is clear that most of Hillman's values and half of Willcox's values would allow farmers to use a smaller proportion of the harvested spikelets as seed than the 20 to 50% of spontaneously shed wild-type spikelets estimated by Zohary to survive in wild stands. This would preclude domestication (in the absence of annual shifts). If we use Zohary's estimate of just 10% survival of spikelets shed from wild-type plants growing on cultivated ground, however, then the percentage sown could easily exceed this figure, and would allow domestication to occur without shifting cultivation. From this spread of values, therefore, it would seem that reuse of old plots which are already partially self-sown with spontaneously shed wild-type spikelets could have either permitted domestication or prevented it.

It could be argued that, with 10% or more of the shed spikelets surviving field predation, the farmer could afford to reduce the amount of sown seed to a level that would (unwittingly) ensure that the mutants (present in the sown seed) were always swamped by self-sown wild types and that domestication would consequently never occur without shifting cultivation. However, it should be remembered that Zohary's 10% survival refers to 10% of that approximately 50 to 60% of the spikelets which are spontaneously shed, that is, just 5 to 6% of the original crop population. The quantities of harvested spikelets that must then be sown to raise this figure to the required 11 to 17% (see above) will thus range from 5 to 12% of the total parent crop (that is, 12 to 24% of the 40 to 50% of the spikelets which got harvested). If we accept Zohary's 10% predation survival rate (and all the evidence suggests we should), domestication would be precluded only at the lowest sowing rates; at all the higher rates, domestication could occur without any shifting cultivation. However, if we assume higher rates of predation survival, the point of balance shifts upward.

Selection Method

It is impossible to know whether the first farmers' methods of selecting their seed stocks from harvested spikelets would have altered the proportion of mutants, and no estimates are offered here.

In summary, therefore, it is clear that at one end of the spectrum of possibilities, reuse of old plots could have precluded all possibility of domestication. Under such conditions, domestication would have occurred only if harvesting with sickles or by uprooting was combined with annual shifts to virgin land using seed stocks from last year's new plots. At the other end of the spectrum of possibilities, domestication could have occurred even if the farmers consistently reused old plots. Present evidence supports Zohary's contention that this last scenario is the most probable. However, it should be noted that if domestication did, indeed, occur under a system in which old plots were consistently reused, it would have proceeded much more slowly than under a system of annual shifts to virgin land.

Once the Mutant Phenotype was Present in the Crop, How Rapidly Will Domestication Have Occurred?

To produce a mathematical model of domestication rate (that is, the rate of increase in semitough-rachised mutants in wild-type crops under primitive cultivation), we needed measurements of mutation rates at the relevant loci, rates of inbreeding/outbreeding in wild einkorn wheat, and the selection coefficients arising from those husbandry methods effective in inducing domestication. Reliable estimates exist for the first two factors (see below), but not for selection coefficient. In initiating this study in the early 1970s, therefore, our primary objective was to measure the selection pressures which can result from combinations of primitive husbandry of the sort likely to have been applied by the first farmers (as outlined above).

Preliminary Measurements of Selection Coefficient

Selection pressure can be affected by several factors. We nevertheless limited our field measurements to selection pressures generated by the different methods of harvesting, because harvesting method is the primary factor determining selective pressure in all systems, it can produce a wide range of different selection values, and these values are easily measured by field experiment. In contrast, annual shifts in cultivation (where these are necessary for domestication) generally either permit domestication or prevent it altogether, and even though different rates of resowing old plots could theoretically produce a range of different values for selection coefficient, we were not in a position to measure them.

We chose to apply the harvesting experiments to wild einkorn, as this particular wild cereal was available in large dense stands throughout much of Turkey where one of us was then based. (We also use wild einkorn in the mathematical

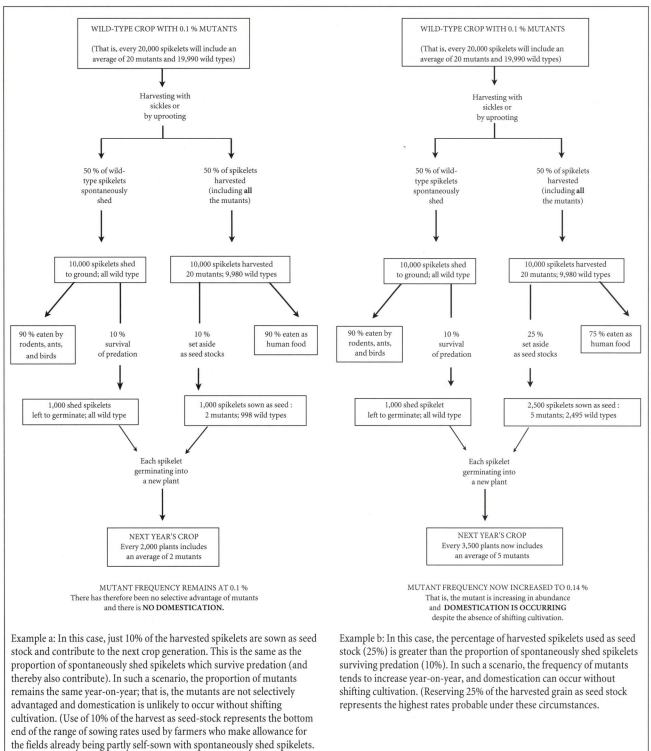

Fig.ure 10.8 Was shifting cultivation of einkorn wheat necessary for its domestication? This figure presents a pair of calculated examples: one where shifting cultivation would have been necessary and another where it would not. In both examples, the same plots are resown every year, the crops initially contain 0.1% of semitough–rachised mutants (a starting mutant frequency of 0.1% [1 per thousand] has been used purely for convenience and in this figure is expressed as 20 per 20,000); they are harvested with sickles or by uprooting (these are the harvesting methods capable of inducing cultivation); 50% of the wild–type spikelets are lost to the ground during harvesting (50% shedding is not too far from our measurements of loss rates with these forms of harvesting); and 90% of these shed spikelets are eaten by rodents, birds, and ants (90% predation loss represents Zohary's [1989] estimate for wild–type cereals on cultivated ground).

Table 10.2 Preliminary measurements of the fitness of two rachis–fragility phenotypes present in populations of wild–type einkorn wheat under the four principal harvesting methods available to early cultivators

HARVESTING TREATMENT		% OF AVAILABLE SPIKELETS HARVESTED WITHIN EITHER PHENOTYPE		RELATIVE FITNESS OF EITHER PHENOTYPE		WILD-TYPE SPIKELETS COUNTED IN COL. III
		WILD TYPE	TOUGH-EARED TYPE	WILD TYPE	TOUGH-EARED TYPE	
1. Beating—repeated passes	a	84%	about 5% (1–10%)	0.84	about 0.05	1280
2. Beating—single pass	a	38				990
	b	48	about 5% (1–10%)	0.44	about 0.05	1100
	c	45				1340
	mean	44%				2330
3. Reaping with sickles	a	35				1050
	b	43	100%	0.40	1	1520
	c	43				860
	mean	40%				3430
4. Uprooting	a	41				2300
	b	37	100%	0.43	1	1240
	c	51				1310
	mean	43%				4850

"Fitness" is calculated as the proportion of that phenotype harvested and represents the probability of its being harvested and thereby contributing to ensuing generations by means of "seed-stocks" taken from harvested spikelets. (Fitness values are expressed as decimals; multiplied by 100 equal percentages.)

model, below.) However, our results are equally valid for emmer wheat and barley, because, as noted by Zohary (1988), the wild types of all three of these Near Eastern founder crops have parallel wild adaptations and have closely similar pollination systems, domestication syndrome, and early prehistory. Indeed, it is on Zohary's advice that we have extended the terms of reference of our chapter to cover all three crops.

After exploratory harvesting (which enabled us to eliminate the most unworkable methods), a preliminary set of simple harvesting trials was undertaken in 1974 in relatively dense stands of near-ripe wild einkorn growing in primary habitats on the Munzur Mountains (near Çemisgezek in eastern Turkey) and on Karadag (near Karaman in Central Turkey). Four areas of the wild stands in either area were simply divided into a series of 1 m², and the different harvesting techniques were applied to a scatter of these. In each, counts were made of the numbers of spikelets harvested and the numbers lost on the ground. The number of spikelets harvested using any one method was expressed as a decimal of the total number of spikelets of the brittle-rachised phenotype produced in the same squares. We thereby obtained a measure of fitness of the brittle-rachised phenotype under each harvesting regime (see table 10.2). (This measure of fitness thus represents the probability that the seed would contribute to the next generation as a result of being incorporated into the harvest from which next year's seed stock is to be taken). To obtain a rough measure of the fitness of the semitough-rachised phenotype, it was necessary to compromise and use a cultivated glume wheat (emmer), as semitough-rachised phenotypes are too rare in wild stands to be measurable. We measured fitness under each harvesting regime exactly as with the wild type, except that we used fewer replicates.

One of the harvesting treatments (treatment 1) involved beating applied repeatedly to the same plots. The first of these passes was timed to coincide with disarticulation of the tops of the earliest ears, and the last with the point when only the bottom third of the spikelets remained on the last ears to ripen. In order to avoid trampling, this treatment was applied to isolated meter squares. In reality, however, early farmers would not have enjoyed this luxury, and trampling would have produced losses which are not reflected in the present result for this repeated passes treatment.

In these preliminary trials, no attempt was made to measure fitness in totally unripe plants in which disarticulation had yet to begin. Exploratory harvestings had suggested that the failure of completely unripe brittle-rachised ears to disarticulate preempted any possibility of positive selection for the tough-rachised phenotype. Thus, no form of harvesting applied to totally unripe crops could lead to domestication (see later discussion), and there seemed little point in including such treatments in the hastily assembled preliminary trials.

The results of the preliminary measurements of relative fitness appear in table 10.2. The most notable features of the results were as follows:

a) the brittle-rachised phenotype showed intermediate levels of fitness under each of the harvesting treatments 2, 3, and 4, and (remarkably) the values were almost the same for each (40%, 43%, and 44% respectively). The exception was a very high fitness of 80% obtained when harvesting by beating was applied in a series of "passes" (but see preceding two paragraphs).

b) In contrast, ripe, semitough-rachised plants (the domestic type) showed a high fitness (tending to 100%) when harvested with sickles or by uprooting, but a correspondingly low fitness when harvested by beating. (Selection coefficient against each type under the various harvesting methods can be calculated as 1-fitness).

A fitness of around 40% for brittle-rachised plants in three of the treatments accords with the recent estimate from Harlan (chapter 1) for recovery rates when harvesting wild grasses; he observed, "I estimate that no [harvesting] method will recover more than half of the potential production." Nevertheless, substantially different values could be expected with different degrees of average ripeness. The extreme fitness values for the semitough-rachised (domestic) plants were as expected, and more rigorous measurement would probably have produced the same all-or-nothing result.

It was never intended, however, that the results of these preliminary trials should be used statistically; the trials were badly designed (from the statistical perspective), and a metal (rather than flint-bladed) sickle had been used. The trials were therefore repeated on a much larger scale using sown populations under controlled conditions with properly randomized treatments (using a split-plot design) and with more ample replication.

Brittle-rachised wild einkorn (collected in the Munzur Mts.: coll. no. GCH 3773) was sown in winter with a controlled admixture of the domestic type at a rate of about 200 spikelets per m² in a field at the Cleppa Park Research Station of University of Wales College of Cardiff. They appeared to germinate well and produced 2 to 3 fertile tillers per plant. This time, we used flint-bladed sickles of three types; the Fayum type, a Natufian type, and a British Neolithic single-piece sickle. (The Fayum type proved to be the most efficient). The first year's trial was ruined by a spring drought followed by an extremely wet Welsh summer. The crop grew (eventually), but the wet conditions at harvest time prevented the ears from disarticulating in any of the harvesting treatments, even in the beating treatment. (Nevertheless, many of the reaped ears disarticulated within two days of the sheaves being allowed to dry in a heated room; figure 10.9).

In the following year, an identical crop was sown under glass (figure 10.10). We sowed, however, too late although the domestic type came into ear, the wild type merely formed grassy tussocks lacking ears. (Ears would presumably have developed in the second year of growth had we left the tussocks to grow on.) In the absence of further opportunities to re-run the trials, it was decided to use the preliminary estimates from the earlier trials in Turkey—albeit merely as a means of obtaining provisional estimates.

Two observations from the abortive trials in Wales are nevertheless of interest:

• In a wet summer, brittle-rachised ears fail to disarticulate when ripe. Indeed, Sharma & Waines (1980:215) and

Figure 10.9 The results of harvesting wild-type einkorn by beating in a wet Welsh summer. The potentially brittle-rachised ears failed to disarticulate properly, and the beating had to become so violent that whole ears were detached in the process, Cardiff, 1979. *Photograph courtesy of Isobel Ellis*

Figure 10.10 Sowing the first of many rows of experimental plots of wild-type einkorn under glass in 1980 at University College, Cardiff, 1980. *Photograph courtesy of Stuart Davies*

Willcox (chapter 11) found that even the morning dew was enough to prevent disarticulation. An equivalent phenomenon was also noted by Kuckuck (1964:99) in crops of Iranian spelt wheat which, under damp conditions, was transformed from a semitough-rachised to a fully tough-rachised state.

• The day length (photoperiod) required for triggering the formation of the embryonic ear (the *inflorescence primordium*) in our wild-type einkorn during the lengthening days of spring was much shorter than in our particular genotype of domestic einkorn. Barring seed vernalization requirements, sowing of this particular domesticate could thus be delayed well into late spring with no more than the usual depression in yields (see chapter 11 for some yield-depression figures obtained from late sowings of primitive domesticates). In our wild type, however, it was totally disastrous. These results further undermine the already untenable argument (for example, in Sherratt 1980:316–21) that early wheat crops must have been spring sown.

Computer Simulation of Domestication Rates

The purpose of recording fitness as outlined above was to provide measurements for a computer model that would simulate the increase in frequency of the semitough-rachised (domestic) phenotype in otherwise brittle-rachised (wild type) crops under primitive systems of husbandry. However, such a simulation also requires measurements (or estimates) of two other determining factors: Firstly, the frequency of selfing or outcrossing; secondly, the frequency of the semitough-rachised allele in the crop population at generation zero, that is, at the start of cultivation (see "Raw materials of domestication" above). The working assumptions of the computer simulation were as follows:

Husbandry methods. The simulation necessarily assumes that the husbandry methods used were those capable of selecting for semitough-rachised phenotypes in a brittle-rachised einkorn crop, namely harvesting when partially ripe by sickle reaping or uprooting (combined, if necessary, with annual shifts to virgin plots using seed taken from the previous year's new plot[s]). Using the fitness values generated by other methods (for example, harvesting by beating) merely produces a situation of zero change, with the crop remaining brittle-rachised indefinitely. We took no account of the lower selective intensities which could result from resowing old plots (in cases where this would not altogether prevent domestication) as no reliable measurements were available.

Fitness levels. In running the simulation, we used the levels of fitness observed with sickle reaping and uprooting in the preliminary Turkish field trials described above, namely 40 to 45% for the wild type and 100% for the domestic type. In view of the preliminary nature of the measurements of fitness in the wild-type and its potential susceptibility to variations in the aptitude of the harvester, and the mean state of ripeness of the crop, however, we also added a broad spread of much more conservative values for fitness of the wild type ranging from 45 to 95%. Values in this range clearly produce slower rates of domestication and correspond to the effect of harvesting the crop when much less ripe. (Selection coefficients against the wild type are 1 fitness.)

Inbreeding frequency in einkorn. For the purpose of this simulation, we have tested the effects of breeding behavior ranging from complete outcrossing to complete inbreeding (selfing). However, Zohary (1981) informed us that the rate of outcrossing in wild wheats is probably below 1%. Thus, for *Triticum dicoccoides* (wild emmer) he notes that

> …there is very little cross-pollination under natural conditions… This is clear from (i) their floral biology (anther dehiscence occurs within the florets prior to lodicule inflation and anther emergence), (ii) the almost complete lack of intermediates when different forms are grown together, and (iii), more recently, from electrophoretically discernable protein markers revealing the predominance of homozygosity in the individuals examined.

He concludes (1988)

> all in all, I think that it is safe to consider *Triticum dicoccoides*, *T. boeoticum* and *Hordeum spontaneum* as predominantly self-pollinated plants. In all three, the amount of cross pollination could vary between 0.5 and 5%.

Willcox (chapter 11) cites what seems to be an aberrant exception to this pattern observed by Boyeldieu (10 to 15% outcrossing under hot conditions in North Africa); however, the broad range of values used in our computer model (0 to 90% outcrossing) clearly allows for such eventualities, and for the unlikely possibility that there has been a major shift in breeding behavior of these cereals during the past 11 millennia.

Allele frequency and mutation rate. It was noted above that, in wild populations growing in primary habitats, the semitough-rachised recessive alleles act effectively as lethals when in homozygous state, since the grains never leave the plant and cannot contribute to the next generation. They therefore occur only in heterozygotes. In an inbreeder such as einkorn, such heterozygotes will be rare and will occur at a nominal frequency only a little above the mutation rate. The same applies to the first crops. In gathering seed stocks from wild stands to sow the initial crops of, say, wild-type wheats, semitough-rachised phenotypes will generally have been left behind if the spikelets were gathered by beating; so, this low frequency of semitough-rachised alleles probably continued into the first crops. Indeed, for the simulation, we have chosen to err on the side of caution and use a mutation rate of the brittle-rachis allele to the semitough-rachis allele of only 10^{-6} per locus per generation. But even at this mutation rate, and given the total area of, say, einkorn crops sown by early Near Eastern farmers (see above), the semitough-rachised mutant will doubtless have been present in the fields of at least some of them from the outset, and soon emerged in most of the others.

Table 10.3 Number of generations required for the semitough-rachised phenotype of einkorn to reach a frequency of 99% at various levels of selection against the wild-type phenotype and with various levels of inbreeding

% INBREEDING	SELECTION COEFFICIENT AGAINST FRAGILE RACHIS PHENOTYPE						
	0.05	0.1	0.2	0.3	0.4	0.5	0.6
0	*	*	*	*	*	*	*
10	4090	1040	860	510	330	220	150
20	2130	1010	450	270	170	120	77
30	1440	680	310	180	120	78	53
40	1070	510	230	140	87	60	42
50	840	380	180	100	71	49	34
60	690	330	150	89	59	42	30
70	580	280	130	76	51	37	27
80	490	240	110	67	45	33	24
90	420	210	95	59	41	30	23
100	360	180	84	53	37	28	21

*No semitough-rachised homozygotes produced in the simulation, even after 8000 generations.

Note: The initial frequency of the semitough-rachis allele was taken as a conservative 10⁻⁶, and the allele was assumed to occur only in heterozygotes in generation.

Results

The results of the computer simulations are presented in figures 10.11 and 10.12 and in table 10.3. Figure 10.11 shows patterns of increase in the semitough-rachised (domestic) phenotype under a range of selective intensities but with inbreeding at a constant 100%. With a selection coefficient of 0.6 against the wild type (fitness = 0.4), as measured in our preliminary field trials, domestication occurs within 20 generations (that is, within 20 years if the crop is sown annually). Even with a selection coefficient as low as 0.1 against the brittle-rachised phenotype (fitness = 0.1), domestication is still complete within 200 generations (that is, two centuries). These lower selection coefficients probably resemble those that would be generated by harvesting the crop when it is less ripe and are perhaps more realistic.

In figure 10.12, selective intensity is set at the measured value of 0.6, but the values used for inbreeding frequency range from 100% to an improbable 10%. At the estimated inbreeding frequency of 99%, fixation occurs within 20 years; and with a mere 70% inbreeding, it occurs within 30 years. Even with 10% inbreeding (equivalent to a strong *outbreeder*), fixation still occurs within two centuries. Total outbreeding (that is, 0% inbreeding) was also tested in the simulation but showed the domestic phenotype remaining at an extremely low frequency at even the 8000-year limit of the simulation program. This last result might be regarded as explaining the supposedly belated appearance in the archaeological record of the domestic form of outbreeders such as rye. However, new archaeological evidence indicates that domestic rye emerged much earlier than hitherto assumed (Hillman 1978; Hillman & McLaren N.D.), and this can be explained only by invoking an inbreeding ancestor such as *Secale vavilovii* as proposed by Miller (1987) and Zohary (1990).

Table 10.3 shows the number of generations required for the domestic phenotype to achieve a level of 99% in the crop population with the full range of values used for both selection coefficient and inbreeding frequency. It could be argued that the figures of practical relevance to studying the domestication

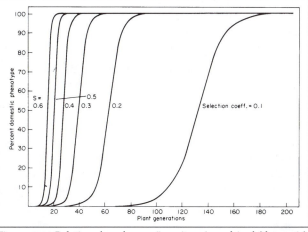

Figure 10.11 Relative abundance of semitough-rachised (domestic) phenotypes in populations of brittle-rachised wild-type einkorn under a range of selective intensities but with a constant 100% inbreeding and with the initial frequency of the semitough-rachis allele taken as a conservative 10⁻⁶. Leftmost curve is closest to the selection coefficients measured in our field trials (see table 10.2). (With annual sowing, 1 plant generation = 1 year.)

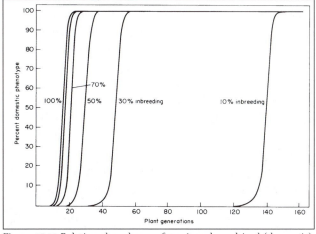

Figure 10.12 Relative abundance of semitough-rachised (domestic) phenotypes in cultivated populations of brittle-rachised wild-type einkorn with a range of levels of inbreeding but under constant selective intensity of 0.6, the value measured in preliminary field trials. The inbreeding rate in wild wheat suggested by Zohary (1980) was "possibly greater than 99%"; that is, close to the first curve. (With annual sowing, 1 plant generation = 1 year.)

rates feasible in wild-type einkorn wheat are those in the bottom right-hand corner, as these figures are based on the value for selection coefficient that was recorded in our field trials (namely S = 0.6) and Zohary's estimate of probable inbreeding frequency (namely > 99%). However, it is equally (or more) realistic to use the domestication rates generated by the lower selection coefficients (0.3 down to 0.1), as these correspond to harvesting the crop when it is much less ripe, and Willcox (pers. comm. and chapter 11) has found the bulk harvesting of crops of wild-type einkorn is much more efficient when they are in this state.

The results of the simulation therefore suggest that domestication (in respect of the fixation of semitough rachis in a brittle-rachised crop population) could be achieved within 20 to 30 years—so long as the crop is harvested when near ripe by means of sickle reaping or uprooting and it is sown on virgin land every year using seed stocks taken from last year's new plots. Even if we use lower values of selection coefficient corresponding to harvesting crops when much less ripe, the process is still complete within two centuries.

This result broadly concurs with the rapid rates of domestication proposed by Zohary (1969, 1984, chapter 6) and Ladizinsky (1987b), although we would argue that somewhat longer periods may be more probable, especially if the effects of unripe reaping were combined with the effects of repeatedly sowing the same plots. Even so, the fact that wild einkorn (and probably also wild emmer and barley) could have been domesticated within two centuries makes domestication an event of such transience that it stands little chance of being recognizable as a clinal process in samples of plant remains recovered from archaeological sites.

Limitations of Computer Model

At a general level, it should be stressed that the computer model is deterministic and takes little account of random processes. Its aim is merely to give a general idea of the time-scale of the domestication process. To this end, we applied a number of simplifications in selecting values for some of the variables. The most obvious simplifications were as follows:

The simulation assumes that the semitough-rachised state in einkorn (the species used both in our field measurements of selection coefficient and in the computer simulations) is determined by a single allele. However, the work of Sharma and Waines (1980:215) demonstrates that two loci are involved in the control of the tough-rachis character in ssp. *monococcum*. The 15:1 segregation ratio they found in the F_2 progeny of crosses between ssp. *boeoticum* and ssp. *monococcum* also indicates that the two genes were assorting independently, that is, they were not linked. The likelihood of fixation of both alleles in a homozygous form in early generations is much less than for a single locus. Once present, and given a high degree of selfing, the genotype would, however, show a similar rapid increase in frequency to the

single gene homozygote. The effects of outbreeding in slowing the rate of increase of the homozygote would, however, be markedly more pronounced than for the single-gene model.

On the other hand, Sharma and Waines suggest that

simultaneous mutations at two loci seem highly improbable. A plant homozygous for the recessive gene at one of the two loci may have arisen first and might have had some degree of rachis toughness. This might have led early humans to select such plants in the course of harvesting. Mutation at the second locus might have been another independent event that occurred later in this already domesticated line, or this second mutation might have occurred in another *boeoticum* line. These two *boeoticum* lines, one homozygous for one locus and the other homozygous for the second locus, by hybridization and segregation might have given rise to present day *monococcum* homozygous for both loci. (1980:215)

Neither possibility conflicts with the basic model presented here, which is concerned merely with indicating the approximate time scale necessary for the primary fixation of increased rachis toughness under unconscious selection. Certainly, with Sharma and Waines' results indicating that even in plants homozygous recessive at only one of the loci, the rachis was tough enough for the ears to remain intact when "left standing in the field for about one month in the dry hot weather," homozygosity at even one locus would have been enough to have achieved domestication as understood in our model. The same would probably have been true if yet more loci had been involved.

The model secondly takes no account of the possible effects of introgression of wild-type alleles from nearby wild stands through occasional outcrosses. (Introgression is the infiltration of genes from one population into another of a different genotype.) Extensive areas of entirely wild-type populations are almost certain to have existed in the vicinity of the incipient domesticates and would have included populations growing on the older cultivated land where the early wheat or barley crops were probably wholly or partially self-sown with spikelets shed spontaneously from brittle-rachised ears. Introgression of this sort could clearly slow down the rate of domestication. Given the high degree of selfing in wheats and barley, however, such introgression is likely to have been relatively modest during the short period involved in the process of domestication (contrast the effect of longer term introgression discussed in the appendix). Indeed, both Harlan (1965) and Ladizinsky (1985b:193) carry the argument still further and suggest that introgression from wild stands into domesticated (or incipiently domesticated) cereals crops serving as pistillate parents was probably insignificant at any stage.

We made no attempt to measure the effect of harvesting crop populations at different stages of average ripeness, as this would clearly have involved much larger trials than those considered here. In any case, the full range of selective intensities likely to be generated by other levels of average ripeness are included within the very broad range of values for selection coefficient that were used in the simulation. In fact, in view of the clear advantages of harvesting wild-type crops when they are significantly underripe (see below, and chapter 11), it is possible that the lower selection coefficients are the more realistic ones, and that domestication required anything between 30 and 200 years (see the right-hand curves in figure 10.11).

We have also disregarded the possibility (however remote) that, when sowing virgin land, the farmers might have incorporated in their seed stocks some wild-type spikelets gathered from old plots where brittle-rachised ears had disarticulated during harvesting. This would clearly have retarded domestication rate. However, the model assumes that these early farmers will (in the early years, anyway) have recognised the value of leaving the shed spikelets to self-seed earlier years' plots, and that they would not, therefore, have wasted time gathering up the spikelets to sow elsewhere. Indeed, the recent field experiments of Willcox (chapter 11) indicate that, with wild-type spikelets, a better germination rate is obtained when they are left to self-implant than when they are artificially buried. Clearly, then, the shed spikelets would best be left where they fell. They would, in any case, be awkward to collect, as they quickly disappear under surface leaf litter and into cracks in the ground.

We have also taken no specific account of the possible effects of modifier genes influencing the expression of the genes determining rachis toughness. If major shifts have occurred during the past eleven millennia in the expression or degree of recessiveness of the semitough-rachised allele, then the present model would need modification. From recent work on cereal breeding at CIMMYT, however, Wilkes (1986) suggests that modifier genes might merely have delayed full fixation of the semitough-rachised phenotype and that the 30 or so years for achieving domestication in respect of major genes (such as those determining rachis fragility) represents one end of the range of time periods probably needed for the full fixation of modifier genes and for the consequent achievement of stability of rachis fragility state. This lack of stability in the final stages of fixation of semitough rachis (or, at least, the first episode of that process) could, he suggests, produce fluctuations at the top end of the sigmoid curve as notionally indicated in figure 10.13.

Fluctuations of this sort could conceivably account for the remarkable mixtures of so called primitive and advanced forms that continued to occur in essentially domesticated crops for a millennium or more—right into the late Aceramic Neolithic—at sites such as Can Hasan III in Turkey (Hillman N.D.), although other interpretations of these mixtures are possible (see appendix). Nevertheless, this should not have

altered the speed with which domestication reached the near-complete state, just short of complete fixation, which is the subject concerning us in this chapter.

Effects of Conscious Selection Imposed Midway Through the Domestication Process

It was noted above that once the frequency of semitough-rachised phenotypes had increased to a level at which they became noticeable in the wild-type crop populations (perhaps around the 1% level), the farmers might have consciously accelerated the process by taking the semitough-rachised ears, sowing the spikelets in a separate plot, and multiplying-up the seed stocks to a level at which they had enough to re-sow all of their cereal fields. From that point onwards, the crop would have been fully domesticated, barring fluctuations owing to changes in modifier genes. If sown thinly, one spikelet generally produces plants with at least 40 spikelets (and generally more); so, the period of multiplying up could have been as short as 3 or 4 years.

From the point at which they sowed the more-or-less pure semitough-rachised seed stocks, the graph would rise near vertically (figure 10.13). However, it can be seen from figures 10.11 and 10.12 that, with even the fastest rate of domestication, the time required to reach the 1% level is at least 10 generations (that is, ten years). Intervention in the manner proposed above would therefore have reduced minimum domestication time by only half at the most.

Testing the Model in Long-term Field Trials

With the computer simulation indicating such a rapid rate of domestication, it was clear that we could test the model over a 20- to 30-year period by cultivating wild-type einkorn (or emmer or barley) under the combination of husbandry systems proposed in the model. However, experience of wild einkorn cultivation at Cardiff indicated that the Welsh climate was too wet for such an experiment, and Patricia Anderson-Gerfaud and Jacques Cauvin of the Institut de Préhistoire Orientale kindly proposed including it in their *Cultures Préhistoriques Expérimentales* program at Jalès, Ardèche, in the south of France. The trial is now in the expert hands of George Willcox and Patricia Anderson-Gerfaud as part of a broad experimental study of early agronomy, and some of their preliminary results are reported in Anderson-Gerfaud (1988), in chapter 12, Willcox and Anderson-Gerfaud 1991, and in chapter 11. If the increase in frequency of the domestic phenotype follows the pattern indicated in our simulation, then this should start to become apparent in about 10 to 15 years.

Such a test can, however, demonstrate merely that it was feasible for unconscious domestication of einkorn (and probably emmer and barley, too) to have occurred in this way. It does not prove that it actually happened this quickly 11 millennia ago.

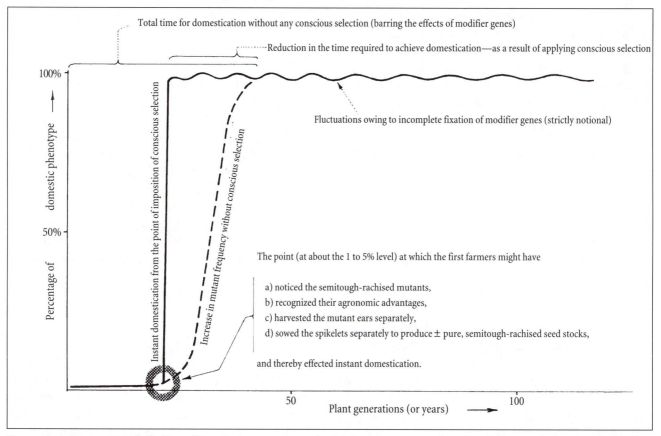

Figure 10.13 Representation of effect of introducing conscious selection favoring semitough–rachised (domestic) plants in crops of wild-type einkorn once their frequency reaches about 1 to 5%. (Compare with figures 10.11 and 10.12.)

Why Should Any Early Farmers Have Used the Required Forms of Husbandry?

The combination of husbandry methods required to achieve domestication may appear impractical. In each case, however, there are sound agronomic reasons why they could have been used by the earliest farmers.[8]

Why Harvest Partially Ripe Cereal Crops with Sickles or by Uprooting?

There are three possible explanations. Harvesting grain from wild grasses/cereals by beating gives the greatest yield per unit harvesting time. For the majority of hunter-gatherers with extensive resources, beating therefore offers the most energy efficient method of procurement. For cultivators expending energy on land-clearance and tillage, however, the pressure to maximize yields per unit area is likely to have favored the harvesting of relatively unripe crops by uprooting or with sickles.

In our field experiments, beating proved to be the most convenient method of harvesting wild cereals, and it was the method favored by most hunter-gatherers when harvesting wild-grass seed (see "Harvesting methods…"). Harvesting by beating is, however, more efficient than other methods only in terms of the amount harvestable per unit time. In terms of the amount harvestable per unit area, beating near-ripe einkorn (with a single pass) is no better than uprooting

and sickling (see table 10.1), and, in practice, could result in much lower returns than other harvesting methods. There are three reasons for this:

- Optimal returns from beating require multiple passes, and this involves trampling the crop before the final passes. (By contrast, hunter-gatherers with very extensive wild stands could probably have afforded to omit the second and third passes.)

- The only way of reducing the number of harvesting passes is to delay harvest until the crop starts to shatter. In practice, however, Willcox (chapter 11) has found that mistiming the harvest by a couple of days can all too easily lead to massive losses through pre-harvest spikelet-shed. Again, when harvesting extensive wild stands as hunter-gatherers, these losses from the shedding of spikelets might have been relatively inconsequential, but on cultivated plots, extra losses mean tilling extra land to get the same net return, and this is energy-expensive.

- If the farmers attempt to limit spikelet shed by harvesting the crop half-green (prior to any spikelet-shed), then harvesting by beating cannot be applied, as beating works only if the ears are disarticulating. Uprooting or sickling then offer the only solution (see chapters 11 and 12).

Thus, despite our observation that harvesting by beating gives the greatest yield per unit harvesting time, for cultivators, the pressure to maximise yield per unit area is likely to have favoured the harvesting of relatively unripe crops by uprooting or with sickles.

This change reflects the substantially altered patterns of energy input and resource distribution that occur with the shift to cultivation. Hunter-gatherers exploit diffuse resources, and pre-processing energy expenditure is limited mainly to travel, harvest, and transport costs. In contrast, cultivators generate their own highly concentrated resources, with heavy pre-harvest energy expenditure on land-clearance, tillage, sowing, weeding, and crop protection. The methods used by earlier generations for foraging diffuse resources clearly had to be altered to maximise energy returns per unit area of tilled land (in which there had been heavy energy investment)—instead of maximizing energy returns per unit of energy expended in harvesting and travel. One obvious way of meeting this requirement was to replace beating by sickle reaping or uprooting. Optimal foraging theory thus offers a partial explanation for shifts in technology which, in turn, can account for crop domestication. [9]

There are two further factors which may have encouraged the first farmers to harvest with sickles or uprooting:

1. The farmers may have wanted a valuable secondary product: straw, which could be harvested only by sickling or uprooting. Straw might have been valued for lighting fires, tempering mud brick or adobe, and, perhaps, as fodder. Straw is invaluable for lighting domestic fires and still serves this role in areas where paper is rare. Straw may well have been needed for tempering mud brick or adobe. If sedentism in southwestern Asia preceded the adoption of large-scale cultivation, as present evidence suggests (see Harris 1977; Hillman, Colledge and Harris 1989; Hillman 1986), then the concomitant storage of crop harvests would have required the construction of storage facilities even before cereal cultivation began. Certainly, complex storage structures of heavily straw-tempered mud bricks are present in even the earliest agricultural level (D) at Ganj Dareh Tepe in the southern Zagros, and they apparently pre-date the construction of equivalent (though larger) adobe structures for human habitation (Smith 1970 for the mud-brick structures; van Zeist et al. 1984 for the earliest evidence of domesticates at the same site. See also Stordeur and Anderson-Gerfaud [1985] and Anderson-Gerfaud [1986, 1988] for evidence that the threshing method used at Ganj Dareh would have necessitated harvesting the straw with the ears.) Either way, straw-tempered adobe structures are common throughout much of southwestern Asia from the Pre-Pottery Neolithic B period onward.

Straw may also have been harvested to fire the harvest. *Sheaf-burning* is an effective way of eliminating much of the chaff and parching the spikelets ready for dehusking and grinding (see Hillman 1984b:141–3). Indeed, we use this method ourselves whenever processing wild cereal grain for consumption, as it saves most of the threshing and winnowing. However, it kills the grain and would not have been used to clean the harvest from those plots providing seed stocks for next year's crop. Nevertheless, if uprooting or sickle reaping (as a prelude to firing) was applied to the rest of the harvest, farmers may have found it convenient to harvest the seed-stock plots by the same method, even though the harvested sheaves from these plots could not have been cleaned by burning.

It might also be argued that the first farmers required straw as fodder for domestic animals, especially for cattle. Certainly, straw is used extensively in this role in the Near East today. However, present archaeological evidence suggests that there were no domestic cattle at this stage in the relevant parts of the Near East and maybe few domestic sheep or goats (see, for example, Legge and Rowley-Conwy in Moore et al. 1999). As for the Bohrer (1972) hypothesis that preagrarian or early cultivator groups fed cultivated fodder to penned wild animals, all the available evidence suggests that this is highly improbable.

If the first farmers suffered a few decades of wet summers. they would have been forced to harvest by uprooting or sickling, even if they had hitherto harvested by beating. Our Cardiff field trials revealed that, in wet summers, brittle-rachised einkorn fails to disarticulate, and beating becomes ineffective. But while domestication could not have occurred for as long as the crop failed to disarticulate, a decade or two of wet summers could have established a tradition of harvesting by uprooting or sickling. It seems unlikely, however, that there was a decade or more of wet summers in southwestern Asia during the terminal Pleistocene (Byrne 1987). [10]

Why Should the Early Farmers Have Annually Extended Cereal Cultivation onto Virgin Land (in Those Cases Where It Might Have Been a Prerequisite for Domestication)?

Two sets of circumstances automatically necessitate annual shifts in cultivation and might account for domestication having occurred in cases where shifting cultivation was a pre-requisite. The first involves shifting cultivation—with regular shifts from old land onto virgin land. Since all the old plots would have been conveniently self-sown with the wild-type crop, deserting these old plots would presumably happen only in the face of serious deterioration of crop yields. Yield might fall because of depletion of phosphates in the calcic soils typical of this region (Bunting 1987) or because of a build-up of weed contaminants.

Annual extensions in the area under cultivation could secondly have occurred without corresponding abandonment of old land. The most obvious reason for adopting such a strategy would have been pressure from expanding populations. Population pressure features in a number of models for the beginnings of cultivation in southwestern Asia (see Bar-Yosef and Kislev 1989; Binford 1968; Cohen 1977; Flannery 1969; Harris 1977; Hassan 1981; Hillman 1986; Moore 1985, 1989; Smith and Young 1983), and present evidence suggests that the population increases accelerated still further after the adoption of agriculture. It is inevitable, therefore, that cultivation had to be regularly or episodically extended onto virgin land. (The later development of intensification practices such as irrigation would have merely reduced the frequency of these extensions).

Why Take Their Stock of Seed (for Sowing) Exclusively from the Grain Harvests of Last Season's New Plots (in Those Cases Where It Might Have Been a Prerequisite for Domestication)?

Such a strategy may again have been adopted to minimise weed infestation. In southwestern Asian steppe, field studies have shown that concentration of most weed species (including toxic-seeded genera such as *Adonis*) builds up rapidly in the first few years of cultivation and then reaches a plateau (Hillman, Colledge, and Harris 1989:253). Weed seed frequencies in harvested grain would therefore have been lowest in harvests from the new plots, and taking all seed stocks from these plots would have assisted weed control.

In summary, therefore, there would have been good grounds for the first wheat and barley farmers applying all of those methods most likely to have resulted in the domestication of wild type crops—even in the event of this necessitating annual shifts to virgin land using seed stocks taken exclusively from last year's new plots. Such methods were probably applied by many of the early farmers of the area, though there were doubtless some who used other methods and whose crops remained in a state of nondomestication cultivation until they eventually obtained seeds stocks of the new domesticates from other early farmers.

Domestication in the Archaeological Record

Our evidence suggests that the process of domestication would have required only 20 to 200 years, with, perhaps, a short period of "domestication delay" owing to the absence of mutants in some of the earliest crops and an additional delay if crops were repeatedly re-sown on the same plots (assuming this would not have prevented domestication altogether). Can we therefore expect to identify stages such as predomestication cultivation or nondomestication cultivation in the archaeological record?

Predomestication Cultivation

Predomestication cultivation is cultivation of wild-type crops from the time of initial adoption of methods that would induce domestication—to the point of eventual fixation of domestic-type mutants in the crop populations. For convenience, it can be taken to include the brief lead-in period during which, in very small crop populations, domestic mutants were provisionally absent (see figure 10.14).

Scholars studying late Mesolithic and early Neolithic sites in southwestern Asia have long hoped for a clear archaeological record of *in situ* domestication. Our simulation suggests that this is unlikely to be realized: the 20- to 200-year set of events involved in the domestication of einkorn (and probably emmer and barley, too) stands little chance of being preserved as a recognizable clinal sequence of morphological changes in archaeological remains from early sites. In Near Eastern archaeology, two decades after the flotation revolution we still have only quite scanty assemblages of wild cereals and early domesticates from late Mesolithic and early Neolithic sites. Even the rich remains from Abu Hureyra appear to represent, on average, one brief event (such as the charring of food residues on a domestic hearth) per approximately 20 years per about 25 m^2 of excavated occupation surface (Moore et al.. 1999; see also Miksicek 1987:221–222). There is therefore little hope that a sequence of morphological changes occurring in a particular crop grown by a particular household would be preserved in recognizable form at, say, 3- to 5-year intervals in clearly stratified deposits; local patterns of on-site deposition are too irregular in the short term, and subsequent disturbance is too common. In most cases, therefore, predomestication cultivation must be regarded as archaeologically invisible—as a clinal process.

On the other hand, an occasional sample of remains from a crop in the very process of domestication (characterised by a mixture of wild- and domestic-type rachis fragments, and representing just one point on the domestication curve) could well be recovered as a chance find. Indeed, the mixed assemblage of wild- and domestic-type rachis remains from PPNA Netiv Hagdud in the Jordan Valley appeared to represent just such a case (Kislev et al. 1986). However, there are alternative interpretations for such a mixture, and after more detailed study, Kislev (1989b, 1990) concluded that the remains were all of the wild type. (These problems are discussed further in the appendix.)

In the absence of remains of demonstrably transitional crops, all we can hope to find is the following. On sites where the pre-agrarian population continued its occupation after starting to cultivate cereals, we will find merely one set of occupation deposits with entirely wild plant foods ("wild" both in terms of plant morphology and in terms of evidence for mode of procurement) and an overlying set of deposits containing remains of fully domesticated (semitough-rachised) crops. From such remains we cannot tell whether the shift from the wild-type cereal to the domestic type represents on-the-spot domestication or the import of domestic seed stocks from elsewhere.

Alternatively, on sites where a preagrarian group moved to a new site when they started cultivating cereals, we will have merely one site (or set of sites) with entirely wild plant foods (that is, typical hunter-gatherer sites) and another site (nearby or far away) complete with domesticates, with the dates of the lowest levels not significantly later than the uppermost level(s) of the first site(s). In such cases, we cannot be certain that it was the same group that moved from one site to the other, and therefore we cannot know whether "on-the-spot" domestication was even a possibility, let alone whether it had actually occurred.

Nondomestication Cultivation

Generally preceding predomestication cultivation and the ensuing cultivation of domesticates, *nondomestication cultivation* is the cultivation of crops (sometimes containing mutants) using methods that cannot induce domestication. It probably persisted at some settlements long after domestication had occurred elsewhere.

At least a few of the earliest farming settlements were probably of this type because harvesting by beating cannot induce domestication, and the technique was probably as popular amongst Mesolithic hunter-gatherers as it was amongst recent hunter-gatherers. It was therefore likely to have persisted among some of the first farmers despite its disadvantages when applied to crops. Such settlements could have continued cultivating wild-type cereals for some years, until they either adopted alternative systems of husbandry of the sort that induced domestication or obtained seed stocks of domesticates from elsewhere. The more isolated the settlement, the greater the possible period of nondomestication cultivation, although cultural conservatism could also have played a critical role.

On sites of this sort, all cereal rachis remains will be of the wild type, whether they were cultivated or not. From the rachis remains alone, therefore, we will have no means of knowing whether the site was occupied by cultivators or by hunter-gatherers who harvested their cereals from wild stands. If the upper levels of such a site contain domesticates, we will again have no means of knowing whether

a) the occupants had eventually adopted different methods of husbandry that induced *in situ* domestication;

b) they had belatedly obtained seed stocks of domesticates from elsewhere; or

c) the original inhabitants had been replaced by cultivators of domesticates from another area.

A range of the ancient husbandry systems identifiable (or unidentifiable) from archaeological remains is outlined in table 10.4.

An Archaeological Example of Some of the Problems: Abu Hureyra in Syria

The late Mesolithic occupations at this site contained charred remains of wild-type einkorn (subsp. *boeoticum*), while the overlying Neolithic occupations produced charred remains of its domestic derivative (subsp. *monococcum*). It was initially thought that the einkorn in the Mesolithic layers might have been under some form of predomestication cultivation which lasted several centuries and culminated in the appearance of the fully fledged domesticates found in the Neolithic levels. However, there appeared to be a break in occupation between Mesolithic and Neolithic, and it was surmized that the final stages of domestication might have taken place at another (undiscovered) site before the occupants returned to Abu Hureyra to establish the Neolithic occupation. This scenario was finally rejected when completion of work on the present simulation showed that our assumed time scale for domestication was far too long.

This still left open two possibilities: the wild-type einkorn was gathered from wild stands; or it was under cultivation of a sort that would never, of itself, induce domestication (Hillman 1975). The matter was finally resolved (Hillman, Colledge, and Harris 1989) using the third of the methods outlined below involving evidence from associated remains of other plants.

Alternative Criteria for Recognizing Cultivation Prior to Domestication

Although domestic-type rachis remains (when present) can provide useful evidence that a crop had been under cultivation, it was noted above that wild-type rachis remains provide no means of distinguishing between wild cereals gathered from the wild stands (as part of hunter-gatherer subsistence) and wild cereals under predomestication or nondomestication cultivation. For this, we have to use alternative criteria.

Use of Micro-morphological Features Observable in Remains of Possible Cultigens

While macro-morphological characteristics such as semitough rachis and increased grain size are advantaged only by specific forms of husbandry, physiological traits such as loss of seed dormancy are advanged by almost any form of cultivation which involves annual sowing. Correspondingly, annual sowing should also select for any histological characteristics physiologically or chromosomally linked with absence of dormancy. Since even the earliest farmers probably sowed their crops annually, these histological changes could serve as markers for the very beginning of cultivation.

In certain legumes, the presence or absence of dormancy has been found to be linked with testa color; and in other legumes, testa color has been linked with differences in testa structure visible under SEM (Butler 1989). There was clearly

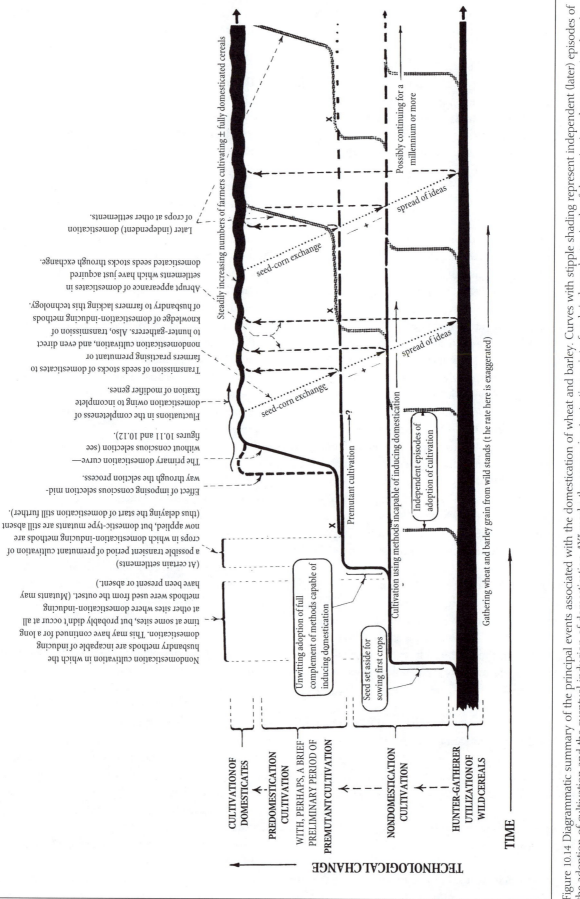

Figure 10.14 Diagrammatic summary of the principal events associated with the domestication of wheat and barley. Curves with stipple shading represent independent (later) episodes of the adoption of cultivation and the eventual induction of domestication. "X" marks the approximate starting point of each independent episode of domestication, thus assuming that the domestication of each of the wheats and barleys occurred independently at a number of different early farming settlements. Whether this was actually the case is still under debate.

Table 10.4 Archaeological remains of potential use in distinguishing foragers from cultivators (A) and nondomestication cultivation (B) from the cultivation of domesticates

SITE (OR PHASE) ECONOMY TYPE	SOURCE OF CEREAL GRAINS	CEREAL HARVESTING METHODS: PRINCIPAL ALTERNATIVES	TYPES OF CEREAL RACHIS LIKELY TO BE FOUND	ARCHAEOLOGICAL EVIDENCE — PROBABLE FORMS OF USE-WEAR ON SICKLE BLADES — WEAR OF TYPES ATTRIBUTABLE TO CEREALS	OTHER TYPES OF PLANT-RELATED WEAR IN SAME TOOL ASSEMBLAGES	CLASSIFICATION APPLIED IN TEXT
A PRE- OR NON-AGRARIAN (HUNTER-GATHERER) ECONOMIES	From wild stands during seasons of einkorn gathering and consumption	1. Harvesting by beating or uprooting	Wild-type (fully brittle-rachised)[1]	No cereal wear/polish	(i) Wear from cutting aerial stems of reeds or rushes;[3] and (ii) wear from cutting edible under-water rhizomes + scratches (?) from grit in the enveloping mud	Cereal foraging (pre- or nonagrarian utilization of wild cereals)
		2. Harvesting by cutting (reaping) — a) Fully unripe cereals	Wild-type (fully brittle rachised)[1]	Wear/polish of types typically generated by cutting green cereals with, perhaps, occasional dust scratches. Such wear could be confused with that from cutting green grasses (for example, as bedding)[3]		
		b) Near-ripe cereals	Wild-type (fully brittle rachised)[1]	Wear/polish of mixed green and ± ripe types (due to uneven ripeness of crop) with, perhaps, occasional dust scratches (as above)[3]		
B AGRARIAN ECONOMIES	Crops in which domestic-type mutants were absent and/or domestication was prevented by the absence of shifting cultivation (in those rare cases where it was necessary)	1. Harvesting by beating	Wild-type (fully brittle)[1]	No cereal wear/polish present	(i) Probably continued wear from cutting reed or rush stems;[3] but (ii) absence of (or sharp decline in) wear + grit-scratches from cutting edible underwater rhizomes	Premutant cultivation and/or non-domestication cultivation
		2. Harvesting by uprooting — a) Green cereals (completely unripe)	Wild-type (fully brittle)[1]	No cereal wear/polish present		
		b) Partially or near-ripe cereals	Wild-type (fully brittle)[1]	No cereal wear/polish present		
		3. Harvesting by cutting (reaping) — a) Green cereals (completely unripe)	Wild-type (fully brittle)[1]	Wear/polish type(s) typically generated by cutting green cereals (or other grasses), often with abundant dust scratches[3]		
		b) Partially- or near-ripe cereals	Wild-type (fully brittle)[1]	Wear/polish of mixed green and ± ripe types (due to uneven ripeness of crop) with abundant dust scratches[3]		
AGRARIAN ECONOMIES involving cultivation of cereals	Crops in which domestic-type mutants were present	1. Harvesting by beating	Wild-type (fully brittle)[1]	No cereal wear/polish present		Nondomestication cultivation
		2. Harvesting by uprooting — a) Green cereals (completely unripe)	Wild-type (fully brittle)[1]	No cereal wear/polish present		Nondomestication cultivation
		b) Partially or near-ripe cereals	Domestic types[2]	No cereal wear/polish present		Cultivation of domesticates
		3. Harvesting by cutting (reaping) — a) Green cereals (completely unripe)	Wild-type (fully brittle)[1]	Wear/polish type(s) typically generated by cutting green cereals (or other grasses), often with abundant dust scratches[3]		Nondomestication cultivation
		b) Partially or near-ripe cereals	Domestic types[2]	Wear/polish of mixed green and ± ripe types (due to uneven ripeness of crop) with abundant dust scratches[3]		Cultivation of domesticates

Table outlines classes of evidence likely to be left by some of the systems of husbandry that might have been applied in the earliest phases of cereal cultivation. However, the table devotes no separate category to crop remains that could theoretically survive from the transient period(s) of pre-domestication cultivation, as they are likely to be archaeologically invisible in most cases. By comparing columns 4 and 5, it can be seen that some forms of husbandry cannot be distinguished from the cereal remains alone, but can (apparently) be distinguished from use-wear analysis. This clearly argues for the two forms of evidence being used in combination whenever possible.

Notes: 1. Fully brittle-rachised refers to the state typical of wild wheat and barley ears in which *a*, all the upper spikelets disarticulate readily, leaving clean scars at the abscission nodes (see figure 10.3), and *b*, the basal few spikelets of each ear disarticulate tardily (if at all) leaving rough scars. (See Appendix to this chapter for discussion of how these basal rachis remains are overrepresented in the archaeological record.) 2. Domestic types rachis remains of glume wheats (einkorn and emmer) will be of semi-tough-rachised type, while those of barley will be of the fully tough-rachised type. 3. Romana Unger-Hamilton (1988) and Anderson-Gerfaud (1989).

a possible link between testa structure and dormancy, and thus a possibility that SEM-observable features of testa histology could be used to identify the point in time when cultivation began, even in cases where the form of husbandry was of a type that would never select for more readily recognizable domestication traits such as tough rachis, (compare the work of Fritz [1986] and Smith [1987] on tests of *Chenopodium berlandieri*; also Ismail [1988] on seed polymorphism correlated with dormancy in *Simmondsia*).

However, early archaeological remains of legumes are rare compared with cereal remains, and it was therefore hoped that equivalent SEM-observable criteria could be found in the cereals and that they would survive in charred remains as evidence of the earliest attempts at any nondomestication cultivation. The necessary histological investigations were undertaken on grain pericarps (particularly the transverse cell layer; see Körber-Grohne 1981) of living wild-type einkorn from both primary and vegetal habitats, and charred wild-type einkorn from Mesolithic Abu Hureyra. Sadly, no criteria could be found in the modern grains which reliably distinguished between wild-type einkorn exposed to cultivation (whether as a crop or as a weed of crops) and wild einkorn gatherered from primary habitats. Similarly, in the ancient grains of wild-type einkorn, no systematic diachronic changes could be detected in pericarp histology that could be attributed to any sort of domestication gradient (Colledge 1989; Hillman, Colledge and Harris 1989:242-243).

Chemical Criteria

The possibility that loss of dormancy could be detected through chemical criteria was tested in 1982 using pyrolysis mass spectrometry (PYMS) as part of a broader exploration of the chemo-taxonomic resolution of this form of analysis. Lack of time has prevented us completing the analysis of the (so far) promising-looking results, but, in the meantime, similar work is being undertaken with the much less expensive (and thus archaeologically more useful) technique of infra-red spectroscopy (IRS). IRS is already proving invaluable in distinguishing charred (modern and ancient) cereal grains of not only different ploidies but also different classical species (McLaren et al. 1990). It is therefore hoped that chemical criteria of this sort might also be able to distinguish between wild-type einkorn grains of the two genotypes concerned here, and thence be used to help identify the start of nondomestication cultivation.

Evidence From Associated Remains of Other Plants

The question of whether or not wild-type cereals were under cultivation can also be addressed through analyses of associated remains of plants of other species which can indicate the sort of plant communities from which the potential cultigens came (for example, whether it was a segetal community or a truly wild one). The rationale, together with detailed examples, is presented in Hillman, Colledge and Harris (1989) in the context of the investigations at Abu Hureyra. At this site, this line of evidence indicated that the wild-type einkorn from Mesolithic levels was gathered from primary habitats (strictly as part of a hunter-gatherer economy) and that it was not under cultivation.

Evidence From Associated Artifacts

When flint-bladed sickles are used to cut reeds, rushes, cereals, or hay, distinctive patterns of wear or polish are generated on the blade surfaces and are observable with epi-illuminating light microscopes (see, for example, Andersen and Whitlow 1983; Anderson 1980; Anderson-Gerfaud 1983, 1986, 1988, chapter 12; Ataman 1989, chapter 22; Keeley and Newcomer 1977; Korobkova 1978, 1981b; Moss 1983a; Newcomer et al. 1986; Stordeur and Anderson-Gerfaud 1985; Unger-Hamilton 1983, 1985a, 1988a, 1989). Korobkova (1978, 1981b) found that when cut low on the culm, cereals grown on cultivated land produced distinctive long scratches on the flint blades. The source of the scratches was thought to be dust or grit blown- or splashed up onto the lower culm from the tilled soil surface. Certainly, relatively few such scratches were produced by wild cereals growing in uncultivated primary habitats. Here, then, was a potentially independent basis for recognizing any form of cultivation which had involved tilling the soil and reaping low on the culm.

Unger-Hamilton (1985a, 1988a, 1989) incorporated studies of this effect in a massive series of field trials conducted in S.W. Asia and Britain and applied the resulting criteria in the interpretation of microscopic studies of flint blades from Mesolithic and Neolithic sites in Palestine. Similar work (though less specifically concerned with the "Korobkova effect") was also undertaken at a range of experimental locations and early sites by Anderson-Gerfaud (1980, 1983, 1986, 1988, chapter 12). In both cases, the Mesolithic sites (locally termed Epipaleolithic) were of the Natufian culture, and the Neolithic sites were of the Pre-Pottery Neolithic A and B cultures (abbreviated as PPNA and PPNB respectively).

Unger-Hamilton interprets her present data as suggesting that cereals were probably cultivated on a very small scale throughout the latter part of the Mesolithic—beginning ca. 10,000 BC, around 2000 years before the earliest remains of domesticated crops. The cereals were reaped while still unripe. (Reaping unripe culms generates a quite different polish on the blades—a point also observed in experiments by Anderson 1980; Anderson-Gerfaud 1986, 1988, and chapter 12; see also Andersen and Whitlow 1983). The cereals were probably cut fairly low on the culms. The cultivation (of this same type) remained small scale throughout the Pre-Pottery Neolithic A (PPNA). At the start of the PPNB (ca. 8000 BC), cereal cultivation began to be practised on a large scale, and the cereals were now harvested in the ripe (or partially ripe) state. At this same point, culm width (as reflected by width of polish on sickle blades) increased from the narrow wild type to the thick domestic type (Unger-Hamilton 1989).

In parallel work by Anderson-Gerfaud (1983, 1988, chapter 12, Anderson 1991), harvesting of cereals in the green state was similarly demonstrated from Epi-Natufian and PPNA sickle blades recovered from Tell Mureybit in Syria and from a few backed bladelets from Epipalaeolithic Abu Hureyra. She also has evidence for cutting cereals fairly low on the culm by the early Neolithic at Ganj Dareh Tepe in Iran (Stordeur and Anderson-Gerfaud 1985; Anderson-Gerfaud 1986, 1988; and chapter 12).

Comparison of Present Evidence From Artifacts and Charred Cereal Remains, in the Context of the Domestication Model

Unger-Hamilton's (1989) evidence for cereal cultivation beginning by 10,000 BC in the southern Levant might appear to conflict with the fact that the earliest finds of domesticated cereals (again from the Levant) date from shortly after 8000 BC (uncalibrated). However, in the context of our domestication model, this apparent disparity makes sense.

Unger-Hamilton has indicated that the cereals apparently under cultivation by ca. 10,000 BC (uncalibrated) were harvested with sickles, thus satisfying a primary precondition for domestication. However, the fact that throughout the first 2000 years these cereals were seemingly harvested in the green, completely unripe state (as they also were at Epi-Natufian and PPNA levels [both essentially early Neolithic] at Tell Mureybit in Syria [Anderson-Gerfaud 1983, 1988, and chapter 12]) would clearly have precluded any positive selection for semitough-rachised mutants, anyway. (Other factors could clearly have contributed here.) Only at around 8000 BC does Unger-Hamilton encounter evidence for the cereals having been harvested in the more mature state which (according to our model) would have allowed domestication to proceed. It is possibly significant, therefore, that it is around this same date that we encounter the first archaeological remains of domesticated cereals (currently dated to ca. 7800 BC [uncalibrated]) and that their earliest appearance (so far) is on sites in this same area of the southern Levant (see Bar-Yosef and Kislev 1989; van Zeist et al. 1972, 1979). It could perhaps also be significant that it was around this same time that Unger-Hamilton's cereals were first cultivated on a large scale, and also acquired a secondary domestic feature (thick culms).

However, it must be stressed that alternative explanations exist for each aspect of the current evidence:

- Any one sickle blade could have been used to harvest both wild and cultivated cereals. Thus, even if the scratches came from harvesting small cultivated plots, as proposed, the bouyant polish attributable to harvesting cereals in the green state could nevertheless have come from using the selfsame blades to cut green wild cereals growing nearby. Present evidence from the blades therefore cannot altogether exclude the possibility that the cultivated plots were harvested in a sufficiently mature state to have allowed domestication to proceed from the outset of cultivation (assuming the other preconditions were satisfied).

- The extreme paucity of charred remains of food plants from early sites in the southern Levant suggests that the current chronology of the earliest finds of domesticated cereals might be purely fortuitous. The absence of charred remains of Mesolithic domesticates could, for example, be blamed on poor preservation of cereal remains on early archaeological sites in the area and the still inadequate standards of their recovery. This dearth of direct evidence therefore offers no proof that the process of domestication did not begin simultaneously with the advent of the sickle reaping identified by Unger-Hamilton from 10,000 BC.

- The dust on the cereal culms which produced the scratches could theoretically have come, not from tillage, but from natural disturbance in or near the wild stands concerned. (Unger-Hamilton [1988a] is currently planning trials to specifically test the extent to which abundance of scratches on flint blades might be correlated with differences in soil type and natural soil disturbance such as nearby mountain screes). Certainly, the work of Anderson (chapter 12; 1991) and of Anderson-Gerfaud et al. (1991) indicates that scratches can be generated without any cultivation, as seems to have been the case at some Mesolithic sites in Europe. However, as noninitiates in this area, we cannot judge whether the European evidence matches the apparently dramatic increase in the abundance of scratches which Unger-Hamilton (1989) records for the transition from Natufian to PPNB in the Levant.

- The Mesolithic blades might have been used to cut both unripe wild cereals (thereby producing the unripe cereal polish), and edible rhizomes of marsh plants such as *Typha* (catstail), *Phragmites* (common reed), and *Schoenoplectus* (bulrush). The occasional scratches on the Mesolithic blades could then perhaps derive from the mud attached to the rhizome surfaces. Rhizomaceous foods were almost certainly staple sources of carbohydrate among local hunter-gatherers in the Near Eastern Mesolithic (see Hillman 1989; Hillman, Colledge, and Harris 1989; Hillman Madeyska, and Hather 1989), but their exploitation probably declined with increased dependence on cultivated cereals. If, therefore, scratches from muddy rhizomes and the dusty culms of cultivated cereals prove to be indistinguishable, it will be difficult to identify the point at which rhizome gathering declined/ceased and the harvesting of cultivated cereals began.

(GCH, Karen Hardy, and their Institute colleagues have now completed the first round of extensive harvesting trials of wild *Typha* rhizomes undertaken, in part, to see whether the flint blades develop characteristic forms of wear)

- The earliest cultivation of cereals might have involved no tillage, in any case, but simply relied on sowing the spikelets by dibbing (that is, in small holes made with a pointed dibber or dibbing stick) or even direct onto soil mulched with uprooted vegetation. Certainly, dibbing has proved very successful with wild-type wheats in the Jalès experiments (Anderson 1989; Anderson-Gerfaud et al. 1991; chapters 11 and 12), just as zero tillage has proved so successful in some ecologically less destructive forms of modern agriculture—especially when combined with generous mulching.

- The husbandry activities that selectively advantaged semitough rachises or plumper grains are unlikely to have been the same as those that favored wider culms. It would therefore be unwise to attach any great significance to the seemingly synchronous appearance in the archaeological record of apparently domesticated grains/rachis remains and independant evidence for thicker culms.

However, despite these alternative explanations, it is clear that use-wear studies of sickle blades offers a potentially useful source of independent evidence for the chronology of cereal cultivation and domestication which archaeobotanists cannot afford to ignore. Nevertheless, much more work is clearly needed in this area (table 10.4).

Was the Domestication of Each Crop a Single or Multiple Event?

It remains uncertain whether each domesticated crop had a polyphyletic or monophyletic origin, that is, whether each was domesticated several times or just once.

Clearly, einkorn, emmer, and barley were each domesticated separately. However, different crop populations of each of these species could themselves have been domesticated independently at each of a number of different early cultivator settlements. If, and how often, any such independent domestications occurred will have depended on three factors. The first factor was how quickly stocks from newly domesticated crops were exchanged/traded across regions where cultivation was being adopted for the first time. Clearly, rapid exchange could have preempted potential cases of independent domestication amongst hunter-gatherers poised to start cultivating. The speed of exchange will, in turn, have depended on the preexisting patterns of social contact between bands, and the potential recipients' perception of the agronomic advantages of the domesticated

forms. The second factor was how big an area of the Near East was witnessing the adoption of cereal cultivation: the greater the area, the greater the chance of some early cultivators being isolated from exchange networks. According to Hillman (1987), the area experiencing primary adoption of cultivation is likely to have embraced a broad sweep of the northern "Fertile Crescent" and the Jordan Valley—at the very least. This area might have allowed ample room for isolation, although the extent and intricacy of the exchange networks of recent hunter-gatherers suggests that any such isolation would probably have been short-lived. The third factor was the density of human occupance in these areas and, thence, just how many different settlements could have independently adopted cultivation and been in a position to independently domesticate the crops concerned.

The lack of evidence relating to each of these factors precludes firm conclusions. Nevertheless, in figure 10.14 we have allowed for the possibility of several different episodes of primary adoption of cultivation and subsequent independent domestication.

But is there any evidence from the domesticates themselves? The answer is a qualified yes. Using a range of morphological and genetic criteria, Zohary (1989a:369–371) argues that because crops such as the wheats, peas, and lentils represent such a limited segment of the full spectrum of variation to be found in their respective wild ancestors, they probably derive from a single domestication event in each case. However, using similar evidence, Ladizinsky (1989a:385–388) argues that the domesticated forms of pea and lentil, at least, must have had a polyphyletic origin; that is, crops of the wild-type ancestors must have been domesticated more than once. For the moment, therefore, the question remains open.

Either way, the narrowness of the genetic base of the initial domesticates (relative to the diversity of the wild types) allows their early establishment to be viewed as a classic example of the founder effect (Ladizinsky 1985b).

A Further Stage of Domestication: The Appearance of Secondary Crops with Fully Tough Rachises

All the foregoing has considered domestication in terms of the fixation of semitough-rachised phenotypes in crop populations of the brittle-rachised (wild) type—primarily using einkorn wheat as our example. This process was justifiably termed *domestication*, as the resulting plants were incapable of surviving in the wild, and were (and still are) dependent on human intervention for their reproduction.

However, domestication in the wheats can (and did) go one step further. Tetraploid and hexaploid wheats that carry mutant forms ("Q") of the speltoid "q" alleles produce a fully tough rachis that fails to disarticulate, even when thoroughly threshed and have thin deciduous glumes which release the grain during threshing (Miller 1987; Muramatsu 1986). Such plants are termed *free-threshing* or *naked-grained* and include both bread wheat (*T. aestivum*) and macaroni wheat (*T. turgidum* var. *durum*)—both now grown worldwide. Because these free-threshing wheats emerged from already domesticated crops (such as emmer and spelt), they can be termed *secondary crops*. This term is most commonly reserved for crops such as rye and oats because they are traditionally thought to have emerged as domesticated weeds (complete with tough rachises, or, in oats, tough rachillas) in fields of primary founder crops, before eventually becoming established as crops in their own right (Vavilov 1917; Sencer and Hawkes 1980; Hillman 1978). Although the domestication of weed rye and weed oats is conventionally thought to be the result of unconscious selection, models for the domestication of free-threshing wheats have yet to be formulated, and conscious selection may well have played a role.[11]

However, new archaeological evidence of very early finds of fully domesticated rye from Abu Hureyra in Syria now suggest that rye was one of the original founder crops and not a secondary crop after all (Hillman and McLaren). As domestic rye is an outbreeder, this new evidence might seem to conflict with our model which suggests that unconscious domestication of an outbreeder like rye would have required more than 8,000 years (see table 10.3). The explanation probably lies in rye having evolved from an inbreeding ancestor: *Secale vavilovii* which formed the first crop and within which domestication occurred, the fully domesticated crop thereafter acquiring the outbreeding habit as a result of introgression from *S. montanum* (Davies and Hillman 1992; Miller 1987; Zohary 1990).

Stability of the new domesticates

This chapter is limited to a discussion of the process of domestication and its archaeological record and does not discuss the stability of newly domesticated crops with regard to introgression (gene infiltration from related genotypes) and the evolution of various isolation mechanisms or the later stages of crop plant evolution. These topics are amply discussed by other authors (see, for example, Harlan [1973] and Ladizinsky [1985b] on introgression and isolation mechanisms).

Conclusions

Domestication of the wheats and barley appears to have occurred under cultivation and not in response to selective pressures arising in wild habitats from the exploitation of wild cereal populations by hunter-gatherers. On the other hand, some form of edaphic preadaptation to naturally disturbed habitats (or, less probably, ruderal habitats) remains a possibility. (Ruderal habitats are those disturbed by human activities other than arable cultivation, that is, waste places.)

Correspondingly, the first cultivated wheat and barley crops were inevitably of the wild, brittle-rachised type.

Although the quantities of grain used to sow these first crops would generally have been too small to have included domestic-type mutants, the crops would probably have been sufficiently large for the mutant to have been generated within the first 2 to 5 years in most einkorn crops, and perhaps a little longer for emmer and barley.

Selection favoring the semitough-rachised types of wheat and barley was necessarily unconscious during the early stages of domestication.

Unconscious domestication of wild-type wheat and barley crops required a combination of specific husbandry methods: the crops had to be harvested by uprooting or sickle reaping; and the crops had to be near-ripe or partially ripe, but not so unripe that none of the ears had started shattering. In certain circumstances, unconscious selection of the domestic mutants might have required annual extensions of cultivation to new plots of virgin land and the seed for sowing these new plots to be taken from last year's virgin plots.

There are agronomically sound reasons why some of the earliest farmers should have used these particular combinations of husbandry methods.

Selective pressures generated by these techniques and favouring the domestic semitough-rachised mutants (relative to the wild brittle-rachised type) might have been intense. Preliminary field trials with wild einkorn gave measured values of about 60% against the wild type—relative to the domestic type; that is, about 60% of the wild-type spikelets were lost per crop generation, but none of the domestic-type spikelets.

Given selective pressures of this order and with the high levels of inbreeding typical of modern wild einkorn, computer simulation indicates that the initially rare semitough-rachised (domestic-type) einkorn phenotypes could have achieved fixation (that is, domestication in the classical sense) within 20 to 30 crop generations (that is, within 20 to 30 years). (Emmer and barley might have needed longer.)

In reality, selective pressures were probably far less intense because the crop was harvested when much less ripe. Nevertheless, the computer simulation indicates that at these lower selective pressures, domestication of wild-type einkorn could still have been achieved within one or two centuries.

In those crops where domestication was able to proceed without shifting cultivation, selective pressures would have been reduced still further—owing to the dilution effect of wild-type plants originating from self-sown spikelets on the re-used plots. However, this is unlikely to have added more than a century or so to the domestication period.

There are other factors which could theoretically have retarded domestication rate: greater outbreeding, heavy introgression from neighbouring stands of wild cereals, and gathering shed spikelets for sowing. It is improbable, however, that they had a very great effect and even less probable that they acted in concert.

The farmers are likely to have applied some form of conscious selection as soon as the domesticates reached frequencies sufficient to attract their attention (perhaps around the 1 to 5% level). From that point, the process of domestication would have been complete within 3 to 4 years (although the first part of the process would have been unaffected).

Such a transient sequence of events is unlikely to be preserved on early sites as a recognizable progression, and we will probably never find a full sequence of charred wheat or barley remains manifesting unequivocal "on-the-spot" domestication. Remains of a transitional crop might occasionally be recovered by chance, but on most sites where domestication occurred we are more likely to find remains of wild cereals in one level and fully domestic cereals in the levels above, with no way of knowing whether the domesticates were imported or generated locally.

If ever found, remains of genuinely transitional crops (resulting from *in situ* domestication) might be indistinguishable from mixtures of wild- and domestic-type rachis remains generated by introgression of wild-type genes from neighbouring wild stands into already domesticated crops or by taphonomic processes affecting the charred remains. (See appendix).

In occupation deposits with remains of wild-type cereals, it is nevertheless possible to distinguish between cases of nondomestication cultivation and gathering from wild stands, albeit not from the cereal remains themselves, but rather by using evidence from associated remains of plants other than cereals which are ecologically diagnostic; and/or perhaps use-wear analysis of associated remains of sickle blades. Chemical markers from the cereals themselves may also eventually prove diagnostic at this level.

It remains uncertain whether each domesticated crop type was domesticated several times or just once.

Acknowledgments. This chapter is based on papers presented in 1977 and 1981 at the Institute of Archaeology, University College London, in 1983 at the Research Laboratory for Archaeology, Oxford University, in 1984 at the Maison de l'Orient Méditerranéen (CNRS) in Lyon, in 1987 at The Vavilov Centenary Seminar – again at the Institute of Archaeology, and in 1988 at the Museum of Anthropology, University of Michigan, Ann Arbor, USA.

We are very grateful to our friend Daniel Zohary (Hebrew University, Jerusalem) for generously providing us with unpublished estimates of outbreeding frequencies in wild einkorn, for many stimulating discussions during the past decade, and for making so many suggestions for far-reaching improvements to this chapter (see various acknowledgements in body of chapter); also to Terry Miller of the Plant Breeding Institute, Cambridge, for helpful comment and advice generously given over many years, and for bringing a number of publications to our attention; to David Lewis of the (then) Plant Science Department, (now School of Pure and Applied Biology), University of Wales, College of Cardiff, for helping us rear and harvest crops of einkorn; also to Jacques Cauvin, Patricia Anderson-Gerfaud and George Willcox of the CNRS Maison de l'Orient Méditerranéen/Institut de Préhistoire Orientale for undertaking the long-term trial domestication of einkorn, and making available unpublished information from their impressive field and laboratory experiments; to David French, Director of the British Institute of Archaeology at Ankara for supporting this and related work undertaken in Turkey; to Garrison Wilkes of the University of Massachusetts, Boston, USA, for helpful discussions on modifier genes; to Professor Hugh Bunting, Barbara Pickersgill, Jack Hawkes, Patricia Anderson-Gerfaud, Bob Whalen, Richard Ford, Gail Fritz, and many others who have made helpful suggestions following the several presentations of this chapter in Britain, France and the USA; and to Daniel Zohary, Wilma Wetterstrom, George Willcox, Jack Hawkes, David Harris, and Richard Hubbard for correcting and commenting on the written version of this chapter. Finally, we should like to acknowledge the influence of Professor Hugh Bunting, John Jones, Roy Snaydon and Barbara Pickersgill (all then of the Department of Agricultural Botany, University of Reading) in establishing our interests in the mechanics of crop plant evolution. (We were both students in their department during the late 1960s.)

The preliminary field trials were undertaken during six years spent (by GCH) in Turkey funded by the University of Mainz (Germany), the Faculty of Agriculture of the University of Reading (UK), and a 3½ year fellowship from the British Institute of Archaeology at Ankara (Turkey). The subsequent field trials in Britain were funded by University College Cardiff, Department of Plant Science, where both of us taught.

Notes

1. There is a second form of wild einkorn—*Triticum urartu* Tum. Although it is near-identical to *T. monococcum* subsp. *boeoticum* in morphology, the work of Johnston and Dhaliwal (1976:1093) and Sharma and Waines (1981:251) suggests that it is today reproductively isolated from *T. monococcum* and that it was not the ancestor of domestic einkorn—*T. monococcum* subsp. *monococcum*.)

2. In domestic emmer and einkorn wheats, the relatively tough rachis nevertheless disarticulates when the ear is threshed, and it is therefore termed *semitough*. However, this semitough rachis is not to be confused with the fully tough rachis of, for example, bread and macaroni wheats which remains intact when threshed, as it does in all the domestic barleys.

3. In the region as a whole, the delay in the start of domestication is unlikely to have exceeded a couple of years, even if the areas sown by each band were minute. For the first cases of domestication in the Near East as a whole, the critical factor was not the size of individual crop populations but the area of all the early Near Eastern cereal populations combined (within each crop species). So long as the combined area exceeded 1 to 2 hectares, there would have been a good chance of the mutant appearing in one of the plots (however small), and this would then have allowed the first cases of

domestication to proceed—just as soon as the mutant was selectively advantaged by the relevant husbandry practices.

4. The "completely unripe" category used here refers strictly to rachis ripeness, rather than ripeness of the grains, and it includes both the "green" and "half-green" categories used by Willcox in chapter 11.

5. There would be no problem in sowing unripe grains – even at the milk-ripe stage, as they are still capable of germinating, a perhaps surprizing fact known to Percival (1921:140) and demonstrated in recent laboratory trials by Willcox and Anderson-Gerfaud using a range of primitive wheats and barleys (Anderson-Gerfaud, chapter 12; Anderson-Gerfaud et al. 1991; Willcox 1988 and chapter 11).

6. Ear stripping with bone tools carved from scapulae as evidenced for Neolithic Ganj Dareh Tepe (Stordeur and Anderson-Gerfaud 1985; Anderson-Gerfaud 1986, 1988) is not included here, as these authors' experiments have demonstrated that the method would have been used for a form of threshing rather than primary harvesting.

7. In referring to the spikelets (or grain) set aside as seed for sowing next year's crop, we have avoided the term *seed corn* used in British English on account of possible confusion to users of American English in which *corn* refers specifically to *Zea mays* and does not serve as a generic term for all the local cereals as it does (or has done hitherto) in British English. Instead, we use the term *seed stocks*.

8. Nevertheless, some farmers doubtless used other methods such that their crops remained in a state of nondomestication cultivation until they obtained seed stocks of domesticates from other farmers.

9. It should nevertheless be remembered that part of the "loss" from spikelet-shed is of benefit to the farmers: the shed spikelets conveniently seed the old plots ready for next year's crop, as noted above. The only problem is that, when harvesting crops in the "near-ripe" state, far more spikelets are lost than are needed to seed the ground for next year, and Zohary (1988 and 1989) estimates that even 90% of them get eaten by ants and rodents anyway. These excessive losses could have been reduced to the desired level by harvesting the crop when less ripe. This would have decelerated domestication, but probably not beyond the level of the right-hand curves of figure 10.11.

10. It is worth adding that sickle reaping was the method used by Harlan (1967) in his experimental harvesting of near-ripe wild einkorn near Viransehir in southeast Turkey.)

11. Barley and rye are different from the wheats in that there is generally no clear intermediate semitough-rachised state, merely fully brittle-rachised wild types and fully tough-rachised domesticates.

Appendix
Problems in using rachis remains to distinguish wild and domestic cereal as evidence of in-situ domestication

It was noted above that, where archaeological remains of wheat or barley rachises survive, it is theoretically possible to distinguish the wild and domestic forms via differences in the morphology of their rachis disarticulation scars. In many cases, however, the distinction can be achieved only by microscopic examination (ideally SEM) of abscission layer histology—as described by Kislev (1989b, and Frank 1964 as cited by Kislev).

In remains from late Mesolithic or early Neolithic sites, a sample containing a mixture of both wild- and domestic-type rachises might seem to offer clear evidence that the parent crop was in the very process of domestication. Indeed, just such a mixture of wild and domestic barley was recovered from PPNA Netiv Hagdud in the Jordan Valley and was initially suspected to come from a transitional crop (Kislev et al. 1986). In reality, however, mixtures of this sort can be

generated by circumstances other than half-complete domestication. One alternative scenario (see "c" below) is advanced by Kislev (1989b, and chapter 7) who suggests that the Netiv Hagdud barleys were probably entirely wild, after all. However, there are certain other circumstances which can also account for these mixtures, and some of these are outlined below:

a) Mixtures of wild and domestic types can firstly result from introgression of brittle-rachis alleles (from wild stands) into nearby crop populations—through cross-pollination. Thus, in the Near East, one commonly encounters crops of six-rowed barley in which a fifth or more of the ears are brittle-rachised. In each case, wild barley can be found growing nearby and would appear to have cross-pollinated earlier generations of the crop—this despite the predominantly inbreeding behaviour of barleys, and despite the recommended isolation distances for plant breeding stations being a mere 180 m (Kernick 1961). Ancient examples of such introgressed crops might include the charred remains of what Helbaek (1959, 1960a, and 1966a,b) described as "transitional crops" of emmer wheat from Neolithic occupations at Jarmo (in Iraqi Kurdistan) and Beidha (in Jordan). We now know that these finds are probably too late to be cases of primary domestication; instead, they are possibly the product of introgression of semibrittle rachis alleles (from stands of wild emmer) into already domesticated emmer crops. Certainly, wild emmer could theoretically have grown spontaneously in the vicinity of both sites. It is therefore safest to refer to such finds merely as deriving from crops of "intermediate" or "mixed" rachis morphology, rather than deriving from a "transitional crop" which implies that it was undergoing change from the wild to the domestic state.

b) Mixed remains of wild and domestic types can also be generated by a related phenomenon, namely the invasion of fully domesticated crops by wild-type plants growing as weeds. Wild emmer is unlikely to have invaded crops in this way, as it apparently lacks weedy tendencies (see, for example, Zohary & Hopf 1988). However, both einkorn and barley are pernicious weeds of domestic cereals in present day S.W. Asia, and probably were in the past, too. (The problem becomes particularly intractible when wild barley invades crops of 2-rowed domestic barley, as it cannot be readily distinguished from the host crop until close to maturity, and thus cannot be weeded out.) The barley remains from Neolithic Beidha (Helbaek 1966a) could conceivably represent the cleanings from just such a crop, although Helbaek's own interpretation remains equally plausible.

A extension of the same syndrome arises in segetally adapted populations of wild einkorn in which disruptive selection has produced a mixture comprising (i) plants which retain their wild characteristics and which disarticulate before or during harvest; and (ii) plants with semitough rachises which get harvested and resown with the host crop (see Hillman 1978:168). Charred remains of such a weed complex can easily be misinterpreted, especially when mixed with remains of the host crop, and especially when this host crop is itself a landrace combining a diverse range of forms.

c) Kislev (1989b; chapter 7) has found that, if wild cereals are harvested green and then threshed (by hand) while still damp, 10% of the rachis nodes produce abscission scars of the semitough-rachised "domestic" type. He further suggests that this could account for the mixture of wild and domestic types from Netiv Hagdud which his novel studies of abscission-layer histology revealed to be entirely of the wild type. However, Willcox (chapter 11) has found that these green-cut wild cereals disarticulate spontaneously when allowed to dry out, and this leaves normal, wild-type scars. The same pattern has also been observed by Helbaek (1961). Both Willcox (chapter 11) and Zohary (chapter 6) have further noted that foragers or farmers are unlikely to have bothered to thresh freshly cut green ears knowing the ears "thresh themselves" by spontaneous disarticulation as soon as they dry out. It is therefore highly improbable that green-cut wild cereals ever left behind charred remains with domestic-type rachis scars (except for the basal spikelets).

d) In even fully ripe wild wheats and barleys, the basal/sub-basal 2 to 4 rachis segments often fail to disarticulate and, if reaped and threshed, these basal nodes can produce rough abscission scars of the semitough-rachised (domestic) type (figure 10.3a). These basal rachis segments are often disproportionately well-represented in any charred remains—partly because they are more robust and more likely to be preserved by charring (see Hillman 1981). Thus, rachis assemblages with a conspicuous component of domestic-type abscission scars might derive merely from wild cereals in which the basal rachis segments are overrepresented rather than from partially domesticated crops. (Clearly, the basal segments will be present only if harvesting was by sickle reaping or uprooting.) In consequence, the validity of claimed identifications of early domesticates based on rachis remains with rough ("domestic type") abscission scars cannot be evaluated without accompanying details of the relative abundance of basal or sub-basal types in the rachis remains concerned. (Fortunately, these basal/sub-basal rachis segments are readily recognised from their greater thickness and heavier venation.)

e) There is finally the problem of forms which appear to be of genuinely intermediate rachis morphology. These invariably derive from botanic gardens; Willcox (chapter 11) cites examples received from the Plant Breeding Institute, Cambridge, and we have accessed examples from botanic gardens/ gene banks at Bordeaux, Budapest, Leningrad, Gartersleben, and Reading. Miller (1987) has suggested that rachis toughness may be determined by different loci in different populations. Some of the intermediates may therefore be the product of unintended crosses between plants of these different populations, and, as such, represent modern "artifacts" of a sort that would perhaps rarely have occurred in the past.

In addition to these problems of interpretation, it was noted above that rachis remains are, in any case, very rare on most early archaeological sites. It is for this reason that often unsatisfactory substitute characters such as grain shape are used in attempting to distinguish between wild and domesticated forms. Nevertheless, it is hopefully clear from this appendix that even when rachis remains do survive, they rarely (if ever) offer a reliable means of distinguishing between cases of genuine *in situ* domestication and those mixtures of wild and domestic types which can result from quite different circumstances. This regrettably reaffirms the conclusion (above) that the sequence of morphological changes involved in domestication is unlikely ever to be archaeologically visible as a clinal process.

Chapter 11 ✒

Archaeobotanical Significance of Growing Near Eastern Progenitors of Domestic Plants at Jalès, France

George H. Willcox

Author's note

This chapter, as published in 1992, described the results of experimental cultivation of cereals at Jalès between 1985 and 1988; the results were presented at the round table held at Jalès in 1988. This was a trial period leading up to experiments on selection rates in wild cereals. Now, over a decade later, important new archaeobotanical results from a number of key sites combined with theoretical results from continued experiments at Jalès have radically changed our understanding of the origins of cereal and pulse agriculture in Southwest Asia. The publications by Kislev on the difficulties of distinguishing wild and domestic emmer wheats (1989b:148), Hillman and Davies' (1990) publication on rates of domestication, and Baruch and Bottema's (1991) and Helmer et al. (1998) work on climatic change, which might be a contributing factor in the emergence of cereal cultivation (Cauvin et al. 1998), have begun to fill in the gaps in our knowledge. In addition, DNA studies on modern cereals (Heun et al. 1997) and a number of collective works such as Harris (1996) and Damania et al. (1999) have contributed to a far more complete understanding of early agriculture. Two recent conferences on the origins of agriculture in South west Asia, one at ICARDA (International Center for Agricultural Research in Dry Areas; Aleppo 1997: Damania and Valkoun 1997, Damania et al. 1999) and another at the University of Groningen (1998), produced a consensus of opinion among researchers who agreed that agricultural emergence was a very slow and gradual process (Pringle 1998, Willcox 1997).

Archaeobotanical data from a number of new early agriculture sites are helping our understanding of the process of domestication: for example, Cafer Höyük (de Moulins 1997), Abu Hureyra (Hillman et al. 1989, Roitel and Willcox in press), Cayönü (van Zeist and de Roller 1994), and Ashikli (van Zeist 1995) have recently been published, and others such as Jerf al Ahmar, Djade, Halula (Willcox 1996, Willcox and Fornite in press), Nevali Cori (Pasternak 1995), Qermez Dere, M'lefaat, Hallan Cemi, Nemrik (Nesbitt 1995), and Göbekli Tepe are now being analyzed. In addition new evidence has come to light concerning the present-day distributions of wild cereals, particularly in Syria (Valkoun 1992, 1997), but also their ancient distribution (Hillman 1996). These new results have added concrete evidence that we can compare with experimental data.

Following the roundtable meeting, and between 1988 and 1993, agricultural experiments at Jalès using wild einkorn (*Triticum boeoticum*) concentrated on an attempt to test the rapidity of the domestication process. A number of researchers had suggested that the selective pressure, under cultivation, for solid rachis cereals would have been high and that domestication would have proceeded so rapidly that the predomestic phase would not show up in the archaeobotanical record. To test this hypothesis in the field we used the model developed by Hillman and Davies (1990) in order to examine a range of possible cultivation techniques. Preliminary results have been published (Willcox 1990, but see also Willcox 1997, N.D.).

Experimental cultivation at Jalès of wild einkorn showed that spontaneous sowing was inevitable and may represent as much as 25% of the crop. Spontaneous seed corn in a harvest results in diminished selection rates (coefficients) for semisolid rachis mutants of inbreeding populations of wild cereals under cultivation. This implies that the lapse in time

Table 11.1 Temperature and rainfall statistics from two weather stations in Jalès region

	JAN	FEB	MAR	APR	MAY	JUN	JUL	AUG	SEP	OCT	NOV	DEC
SALINDRES (altitude: 195 M), 1956–1985												
Avg. monthly max. temp. (overall mean = 18.1 C)	9.2	10.7	13.06	17.1	20.9	25.0	28.7	27.5	24.1	18.6	12.8	9.5
Abs. max. temp.	18.8	23.0	25.0	28.2	31.2	35.6	39.5	39.8	36.0	28.2	24.2	20.0
Abs. min. temp.	-13.6	-14.5	-9.0	-1.9-	0.2	4.4	4.8	7.8	2.0	-0.5	-7.9	-13.0
Avg. monthly rainfall: mm (1042 total)	82.0	67.3	94.4	78.7	89.0	68.5	39.8	62.7	18.9	142	109.5	99.2
COURBESSAC (altitude: 57 M) 1946–1987												
Avg. monthly max. temp. (overall mean = 19.3 C)	10.1	11.7	14.8	18.1	21.9	26.4	29.8	28.8	25.4	19.9	14.2	10.8
Abs. max. temp.	20.9	23.4	25.5	30.6	33.2	37.4	38.6	40.6	35.0	28.7	26.1	20.6
Abs. min. temp.	-12.	-14.	-6.4	-1.1	-1.1	5.4	10.0	9.3	5.4	0.8	-3.3	-9.7
Avg. monthly rainfall: mm (739 total)	58	63	67	51	66	41	25	49	71	109	71	68

between the beginnings of cultivation and morphological domestication (predomestic agriculture) may be longer than suspected. These results are inevitably hypothetical. However the archaeobotanical record, now better understood, does to some extent endorse the hypothesis. First, we are beginning to identify predomestic agriculture several centuries before the appearance of domestication at a number of sites from the associated weed taxa (Willcox 1996, Colledge 1997). Second, wild types persist for long periods after morphological domestication, for example at Aswad, Cayönü, and Halula. This indicates that it was not possible to keep the two populations apart well after domestication. The wild types could have been gathered in the wild, or been part of the field harvest as weeds or as part of the crop. In all cases the wild types because of their similar (almost identical) morphology would be difficult to keep separated from their domestic counterparts. In the initial stages of domestication, this would lower selection rates.

New evidence also suggests that there were multiple domestication events, for example, Hillman's evidence for rye domestication and Willcox's assessment of cereal assemblage variation which were both presented in papers at the Groningen conference in 1998. In addition, a number of sites indicate that wild types were replaced progressively by their domestic counterparts. Finally, in order to try to understand these new results experiments now under way at Jalès are testing different cereals such *T. urartu*, wild emmer, and wild barley.

THIS CHAPTER DESCRIBES SOME OF THE RESULTS obtained from growing wild progenitors at the Institut de Préhistoire Orientale at Jalès in southern France. The project, under the name of "Cultures Préhistoriques Expérimentales," was established in 1985 by Patricia Anderson, a member of the "Équipe de Recherche Archéologique 17," under the directorship of Jacques Cauvin, of the Centre National de Recherche Scientifique.

The domestication of plants was a consequence of their cultivation. The first signs of cultivation appear in the Middle East at the end of the Epipaleolithic and the beginning of the Neolithic, some 10,000 years ago (van Zeist and Bakker-Heeres 1984). This can be variously described as proto-agriculture or, preferably, pre-domestic cultivation, because at the beginning the plants under cultivation were morphologically wild and not yet domesticated.

This period of prehistory is still poorly understood, yet the transition from hunter-gatherers to farmers was fundamental to the history of mankind. The transition may have been gradual, yet the actual domestication appears to have been rapid (see chapter 10). Carbonized plant remains which morphologically resemble wild progenitors have been recovered from a number of sites, but it is difficult to determine whether they were cultivated or gathered from the wild (Hillman et al. 1989; van Zeist and Casparie 1968; van Zeist and Bakker-Heeres 1984). Our aim at Jalès is to elucidate the economy of this period by a process of simulation and experiment, through the cultivation of the very same plants, that is, the wild progenitors of the Old World domestic plants. On the one hand, we can set up experiments, and on the other hand, the act of growing these plants under primitive conditions is an apprenticeship which leads to increased knowledge of how Neolithic man might have cultivated these plants, which have not been cultivated on a large scale since the Neolithic. This project was inspired by Gordon Hillman, who started similar experiments in Wales but was thwarted by unfavorable climatic conditions (see chapter 10).

The wild ancestors of domestic plants have not been cultivated on a large scale since the early Neolithic because they could not compete with domestic crops which have evolved from them. The wild progenitors retained three basic characteristics which are disadvantageous to the prospective farmer, but essential for survival in the wild:

- Dormancy
- Uneven ripening
- Natural dispersal at maturity

These three features constitute the most important difference between wild and domestic Old World cultivars. According to a number of authorities (Harlan 1975; chapter 10; Zohary and Hopf 1988) these features were eliminated soon after the beginning of agriculture, or, more precisely, the beginning of cultivation.

Climate of the Region as Compared with That Occurring in the Natural Habitat

Both wild diploid wheats and wild barley show great climatic tolerance in terms of their natural distribution. Their habitats vary greatly in both latitude and altitude. Einkorn, for example, is found growing from 0 to 2000 m altitude and from Macedonia through eastern Turkey to Iran and Iraq; the most dense stands occur today in southeast Turkey, at altitudes between 900 and 1500 m. Wild emmer is found at 100 m below sea level in the Jordan valley and at 1500 m on the slopes of Mount Hermon (Zohary 1969). According to Zohary, the three Near Eastern wild cereals are important constituents of the sub-Mediterranean oak-park forest vegetation belt, which receives between 400 and 1000 mm of rainfall annually, falling mainly in the winter. In reality the different climatic zones are occupied by different ecotypes adapted to those particular conditions. Thus, it is not simply a question of comparing the different climates but more of finding ecotypes most suitable to the environment at Jalès.

The broad botanical and climatic similarity of the two regions tends to rule out the possibility of bias in our experiments at Jalès. The southern Ardèche, eastern Mediterranean, southeast Anatolia, and Zagros mountain region are in the same general climatic and vegetation belt. The climate of the southern Ardèche is classic Mediterranean. Jalès is situated at 130 m but there is a modifying continental influence of the Massif Central to the west and of the Alps to the east. Table 11.1 gives some statistics from two local weather stations in the region.

Vegetation in the Area of Jalès

The natural climax vegetation of the surrounding hills includes the following species: *Quercus ilex, J. communis, Q. pubescens, Pyrus pyraster, Buxus sempervirens, Celtis orientalis, Juniperus oxycedrus,* and *Phylliria media.* Olive groves are also frequent. On the plain of Beaulieu where Jalès is situated, the original flora has been totally replaced by agriculture. The cultivated fields at Jalès are situated on what was meadow grassland, cut for hay, which accounts for such species as *Medicago sativa, Onobrychis viciafolia* and a number of grasses (see section on weeds below). Inevitably the assemblage of plants making up the meadow determined some of the weeds present in the fields.

The Crops

During the first year we planted a large variety of different progenitors and crop plants, in order to build up a reference collection and gain experience in the behavior of a wide selection of plants. At the time of writing we have built up a grain stock for replanting which allows us to cultivate plots large enough to evaluate our experiments. These consist largely of wild progenitors of Old World cultivated plants, but in addition we are growing four other crops of cultivated wheats: *Triticum aestivo-compactum* #13, *T. dicoccum* #82; *T. spelta* #9, and *T. monococcum* #12.

More importantly, we have five populations of wild diploid wheats composed of *Triticum boeoticum* var. *aegilopoïdes* #55 Plant Breeding Institute; *T. b. aegilopoïdes* #77 Asia minor; *T. b. urartu* #59 Armenia; *T. b. thaoudar* #38 Crimea; and *T. b. thaoudar* #122 Eastern Anatolia. Of these five, our main population, grown on a larger scale than the others, is #122. This population was collected in 1986 in eastern Anatolia near Karaçadag (#7 collection M.-C. Falkowitz and D. Vaughan) between Diyarbakir and Siverek at an altitude of approximately 800 m and in a region where there is an annual rainfall of approximately 600 mm. The winter mean average temperatures are lower than at Jalès, while the summer means are more comparable. This population appears to be well adapted to the climate at Jalès and shows all the signs of being a truly wild species, which is not the case with certain other populations we have acquired from plant breeders.

In 1987 I collected the following wild progenitors in southern Syria: *Triticum dicoccoides* #124; *Hordeum spontaneum* #123; *Pisum humile* #127; *Lens orientalis* #130; *Vicia ervilia* # 131. These plants were gathered from localities in the Jebel Druze, an igneous volcanic massif predominantly of basalt, in contrast to the calcareous substratum at Jalès. The wild cereals were collected at an altitude of 300 to 400 m while the legumes came from a considerably higher altitude, between 900 and 1000 m.

These plants were sown at Jalès in the autumn of the same year, with very poor results, both in germination and in development. The reasons for these failures are no doubt multiple—for example, the absence of the specific *Rhizobium*, the nitrogen-fixing bacteria, in the case of the pulses—but the overriding reason is poor adaptability to the soil and climate of Jalès. We intend to continue planting these populations in the hope of selecting traits that would render them more adapted to this environment. However, it is possible that we could collect other ecotypes of the same species which would be suitable for this region from areas with more similar soil and climate. While wild emmer and barley may occur in or near cultivated areas, they do not to my knowledge show the intermediate morphology that can be seen in einkorn.

Landrace populations

In traditional farming communities the crops are highly variable, being made up of many different lines or genotypes. These are called landrace populations (Harlan 1975), and this built-in variability is an advantage to the farmer in that the various lines are resistant to different hazards in nature. It is only within the last century that landraces have been replaced by uniform true-breeding crops of controlled parentage. The populations we have gathered in the natural habitat show variability even to the extent of having some wild emmer and *Aegilops speltoides* mixed in, these having been accidentally harvested at the same time, which could, at the limit, be considered part of the same gene pool. The populations we obtained from plant breeders, in contrast, are single-line, true-breeding populations and are therefore less representative of early farming practices, despite the fact that they are wild progenitors.

Self-fertilization and its implications for crop plants

The Old World crops are all predominantly self-fertilizing. The rate of selfing may vary depending on a variety of factors. Boyeldieu (1980) reports that in wheat grown under hot conditions in north Africa, the spikelets open prematurely, raising the rate of cross-fertilization to ten or fifteen percent. However, the fact that these plants are predominantly self-fertilizing means that as a population they are made up of numerous true-breeding lines which makes selection of mutants (recessive or not) a straightforward process. For a detailed discussion on how this affects the rates of domestication, see chapter 10.

Time of Planting
Summer sowing

In their natural habitat the wild cereals sow themselves immediately after ripening. Thus the time of sowing is dependent on the altitude and latitude of the particular ecotype. Natural dispersion will therefore vary from May to August, following the relative ripening times in different geographical areas. It is possible that the first farmers copied the course of nature not just because it seemed the most obvious but to eliminate the problems of storage which could lead rapidly to total loss of viability.

During the first year our stocks were attacked by moths whose larvae consume grain; if the stock had not been quickly treated with insecticide we would almost certainly have lost our crop. The spikelets are adapted to survive the hazards encountered when dispersed naturally, that is, as soon as the plants are ripe. The only major danger we have experienced in the fields is from rodents.

There is another important advantage in planting early, though this remains to be proven, and that is to eliminate as much as possible the effects of dormancy. Finally, early planting may considerably increase tillering, a distinct advantage in that yield in terms of grain sown to grain harvested can be increased in this way.

The advantages of early planting are: no loss of viability through storage, increased tillering, and reduction of the effects of dormancy.

Planting dates for Jalès

The planting dates for the crops sown at Jalès are the following:

1985   15 to 20 October
1986   10 to 15 November
1987   25 to 27 November
1988   July to August and November

Until 1988 we planted according to the traditional times, variation from year to year resulting from varying climatic conditions and availability of labor. Spring planting always produced a diminished crop. Our domestic emmer crop produced twice as much from winter sowing when compared with the spring sowing for a given area. We are now in the process of experimenting with summer sowing techniques, that is, in July and August. Hillman observed Turkish farmers planting in early September.

Spontaneous sowing

Following the 1987 harvest the spikelets that were lost by natural shattering (those that fell to the ground), were left to geminate. Many germinated after the first rains during the second week in July and subsequently developed nominally; not a single plant flowered until the following year due presumably to lack of vernalization. The stand produced in 1988 was as extensive as the planted crop of 1987 which appeared to reproduce itself despite cropping. In 1988 we would have liked to continue harvesting this spontaneous crop, but unfortunately we arrived too late, the majority of the crop having already fallen; at the time of writing much of the crop has been lost to rodents, which reached epidemic proportions this year, apparently because of two successive mild winters.

Spontaneous sowing under cultivated conditions

During the Neolithic it is possible that a method of spontaneous sowing was used under conditions of cultivation: that is, the crop was harvested at a time when a proportion of the crop had already fallen. This method would not select for a solid rachis and is a major argument against rapid selection (for more detailed discussion, see chapter 10).

Spring planting and vernalization

Apart from the problems of storage, vernalization is the major factor controlling the season for planting, whether spring or winter. All Old World cereals can be planted in the winter but only those lacking the vernalization factor may be planted in the spring. We have not as yet tested all our crops for vernalization. *T. boeoticum aegilopoïdes* was both spring and winter-sown in 1987/8 and exhibited poor tillering for the spring-sown crop. In general, the wild wheats exhibit varying degrees of vernalization requirement and this almost certainly depends on the geographical distribution of different ecotypes. This kind of study is beyond the scope of this project but those interested should refer to Mathon (1985) who found a need for vernalization in all the wild einkorns he tested. It would appear that in the case of wild einkorn the vernalization factor would have made spring planting improbable for Neolithic farmers.

Both modern and primitive farmers today traditionally plant winter wheat crops because they give a much higher yield; only when the winter crop fails or they lack the right weather conditions for planting are they forced to plant in spring. In semiarid regions the lack of precipitation in spring results in an even greater difference between yields of winter and spring crops. On the other hand, some crops are frost sensitive or have a very short life cycle, as in the case of *Panicum miliaceum* and certain modern barleys and pulses, and so may be planted in the spring.

Methods of Planting
Sowing naked or hulled
Germination tests show that when wild einkorn is sown naked the effect of germination inhibition is removed. It would therefore be logical to sow naked grains; however, the problem is that during removal of the glumes the grain is frequently damaged. For this reason, we sow hulled grains.

Sowing with or without awns
While it is not possible to throw the spikelets of awned cereals in the same way as one can broadcast naked grains it is perfectly possible to sprinkle the awned spikelets evenly over the soil. At first we removed the awns, but now this does not seem necessary. Contrary to what one might expect, the spikelets do not enter the cultivated soil more easily with the awns, whose function seems to be to help the spikelets penetrate a mat of vegetation and cracks in the ground in the wild situation, which they do very effectively. The awns serve an important purpose during separation of the straw and the spikelets because they burrow under the straw.

Depth of planting
Modem varieties of wheat are planted at a depth of between 2 and 5 cm. Wild wheats on the other hand have a much smaller grain and therefore need to be planted at a more shallow depth. The reason for poor germination in the field in 1986 was probably in part owing to the fact that the grains were sown too deeply.

Density of sowing
The optimum density given for modem wheats is 250 to 300 plants per square meter. However this is within the context of giving maximum yield per acre, as opposed to the return from a given amount of grain sown. It is the latter method of measuring the success of a given crop which would have been of interest to Neolithic farmers. Sowing at a low density may

Table 11.2 Germination tests for 7 to 21 October 1987

SPECIES	REF. #	NAKED GRAIN %	HULLED %	DOUBLE %	COMMENTS
T. monoccoum	12	92	80	0	
T. dicoccoides	18	56	17.5	0	Only 40 spikelets
T. thaoudar	122	82	80	0	Green
T. thaoudar	122	62	42	0	Half green(moldy)
T. thaoudar	122	92	90	0	Ripe
T. thaoudar	77	94	94	0	Green
T. thaoudar	77	98	96	18	Half green
T. thaoudar	77	92	84	46	Ripe
T. thaoudar	38	92	98	16	Green
T. thaoudar	38	100	95	10	Half green
T. thaoudar	38	100	100	20	Ripe
T. urartu	59	82	94	6	Ripe
T. compactum	13	90	-	-	Free threshing
H. spontaneum	33	97.5	58	-	Ripe
	52	54	-	-	Green

have been to his advantage because of increased tillering per plant. Having said this we have noted several important advantages when sowing wild wheats as densely as possible, which are:

- Elimination of weeds through increased competition
- More uniform ripening
- Ease of harvesting
- Elimination of sterile tillers
- Less tilling required

In fact, dense sowing produces a population which is much easier to harvest, and competion may cause it to ripen more uniformly. For this reason dense sowing is seen as a possible advantage to a farmer of wild cereals. It would also increase the chances of cross-pollination in what are basically selfers.

Broadcast as opposed to furrow sowing
Both techniques have certain advantages. Broadcast sowing undoubtedly requires more grain, although in our case the figures may be exaggerated through lack of experience. Agricultural manuals give the following figures for the number of kilos of wheat to be planted per hectare: 150 to 225 for broadcast by hand and 150 to 200 for furrow using seed drill. Our main crop of wild einkorn gave the following figures: 200 to 250 for broadcast by hand and 60 to 100 for furrow using seed drill. In terms of the number of stems per square meter we have the following figures for *Triticum boeoticum thaoudar* 122b: 402 broadcast and 436 furrow. Thus there is little doubt which is the most efficient in terms of yield. However, on a subjective level the ease of broadcast sowing and its efficiency makes it preferable. The gesture of throwing the seed, allowing it to slide out of the palm of the hand creating an even spread over a wide surface, seems the most

natural of actions. Sowing in furrows is best suited to mechanical farming. We intend to continue using the two methods. In future, it will be important to record the number of spikelets per square meter and the number of plants.

Fallow system

The fields at Jalès have not been under cultivation long enough to determine whether or not we will adopt a fallow system. In terms of simulating the domestication process, there is little doubt that a fallow system would favor the domestic trait of the solid rachis, because there would be no chance of spontaneous sowing of the crop. Thus 100% of sown seed would have been harvested with no germination of fallen grain from the previous harvest (see also chapter 10).

In the Middle East the open nature of the landscape lends itself to the fallow system. For example, in southern Syria before the introduction of fertilizers, fields were only cultivated once every four years (Delbiet 1856). Hillman reports that in eastern Turkey the fallow system increased relative to the distance of fields from the village (Hillman 1973c). A further extension of the fallow system is to open new land every year. This would be useful in keeping agricultural weeds at bay and also avoid depletion of soil nutrients (for further discussion, see chapter 10).

Preparation of the soil

The soil before planting was prepared by ploughing with a tractor and then by passing a rotavator in the conventional way. This aggressive tillage does not resemble the possible methods of tilling available to Neolithic man and will in the long term affect the weed species present in our fields. On the other hand it should not greatly affect the behavior of the wild progenitors.

Germination
Germination in the laboratory

This is carried out systematically every year by the local agricultural college at Aubenas on samples of our seed grain, in order to compare germination in the field with that in the laboratory; test the levels of dormancy exhibited by our crops; and test the viability of wild cereals harvested before maturity. Table 11.2 gives the results of germination tests for October 7 through 21 in 1987. Four important conclusions can be tentatively drawn from these results: in the case of wild einkorn, a crop harvested before maturity gives viable seed for planting the following autumn; the glumes in the twinned-grained einkorns tend to inhibit the germination of the "second grain;" no twinned germination occurred in # 122; wild emmer and wild barley gave poor results, perhaps because of strong germination inhibitors; and #77 appears to lack the dormancy factor when harvested ripe. This population, which appears to be a single line (true-breeding), also tends to a more solid rachis. These results should be treated with caution until further tests have been carried out to confirm them. The

Table 11.3 Optimal harvest period

#	1986	1987	1988
122	1–5 July	1–5 July	1–5 July
55	5–10 July	10–15 July	10–15 July
59	25–30 June	5–10 July	10–15 July
77	5–10 July	5–10 July	10–15 July
38	5–10 July	5–10 July	10–15 July
124	–	*20–25 May*	15–20 June
123	–	*15–20 May*	10–15 June

Italic type is used to indicate collection in natural habitat.

choice of heads at different stages of ripeness is not based on the development of the grain but on the following features:

green	=	all glumes green, unshattered
half green	=	top-most glumes dry, unshattered
ripe	=	glumes dry, top of ear shattered

The reason for this method rather than the more conventional method as used by agronomists, who use a scale based on the hardness or softness of the grain, is that in the wild cereals, the spikelets on any one ear will not all be at the same stage of development.

To further test the effects of regulation of germination, that is to test the dormancy factor in hulled wheats, we will be carrying out tests over longer periods. Until now we have only been testing for 14-day periods.

Germination in the field

Germination in the field has proved to be far more difficult to assess, for two reasons: 1) when planting spikelets one is not always sure how many grains are present, and 2) our methods of planting are such that it is not always easy to compare the number of plants with the number of grains sown. In addition, germination in the field is a function of many different factors, including:

- Depth
- Relative humidity
- Temperature
- Time of planting

In many cases germination in the field was extremely variable from area to area, but the reasons for this are difficult to determine. Depth of planting and waterlogging are the most probable reasons. From the archaeological point of view it is obvious that it is the field germination which is relative to the evolution of crop plants and the eventual loss of dormancy. For this reason we will be including a program of field experiments in the future: for example, to test whether summer sowing decreases the effects of dormancy.

The fact that our population of single-grain wild einkorn, *Triticum boeoticum aegilopoïdes,* does not exhibit dormancy suggests it is perhaps more predisposed to domestication. The majority of domestic einkorns are of course single-

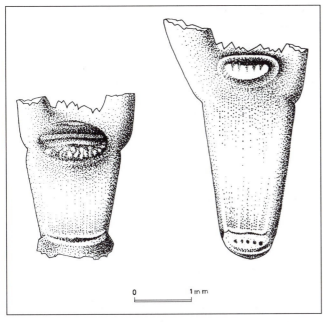

Figure 11.1 The abscission scars on the internodes of modern domestic and wild einkorn. While the morphological difference is clear in modern material 10,000 year after domestication, this is not always the case with archaeobotanical material.

grained. However it could be misleading to make conclusions from a single population.

Dormancy in the field

At present we have no accurate data on dormancy in the field, except to say that in a number of cases the emergence of the seedlings in wild cereals is later than in their domestic counterparts. Emergence under field conditions will be determined primarily by the weather conditions in any one year. Preliminary results show that in two-grained wild einkorn, grains do not remain dormant in the soil for more than the winter season.

Relative Ripening Times

One of the features of annuals in their natural habitat is that there is no uniform ripening of seeds from one plant to another or within the inflorescence. This is true for the wild cereals and pulses. It is also true for some of the more primitive domestic cereals such as einkorn, emmer, and spelt. For this reason it not always easy to estimate the time of ripening. In table 11.3 I have estimated the relative optimal five-day period during which a harvest was carried out with minimum loss through shattering and yet with a minimum number of immature heads.

These figures represent crops sown in the winter: those sown in the spring mature five to ten days later. The same population in different plots may vary up to five days, apparently depending on soil conditions; poor soil conditions retard the development of the plants by a period of approximately five to ten days. In 1986 we sowed #38 and #77 very densely on rich soil. There was good germination and

the plots developed in a thick stand which appeared to force them into maturing more uniformly. These two samples both come from the Cambridge Plant Breeding Institute and have a rachis which behaves as an intermediate between wild and domestic plants.

Once the crop plants retain their seeds, irregular ripening becomes a harmless trait, and indeed remained with many crop plants. However, from our experience irregular ripening is disadvantageous when cultivating nondomestic cereals, this being an argument for rapid selection of a semisolid rachis once cultivation began.

Natural Dispersal Mechanism in Predomestic Crops
Abscission layer and disarticulation of rachis

Before discussing the details of our observations it should be noted that four different morphological types can be distinguished as far as the rachis is concerned:

1) Wild einkorn, fragile rachis
2) Segetal einkorn, and many populations from plant breeders, intermediate between 1 and 3
3) Domestic einkorn, emmer, and spelt with semibrittle/ solid rachis
4) Hard and soft free-threshing wheats with a solid rachis

In wild cereals the ear matures progressively with the uppermost spikelets ripening first. As they dry out, the abscission layer, which is already formed, separates on drying and the segments fall. That the abscission layer in wild barley is formed early in the development of the plant can be shown by cutting an ear at an early stage, for example when it is in flower, then allowing it to dry in the sun; eventually the ear will break up just as it does at maturity, though not having formed grain. Thus the danger of confusing the remains of a green harvest of a wild cereal with that of a solid or semirachis population under the conditions of carbonization (pseudo-solid rachis) would be extremely unlikely, since any crop harvested green would be immediately dried, an almost unavoidable process in a Mediterranean climate. In the case of wild einkorn the same experiment was conducted for #122 with the same results.

Weather conditions, or more specifically relative humidity, greatly affect the shattering of the rachis. Thus if a wild crop is ripe, it is an advantage to harvest early in the morning, while the dew is still on the plant, to avoid shattering.

According to Zohary the evolution of the semisolid rachis involves only one gene (see chapter 6); he suggests that theoretically the shift from brittle to nonbrittle rachis should have been fast, and if the planted populations were large enough it could have been accomplished in a matter of a few generations (Zohary 1969, 60). The presence of intermediate types indicates the possibility of other genes being involved. However these intermediate types have not been identified in archaeological sites.

Hillman and Davis (chapter 10) have measured selection coefficients and on this basis have estimated the time between the beginning of cultivation and the appearance of a semisolid rachised population. In 1984, Hillman suggested that we should attempt a simulation of the domestication process in order to test the theory at Jalès. This experiment has already been set in motion as part of the project. However there remains, in the experimental situation, the problem of population size, which in the Neolithic was ample enough (see chapter 10). Green harvesting, if this was indeed an ancient harvesting technique, would be less selective in terms of a population with a semisolid rachis population and may tend to select for late ripening (see Willcox and Anderson, "The effect of different harvesting techniques on mutant frequency," 1991).

Possible intermediate types

Two populations of wild einkorn, #77 and #38, retain their spikelets more readily than the other populations, yet not as efficiently as the true domesticates. These populations were sent to us from the PBI in Cambridge, England, and their history since they were collected has not been established at the time of writing. Indeed this phenomenon could be explained if the plants were collected from weed populations where intermediate forms had evolved. For weedy ecotypes this intermediate stage appears to be an advantage because part of the population remains with the crop and part falls to the ground (Harlan 1975). All the populations which were obtained from plant breeders are true-breeding single-line populations and two of these populations must have originated from an intermediate type of parentage or from a cross between wild and domestic forms which occurred during breeding.

Rachis fracture in wild and domestic einkorn

The difference at the point of the break between wild and domestic einkorns after shattering can be clearly distinguished (figure 11.1). Our conclusion is that the internodes from a green harvest will break up after drying, but that intermediate varieties such as we have seen in populations obtained from plant breeders could complicate the issue. Whether these types existed in antiquity has not been demonstrated.

Selection for the semisolid rachis

Because the Old World cereals and the pulses are all "selfers" the selection rates for nonshattering heads would have been relatively quick, unlike cross-pollinators where recessive traits would not be manifest so frequently. Domestic plants which are cross-pollinating are often vegetatively propagated; thus as with "selfers" advantageous mutants are not lost through segregation and introgression, According to Harlan (1975) tribes in Africa do consciously select seed from sorghums

and broomcorn millet. It is doubtful that this was an important factor in the development of Near Eastern cereals. However, once the semisolid rachis genotype became obvious, then it is possible that Neolithic man could have consciously kept back grain which to him seemed most suitable for cultivation. For the evolution rates of the domestication of wild einkorn in respect to the semisolid rachis, see chapter 10.

Methods of Harvesting

For a detailed discussion on the implications of different harvesting techniques see chapter 12. The following observations were found to be significant for interpreting the archaeobotanical record:

- A harvester will attempt to avoid weeds, particularly spiny plants such as thistles;

- Shaking ripe heads into a container was unsuitable for wild einkorn in our densely sown plots. However it may be more suitable in the wild situation, especially in the case of panicled grasses;

- Uprooting contaminates grain stock with soil and so may be more suitable for fodder crops such as hulled barley and bitter vetch;

- A green or premature harvest provides a viable crop with less seed loss than a ripe harvest.

Threshing
Fragile rachis

At present we can only report on our experiments in separating the spikelets from the straw, which is the first stage of threshing (Hillman 1984a), and one that would be eliminated if the harvest was carried out by shaking. For wild einkorn the crop must be left to dry, which starts the process of shattering the ears. Beating, trampling or flailing are all effective methods (many others exist, Hillman 1984a). The most efficient method is to beat small sheaths against a wall in order to break up any ears which are not completely shattered. Any straw that falls or becomes mixed with the spikelets is automatically separated because the arrow-shaped spikelets with their barbed awns always burrow down so that the straw simply has to be raked off the surface from time to time.

Semifragile rachis (as seen in T. monococcum and T. dicoccum)

These crops have a semifragile rachis. The process of separating the spikelets from the straw is exactly the same as for wild einkorn. For this reason it would appear that the semifragile rachis is indeed an advantage when threshing hulled wheats, and this no doubt is why it was retained in the hulled wheats since the Neolithic.

Table 11.4 Weed species found among crops

Salicaceae	Populus alba (suckers)	Umbilliferae	Daucus carota
Polygonaceae	Polygonum aviculare		Eryngium campestra
	P. persicaria	Rubiaceae	Galium verum
	Fumex crispis		G. aparine
	Bilderdykia convolvulus	Convolvulaceae	Convolvulus arvensis
Chenopodiaceae	Chenopodium alba	Boragonaceae	Heliotropium europaeum
	Atriplex patula	Verbenaceae	Verbena officinalis
Amaranthaceae	Amaranthus retroflexus	Labiatae	Galeopsis segetum
Caryophilaceae	Stellaria media		Calamintha nepeta
	S. sp.		Prunella vulgaris
	Silene alba		Salvia sclarea
Ranunculaceae	Ranunculus bulbosus	Solanaceae	Solanum nigrum
	Nigella damascena	Scophulariaceae	Linaria sp.
Papveraceae	Papaver rhosas		Kickseia sp.
	P. somnifera	Plantaginaceae	Plantago major
	Fumaria officinalis		P. lancelata
Crucifereae	Sisymbrium officiale		P. media
	Capsella bursa-pastoris	Campanulaceae	Legousia speculum veneris
Resedaceae	Reseda phyteuma	Compositae	Cirsium arvense
Rosaceae	Potentillia reptans		C. vulgaris
	Agrimonia euphatoria		Sonchus arvensis
	Sanguisorba minor		S. oleraceus
	Fragaria vesca		Senecio vulgaris
Leguminoseae	Medicago arabica		Helianthus annuas
	M. sativa		Carthamus lanatus
	M. lupulina		Lactuca serriola
	Ononis spinosa		L. verminea
	Melilotus altissima		Picris echioides
	M. officinalis		P. hieracoides
	M. alba		Taraxacum vulgare
	Trifolium pretense		Tragopogon porifolium
	T. dubium		T. pratensis
	Vicia sativa		Achillea millefolium
	V. benghalensis		Centaurea nigrum
	V. hirsuta		Chrysanthemum leucanthemum
	Lotus corniculatus		Cichorium intybus
	L. tenuis	Liliaceae	Muscaria sp.
	Onobrychis viciifolia	Gramineae	Lolium rigidum
	Lathyrus hirsutus		Bromus tectorum
	L. sp.		B. erectus
Geraniaceae	Geranium robenianum		B. sterilis
Euphorbiaceae	Mercurialis annua		Festuca pratensis
	Euphorbia sp.		Cynodon dactylon
Polygalaceae	Polygala vulgaris		Setaria viridis
Malvaceae	Malva sylvestris		Gramineae spp
	Althaea cannabina		

Solid rachis

This morphological feature occurs only with free-threshing wheats where the chaff and the straw are separated from the naked grains in the same operation. Why this labor-saving characteristic was not adopted on a wide scale since solid rachis forms were present during the Neolithic, is a mystery.

Weed Species

Not all the species found growing among our crops are true weed species; some come from the meadow flora which had

existed before we ploughed. Over the first three years we have already seen some of these species diminish and the ruderals increase, but it is difficult to draw any conclusions over such a short period. In the first year the most dominant weeds were *Bromus tectorum* and *Cirsium arvense*. The second year was similar, but in the third year there is a predominance of *Lolium rigidum*, *Daucus carota* and *Melilotus officinalis*. Table 11.4 is a list of the plants that have occurred in the fields to date and have been noted during the time of the harvests of 1986, 1987, and 1988. As can be seen

Table 11.5 Threshing floor residues

	SEEDS	TYPE
122B H1 1988 COURTYARD JALÈS		
Ononis spinosa	28	W
Onobrychis vicilfolia	1	W
Trifolium dubium	31	W
Lolium sp.	5	W
Mercurialis annua	3	W
Bromus sp.	10	W
T. boeoticum	5	C
Tilia cordata	3	ct
122B H7 1988 BARN		
Vicia sativa	5	W
V. bythynica	3	W
Melilotus sp.	16	W
Galium aperine	25	W
Rumex crispis	17	W
Bromus sp.	4	W
Lolium sp.	5	W
Aegilops speltoides	2	W cont.Turk
T. boeoticum naked grains	3	C
T. boeoticum internode frags	2	C
T. aestivo-durum	3	ct
Stem base	2	C
Mouse droppings	3	ct
Vitis vinifera	1	ct
Helianthus annuus	6	ct
Fragments of wood	1	ct

W = weed; W cont. Turk = weed from collecting area; C = part of crop; ct = contamination at the threshing floor

Table 11.6 Dimensions and index values for crops at Jalès, 1988

		L	B	T	L/B	T/B
122	Max	8.9	1.8	3.0	778	227
	Min	5.6	9	1.2	444	100
	Avg	7.3	1.3	1.8	558	141
122	Max	8.8	1.9	2.5	714	220
	Min	5.0	7	1.3	381	100
	Avg	6.7	1.3	1.8	513	137
55	Max	8.8	1.9	2.5	714	300
	Min	5.0	7	1.3	381	125
	Avg	6.7	1.	1.8	513	208
77	Max	8.0	1.8	2.5	681	211
	Min	5.1	0.9	1.3	387	100
	Avg	6.6	1.3	1.8	487	132
Percival		6-7.5	1-1.5	2.1-2.6	-	-
Mureybet	Max	6.5	1.7	1.7	570	155
carb.	Min	3.4	0.8	0.9	232	68
	Avg	4.6	1.2	1.3	394	107

Lens					1987	1988
orientalis		Diam.	Thickness		Diam.	Diam.
1987	Max	3.5	1.7	*Pisum*	5.8	5.0
	Min	2.2	0.8	*humile*	3.5	2.6
	Avg	2.9	1.5		4.6	4.0

		L	B			
Vicia	Max	3.4	3.2			
ervilia	Min	2.5	2.3			
1987	Avg	2.9	2.7			

from the list there are at least ten perennials present despite our aggressive tilling methods. Thus the presence of perennials associated with a crop is not indicative of gathering, especially when one considers that during the early Neolithic the tilling was almost certainly very shallow.

Table 11.4 includes many species that reflect the surrounding vegetation rather than a field cultivated under primitive conditions. For example, the sunflowers were brought in by birds from surrounding fields. *Setaria viridis* is typical of the irrigated fields around Jalès, as is amaranth which is found on the more sandy soils in the region. How much of a problem weeds were to the farmer of primitive crops can not be determined from our experiments, because the type of tilling would greatly affect the weed population.

Described in the section below are the weeds present in the residues from threshing areas sampled during harvesting. So far our experience shows that by sowing early and densely, the weed problem can be greatly reduced. Some of the weeds in the fields are of course edible and it is possible that primitive humans may have encouraged certain field weeds.

Threshing Areas
Self-seeding

The presence of self-seeded cereals occurring in and around threshing areas at Jalès is common, and no doubt this almost unavoidable phenomenon also occurred during the Epipalaeolithic at the gathering stage. Could this natural process have heightened man's awareness of plant potentiality? In other words, when he inadvertently displaced wild einkorn, it may have introduced him to the idea of cultivation.

Analysis of threshing floor residues

Archaeobotanical finds from early Neolithic sites frequently contain a large number of weeds (see Hillman et al. 1989, 1984a, 1985, and van Zeist and Bakker-Heeres 1984). The exact origin of these carbonized seeds is not always clear. We have analyzed residues after threshing in order to determine what weeds are contaminating our harvests, in the hope of aiding the archaeobotanical interpretation. Table 11.5 includes two lists of seeds from a sickle harvest, from two separate threshing areas, excluding spikelets of the main crop.

When compared with the results from archaeological sites this assemblage of weeds appears rather poor in number of species. This may be more apparent than real, since in the archaeological context there is a much richer concentration of residue, representing possible buildup over many years of harvesting. Hillman reports that on modern Turkish threshing floors he has recorded up to seventy species (Hillman 1984a).

The most common weeds are represented by species which are medium to tall, the weeds of less than 20 cm being less represented. During the harvest the harvester tried to avoid

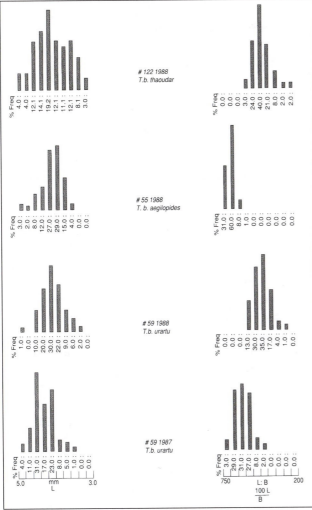

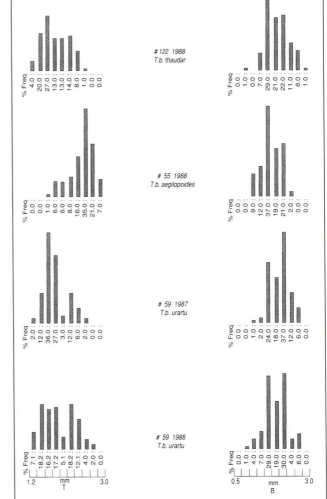

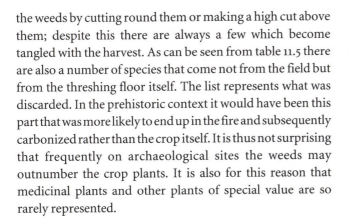

Figure 11.2 Histograms giving length and length/breadth index for four wild einkorns cultivated at Jalès

Figure 11.3 Histograms of thickness and breadth dimensions from four cultivated wild einkorns. Note double peak for the twin-grained varieties.

the weeds by cutting round them or making a high cut above them; despite this there are always a few which become tangled with the harvest. As can be seen from table 11.5 there are also a number of species that come not from the field but from the threshing floor itself. The list represents what was discarded. In the prehistoric context it would have been this part that was more likely to end up in the fire and subsequently carbonized rather than the crop itself. It is thus not surprising that frequently on archaeological sites the weeds may outnumber the crop plants. It is also for this reason that medicinal plants and other plants of special value are so rarely represented.

Biometrical Analysis
Grain size
Measurements of grain size and relative shape are frequently used to aid in the identification of cereal remains from archaeological sites (Renfrew 1973; van Zeist and Bakker-Heeres 1984; Helbaek 1963; Percival 1921). Between very similar

subspecies, environmental variation may be as great or greater than variability at the genetic level. While this is almost always the case with stem height, it does not appear to be true of grain size. Within a crop a wide variation in the genotypes is also possible, as seen in variability in the population, in a number of landrace lines (see above). In addition to the variables already mentioned in the archaeobotanical material there is the process of carbonization, which distorts the grain (Renfrew 1973; Helbaek 1963).

It should be pointed out that measurements of grain size are only one way to describe populations recovered from archaeological sites. Others include embryo shape, hilum form, testa histology, and chemical indicators. However, here we are especially concerned with grain size. The most convenient method to describe grain size/shape is by scatter diagrams and histograms. Measurements of the crops we have grown at Jalès were taken from 100 grains. These are given below for reference to archaeological material. For the twinned einkorns we opened the necessary number of

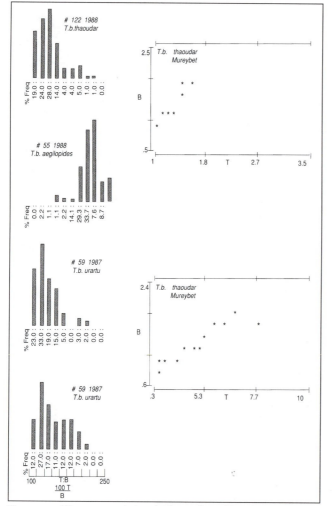

Figure 11.4 Histograms giving thickness/breadth index. Note difference in the single-grained variety #55. Scatter diagrams of carbonized grains from Mureybet taken from van Zeist (1984).

spikelets in order to arrive at 100 grains; some spikelets only contained one grain. The proportions are:

			DOUBLE	SINGLE
T. thaoudar	122	1988	84	16
T. thaoudar	122	1988	88	12
T. urartu	59	1988	66	33
T. urartu	59	1987	90	10
T. aegilopoïdes	55	1988	0	100

Notice the strikingly different figures for #59 from one year to the next. In 1988 the crop did very poorly and, significantly, produced far fewer twinned-grain spikelets.

Table 11.6 gives the dimensions and index values for the crops at Jalès for 1988. The measurements obtained from wild einkorn grown at Jalès are greater than those of the modern grains reported by van Zeist and Casparie (1968) and considerably larger than the carbonized grains reported from the archaeological site of Tell Mureybet in northern Syria. The process of carbonization may account for these differences. On the other hand, these measurements are not so different from those given by Renfrew (1973).

In figures 11.2, 11.3, 11.4, 11.5, and 11.6, the morphology of the grains are described in the form of scatter diagrams and histograms, in order to determine the possibility of distinguishing the three races of wild einkorn on the basis of grain size. Measurements for #77 are given for 1987 and 1988 in order to see whether environmental differences would show up, since in 1987 this crop was very successful, having been grown on rich soil in the garden area. The following year, 1988, it was grown on poor soil. While certain differences can be seen, they are not as great as those between *T. aegilopoïdes* and *T. thaoudar,* which show up clearly in thickness and the TB and LB index as well as in the scatter diagrams. On the other hand, the distinction between the two twin-grained races, *T. urartu* and *T. thaoudar,* is not apparent. These two types can only be securely separated on the basis of their glumes.

Ear Lengths

The height of the ear in the diploid wheats is a feature that distinguishes truly wild forms from their domestic counterparts. This reduction in ear height may be related to the less fragile rachis seen in domestic wheats and is caused by the compactness of the spikelets rather than a reduction in the number of spikelets per ear. This compactness may also influence the relative ripening of the ear. As the height of the ear may be a determining factor for domestication, we measured relative heights and these are given below. Although the length of the internodes is of more use for comparison with the archaeological material, the length of the ear gives a relative measure and in the future we will be giving exact dimensions for the internodes.

The length of ears before shattering, mean average from

Table 11.7 Aubenas measurements

#	WT SAMPLE	WT GRAIN	WT CHAFF	% GRAIN	% CHAFF	WT 100 GRAINS
122	4.40	1.91	2.49	43.4	56.6	1.27
55	0.82	0.27	0.55	32.9	67.1	1.66
77	0.98	0.51	0.47	52.0	48.0	3.50
59	2.57	1.26	1.31	49.0	51.0	1.54
38	4.07	1.88	2.19	46.2	53.8	1.40
12	1.82	1.30	0.52	71.4	28.6	2.50
82	2.48	1.55	0.93	62.5	37.5	3.35
9	11.06	7.33	3.73	66.3	33.7	4.08

Table 11.8 Weights and surface areas for Jalès crops

#	SOWN 1986	M²	HARVEST 1987	SOWN 1987	M²	HARVEST 1988
122	0.75	130	6.5	6.5	501	17.4
77	0.130	14	2.5	2.0	61	3.8
59	0.08	15	2.5	2.0	58	2.1
55	1.36	180	10.0	5.5	150	5.5
38	0.18	35	6.0	2.5	96	7.0
123	-	-	-	0.65	115	0.9
12	0.46	70	11.0	6.0	146	10.1
13	1.09	66	14.0	13.5	576	22.0
82	1.4	100	12.0	7.0	150	11.07

100 heads, is as follows:

Triticum boeoticum thaoudar	122b	8.65 cm
Triticum boeoticum thaoudar	122b	9.12 cm
Triticum boeoticum aegilopoïdes	55c	8.38 cm
Triticum boeoticum aegilopoïdes	77c	7.43 cm
Triticum boeoticum urartu	59c	7.05 cm
Triticum monococcum	12c	6.14 cm

The above measurements show that the domestic population has the shortest ear. Also, the populations that are thought to be intermediate are shorter than the population of #122.

Other biometrical data concerning the ear

The results in table 11.7 are based on measurements made by the agricultural college at Aubenas. As shown, *T. boeoticum aegilopoïdes* #77 gives a very high figure for the weight of grain, although this sample, supplied from plant breeders, should be treated with caution. The table also shows that for the wild einkorns the weight of grain is less than the weight of the chaff. This is relevant in terms of the possibility of long-distance transport of cereals because there would be a distinct weight advantage in transporting threshed grains. In terms of bulk the removal of the envelope would also make a great difference (van Zeist 1984; Hillman et al. 1989).

Yield

The relevance of crop yield in the modern sense is of limited interest to the archaeobotany of the early Neolithic in the Middle East. The primitive farmer would have been less interested in how many tons he obtained per hectare than in the return from a given amount of grain, regardless of the surface area. He would also favor a constant return, despite natural environmental fluctuations. Even in Europe, up to the turn of the century farmers still measured their harvests in this way (see chapter 28). In drier areas, as in the Middle East where the ground naturally has very little vegetation cover and is easily tilled, there is far more tillable land compared with northern Europe. It is for this reason that in many areas of the Middle East there is an extensive fallow system (Delbet 1856).

Table 11.8 gives the various weights in kilos and surface areas in square meters for some of the major crops at Jalès.

Interpretation of the yield

The difference between 1987 and 1988 is very marked. This difference can be accounted for by the following variables:

- Differing weather conditions
- Spring planting in the case of #82 and #55 in 1988
- For #59 and #77 the tillering was very poor: this may have resulted from an exceptionally mild winter which did not provide the necessary vernalization

- Plants were generally grown on poorer soil in 1988
- Harvesting techniques for the 1988 season were less efficient, and in some cases there was unnecessary loss
- In 1988 the fields became infested with harvest mice and other rodents which in some cases, particularly the wild barley crop, led to large losses
- In the case of # 122 and #55 we did not harvest early enough so many of the ears had already begun to shatter and had therefore lost their upper spikelets

The results from 1987 show that it is possible to produce a viable harvest from wild einkorn. Yet the results from 1988 alone would not be encouraging. By experience we hope to learn how to increase the yield of these wild plants.

Storage

While early planting may ease the problem of storage, there is still a need for storage, not just for consumption but also as an insurance against years with catastrophic harvests. At present we are not at the stage where we can experiment with copies of so-called storage structures found on early Neolithic sites, but it is our intention to investigate the possibilities of storing wild progenitors in future experiments. It might also be useful to compare hulled and naked wheats.

Conclusion

After three seasons of growing the wild progenitors of domestic plants it is clear that there is a great deal to learn about pre-domestication cultivation and the beginning of agriculture, which occurred at the interface of the Epipaleolithic and the Neolithic. The results are beginning to give us a more complete view of the problems faced by the first farmers, and the observations and data we are collecting are proving useful in interpreting the archaeological and archaeobotanical record.

The most important archaeological question is to determine the duration of this period, in order to accurately distinguish between the gathering stage and the cultivation stage, when the plants were morphologically identical. Hillman has provided extremely convincing data which indicate that under certain conditions selection for domestic characteristics would have been very rapid. By establishing the probable agricultural techniques wild plants require, we hope to be able to show how they might affect the rates of selection of domestic traits occurring as natural mutations in a given population. The rates of evolutionary domestication based on measurements of selection coefficients generated by primitive forms of harvesting are discussed in chapter 10. One outcome of growing these plants is that we find ourselves attempting to discover ways of eliminating the problems posed by their undomestic behavior. The first farmers faced the same problems and would have sought to overcome them too. We are not yet at a stage where we can demonstrate that

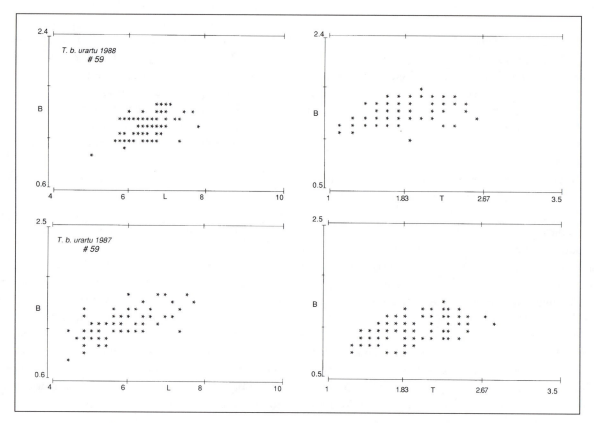

Figure 11.5 Scatter diagrams plotting length against breadth and thickness against breadth for different populations of einkorn

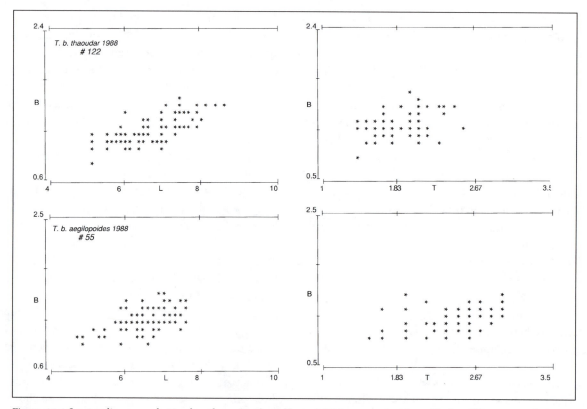

Figure 11.6 Scatter diagrams plotting length against breadth and thickness against breadth for different populations of einkorn

by using certain techniques the wild characteristics which are disadvantageous to agriculture can be overcome, but we can suggest possible methods; regulation of germination—summer planting; cultivation of one-grained einkorn; uneven ripening—dense sowing; and dispersal of grain—harvest before maturity. If these techniques prove successful in overcoming the difficulties of cultivating wild crops, we could then envisage reduced selective pressure for domestic mutants. This would imply a prolonged stage of predomestic cultivation. However our initial and inexperienced attempts at simulating the plant husbandry of the neolithic farmers suggest, on the contrary, that selection pressures were very high. The question is, can we adapt to these plants before they adapt to our manipulation?

Acknowledgments. I am very grateful to P. Anderson, J. Cauvin, G. Deraprahamian, D. Helmer, M.-C. Cauvin, and all the members of the ERA 17 for their kind help, intellectual stimulation, and practical participation in the work which led to this article. I owe special thanks to G. Hillman, whose idea it was to create such an experimental situation, whose original research made this project possible, and who has enthusiastically motivated many researchers in the field of archaeobotany. He read this article meticulously in its first draft and made many useful comments. Special thanks are also due to D.C. Anderson, M.-F. Diot, D. Vaughan, M.-Cl. Nierlé, J.-P. Mandin, and members of the Lycée Agricole at Aubenas whose participation in the project was indispensable, and to all others who gave help in many different ways.

Chapter 12 ✍

Experimental Cultivation, Harvest, and Threshing of Wild Cereals

Their Relevance for Interpreting the Use of Epipaleolithic and Neolithic Artifacts

Patricia C. Anderson

HARVESTING, SOWING, AND PROCESSING OF wild then domestic cereals first developed in the Near East. Since 1985, at the CNRS Institut de Préhistoire Orientale, Jalès, Ardèche, France, G.H. Willcox (see chapter 11) and I have been experimentally simulating the cultivation of wild cereals,[1] along with domestic cereals relevant to the Neolithic in the Near East. Analyzing harvesting and processing tools used in these experiments for characteristic microscopic traces of use, we have then looked for similar traces on prehistoric tools. This chapter outlines our observations on the various experimental techniques and on the prehistoric harvesting methods used for wild cereal, as indicated by microwear traces on certain tools from two northern Levantine sites with wild cereal remains, Abu Hureyra (Epipaleolithic) and Mureybet (Natufian and Neolithic). Based on experimental observations, this chapter intends to show the sowing technique best adapted to wild cereals and the necessity of hoeing or tilling in cultivation; he effectiveness of sickles in harvesting experiments in different field conditions, and the precise use of sickles from prehistoric sites with wild cereal remains; and the probable impact on the domestication of wild cereals of different cultivation techniques we have tried and of harvesting techniques documented by use-wear traces on stone tools from prehistoric sedentary sites.

Findings and Hypotheses on Wild Cereal Exploitation
Cultivation and domestication of wild cereals
Location of earliest domesticates. Recombinant DNA techniques have been used to reveal genetic properties of the earliest (domestic) cultivars identified in Near Eastern sites.

The genotypes of the early cultivars show that wild cereals, which are their potential progenitors, are found only in the Levant, indicating that domestication of emmer, einkorn, and barley indeed occurred at one or very few locations in this region (Zohary 1989a, chapter 6). Recently, infrared spectrometry analysis has shown rye may have been among the earliest domesticates in the Northern Levant (McLaren et al. 1990).

The finds of morphologically domestic cereal grain from Aswad in the Northern Levant date from approximately 7800 BC (van Zeist and Bakker-Heeres 1984). It was thought that cereals arrived at the known early agriculture sites of the seventh and eighth millennium in domestic, cultivated form because the directly underlying levels of the sites showing no remains of the ancestral wild cereals that needed to be cultivated before selection for domestic forms could occur (see chapters 7 and 10).

At Abu Hureyra, grains of wild einkorn (*Triticum boeoticum*) and wild rye (*Secale cf. montanum, Secale cf. cereale*) and a very small amount of wild oats (*Avena sterilis*) have been identified by Hillman (in Moore 1985; Hillman et al. 1989). At Mureybet wild einkorn and wild barley (*Hordeum spontaneum*) were identified by van Zeist (van Zeist 1970A, van Zeist and Bakker-Heeres 1984).

Analyses of the overall composition of the macrobotanical remains from these two sites do not show whether cultivation occurred. Plant remains are not associated in such a way as to suggest they were harvested from cultivated fields as opposed to being gathered from the natural environment (Hillman et al. 1989; van Zeist and Bakker-Heeres 1984). The finds of morphologically wild cereal grain are therefore considered by the archaeobotanists studying them as coming from gathered, spontaneous populations (Hillman et al. 1989; van Zeist and Bakker-Heeres 1984). However, recent studies of grains using infrared spectrometry may shed new light on the question; reexamination by this technique of several grains from Mureybet appears to indicate the presence of both wild and domestic rye (McLaren et al. 1990). The idea that wild cereals may have been cultivated by the site inhabitants has been advanced for the Abu Hureyra Epipaleolithic (Moore 1982), and beginning at Mureybet in the Neolithic Phase III (see chapter 18; Cauvin 1977, 1989) based on features recalling agrarian sites. These include a certain level of development of symbolism, material culture, social organization, and sedentism as well as the presence of structures so small as to seem appropriate for (grain ?) storage and a marked increase in bones of rodents found in these levels (Helmer 1978). This idea was suggested to some by the sheer abundance of wild cereal grain at Abu Hureyra (Moore 1982) and the increase in remains of wild cereal grain (van Zeist and Bakker-Heeres 1984) and Cerealia-type pollen (Leroi-Gourhan 1974) from the Natufian to the PPNB levels at Mureybet.

To date, study of the use of prehistoric stone tools has not turned up evidence of cultivation of wild cereals. For example, no artifacts used for soil preparation (hoeing, digging, and so forth) have been identified from sites containing wild cereals (or even early agriculture sites in Mesopotamia prior to fifth millennium sites in southern Mesopotamia); stone tools shaped like these later hoes were found at Mureybet, but a microwear analysis found most were used to work wood, or less frequently bone or hide, and none had detectable traces of soil working (Coqueugniot 1983). It could be argued that soil was prepared using tools of organic materials such as wood which were not preserved, or that they were not found due to their abandonment in unexcavated areas such as the cultivated field, for example. Our experimental observations, however, suggest that preparing the soil is not only unnecessary but can actually be disadvantageous to germination of wild cereals. Therefore it is very unlikely that the gathering or management pattern of wild cereal by the inhabitants of the site involved working of the soil or regular sowing.

Ethnobotanical studies of modern wild cereal distribution and analysis of pollen cores (see chapter 8) do not offer certainty as to the minimum distance from these sites to the places where wild cereals could have been gathered. If their present distribution is considered to be the same as in the past, gathering einkorn could have required travel of as much as 100 km or so in each direction. If this were the case, at some point site inhabitants (being sedentary) may have cultivated the morphologically wild einkorn or barley nearer to or on the site, rather than repeatedly gathering grain at such a great distance. If the wild cereals grew nearby, on the

other hand, site inhabitants could well have continued to gather them from natural stands until some inhabitants moved out of the natural range of these plants.

Domestication by unconscious selection

Hillman and Davies (chapter 10) suggest that either sickle harvesting of wild cereal or uprooting the plants by hand could have played a decisive role in selection leading to domestication. The harvesting motion of these two techniques would cause the grain to be gathered from the rare mutant plants with a semisolid rachis which hold grain at maturity (for example, domestic type). However, according to Hillman and Davies, both techniques would cause mature grain from wild-type, fragile-rachised plants to spill. Therefore the mutant plants would be unconsciously selected (assuming the latter would at first be too rare to be distinguished from wild-type plants in a large stand). This could occur using either harvesting method, in conjunction with certain conditions of cultivation such as annual sowing of grain from the harvest. The use of these techniques would lead to an increasing proportion of domestic-type grain in each year's harvest, and this grain would continue to increase in the seed stock from year to year. Earlier, Hillman thought there would also have to be use of a fallow system or a change in the sowing area every year (G. Hillman, pers. comm.), but here he proposes that this was not a necessary requisite for domestication.

Presumably, harvesting by picking seed heads by hand would result in slower selection of domestic-type mutants than sickle harvesting (see chapter 10; Anderson-Gerfaud 1988). However, selection would occur in the opposite direction for wild-type plants if other harvesting techniques more common in hunter-gatherer populations (Harlan 1989; Allen 1974) such as beating of grains by hand were used. These techniques would not detach grains of mutant plants with semisolid rachises. They are therefore called nondomestic agriculture techniques by Hillman and Davies. Hillman and Davies go on to state that if harvesting and sowing techniques inducing selection for solid-rachised mutants had been practiced yearly, a domestic population would have been produced in just 20 to 200 years.

Sickle harvesting and selection.
If the conditions and the technique of harvest of the wild cereals can be read from special microscopic traces of use on prehistoric stone tools, we can show whether cereal stems were gathered with the grain and whether this occurred at a green or at a ripe stage of the plants' development. This, then, would suggest what proportion of the grain was taken and what was lost during the harvest (Anderson-Gerfaud 1983, 1986, 1988). If the hypothesis of cultivation is adopted, selection pressure in

favor of any domestic-type mutants can be estimated, using field measurements and mathematical models such as those in chapter 10.

Instrumentation and microwear traces

Sickle gloss and analysis of use-wear traces using optical microscopy. Optical microscopes, particularly metallographic or petrographic microscopes at 100 and 200x magnifications, allow close viewing of features of use-wear traces such as polish and striae. Experiments have shown that using this technique to identify distribution, orientation, linearity, and degree of smoothness or brightness of traces, one can deduce the particular motion of the tool, its penetration into the worked material, and properties of the contact material. These attributes occur in different combinations after different uses but produce recognizable patterns. When microwear traces have been independently reported by various researchers after the same experiment, consistent results were obtained (chapter 10.; bibliography in Juel-Jensen 1988b; Anderson-Gerfaud et al. 1987; Anderson-Gerfaud 1981, 1983, 1986, 1988; Moss 1983a; Korobkova 1981b; Vaughan 1985; Plisson 1985). Precise experimental tool use and microscopic analysis of traces of use are particularly crucial for correctly identifying sickles. I emphasize that prehistoric tools with gloss on their edges cannot be assumed to have been used as sickles (for example, to obtain grain) in the absence of further analysis, because many other uses can cause wear on the tool edge like that traditionally described as sickle gloss. Some tools with gloss have been shown to have been used neither for gathering of cereal grain nor for other agriculturally related activities (Anderson-Gerfaud 1983, 1986, and 1988).

In order to differentiate the various uses of tools possible, researchers have studied accounts of ethnographic tool use and analyzed macroscopic and microscopic traces of use produced on copies of tools used in various experiments. These observations have been compared with observations from a careful microscopic analysis of alleged sickles from archaeological sites. The wear features detected microscopically, such as the appearance of the polish and the striations and orientation of these features, show that some tools with gloss were used not as sickles for cereal harvesting but for other purposes.

One was to cut stems of the noncereal plants that can produce use-wear traces generally similar to those from cereal harvest because they are also humid and silica-rich. Such plants include grasses, reeds, rushes, or sedges. Another was to split or peel stems of use similar noncereal plants (Anderson-Gerfaud 1981, 1983, 1986; Anderson-Gerfaud et al. 1987; Vaughan 1985; Juel-Jensen 1988a; Van Gijn 1988 and chapter 25, Keeley 1980; Moss 1983b). More complex combinations of traces on other tools have been shown to correspond to combing or stripping of grain from the stem

(Anderson-Gerfaud 1988; Stordeur and Anderson-Gerfaud 1985) or to flint inserts from threshing sledges (see chapters 21 and 22).

Finally, experimentation has shown that certain nonvegetal contact materials produce gloss that on a microscopic level resembles archaeological tools alleged to be sickles. Examples include sod cutting, the proposed use of Dutch crescentic "sickles" (chapter 25); and shaving off slivers of humid clay with a flint blade to shape an object while it was turned on a wheel, the use shown for Harappean blades with gloss found in a potters' workshop (Anderson-Gerfaud et al. 1989).

Sickle gloss can therefore be produced by using a tool on a number of materials of a similar humidity or suppleness, particularly if they comprise silicon or other mineral particles of a fine grade (Anderson-Gerfaud et al. 1989). Even flint polished mechanically, using human-made materials with these properties, can show a similar gloss to that obtained by harvesting (Levi-Sala 1988; Kamminga 1979). It therefore became evident that a separate set of experiments was necessary in order to replicate the traces corresponding to different techniques of the harvest and processing of wild cereals, in particular in a cultivation context.

Scanning electron microscopy and chemical analysis of residues on tools.

The kind of information described above can be complemented by study of the tools' edge surface at higher magnifications, using the scanning electron microscope. In earlier research, I have studied tools using the SEM at magnifications up to 3000x (500 to 1500x appears to be the most useful range of magnification). The SEM and energy-dispersive analysis show that mineral components of the worked material can survive as microscopic residues adhering to the surface of the working edge of glossed tools (Anderson 1980; Anderson-Gerfaud 1983, 1986, see ref. in Anderson-Gerfaud et al. 1987).

I was able to identify some of these residues as phytoliths by comparing their morphology with phytoliths extracted from known present-day plant samples. Phytoliths (see chapter 20, and Anderson-Gerfaud 1985/1986) are silicifications of cellular and intercellular areas in certain plants. Alone they measure about 10 to 50 microns in largest diameter, but they are only angstroms in thickness. They therefore can adhere to the surface of the working edge of plant processing tools (we have seen them on stone, bone and metal tools using the SEM) as thin sheets of a number of connected cells (or silica skeletons). Phytoliths have been most often preserved on archaeological tools in this manner, with discrete residue size depending upon the fragment torn from the plant and the friction and wear and tear on the fragment once it attaches to the tool edge.

Some phytolith residues have a characteristic morphology which can lead to the identification of the general type of plant harvested or indicate the part of the plant processed with the tool (for example, the culm as opposed to the glumes, Anderson-Gerfaud 1986; Stordeur and Anderson-Gerfaud 1985). The amount of phytolith material preserved on individual tools may be adequate to indicate that the plant harvested was one of the *Gramineae* family, which have very characteristic forms, but would very seldom point to a plant within that family, particularwhich includes grasses, cereals, and reeds. (These distinctions can often be made if use-wear traces are viewed in optical microscopy as well).

The chemical (energy-dispersive) analysis technique we used could not separate the silica from plant residues from silica (flint) comprising the tool surface. We know the phenomenon of residue deposition exists after use from a chemical standpoint because the chemical analysis was able to clearly distinguish siliceous plant residues on experimental threshing tools made of bone as well as on prehistoric tools with analogous wear and residue traces (Stordeur and Anderson-Gerfaud 1985). Residues are usually found only in microscopic depressions of the contact area of the tool edge (Anderson-Gerfaud 1986, Stordeur and Anderson-Gerfaud 1985; Karol Szymczak, pers. comm). These observations have also been made for metal sickles from an ethnographic context (Vaughan et al. 1987). Chemical analysis of some experimental harvesting tools used to cut near the soil show calcium residues located in the working area that could correspond to soil or, less likely, to calcium-rich weeds repeatedly contacted during use along with cereals. Such residues have been observed on Epipaleolithic and Neolithic tools with traces from harvesting cereals or grasses (Anderson-Gerfaud 1986, 1988). Perhaps further investigation of these residues will show they correspond to proximity of the tool to soil and calcium-rich plants during the harvesting motion, showing whether crops were harvested low down rather than high up from the ground.

It is ideal to combine these approaches to tool use. Investigating variation or evolution in plant treatment techniques provides a means to better understand the development of agricultural practice and the process of domestication.

Results of Research on Cultivation and Harvesting Techniques of Wild Cereals
Tools used and studied in experiments

Harvest or processing of wild cereals has been carried out using approximately 50 tools to date, all with a view to building up a body of reference data for interpreting micro-traces of use on archaeological tools and evaluating the results and impact of such tools' use in a prehistoric context as accurately as possible. The flakes and blades used in experiments were similar to the archaeological tools from sites with wild cereals and from early agriculture sites. However, these tools are found as isolated flakes and blades, often in fragmented form. Some experimental tools we used as harvesting knives and sickles were held in the bare hand,

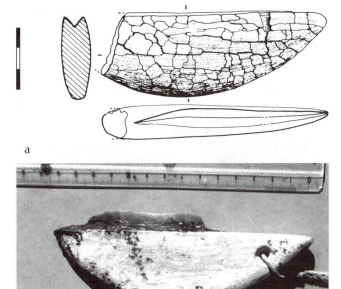

Figure 12.1 Reconstructed hafted sickles used in experiments to harvest wild cereals which could correspond to the distribution of gloss observed on archaeological sickle inserts: *a*, object with shallow groove carved from soft limestone, thought to be a haft, from the PPNA of Mureybet; *b*, Reconstruction of *a* as handle with blade like those found in the PPNA level (see figure 12.19a) hafted in the groove using bitumen and grit. Reconstructions such as these were less practical to use than others with longer handles (see following figures). *Photograph courtesy of author*

but most were hafted according to simple reconstructions, devised using copies of rare known hafts (figures 12.1a and 12.1b) and as deduced from the distribution of the wear traces and, occasionally, of adhesive traces on the archaeological tools which were inserts (figures 12.2 and 12.3). Such reconstructions were made to learn to use different tool forms, evaluate their efficiency for the task, see microwear traces left on their flint inserts, and compare copies of the same tool forms used over several seasons of harvest. Observations have been in the form of qualitative evaluations, video films, photographs, slides, measurements, and microscopy. Particular attention was given to microscopic traces of use on the various tools in order to determine whether traces were sensitive enough to be characteristic of use of a tool for harvest of cereals in particular, for harvest of wild cereals at the green vs. the ripe stage of maturity, for harvest high vs. low on the stem, for differentiating harvesting motions (sawing, cutting, stripping), hafting arrangements, and durations of use.

In other experiments, approximately 30 tools were used to harvest other wild, nonwoody plants (reeds, various small-seeded grasses, sedges, cattail, rushes, and so forth), and another 100 tools to harvest domestic plants, including primitive cereals (emmer, einkorn, spelt, barley) at Butser Farm and at Jalès (Anderson-Gerfaud, 1986). Several hundred

Figure 12.2 Curved wooden handle we used with 2 to 3 elements hafted with bitumen and grit. It was the most practical sickle form and was used from year to year without retouching or renewing blades.

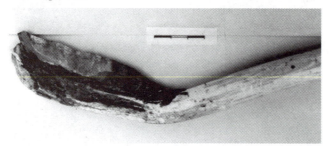

Figure 12.3 Blades hafted alone in hafts such as these were used in experiments comparing ripeness and height of harvest. Their simplicity held variables to a minimum, but they were thought to be somewhat less efficient than the one in figure 12.2, although preferred to the hafts in figure 12.1. *Photograph courtesy of author*

other tools were used to cut or process woody plants (Anderson-Gerfaud 1981; Anderson-Gerfaud 1990), to work soil (Nd), clay (see above and Anderson-Gerfaud et al. 1989), and stone, wood, and various animal materials (shell, bone, antler, ivory; Anderson 1980; Anderson-Gerfaud 1981). Traces from the various other uses were found to be microscopically and often macroscopically distinct from traces from harvest of wild cereal discussed in this chapter.

Limitations of prior experiments and ethnographic data

An additional reason it was felt experiments were needed is that, to our knowledge, wild cereal utilization is not attested to in the ethnographic record. The closest related activities documented are intensive gathering (chapter 1) and occasional sowing of wild grass seeds other than cereals (chapter 2; Keeley, pers. comm.; Allen 1974). Experimental cultivation of other grasses also has been carried out by agronomists but on a small scale (Harlan 1967; Zohary 1989a). Wild cereal cultivation needs to be dealt with experimentally on a large scale and in an ongoing fashion in order to continue Harlan's (1967) and Hillman's (chapter 10) experiments. Repeated experimental simulations over a number of years reveal patterns showing how wild cereals may have reacted to different cultivation techniques.

Seeds and sowing

Origins of seed stock. In order to carry out long-term observations and experiments with wild cereals, two-grained wild einkorn wheat indigenous to the Anatolian region of Eastern Turkey (*Triticum boeoticum thaoudar*) was gathered there, then imported for cultivation and harvesting in controlled conditions on the grounds of our research laboratory (CNRS Institut de Préhistoire Orientale, Jalès, Ardèche) in a Mediterranean region of southern France, to which it is well adapted (see more details concerning cultivation in chapter 11).

Special cultivation techniques for wild cereals. In the first years of experiments, different sowing times, techniques and fields were tried, over an area of about one hectare. Experimental results show that the cultivation of wild cereals differs from that of domestic cereals sown in tilled fields in many ways, one being that wild cereals do not require tilling.

Near Eastern landscapes would not have needed to be cleared before sowing, as is the case today, where soil has been long subjected to tilling. Moreover, our experiments suggest that tilling tends to discourage wild cereal germination: experiments involving burying the grain in furrows were less successful than those where the grains were broadcast, then the ground trampled or a stick used to barely cover the grains with soil. This is because spikelets of wild cereals are perfectly adapted to penetrating the vegetative mat near the soil, such as stems from the previous year's plants, and so forth, and germinating barely below or at the soil surface (Anderson-Gerfaud 1988; Anderson-Gerfaud et al. 1991).

Our experience has shown the best results are produced from broadcast sowing (we now sow 1200 g of spikelets per 25 m^2) takes place near the time of natural grain dispersal, between late June and August (rather than autumn or spring); in this case the grains do not need to be buried. In this particular region, the wild einkorn and barley is ready to harvest between early June and mid-July, depending the year's climatic cycle.

Observations on different techniques of harvest

Our harvesting techniques derived from ethnographic examples of techniques observed for other wild plants or for domestic cereals, adapted as information was gleaned from successes and failures from year to year. We therefore believe that these methods (with certain reservations, below) could have been used in the past to gather grain from wild cereal in its natural environment as well as that sown intentionally in fields. We realize that some techniques such as sickle harvesting would be far more likely to have left identifiable traces in the archaeological record than others such as hand picking of seed heads or beating, therefore the archaeological record represents at best a skewed version of the reality of harvesting techniques used. Qualitative description of our experience with each technique for harvest at the green or ripe stage, indicating the practicality or impact of the use of each one, was thought to be another means of judging whether it was likely to have been employed in the prehistoric past.

Beating of seed heads. This technique is used for gathering wild grass seed in Africa and America (Harlan 1989), and Australia (Allen 1974). Beating seed heads into a container did not meet with success in our experiments, despite its use ethnographically and the reported success harvesting wild einkorn in Turkey (Hillman chapter 10; Harlan 1967). We did find beating the seed into a container the most rapidly executed technique of all tried, but it was also clearly the one that resulted in the least wild einkorn or wild barley grain, whether green or ripe. This was apparently because grain was either too green to be detached by beating or, if ripe, fell to the ground before we could catch it.

Harvesting by beating is customarily carried out several times as the wild grains ripen so as to gather grain stock that is ready at that moment. Successive passes through the stand, unless extremely sparse, resulted in trample stems and spoiled stems and grain. Our fields varied in density (150 to 300 stems per square meter); it would be interesting to compare these densities with those of einkorn stands growing in their natural habitat. Perhaps the technique is less adapted to spike grasses such as wild einkorn or wild barley than to panicled grasses (the only kind cited in ethnographic examples known to us). Our results may differ from prior experiments in Turkey because the technique may have varied in some undefined way, or conditions may have been significantly different, that is, our plants may have been of a different height (Hillman, pers. comm.) or density than those he and Harlan (Harlan 1967) successfully harvested by beating. Our experimental attempts strongly suggest therefore that harvest by beating would not select for grain of domestic-type plants but only some of the ripe wild-type grain.

Picking or stripping seed heads without tools. This method of harvest can work well for domestic cereals at half-green or ripe stages. Reynolds (pers. comm.) finds separate head harvests (by picking) and straw harvests (by cutting with a metal sickle) to be efficient for the domestic emmer, einkorn and spelt he grows at Butser Experimental Iron Age farm in Southern England.

Picking heads of wild cereals (figure 12.4) is effective at the half-green stage of maturity, but if the seed head is picked too green the pulling motion can cause uprooting of the plant. In all harvesting of wild cereals, ripe spikelets often fall before the harvester can reach them (figure 12.5), the very motion of passing through the cereal stand causing spillage. The most successful harvesting motion is to gently pull or bend the seed head, causing spikelets nearest ripeness to detach in the hand, repeating the procedure as necessary as remaining

Figure 12.4 Hand-picking of seed heads of wild wheat at the ripe to half-green stage of maturity. In experiments we carried out this harvest took place in late May or early June in the southern Ardèche. This technique was practical in this instance because these seed heads are particularly fragile and plants were sparsely distributed. *Photograph courtesy of author*

Figures 12.5 Wild einkorn sown in the experimental field. (Note differences in height and in stage of ripeness of ears.) This corresponds overall to the half-green stage, when we usually carry out sickle harvesting. *Photograph courtesy of author*

grains ripen. As for beating, trampling from multiple passes through the cereal stand causes problems described above. Often seed heads were inadvertently missed and left in the field. This method is the slowest we used, even when only one pass was made.

When cereals are picked in one pass at the half-green stage, wild-type grain (except that too green to be removed at the base of the spikelet, or so ripe as to fall) would be taken, as well as the grain from any mutant, semisolid rachised plants in the field. Repeated use of this technique should lead slowly to domestication of the population if mutant plants are present and the appropriate agricultural regime is practiced (ie the seeds are intentionally planted in another location). In our experiments, the old field regrows the following year from fallen grain left behind (figure 12.7), but this grain must be only the wild kind, so it would not be enriched by grain of any mutant plants from the prior year. New mutants may appear that year in the spontaneous field, however, according to the mutation rate for natural populations (chapter 10).

Pulling off or cutting off seed heads using tools. Detaching heads one by one just below the rachis or seed head by cutting or pinching the stem between the thumb and blade of a tool, a variant of the above technique, is used to harvest grain of millet and sorghum (Sigaut 1978, in Japan; E. Takei, pers. comm., and traditionally in western France as demonstrated at the "Fête du millet" in Aizenay, Vendée). This was a slow method of harvesting domestic cereals. Our experiments using it to harvest wild cereal found it to be ineffectual, with hand harvesting without tools being more effective for harvesting seed heads individually.

Mesorias, still used in Asturias, are two long sticks that one or two workers press firmly together around groups of stems of spelt wheat in the field. The workers then pull upwards while holding the stems pinched between the *mesorias*. This has the effect of neatly detaching the ears (seed heads) from the stems. The workers step on the base of the stems to prevent uprooting of the plants (Sigaut 1978 and unpublished film shown at the 1988 Jalès conference). Similar but shorter sticks are used in Georgia by only one person to harvest a glume wheat (einkorn?; Bregadze 1982b:86–87).

Our microwear study of hafted tools from the Swiss Neolithic showed that some harvesting knives from the Horgen period may have been used to harvest using a similar motion. The tools in question had peculiar traces of plant harvesting, oriented perpendicularly to the tool edge. We tested and replicated the traces on the Swiss tools by using hafted stone tools in a motion similar to the instruments above: to comb ears from stems of spelt, einkorn and emmer wheat at Jalès. We accomplished this by pinching several stems of wheat between our thumb and the blade of the tool (see illustration on cover of this volume and Anderson-Gerfaud 1988; Anderson-Gerfaud et al. 1991) and removing

the seed heads from the straw using an upward pulling motion. Our experiments showed this technique to be efficient for emmer, spelt and einkorn wheats, and traces on the experimental tools were similar to those on the particular Horgen knives mentioned above.

However, when we expanded our experiments to include use of this technique for wild cereals, the results were very poor, causing ripe seeds to spill to the ground and greener seeds nearer the spikelet base to catch, uprooting the plants. These poor results were due to fundamental differences between wild and domestic cereals: the wild cereals ripen unevenly and their rachises are fragile.

The evidence from microwear analysis of prehistoric tools to date reinforces the above observations that these head-harvesting techniques were not used for wild cereal. Microscopic use-wear traces we have seen thus far on tools from the Epipaleolithic and the Neolithic of the Near East which appear to correspond to harvesting of cereals, are oriented parallel or at a slightly oblique angle to the working edge of the tool, and in general do not ressemble traces obtained in our experiments using tools to comb or pull off seed heads, which are oriented perpendicularly to the edge. When plant-working gloss traces on Near Eastern tools are oriented perpendicularly to the cutting edge they have thus far proven to have microscopic features like those produced in our experiments by scraping or splitting of reeds.

The possible advantage of these techniques over others is they save having to separate the spikelets from the straw after harvest, although if the straw is desired it still must be harvested in a separate operation. Furthermore, we doubt its advantages in efficiency in the case of wild cereals because our experience at Jalès has shown that most of the wild grain detaches from the straw naturally within several hours after harvest (the seed head separates into spikelets), particularly if the sheaves are laid or stacked to dry in the sun.

Uprooting the entire plant. This technique harvests grains and straw by pulling up the stems by hand, or by striking them with an object such as a stick or the back of a sickle (Hillman 1984a; chapter 5). This can cause seed loss and tearing or cracking of the stems, as can sickle harvesting, if it is carried out when the plants are too ripe. It is best done at green or half-green stages of maturity. This was the fastest successful technique we used (beating was quicker, but gave a disastrously poor yield, see above). This technique can be the most practical at harvest when green stands or fields are sparse, because stems are too far apart to be grouped together for harvest by cutting with a sickle. However, roots and soil (Hillman 1984a), and the humidity of soil adhering to roots may cause rotting of the sheaves or require additional separation during threshing. We found that if stems are widely spaced, uprooting can inadvertently occur when hand picking or sickle harvest are attempted (see above and Anderson-Gerfaud 1988). Because this technique shakes the stem, we have found (Willcox and Anderson 1991), like Hillman and Davies (1990a), that it induces grain loss similar to that for sickle harvesting. The latter authors consider it, like sickle harvesting, to be a predomestication technique. Uprooting of cereals may be inferred from the presence of roots and weeds in plant remains (Hillman 1984a).

Sickle harvesting by cutting groups of wild cereal stems. Any harvesting procedure involving cutting through groups of stems at once is effective if carried out at a time most grains will not shatter from the stem. This time is variable in wild cereals and even from one plant to another or one grain to another in the same seed head. Therefore some upper spikelets, which mature first in an individual seed head, will be detached and lost (figures 12.6, 12.7). This grain loss may be the reason this technique is rarely used in ethnographic accounts to obtain seeds of wild grasses (Harlan 1989; see chapter 10 for exception), and beating, picking, and combing of seed heads (of panicled grasses) or uprooting of the plant are preferred techniques.

Our experience has shown that sickle harvesting is a rapid way to obtain straw and grain of wild cereal and will produce a good yield of viable grain in certain precise conditions: first, if the plants are growing close enough to one another to be gathered in handfulls before cutting and second, if the harvest takes place during the the green or half-green stages of maturity. The motion we used is first to gather stems toward the harvester, using the sickle if the haft is long enough, or with the hands. With the stems grasped in one hand, the sickle is used to cut them by drawing or pulling the blade, handle end first, toward the harvester.

Height of harvest. A low cut (usually 20 to 30 cm above the ground, figure 12.8) was chosen to harvest straw as long as possible. The distance above the soil depended on practical matters such as the height of prickly weeds the harvester wanted to avoid (either because of seed contamination or discomfort to the hand if no protection was worn). The high cut (figure 12.9) consisted of grasping the stems (not the ears, which would cause grain to fall) at the level of the base of the lowest ears to be harvested and cutting below hand level. In our experiments using techniques to pick seed heads or to cut high on the stem, the straw was left standing in the field, the growing back of the field the following year without resowing, as the seeds that fall germinate through the vegetative ground cover. The new, unsown field would be of wild type plants except for domestic-type mutants (chapter 10) that might appear in the new population.

Straw could have been cut after the seed heads had been gathered, for example by hand picking or beating. Sigaut (1978) cites similar examples for domestic glume wheats, concluding that sickle harvesting is carried out in

Figures 12.6 Close view of seed heads of wild einkorn sown in the experimental field. Note differences in ripeness of different spikelets (green spikelets appear darker). Some of the uppermost, ripest spikelets are beginning to fall to the ground. *Photograph courtesy of author*

Figure 12.7 Spikelets which have fallen to the ground in the harvested field. They will germinate after the first rains, usually beween August and October, and the following year, constitute a "spontaneous" field. *Photograph courtesy of author*

ethnographic examples because the straw is needed, and not necessarily at the same time as the grain harvest.

Harvesting rate. Where sickles and harvesting knives were used, the number of plants cut with each motion of the tool was noted as well as the approximate number of stems in each handful. This was dependent on tool type and harvesting motion, green or dry nature of stems, and denseness of plants in the field. Where distribution was very sparse, only one or two stems could be grasped and cut at one time, and uprooting sometimes inadvertently occurred. Where density was greater, we estimated the harvester could hold up to 40 or 50 stems in his hand and five stems on the average could be severed with each motion, as long as the cutting edge was at least 8 cm or in length. The number of stems cut in a given time depended on individual factors such as force applied, rhythm, and motion of work; therefore specific estimates of efficiency for different sickle types are of questionable archaeological relevance.

Stem density and size of seed heads vary from one year to the next. To cite an example based on different 25 m² plots for a given year, yield was estimated to vary between 416 and 902 kilos per hectare and sickle harvesting of 25 m² took anywhere from 45 minutes to two hours with a one-bladed harvesting knife (figure 12.4), uprooting the plants took 40 minutes, and picking seed heads by hand took seven hours! These figures do not take seed loss into account, which is in the process of being quantified in the experiments.

Figure 12.8 Sickle harvesting of wild einkorn wheat near the ground, Jalès, France. *Photograph by E. Tengberg*

Effect of stage of maturity at harvest on successful collection of viable grain

We have attempted to describe a green or half-green time of harvest, as opposed to a ripe harvest, using qualitative (color of spikelet glumes and grain) and quantitative criteria (percentage of rachis intact and not fallen to the ground, measurement of average humidity of the green vs. ripe grains).

Several years of germination tests in the laboratory (carried out by standard agronomical procedures by the Lycée Agricole d'Aubenas, see Anderson-Gerfaud et al. 1991; chapter 11), have shown that even green immature grains, harvested before the shattering of the rachis, were indeed viable, with germination scores generally in the 85 to 95% range, like those for half-green and ripe grains. Seed heads harvested green dry quickly in the sun; then spikelets usually break up spontaneously.

Sickle harvesting was the most efficient when carried out in the half-green and green stages, rather than at the ripe stage, both in terms of effectiveness of the cutting action of the tool and the amount of viable grain harvested. At the former stages, some seed heads have lost their uppermost spikelets and comprise a mixture of dry and green spikelets, green at the base (figures 12.5, 12.6, 12.9), and harvesting does not cause much seed loss. Almost all stems were green at the

Figure 12.9 Sickle-harvesting of wild einkorn ears, cutting fairly high on the stems (a "high cut"), using the tool in figure 12.2. *Photograph courtesy of D. Stordeur*

Table 12.1 Stem humidity: green, half-green, and ripe sickle harvesting

LOW CUT (APPROXIMATELY 20 CM FROM SOIL SURFACE)

SAMPLE	JUNE	GREEN HARVEST			HALF-GREEN HARVEST			RIPE HARVEST			DIFFERENCE: AVERAGE GREEN VS. HALF-GREEN		
		FRESH	DRIED	DIFF.	FRESH	DRIED	DIFF.	FRESH	DRIED	DIFF.	FRESH	DRIED	DIFF.
1a	12	0.08	0.03	0.05	-	-	-	-	-	-	-	-	-
1b	13	-	-	-	0.06	0.03	0.03	-	-	-	-	-	-
2	12	0.12	0.05	0.07	-	-	-	-	-	-	-	-	-
3	19	0.10	0.05	0.05	-	-	-	-	-	-	-	-	-
SUM		0.30	0.13	0.17	0.06	0.03	0.03	-	-	-	-	-	-
AVERAGE		0.10	0.04	0.06	0.06	0.03	0.03	-	-	-	0.04	0.01	0.03

HIGH CUT (APPROXIMATELY 60 CM FROM SOIL SURFACE)

SAMPLE	JUNE	GREEN HARVEST			HALF-GREEN HARVEST			RIPE HARVEST			DIFFERENCE: AVERAGE GREEN VS. RIPE		
		FRESH	DRIED	DIFF.	FRESH	DRIED	DIFF.	FRESH	DRIED	DIFF.	FRESH	DRIED	DIFF.
4a	13	0.06	0.03	0.03	-	-	-	-	-	-	-	-	-
4b	20	-	-	-	-	-	-	0.04	0.03	0.01	0.02	0	0.02

Notes: For each sample (N = 100), average weight (in grams) for one 5-cm stem segment.

point cut. Because germination tests have shown that green grain of the wild cereals is largely viable, we can abandon our earlier hypothesis (Anderson-Gerfaud 1983, 1988) that sickle harvesting of wild cereal would give poor results in an agricultural context.

When wild einkorn was harvested at the ripe stage (glumes and stems are yellow to light green in color) both low and high cutting of the stems was ineffectual for procuring grain, because it commonly produced considerable shattering of those spikelets still on the rachis (Anderson-Gerfaud 1988). The sickle would often not so much cut through dry stems as bend, break, and tear them and uprooting of the plant sometimes occurred.

For these reasons, microwear traces develop somewhat differently on the tool edge during a ripe harvest, appearing less smooth and bright than traces produced by a green harvest. Stems seem to be more firm and resistant when they are green at the point of the cut, with the sickle edge surface in more intensive contact with stems—that is, biting more—than is the case when stems are dry.

As the grains matured, gradation in color of a given stem occurred from the ground up, the stem remaining greenest the longest nearer the seed head and going from yellow, yellowish green, and green from the ground up. To quantify our observations that humidity content varied according to these observed stages of maturity and stem greenness, we measured the humidity of stems near the point they were harvested. This measurement was carried out for three groups, each comprising 100 stem segments of 5 cm. The stem segments (figure 12.10) were weighed within two hours of harvest, then put in a drying oven at 100 °C. and reweighed at intervals until their weight stabilized. This dry weight was usually obtained after 24 to 48 hours in the oven.

We felt this measurement was useful for two reasons. First, we wished to quantify the differences in overall humidity,

Figure 12.10 Stem segments of wild einkorn wheat—some green, some yellow—cut from the base of the sheaves just after a half-green harvest. The segments are weighed just after harvest, then again after complete drying, in order to determine average humidity content of stems at this time of harvest. *Photograph courtesy of author*

despite extreme irregular ripening in the population, between harvests which we called green, half-green, or ripe. Second, we hoped to see whether the differences in average greenness and resistance of the stems already observed between two harvests of a same area, harvested as little as 24 hours apart, would correspond to a measurable difference in the humidity of the stems and would account for the fact that microwear traces appeared different on the harvesting tools used on the two different days.

Stem humidity was measured for a high and a low harvest carried out on the same day in order to quantify our impression that stems cut higher were greener, and therefore more humid, than those cut nearer the ground. The dry weight of the stem material was subtracted from its weight just after harvest, shown in table 12.1, for the calculated value of one stem segment, by dividing the total weight difference by 100. These measurements confirm our observation that time of harvest can make a significant difference in the humidity encountered by the tool. For example, in the same plot, one day apart, harvesting low on the stems at about 20 to 30 cm from the ground corresponded to a weight loss after drying stems of 0.05 g one day and only 0.03 g the following day. This confirmed our impression that stems were green at the level in a green low cut, a time some upper spikelets had fallen to the ground on one day, but at the same point on the following day, the stems of plants still in the field became dry or yellow and the low-cut harvesting corresponded to a half-green to ripe stage, and a time of greater grain loss. This correlates with the humidity content of the grains at various stages of ripening (Willcox and Anderson 1991).

It is assumed the material lost by drying was water vapor. These measurements support the idea that differences in humidity content of stems can explain subtle differences in appearance in microscopic wear polish according to whether most of the cereal stems harvested are green or dry where cut. As this corresponds to grain maturation, it can give an idea of loss from spillage (and thus yield) of the harvest.

Our earlier experiments with other materials had suggested that humidity apparently influences not only the optical brightness of microscopic polish but also the extent of alteration by localized hydrolysis of the flint microsurface (Anderson 1980; Anderson-Gerfaud 1986, 1988). Chemical analyses of the traces using RBS techniques (Andersen and Whitlow 1983) greater humidity or water in areas of tools altered by use on humid materials than on dry materials. It therefore appears reasonable that harvest of green, wetter stems produce traces that appear brighter and smoother than those from harvest of dry stems.

The measurement did not quantify the observed phenomenon of greater humidity (greenness) of the stems near the top than at the base. I suspect this occurred because the 5-cm segments of stems cut near the base proved to be significantly wider (and heavier) than those higher up on the stem, under the ears. This may have hampered comparison of humidity content by weight of segments taken at the two levels. The measurement will be retried at a later time using a different sampling procedure.

Processing tried in the field experiments
Threshing. Threshing of the grain (see Hillman 1984a), was

accomplished most effectively by beating sheaves against a wall (causing breaking up of the rachis, separating of spikelets and stems for the wild crops and glumed wheats, or separating of grain from seed heads and stems for free-threshing wheats). This technique was facilitated by leaving a length of straw. Grain or spikelets were caught on a plastic sheet below; then the macroremains were studied by Willcox (chapter 11) and the pollen remains by Diot (chapter 9). However, for the wild cereals such as the wild einkorn described here (no. 122 in chapter 11), prior to threshing many spikelets had separated from the rachis after simple drying of the sheaves in the sun for several hours following the harvest.

Other threshing techniques were tried, including flailing and trampling. They worked less well than the technique of beating against a stone wall for wild cereals and for semisolid rachised domestic spelt, einkorn, and emmer; however, in addition to the wall technique, flailing and trampling were effective for separating the grain from the seed head of free-threshing wheat (*Triticum aestivo-compactum*). It seems that the *tribulum* (threshing sledge) would be effective only for free-threshing plants for similar reasons. Threshing sledge flints, whose wear traces are described by Ataman (chapter 22), are thought to exist on the basis of ethnographic parallel and microwear analysis by Skakun (chapter 21) as early as the Chalcolithic of Eastern Europe and perhaps the Neolithic but are found where grain of free-threshing cereals is present.

We tried pulling off seed heads from sheaves of harvested cereals. We did this for small bunches of cereal stems at a time, by jamming them between a tool edge or surface we pressed against another surface or object, then pulling the stems toward us, effectively stripping seed heads cleanly from the straw. This technique involved using either special notched sheep/goat scapulae (like those found at Ganj Dareh)[2] or flint flakes pressed against sheaves placed on the ground or a flat surface. As before, these techniques were effective for semifragile-rachised domestic cereals, green or ripe. However, they were not effective for wild cereals. This was mainly because a certain number of seed heads were in the process of breaking up at all times from drying of the plants after harvest, so that the motion of combing was not only ineffectual but also caused seed loss during use or during transport of sheaves to the area of tool use.

For wild cereals, it appears likely that no special threshing tools would be used for separation of spikelets from the straw or breaking up of the rachis. Indeed, this stage may not have entailed anything more complicated than drying sheaves (or seed heads, if harvested separately), in the sun, and it appears unnecessary to apply forcible breaking up (hand breakage, beating, trampling, flailing, and so forth) to the rachis of wild cereals that have dried, even if they were harvested at the green stage (see discussion in chapter 7 and postcript in chapter 6).

Dehusking. Groundstone tools have the potential of providing evidence for intensity of wild cereal exploitation and techniques used to process grain, in turn giving an idea of how a plant was used. Can we expect to find tools corresponding to dehusking of grain in prehistoric sites? Dehusking of cereal grain could have been carried out using nonlithic tools. A wooden mortar and pestle were found to be far more effective for dehusking of emmer, einkorn, and spelt than a groundstone handstone and saddle quern from the Bandkeramik, which caused significant grain crushing (chapter 24). Foxhall (1982) showed a wooden upper manos and stone quern to be effective for this. No tools other than a wooden stick may be needed, for example if dehusking is carried out in a hole in the earth and using heated pebbles, as reported in ethnographic examples observed in Australia by Cane (1989). Therefore this activity could certainly pass unnoticed in the archaeological record.

Grinding and crushing. Grain was not necessarily ground on stone tools for consumption; it could have been boiled or fried (*friké* as today in the Middle East). Again, characteristic microwear traces showing crushing of grain or grinding of grain into flour needs to be shown experimentally before prehistoric tools can be interpreted. If data for making flat cakes and breads are sought, experimental design can be guided by procedures (tools, motions, times) which achieve different grades of flour (extraction ratios). These are detailed in Sumerian texts (chapter 23) and were found from analyses of bread remains from Neolithic Twann in Switzerland (Währen 1984) coupled with experiments with prehistoric tools from this site (chapter 23) and from experiments using a Bandkeramic grinding stone (chapter 24).

Use-wear traces obtained in experiments and their relevance in identifying type of wild-cereal exploitation
Techniques of observation used. In the present study, as in earlier work (Anderson-Gerfaud 1981, 1988), and based upon that of Semenov (1964), Schelienski (1983), and Keeley (1980), all tools, experimental and prehistoric, were studied for identifiable traces of use using a stereoscope to 40x, and as the principal tool, a metallographic (reflected light) microscope at 100x, 200x, or 400x magnification. The various features of use-wear traces seen with this technique (smoothness, brightness, distribution, and linear appearance and directionality of polish or gloss, occurrence of striations), were shown by experiments to be relevant for discriminating among different uses of tools with very slight or pronounced gloss which were of interest to this study (figures 12.11 to 12.14).

General observations. Harvesting plants using sickles and harvesting knives produced a characteristic distribution of microscopic traces, clearly mapping the direction of motion of the tool and the hafting arrangement. We found that

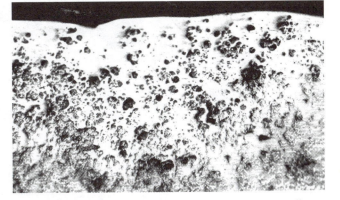

Figure 12.11 Microwear traces on a blade used experimentally in sickle in fig. 12.2 to harvest green to half–green wild einkorn wheat sown in our field, cutting at 20 cm from the ground, for approximately 5 hours. Note smooth appearance of polish, related to humidity of stems, and fine, short striations (probably from soil abrasion) that are just visible in the brightest areas. *All photomicrographs taken by author.*

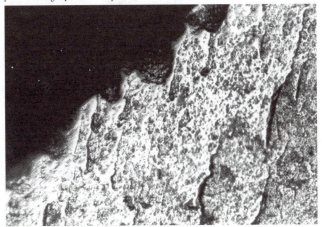

Figures 12.12 Microwear traces on ventral face of a blade used for several hours to harvest wild einkorn wheat when stems are fairly dry, cutting at about 30 cm from the soil. All micrographs are at 100x magnification of used tool edge surfaces using a metallographic, reflected–light microscope.

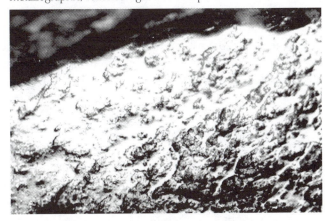

Figure 12.13 Microwear traces on dorsal face of a blade used for several hours to harvest wild einkorn wheat for a mixture of green and dry stems, cutting at about 30 cm from the soil. Compare traces on this blade and the one in figure 12.12, used alone and oriented at an oblique angle in relation to the haft (like the Egoswill sickle), to those in figures 12.11 and 12.14, mounted parallel to the haft.

Figure 12.14 Microwear traces on edge of blade used as in figure 12.4, to harvest approximately 125 m² of wild einkorn wheat at green stage, from "grownback" fields at 30 cm from the ground during approximately 5 hours. Note smooth, bright polish and beginnings of linear features parallel to the edge. It is thought blade in figure 12.11 exhibits clear striae because it was used closer to the soil.

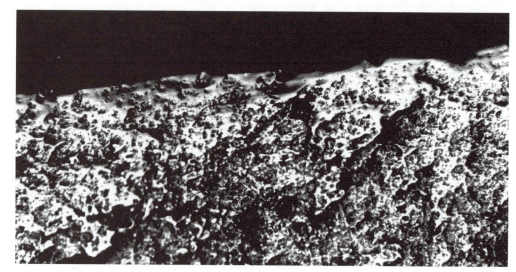

particular types and combinations of use-wear traces on tools reflect variables such as whether one or several stems were reaped with each tool motion and angle of penetration into stems (oblique, perpendicular, and so forth), the humidity, hardness, and siliceous nature of the stems, and whether (soil) abrasives were in contact with the tool during use. These microwear features become more accented as the time of use of the tool increases. Therefore in the case of an archaeological tool, when plant material is identified as the category of material worked, the general type of plant and the plant part contacted or processed can be inferred in many cases from the appearance of the microwear traces. This in turn gives information pointing to whether wild cereals (or edible grasses) in particular were the type of plant harvested.

Striations. Striations occurred on experimental tools when they were used to harvest near ground level (20 to 30 cm from the soil, figures 12.8 and 12.11) but rarely on tools used to harvest the cereals high on the stems (figure 12.9), just under the seed heads. Therefore the proximity of the tool to the soil during use appeared to be the major cause of striations at Jalès (in a semiarid climate). The duration of tool use and development of smooth, bright polish were also important factors in striations becoming apparent; although the tool edge surface is striated as it is used for longer periods of time, as the polish forms visually it provides a background against which the dark, tiny striations are more easily visible than at earlier stages of use when the tool surface is still dark and matte appearing. Striation formation also seemed dependent to some extent upon the type of climate, specifically the dryness of the climate at harvest time: for example, at Little Butser Farm in England, striations were rarely found on tools used to harvest domestic cereals (einkorn and emmer wheat) at about 20 cm from ground level for equivalent amounts of time as at Jalès, but where precipitation during harvest time was frequent (Anderson-Gerfaud 1988).

Another study (Unger-Hamilton 1985a, 1989; chapter 13)

hypothesizes that southern Levantine sickles from the Natufian were used to harvest cultivated wild cereals, because microscopic striations were seen on the tools and were said to have occurred because the ground was tilled.

This study failed to address contrary experimental research. Our experiments (Anderson-Gerfaud 1988) showed that whether or not soil had been tilled, whether the context was agricultural or wild, striations occurred on tools according to the factors listed above. In fact, we found sickle gloss with striations on Paleolithic and Mesolithic tools from France that were clearly used for cutting the stems of siliceous plants, presumably near soil (Anderson-Gerfaud 1981).

Experimental sickle harvesting with stone tools was carried out in Moldavia (Korobkova 1981b). Wild grasses were harvested green (but not wild cereals), as compared with cultivated domestic cereals (undoubtedly harvested when stems were drier, cutting closer to the ground). The latter use produced more striae on the tools than the former. However, these experimental criteria do not address and cannot be directly applied to a period and context as different as the beginnings of incipient cultivation in the Near East, where the question is whether wild cereals were intentionally sown in certain specific locations. A similar observation can be made for experiments Unger-Hamilton (1985a and chapter 13) used in her interpretation of Near Eastern artifacts. Although she carried out important experiments harvesting wild cereals and other wild plants in their natural habitats in the Near East, her other set of experimental data concerned experiments with harvesting of domestic cereals cultivated using modern methods. She did not experiment with cultivation of wild cereals. She found harvesting of wild cereals produced few striations as compared with harvesting domestic ones.

Our experiments give us reason to believe that techniques of wild cereal cultivation are significantly different from those of domestic cereals, even in the case of so-called primitive techniques carried out today. We do not think soil preparation would have been needed to cultivate wild cereals in the Epipaleolithic and Neolithic. Even if we consider the possibility tilling was used for the cultivation of wild cereals in the past, according to our experiments this soil preparation would have been carried out a year before harvest, followed by winter rains and then by months of dryness. It was necessary for us to clear the prairie for our experiments in a far more violent way than was done in the Levant 10,000 to 8,000 years ago; nonetheless, the soil was hard packed a full year later, at harvest time. It seems unlikely that soil of this prehistoric period, even if tilled, would still be loose at the time of harvest (Unger-Hamilton 1985a, chapter 13), and thus striate tools more than harvest over unprepared ground.

These observations suggest that the two groups of experiments used by Unger-Hamilton (chapter 13)—harvest of wild plants vs cultivated domestic cereals—do not provide adequate information for distinguishing tools used to harvest cereals in the wild habitat from those used to harvest cultivated wild cereals. Other variables that may explain the difference in striation occurrence she observed, corresponding to the difference in the extent to which tools were brought into contact with soil abrasives, are the denser nature of the cultivated fields, more intensive tool use for harvest of domestic cereals, or harvest of wild cereals at a level higher from the soil than cultivated domestic cereals. These factors can vary independently of whether or not cultivated plants are harvested. Therefore, although experimenters agree striations are more frequent the closer the tool is used to abrasives (soil), striations on harvesting tools can be better attributed to many other experimentally supported causes than to use over tilled soil.

Humidity of stems at harvest: Height of harvest or state of maturity? The height of harvest at the critical phase of green and half-green grain development will influence the appearance of microwear traces on the tool. If stems are cut near the ground, as discussed earlier, which is particularly convenient when straw is desired and denseness of the stand allows gathering bunches of stems at one time, the microwear trace will appear to correspond to a drier harvest than when stems are cut higher. This leads us to question whether traces of cutting drier stems on an archaeological tool should be interpreted as a later harvest corresponding to a time much wild cereal grain is falling, as opposed to a harvest of grain at at the half-green stage cutting at two different levels on the stem, where the drier-appearing traces would be caused by cutting low, where the stem has already lost humidity, and the greener or more humid traces caused by cutting higher on the stem, where there is still greater humidity. The presence of striations can be used a guide to decide between these alternatives, showing whether the tool was used close to the ground.

All these alternatives were not considered in Unger-Hamilton's interpretation of Southern Levantine lustred tools in contexts of wild-type cereals, for which she observes both an increase in striations and cutting of drier stems, as time goes on (1989; chapter 13), showing increased cultivation and harvests of wild cereals at later and later stages, which would cause increasing grain loss. If our experimental data is taken into account in interpreting her observations, it would suggest a different scenario than the one she puts forth. In her sites harvesting may be occurring at the same ripeness stage, minimizing grain loss, but at lower and lower levels on the stems, implying the stands are denser; this also suggests the straw itself is more systematically harvested. This harvesting technique, and densification, could be occurring in a natural wild stand or where wild cereals are cultivated, but this particular distinction is not demonstrated by the observed data.

Distribution and development of traces of cereal harvesting. Factors long-recognized by typologists such as proximity of adhesive to the tool edge can make the gloss width vary by obstructing its extension away from the very edge. In the absence of such obstruction, we have also found that the most intensive area of contact is between the plant stems and a narrow band along the edge of the tool, and this area is where visible gloss appears first, extending farther from the edge as the work progresses. If harvest is carried out near the ground, the number of visible striations also increases with use. These two variables cannot be translated into a quantification of tool use, unfortunately, as our experiments have shown that the hafting of a sickle element (single or multiple elements, angle, area exposed) as well as the direction and force of the harvesting motion itself can produce variation in rapidity of gloss development. Also comparisons of use duration require that the plants harvested be of the same kind, the same ripeness, and the stems therefore of the same humidity.

Unger-Hamilton observes an increase in width of the gloss trace on harvesting tools from the Levant from earlier to later periods (chapter 13) and interprets this as an evolution toward an increase in cereal stem width with cultivation. This interpretation ignores certain experimental and ethnobotanical data. Data showing that an overall change in width of cereal stems would not be directly correlated with change in gloss width include our observation that the width of wild cereal stems can vary within one population from year to year and from one area of the field to another, presumably owing to such factors as soil type and rainfall (Willcox, pers. comm, and my own unpublished measurements of stem width). The height of the cut would also be a major factor in stem width; I have observed that both wild and domestic einkorn and emmer stems are wider near the soil, at the base, and gradually become much narrower at the top of the stem; they are also wider at nodes than in internode areas. Therefore, in direct relevence to harvesting with a sickle, the tool would actually come into contact with different stem widths according to the height at which the cut was made and the particular nature of each stem where the tool happened to contact it (nodes, internodes, and so forth).

Our observations are that for a harvesting motion, gloss width increases with use of the tool. If more stems were cut with time, this agrees well with the observed increase in number of striations on tools later in time (chapter 13 and see above section). Harvesting of cereal in our experiments does not cause individual stems to contact the tool edge repeatedly; rather, at least five stems are severed with each stroke (unless the field is very sparse, in which case the sickle motion loses effectiveness and regularity). The trace width varies according to factors cited above, as well as the shape of the tool, position of the harvester, and oblique angle of penetration of the tool edge. Sawing thick stems of reeds with a sickle, on the contrary, involves a different motion and stem morphology, which could, after long enough tool use, be reflected by a certain gloss width on the tool edge.

Reexamining prehistoric tools for plant harvesting

Sampling. Research prior to the present experiments has been devoted to optical microscopic study of stone tools (sickles) from the Levant (Anderson-Gerfaud 1983, 1986, 1988; Anderson-Gerfaud et al. 1991, Unger-Hamilton 1985a; 1989). This study involved reexamination of tools published earlier (Anderson-Gerfaud 1983) in light of our experimental results from harvesting of wild cereals, which had not been carried out at that time, and study of other tools from samples we examined since the prior research. We could more effectively sample for potential sickles as our experiments progressed. Tools discussed here are from Abu Hureyra, Epipaleolithic II and III, tenth to ninth millennium BC (Moore, pers. comm.), and from Mureybet, Final Natufian, Epinatufian, Khiamian, and Mureybetian, late ninth millennium to eighth millennium BC (Cauvin 1977).

Experiments showed that the repeated use (several hours to several days) of a tool edge for harvesting wild cereals at the green or half-green stage (a time when most to half of the grain has not yet fallen) will always produce a very narrow but usually highly reflective band of marginal gloss, extending 1 to 3 mm from the edge.

We therefore examined all archaeological tools we could find with such a reflective band of gloss, as well as others similar in morphology to those with gloss. Sampling involved several visits to the archaeological collections and repeated study of the artifacts with the microscope as we became more familiar with ways of distinguishing among subtle differences in use of the glossed tools according to their microscopic traces. Although this sampling procedure resulted in including tools with gloss produced by use for other than

cereal harvesting, we think it allowed us to find tools used systematically to harvest wild cereal grain, which was our goal in this stage of the analysis. The overall sample we have examined is not adequate at this writing to allow us to quantify the number of harvesting tools from each level discussed; we wish only to highlight general tendencies seen thus far. A more complete analysis is in progress.

Overall characteristic of tool use. A small number of tools in our samples from the three sites studied had traces like those from our experiments harvesting wild cereals (figures 12.11 to 12.14). These have several characteristics in common. As stated above, their edge has a band of macroscopically visible, highly reflective gloss of 1 to 3 mm in width, like that which occurred on our experimental tools used for approximately 5 hours to harvest wild cereals at the green and half-green stages. Adhesive material did not influence polish development in these experiments because it was not used or it came up only as far as 1 cm from the tool cutting edge and therefore did not overlap with gloss formation.

As we saw earlier, gloss width and striations increase as the tool is used for longer and longer periods to harvest in a low cut. Therefore gloss width on the archaeological tools seems to correspond simply to length of time of use of the edge, angle of penetration during use, and so forth with the exception of two or three cases of tools from Abu Hureyra. Microwear traces show the tools were used to cut, in one direction, held perpendicularly to the stems, and not to saw. This agrees with our experimental observation that if a back-and-forth motion is used to harvest cereals, it tends to destabilize the hafting arrangement and cause sickle elements to be pulled out. Some tools with gloss had microscopic traces showing that the tool moved in a direction perpendicular to the its long axis, but further analysis showed this corresponds to traces of scraping or splitting of reeds and not to combing off seed heads during or after harvest.

It seems that tiny edge damage seen on experimental tools and ones from Mureybet and Abu Hureyra had the effect of stabilizing the edge for harvesting. In our experiments, some flint blades have been used for several years of wild cereal harvest as described here, totalling up to 20 hours of continuous use, but neither these blades nor others have ever needed to be retouched in order to function effectively.

Abu Hureyra Epipaleolithic. The tools we describe here from Abu Hureyra could not chosen from a complete sample. We intend to pursue the study. The tools we chose for this study include one backed tool published in 1983 and others (backed pieces, small flakes, and blades) we selected from a more recent sample of approximately one hundred elongated flakes, blades, and backed pieces from the collections in Aleppo, transmitted to us by Dr. Andrew Moore. Olszewski (pers. comm.) has informed us that she has seen nineteen complete

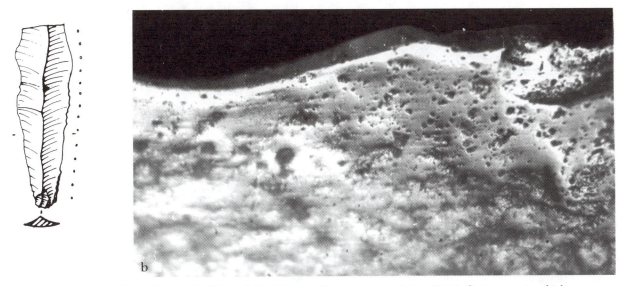

Figures 12.15 *a*, Drawing of tool from the Epipaleolithic of Abu Hureyra (drawing is actual size. Dots indicate areas in which macroscopic gloss is visible and where micrographs were taken at 100x); *b*, micrograph of used edge. Striations like linked depression dots and polish are like those in our experiments harvesting wild cereals, cutting low on the stems. Micrographs are intended to give an idea of the variability in appearance of microwear polishes from plant harvesting. *All photographs in figures 12.15 to 12.23 by author*

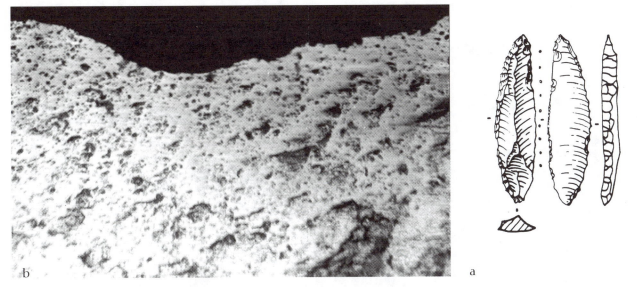

Figures 12.16 *a*, Drawing of backed piece from Abu Hureyra Epipaleolithic; *b*, micrograph of used edge. Note polish development and linear traces like those in our experiments harvesting wild cereals, cutting low on the stems.

lunates with visible gloss in other samples; these are potential harvesting tools which are not included in our sample, which may therefore include less than half of the excavated harvesting tools. We feel nonetheless that the tools we have seen give a qualitative idea of the type of sickle harvesting occurring at the site, despite our inability to draw any quantitative conclusions (Anderson 1995b).

Six tools have traces truly similar to those produced in our experiments harvesting wild einkorn. They include unretouched blades (figures 12.15a and b) and backed pieces (figures 12.16a and b).

Tool edges have 1 to 2 mm of visible gloss and show some striations. The lunates with gloss were particularly intensively used to harvest wild cereals in a low cut. The tools were used

hafted to harvest cereals in a green or semigreen state, when the majority of the grains would be intact on the rachis.

As noted earlier, our experiments harvesting wild barley and einkorn show the rachis shatters very quickly after the green stage. Thus viable grains would have been obtained (only) by harvesting as here: in our experience grains can be harvested when green only by using sickles or by uprooting; therefore seed heads would not have been gathered prior to the sickle harvest of the plants cut using these tools. These traces are similar overall to those on Neolithic tools from Mureybet. Processing tools may correspond to treatment of these grains, but this cannot be shown without further experimentation and analysis.

It seems that gloss width corresponds in some cases to

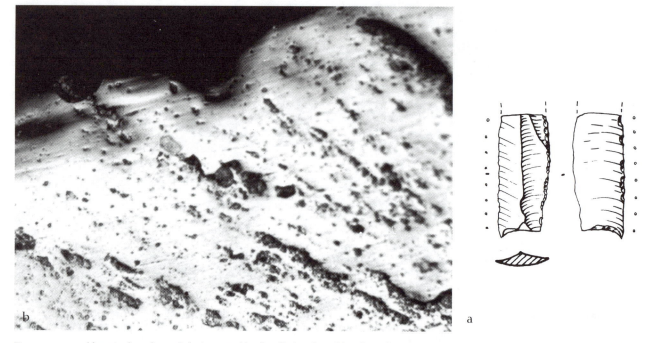

Figures: 12.17*a* (drawing) and 12.17*b* (micrograph) of well-developed bright, striated use-traces on a tool from the Epinatufian level of Mureybet. Note similarities of traces to experiment in figure 12.11. Actual size.

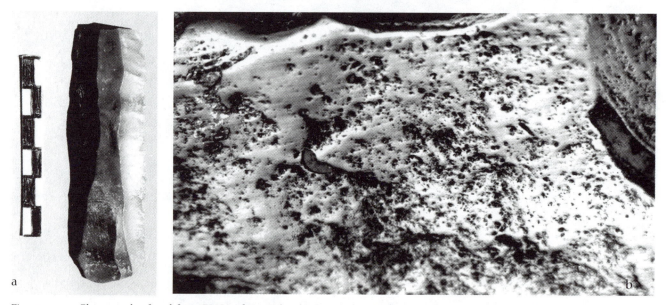

Figure 12.18 *a*, Photograph of tool from PPNA of Mureybet (scale: 6 cm) with "gloss"; *b*, of microwear traces like those obtained experimentally harvesting wild cereals at green to half-green stage, cutting near the soil (compare with figure 12.11)

adhesive material's coinciding with part of the contact area of use of the tool working edge, particularly in the case of two small blades. When viewed with a microscope, the boundary between the gloss on these tools and the unused surface appears abrupt (outlined by the adhesive boundary). Our experiments show *small* blades are effective for harvesting if hafted, but they can be pulled out of the haft during use if adhesive does not come up very near to the edge, as it must have here, therefore regularizing and strengthening the sickle cutting edge and anchoring the elements more firmly in the haft. Sometimes minute, macroscopically visible traces of probable adhesive material were seen, but they were not

sufficient to show the total area covered by the adhesive material in the past.

Mureybet. The tools from Mureybet were selected from approximately half of the excavated material, housed at the Institut de Préhistoire Orientale at Jalès (Ardèche, France). Most were part of the sickle-blade category, although a few had not been noticed in typological analysis because of the extremely limited nature of the macroscopic traces. Not all the tools classified as sickles at Mureybet had microscopic traces of use matching ours obtained in experiments harvesting wild cereals. Some, with diffuse sheen on their

a   b

Figures 12.19 *a*, Drawing of tool with gloss from PPNA level of Mureybet and *b*, bright, highly striated microwear traces on this tool. This would indicate lengthy use of tool in sickle used to cut wild cereals near the ground.

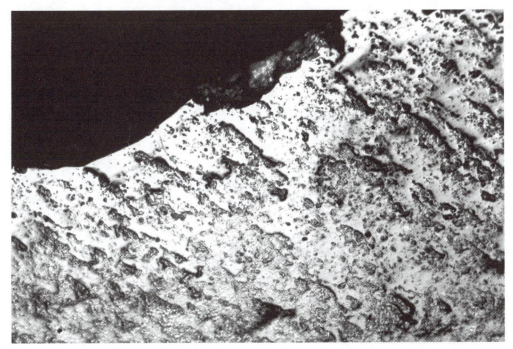

Figure 12.20 Traces on a glossed tool from Abu Hureyra with traces showing PPNB, reminiscent of harvest near the ground of wild cereals or reeds

edges, were used to cut types of plants other than silica-rich grasses, reeds, cereals, and sedges—perhaps other plants common in the archaeobotanical samples such as *Polygonum*.

Natufian. Our analysis showed the majority of the Natufian tools classified as sickles were used for cutting plants other than cereals (8 tools); one other seen was used to scrape reeds, and a few others were used to cut skin and hide. The remainder were not interpretable due to soil damage, but we do not think this could have obscured the very bright, narrow band of gloss characteristic of harvesting cereals had it been present.

To date, we have seen three blades from the Natufian of Mureybet with microscopic traces (Anderson 1995b) like those obtained in our experiments harvesting wild cereals for very short periods of time (Anderson-Gerfaud et al. 1991:211, 213). Macroscopically visible polish is only about 1 mm in width on these tools, but only very small portions of the edge located near an extremity are preserved in two cases. The traces suggest the plants were cut at the half-green stage. The one complete blade shows some striations, suggesting harvest in a low cut like the Epipaleolithic tools from Abu Hureyra.

Epinatufian. Although archaeobotanical remains recovered are similar to those from the Natufian (van Zeist and Bakker-Heeres 1984), from the Epinatufian on to the Neolithic, harvesting tools from the later levels are far more intensively used than these Natufian ones. The Epinatufian level yielded more (six) tools with gloss extending 1 to 2 mm from the edge (figures 12.17a and b), corresponding to traces we obtained in experiments harvesting wild cereals green or half-green, for 5 to 10 hours. Microwear traces include striations, indicating harvest low on the stem.

Traces on Epinatufian harvesting tools are far more developed than those on the Natufian tools; therefore the former were used over a longer period of time than the latter. The microwear traces on the Epinatufian tools represent either a more developed version of the same use as for the Natufian sickles or are actually the first examples of harvesting of wild cereals near the soil from Mureybet; it is possible that the traces on the Natufian tools were from harvesting of plants other than cereals (such as other grasses, but also for food purposes).

PPNA and PPNB. In phase III in the PPNA levels, macroremains of cereal found were more abundant than earlier, as were pollen which Leroi-Gourhan (1974) interprets as Cerealia type. In these same levels, small structures occur which Cauvin interprets as used for storage. Microscopic traces have thus far been studied for some of the above sample of tools, that is, from the PPNA, phases II (Khiamian) and III (Mureybetian; figures 12.18, 12.19), and the early PPNB (figure 12.20), phase IV (Cauvin 1989). We found that the traces on some tools best match experimental tools used for cutting or scraping reeds whereas others have microscopic traces of use very similar to ones we obtained in experiments harvesting wild cereals green and near the ground (figures 12.11 to 12.14 vs. figures 12.18 to 12.20). Furthermore, these traces are of the same general types (showing parallels in harvesting techniques) as those seen on some tools we are presently examining from the Neolithic of Abu Hureyra (figures 12.21, 12.22) and of Aswad Ia (figure 12.23), where in each case domestic cereal remains are attested.

Groundstone tools. At Abu Hureyra, the Epipaleolithic assemblage includes handstones as well as querns, mortars and pestles (Moore 1975:56). At Mureybet, a handstone was found in the Natufian levels; Epinatufian levels contained handstones and pebble mortars; and these tool types as well as pestles and saddle querns were found in Neolithic levels (Nierlé 1982). Some handstones from Mureybet are reportedly "lustred" (Nierlé 1982; see also Anderson-Gerfaud 1983); thus it was hoped this might result from contact with the silica-rich glumes and be an indication of dehusking of cereals, but I was unable to show this by chemical analysis.[3].Similarly, many of the above tools could have been, but have not been shown to have been, used for processing of wild cereal grain in particular. Demonstrating the function of these groundstone tools will require experimentation and comparative study of both traces of wear and residues from the material processed. Methods of study may include those used by Hillman[4] for a prehistoric tool, by Fullagar for ethnographic tools (chapter 3), and infrared spectrometry, currently being developed by Evans and McLaren (McLaren

et al. 1990).

Wild-cereal use and limitations on the representativeness of this sample. Much information concerning cereal exploitation is invisible and not quantifiable. First, cereal harvesting tools (or processing tools, when we will be able to identify them with greater confidence) represent examples of a kind of activity but not the amount of cereal harvesting (or processing) carried out using tools. This is because they may not all have been found in the excavation and because the present sample was not drawn from the half of the excavated artifacts which remained in Syria. Relative numbers of tools related to cereal use from one level to the next may be biased because different amounts of surface area were excavated (J. and M.-Cl. Cauvin). Second, our experiments show cereals can be effectively harvested and processed using archaeologically invisible techniques. Cereal harvesting could have occurred without the use of any (identifiable) implement, by beating or picking of the seed heads or by uprooting.

Concluding Comments

Data from analysis of archaeobotanical remains and artefacts cannot at present directly prove cultivation occurred at sites containing wild cereal remains. However, data suggest that the transition to cultivation of wild cereals would have been evolutionary rather than revolutionary in nature:

Technology

The basic technology involved in wild cereal harvest undoubtedly dates from Paleolithic times. Stems of grasses and rushes could have been uprooted and wild plant seed effectively gathered by beating, as occurs in ethnographic contexts for wild grasses (see chapter 1). Our experiments show reeds and perhaps sedges would have been far easier to gather using a stone tool than by uprooting of the plant, and these siliceous, humid plants produce a sickle gloss. Examples of such tools have been found in the Lower Paleolithic of East Africa (Keeley and Toth 1981) and the Middle Paleolithic and Upper Paleolithic of France (Anderson 1980; Anderson-Gerfaud 1981, 1990). Flakes with gloss and striations from the Mesolithic of Rouffignac in the Perigord (France) could easily be mistaken for Neolithic sickle elements (Anderson 1995b). However the latter tools seem to correspond to sawing of stems such as reeds (*Phragmites*), possibly for making objects or for building material. We suggested earlier (Anderson-Gerfaud 1983, 1988) that sickle harvesting might be linked to increased need for stems for building or fuel, for example, which could be associated with increasing sedentary nature of Epipaleolithic and Neolithic sites, and we see tools used for exploitation of plants such as reeds become more common beginning in the Natufian and Epipaleolithic through the Neolithic. This suggests that the overall increase in sickle use is not wholly due to the obtaining of grain.

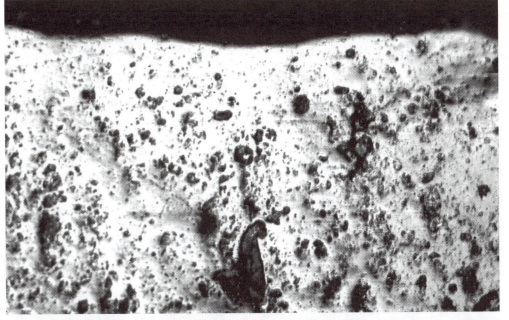

Figure 12.21 Microwear traces on glossed edge of tool from Abu Hureyra Neolithic (PPNB) level, where cultivated domestic cereal is attested, used to harvest cereal or possibly reeds near the ground. Compare with traces illustrated in figures 12.15a and 12.15b on Epipaleolithic tools from the same site, and on experimental tool in figure 12.11.

Figure 12.22 Traces on another glossed harvesting tool from Abu Hureyra Neolithic level, with more marked polish than in figure 12.21 and showing linear "corrugations" or undulating texture, parallel to the tool edge. The traces appear to be from harvesting hard, green stems, probably of cereal, possibly of reed.

Hillman and Davies (chapter 10) suggest some glossed, striated stone tools may have been used to obtain tubers or rhizomes, and the microwear characteristics of this use will need to be documented by experiments (chapter 4). Although the probable motion and raw material are different enough from cereals to avoid confusion with the microscopic attributes observed on our tools used to harvest wild cereals, we may have been overlooking such tools.

However, our experiments show that once intensive wild cereal exploitation was underway, there would have been other pragmatic reasons different techniques would be best suited to obtaining grain at a particular phase of maturity or in a dense or sparse stand or field and that sickle harvesting of

wild cereal for grain may have become increasingly practical.

This experimental study has allowed us to show that certain tools from Epipaleolithic (or Natufian) and Neolithic levels containing wild cereal were used, like those in our experiments at Jalès, to harvest groups of stems of wild cereals in a green or semigreen state (shown by brightness and development of the microscopic polish), often close to the ground (shown by presence of striations). Experiments show that this means edible and viable grain of wild cereals (as well as stems) were the products obtained. Both our data and Unger-Hamilton's indicate that with the beginning of the Neolithic, there appears to be more intensive use of harvesting tools (traces more highly developed, striations present) and of harvesting closer

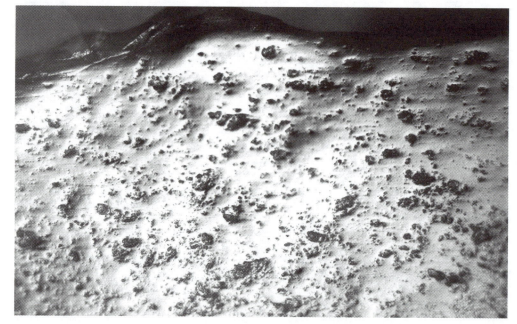

Figure 12.23 Microscopic usewear traces showing polish on a harvesting tool from Aswad level 1a, the earliest known with domestic cereal remains. Compare with figure 12.11.

to the ground of many stems at one time, which suggests fields may have been denser in the Neolithic sites with wild cereal remains than in the Natufian ones. These harvesting traces, although encountered in wild cereal contexts, resemble traces on tools we have studied from the Northern Levantine early agriculture sites [Aswad 1a (figure 12.23) and Abu Hureyra Neolithic (figures 12.21, 12.22)], therefore showing that the techniques (motion, stage of harvest, level cut, general number of stems cut with each motion) were similar in the two contexts.

If we hypothesize that sowing of wild cereal grain was occurring, summer (early) sowing can produce denser fields than autumn sowing (see chapter 11), and denser fields appear to be more even ripening than sparse ones in our experiments. This would increase the practicality of sickle harvesting, gathering all grain at once, and densely growing stems are more easily cut close to the ground than those spaced farther apart.

Other methods shown to be ineffective for wild cereals may have become effective as the fragile-rachised or uneven-ripening character of the crop population diminished. For example, when cereals become even-ripening and semisolid rachised, harvesting with a sickle and by uprooting become effective at the ripe stage as well as the green and half-green stages. Harvesting by combing with tools, as we think occurred in the Swiss Neolithic and threshing by combing or pulling grains from the stem, as in the Near Eastern Neolithic at Ganj Dareh (Stordeur and Anderson-Gerfaud 1985; Anderson-Gerfaud 1988) can also be effectively practiced once domestic cereals are present. The appearance of such tools in transitional contexts where the presence of domestic grain is uncertain may help guide interpretation as to cereal morphology (that is, rachis fragility).

Tilling

Cultivation of wild cereals would not have required invention of new tools or technology. Our experimental cultivation and harvest of wild einkorn wheat has shown that the wild cereals grow well when they are sown in the simplest possible way, broadcast over unprepared ground in the summer, much as they disperse in their natural habitats. This has led us to propose that soil preparation such as hoeing or tilling was unlikely to have been used in conjunction with cultivation of wild cereals in the Near East. Striations occurred on the edges of the experimental sickles when they cut near to the ground after long enough use, whether the soil had been prepared with tools or not. Therefore we interpret archaeological harvesting tools with striae as used near the ground, but the traces do not show the ground was tilled.

Spontaneous sowing and domestication

After the cereals were harvested, the field nonetheless grew back the following year from grains that fell and germinated, making resowing unnecessary. This spontaneous regrowth has occurred over a period (thus far) of three annual growing seasons, after yearly harvest of the area. We observe that, in the past, according to the microwear analysis of some of the blades, selection potentially occurred because sickle harvesting of wild cereals was occurring. However, this effect would be negated if the yearly harvests were of grownback fields, as this would halt any effect of the selection for domestic-type cereals. Grownback fields may have been exploited by practical-minded sedentary populations, in particular because they provided grain for the following year's harvest, with no sowing required. Whether the cultivated field is closely cropped (even by sickle harvesting at the green stage) or let to fall naturally, in our experiments the plots have grown back densely over a period of years, with no tending or further episodes of sowing required. Thus, a gathering strategy (without soil preparation or sowing) could continue until sowing needed to be repeated; then this would occur without soil preparation being needed, to enrich or to extend existing fields. Sowing patterns sufficient to produce selection leading to domestication (that is, keeping the domestic-type grain unconsciously selected for, from mixing with with wild-type grain from spontaneous or grown-back fields) may have occurred only when a human group cultivated while physically moving away from the area in which these resources grew already, and kept moving frequently until the selection for domestication had occurred.

Therefore, ironically, despite the potential selective effect of harvesting wild cereals using sickles (chapter 10), an activity we see represented in sedentary sites by study of microscopic use-wear traces on tools, either lack of cultivation of wild cereals, cultivation in one area, or harvest of grain from grown-back fields of wild-type cereals (or of course original wild stands) would have the effect of diluting and halting any unconscious selection of domestic-type cereal occurring.

Although this study cannot prove when and where agriculture began, we think it gives us the means to better understand possible stages of wild cereal exploitation which may have lead to agriculture and domestication. Tracing the beginnings of cultivation and the process of domestication will entail further archaeological data and new field and experimental observations of wild cereals, using methods described here as well as others yet to be discovered.

Figure 12.24 Experimental harvesting in a spontaneous, uncultivated stand of wild einkorn wheat, in 1996 in northern Syria, near Ain al Arab. Note the density and homogeneity of the stand. *Photograph by author*

Acknowledgments. I would like to thank Jacques and Marie-Claire Cauvin and Andrew Moore for allowing me to study material from their excavations. Gérard Déraprahamian kindly made the drawings in this article, and he, Daniel Helmer and Frédéric Abbès made the tools. George Willcox and G. Déraprahamian have provided invaluable assistance in the tedium of sowing, harvesting, and threshing grain; I thank them and all the others involved at some stage or another, and I am also grateful to Gordon Hillman, Sytze Bottema, Peter Reynolds, Terry Miller, Marie-Claude Falkowitz, and Karen Lundstrom for their practical support and to Daniel C. and Joan Anderson for improving the form of this manuscript. Work described here was funded by an ATP of the CNRS and the "Paleoagriculture" theme of the CRA (Valbonne). Later work could not have occurred without help of the Direction of Antiquities in Damascus and the ICARDA in Syria and Danny Zohary's and Gordon Hillman's guidance in Turkey.

Notes

1. M.-Claude Nierlé-Falkowitz (Geneva, Switzerland) and Dominique de Moulins (Institute of Archaeology, London) did the collecting of *Triticum boeoticum thaoudar* grain in Anatolia for our experiments. Most of the experiments reported here were carried out on this crop when cultivated in the southern Ardèche.

2. Experimented with earlier by ourselves and Peter Reynolds at Butser Farm, see figures in Stordeur and Anderson-Gerfaud 1985 and in Anderson-Gerfaud 1988.

3. An alternative use would be grinding of siliceous stems, as we found both stems and glumes of grasses in mud-brick, and phytolith structure of very minute fragments showed them to be from grasses or cereals (Anderson-Gerfaud 1983, N.D.). However, SEM and EDS analysis for silicon we carried out for two basalt handstones from Natufian and PPNA levels of Mureybet (Anderson-Gerfaud N.D.) were inconclusive due to the heterogenic nature of the basalt: silicon was concentrated in small areas of the tool surface which were worn and bright, but it could not be shown this was from residue material (for example, from cereal glumes), rather than naturally occurring inclusions (some siliceous inclusions were found in complimentary analyses we carried out on fresh breaks of the same tools).

4. Pyrolysis mass spectrometry carried out for organic residues from a grinding stone from Wadi Kubbaniya (CER Jones, in Hillman 1984a) showed high-cellulose, low-protein material was processed on the tool (suggesting not seeds, but materials such as tubers of nut grass or club rush.). Examples of processing of tubers using tools are cited by Hillman (1989a), Cane (1989) and Sievert (chapter 4).

Postscript: October 1998
Update on techniques used to exploit wild cereals and implications for cultivation and domestication
Still no tools (other than groundstone) have been shown to have been used for processing wild cereals, and more recently identified harvesting tools testify to the technique described in this article. Therefore my suggestion in the "technology" section of the concluding comments, that we might find new tools from later wild cereal sites which would show progressive adoption of agricultural techniques, found in developed form later, and that these very techniques could have induced unconscious selection for domestic-type cereals during this period (see chapter 10) is unsupported by data. Domestication was apparently not driven by technical evolution.

At the time of this writing, one issue was whether observation of striations in microwear traces from harvesting could show that wild cereals were under cultivation (Unger-

Figure 12.25 Experimental harvesting of wild einkorn wheat in another spontaneous, uncultivated stand, in 1996, in southern Syria (Jebel Arab area). The wooden sickle, with flint inserts, is effective for cutting groups of stems near the ground. *Photograph by author*

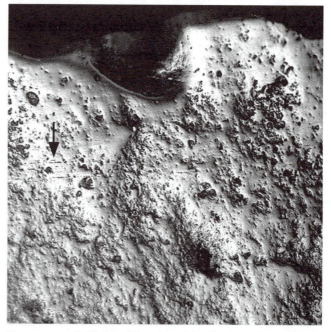

Figure 12.26 *a, b,* Views of the edge of the flint blade inserts in the sickle in figure 12.25 after approximately ten hours of use. Traces, seen at 100X magnification, show in both cases development of a smooth, bright polish as well as striations (see arrow) parallel to the edge and just back from it. *Images by author*

Hamilton 1985, 1989). New data were obtained during 1992 to 1996, from harvesting wild cereals with flint and obsidian sickles in natural stands in "relict" primary environments in the Near East, wild einkorn (*T. boeoticum thaoudar, T. aegilopoïdes, T. urartu*), wild barley (*Hordeum spontaneum*), wild emmer (*T. diccoides*), and wild rye (*Secale cereale vavilovii*) in north, central, and south Syria, and east Turkey (Anderson and Valla 1996; Coqueugniot and Anderson 1996; Anderson 1999). I found that in most cases, the wild cereals grew naturally in dense stands (figure 12.24), like the best of cultivated fields, making it simple to cut handfuls of the plant stems near ground level (figure 12.25). The microwear traces produced on the experimental sickles used to harvest in these areas, where the land is not worked, include striations, (figure 12.26ab) and in every respect resemble both tools from our experiments harvesting wild cereals we cultivated in France (see figures 12.11 to 12.14), and traces observed on glossed tools from sites with wild cereal grain cited here, Mureybet (Natufian, PPNA and early PPNB; see figures 12.17 to 12.20) and Abu Hureyra Epipaleolithic (figures 12.15, 12.16). Furthermore, my study of many more tools from Levantine sites with wild cereal remains from the Natufian and the PPNA through early PPNB contexts, Hayonim Terrace in Israel (Anderson and Valla 1996), Hatoula in Israel (Anderson 1994a), Jerf al Ahmar and Djade in the Upper Euphrates Valley, Syria (Anderson 1996), and El Aoui Safa in the Black Desert, Syria (Cocqueugniot and Anderson 1996) also gave results resembling the above experiments. This shows tools

Figure 12.27 Traces (100x) on blade (figure 12.28), from Kutan in northern Iraq, third millenium BC (fifth millennium before present, see figure 12.30), interpreted as a threshing sledge blade used in a construction as in figure 12.29. Note abrasive polish and removals (dark areas) of the abraded flint surface, resembling traces on traditional threshing sledge elements and characteristic of pressure from use, dragging over sheaves of dry, silica-rich plant materials on the threshing floor. *Image by author*

Figure 12.28 Dorsal and ventral faces of a blade, showing on one edge extensive gloss from use and on the other traces of bitumen used as adhesive, interpreted as a threshing sledge element fixed with bitumen in a structure like that in figure 12.29. *Photograph by B. Bireaud*

Figure 12.29 Underside of an experimental reconstruction of a "Sumerian" threshing sledge, interpreted according to texts concerning its raft-like structure and according to traces of use-wear and adhesive traces on flint inserts, fragments of Canannean blades, from this period (third millenium BC). *Photograph by author*

were used cutting with a longitudinal motion and near the ground. From stem humidity data translated into use-wear, the harvest occurred when some shattering of the ripe spikelets at the tops of the seed heads had begun, but the slightly unripe caryopses in spikelets remaining on the stem would have already been viable (see article). Both in the Middle East and in our cultivation experiments in Mediterranean France, we found this stage lasted only several days in one area and altitude. How far above the soil the harvester works and how long the tool is used determines how much abrasion of the tool occurs, but whether I harvested the wild cereals in natural stands still in existence today, or after cultivation in southern France, the appearance of microwear traces did not vary if these other variables were approximately the same.

Therefore, no data argues for the contention that cultivation of wild cereals regularly occurred and constituted a widespread stage of development of agriculture prior to domestication of cereals. The probability is that sowing to transplant or enrich stands or fields occurred in a discontinuous fashion, constituting a nonagricultural management strategy like that observed for hunter-gatherers in the recent past, involving maintenance or tending of wild plant resources (chapter 1 and Harlan 1995). I still believe that it was behavior inhabitual in the sedentary patterns of the time, involving seasonal or progressive displacement of persons and grain, that made annual planting expedient and influenced selection for domestic grain.

Update on harvesting and separation techniques used in early agricultural contexts

Flint tools we have identified as used as sickles from middle and late PPNB sites where morphologically domestic cereals are present are used in the same way as those in the prior period, for wild cereal exploitation. This observation can be made for the following sites where domestic grain has been identified: Magzalia in Iraq (Anderson 1994a), El Koum in Syria (Anderson 1999), Aswad (Anderson 1995), and Halula in Syria. I have identified obsidian blades with clear microscopic harvesting traces at Asikli in Turkey (Anderson 1996). It appears in general that the traces on sickles show more variability in domestic cereal sites than on sickles used to cut wild cereals, which tend to have been used in similar conditions due to the nature of the behavior of the plants (fragile rachis, uneven ripening, and so on). The variation in stage of harvest for domestic cereals (cutting plants when stems are drier, reflecting the greater choice for even ripening and semisolid or solid rachised, domesticated cereals) or in height of cut from the ground (the high cut is a viable option for domestic cereals; figure 12.20).

As concerns processing tools, I found notched scapula bone tools at Cayonu in Turkey like those studied earlier from Ganj Dareh in Iran for microwear traces and found by Skakun (chapter 21 and 1993) in Chalcolithic and Bronze Age

Table 12.2 Cereal treatment from the Natufian to the Bronze Age

Symbol key used in the data cells below (see full legend under "Note"):
● = morphologically wild cereal grains · ⊟ = morphologically domestic cereal grains · S = sickle harvesting · St = strip seed from stems · Sl = threshing sledge · Tr = tribulum (Bronze Age) · ? = presence not certain · N/A = information not available · blank = not found.

SITES	DATES*	WILD EINKORN WHEAT	WILD EMMER WHEAT	WILD BARLEY	EINKORN WHEAT	EMMER WHEAT	NAKED WHEAT	HULLED 2-ROW BARLEY	HULLED 6-ROW BARLEY	HARVEST CEREAL WITH SICKLE	STRIP SEED FROM STEMS	SLEDGE: THRESH CHOP	CUT-UP STRAW USED
ARCHAEOBOTANICAL REMAINS													
Hayonim (Syria)	12,360–11,920	●		●									
Abu Hureyra (Syria)	11,050–10,000	●		●						S			
Mureybet I–III (Syria)	10,250–9,500	●		●						S			
Jerf el Ahmar (Syria)	9,800–9,700			●						S			
Tell Aswad Ia (Syria)	9,700–9,600	●		●		?		?		S			
Dja'dé (Syria)	9,600–9,000	●		●		?				S			
Mureybet IV (Syria)	9,400–8,500	●		●						S			
Cafer Höyük XIII–X (Turkey)	9,400–9,000	●	●	●	⊟	⊟				S			
Çayönü (Turkey)	9,200–8,500	?	●	?	⊟	⊟		?		S	St	N/A	N/A
Nevali Cori (Turkey)	9,200				⊟	⊟		⊟		S		N/A	N/A
Ain Ghazal (Jordan)	9,000–8,500					?		⊟		S		N/A	N/A
Cafer Höyük IX–VI (Turkey)	9,000–8,400	●	●	?	⊟	⊟		⊟		S	St	N/A	N/A
Beidha (Jordan)	8,900–8,700				⊟	⊟		⊟		S		N/A	N/A
Ganj Dareh (Iran)	8,900–8,200							⊟		N/A		N/A	N/A
Asikli Höyük (Turkey)	8,800–8,400	●		●	?	⊟	⊟	⊟	⊟	S		N/A	N/A
Abu Hureyra PPNB (Syria)	8,800–8,000	?	●	●	⊟	⊟	⊟	⊟	⊟	S		?	?
Halula (Syria)	8,700–8,000	?		●		⊟	⊟	⊟		S		Sl	Tr
Magzalia (Iraq)	8,600–7,800			●	⊟	⊟	⊟	⊟		S		Sl	Sl
El Kowm 2 (Syria)	7,760–7,400				⊟	⊟	⊟	⊟		S		Sl	N/A
Tepe Sabz (Iran)	7th millennium					⊟			⊟	?		Sl	Tr
Tell Atij (Syria)	5th millennium					⊟	⊟		⊟				
Tell Gudeda (Syria)	5th millennium					⊟	⊟						
PUBLISHED SOURCES													
Kashkashok (Syria)	5th millenium				⊟	⊟	⊟		⊟			Sl	N/A
Amuq Judaideh (Syria)	5th millenium				⊟	⊟	⊟		⊟			Sl	N/A
Meggido (Israel)	5th millenium				⊟	⊟	⊟		⊟			Sl	N/A
Tell Leilan (Syria)	5th millenium				⊟	⊟	⊟		⊟			Sl	Tr
Ain Dara (Syria)	5th millenium				⊟	⊟	⊟		⊟			Sl	N/A
Kutan (Iraq)	5th millenium									?	St	Tr	N/A
Dolnoslav, Durankulak (Bulgaria)	5th millenium									?		Tr	

Note: Identified from microwear traces as used for harvesting, stripping off seed heads (only notched bone tools), or as inserts in a threshing sledge–like structure (Skakun for last two sites), as opposed to presence of chopped remains of stems in temper and ash deposits in the same sites. These data are compared with plant remains, adapted from Willcox (in press).

* = Uncalibrated BP

? = Presence not certain

blank = Plant, tool, or attribute not found at site

N/A = Information not available

● = Finds of morphologically wild cereal grains in sites

⊟ = Finds of morphologically domestic cereal grains, according to published sources

(dark oval) = Sickle harvesting

(grey oval) = Kind of threshing sledge used

(hatched oval) = Tribulum from the Bronze Age, inserts made from large Cananean blades contexts in Bulgaria (figure 12.30). These instruments would be interesting to trace further and represent the technique of combing off seed heads, after harvest using a low cut.

Evidence for early use of threshing sledge or tribulum

Since this writing, the existence of new tools from Middle Eastern sites with early domestic cereal agriculture have been demonstrated, using reliable criteria from microwear analysis supported by experimental replication and observation of traditional tools. These new tools, flint blades used to arm a kind of threshing sledge, processed cereals after harvest but prior to treatment with groundstone tools. We have extensively studied these tools, which were missed in earlier studies because they have gloss and were therefore assumed to be sickles (see chapters 22 and 21). The fact that their microwear traces, with abrasion and wide, often comet-like gouges and grooves (figure 12.27) are unlike those from harvesting traces anyone has obtained in experiments, but were nonetheless identified as caused by harvest, occurred due to lack of experience of many researchers in harvesting and lack of knowledge of other traces such as those from the threshing sledge and other uses causing gloss (see van Gijn, chapter 25, Juel-Jensen 1994). In fact, this situation was predicted by Ataman (chapter 22) and by Kardulius and Yerkes (1996), both microwear analysts having studied the traces on ethnographic threshing sledge inserts, aware of the great antiquity of this instrument. Skakun (chapter 21), who was the first to reliably identify traces on flint blades corresponding to use of the threshing sledge in the Chalcolithic of Bulgaria, enriches descriptions of traces on these blades and numbers and geographical extent of archaeological finds. Her research, as well my own unpublished observations of traditional threshing sledge flints, lead me to hypothesize use in a threshing sledge as the origin of characteristic traces on large numbers of Canannean blade segments from sites in Syria, Iraq, and Israel (Anderson and Inizan 1994). Several years of experiments using a threshing sledge we reconstructed from location of the use-wear traces on these blades (figure 12.28) and from descriptions in Sumerian texts of this instrument (figure 12.29) have refined and confirmed our hypothesis that standardized blades from the Bronze Age were used to arm the underside of an early form of the threshing sledge (Anderson 1994b, 1999). Our experiments show that it can rapidly process cereals in massive quantities, separating seed heads from stems and threshing grain and chopping straw, and that the degree of wear on the ancient blades indicates at least 10 to 50 hours of use.

Moreover, since then, we have been able to interpret the traces on several glossed blades above from Middle and Late PPNB sites (Anderson 1994b, c) as having been used as in a primitive threshing sledge. I have seen others from Pottery

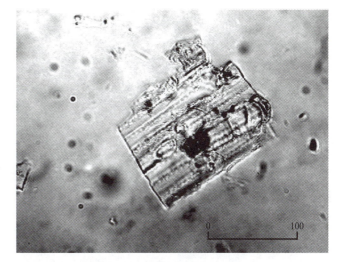

Figure 12.30 Phytolith sheet (epidermal silica cells) remains from the leaf of cereal/grass, like those making up all of a thick ash deposit in a structure from the Late Neolithic at Halula, Syria, circa 8500 BP. Note smooth, slightly curved cuts of the edges of this fragment, common at the site and thought to be due to the action of a kind of threshing sledge on the plant material (Compare with figure 12.31). Magnification 400X, Nomarski lighting. *Image by author*

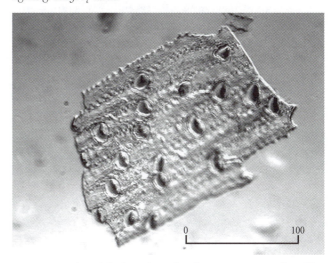

Figure 12.31 Phytolith sheet from threshing remains produced by the use of a traditional tribulum (threshing sledge, see chapters 21 and 22), together with one like that in figure 12.29. Note smooth, curved cuts of the edges of the fragment, similar to that in figure 12.30. Smooth, straight, and curved cuts are found only with use of the threshing sledge and were not produced by other processing and cutting methods tested in experiments, or by natural fragmentation of plant material. Magnification 400X, Nomarski lighting. *Image by author*

Neolithic and Chalcolithic sites from various areas of the Middle East. It is not clear why fewer blades used as in a threshing sledge have been identified in Neolithic-Chalcolithic sites than in the Bronze Age sites, but the sample needs to be increased before any statements can be made concerning the structure, size, or ubiquity of this early instrument. Whatever its size and number of flint blade inserts, these finds show that a weighted tool with multiple stone blades was pulled, by newly domestic oxen or humans, chop them (Anderson 1994b, c), here and there shortly after cereal and oxen domestication, as a virtually immediate response to the change from fragile rachis to semisolid and solid rachis in cereals (table 12.2). This instrument would have provided first, threshed grain to feed populations of persons and newly domestic animals and second, chopped straw for animals, bedding, and temper for wattle-and-daub architecture. Its adoption or diffusion with the first spread of agriculture appears to have been rapid (see chapters 6 and 15), as attested to in Bulgaria only about 1000 years after its first occurrence in the Middle East, from clear microwear traces on blades (Gurova 1997–1998).

Phytolith data that I have been able to examine thus far support the idea of the antiquity of the threshing sledge, both in the Near East and in Europe. Phytoliths entirely comprising a thick ash deposit found in a structure from the Late PPNB at Halula (an early domestic cereal Neolithic site also having flint blades with traces from use in a threshing sledge, see above and table 12.2) had an unusual appearance under the microscope: the siliceous epidermal sheet phytoliths were cut in an unusual manner, producing smooth, curved profiles (figure 12.30; Anderson 1999). I recently studied phytolith data sets produced in our experiments cutting cereals with a threshing sledge, and from plant material cut with traditional threshing sledges in Spain. Apparently the peculiar pressure involved in rolling plant material against threshing sledge blades cuts the plant material and therefore the phytoliths in the way described above (figure 12.31), whereas we have shown that such cut profiles do not occur for natural breakage, trampling, passage through the digestive tract of herbivores, or even other cutting process using sickles we experimented and studied (Anderson in prep). This data supports our observation of the use of this instrument in the Late Neolithic Levantine context at Halula. Such phytoliths, interpreted in comparison with material from a traditional threshing floor, as produced by use of the threshing sledge, had been found in earlier studies of Bronze and Iron Age contexts from Spain (Juan Tresseras 1997) Similarly, other studies have turned up the same kind of phytolith data (Cummings 1998) at Tell Leilan in Syria, a site where microwear study of Bronze Age Canannean blades (van Gijn 1996) showed traces of use in a threshing sledge. The threshing sledge, shown by multiple data sets to have been used with the beginning of cultivation of domestic cereal forms and found with the adoption of agriculture thus far in southeastern and southern Europe (chapter 15), should be added to the common "package" of founder crops and domestic animals in the Neolithic Near Eastern assemblage (chapter 6), so as to help trace the nature of the rapid development across time and space of agriculture and to elucidate the nature of this lifestyle shift.

Chapter 13 ✎

Harvesting Wild Cereals and Other Plants
Experimental Observations

Romana Unger–Hamilton

THE EXPERIMENTS REPORTED HERE WERE carried out as part of a three-year research project (Unger-Hamilton, 1988) the major aim of which is to establish the function of about a 1000 lustered flint so-called sickle blades recovered from the Natufian (ca. 10,000 to 8000 BC), Pre-Pottery Neolithic A (PPNA) (ca. 8000 to 7000 BC) and Pre-Pottery Neolithic B (PPNB) (ca. 7000 to 6000 BC) levels at various sites in the Southern Levant (Weinstein 1984). A total of 761 so-called sickle blades has so far been studied from the following sites (table 13.1): Mugharet el Wad B, B1 and B2 (Garrod and Bate 1937; Valla 1984), Mugharet el Kebara B (Turville-Petre 1932), Hayonim Cave (Bar-Yosef and Goren 1973) , Nahal Oren VI, V and III (Noy et al. 1973; see Valla 1984), Jericho Area E (Crowfoot Payne 1983), Gilgal (Noy et al. 1980), Netiv Hagdud (Bar-Yosef et al. 1980), Gesher (Garfinkel N.D.), and Yiftahel (Garfinkel 1985).

The function of the earliest flint so-called sickle blades has been much debated (Vayson 1919; Sauer 1958; Vita-Finzi and Higgs 1970; Cauvin 1983), yet no one has as yet been able to establish whether they had been used to harvest cultivated cereals, wild cereals or other plants. In this study, a new approach, namely that of "high-power" microwear analysis (Keeley 1980) was used. This method—although affected by considerable problems (Unger-Hamilton 1988a)—appears to be a reliable indicator of use motion as well as of the worked material provided that use was strong, variables are limited, and natural surface mod-ifications are not apparent (Unger-Hamilton et al. 1987). Such was the case with the majority of the ancient sickle blades.

Microwear Analysis
The method of microwear analysis and also the results of this analysis are fully described (Unger-Hamilton, in press and forthcoming). This chapter presents the experimental observations. However, the results of the microwear analysis are also incorporated as they are integral to the project.

Method
Blades and sickles
Two hundred and ninety-five experimental blades were

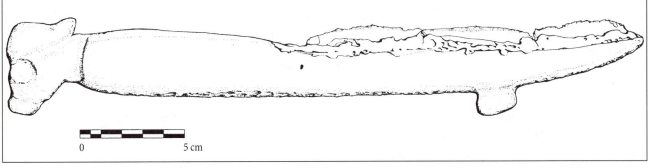

0   5 cm

Figure 13.1 Experimental sickle

145

Table 13.1 Sites and numbers of archaeological sickle blades

NATUFIAN	379
Mugharet el Kebara B	185
Mugharet el Wad B2	63
Mugharet el Wad B	49
Hayonim	46
Nahal Oren V, VI	23
Mugharet el Wad B1	8
Jericho	5
PRE-POTTERY NEOLITHIC A	116
Nahal Oren III	4
Gesher	11
Gilgal	11
Netiv Hagdud	47
Jericho	43
PRE-POTTERY NEOLITHIC B	266
Jericho	218
Yiftahel	48
TOTAL	761

knapped from a variety of flint, including local flint from the vicinity of the archaeological sites. The blades were used unhafted and hafted in copies of a Natufian bone sickle haft from Kebara B (figure 13.1; Turville-Petre 1932), b) an antler haft from Haçilar (Unger-Hamilton 1988a: Fig. 7b) and c) a wooden haft from the Fayum (Unger-Hamilton 1988a: Fig. 7a).

Plants

The blades and sickles were used to harvest different wild and cultivated plant species (table 13.2), the carbonized remains of which commonly occur on Levantine Epipaleolithic and Neolithic sites (for example, van Zeist 1970b; Hillman 1975; Hopf 1983). Forty-five of the blades were used to cut the wild progenitors of domesticated cereals (Harlan and Zohary 1966; Zohary 1969) emmer wheat (*T. dicoccoides*), einkorn wheat (*T. boeoticum*) and barley (*H. spontaneum*). Also cut were plants that grow amongst the wild cereals, such as brome grasses (*Bromus* spp.), wild oats (*Avena sterilis*), *Hordeum bulbosum* and vetches (*Viciae* spp.), growing amongst emmer in Palestine, and *Aegilops speltoides* growing amongst einkorn in Turkey.

Locations

Previous experiments had demonstrated that the same plant species harvested in different areas produce virtually similar microwear polishes (Unger-Hamilton 1988a: 253). However, experiments also demonstrated that different pedological contexts (tilled, untilled or no soil, see Unger-Hamilton 1988a; 1985a) produce different numbers of striations. This was the initial reason why the experiments were carried out as near as possible to the archaeological sites studied. Where this was not possible—for instance, in the case of wild einkorn

Table 13.2 Near Eastern plant resources likely to have been harvested during the Epipaleolithic and Neolithic and which were harvested with experimental flint sickle blades

A. WILD PLANT SPECIES
1. Wild emmer (*Triticum dicoccoides*)
2. Wild einkorn (*Triticum boeoticum*)
3. Wild barley (*Hordeum spontaneum*)
4. Wild mountain rye (*Secale montanum*)
5. Wild oat (*Avena sterilis*)
6. *Stipa* spp. (*S. barbata, S. capensis, S. gigantia*)
7. *Phragmites communis*
8. *Saccarum* sp.
9. *Scirpus maritimus*
10. *Schoenoplectus lacustris*
11. *Typha* spp. (*T. angustifolia, T. latifolia*)
12. *Cyperus longus*
13. *Sparganium ramosum*
14. *Juncus* spp. (*J. inflexus, J. effusus*)
15. *Vicia* spp. (*V. palaestina, V. narbonensis*)*
16. *Lathyrus* spp. (*L. L. sphericus, L. sativus, L. cicera*)*
17. *Lens orientalis* *
18. *Equisetum fluviatile*

B. CROP SPECIES
19. Domestic emmer (*Triticum dicoccum*)
20. Domestic einkorn (*Triticum monococcum*)
21. Bread wheat (*Triticum aestivum*)
22. *Triticum durum*
23. Domestic barley (*Hordeum vulgare*)
24. Domestic oat (*Avena sativa*)
25. Horse bean (*Vicia faba*)*
26. Bitter vetch (*Vicia ervilia*)*
27. Common vetch (*Vicia sativa*)*
28. Lentil (*Lens culinaris*)*
29. Chickpea (*Cicer arietinum*)*

C. WEEDS (abundant in Near Eastern crops and likely to have been harvested with ancient crops if unweeded)
30. *Buglossoides tenuiflora*
31. *Bromus* spp. (*B. fasciculatus, B. rubens, B. madritensis*)
32. *Aegilops speltoides*
33. *Hordeum bulbosum*
34. *Papaver* spp. (*P. orientale, P. rhoeas*)
35. *Polygonum* sp.

which is not found at present in the Southern Levant—the plants had to be harvested elsewhere. The harvests of wild cereals (as well as of the other plant species shown on table 13.2; see also Unger-Hamilton 1988) took place mostly in the spring and summer seasons of 1985 to 1987 in the following:

- Carmel area, at Haifa Technion campus (figure 13.2; table 13.1; plant species nos. 3, 5, 33; April 1985)
- Eastern Galilee, between Tabha and Safad (species nos. 1, 3, 5, 15, 31, 33, May 1985 and 1987)
- Golan Heights, near Yahoudiyah (species nos. 1, 3, 5, May 1985)
- Jerusalem, at Ein Kerem, Sheikh Jarra, and the Jerusalem

Forest (species nos. 1, 3, 5, 6, 15, 30, 31, 35, April 1987)
- Central Syria, at Arjoune (species nos. 7, 8, 13, April 1987)
- South, Central, and Southeastern Turkey, between Darende and Malatya, at Tunceli, Çemisgesek, Hazar Golu, and Akdamar (species nos. 2, 4, 6–8, 10, 15–7, 24, 26–9, 32, June and July 1986)
- England (Sussex, Bedford), Wales (Rumney Levels), and Germany (Sylt) (species nos. 6, 7, 9, 11, 12, 13, 14, 18, 19, 20, 23, 34, 1982, 1983, 1987, and 1988)

Problems

There were a number of problems inherent in this type of work. The most important are that only blades from the Southern Levant were available for study and harvesting had to be confined to certain areas. The results of this study, therefore, can only be applied to these regions and should be regarded as preliminary. They need to be compared with results from similar work elsewhere in the Near East, for instance the Jordan Valley and, further afield, the Zagros.

It was only during the course of the harvesting experiments reported here that I realized the importance of certain observations made in the field, for instance, with regard to year-to-year variations in yield. This arose from my observations not having been preconceived, but it does also mean that certain useful quantitative measurements have not been made. Nevertheless, independent observations made by the Institute of Evolution, Haifa University, confirmed the observations on seasonal variations in yield.

Results

During the course of the harvests a number of observations was made; these had substantial implications for Natufian plant husbandry and the Origins-of-Agriculture models (see Unger-Hamilton 1985b).

Need for sickle blades. Sickles could be used with ease to cut wild cereals. This proved not to be the case with some other plant species for example, the legumes asterisked in table 13.2, *Stipa*, *Typha*, and *Scirpus*. These wild legumes had very thin and tough stems which with ripe plants were fragile. Such stems could not be cut with flint blades, but the shallow roots were pulled out cleanly and easily. The same applied to most of the cultivated legumes, the *Viciae* and lentil, while the stem of the chickpea was too thick and tough. All these species were uprooted easily and cleanly. Furthermore, the drying of lentils for instance (in Central Eastern Turkey on roofs of bus shelters) necessitates harvest of the entire plant, as severed branches would blow away (also Hillman, pers. comm.). Butler (pers. comm.) reported the use of sickles and scythes for uprooting lentils in Diyarbakr in mid-June 1986, and Hillman (pers. comm.) that of a blunt sickle-like tool (also Dorrell, pers. comm.). (Wear traces from this activity, however, would certainly differ from those from cutting, if only in their orientation.) Flint blades could be

Figure 13.2 Wild cereals on Mt. Carmel

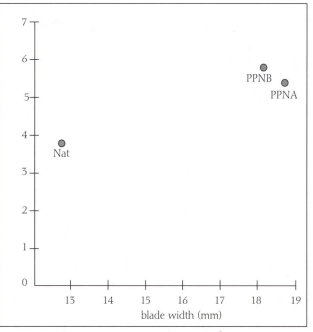
Figure 13.3 Width of the ancient blades

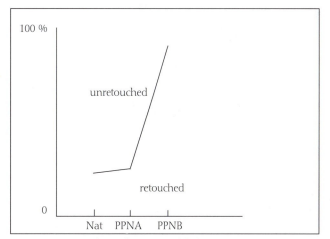
Figure 13.4 Retouch on the ancient blades

used for the removal of legume pods; however this was easily be done by hand. To cut the tough stems of *Stipa barbata* and *S. capensis* proved difficult. The plants were most efficiently harvested by pulling the stems cleanly from the basal nodes.

Figure 13.5 Wild barley, oat, and *Hordeum bulbosum*

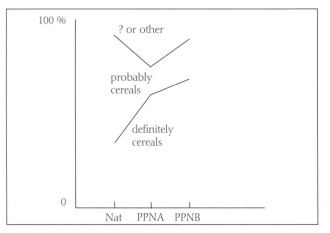

Figure 13.8 Polish on the ancient blades

Figure 13.6 Experimental polish from wild barley, original x100

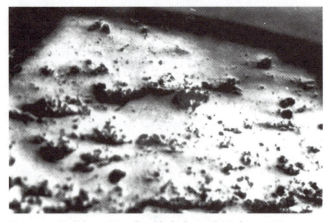

Figure 13.7 Polish on Natufian blade from El Wad B2, MWB 1.7388, x100

Figure 13.9 Wild cereals and undergrowth

Harvest by pulling was not tested on *S. gigantia* which could be cut again with difficulty with a serrated blade. *Typha* could be harvested in several ways, the head by snapping off by hand, and the rhizomes dug out from the mud. Sickle blades did not prove useful for either operation. The stems (10 to 20 mm) were too thick and hard to be cut with the small Natufian-type blades (around 13 mm, see figure 13.3), although the later PPNA or PPNB blades would be more suitable (figure 13.3).

The heads of *Scirpus* could equally well be snapped by hand although the stems could be cut. However the latter are

perhaps too sharp for use as bedding or basketry (Hillman, pers. comm.). *Saccarum* and the big *Phragmites* stems were far too tough to be cut with small Natufian type blades, although the wider and more frequently serrated PPNA and PPNB blades would have been more useful (figures 13.3, 13.4). Equally, some of the weeds (see table 13.2) could not be harvested with sickles, as their stems were either too woody (*Polygonum*), or else too small (*Buglossoides*). The above findings narrowed down considerably the plant species possibly harvested with sickle blades.

Conversely, other methods (hand collecting, uprooting)

of harvesting wild cereals proved not so easy. Hand collection was in my experiments a painful process as the awns are very sharp. Hillman (pers. comm.) reported that uprooting was only easy when the soil was friable.

Wild emmer and barley in the Galilee and the Carmel were rarely the highest plant but were surrounded by dense stands of the taller *Avena* spp., and *H. bulbosum* (figure 13.5). This means that they could not be harvested selectively by beating. Wild einkorn in the locations in SE Turkey where I harvested, on the other hand, was—together with, for example, *Aegilops*—the tallest plant. This means it could easily be harvested by beating (Hillman 1989b).

Implications. These findings suggest that only some of the species listed can be harvested efficiently with sickles, particularly with the small, mostly unserrated Natufian blades (figures 13.3, 13.4).

The findings also suggest that sickle blades might have been more necessary for the harvest of wild emmer and barley in the Southern Levant than for that of wild einkorn further north. This difference may well be reflected in the archaeological record: over 1000 lustered "sickle"-blades (see Unger-Hamilton 1983; 1985b) have been recovered from Natufian sites in the Southern Levant compared to a few lustered implements from Epi-Natufian and "Mesolithic" sites in Northern Syria (see Anderson-Gerfaud 1983).

The microwear study (Unger-Hamilton 1989) suggests that the majority of the Natufian sickle blades were used to harvest cereals (figures 13.7, 13.8).

Presence of soil during harvest. The wild cereals could not usually be cut close to the ground. This was because they grew from under stones, as was the case with wild einkorn in Southeastern Turkey, and/or from a "hostile" undergrowth containing prickly plants, scorpions, and so forth, as was the case with wild emmer and barley in the Southern Levant (figure 13.9). Thus, no soil material came in between sickle blades and culms. Even when I did manage to harvest wild cereals close to the ground very little soil material came into contact with the blades because of the grassy cover of the undisturbed soil surface. On the other hand, domesticated cereals are most efficiently cut close to the ground, and in my experiments, a lot of loose soil from the tilled ground came between sickle blades and culms.

Implications. This suggests that a large number of soil particles come between sickle blade and culm *regularly* only when plants are harvested from tilled ground (see also Korobkova 1981b); the same may happen in other edaphic situations such as screes (see Unger-Hamilton 1988), though such situations are unlikely to occur with regularity.

Using microwear analysis, a correlation between tilled soils and microstriations on experimental flint sickle blades has been demonstrated (figures 13.10 to 13.11; Unger-Hamilton

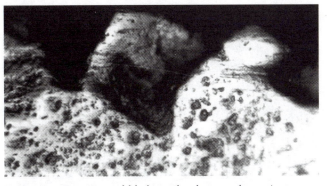

Figure 13.10 Experimental blade used to harvest domestic emmer wheat, Mx 200

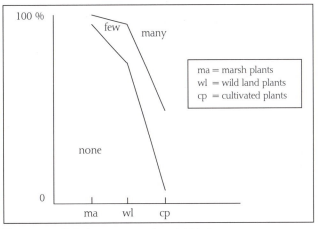

Figure 13.11 Striations on experimental blades

1985a 1988a, 1989). The number of striations found on the ancient sickle blades which I studied appeared to vary with time: 22% of the Natufian (including 24% from the Early Natufian), 53% of the PPNA and 73% of the PPNB blades were heavily striated (figures 13.12 to 13.13). This suggested that loose soil must have been present increasingly during harvests from the Early Natufian onward.

Weeds and microstriations. It has been proposed that microstriations are caused not by soil but by weeds (for example, Anderson-Gerfaud 1983). However, in the Near Eastern fields I harvested most of the weeds were thistles and could therefore not have been harvested. Also, experiments demonstrated that other types of weeds did not cause striations (Unger-Hamilton 1988a: Pl. 25g).

Ripeness of the wild cereals. The wild cereal seeds could not be harvested by cutting unless still unripe (or wet), as the ears shattered when the plants were ripe (or dry) (Hillman 1989b).

Implications. This suggests that wild cereals must have been sickle-harvested when still unripe or when wet.

The experimental microwear analysis demonstrated slight differences in polishes from harvesting the same plants dry or ripe and moist or unripe (figures 13.14–13.16). There appeared to be a chronological shift in the use of the ancient

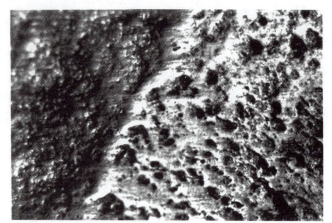

Figure 13.12 Polish on Natufian blade from El Wad B2, no number, Mx 100

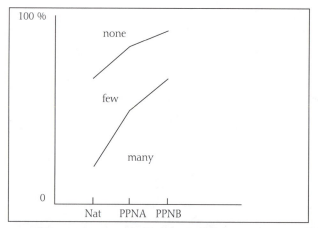

Figure 13.13 Striations on the ancient blades

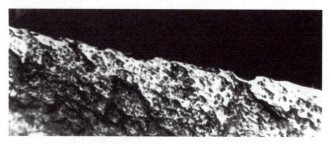

Figure 13.14 Polish from harvesting green *T. durum*, Mx 100

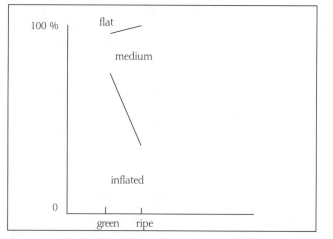

Figure 13.15 "Inflated" polish on the experimental blades

sickle blades (figure 13.17): the evidence suggests that the majority (68%) of sickle blades were used to cut relatively green (or wet) cereals during the Natufian, with a shift towards the harvest of dryer or riper cereals (59% of the blades) during the PPNA and even more so the PPNB (68% of the blades).

Sickles and retouch

Observations. The harvest of wild cereals was most efficiently carried out with the short, slightly curved copy of the Natufian sickle from Kebara (figure 13.1).

The blades were best left unretouched as blades with serrated edges caught the thin culms (see below) of the wild cereals and uprooted them. However, after about 10,000 strokes through wild emmer and barley the blades became blunt and had to be sharpened through retouch. Domesticated cereals on the other hand had generally thicker culms (Unger-Hamilton 1988a; Bor 1968: Pl. 87 (1) and Pl. 88 (1)), and blades with serrated cutting edges could easily be used while proving more durable (see Unger-Hamilton 1988a: Ch. 17).

The cutting of thicker and tougher-stemmed plants such as most reeds and *Typha* demanded a strongly serrated cutting edge, or else the edge became unusable after a short time (Unger-Hamilton 1988a:Ch. 17).

Implications. Finely serrated sickle blade edges are best used for the harvest of thick-stemmed, that is, usually domesticated cereals. This is reflected in the archaeological record (figure 13.4): about 30% of the Natufian and of the PPNA blades, but around 90% of the PPNB blades have retouched (mostly serrated) cutting edges. This sharp increase in the retouch on the cutting edges of sickle blades from the PPNA to the PPNB might well reflect the transition to full-scale agriculture.

Coarsely serrated blades on the other hand are best suited to the harvest of very thick and tough stems such as those of *Typha* or large reeds.

Wild cereals

Observations. The culms of the wild cereals were *generally* (but see below) much thinner than those of the domesticated cereals (see Unger-Hamilton 1988a; Bor 1968).

Implications. Experimental microwear analysis demonstrated that micropolish width is directly related to culm thickness (figure 13.18; Unger-Hamilton 1988a). A considerable increase in polish width could be detected from the Natufian to the PPNA, and from the PPNA to the PPNB (figure 13.19). A corresponding increase in blade width is noticeable (figure 13.3). However, the restricted polish width in the Natufian was probably not related only to restricted blade width as on these tools there is not the sharp demarcation between polish and unused flint surface which would be detectable if the blade had been affected by use right up to the haft or hafting agent.

Observations. The wild cereals in the Southern Levant did not grow in pure stands but had a considerable admixture of *for* example, brome grasses, the grassy species of *Hordeum*, wild oat and vetches which would probably also have been found amongst the wild cereals in the Natufian.

Implications. Not only wild cereals but also some other plant species would have been harvested with the same sickle blades. Microwear analysis demonstrated that the Natufian cereal polishes exhibited more variety than did the cereal polishes in the later periods (figure 13.8).

Observations. Wild large-seeded barley grew together with wild emmer in the Southern Levant. At the time of their harvest, that is, when still unripe, they looked similar at a first glance. The difference between these two species (number of awns and the fan-like spread of emmer) became obvious only when they were ripe and when it was consequently too late for sickle-harvest.
Implications. This fact may be one of the reasons why barley and emmer were cultivated together (Helbaek 1959).

Available harvesting time
Observations. A number of observations suggested that the time available for harvesting wild emmer and barley in the Southern Levant was very short. In the Galilee (where both species were harvested) and the Carmel area (where only barley was harvested) the plants of each species appeared to ripen at the same time at the same elevations (although this time was about three weeks later for emmer than it was for barley). Only a few days interval was noticed between the ripening and the shattering of the ears (also Zohary 1969) which appeared to be precipitated by the effect of local hot winds ("hamsins" or "sharafs"). The elevation range and steepness of slopes in the Southern Levant (ranging up to 1208 m in the Galilee, less in the Carmel) appear not to be as dramatic as at for example, the Karaçadag (Harlan 1967) or the Munzur mountains where einkorn was harvested for the present study.

Implications. This means that in the Southern Levant it would have taken a considerable time to walk to a sufficiently different elevation to increase the period of time available for harvesting ripe wild cereals such as wild emmer and barley.

Observations. In contrast, a number of observations suggest that the period available for harvesting wild einkorn in Southeastern Turkey was much longer (Harlan 1967, cites several weeks; also Hillman 1989b): the wild einkorn appeared

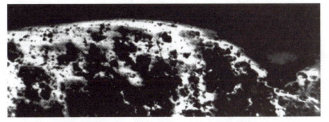

Figure 13.16 Polish from harvesting ripe *T.durum*, Mx 100

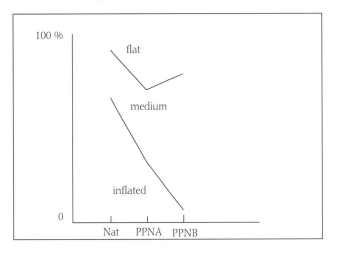

Figure 13.17 "Inflated" polish on ancient blades

to be at varying stages of ripeness at the same elevations. The difference in elevation, over a given horizontal distance, and thus the difference in crop maturity, is generally much greater than in the Southern Levant.

Implications. These findings suggest that far more time is generally available for the harvest of wild einkorn in SE Turkey than is available for the harvest of wild emmer and barley in the Southern Levant.

Beginnings of cultivation
Observations. Considerable differences in the biomass yield (also Nevo, pers. comm.) of the wild emmer and barley in the same area of the Southern Levant were noticed between 1985 and 1987. In 1987, after a humid winter (around 700 mm rainfall), the emmer and barley stands were dense with thick (about 4 mm) and tall (about 1 m high) culms. However, this was not the case in 1985, when, after a dryish winter (around 400 mm rainfall) the stands were sparse with the culms thin (about 3 mm) and short (about 40 cm high). Although grazing animals and/or rodents may have played their part (Gill and Vear 1980), such differences were nevertheless observed for many plant species and for the country as a whole.

Implications. This suggests that the availability of wild cereals and other wild plants (and not only of the domesticated cereals, see Redman 1978: 107) can vary dramatically from year to year within the same climatic cycle.

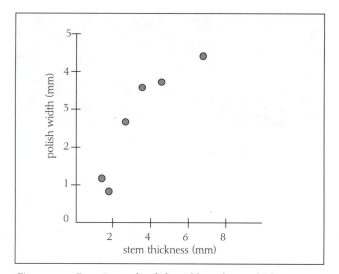

Figure 13.18 Experimental polish width and stem thickness

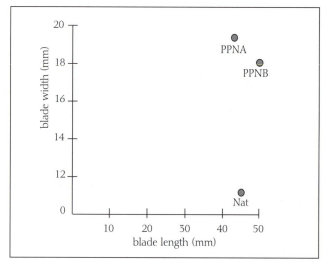

Figure 13.19 Width of ancient blades

Conclusions

From the experimental observations and their implications, as well as from the microwear studies of the experimental and the ancient sickle blades I came to the following conclusions:

Several plant groups, the legumes, some species of *Stipa*, as well as *Scirpus, Typha,* and *Saccarum,* could not be harvested efficiently with sickles. The same applied to some of the weed species. Tougher-stemmed large reeds could only be cut with strongly serrated large blades, which are absent from the Natufian levels I studied. This leaves, given the vegetation near the sites, mainly the cereals as harvesting "candidates" for sickle blades. The microwear traces on most of the Natufian sickle blades were compatible with those obtained from harvesting cereals. (For exceptions, see Unger-Hamilton 1988a: 271–272; this analysis was carried out before harvesting

in the Levant and, in particular, harvesting wild cereals.)

Weeds could rarely be harvested from the Near Eastern fields as most of them were thistles. Also, the weeds harvested on their own did not cause striations. This leaves the soil as the main cause for microstriations on the harvesting blades (laboratory tests of this correlation will be published in Unger-Hamilton 1989). The soils striation correlation, and in particular the presence of 24% of heavily striated blades from the Early Natufian onwards, could be indicative of a number of possibilities: small-scale cereal cultivation may have been practiced from the Early Natufian onward, wild cereals may have been harvested from rubbish tips or screes; there may have been different pedological contexts; or aridity may have increased during the Natufian. It seems that at present, the most plausible explanation is the first, perhaps the most significant alternative.

The findings suggest that there may be considerable differences in the harvesting methods of different wild cereals in different areas of the Near East, and thus perhaps different processes of cereal domestication.

The evidence also suggests that far more time is generally available for the harvest of wild einkorn in Southeastern Turkey than is available for the harvest of wild emmer and barley in the Southern Levant and that the extension of the period of harvesting through the cultivation of plants would have been more necessary in the Southern Levant than in Southeastern Turkey and perhaps neighboring countries. It also means that Harlan's experiments (1967) should not be used as evidence for Origin-of-Agriculture models concerning the entire Near East.

The observations concerning the considerable year-to-year differences in the vegetative mass yield in one wild cereal nuclear center of the Southern Levant—the Eastern Galilee—also suggest that emmer and barley cultivation may well have started in the nuclear centers (*contra* Harlan and Zohary 1966) rather than the adjacent areas. The differences in mass-yield were observed with many plant species which means that there might have been plant food shortages even where reliance was not mainly on cereals but on a broad-spectrum diet (Flannery 1969). By means of cultivation this mass yield could have been increased.

Vital information can be gained through harvesting in the same regions as the archaeological sites.

Acknowledgments. I would like to thank amongst many others (see Unger-Hamilton 1989) G.C. Hillman and P. Dorrell for their help. This project was funded by the Science and Engineering Council of Great Britain.

Chapter 14

Reflections on Paleobotanical Remains from Hayonim Terrace (Upper Galilee)

Ramon Buxó i Capdevila

WE ARE STILL FAR FROM PRECISE KNOWLEDGE of the Natufian diet. Archaeological remains indicate that Natufians ate meat (gazelle, deer, roe-deer, and boar) as well as snails and fish. There are still unresolved questions as to plant diet, although plants were undoubtedly a considerable part of the diet.

In the middle Euphrates, wild einkorn (*Triticum boeticum*) and wild barley (*Hordeum spontaneum*) were gathered during the late Natufian, at Tell Mureybet (van Zeist and Casparie 1968; van Zeist and Bakker-Heeres 1984) and at Mesolithic Abu Hureyra (Hillman 1975). From the beginning of the ninth millennium BC, Abu Hureyra shows evidence of wheat and wild barley cultivation. Other plant remains were also found, especially pulses (wild lentil, fruits from bushy plants [caper]), and Herbaceae (for example, *Lithospermum* sp., *Atriplex* sp., *Alyssum* sp., and *Stipa*) (Hillman 1975). A phase of protoagriculture at Mureybet was hypothesized by J. Cauvin (1977), and A. Moore (1979)suggested there was harvesting of wild grain at Abu Hureyra.

In the Jordan Valley, Jericho appears to be a possible center of agricultural innovation while in the south, plant remains are often scarce. In the Jordan Valley, Wadi Hammeh 27 had remains of Gramina: very abundant wild barley (*Hordeum spontaneum* L.) and feather grass (*Stipa* sp.). But Leguminosae made up most of the remains: lentils (*Lens* sp.), particularly *Cuscuta* sp., and fragments identified as the Liliaceae family (Edwards, Bourke, Colledge, Head, and Mucumber 1988).

At Mallaha (Eynan), most remains are of almond (*Amygdalus communis* L.) and pistachio (*Pistacia atlantica*). In Hayonim cave, most remains are of lupine (*Lupinus pilosus* L.), but there are also two grains of wild barley (*Hordeum spontaneum* L.), some wild almond (*Amygdalus communis* L.), and a few Leguminosae of spherical shape, probably *Pisum* sp.; these were indigenous to the region, so they were very likely collected from around the site (Hopf and Bar-Yosef 1987) (figure 14.1).

Carbonized Plant Remains from Hayonim Terrace

Systematic research begun at Hayonim terrace appears promising in showing changes in and the nature of the exploitation of plant resources, including their role in the process leading to agriculture.

Hayonim terrace and cave constitute a large Natufian unit on the right bank of the Nahal Yizhar, 14 km from the present Mediterranean shoreline, in a rather open valley which slopes down from the mountains of western Galilee to the Mediterranean coastal plain (figure 14.1). Since 1965, the partially collapsed cave has been used for sheepherding and was the object of excavations supervised by O. Bar-Yosef, from the Hebrew University of Jerusalem, until 1979. The excavations show a stratigraphic sequence from the Mousterian, Levantine Aurignacian, Kebarian, and Natufian, overlain by deposits from historic periods (Bar-Yosef and Tchernov 1966; Bar-Yosef and Goren 1973).

A rock blocks access to the cave from the four terraces, which extend down to the bottom of the valley. The upper terrace, 60 m long by 13 m wide at its widest point, shows surface traces of plowing and olive cultivation. I have observed that the surrounding maquis consists mainly of *Ceratonia siliqua* and *Pistacia lentiscus*, with *Sarcopoterium spinosum* over all the wadi's small valley, *Capparis spinosa*, *Echinops*

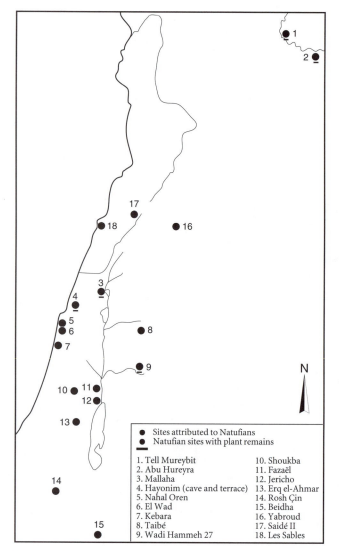

Figure 14.1 Archaeological sites

Legend within figure:

● Sites attributed to Natufians
● Natufian sites with plant remains

1. Tell Mureybit
2. Abu Hureyra
3. Mallaha
4. Hayonim (cave and terrace)
5. Nahal Oren
6. El Wad
7. Kebara
8. Taibé
9. Wadi Hammeh 27
10. Shoukba
11. Fazaël
12. Jericho
13. Erq el-Ahmar
14. Rosh Çin
15. Beidha
16. Yabroud
17. Saidé II
18. Les Sables

viscosus, Silybum marianum, Smilax aspera, Glaucium oxylobum, Salvia judaica, Ononis, Artemisia herba-alba, Echium judaicum, Malva nicaensis, and other Herbaceae. Annual rainfall is about 500 to 600 mm.

The first explorations on the terrace were in 1966 and 1969 by O. Bar-Yosef. These were followed by two excavation seasons by D. O. Henry over an area of 25 m² which showed a Geometric Kebaran occupation beneath the Natufian (Henry, Leroi-Gourhan, and Davis 1981).

Systematic excavations undertaken in 1980 by a French team directed by F. R. Valla (CRFJ) of a surface at the edge of the site revealed circular structures, knapped flints, and burial sites attributed to the Natufian (Valla 1989; Valla, Plisson, and Buxo i Capdevila 1989).

Open-air sites have contributed new information concerning Natufian diet. Pollen analyses from Hayonim terrace indicate that the Natufians who occupied the area between the second half of the eleventh and the end of the ninth millennium BC experienced a period of relative humidity and warming, followed by a drier period. Cereals appear only

rarely in the pollen diagrams of the period (Henry and Leroi-Gourhan 1976).

We used all means possible to recover plant remains in the field. Botanical samples were processed at the site, using manual flotation. Priority was given to sediments with high organic content and to those from structures, in particular one pit and the interior of the houses. The volume of soil sampled was 10 liters (1 pail) per artificial unit of excavation to 5 cm in depth in order to recover the entire sequence found in the structure contents.

The initial results of the analyses are limited because of the paucity of remains. They represent plants, mainly wild barley (*Hordeum spontaneum*), whose state of conservation was poor and a few fragments of small pulses. The barley caryopses were fragmented and the upper part of all the grains was missing. The germ was not preserved, and the scutellum was much reduced compared with cultivated specimens. Wild barley is characterized by extreme flatness and thinness at the apex, which was not preserved in this case. Remains of hulled barley with fragile rachises were symmetrical, characteristic of two-row barley. Remains of dodder (*Cuscuta* sp.), a small parasitic vine, comprised the rest of the assemblage. These results are still preliminary; however, the presence of plant remains in the pit suggests it had a specific function (figure 14.2).

There is no doubt that the wild barley and other plant remains recovered represent plants collected in the vicinity of the site. There is no detectable modification in caryopsis morphology, though intensified gathering perhaps occurred. This region is situated within the natural zone of wild barley distribution, which is very wide, principally the part that includes the mountains of Judaea and Ephraim, Galilee, the Jordan Valley, the Damascus Basin, and the Golan Heights, a zone which extends south to the Negev and north over the entire Fertile Crescent (Harlan and Zohary 1966). Wild barley does not withstand very low temperatures and disappears above 1500 m. We assume that the natural habitat of barley during the Natufian resembled its present-day distribution.

Conclusion

Present data lead us to consider Natufian communities as founded in the Upper Paleolithic, as Valla suggests (1988). These results show a discontinuity in the transition from Natufians to their successors and consist of certain archaic characteristics mixed with other innovative ones. Natufians were mainly hunters, but the plant resources show that they were diversified foragers, collecting not only cereals but also fruits and pulses, the latter represented most among the archaeobotanical remains.

Recent studies clearly show plant exploitation by Natufians, as the archaeological data also suggest: from the earliest phase of Hayonim, abundant glossed flint blades, mortars, and pestles are found. The Str/Ca ratio in bones

Figure 14.2 Fragments of wild barley (*Hordeum spontaneum*)

indicates that a high percentage of plant food was consumed (Sillen 1984).

In a more recent phase, storage in silos may have occurred, though the diet became more carnivorous. This phenomenon increases in the final phase (Valla 1987).

Valla wonders why we lack remains of morphologically domestic grain in some regions, whereas they seem to occur as early as the first half of the eighth millennium BC in the Jordan Valley (Jericho) and the Damascus Basin (Aswad). He also wonders whether the Natufian plant diet in the Mediterranean area consisted mainly of noncereal species. Pulses, whose grains are not easily separated from the pod, could have been pounded in deep mortars; cupstones, then querns replaced this kind of mortar when wheat and barley became commonly used (1987). In fact, the majority of the plant remains identified in Palestinian sites testify mainly to the presence of seasonal fruits and pulses, and to the scarcity of harvested grasses or cereals (only feather-grass and wild barley are present). Important data concerning the role of pulses is the presence of dodder, at Hayonim Terrace and Wadi Hammeh 27, as parasites affecting the growth of cultivated plants, particularly pulses.

These hypotheses and questions concerning Natufian plant diet will need to be checked in light of future data.

Acknowledgment. This chapter was translated from French by Jacqueline Gaudey, CRA, CNRS, France.

Chapter 15

Franchthi Cave and the Beginnings of Agriculture in Greece and the Aegean

Julie Hansen

IN NUMEROUS RECENT PUBLICATIONS ON the origins of agriculture in Europe and the eastern Mediterranean, Franchthi Cave in the southern Argolid, Greece, (figures 15.1 and 15.2) figures prominently as an example of a site with a depositional sequence spanning the transition from hunting and gathering to agricultural subsistence. Of critical importance for a discussion of the development of agriculture at Franchthi Cave are the presence of wild lentils and barley in Upper Paleolithic and Mesolithic levels, since it is the presence of domesticated forms of these plants later in the botanical sequence, along with the appearance of emmer wheat and domesticated ovicaprids, that helps define the beginning of the Neolithic at this site.

In previous papers (Hansen and Renfrew 1978; Hansen 1978; Hansen 1980), it was intimated that the increase in size of the wild lentils from the Upper Paleolithic and Mesolithic to the Neolithic at Franchthi Cave provided evidence for the beginnings of domestication of this plant. It was further suggested that it may have been possible for the wild oats and barley to have been cultivated prior to the Neolithic without necessarily resulting in selection for morphological changes associated with the domesticated species. The botanical data from Franchthi Cave have been used by others as well to support theories on the indigenous origins of agriculture, or at least experimentation with potential domesticates in southeast Europe (Dennell 1983; Barker 1985).

In this chapter I will briefly examine the current theories on the origins of agriculture in southeast Europe. I will then re-examine the botanical remains from Franchthi Cave, with special attention paid to the transitional period from the Upper Mesolithic through the Early Neolithic, and the

evidence for the indigenous domestication of lentils and barley. Although the rapidly rising sea level and decreasing coastal plain could have provided the impetus for intentional increase in resources through cultivation, the apparent paucity of remains of all categories of material at Franchthi in the latest Mesolithic levels suggests a decrease in intensity of occupation or even abandonment of the area for a brief time before the appearance of domesticates. In addition, there is no positive evidence of cultivation before the sudden appearance of domesticated emmer wheat and two-row barley. The increase in lentil size apparently also coincides with the appearance of these domesticates. I conclude, therefore, that agriculture was introduced to the site around 8000 BP and was not an indigenous development at Franchthi Cave. Elsewhere in Greece, the lack of evidence for a Mesolithic population precludes the possibility of a productive discussion of indigenous development of agriculture at this time.

Current Theories on Origins of Agriculture

The current theories on the origins of agriculture in Europe can be divided into two basic schools of thought: diffusion from the Near East and indigenous development. Diffusion is further subdivided into *demic*, the movement of groups of people, and *cultural*, the movement of ideas and crops without the need for human displacement (Ammerman and Cavalli-Sforza 1984:6).

A major proponent of independent invention is Robin Dennell (1983) who suggests that the existing Mesolithic population in southeast Europe was predisposed toward the acceptance of novel resources, such as emmer and bread

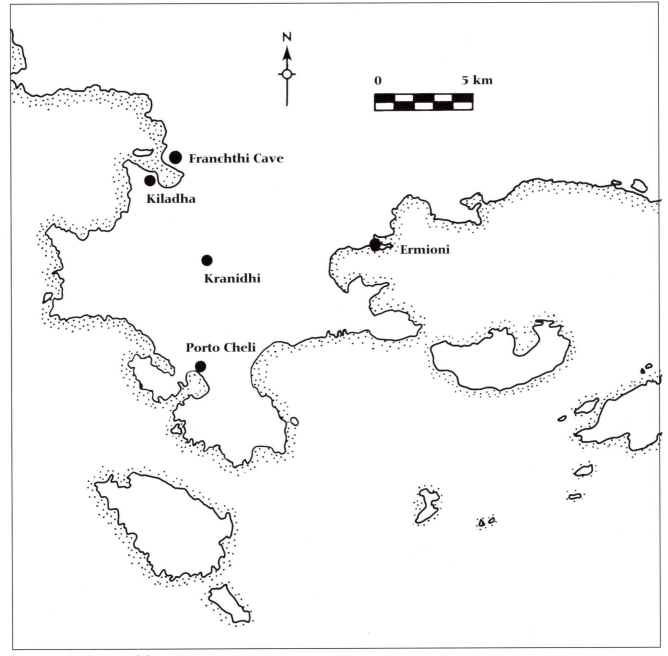

Figure 15.1 Southern Argolid

wheat, because they had been exploiting and perhaps cultivating the local resources such as einkorn wheat and barley (1983:165–167). This, Dennell feels, better explains the appearance of the earliest farming villages on the prime arable land in northern Greece and Bulgaria (1983:168). In order to support this theory we need to identify small Mesolithic sites occupied for short periods of time and containing artifacts for harvesting and processing grain and legumes, along with the plant remains themselves.

Lewthwaite (1986:64), on the other hand, sees no evidence that the Mesolithic populations of the Mediterranean were on the verge of developing a farming system based on local resources. In particular he notes "where the Mesolithic population appears to have been particularly sparse, as in

Greece and the Aegean Sea, it is difficult to envisage a nondiffusionist model of the introduction of food production" (1986:64). Ammerman and Cavalli-Sforza support the theory of demic diffusion of agriculture from Near Eastern centers with a model suggesting a wave of advance at the rate of about one kilometer per year (1984:57). In this way the natural growth of the population and gradual movement of small groups away from the periphery of the larger settlements would result in the spread of agriculture. Thus, "the model of a population wave of advance would be one of slow, continuous expansion, involving the frequent formation of new settlements at short distances from previous places of occupation" (Ammerman and Cavalli-Sforza 1984:62). In support of this model we should see nuclear

Figure 15.2 Excavated areas of Franchthi Cave

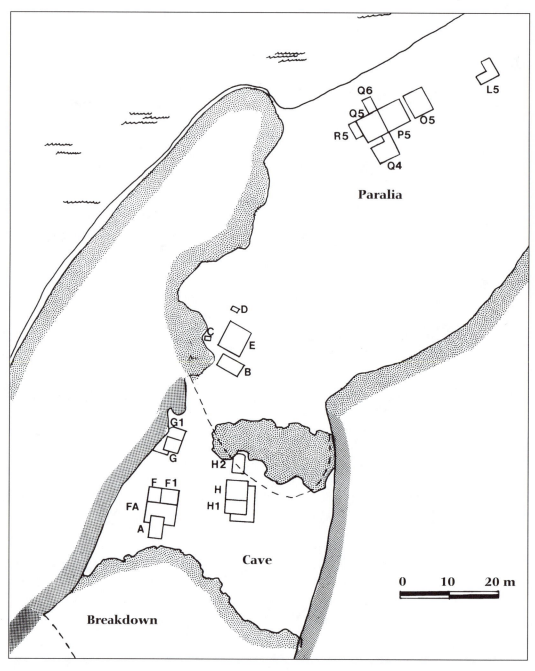

centers in southwest Asia dated to about 9500 BP with numerous progressively later sites radiating out from these centers through western Turkey.

The theories for the appearance of agriculture in southeast Europe, specifically Greece, can be summarized as follows (see Barker 1985:71):

* Agriculture based on emmer wheat was readily accepted by the existing Mesolithic population because they had already been harvesting and processing local cereals and legumes in those areas of prime agricultural land where the earliest farming settlements were established. The idea of agriculture and the necessary crops spread to southeast Europe either through cultural diffusion via exchange networks without any movement of people or through natural means (for example, rodents, birds, and ungulates) and were then adopted by the indigenous population.

* Agriculture was diffused from the Near East either by people who rapidly colonized those areas where early farming villages are now found or through a slow process of demic diffusion from Near Eastern centers over a period of about one thousand years.

For each of these models there are specific archaeological data that must be identified to test it. In the case of indigenous development we need small Mesolithic sites in areas that are later occupied by agricultural villages. These sites must be continuously occupied in areas of arable land and should provide evidence of harvesting and processing wild cereals and legumes. In the case of diffusion, we should find an abundance of Neolithic sites in western Turkey that would point to population pressure and a sudden appearance of comparable fully developed agricultural sites in Greece or an abundance of agricultural sites radiating from the older centers in the Near East through western Turkey to Greece should be identified.

Each of these models must be tested by an examination of the archaeological evidence of Mesolithic and early Neolithic occupation from Greece and western Turkey. A key site in this process, indeed the only Mesolithic site to have produced any botanical evidence, is Franchthi Cave in the Southern Argolid. Before looking at the data for the rest of Greece, therefore, I will present the botanical data from Franchthi Cave to determine how this site fits the proposed models.

Botanical Sequence at Franchthi Cave

The plant macrofossil assemblage from four deep trenches in the Franchthi Cave has been divided into biostratigraphic zones based on the changes in the frequency of various species (Hansen 1980). In this discussion, material from trenches FAS and FAN only will be considered, given that no botanical remains from the Neolithic levels of H1A or H1B were recovered. Six biostratigraphic zones have been delineated by an analysis of the remains in trenches FAS and FAN. Zone I, the lowest units in the trenches covering the Upper Paleolithic during the glacial maximum from before 23,000 to 15,000 BP, can be ignored for the purposes of this discussion since no species of obvious economic importance were recovered. Zone II is best represented in trenches H1A and H1B and is characterised by the appearance of carbonized plant remains including lentil, pistachio, and almond but with the continued presence of substantial numbers of Boraginaceae. Only the very end of this zone is present in trench FAS.

In FAS and FAN zones III through V comprise the biostratigraphic units of the remainder of the Upper Paleolithic through the Mesolithic deposits and date from about 9500 to 8000 BP. The cultural designations, defined by the lithic industry at the site (Perlès 1987, 1991), cannot be distinguished in the botanical sequence. Rather, there is a continuation of the same species throughout the sequence with the addition of a few new plants, and an overall increase in density of plant remains through zone III. The primary species represented are wild oats, lentils, pistachio, and almond, while wild barley and various legumes occur in smaller quantities. Zone IV is characterized by an overall decrease in diversity of plant remains from the previous zones and the presence of large quantities of *Lithospermum arvense*, as in zone I. These seeds are badly eroded and

covered with a reddish clay, like those found in the lowest zone, and may be the result of redeposition of earlier material. All species decrease in zone V to a level of about 0.19 seeds per liter of excavated deposit. This decrease has also been noted in other materials such as animal bones and lithics from the same units. Around 8000 BP, the domesticated cereals emmer wheat and two-row hulled barley appear while the wild cereals virtually disappear from the sequence and mark the beginning of zone VI. Several resources such as pistachio, almond, and various legumes continue to be exploited, although they occur in reduced quantities.

Lentils were recovered from most deposits beginning with the Upper Paleolithic around 9500 BP and ending with the Final Neolithic around 5000 BP, although they appear as early as about 13,000 BP in trench H1A. The question of local domestication of this legume was addressed through an examination of the change in diameter of the seeds (figures 15.3, 15.4, 15.5, 15.6; 15.7, and 15.8; table 15.1). Although recent work by Ladizinsky (1978) has suggested that seed dormancy is the primary characteristic that distinguishes wild from domesticated forms, this trait cannot be identified in an archaeological population, and attribution of lentils to the domesticated species has generally been based on increased seed diameter (Zohary and Hopf 1973:891).

The small-seeded *Lens orientalis* is the wild progenitor of the domesticated lentil and in modern populations has a diameter of 2.0 to 3.2 mm. This and two other species, *Lens nigricans* and *Lens ervoides*, are common to the Mediterranean and are known to exist today in Greece. The size range of the latter species is approximately 2.5 to 3.0 mm. With such an overlap there is no way to distinguish one species from another on the basis of size, nor can they be identified by other morphological characteristics in the carbonized state.

The natural habitats of the three species also overlap: *L. nigricans* and *L. ervoides* are found from sea level to 600 and 900 m, respectively; *L. orientalis* does not occur below about 450 m and has been found as high as 1300 m. Since much of the terrain around Franchthi Cave falls below 400 m and the inundated coastal plain was relatively flat, (van Andel et al. 1980:399), it seems more likely that *Lens nigricans* or *Lens ervoides* would have been more readily available in the area and collected by the inhabitants of Franchthi Cave. If this were the case, the possibility of local domestication of lentils is eliminated. If *Lens orientalis* was exploited, the increase in seed size from the Mesolithic to the Neolithic levels may indicate local domestication. The domesticated lentil *L. culinaris* ranges from 3.0 to 9.0 mm in diameter and is divided into two subspecies on the basis of seed size—ssp. *microsperma* from 3.0 to 6.0 mm and ssp. *macrosperma* from 6.0 mm to 9.0 mm. The average diameter of the lentils in FAS at Franchthi Cave increases from 2.26 to 2.47 mm in zones III to V (the Upper Paleolithic through Mesolithic) and to 3.02 mm in zone VI (the Neolithic; figure 15.5; table 15.1). In FAN

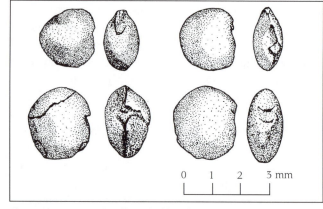

Figure 15.3 *Lens* sp. Small-seeded lentils from Upper Paleolithic and Mesolithic levels

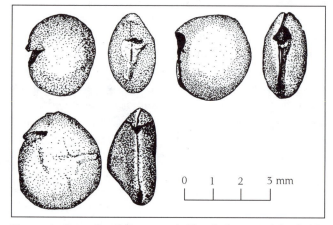

Figure 15.4 *Lens culinaris.* Large-seeded lentils from Neolithic levels

Table 15.1 Lentil measurements for FAS and FAN

	TOTAL SEEDS	X	MIN (mm)	MAX (mm)	SX	SX^2
FAS						
Zone VI	103	3.02	1.9	3.9	0.39	0.15
Zone V	16	2.47	1.7	3.6	0.48	0.23
Zone IV	24	2.34	1.9	2.8	0.24	0.06
Zone III	214	2.26	1.0	3.1	0.36	0.13
FAN						
Zone VI	55	3.07	1.8	4.2	0.43	0.19
Zone V	15	2.72	1.9	3.3	0.45	0.20
Zone IV	30	2.42	1.9	3.3	0.27	0.07
Zone III	483	2.32	1.5	3.5	0.36	0.13

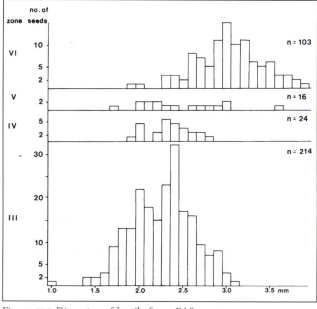

Figure 15.5 Diameter of lentils from FAS

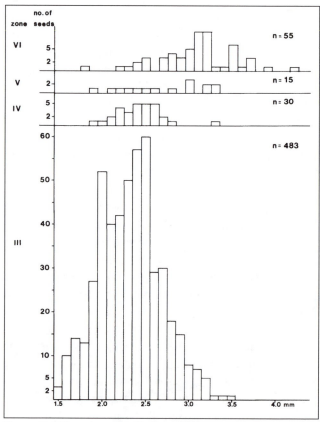

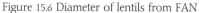

Figure 15.6 Diameter of lentils from FAN

the average diameter of the lentils ranges from 2.32 mm in zone III to 2.72 mm in zone V and is 3.07 mm in zone VI (figure 15.6; table 15.1). (It should be noted that lentil measurements were not used as a factor in determining zones.) The major change occurs between zones V and VI and suggests that a larger-seeded lentil appeared suddenly at this time. Zone VI is characterized by the first appearance of domesticated emmer wheat and barley, as well as the disappearance of wild oats and barley, and it would thus

seem likely that the larger-seeded lentil was introduced with the domesticated cereals. It may be possible, however, that the increase in size of the lentil seen in the Neolithic levels could be the result of wild plants grown in fields prepared for cultivation and thus in less competition with other wild species.

Part of the problem in analyzing the lentil data from zones IV and V and showing conclusively that there was or was not a gradual change in diameter stems from the fact that very few seeds were recovered from these units. The units composing zone V in particular are extremely poor in remains of all kinds and the impression is that of decreased use of the cave, perhaps from year-round to seasonal occupation, or even more sporadic visiting. Although some continuity can be traced between these and succeeding levels with respect to lithics, botanical remains, and animal bone, the sudden appearance of domesticated plants and animals and the decrease or disappearance of certain wild species strongly suggests at least the introduction of new resources if not the immigration of new people at this time.

A second species, wild barley (*Hordeum spontaneum*) (figures 15.9, 15.10) presents the possibility of discussing local domestication at Franchthi since domesticated barley, *H.* cf. *distichum* (figure 15.11, 15.12), occurs in the Neolithic levels. The wild species is very badly preserved, most grains having one or both ends broken off, and a total of only 167 grains were identified from the sorted botanical remains. They have been identified as *H. spontaneum* on the basis of their similarity to the illustrations of wild barley reported from the site of Tell Mureybit in northern Syria (van Zeist and Casparie 1968:51, Fig. 8; van Zeist 1970:176, Fig. 6) and with the modern *H. spontaneum* in the comparative collection at the University of Southampton, grown in the Plant Breeding Institute (PBI) at Cambridge, England. Table 15.2 gives the dimensions of the Franchthi grain, Mureybit grain, a sample of modern *H. spontaneum* from Damascus collected by van Zeist, and the sample from the collection at Southampton.

The Franchthi grain is substantially larger than that from Mureybit, especially considering that the full length of the Franchthi barley is not always preserved. Instead, the barley from Franchthi more closely resembles that from Damascus or the PBI. Van Zeist (1970:176) notes that the modern grains from Damascus belong to a race characterized by extremely large seeds, abundant in southwestern Syria and northern Jordan and Palestine. After carbonization these seeds measured on average 7.67 mm in length, 2.90 mm in breadth, and 1.90 mm in thickness, indicating that with carbonization the grains decrease in length and increase slightly in breadth and thickness. With respect to the Franchthi sample, this means that the grains more closely approximate the size of the modern Damascus and PBI grains and thus may be of the large-seeded race.

Wild barley is spread throughout the Eastern Mediterranean basin and Western Asia (figure 15.13). According to Zohary (1971:246) its distribution center lies in the fertile arc from Israel and Transjordan in the south west, to the north as far as southern Turkey and southeast toward Iraqi Kurdistan and southwest Iran. It grows from sea level to 1500 m. Rechinger noted *H. spontaneum* from Crete (1943:768), and Harlan and Zohary (1966:1075) identified a population from northern Greece, near Thessaloniki. The Franchthi grain enhances our knowledge of the natural

Figure 15.7 *Lens* sp., Upper Palaeolithic and Mesolithic

Figure 15.8 *Lens culinaris,* Neolithic

distribution of this species.

Hordeum spontaneum is believed to be the wild progenitor of domesticated barley, both two-row *H. distichum* and six-row *H. vulgare* (Nilan 1964; Harlan 1968, 1977; Harlan and Zohary 1966 ; Zohary 1960, 1963, 1971). The presence of *H. spontaneum* in the lower levels of the Franchthi sequence requires that the question of local domestication at Franchthi must be raised again, as it was for the lentil. According to Hillman and Davies (1990; see also chapter 11), the change from wild to domestic type could take as little as 19 years and the process of domestication would thus not be expected to be visible in an archaeological sequence. More striking evidence for the introduction of domesticated barley in the Neolithic at Franchthi Cave is the complete disappearance of the wild type before the appearance of the domesticated

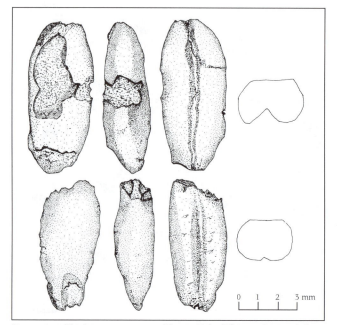

Figure 15.9 *Hordeum spontaneum*, Upper Paleolithic and Mesolithic

Figure 15.10 *Hordeum spontaneum*, Upper Paleolithic and Mesolithic

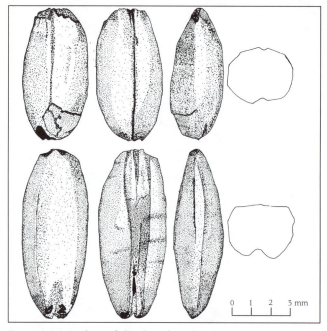

Figure 15.11 *Hordeum* cf. *distichum* from Neolithic levels

barley. More than one meter of deposit separates the last occurrence of wild barley from the first appearance of the domesticated grain.

I suggested earlier (Hansen 1980) that the wild oats and barley in the Upper Paleolithic and Mesolithic levels at Franchthi Cave could have been cultivated without resulting in the selection for morphological changes, such as tough rachis, that are associated with domestication. A harvesting method that favored brittle-rachised plants would not have selected for the tough rachis. Beating the grain into a sack or basket is a method used for a variety of cereals, both wild and domesticated, worldwide (see chapter 1). Such a harvesting method would select against the tough-rachised form, and the sowing of the harvested grain would serve to favor the wild species. The panicle form of the oat plant lends itself more to this type of harvesting technique than does the spike of barley. The latter would be more efficiently collected either by pulling off the whole ear or cutting the culm. Since the brittle rachis shatters as it ripens from the top down, grasping the ear or head in one hand and pulling or cutting will prevent much of the grain from falling to the ground. Harvesting the grain just prior to ripening, in the green, waxy stage, would also ensure maximum recovery of viable grain (Zohary 1988). These unripened ears or heads could then be left to dry before threshing and further processing.

In the absence of morphological characteristics to identify cultivated plants, however, there will be little archaeobotanical evidence of primitive cultivation. The technology available, digging stick and hoe, would not have produced a dramatic change in the weed flora that might show up in the botanical remains from the site (Hillman 1981:145); nor is it likely that areas of forest or bush would have been cleared to the extent that the vegetation change would be visible in the pollen record or in wood remains from archaeological sites. It could be argued that the lack of positive evidence for cultivation does not preclude the possibility that it was practiced. Decreasing coastal plain owing to eustatic rise in sea level may have resulted in a significant decrease in resources such as wild oats and barley (figure 15.14; van Andel et al. 1980). In an attempt to retain these resources in sufficient abundance the inhabitants of Franchthi Cave may have resorted to planting them further inland. In the absence of any corroborative evidence, however, there is little point in pursuing this argument.

Looking back to the models proposed earlier we see that the botanical remains from Franchthi Cave cannot be used to support Dennell's indigenous development hypothesis but rather more strongly support the model of diffusion of agriculture from the Near East. No positive evidence of cultivation of the cereals or legumes can be identified in the Mesolithic and the absence of wild barley for more than a meter of deposit before the appearance of the domesticated species points to either the disappearance of the wild plant from the region or abandonment of its use in the Mesolithic at Franchthi Cave. The paucity of botanical remains and other kinds of material in zones IV and V strongly suggests a decrease in occupation, if not abandonment of the cave, in the later Mesolithic. The appearance of domesticated animals and plants, as well as architecture and other artifacts at the same time, point to an intrusion of new people into the area around 8000 BP. Only one other Mesolithic site (figure 15.14; F35) and no other Early Neolithic sites have been identified through survey of the southern Argolid (Runnels and van Andel 1987:309), and so it is not possible to suggest that these traits were being developed elsewhere in the region and were moved to Franchthi around 8000 BP. The absence of possible coastal sites makes drawing firm conclusions impossible. Despite this, however, I believe the data available from Franchthi Cave and the southern Argolid most strongly suggest an immigration of new people with an agricultural economy based on a Near Eastern complex of emmer wheat, barley, lentils, and ovicaprids.

Greece and the Aegean

Although recent survey data suggest that Franchthi Cave was a unique site in the southern Argolid through the Early Neolithic period (Runnels and van Andel 1987), elsewhere in Greece, especially in central and northern Greece, the period beginning about 8000 BP was one of apparently rapid development of settled agricultural villages. Figure 15.15 shows many of the Early Neolithic sites known in Greece, and although relatively few of these have produced plant remains, there is a consistency in the species that are represented: emmer and einkorn wheat, lentils, and barley, all dating to approximately the same time (8000 BP; table 15.3). The plant assemblage is that of the Neolithic Near East and it has been widely accepted that these sites were established by peoples immigrating from the Near East (Runnels and van Andel 1988). We should, however, look at the evidence for indigenous development of agriculture.

According to the model of indigenous development, we would expect to see in this area small Mesolithic sites with harvesting and processing tools along with wild einkorn wheat, barley, and legumes. Dennell (1985:157) points out that most of the Early Neolithic sites in Thessaly are located on prime agricultural land and it is unlikely that new arrivals from a different country would have known where such arable land existed and been able to go directly to it upon arrival. Surveys done in the past ten years (Özdogan 1979; Fotiadis 1985; Bintliff and Snodgrass 1985; Chapman et al. 1987; Runnels 1988), have, however, failed to identify conclusively any Mesolithic sites in central or northern Greece, southern Yugoslavia, or northwest Turkey. One might account for the lack of sites by arguing that they were coastal and are now submerged, but we must then wonder what happened to the population? Would they not have moved

Figure 15.12 *Hordeum* cf. *distichum*, Neolithic

Table 15.2 Comparison of measurements for *Hordeum spontaneum*

	LENGTH (mm)	BREADTH (mm)	THICKNESS (mm)	L/B	T/B
MUREYBIT (N=8)					
Average	5.44	1.89	1.26	290	67
Minimum	3.8	1.5	1.0	252	61
Maximum	6.7	2.1	1.6	372	76
DAMASCUS (N=20)					
Average	9.20	2.84	1.55	325	55
Minimum	8.3	2.5	1.2	295	48
Maximum	10.4	3.2	1.8	357	64
PBI (N=30)					
Average	9.81	3.29	2.41	303	73
Minimum	8.5	2.6	1.7	260	63
Maximum	10.6	3.6	2.7	353	79
FRANCHTHI (N=23)					
Average	(6.78)*	3.03	2.09	(229)	70
Minimum	(5.5)	1.9	1.5	(170)	59
Maximum	8.6	4.4	2.6	316	92

* Parentheses indicate incomplete measurement on a broken grain.
Sources: Mureybit and Damascus (van Zeist and Casparie 1968:51); Franchthi (Hansen 1980:181)

further inland as the sea level rose, in which case we should find Mesolithic sites in those very areas where Dennell suggests we should find them and where the Neolithic agricultural villages later appear. Although it is an argument *ex silentio*, I believe enough area in northern and central Greece has been surveyed to be able to say that if the Mesolithic culture existed in these regions, it was sparse to the point of invisibility.

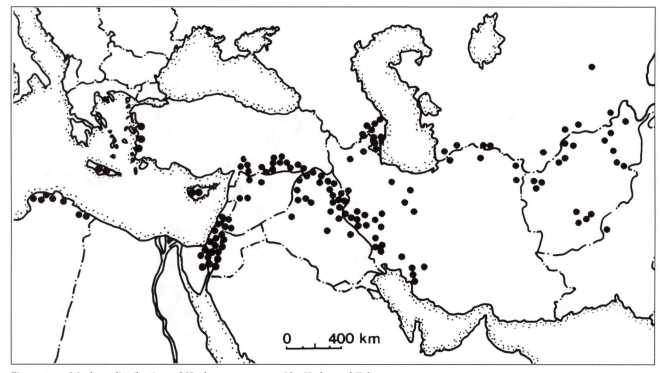

Figure 15.13 Modern distribution of *Hordeum spontaneum. After Harlan and Zohary 1966:1075*

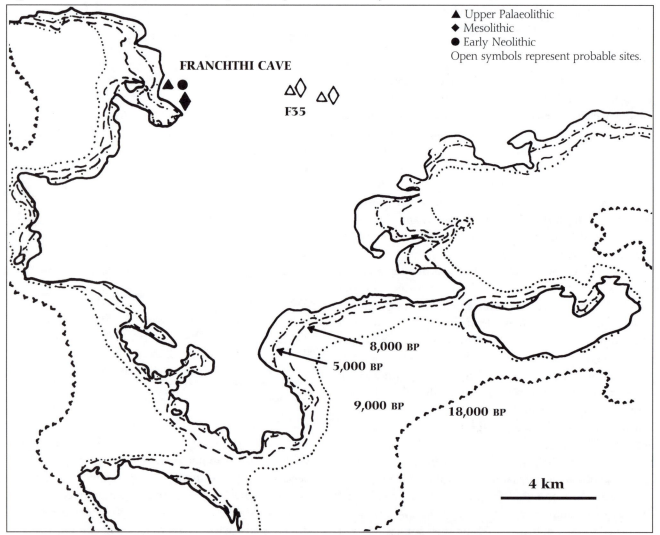

Figure 15.14 Shoreline change and Upper Paleolithic, Mesolithic, and Early Neolithic sites in the southern Argolid. *After Runnels and van Andel 1987*

Table 15.3 Some plant remains from Early Neolithic sites in Greece and Crete

SPECIES	NEA NIKOMEDEIA	ARGISSA	SOUFLI	GEDIKI	SESKLO	ACHILLEION	FRANCHTHI CAVE	KNOSSOS
Vitis sp.							X	
Pistacia sp.				X	X		X	
Vicia ervilla	X			X			X	
Vicia sp.				X			X	
Vicia/Lathyrus sp.							X	
Lathyrus cicera							X	
Lens culinaris	X	X	X	X			X	
Pisum sp.	X	X	X	X	X			
Astragalus sp.							X	
Prunus amygdalus					X		X	X
Pyrus sp.							X	
Triticum monococcum	X	X	X	X	X	X	X	
Triticum dicoccum	X	X	X	X	X	X	X	X
Triticum aestivum								X
Hordeum distichum				X	X	X	X	X
Hordeum vulgare	X	X						

Sources: Nea Nikomedeia (van Zeist and Bottema 1971); Argissa (Hopf 1962); Soufli, Gediki, Sesklo, Achilleion (Renfrew 1966); Franchthi (Hansen 1980); Knossos (Evans 1968)

Along with the absence of Mesolithic sites is the lack of any wild einkorn, barley, or legumes, as well as harvesting or processing tools for this period. In addition, it would seem probable that if these wild botanical resources had been exploited up to the time of the introduction of the emmer and bread wheat, then we should logically expect to find some vestiges of the wild plants on the Early Neolithic village sites. This is not the case. To date, except for the wild barley and lentils in Mesolithic levels at Franchthi Cave, no remains of these plants or wild einkorn have been identified from any site in Greece (table 15.3). As at Franchthi, their complete absence from the Neolithic levels strongly suggests the introduction of agriculture by new people moving into the area rather than being adopted by an existing Mesolithic population.

Thus, the model of indigenous development of agriculture in Greece cannot be supported by the existing evidence from central or northern Greece and is not at all supported by the evidence from Franchthi Cave. The possibility of the cultural diffusion of agriculture from the Near East adopted by an indigenous Mesolithic population is equally untenable owing to the apparent absence of any Mesolithic population in most of the country. While further survey and excavation may reveal this missing culture, for the moment we must turn to a diffusion model.

The diffusion of agriculture as the result of a rapid colonization movement of people from the Near East has gone out of favor largely owing to the lack of evidence for any impetus for such a movement. It was initially thought that the advent of agriculture resulted in population increase to the point that groups of people would break away from the center and move to available arable land, reaching Greece and the Balkans around 8000 BP. Ammerman and Cavalli-Sforza (1984) have suggested a more gradual wave of advance with small groups moving away from the periphery of the larger settlements. These waves, more like ripples, eventually either spread across the Aegean or spilled over into Thrace and northern Greece as they expanded beyond western Anatolia. The latter hypothesis, we have seen, is not supported by the available data. The primary problem with either of these models is the lack of evidence of large numbers of Early Neolithic farming communities in western Anatolia dated to just before about 8000 BP (figure 15.15). Certainly systematic survey in these areas will either support or refute the hypotheses.

It must also be remembered that much of the former coastlines of Anatolia and Greece, have been inundated (van Andel and Shackleton 1982). This should not be a problem for determining from where and when the farming communities left Anatolia, since there should still be a buildup of sites far enough inland that they would not have been drowned. The rise in sea level might have inundated some sites on the Aegean islands or coastal Greece, however.

Although there are as yet no identified Mesolithic or Early Neolithic sites on the west coast of Anatolia, nor in the Aegean Islands to support the notion of intercontinental movement, the presence of Melian obsidian at Franchthi Cave by 9000 BP indicates some level of sea travel at this time. The Aegean islands do not, as a rule, provide arable land in great abundance, but following perhaps well-known exchange routes travellers would have been led to the east coast of Greece. The arrival of the first farmers by sea would explain the absence of earlier Neolithic villages in Thrace and Macedonia (Özdogan 1979; Fotiadis 1985) and the previous, perhaps long-standing contact with the Greek mainland would explain the appearance of settled agricultural villages in areas of the best and most abundant arable land. As for the preceding Mesolithic people it is possible to envision a population so reduced and scattered that they could be easily overcome or, more likely, absorbed by the arriving farmers.

Figure 15.15 Early Neolithic sites in Greece and Crete. *Sources: Theochares 1973; Weinberg 1970, Map 15; Pendlebury, 1965*

1. Nea Nikomedeia
2. Nissonis
3. Gediki
4. Soufli
5. Otzaki
6. Argissa
7. Magoulitsa I
8. Achilleion
9. Sesklo
10. Pyrassos
11. Ayios Petros-Kyra Panayia
12. Skyros
13. Elateia
14. Ayia Marina
15. Halai
16. Polyghyra
17. Chaeronea
18. Orchomenos
19. Pyrghos
20. Asmini
21. Aidipsos
22. Varka
23. Chalcis
24. Dystos
25. Marathon, Cave of Pan
26. Mea Makri
27. Athens
28. Glyphada
29. Kaza Pavakton
30. Gonia
31. Corinth
32. Nemea
33. Tiryns
34. Lerna
35. Lorka
36. Ayiorytika
37. Asea
38. Malthi
39. Franchthi Cave
40. Koufovouno, Sparta
41. Astiri
42. Ayios Strategos
43. Goulas
44. Epidauros Lithera
45. Sidari
46. Knossos
47. Katsamba

Another hypothesis for the arrival of agriculture into Europe has recently been presented. Runnels and van Andel (1988:86) suggest that the rise of agriculture in the Near East was a response to a long-standing trade network in which farming, along with the concentration on producing a surplus of a narrow range of crops, was a means of accumulating wealth that could then be traded for other commodities, either necessary raw materials or luxury items. Such a network undoubtedly goes back to the Upper Paleolithic and can perhaps be seen in the appearance of such items as Melian obsidian at Franchthi Cave, and the movement of flint and shell in Europe. (Gamble 1986:336; Runnels and van Andel 1988:97). With the growth of this network in the Near East around 8000 BP, the strong incentives (accumulation of wealth) necessary for dispersing the primary crops—emmer and einkorn wheat, barley, and lentils—to new regions were established. In this way it is fairly easy to imagine a group from western Anatolia or the Levant travelling through the Eastern Mediterranean and Aegean to mainland Greece, Cyprus, and Crete both to procure exotic goods to trade in their homeland, as well as to look for additional areas for producing the cash crops.

This would account for the appearance of well-settled agricultural villages in areas of prime arable land such as the Thessalian Plain. This was not an area that was stumbled upon by footsore travellers but was consciously sought out by colonists seeking to expand their production. They may have traded some of these crops with an indigenous population of hunter-gatherers who may or may not have adopted the sedentary farming mode of life. It is not necessary to this model, however, that an indigenous population be present or familiar with agricultural techniques or products.

Conclusions

The botanical remains from Franchthi Cave indicate that wild oats, barley, and lentils were utilized by the Mesolithic inhabitants, although there is no positive evidence that any of these plants were cultivated. After a period of either discontinuous or, sporadic occupation of the site, domesticated emmer wheat, barley, and lentils appear and wild oats and barley disappear. The domesticated lentils and barley are apparently not derived from the preceeding wild species, and the disappearance of the wild cereals may be attributable to the decrease in available habitat owing to rising sea level.

Elsewhere in Greece and the Aegean islands there is virtually no evidence for any Mesolithic population and the sudden appearance of a well-developed Neolithic with the Near Eastern agricultural complex would seem to argue most strongly for an introduction. Whether this was the result of a colonization movement across the Aegean or slow diffusion through a wave of advance is not possible to say because both models require large populations and numerous earlier Neolithic sites in western Anatolia than have yet been demonstrated. From the presence of these Early Neolithic sites in the areas of prime arable land it is possible that the immigrants were aware that this land existed prior to their arrival. This can perhaps best be explained by the exchange or trade network that would undoubtedly have brought travellers from the Near East to the Greek mainland before 8000 BP, and later perhaps in search of additional land to increase production of cash crops.

In order to test these models more accurately it is imperative that additional Mesolithic sites be found in Greece, Macedonia, and Thrace and Early Neolithic sites in western Turkey. Much of the eastern Aegean coast has not been thoroughly surveyed and more work could certainly be done in Greece as well. We need to find more complete versions of Franchthi Cave where the transition can be accurately identified and the economic processes can be evaluated in terms of subsistence, exchange, and interaction within the Aegean and Eastern Mediterranean sphere.

Chapter 16 ❧

A Cautionary Note on the Use of Morphological Characters for Recognizing Taxa in Wheat (genus *Triticum*)

Terry E. Miller

THE EVOLUTION OF THE WHEATS, GENUS *Triticum*, has been a process of hybridization and polyploidization involving the wild diploid *Triticum* species and diploid species of the closely related goat grasses of the genus *Aegilops* (figure 16.1; see also Miller 1987a).

Three levels of ploidy exist: diploid, tetraploid, and hexaploid. At the diploid and tetraploid levels there are wild and cultivated forms but at the hexaploid level there are only cultivated forms, although a semiwild form, possibly an escape from cultivation, has been reported from Tibet (Shao 1980).

The nomenclature and classification of the wheats is both varied and confused. Percival (1921) wrote, "The nomenclature of wheats in all countries is in hopeless confusion; the same form is frequently found under many different names; totally different forms are often given the same name. The trouble is not modern, for medieval names for the same form of wheat are abundant: it has, however, increased in recent times, and there is no prospect that it will ever cease." Nearly seventy years later the problem is still with us. In this chapter a relatively simple nomenclature (Miller 1987a) will be used (table 16.1). The descriptive nature of nomenclature, particularly common names, should always be treated with caution. For example, the Polish wheat, *T. polonicum*, is of Mediterranean not Polish origin; it was not grown in Poland before 1870. Similarly cone wheat, *T. turgidum*, is not cone shaped, although the spike may be slightly tapered. The origin of the name is unknown but it

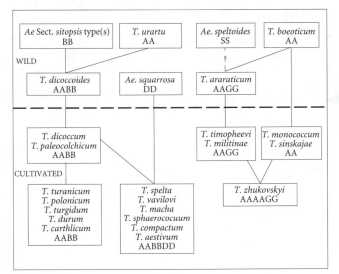

Figure 16.1 The evolution of the polyploid wheats

Figure 16.2 Spikes of the ABD hexaploid wheats: *Triticum spelta*, *T. vavilovi*, *T. macha*, *T. compactum*, *T. sphaerococcum*, and *T. aestivum* (*left to right*)

Table 16.1 The wheats, genus *Triticum*

SPECIES NAME	COMMON NAME	GENOME FORMULA
DIPLOIDS		
T. urartu TUM.	Wild einkorn or small spelt wheat	AA
T. boeoticum BOISS. ssp. *aegilopoïdes*	Wild einkorn or small spelt wheat	AA
ssp. *thaoudar*	" " " " "	AA
T. monococcum L.	Cultivated einkorn or small spelt wheat	AA
T. sinskajae A. FILAT. & KURK.	Cultivated einkorn	AA
TETRAPLOIDS		
T. dicoccoides (KOERN) SCHWEINF.	Wild emmer wheat	AABB
T. dicoccum (SCHRANK) SCHUBL.	Emmer wheat	AABB
T. paleocolchicum MEN.	Georgian wheat	AABB
T. carthlicum NEVSKI	Persian wheat	AABB
T. turgidum L.	Rivet or cone wheat	AABB
T. polonicum L.	Polish wheat	AABB
T. durum DESF.	Macaroni wheat	AABB
T. turanicum JAKUBZ.	Khorasan wheat	AABB
T. araraticum JAKUBZ.	Wild emmer wheat	AAGG
T. timopheevi ZHUK.		AAGG
T. militinae ZHUK. & MIGUSCH.		AAGG
HEXAPLOIDS		
T. spelta L.	Spelt or dinkel wheat	AABBDD
T. vavilovi (TUM.) JAKUBZ.		AABBDD
T. macha DEK. & MEN.		AABBDD
T. sphaerococccum PERC.	Indian dwarf or shot wheat	AABBDD
T. compactum HOST.	Club wheat	AABBDD
T. aestivum L.	Bread or common wheat	AABBDD
T. zhukovskyi MEN. & ER.		AAAAGG

Figure 16.3 Representative spikes of the AB genome tetraploid wheats. Left to right: *Triticum dicoccoides, T. dicoccum, T. paleocolchicum, T. turanicum, T. polonicum, T. turgidum, T. durum, and T. carthlicum*

goes back to at least the seventeenth century.

The cultivated polyploid wheats, in evolutionary terms, are all of recent origin, and with the exception of *T. timopheevi* (figure 16.1) have arisen from emmer wheat, *T. dicoccum*, since its domestication.

The resultant distinct forms of today have arisen by adaptation and selection to meet the changing needs of humans and their environment. It is important to keep in mind the fact that today's wheats are the product of what

must have been a continuum of change, and one should not necessarily expect to find identical forms in early archaeological contexts. Moreover, the nomenclatural divisions of today are in many cases based on distinct morphological differences that are often the result of changes in a few genes, and within the divisions extensive genetic variation still exists.

The AABBDD hexaploids (figure 16.2) are mainly distinguished by single genes affecting the shape of the spike.

These are: *q*, the speltoid gene and its allele *Q* which confers free-threshing grain and a tough rachis; *c*, and its dominant compact-ear-producing allele *C*; *S*, and its recessive allele *s* for spherical grain and *V* for a branched spike (elongated rachilla) (Swaminathan and Rao 1961). The hexaploid forms are thus characterized as follows:

T. spelta	qq	cc SS
T. vavilovi	qq	cc SS VV
T. macha	qq	CC SS
T. compactum	QQ	CC SS
T. aestivum	QQ	cc SS
T. sphaerococcum	QQ	*cc ss*

Despite the phenotypes produced by these genes of major effect there is still considerable variation within each hexaploid species, such that it may not always be easy to differentiate them. For example, care is needed when differentiating *T. compactum,* with its short uniformly dense spike, from forms of *T. aestivum,* with dense or clavate (club-shaped, more dense at apex) spikes. Similarly, with the speltoid species, *T. spelta* and *T. macha*, if only spikelets are compared it is very difficult to determine the compactness of the ear, especially as *T. macha* is a polymorphic species.

The cultivated tetraploid wheats show a wide range of divergence from the more primitive emmer (*T. dicoccum*) type (figure 16.3). The major forms are given specific status, but again the divisions are based on small genetic differences. *T. polonicum* is separated by large ears with long, narrow empty glumes which extend beyond the rest of the spikelet. However, a similar long-glumed character is also found in a form of *T. dicoccum* (*T. ispahanicum* HESLOT). *T. paleocolchicum* is a monomorphic wheat and is distinguished from *T. dicoccum* by a compact laterally compressed spike with a zig-zag rachis. It is only found cultivated as a mixture with the hexaploid *T. macha*, which has a similar spike morphology. Both forms presumably are the result of strong selection for this particular spike from within these populations. The Persian wheat *T. carthlicum* is distinguished by being truly free-threshing and by the presence of an awn on both the lemma and the outer glume. Its free-threshing is due to the presence of the gene Q, which was thought to have been introgressed from hexaploid wheat (Morris and Sears 1967; Kuckuck 1979), but Muramatsu (1986) has shown that other tetraploids including *T. durum* and *T. dicoccum* can also contain the Q gene. Also *T. militinae*, a single specimen derivative of *T. timopheevi* is free-threshing and has an awn on the outer glume like *T. carthlicum*. It seems likely, therefore, that Q arose at the tetraploid level. A free-threshing einkorn, *T. sinskajae*, also exists, showing that this character can arise at all levels of ploidy. For more detailed descriptions of the morphologies of the tetraploid wheats see Percival (1921) and Miller (1987A).

The diploid wheats all have very similar morphologies

Figure 16.4 Representative spikes of the diploid wheats. Left to right: *Triticum urartu, T. boeoticum* ssp. *thaoudar, T. boeoticum* ssp. *aegilopoides, T. monococcum,* and *T. sinskajae*

(figure 16.4). The wild forms which have similar geographic distributions are separated into two species, *T. urartu* and *T. boeoticum* on the basis of genetic sterility of hybrids between them. *T. boeoticum* is further divided into two subspecies or races: one, ssp. *aegilopoïdes*, with a single fertile floret in each spikelet and a single awn on the lemma of that floret; and the other, ssp. *thaoudar*, with two fertile florets per spikelet each with an awn on the lemma. *T. urartu* also has two fertile florets each with an awn, but it can be distinguished from *T. boeoticum* spp. *thaoudar* by the presence of a small third awn on the rudimentary third floret of each spikelet, and by the three-dimensional spreading of the main awns compared to the two-dimensional spread of the awns of *T. boeoticum*. The cultivated *T. monococcum*, like *T. boeoticum* ssp. *aegilopoïdes* from which it is presumably derived, is single-seeded and single-awned. *T. sinskajae*, which is also cultivated, is assumed to be a free-threshing derivative of *T. monococcum*. Difficulties in distinguishing the wild diploids can arise when studying incomplete specimens. On ripening the awns are frequently lost, and well-grown specimens of single-seeded forms frequently produce two fertile florets per spikelet at the center of the spike. Thus a sample of spikelets containing one or two seeds, where it was not possible to determine if awns had been present, could either be a mixture of one- and two-seeded forms or a single sample of a well-grown single-seeded form.

Brittle rachis is another difficult character as it is controlled by more than one gene. All diploid wheats have brittle rachis, the cultivated *T. monococcum* can be less brittle than the wild forms and may not disarticulate prior to harvest, but when fully ripe it will do so with the slightest mechanical pressure.

The same situation exists between the wild emmers, *T. dicoccoides* and *T. araraticum*, and the cultivated emmer, *T. dicoccum*, and to a lesser extent *T. timopheevi*. At the hexaploid level both *T. spelta* and *T. macha* have a brittle rachis, but there is a considerable range in the fragility of the spike within both species.

In the past a number of patently incorrect statements about wheat have been made by archaeologists. To take just one example, it has often been stated that spelt wheat replaced emmer wheat in Britain because the former is a winter wheat which is more hardy and produced a better crop than the spring emmer wheat (Applebaum 1954). Both *T. spelta* and *T. dicoccum* have both winter and spring types. The winter type is in all probability the normal type. The wild emmer,

T. dicoccoides, is basically a winter wheat; like many of its wild annual relatives that grow in a Mediterranean-type climate it germinates in the autumn, grows vegetatively during the cooler wet winter, and flowers and ripens rapidly with the onset of the hot, dry summer. The early cultivated emmer would presumably also have been of this type.

In highlighting the problems associated with just a few of the morphological characters that distinguish wheat species it should be clear that the inheritance of many of these characters and hence the classification of the genus into distinct taxa is complex. More is probably known about the genetics of wheat than any other group of plants and archaeobotanists would be well advised to take full advantage of this knowledge.

Chapter 17 ❧

A Carpological Approach to the Neolithization of Southern France

Philippe Marinval

AGRICULTURE EXISTED FROM THE EARLIEST impressed-ware ceramic Neolithic of the western Mediterranean (Cardial) in southern France, as shown by anthracological, palynological, and carpological data. (*Carpology* is the discipline which studies fossil grains and fruits, in the form of paleoseeds or carporemains preserved in archaeological sediments.) During the Cardial, a variety of plants were cultivated or gathered for food purposes (table 17.1; Marinval 1988). Collecting of pistachio (*Pistacia* sp.) nuts has been recently revealed. Harvesting of these small fruits was prevalent in the Mediterranean Basin, and their remains are found in some Neolithic levels of the Near and Middle East as well as Greece (van Zeist and Bakker-Heeres 1985; notably Renfrew 1979; Kroll 1981). For cultivated plants, some evolution is perceptible, although this issue can be controversial.

Table 17.1 Plants cultivated and collected during the French Cardial

CULTIVATED PLANTS
Compact bread wheat (*T. aestivo-compactum*)
Naked polystic barley (*Hordeum vulgare* var. *nudum*)
Emmer (*T. dicoccum*)
Einkorn (*T.* cf. *monococcum*)
Peas (*Pisum sativum*)

COLLECTED PLANTS
Hazel (*Corylus avellana*)
Wild rose bush (*Rosa* sp.)
Pistachio (*Pistacia* sp.)
Wild vine (*Vitis sylvestris*)
Oak (*Quercus* sp.)
Dogwood (*Cornus sanguinea*)

Origin of the Introduction of New Cultivated Plants

Emmer (*T. dicoccum*), and perhaps einkorn wheat (*T. monococcum*) if it is this species, is cited only from the Epicardial (towards 6500/6300 BP) onwards. The data concerning these taxa are still limited, but it is highly probable that southern European agriculture was enriched with these new species at this time. These data suggest that an additional arrival of cultivated plants took place during this period.

This introduction of new species into the southern French context may have resulted from contacts established between the Cardial society living in the south of France and other Mediterranean groups. Indeed, emmer is mentioned at Peiro Signado, Portiragnes (Hérault), dating from 6500 BP, of a Tyrrhenian facies (Roudil and Soulier 1983; Guilaine et al. 1984). Moreover, emmer and einkorn are frequent in the early and middle Neolithic of Spain (Hopf 1966; Buxo 1985) and Italy (Coppola and Costantini 1987; Follieri 1987).

The possibility of contact also with groups of cultivators from the Danubian civilization cannot be excluded. A series of data speak in favor of the existence of such relations:

• The peculiarities of La Baume de Gonvillars (Haute-Saône), dating from 6000 BP (Pétrequin 1974), are surprising. Indeed, the site lies in a natural rock shelter, unusual for a settlement situated in the outlying area of linear ceramics. Also, this deposit concealed caryopses of compact bread wheat (*T. aestivo-compactum*) (Villaret-von Rochow 1974)[1]. This taxon is not generally attested in Danubian sites. K. H. Knörzer (1974) even defined the LBK civilisation as characterised by the use of hulled wheats: emmer (*T. dicoccum*), einkorn (*T.*

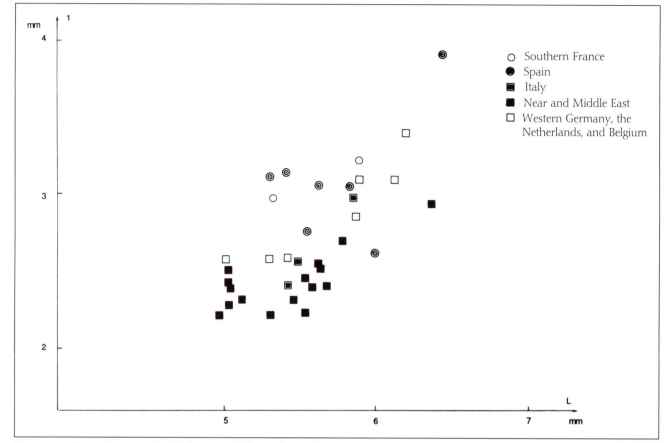

Figure 17.1　Biometric comparison of emmer (*T. dicoccum*) populations

monococcum), and perhaps spelt (*T. spelta*), found only in southern Poland and Moldavia (Willerding 1980).

- The existence of a rock-shelter site in the LBK area and the presence of *T. aestivo-compactum* at that time—even though the latter had mainly Mediterranean characteristics during that phase—have allowed P. Pétrequin (1974) to envisage a relationship between Jura and southern France as early as 6000 BP.

- Many Rhenan LBK sites have yielded poppy (*Papaver somniferum*) seeds (Bakels 1982). In fact, this plant is of Mediterranean origin. Thus, C. C. Bakels (1982) also thinks that southern species may have reached the Rhenan regions by the early Neolithic.

- According to M. Lichardus-Itten (1986), certain parallels exist in pottery decoration between the Cardial and the recent Bandkeramik of the Paris Basin, perhaps showing a Mediterranean influence on pottery decoration.

Biometric data do not provide additional arguments in favor of either hypothesis. The southern French varieties of emmer (*T. dicoccum*; figure 17.1) are as close to Spanish ones as to those from Northern Europe (Netherlands, Belgium, and Western Germany), and also to an Italian population.

Conversely, they differ from grains belonging to the Near and Middle Eastern excavations.

In the present state of knowledge, it is impossible to determine whether the development of emmer (*T. dicoccum*) in the French Epicardial was based on an exclusively Mediterranean supply or from contacts established between the Danubian world and the French Mediterranean area. Insofar as it is highly probable that Mediterranean plants were cultivated by human groups of the LBK civilisation, the reverse may have occurred. Finds of *T. dicoccum* in the Cardial context are mainly in river basin areas (figure 17.2), whereas bread wheat is distributed over the whole geographical area as shown in figure 17.3; this occurrence may indicate that this wheat came from countries to the north, with the Rhône Valley as the likely vector.

Origin of Cereal Cultivation in Southern France

With the emergence of emmer wheat (*T. dicoccum*) in the French Mediterranean area, the Cardial begins to connect with more eastern Mediterranean areas. This raises the problem of the origin of cereal cultivation in southern France. Concerning the cereals sown in the early Neolithic, the Mediterranean Basin seems to be divided into two areas:

- The western part (Spain and southern France) appears to have been a cultivation area for compact bread wheat

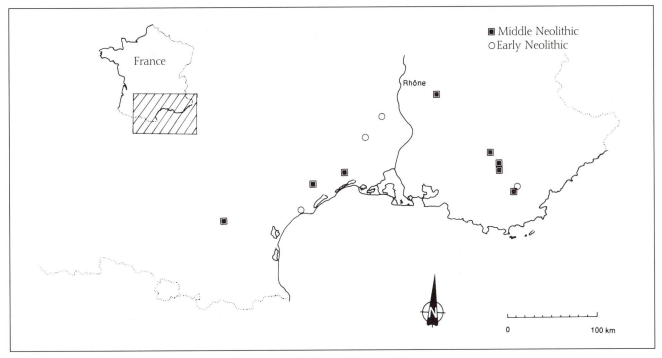

Figure 17.2 Early and Middle Neolithic sites where emmer (*T. dicoccum*) is attested

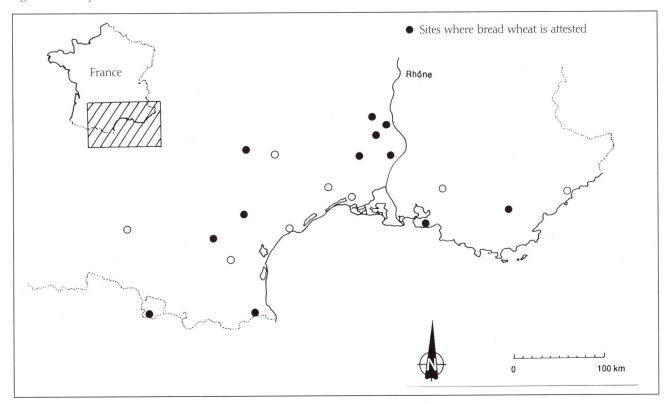

Figure 17.3 Map of the distribution of palaeoseeds from the French Cardinal

(*T. aestivo-compactum*) and naked polystic barley (*H. vulgare* var. *nudum*); Spain exploited in addition hulled polystic barley (*H. vulgare*) as well as emmer and einkorn wheat (*T. monococcum*; Hopf, 1966; Buxo, 1985; figure 17.4). The Spanish finds are, however, slightly more recent (6000 BP at La Cova de l'Or).

• In the central part of the Mediterranean basin (Italy and Greece), agriculture seems to have focused on emmer (*T. dicoccum*) and einkorn (*T. monococcum*). Barleys (*H. vulgare* and *H. distichum*) would have occupied only a secondary position (Coppola and Costantini 1987; Follieri 1987; Renfrew 1979; Kroll 1981). This situation is like that in the Near and Middle East (van Zeist and Bakker-Heeres 1985; van Zeist 1980; figure 17.4).

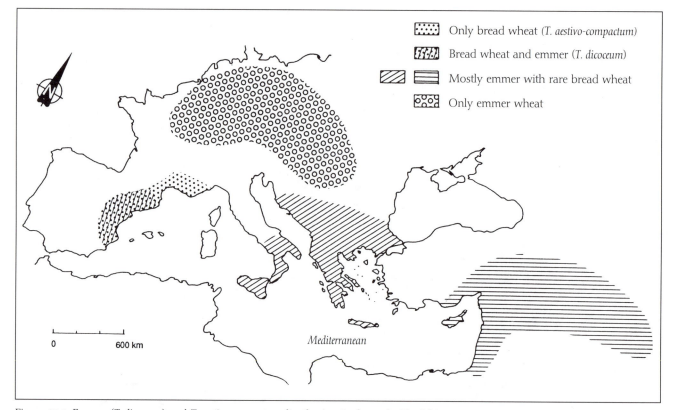

Figure 17.4 Emmer (*T. dicoccum*) and *T. aestivo-compactum* distribution in the early Neolithic

In the Near and Middle East, *T. compactum* is known as far back as 9000 BP, notably at Tell Aswad phase I (van Zeist and Bakker-Heeres 1985), and it would have developed during the sixth millennium only, while remaining in a secondary position of importance to emmer.

In Greece, naked wheat is found in few sites. It seems that it developed—while remaining secondary compared with emmer—no sooner than in proto- and pre-Sesklo levels (towards 6500 BP; Renfrew 1979; Hansen 1980; Kroll 1981).

In the Italian peninsula, *T. aestivo-compactum* is cited in phase I of Rendina, dating from 7100 BP (Follieri 1977; 1982) and also at Uzzo Cave, levels 7 and 8 (6850 BP; Costantini, 1981). It does not actually appear before 6500 BP (Coppola and Costantini 1987; Follieri 1987) and, moreover, it would have rarely been sown during the Early Neolithic (8150–7250 BP). It remained rare during the Middle Neolithic (7250–6250 BP).

In Yugoslavia, this wheat existed in the Starcevo culture (7300–6500 BP) but not abundantly, with emmer and einkorn far more common in this region.

At the biometric level,[3] the geographical bipartition of the Mediterranean Basin is also shown, although statistical investigations are limited by the fact that foreign carpologists do not give the standard deviations of the populations they measure. Indeed, French populations of naked barley (*H. vulgare* var. *nudum*) and of *T. aestivo-compactum* dating from 6000 BP or earlier resemble Spanish specimens (figures 17.5 and 17.6), or else fit completely into their scatter-diagram.

They seem to be more distant from the distribution of Italian as well as Near- and Middle-Eastern individuals (except for one Italian population). However, French data come from sites in Provence (La Font-aux-Pigeons, Châteauneuf-les-Martigues [Bouches-du-Rhône] and La Baume de Fontbrégoua, Salernes [Var]), relatively far from Spain.

The division of the Mediterranean on the basis of carpological results is surprising owing to the apparent predominance of *T. dicoccum* in Italy, Greece, and the Near and Middle East, whereas it seems to have been more recently cultivated in the French Mediterranean sphere. The preference for *T. aestivo-compactum* cultivation in southern France dates from the earliest phases of the Cardial (7500/7000–6500 BP), whereas it only appears in the Italian peninsula around 6500 BP only and seems to have been very rarely sown during the Italian Middle Neolithic. The biometric similarity of southern French wheats and barleys to Spanish populations are in contrast to their relative difference from Italian and Eastern ones.

Since the Cardial phenomenon has its origin in the impressed-ceramic Neolithic cultures that developed in southern Italy during the sixth millennium (Guilaine 1976; 1986), we might assume that the plant species cultivated in France were the same as the ones that were sown and harvested in this area. In fact, the agricultural economy between these two regions is based on different taxa. Moreover, the fact that the development of *T. aestivo-compactum* in the Near and Middle East is contemporaneous (sixth millennium BC) with

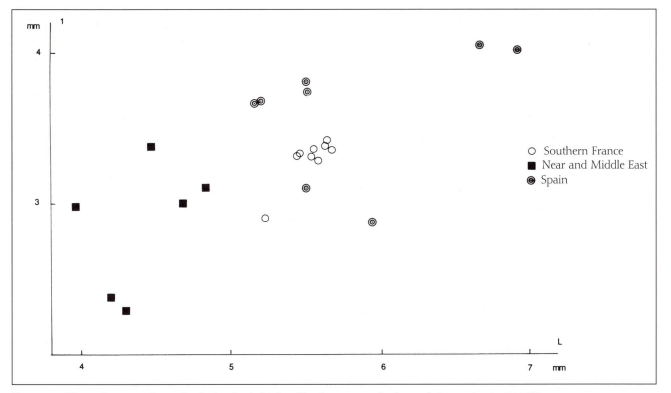

Figure 17.5 Biometric comparison of naked polystic barley (*H. vulgare* var. *nudum*) populations prior to 6000 BP

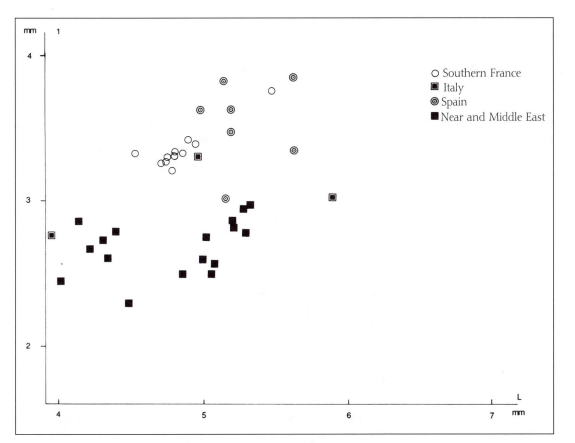

Figure 17.6 Biometric comparison of *T. aestivo-compactum* populations prior to 6000 BP

the emergence of agriculture in southern France (based on the cultivation of this same wheat, among others) is also unexpected. In view of the progression of early agriculture, we prefer to consider that this sort of wheat arrived in France much later. The biometric similarity between French and Iberian grain populations is surprising as well.

The following cultural, technical, and ecological disparities among these regions cannot completely justify such differentiation:

- These regional specificities (for example, ceramic and lithic styles) show the existence of some partitioning between regions from the earliest phases of the Neolithic (Guilaine 1985)

- Disparate agricultural techniques are attested from one country to another; however, they must have been relatively simple and flexible to adapt to the various cultural situations and the environmental conditions of each area (Guilaine 1985);

- Different ecological situations exist among all these regions, even though they belong to the Mediterranean ecological complex (except for the most continental areas of the Middle East). However, these differences are not obstacles to wheat cultivation; in fact, T. aestivo-compactum, T. dicoccum, and T. monococcum were all grown in these regions.

The Cardial developed in North Africa, which also shows constant exchange between Spain and the early coastal Neolithic of Morocco (Camps 1974; Guilaine 1976). However, the oldest dates of the Moroccan Cardial are controversial: end of the sixth millennium bc (Camps 1974) or middle of the fifth (Guilaine, 1976).

There also exists the Saharo-Sudanese Neolithic, which has pottery as early as the ninth millennium BC, and this in an environment appropriate for the appearance of agriculture (Robert-Chaleix 1985). G. Camps (1974) predicted this culture was a source of Neolithization, but it seems that no contact between the Saharo-Sudanese Neolithic and the coastal Cardial was established (Camps 1974).

Carpological data are dramatically lacking in North Africa. In Spain, they exist only in the levels from 6600 BP. This greatly restricts our research capabilities, but it does seem that the existence of cereal diffusion from North Africa cannot be excluded.

Our data do not allow either an assertion, or a conclusion, concerning these theories. It is clearly indicated that a program of carpological research should be undertaken on these issues in Spain and the Maghreb. New and perhaps surprising data from these geographical areas are liable to clarify the Neolithization process for southern France.

Acknowledgement. This chapter was translated from French by Jacqueline Gaudey, CRA, CNRS, France.

Notes

1. A problem of terminology and identification is raised for naked wheats. I opted for the term *Triticum aestivo-compactum* as a result of an argument developed in my thesis (1988), to describe caryopses of naked wheats, which have a rather small length in southern France (4.81 mm on an average) and are more or less round-shaped.

   F. Schiemann (1948), after studying the morphology of naked archaeological wheat grains (short and round), had proposed the term of *Triticum aestivo-compactum*, which combines under the same nomenclature *bread wheat* (*T. aestivum*) and *compact wheat* (*T. compactum*), both hexaploid, because analysis of burnt caryopses does not allow us to distinguish the two species. This term replaced the old name of *Triticum antiquorum* suggested by O. Heer (1885, in Jacomet and Schlichtherle, 1984).

   In the last few years, M. E. Kislev (1980b; 1984ab), notably, and W. van Zeist (1976, *in* van Zeist & Bakker-Heeres, 1985) have newly examined the specific attribution of these grains in the Near East and Mediterranean Basin.

   According to these authors, it is not possible to distinguish the three following species from burnt archaeological grains or even in recent material: macaroni wheat (*T. durum*), bread wheat (*T. aestivum*) and compact wheat (*T. compactum*); this is fully admitted by J. Erroux (1979) and D. Zohary (1973). W. van Zeist (van Zeist & Bakker-Heeres, 1985) even specifies that the rachis of modern or archaeological ears does not enable a specific identification either.

   G. C. Hillman (1978) and S. Jacomet & H. Schlichterle (1984) think that rachis and ears allow a differentiation of these species of wheat.

   It seems more logical to W. van Zeist (1976, in van Zeist & Bakker-Heeres, 1985), on the basis of ecological criteria, to link these caryopses of naked wheats to the species of tetraploid durum wheat (*T. durum*). Indeed, the latter is well-adapted to the Mediterranean climate (with moderate rainy winters and hot dry summers). Besides, it is the wheat most cultivated in the Mediterranean Basin. *T. aestivum* grows in slightly more northern and continental areas (Western Asia, temperate Central Europe, and Western Europe). This is why he proposes the term of *Triticum aestivo-durum*, even if it merges a hexaploid wheat (*T. aestivum*) and a tetraploid wheat (*T. durum*), a solution which may be surprising, but presents the advantage of clearly showing the difficulty in diagnosis.

   I believe that, *T. aestivum* results from a hybridation of *T. dicoccum* and/or *T. durum* with *Aegilops squarrosa*, hence it would be later than *T. durum*. M. E. Kislev (1980b; 1984ab) thinks that, on certain sites in the Middle East and the Balkans, archaeological naked wheat grains should be attributed to *T. parvicoccum*, which he determined from carbonized remains (caryopses and ears).

   T. parvicoccum is thought to be a tetraploid wheat. (Thirteen features bring it closer to tetraploid wheats, among them rachis and glumes.) Six features bring it closer to an hexaploid wheat, notably its distribution over the Mediterranean Basin and the Middle East. *T. dicoccum* as would have been its direct ancestor.

   It produces grains shorter than 5 mm. The average caryopses vary between 3.6 and 4.9 mm (hence being quite comparable to French samples).

   According to J. Erroux (1979, pers. com., in Buxo 1985), the morphological features of French carbonized naked grains do not correspond to *T. durum*, but rather to *T. compactum*. This is why he prefers to include them in *Triticum aestivo-compactum*, proposed by E. Schiemann (1948). J. Erroux considers (1979) that the phylogeny of tetraploid wheats (for example, *T. durum* and *T. turgidum*) remains to be determined. Are they mutations or hybridations of certain types of *T. dicoccum*? In J. Boyledieu's opinion [1980; pers. com.], *T. durum* is typically Mediterranean (in fact North-African), and its cultivation extended to France only in 1955 (from 1962 in the Northern Loire).

S. Jacomet & H. Schlichtherle (1984), having reexamined the wheats found in Swiss lake dwellings in the nineteenth century (in an ecological zone different from the Mediterranean area) and determined by O. Heer, have shown, from analyses of ears, that there was a high percentage of tetraploid wheat (*T. turgidum* or *T. durum*).

According to M. Feldman & E. Sears (1981), who used cytogenetic studies of present-day populations, these wheats correspond to *T. aestivum*, whose origin would be clearly established. This species would arise from a natural hybridation between a *T. turgidum* (no doubt the cultivated variety: *T. turgidum dicoccum* = *T. dicoccum* in our terminology) and a wild species, *T. tauschii* (= *Aegilops tauschii* = *Aegilops squarrosa*). Spontaneous hybridation would have occurred in fields in western Iran, when cultivated emmer (*T. dicoccum*) was introduced into areas where wild grass (*Aegilops squarrosa*) was growing.

Therefore, the debate concerning these naked wheats remains open. In this complex situation, I prefer to stand by the term *Triticum aestivo-compactum*.

2. As the size of plant individuals not only results from external factors (for example, edaphic and hygrometric) but also is expressed according to a genetic determinism, biometry can be a criterion for population characterization. Besides, morphological and biometric studies (foundations of comparative anatomy) are the basis for taxon identification and species determination, when grains are fossilized—in this case, burnt—for the majority of carporemains. We must assess the degree of statistical reliability of such criteria. This is characteristic of any archaeological object, which is, by definition, submitted to taphonomic distortions .

Chapter 18 ✒

Problems and Methods for Exploring the Beginnings of Agriculture

The Archaeologist's View

Jacques Cauvin

AT THE ROUNDTABLE CONFERENCE ON NEW methodological approaches to prehistoric agriculture held at Jalès, I was asked by the organizer to evaluate this confrontation of disciplines and to consider how it contributes, through different channels, to elucidating the problems raised by excavations. Increasing recourse to natural and physicochemical sciences is an essential advance in the study of prehistory today.

The central problem concerned the origin of agriculture in the Near East and in Europe—that is, plant domestication in these two geographical areas. Those studying archaeobotany (macroremains and pollen), pedology, experimental archaeology, and microwear (functional) analysis of tools were requested to evaluate potential and progress in this field. Researchers in ethnology, another discipline now very much in demand by archaeologists, were also asked to give us the benefit of their inquiries and models.

Discussion was mainly about methods and between specialists. Given the questions addressed, the exchange of information between specialists was important, since each area has become essential to us. It now falls to me, an archaeologist and anthropologist, to try and evaluate some of their results. My excavations in the Near East have led me to study the Neolithic revolution in its earliest phase; therefore, I would like to make a few comments on the question of the Near Eastern origin of agriculture.

First, it is useful to recall that the emergence of agriculture is but one aspect, however important, of Neolithization. By the time this change occurred, about 11,000 years ago, humans already had two million years of experience hunting and gathering, during which any agricultural behavior was absent.

What would change first would be humans themselves, and plants would follow. Before exploiting their environment, and plants in particular, differently, humans need to perceive their environment, and themselves, differently.

It is therefore not surprising to find—on the verge of the first agricultural experiments—sociocultural changes modifying the human environment. In the Levant, these changes include the development of sedentism, which occurred among hunter-gatherers at the end of the Pleistocene. It began in a subdued manner from 15,000 BP, as far back as the Kebaran, then the geometric Kebaran, until it was achieved in the Natufian, between 12,000 and 10,200 BP.

Such grouping into villages was above all a sociological phenomenon because at the economic level, Natufian villagers were still traditional hunter-gatherers who had settled in environments that were sufficiently rich and varied as not to require their movement for food procurement. Here we regret an error of perspective, for which we archaeologists are primarily responsible, owing to observation of a few glossy blades and mortars, and a few pits (at Mallaha) supposed to have served as silos, and the fact that the Natufian sites excavated, otherwise very rare, first seemed to all be found in the so-called nuclear area of wild cereals. We concluded too rapidly, in the absence of any botanical studies, that they were specialized gatherers of cereals who were somehow preparing, through this choice, the future cultivation of these plants. At present, there exist a few botanical studies that do not seem to indicate this. The late Natufian people of Abu Hureyra did gather wild einkorn intensively, but not far from there, in the final Natufian of Mureybet, where macroremains of cereals are rare, it is polygonum and astragalus that were gathered in huge quantities. Van Zeist thought that such differences reflected merely some dissimilarities in the immediate environment of human settlements (van Zeist and Bakker-Heeres 1984). The Natufians of Hayonim Cave mainly gathered lupine, even though there was also some barley available. At Abu Hureyra at the very end of the Natufian occupation, we now know (Moore and Hillman 1992) that cereal exploitation greatly diminished as that of small pulses increased. This change occurred because the aridity brought about by the late Dryas modified the natural landscape. The difference between Mureybet and Abu Hureyra is therefore chronological (hence climatic), with Mureybet being more recent than Abu Hureyra. It is not suprising therefore that the study of microtraces on tools reflects this difference: Anderson (1983) found, for example, for the rare glossy blades of Mureybet a use completely other than harvesting of cereals, whereas Unger-Hamilton (chapter 13) thinks that an intensive gloss on the Natufian sickles of some older Palestinian sites is attributable to cereal harvest. It is advisable to refuse to ascribe any general significance to these specific observations.

Indeed, most of the Natufian diet appears to have reflected, in a rather passive manner, as is the general case for prehistoric hunter-gatherers, the full spectrum of edible species present in the neighboring environment. Apparent specializations express ecological peculiarities rather than cultural choices. Therefore, we should utilize with caution the ethnological models concerning traditional specialized gatherers, to whom Natufian people have sometimes been compared. The gatherers described by Harlan (chapter 1) are truly specialized; for them, a particular plant species is the object of a selective search, "a gourmet choice," according to Harlan, not at all imposed by the environment and, moreover, accompanied by a marketing system of fairly modern inspiration. The model therefore remains valid, but for types of societies more advanced than the Natufian.

On the other hand, the Natufian passivity, which may have resulted in occasional pseudospecializations, should cause us to reconsider analogous cases outside the Near East, where, under sociocultural conditions that do not appear suitable and in the absence of convincing morphological arguments, cultivation of a species has been proposed, based upon its mere quantitative prevalence among plant remains. Such inferences are at the heart of the debate now opposing, in the Mediterranean area, the diffusionists of Neolithization and the supporters of indigenous agricultural practices supposed to predate Near Eastern influence. We must therefore attach much importance to Hansen's current conclusions (chapter 15) concerning the Greek site of Franchti, where the marked abundance of wild lentil in Mesolithic levels seems to be now unrelated to that of domestic lentil (Lens culinaris), which arrived on the site from the Near East

in the Neolithic, together with cereals: we know how often the example of Franchti was cited in support of a Mesolithic protoagriculture in the Mediterranean area.

Indeed, we cannot invent agriculture in any sociological and cultural context. The archaeologist regrets that the archaeobotanist sometimes relates its emergence to only favorable ecological factors, although such factors are necessary. When we speak about plant exploitation, we have to define what "exploitation" means. Any human predatory group, even in the Paleolithic, just as any herbivore, subsisted on the edible plant species available in the environment and therefore exploited them. The meaning of an agricultural "exploitation" is quite different: it concerns certain species only, chosen by humans to be artificially reproduced, whatever the quantity of wild forms that may have already existed in the environment. The change in human attitude was the true revolution, because it gave humans for the first time great initiative in choice of diet, given that they "produced" it. Whereas the selection of characters which led at the morphological level to the emergence of new species considered to be domestic was essentially unconscious, the cultivation of plants could be nothing other than a conscious decision. When searching for the causes of agriculture, the anthropologist will mainly search for the causes of this new behavior.

This behavior, whether or not it had immediate morphological consequences entailing the emergence of domestic species, is the issue here. The possibility, suggested by Hillman (chapter 10), of a nondomestic agriculture emphasizes the importance of experimental data able to confirm this hypothesis (chapter 11) and of a field approach that is more archaeological than strictly archaeobotanical, meant to detect what Zohary (chapter 6) calls the "circumstantial evidence" in the technical and cultural context.

Recent research in the Levant has shown the gradual evolution of the sociotechnical environment that made agricultural activity possible. The first change was the development of sedentism and villages, where the descendants of Natufian people would invent agriculture. The second was the transformation of the psyche itself, expressed in the Khiamian culture just before 10,000 BP, in the Jordan Valley as well as in the middle Euphrates region, by a "revolution of symbols." I have attempted (1987) to emphasize the historically dynamic nature of this as well as its repercussion on humanity's past conceptions of nature and itself and perhaps, consequently, on strategies of exploitation. The third change, between 10,000 and 9500 BP, at the time of the very first experiments in agriculture, enables us to define the economic context of these experiments, the context of ongoing predation. The example of Mureybet shows the end of the eclectic nature of the Natufian and Khiamian, with their "large spectrum" economy (Flannery). Certain abundant resources, heavily exploited previously (for example, fish, small herbivores, and various plants) appear to have been neglected in favor of others (including cereals), which were specially chosen by the village group for extra technical investment devised with this end in view. The first agricultural practice appeared at this stage only as a special case of this intelligent selection, where the species chosen cannot be dissasociated from the techniques devised to exploit it as a basic resource.

This is no doubt why we have not yet found any first agricultural village, dating between 10,000 and 9500 BP, within the nuclear area of wild cereals, but rather only in the western part, the Levant, between the Dead Sea and the Eastern Taurus. We find these villages where cultures derive from the Natufian (Sultanian, Aswadian, and Mureybetian: see *Colloque Préhistoire du Levant II*), with their necessary mental and technical mutations.

Finally, I consider particularly positive and hopeful that these few cultural observations that I have attempted to describe are in fact fairly convergent with the new hypotheses expressed by the archaeobotanists themselves at this conference, derived from approaches peculiar to their discipline. Zohary's belief that, mainly for genetic reasons, eight plants were domesticated both during a limited time period and in a limited geographic area, despite the present-day location of their wild progenitors, ties in well with what I am proposing.

On the other hand, Zohary is thus led to consider as cultivated some plants whose domestication is not yet shown by any physical change, by referring to determinant "circumstantial evidence" (for example, the absence, for climatic reasons, of wild chickpeas in Jericho). While he draws such "circumstances" from the ecological context, the archaeologist only wishes that the cultural context be included as well. A problem such as the one we are treating here is an ideal area for close intellectual exchange between the natural scientist and the anthropologist.

Chapter 19 ❧

Cycles of Agricultural Economy as Seen from Experimental and Use-wear Analyses of Tools

Galina F. Korobkova

IT IS VERY IMPORTANT TO RECONSTRUCT THE characteristics of economy and production in early societies, especially in societies where, within a hunter-gatherer economy, elements of a new economic pattern begin to emerge. This is apparent from discussions of the Epi-Paleolithic sites of the Natufian culture and the economic origin of their inhabitants (for example, Garrod 1957; Hillman 1975; Moore 1989; 1991; Korobkova 1994; chapter 12). However, it is very difficult to determine these factors, particularly on sites where no plant remains are found. In that case, tool assemblage, which preserves characteristic use-wear traces, plays a decisive role in identification of the economic pattern. Micro traces are relatively reliable criteria for this identification, because they allow use of tool function as a basis.

Naturally, relevant criteria include the different plant residues present in the cultural layer as well as on the tools themselves. For their study, chemical, archeobotanical, pollen, and phyto-use-wear analyses must be carried out. The problem of agriculture should be tackled from different angles: nature of soils, range of cultivated plants, irrigation, and tool assemblage. In Russia, to reconstruct the economy of past societies a wide range of methods was used: pollen analysis, paleobotany, paleogeography, pedology, charcoal analysis, aerial photography, micro and macro use-wear analysis, experiments, and micrometric study. In the absence of plant remains, the results of the analyses verified by experimental and ethnographic data play a major role.

I have studied the late Paleolithic, Mesolithic, and Neolithic material from three regions in southern ex-USSR: Central Asia, the Caucasus, and the northwestern Black Sea area

(1987). The essential equipment used for the study was a stereoscope giving 10 to 85 times magnification. Where traces were indistinct, a metallographic microscope MIM-6, which magnifies up to 400 times, was used, with a FMN-2 camera to record traces up to 200 times magnification.

To differentiate agricultural tools, I relied on detailed study of use-wear traces from many experiments, whose study revealed the rules governing trace formation (Korobkova 1978; 1981; 1993). Experiments with harvesting implements were carried out over more than 12,000 m² and repeated every year. Study of digging tools was performed on various soils, the total area of plots exceeding 3000 m². On stone querns, nearly 100 kg of grains, acorns, roots, and plants were crushed. Wild and domestic wheat, other cereals (oat, barley, rye), pulses, grasses, reeds, and nettle, among others, were harvested. Primitive varieties of wheat were especially studied: einkorn, emmer, compact wheat, and spelt were cultivated on a plot in the botanical garden of the Moldavian Academia of Sciences by the paleobotanist Z. V. Yanushevich. To compare the efficiency of the various types of harvesting tools found on early agricultural sites in ex-USSR, we tested nearly a hundred harvesting knives and sickles (now more than 650), including a modern sickle with a metallic blade.

These large-scale experiments allowed us to better understand the microwear traces on tilling or harvesting implements and to correlate them with tool function. The topography of microwear, its texture, removal scars, polish, and combination of these factors exhibits differing characteristics. "Standard" micro-use-wear was defined according to whether the tools were used for cutting wild or cultivated cereals, grasses, or reeds or for crushing grain, acorns, roots, coloring materials, or metal. The tools (more than 6000 specimens) are stored in the Laboratory of Experimental Use-wear Analysis of the Saint Petersburg Institute of Archaeology.

Central Asia

The material submitted to use-wear analysis was found in sites from the Upper Paleolithic: Samarkand (Korobkova 1972A) and Tutkaul village level 3 (Ranov and Korobkova 1971); the Mesolithic: Tashkumyr and Obishir caves 1,5 (Obishir culture), Kushilish (Islamov 1980), and Tutkaul level 2a; and the Early Neolithic: all sites of the Djeitun culture, Kavat village 7, 32 sites of the Kel'teminar culture in Greater and Lesser Tuzkan (Korobkova 1969; 1987), Charylli 25 (Korobkova and Yusupov 1977), levels 2 and 1 of Tutkaul, of the Hissar culture (end of the seventh to fifth millenia) (Ranov and Korobkova 1971; Korobkova 1996b); and many other sites.

Djeitun culture (end of the 7th-6th millennia BC)

Use-wear analysis has demonstrated the agricultural nature of the Djeitun culture, to which concerns 25 to 40% of the tool assemblage belongs (Korobkova 1969; 1996a). In most cases, it includes harvesting knives, fitted with two or three elements, generally made of flint prismatic blades. Micro- and macro-use-wear traces as well as the texture of striae testify that all tools were used for harvesting cultivated cereals; indeed, the mirror-polish, equally distributed on both working surfaces, and slight "comet"-shaped striae (oriented, like the polish, parallel to the edge) are typical; these striae are often close to one another and sometimes overlapping (Korobkova 1987:Fig. 5,3-5; 1994, table 1:1,2). The edge damage is microscopic, deep, steep, regular and irregular, most often unilateral with single edge damage scars on the opposite side. The edges of microscars are levelled. The nature of the use-retouch depends on cereal ripeness, stem thickness, angle of edge sharpening, and duration of use. The working edge is rounded in the transversal plane. It can be smooth, uninterrupted (when the sharpening angle is large) and slightly denticulated. Other agricultural tools include the stone rings which may have been weights for digging sticks, as well as various sorts of querns, handstones, mortars, and pestles.

The material excavated was related to three types of agricultural activities: soil working, harvesting, and grain-grinding.

The villages of the Djeitun culture are located near alluvial cones (in which sands accumulate rapidly) or in middle river valley areas (Lisitsyna 1978:40). According to G. N. Lisitsyna, soils were fertilized by flood waters once a year, which is a primitive method of irrigation (Lisitsyna and Kostiouchenko, 1973). Research by D. Harris and S. Limbri showed that flood

water irrigation was not reliable and that Djeitunian fields were preferentially located on plots with a high level of groundwater (1992:11). The surrounding lands were fertile and easy to work. Ethnographic data (Bukinich 1924:110) indicates that flooded fields were not even tilled but that wheat was sown on their surfaces when still wet. Loess belonging to former oases had low salinity and high "humidification" (Minashina 1974). Pointed sticks may have been used to prepare the soil, suggested by large stone rings with a strongly worn hafting hole, which were probably used as weights. They were discovered in villages from the second phase of the Djeitun culture, Mondzhukli tepe, and Gadymi tepe. Sowing took place on flat plots in the areas flooded by rivers and brooks. Near the village of Djeitun, we discovered a level with traces of artificial irrigation (Lisitsyna 1978:206).

Thus, in the sixth millennium, there existed an "oasis" type of agriculture which was irregularly irrigated. The archaeological record shows that Djeitun inhabitants cultivated two varieties of wheat (bread and compact) and also two-row barley. The first is of Near-Eastern origin; the other two could be endemic (Vavilov 1960:42; Sinskaia 1969:18). After experimentation, bread wheat showed strength, resistance, and "defensive" capacity against birds. Research in 1989-1991 showed that the main crops were einkorn wheat and naked or hulled barley. According to G. Hillman's observations, Djeitun inhabitants practiced double harvesting: they first cut the ears, then the stems (Charles and Hillman 1992:86). Harvesters used harvesting knives fitted with prismatic flint blades with smooth, unretouched edges. Tools from the second and third phases of the Djeitun culture had a thinly denticulated edge, which highly increased their harvest productivity, from 0.4 to 0.9-1.1 m² per minute (Korobkova 1987:219,figure 54). Harvesting implements are regularly distributed among the different houses and seem to have constituted the main tool kit of each family.

No threshing implements were found. Flails may have been used to thresh sheaves in small adjoining courtyards, then grain was wind-winnowed, dried, and roasted to facilitate its treatment and preservation. Each dwelling contained a large hearth of clay blocks with an area of burnt clay encircled by a rim in front where grain was dried and roasted. Grain was hulled with wooden pestles and mortars, according to experimental observation.

Winnowed grain was stored in large pits with clay-covered walls; several were found in houses at Djeitun (Masson 1971:167,Pl.3). There were also a few storage structures for grain: in level 2, seven were found near different houses (Masson 1971:14, Fig. 5). A particularly large one may have been shared by all the villagers, according to V. M. Masson.

For utilization as food, grain was partly ground on querns with stone pestles. These implements have retained characteristic use-wear traces. The working surface is glossy, edges of circular depression are worn, and the polish appears only on the working surface. Concentric, discontinuous striae traces with a slight rim were observed which show the pestle's working motion. The working area is worn mainly in the center and therefore has a concave profile. Striae are the most marked in this area and grow dimmer, in the same way as the polish, in the peripheral area. Experiments on stone querns indicate the work was laborious; crushing 500 g of grain, for instance, requires some 10 hours of uninterrupted labor. This fact, and a particular method of processing, may explain why the early and middle phases of the Djeitun culture have yielded only a few querns, whereas the recent phase, Chagilly tepe, yielded several dozen. Indications are that coarse grain cooked into a liquid paste (kasha) was used as basic foodstuff. Small high-edged bowls were heated from inside by red-hot stones, as indicated by the stones, split by heating, found near each hearth.

Judging from paleogeographical and demographic estimates, the land area cultivated by Djeitun inhabitants could have been as much as 15 to 20 ha (Lisitsyna 1978:206). Similar results were deduced from experiments (Korobkova 1974; 1980). These paleo-economic estimates were based on the complete excavation of level 2 in Djeitun; the use-wear analysis of all the material, including waste products (6000 items for Djeitun); and classification of harvesting tools and determination of their degree of use-wear, using quantitative parameters produced by the data bank concerning the number of plots worked during a unit time and by the life threshold indicated by the implements studied:

$$S_1 xt = S_2 \quad S_2 xM = S_3$$

where S_1 is the mean surface of the plot worked with a sickle in 1 hour; t is the time of the sickle's extreme wear; S_2 is the surface worked by 1 sickle during its life without edge rectification; M is the quantity of sickles in the village; and S_3 is the total surface of the harvested plots. Consequently, agriculture in the Djeitun Neolithic culture appears to have been fully developed, and its origin should be sought in earlier Epi-Paleolithic levels, even if they have not yet been discovered in Central Asia.

Hissar culture (end of the 7th–5th millennia BC)

The early Neolithic culture of Hissar in the mountains of Tadzhikistan (Ranov and Korobkova 1971; Korobkova 1996b) shows another form of economy. This culture is represented by two types of sites: temporary camps, with a scattered cultural layer, and long-term villages, with thick cultural layers (for example, the two upper layers of Tutkaul and Saï-Saïed), with stone floors and hearths, with isolated burials lacking special monuments and grave goods. The villages are situated around large piedmont cones at the outlet of lateral gorges 20 to 50 m high, particularly suited to the breeding of small cattle. They occupy areas from 0.4 to 0.5 ha (Saï-Saïed and Kouï-Boulien) to 1 ha (Tutkaul and Ak-Tangui). We also found small temporary camps, below 0.01 ha (for exapmle, Koum-tepe and Koktcha), which, in my opinion, are litovki (centers) used during small-cattle displacements (1996b:111).

The question of the subsistence base is controversial. Some researchers (A. P. Okladnikov 1958) proposed that Hissar tribes practiced agriculture and breeding. Others (V. M. Masson 1966; 1970) considered them to be nomadic hunter-gatherers. I analyzed the materials from the two upper (Hissar) layers of Tutkaul (over 50,000 objects) under the microscope and concluded that Hissar economy was multiple: it consisted basically of breeding and incidentally of hunting; there were also complex patterns of wild grass gathering (1987:117). This is indicated by the variety of tools, the saturation and thickness of cultural layers, the favorable ecological environment, the presence (Tutkaul and Saï-Saïed) of bones from domestic animals in the fauna, and the absence of hunting weapons.

Inserts from harvesting knives are rare in the tool assemblage, and they bear traces from use on grass. On these blades, as on all harvesting tools, there is gloss-type polish, particularly on surfaces adjacent to the cutting edges. As opposed to sickles used to cut cultivated cereals, the polish here is more pronounced and even. All roughness on the microrelief is smoothed. The polish sometimes takes on a linear direction; fine striae are either missing or found only on corners of inserts in contact with the ground or sparsely distributed along the working edge (Korobkova 1987:43, Fig. 5,6; 1994:170,171, Table 1:6; Table 2:1,2).

When wild grasses are cut at a "green" stage, thin scratches may either be missing (in this case, the polish takes a linear direction) or observed on the edge's cutting area on both sides. Striations are more characteristic of tools used for half-ripe or ripe wild grasses. However, contrary to sickles for cultivated grasses, the working surface of these tools has no comet-shaped traces, and the length of scratches is only 1 to 2 mm (Korobkova 1994, Table 1:3-5). The existence of a diversified plant gathering strategy is confirmed by the data from palynologic and paleogeographic analyses.

The low-grass region of Tadjikistan is part of the natural distribution area of aegilops and wild barley, which may have been cut using the inserts of harvesting knives we found. Two stone hoes found at the base of the second level of Tutkaul (Korobkova and Ranov 1971) may be considered earth digging tools, used for constructing underground huts in this same level. Here there was no transition towards agriculture in progress.

Kel'teminar culture (end of the 6th–4th millennia BC)

The north of central Asia abounds in sites belonging to the Kel'teminar cultural community (Vinogradov 1981) from the end of the sixth to fourth century, which are found grouped in present-day Uzbekistan and Northern Turkmenistan. These sites had predatory forms of economy. The assemblage of tools, the paleoethnobotanical, pollen, paleozoological, and palaeoecological data testify to the prime role of hunting and fishing in the economy of Kel'teminar tribes, who had various weapons: hafted spears and javelins, bow and arrows. *Touga* and bush in the former delta areas where the sites are located, combined with steppe and desert landscapes, represented rich hunting territories. They hunted Bukhara deer, wild boar, *djeïran,* and *kulan* (proto-horse).

The main economic sector was fishing, a stabilizing factor for the culturo-economic type of sedentary fisher-hunters. Certain dune sites in the Zeravshan plain have produced a few harvesting knife blades with a denticulated edge which, according to trace analysis (Korobkova 1969; 1996b:107), were used to harvest cultivated grasses, a use which shows influence from the Djeitun Neolithic culture. They are completed by querns, pestles, and weights for digging sticks. In addition, two bone hafts for harvesting knives bearing traces characteristic of use-wear were found on the site of Tolstov (Vinogradov 1981) and in the early Neolithic level of Machai Cave in Uzbekistan (Islamov 1975). Almost no other data show agricultural practice. All this suggests the appearance, in several sites of the Kel'teminar culture, of an agriculture under the influence of neighboring Djeitun tribes from the late period of this culture.

Thus, in the main areas of distribution of the Kel'teminar culture, hunting-gathering prevailed and varied according to the different forms of economic activity. At the same time, traditional economy underwent a change, and elements of a production economy were forming, under the influence of neighboring tribes.

In summary, during the sixth century in Central Asia, three historico-cultural communities were developing: to the south, the Djeitun and Hissar communities; to the north, the Kel'teminar. They had diverse technical traditions and economic bases as well as a varied assemblage of tools and related objects.

Djeitun culture is distinctive in its agro-pastoral economy. The Hissar retained old forms of pastoral economy, despite the appearance of husbandry. Being confined in the mountains, they were not able to open in to the vast steppic areas which would have facilitated the development of herding. Goat (preferentially) and sheep breeding developed slowly in the Hissar culture and remained far behind the agro-pastoral cultures of Western Central Asia. The tribes of the Kel'teminar culture had a much different economic base: specialized hunting-fishing.

It appears that the balance and stability provided by these economies guaranteed a minimal subsistence and precluded adopting new methods of game procurement or food production. Only close neighboring and cultural relationships with Djeitun caused the Lower Zeravshan peoples to adopt agriculture. This is attested by the similarity of their harvesting instruments and earth digging tools. The Lower Zeravshan was receptive to innovation and drawn into the spreading sphere of the agricultural cultures of Central Asia.

Thus, in Neolithic Central Asia, we see concretely the heterogeneity of the culturo-historic and paleoeconomic process after the transition of several tribes to a production economy: when one group (Djeitun) experienced a boon in material culture, the other (Hissar) remained at an archaic level of development, and the third (Kel'teminar) evolved slowly towards food production at the end of the sixth century in the Lower Zeravshan, only at the end of its development in other regions.

Based on these data in Central Asia, we do not know of any site showing transition toward a production economy. Mesolithic level IV in DamDam-Cheshme 2 (Markov 1966) on the Eastern shore of the Caspian Sea may have potential, as it has remains of domestic goat. We have no information about the first steps of true agriculture, becausethe available materials bear witness only to a fully developed agricultural economy and its evolution.

Caucasus

Centres of origin of production economy have their peculiarities, determined above all by physiogeographical conditions, the presence of wild ancestors of domestic plants and animals, the level of tool development, and the technology of production. The complex study of the Caucasus is only just beginning, therefore complete data on early levels are not yet available. On the contrary, archeobotanical as well as use-wear and experimental data are quite circumstantial for this region.

The Caucasus is distinctive in the variety of its natural contexts, economic complexes, and tool assemblages. It contains a large genetic range of cultivated plants, closely related to local climate, hydrology, soils, plants, and geological structure (Lisitsyna and Prishchepenko 1977:13). The species cultivated between the sixth and second millennia include bread wheat, hard wheat, compact wheat, einkorn, emmer, spelt, English wheat, and Persian round wheat. Endemic plants were similarly grown: *Macha* wheat, *Zanduri* wheat and others. We can add barley (two- or several-row, hulled or not), millet, oat, legumes, and flax. The cultivation of fruit trees developed extensively; Transcaucasia is an area of wild vine diffusion and domestication (Lisitsyna and Prishchepenko, 1977:19).

Thus, because of its botanical antecedents, the Caucasus appears to be one of the autonomous centers of origin and development of various cultivated species.

The variety of the paleoecological situation is reflected in the formation of different cultures, and their specificity and ways of development. The most surprising is that the variability within this region is maintained during all stages in the historic process.

Settlement in the Caucasus was irregular, much dependent on the landscape/climate changes that occurred as a result of the Caspian Sea transgressions. Following the Novocaspian transgression some nine thousand years ago (Leontev and Rychagov 1982), many Caucasian areas were occupied: the Black Sea and Caspian shoreline (western Georgia and southeastern Azerbaijan), the mountain areas of Dagestan and the valley plains of the central and southern Caucasus. Therefore, in various ecological zones, sites and villages of Neolithic hunter-gatherers existed simultaneously with farmer-breeders.

The complexes that first adopted an agro-pastoral economy are represented by westtranscaucasian sites (Anaseuli 1 and Darkvetski caves (layer IV); (Nebieridze 1972; 1978), Kholodny Cave (layer B-1), and the east Transcaucasian multilevel site of Chokh (Amirkhanov 1982; 1985).

Chokh culture, in Daghestan (end of the 7th–beginning of the 6th millennia)

The Chokh culture, spaning the period from the Late Mesolithic to the Early Neolithic, was first defined by Kh. A. Amirkhanov based on the type-site Chokh (1982; 1985; 1987) and the open-air single-level site of Kozimanokho (Kotovitch 1964). According to sporopollen diagrams, the lower part of Chokh can be correlated with the Tardikhvalyn regression of the Caspian Sea (10,000 to 9000) and the upper part with the Novocaspian transgression (8000). C14 dates are for the end of the seventh to the beginning of the sixth millennia BC.

Chokh is located in a horseshoe gorge, 1600 to 1800 m above sea level. It is on a small sunlit terrace protected from cold winds. Its propitious location includes the proximity of a river.

It contains the earliest permanent houses in the Caucasus, each with a corridor-like entrance and hearth in the center, fitted with unknapped blocks of limestone. They are half-circular, and adjacent to the bed-rock on one side. The surface of one house (No. 2) is 60 m². The 800 km² village covers an area of about. According to ethnographers, this type of small mountain village is traditional in the Caucasus (Islammagomedov 1967:113).

The most abundant artifacts are lithic, generally made of black and light-gray flint. Schist and limestone were more rarely used. In the tool assemblage, microbladelets prevail (27%). Inserts of harvesting knives have been identified in schist, bone, and apparently wood hafts. The schist haft was discovered in Chokh and is unique in the Caucasus. We can find analogs in the materials from Sialka 1 (Ghirshman 1939).

Chokh evidences an early form of agriculture. Through flotation, we identified einkorn and emmer, bread wheat, compact wheat, naked and hulled barley, millet, a few wild grasses, and vine. There are also fragments of querns and handstones, bone hafts from harvesting knives, and their blades which, according to use-wear analysis, were used to cut domestic cereals. Apart from wild varieties of cereals (wheat, barley, and millet), which can be considered weeds, we find transitional forms to cultivated varieties. The findings from the early agricultural complex of Chokh testify to origins in the Mesolithic. Fauna includes wild and domestic cow, sheep, and perhaps goat.

Data from the study of Chokh and the Chokh culture in general testify to a transition toward agriculture and herding. So far, this is the only trace of an initial phase of agricultural economy in the Caucasus, but there is no data for the origin of agriculture. We need to seek such data in earlier Mesolithic complexes. The Caucasus, according to many researchers, is one of the centers of domestication of many cultivated plants (Vavilov 1960; 1965; Yukovski 1971). I. I. Vavilov's long and fertile research allowed him to deduce that "due to varied forms of cultivated and wild wheats, the Caucasus is the world leader, even before Anatolia" (1957:116). *Hordeum spontaneum C. Covh* (Bakhteev 1966:19) was found at Chokh along with its domesticated form (Lisitsyna 1984). Domestic rye, found by G. N. Lisitsyna at Arukhlo 1 and 2, suggests initial domestication of this cereal in Transcausia (Lisitsyna and Prishchepenko 1977:79).

West Transcaucasia (end of the 7th–6th millennia BC)

A similar phenomenon can be seen in west Transcaucasia, which contains several sites belonging to the preceramic Neolithic from the end of the seventh to the sixth millennia BC (Kushnareva 1986; Byanya 1996). This territory was intensively exploited during the transition from the Mesolithic to the Neolithic. People first settled on river terraces and hills, then on the hilly piedmont of west Transcaucasia. This zone is characterized by a subtropical climate, endemic forms of plants and animals, and, according to one researcher, cultivation techniques with common technological traditions and a well marked sequence (Nebieridze 1986). Sites which are transitional from the Late Mesolithic to the Early Neolithic show uninterrupted development.

The Neolithic of west Transcaucasia is represented by two groups of sites related to its different periods and cultures (Neberidze 1972). They are single-level open-air occupations. The first group is comprised of sites from the Aceramic Neolithic (for example, Anaseuli 1, Apiancha, and Darkvetski naves). The second includes Tardineolithic sites of the Odichi culture (for example, Anaseuli 2, Odichi, Kistrik, and Nijnyaya Chilovka). Some are found in the southeastern Black Sea area, and the others the northeastern area (Odichi culture).

Among the first, the most significant is Anaseuli 1, located in western Georgia (Nebieridze 1972; 1978; 1986). Tool production is mainly from imported obsidian (76%), more rarely using local flint and pebbles.

I identified inserts of harvesting knives through use-wear analysis. A high percentage of other agricultural tools derive from the local Epipalaeolithic. Perhaps subsequent study of Paleolithic and Mesolithic complexes will supply new data concerning the origin of agriculture in the Caucasus.

The first steps in the transition to food production are indicated by the multilayer site of Darkvetski caves (Nebieridze 1978). In layer IV (Aceramic Neolithic), remains of domestic animals, harvesting knives, stone hoes, querns, and pestles were found. We could raise the question of the emergence of agriculture except that the plant remains contain only wild millet. We assume that this was the first plant cultivated, even though it had not yet acquired the morphological features of domestic cereals. We also think this was the case for the Natufian culture of the Near East, for example at Kebara (layer B), Abu Hureyra, Nahal Oran, and Beidha, where we believe harvesting tools show traces from harvesting cultivated (wild) cereals, although plant remains show no morphological features of domestication (Korobkova 1994).

For tilling, early Neolithic peoples used bone, horn, or stone hoes. The first two types are characteristic of Chokh, the latter of Anaseuli I, and the rest of west Transcaucasia. Small stone hoes were inserted in horn hafts by means of a sharpened butt area. Experiments indicated these tools were effective for working the stony soils surrounding the village. Digging and softening of the soil as well as sowing were carried out using the same hoes. The humid climate, with heavy rainfall, was suitable for a nonirrigated agriculture. While Chokh yielded a wide range of cultivated species, this was hardly the case for western Georgian sites. However, economic differences existed among the different sites: cave inhabitants practiced animal husbandry, while village and camp inhabitants practiced agriculture.

Collecting was done using harvesting knives whose blades were made of obsidian or flint with no particular retouch. Use-wear traces on obsidian blades are different from those on flint blades (Korobkova 1987:43,Fig. 5,2). The edges of obsidian blades take on a matte appearance, while the edge of flint specimens is glossy. Parts formerly held in the haft are well marked, as they have traces of tar. The width of the working area varies according to the amount the blade protrudes from the haft, and its length is generally that of the blade (for harvesting knives). Microtraces in the form of unequally deep striae follow the tool's use-motion. In places, striae meet to form deep grooves. Macro-use-wear is insignificant; it lies mainly on one side and sometimes forms small denticulations.

Grain grinding was performed on small circular querns with one or two concave faces, with pestles made of porphyrito-diabasic rock. Grain was stored in pit silos close to houses.

To conclude, the materials from this group of sites show the existence in the Aceramic Neolithic of a complex mixed economy. Based on advanced hunting, sophisticated gathering of wild grasses (millet), and favorable ecological conditions, the beginnings of agriculture and animal (first, pig) husbandry appear to exist. The first is indicated by harvesting knives and hoes from Anaseuli 1, Darkvetski Cave, and Kholodny Cave (layer B-1), among others. At Apiantcha a harvesting knife inserted into a straight haft was found (Tsereteli 1978). Grain from wild millet was found in Kholodny Cave.

From tool use-wear analysis, we consider the materials from layer IV in Darkvetski Caves and Anaseuli 1 as indicative of the first stages of agriculture in Western Transcaucasia, based on the cultivation of endemic millet. The ecological environment allowed for dry farming.

Shomu tepe-Shulaveri culture (6th–4th millennia BC)

The central and southern parts of Transcaucasia were occupied by the sedentary, agro-pastoral culture of Shulaveri-Shomu tepe (Narimanov 1987; Dzhaparidze 1976; Kiguradze 1976). It is represented by compactly grouped open-air sites (2 to 5 villages in each group) in the Kura Valley, in the plain of Kvemo-Kartli as well as in intermountain and foothill valleys. The villages are either tells, mountains, or tepe between 2.5 and 8 m high, with several building levels. Their surface varies from 0.5 to 5 ha. They are linked, and separated from each other by 500 to 2200 m (Kushnareva 1993). The main sites are Shulaveri-gora and Shomu-tepe (earliest cultural complexes), Arukhlo 1 and Tsopi, among others (late). The blade industry has preserved unretouched inserts of sickles (10.5 to 13.5%). We find horn hoes and digging spades, bone awls, needles, smoothers, and spoons.

Apart from the agricultural assemblage of instruments, agriculture is evidenced by several artifacts and by the ecological situation.

The territory occupied by this culture was an open landscape covered with meadows and bushes (Golichaĭshvili 1979:65-67) containing sagebrush, Labiae species, and grasses. From the sedimentation rate, researchers have deduced use of dry farming. In river valleys, an alternate agricultural system was practiced using primitive irrigation, attested by remains of ditches at Arukhlo 1, Imiris-gora, and Chakh-tepe, interpreted as reservoirs for single-phase watering of sown plots (Chubinishvili and Chelidze 1978:60). The existence of artificial irrigation is also indicated by the data from buried soils near Arukhlo 1. By their composition, the latter are identical with modern irrigated soil (Mardaleshvili and Dzhanelidze 1984:91). According to G. N. Lisitsyna, irregular irrigation occurred during plant vegetation (Lisitsyna and Prishchepenko 1977:47).

In this culture, agriculture is at a more advanced stage (Narimanov 1966; Dzhaparidze and Dzhavakhishvili 1971). This is confirmed by the range of domestic species: eight varieties of wheat, several forms of barley, as well as millet, oat, rye, lentils, peas (Lisitsyna and Prishchepenko 1977:76); the existence of remains of an irrigation system near Arukhlo I, Imiris Gora, and Shomu tepe; and the diversification of tools.

Bread (naked) wheats are predominant, sown separately from hulled varieties (Bregadze 1988:13), which testifies to a high level of agricultural technology. The range of wild species suggests winter and spring sowing. Thus, at that time, sowing was done in two stages to protect cereals from dryness; to this was added vine, fruit, and melon cultivation. At Dangreuli-gora and Gadachrili-gora, we discovered melon seeds and sorrel remains. Agriculture was practiced over most of the Caucasian countryside.

The land was worked with bone and horn hoes. They were inserted in horn hafts and attached with straps (Korobkova 1979B). Weighted digging sticks were probably used as well as bone scoops for grain and small horn planting tools for gardening. Cereals were harvested with sickles (rarely harvesting knives) with obsidian or flint blade inserts (18 to 35% of the stone tool assemblage). There were two types of sickles, one with carefully set elements forming a continuous blade and the other with obliquely hafted flakes or blades (like Karanovo sickles). Certain sickles had hafts made from animal jaws. Experiments have shown that sickles were much more efficient than harvesting knives (from 0.9 to 1.1 m²/mn). Use-wear traces on obliquely-hafted blades were diagonal, forming an oblong triangle with mirror-polish and striae oriented in the same direction.

Grains were separated with *tribulums* (threshing sledges) in which obsidian or flint flakes and blades were inserted; these tribulums were pulled by animals. Such implements did not appear before the end of the Neolithic-Chalcolithic. They were revealed by use-wear analysis of inserts, on the sites of Garakepek tepe and Gjunesh tepe (Korobkova 1987:149-150). The use-wear traces resemble those on sickles in some ways, but the blade edges are quite different: massive and flattened, they have a *P*-shaped transverse section. The rims of the small flake scars due to use are leveled from abrasion. The polish is more abrasive, with a more worn surface, than on sickles. Reconstruction of the function of these items is shown by ethnographic data (wooden tribulu*m* with flint elements) and by the study of experimental standards. Grain was ground on stone querns, which were larger and more numerous than in early Neolithic sites.

The ecological situation in southern Transcaucasia, adjacent to the Araks Basin, is different. The sites were located in the steppe, with a dry, continental climate and little soil cover. Agriculture could develop only with the help of artificial irrigation, as indicated by the location of agricultural villages in the area of dried watercourses remaining from an ancient hydrosystem. The most significant sites are Khatunarkh and Tekhut, Alikemektepesi and Ilanly-tepe, Kiol-tepe 1. They are all dated from the sixth to the middle of fourth millennia

BC and form three autonomous culturochronological complexes. Khatunarkh and the lower layers of Kiul-tepe are earlier and contemporaneous with sites of the Shulaveri-Shomu culture. Agriculture was indicated by bone and horn hoes, composite sickles, and harvesting knives made from big obsidian blades, inserts from a threshing sledge, many querns, handstones, mortars, and pestles.

According to researchers (Kushnareva 1993:191), an alternate sowing system was practiced. Regular irrigation is indicated not only by analysis of buried soils but also by the composition of cereal crops that could be grown by artificial watering (soft bread wheat and six-row barley). At Tekhut, Kiol-tepe 1, and Khatunarkhe, one-blade sickles were fixed into a concave handle. In early stages, grain was probably threshed by beating cereals with sticks, as shown by the complete absence of specialized instruments. Later (in the fourth millennium BC), threshing was done using threshing sledges (for example, Garakepek-tepe).

To conclude, the sites in the Middle Kura Valley belonging to the Shulaveri-Shomu culture and the dry steppe areas of southern Transcausia from the sixth to the fifth millennia BC, represented by the lower-level type of Kiul-tepe 1 and the types of Alikemek-tepesi, Tekhuta, Khatunarkha, bear witness to advanced agricultural economy, first based on irregular irrigation of sown areas (Lisitsyna and Prishchepenko 1977:47) (for example, Shulaveris-gora and Shomu-tepe). This is indicated by remains of clay works (outside the built-in area), interpreted as water reservoirs (Dzhavakhishvili 1973:100).

Later (in the fifth millennium BC), there appeared traces of an initial irregular artificial irrigation of fields. Sedimentary alluvium found in a ditch results from the action of running waters, at Imiris-gora (Dzhavakhishvili 1973:40) and, well marked, at Arukhlo 1 (Kushnareva 1993:199). These last years, we discovered in the vicinity of Arukhlo 1 a complete irrigation system (Mardaleshvili and Dzhanelidze 1984).

The progress of agriculture is attested by the variety and composition of cultivated plants, the complex technology of their treatment, and double cropping as well as the high percentage and wide range of agricultural tools. Thus, remains from the Early and Late Caucasian Neolithic are clear proof that these regions, like Central Asia, are early centers of agricultural emergence and development.

Contrary to the Djeitun culture, where no initial stage of agriculture was established, Chokh and west Transcaucasian cultures contain all the features of a transition from food procurement to production. The Caucasus abounds in sites showing the development of agricultural economy, such as the villages of the Shulaveri-Shomu culture and, for instance, of the Kiol-tepe 1, Khatunarkha, Tekhuta, and Alikemek-tepesi cultures. The different paleoclimatic and landscape areas, and the technical level of societies and other conditions were reflected in agricultural techniques. They point to the use of dry agriculture (west Transcaucasian culture) and a transitional stage from dry irrigation to primitive artificial irrigation (for example, Shulaveris-gora and Shomu-tepe).

The differentiation of endemic domesticated cereal crops reflects the choice of plants in the economy of particular pre-agricultural cultures of the Caucasus. The passage to artificial irrigation of fields involved change in the agricultural assemblage of tools. The percentage of digging and harvesting instruments rose, the first threshing sledges appeared, and the variety of tools for grain processing increased. These tendencies, despite the presence of techno-morphological peculiarities in each cultural complex, characterize all Caucasian agricultural villages.

Northern Black Sea

In the northern Black Sea area (territories of Ukraine and Moldavia), the origins of an early agricultural economy are less discernible. This region is characterized by a wide range of cultures and subsistence economies, but none can be considered characteristic of an emerging production economy.

Neolithic sites from the sixth to the fifth millennia belong to the cultures of Bug-Dniestr (Markevich 1974; Chernysh 1996a), Sursk-Dniepr (Danilenko 1969; 1985; Chegin 1996a), Dniepr-Donets (Chegin 1979; 1985), Cris (Potushnyak 1985; 1996), and Linear Band Keramik (Passek and Chernysh 1970). They had complex economic systems with various combinations of hunter-gathering and husbandry. It is generally thought that agriculture was introduced to the northwestern Black Sea area from the Near East, through the Balkans. The argument is that it appeared in an elaborate form, with diversified agricultural tools.

The high density of population in the Upper Palaeolithic (Masson 1976:104) and the beginning of a crisis of traditional hunting economy in many regions led people to search for new sources of subsistence. Then some reorientation of the economic systems took place. This was an essential preliminary stage in production economy in the northwestern Black Sea. This is the place where, in the eleventh to the tenth millennia, late Paleolithic societies showed new tendencies, which are reflected not only in the modified nature of villages, houses, and mode of life but also, above all, in tools. Change in the ecological situation at the end of the Pleistocene and beginning of the Holocene brought about change in hunting techniques. Fishing and plant gathering (then based on various wild grasses) increased (Korobkova 1989).

Microscopic analysis of tools shows that the first blades of harvesting knives used for cutting grass and wild cereals appeared in the Late Mesolithic villages of Mirnoe and Abuzova Balka (eighth to the seventh millennia). Pollen analysis supports functional deductions. In the occupation levels of Mirnoe, we found pollen of wild grasses/cereals (Pashkevich 1982). The percentage of harvesting implements

is low: 18 blades out of 22,000 tools, or 0.2 to 0.3%, but it is undoubtedly significant.

We can assume that the Mesolithic village of Mirnoe was on the threshold of a transition to agriculture. We think it had already taken a step toward cereal domestication. However, we found only two sickle blades with an oblique polish, used for harvesting domestic cereals (Korobkova 1987:43, Fig. 5,1). They do not appear in this area by chance. In the late Paleolithic village of Ivashkovo VI (twelfth to the eleventh millennia BC), I discovered five blades for cutting wild cereals and grass (Korobkova and alii 1995:57,58) and seven blades at Kamenka (Korobkova 1993:370). A similar insert was discovered by V. E. Shchelinskij in a Bulgarian site dating to the late Paleolithic, Temnata Dubka. This kind of tool is also identified in the Late Palaeolithic site Bolchaia Akkarja. It is still difficult to explain; subsequent research should elucidate the origin of these tools. Nevertheless, the Mesolithic and perhaps Late Paleolithic hunter-gatherer economy of the populations living in the northwestern Black Sea area shows some signs of change from the previous system: the emergence of complex gathering, which later developed in Neolithic sites.

The Neolithic sites of this region have a complex economy, with mainly hunter-gatherer activities (Bug-Dniestr culture: site of Matveev Kurgan I and II) and husbandry (Cris and LBK cultures). Agricultural tools are less than 1% of total tools in the Cris and vary from 3 to 10% in the LBK.

The influence of agricultural centers such as the Balkans and the Near East on the development of the northwestern bank of the Black Sea appears in the material from Soroki I and V in the Bug-Dniestr culture (end of the sixth to fifth millennia BC), as well as in Selishte I and Sakarovki in the Cris culture (end of the sixth to fifth millennia). It corresponds to introduction of hulled wheats (emmer and einkorn) (Yanushevich 1976:199, Pl. 41) as well as of barley, oats, and legumes (idem 1986:4–14), into this region.

The climate and landscapes are varied. According to researchers, we find all the pedological zones of European Russia except tundra (Dooushaev 1950:20). We can observe lixiviated chernoziums, and gray and brown forest soils as well as flooded chernoziums. Chernoziums are more fertile but also heavy, difficult to work, and more sensitive to dryness (Krupennikov et al. 1960:134). Because of the low technical level of their tools, past cultivators preferred light loessic soils, forest soils, and, above all, foliated soils of flooded grasslands better suited to cultivation of cereals, pulses, and gardening. Steppe soils were not well adapted to primitive agriculture. It may be for that reason that the successors of the inhabitants of Mirnoe and the early Neolithic site of Matveev Kurgan (in the steppic area) (Krizhevskaya 1974) did not make agriculture the key sector of their economy and continued to gather wild cereal and breed livestock.

Specialists think the Holocene climate was more humid

and mild than the present one (Dolukhanov 1984:15; Kremenetski 1987:9). A variable climatic situation influenced the development of agriculture and was determinant in local economic changes, including those within individual cultures.

Bug-Dniestr culture

The territory of the Bug-Dniestr culture was ill suited to agriculture (Dolukhanov 1984:24), confirming my opinion about the relative nonprofitability of agriculture among Bug-Dniestr populations. This conclusion is supported by the composition of the tool assemblage, of which agricultural implements comprise less than 1% (Korobkova 1972b).

The land was worked with horn hoes which had a conical blade or the shape of a flat ax. They showed a fairly high efficiency for all types of soil and appear to have been multifunctional tools, used for spreading seed as well as softening soil (Korobkova 1975). Three varieties of hulled wheat were sown (einkorn, emmer, and spelt), and *Phalaris paradoxa* (canary grass) was gathered (Yanushevich 1976:32, Pl.6); transitional and hybrid forms of hulled wheats were identified (Chernysh 1996a:26). Harvesting was done using composite Karanovo-type sickles whose obliquely hafted elements formed a tooth-shaped blade area. We cannot distinguish the tools used for plant gathering from those used for actual agriculture. To remove the glumes from hulled wheats, apparently wooden mortars and pestles were used. Stone querns are rare, and small (10 to 12 cm), suggesting the use of coarse grain, not flour, as a foodstuff.

Cris culture

The sites occupy the Prut-Dniestr plain, with flooded lands (Chernysh 1996a:22) which could be easily worked with horn hoes (Sakarovka and Selichte), and the mountain areas of Transcarpathia (Zastavnoe and Rovnoe). Main crops were emmer, spelt, and naked barley. More rarely, einkorn, oats, and pulses were sown (Yanushevich 1976:4-14). Emmer was sown only in the form of spikelets. Harvesting was done using Karanovo sickles.

No threshing implement has been found. This operation may have taken place using flails, like those known ethnographically. Dehusking of hulled wheats with wooden pestles and mortars is only a hypothesis, although suggested by our experiments. Grain was kept in large vases and in pits; it was crushed on querns using pestles. People lived in underground huts and small above-ground houses made of wood and clay close to rivers and streams. They bred pigs as well as large and small cattle.

The location of sites in different ecological areas was reflected in the peculiarities of the tool assemblage and the economic production of the population. On the plain, tools were made mainly of flint; in Transcarpathia, of obsidian (85%) and more rarely of opal and andeso-basalt (Potushnyak 1996:37). In the first region, agriculture was preferred, in the

second, cattle breeding. Apart from one- and two-row barley, Transcarpathians sowed millet and vetch.

The materials from the plain, in the fifth millennium BC, testify to close relations between the Cris and Bugo-Dniestr cultures.

The most polyfunctional and advanced agriculture is that of the LBK culture. According to researchers (Passek and Chernysh 1970), villages of this culture appeared in the Dniestr and Prut areas after the immigration of communities from the Upper Visla.

LBK culture (second half of the 5th millennium BC)

So far, more than 60 villages of the LBK culture have been found in Moldavia, and somewhat fewer in Ukrainian Transcarpathia. The main sites are, for instance, the lower layer of Florechty, Dancheny, and Nezvisko. The houses were different-sized underground and above-ground buildings (Chernysh 1996c:29). Villages were found on the layered soils of flooded grasslands or on low-salinity soils, which were worked with horn hoes. There were wild grasses, such as aegilops, and a fescue grass (Kremenetski 1987).

Five varieties of wheat were cultivated, including bread wheat, naked and hulled barley, millet, and oat (Yanushevich 1986: Pl.2). Gardening was practiced. On the sites of Floresti I and Dancheni I, we identified remains of mirabelle plums, cherries, cornouillers, and (at Dancheni) hemp imprints. Sickles of Karanovo type, used by farmers in the preceding cultures, were also characteristic of this culture. Grain was kept in large vases and in storehouses, either buried or raised above ground. The village of Dancheny I has yielded remains of ovens (clay areas encircled by a rim), where grains were roasted and dried (Larina 1988).

Querns found on site were situated in economic actiivity areas only (for example, near storehouses, pit silos, and especially arranged areas), where grains were crushed and pounded. Querns were larger (48x48, 54x26, and 38x32cm) and elongated and required heavy two-handed rubbers for grain grinding.

Thus, the tools yielded by this culture concern all stages of the agricultural cycle: soil working, harvesting, and grain transformation. Digging implements are of two types: universal horn hoes with conical or trapezoidal blades, for field preparation; and digging sticks, for gardening.

Obviously, agriculture was well developed and diversified. Cattle breeding was apparently also developed, based on large, horned cattle.

Conclusion

From analysis of the materials from the Bugo-Dniestr culture, the Cris culture, and the LBK, it is evident that the ecological situation in the area of their diffusion (Moldavia and Ukraine) was appropriate for the development of husbandry. However, the landscape and climate are quite varied, which is reflected in the differentiation of the economic systems of these societies (Korobkova 1987). A settled economy, with specialized hunting and fishing as the mainstays and, in a secondary role, gathering, cattle breeding, and partial agriculture (evolved forms of wheat and harvesting tools arrived here) of a nonindigenous type, are characteristic of the sites of the Bugo-Dniestr culture. During its development, the latter tended to strengthen the role of herding (preferently of pigs and big horned cattle).

The materials of the Cris culture indicate a similar type of economy, but the breeding and hunting sectors began to play a leading role; agriculture, judging from the presence of a more varied assortment of cereal and other crop plants and from the varied assemblage of agricultural tools and their relative quantity, became more important and polyfunctional.

In the LBK, the leading role seems to have been played by agriculture and herding. The population cultivated various forms of wheat, barley, millet, and peas, among others. Agriculture was polyfunctional and developed but was not extensive everywhere (the plots suited for sowing are too small in several villages Florechty, Rogojany, and Nezvisko). A large part of the territory was occupied by forest. At the same time, villages such as Dancheny presented all the features of well developed agriculture, supplying basic food products. The economic variability, which I studied through the lithic tool industry, and my conclusions (1972b; 1987) are supported by data from ecological research.

This general survey allows at least three major conclusions:•

- Microwear analysis provides evidence for the origin and nature of agricultural economy, and this evidence is not accessible through other methods.

- The origin and early stages of this new economy, in particular the predecessors of the functional types of tools emerging at this time, are prior to the Neolithic.

- The more material we study, both on a general and on a detailed level, the more variability we observe in the agricultural economy of cultures which followed the same basic process of transition to a production economy; economic pluralism dominates in the strategies of early agricultural societies.

Acknowledgment. This chapter was translated from French by Jacqueline Gaudey, CRA, CNRS, France.

Chapter 20

Phytoliths as Indicators of Prehistoric Irrigation Farming

Arlene Miller Rosen

PHYTOLITHS FORM IN LIVING PLANTS WHEN silica is deposited within the cells of the epidermal tissue. In some cases silicification occurs only in single cells and in others whole sections of contiguous cells are silicification-producing forms called silica skeletons. The extent of cell silicification is in part related to growth conditions of the plant. With dry-land farming, only a small amount of silica is available to the plant due to good drainage and the rapid drying of the soil after rainfall events. In contrast, irrigation agriculture on alluvial plains or on moist soils near springs, creates a situation where drainage is poor, and soil water provides additional silica to the plant over a longer period of time. This excess concentration of silica may contribute to the silicification of multiple contiguous cells. The process is further enhanced in hot, arid environments with high transpiration rates. The relationship between moist alluvial soils; hot, arid habitats; and production of silica skeletons provides paleobotanists with a tool for identifying the use of irrigation in ancient Near Eastern farming systems (Rosen and Weiner 1994).

In studies concerning the early evolution of village farming systems, the development of irrigation systems plays an important role in understanding the structure of labor organization and the formation of stable agricultural economies. However, the identification of early irrigation is sometimes problematic. In the absence of possible macro-botanical indicators, it often depends on remnants of land forms such as canals, check dams, and enlarged floodplain basins which are difficult to date and often modified or destroyed by later earthworks.

Another possible method of identifying early irrigation

agriculture is by the analysis of silica bodies. Research has shown that phytoliths are useful in archaeological studies for the identification of cultigens and other economically useful plants from archaeological sites and prehistoric fields (Rovner 1971; 1983; Pearsall 1982; Piperno 1988). The purpose of this chapter is to explore the use of phytoliths for identifying whether plants cultivated by Neolithic and Chalcolithic farmers were irrigated or dry farmed.

Background to Silica Uptake in Cereals

Phytoliths are composed of amorphous silica (Yoshida et al. 1959a; Jones and Milne 1963) which is a substance absorbed by the plant from soil water. The amount and distribution of this silica in the cultigen reflects the conditions of the farming environment. It is therefore possible to distinguish between grasses that were dry farmed and those that were irrigated, by the nature of the silica bodies they contain.

In temperate climates, grasses typically deposit silica in several special silica cells. When plants decay, these cells retain their distinctive shapes and can be identified when separated from the sediment. There is also a less common pattern of silica deposition. Atypical silica bodies, or silica skeletons, have been reported in archaeological samples (Schellenberg 1908; Helbaek 1960B; Renfrew 1973: 204; Rosen 1987) as well as in living plants (Parry and Smithson 1964; Blackman and Parry 1968; Jones and Handreck 1965; Hodson and Sangster 1988). These abnormal phytoliths are silicified cells of epidermal tissue not ordinarily used by plants as a repository of silica.

Analyses of archaeological sediments from low latitude desert and rainforest environments have shown that in some

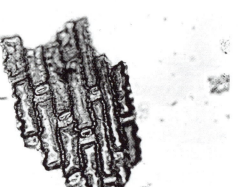

Figure 20.1 Multicell phytolith (silica skeleton) from the ancient
Maya site of Cuello, Belize. Scale bar = 10 μm

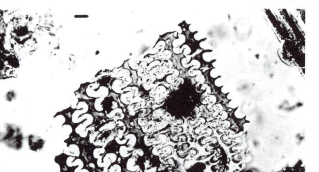

Figure 20.3a Multicell phytolith from a wheat (*Triticum* sp.) husk,
collected from the Chalcolithic site of Gilat. Scale bar = 10 μm

Figure 20.2 Multicell barley (*Hordeum* sp.) husk phytolith
collected from ash deposits at the Predynastic site of Merimda
Beni Salama, Egypt. Scale bar = 10 μm

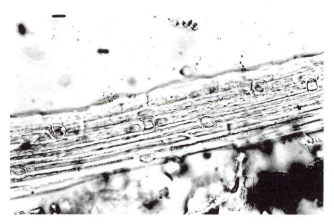

Figure 20.3b Multicell phytolith from the stem of a cereal,
Chalcolithic Gilat. Scale bar = 10μm

circumstances silica skeletons are far more numerous than
the typical single-celled phytoliths. Not only are atypical
individual cells silicified but also whole sections of intact
epidermal tissue. Something in the nature of the growing
environment favored this type of development. Abundant
remains of these silica skeletons were found by the author in
archaeological middens from the Mayan lowlands of El
Salvador and Belize (Hammond et al. 1979), two Egyptian
Predynastic sites in the Nile Valley, and several Chalcolithic
sites along the Wadi Beersheva in the Negev desert of Israel
(Rosen 1987, 1996; figures 20.1, 20.2, and 20.3).

At first consideration, the farming environments of lowland
Central America and the Nile Valley appear very different.
However, they do share two important features: high
temperatures and an abundance of water. In Central America
the water comes from heavy rainfall; in Egypt, the annual Nile
flood. These two variables might therefore be responsible for
the increased uptake and deposition of silica by cultivated
grasses. Therefore it is possible that in warm semi arid
environments with low rainfall, such as the Near East and
North Africa, silica skeletons form primarily in cultigens that
have been irrigated or grown in poorly drained soils.

This hypothesis rests on several assumptions that can be
supported by previous experimental studies on silica uptake
in plants. These assumptions are as follows: First, a greater
amount of silica in the plant leads to greater deposition and
formation of the silica skeletons; second, plants at least
partially absorb silica passively and in proportion to the
amount available in soil solution; and third, an increase in
soil water by irrigation leads to larger amounts of soluble
silica that would then be available to the plants. Let us examine
the assumption that a greater amount of silica in the plant's
transpiration stream leads to increased deposition as atypical
silica bodies. Silica is absorbed by plants as monosilicic acid.
It is gelled by either catalyzation by organic molecules
(Gangster 1970), changes in pH after initial formation of
polysilicic acids, or simply increased silica concentration
because of evaporation of water by transpiration (Iler 1955;
Krauskopf 1959; Blackman, 1969; Yoshida et al. 1959b). It is
then normally deposited in typical silica cells. Yoshida et al.
(1959b), Blackman (1969), Sangster (1970), and Hayward
and Parry (1980) suggested that the process of deposition is
passive, and probably not enzymatic. This implies that greater
deposition is proportional to greater amounts of silica in the
plant. Blackman found that as cells age, they first lose their
contents and are then passively filled with silica gel. Sangster

(1970) hypothesized that degraded organic material in senescent leaves provides a matrix for the polymerization of silica after leaching of other cell contents.

It has been postulated by several researchers that large amounts of silica in the plant will in fact lead to silicification of cells other than the normal silica cells, thus forming silica skeletons (Yoshida et al. 1959a; Parry and Smithson 1964; Blackman and Parry 1968; Blackman 1968, 1969). Parry and Smithson (1964) found this to be true in pot-grown grasses which had heavy applications of sodium silicate. Conversely, plants grown in a silica-poor medium produce fewer phytoliths (Yoshida et al. 1959a; Blackman 1969) which are restricted in form to the shapes of the typical silica cells. This implies that there may be an order by which different atypical cells are silicified, varying with the age of the plant and the amount of silica available. Grasses first deposit the substance in normal silica cells, then other cells are silicified sequentially.

Parry and Smithson (1964) observed that stomata cells were only affected after the leaf was old and many long cells had been silicified first. Blackman (1969) noted a characteristic pattern of silica deposition which may result from the order by which cell varieties die and become empty receptacles. Sangster (1970) also found that characteristic phytolith types develop during different stages of leaf growth. The long cells, stomata cells, and bulliform cells are last to silicify. Therefore, it is possible that with a constant supply of silica, mature and senescent plants produce more varied types of phytoliths.

The second assumption is that plants absorb silica from the soil solution in larger amounts if the concentrations of silica are higher in the soil water. In order for this to be true, silica absorption would have to be passive or involve no metabolic process that would filter out excess silica. Barber's and Shone's research (1966) contradicts this assumption. From experimental data on beans and barley, they concluded that metabolic processes did maintain a constant level of silica, despite the concentration in the soil solution. Although they varied the amounts of silica available to the beans, Barber and Shone did not increase the silica in plots of barley. They observed that larger quantities of silica had no effect on amounts absorbed by beans and assumed this to be true of barley as well. However, grasses are much more effective silica absorbers than legumes, so that a simple comparison cannot be drawn. Another weak point in their research is that they used bean and barley seedlings which were grown for only one week, which added a bias to their experiment. Blackman (1969) has shown that silica uptake by wheat increases dramatically after 19 days growth, when the leaves are fully expanded. It is possible that grasses absorb silica less discriminately after this critical point in their growth.

Perry et al. (1984) examined the inorganic elements in the macrohairs from the lemma of *Phalaris canariensis* and found evidence suggesting that silica deposition in the macrohairs was controlled by cellular activity. This, however, does not show that all the silica deposition is metabolic. Hayward and Parry (1973) propose that silica deposition in barley may be partially metabolic and partially passive, depending upon the plant part and cells involved.

In other research, Jones and Handreck (1965) found that the concentrations of silica in oats were in fact roughly proportional to the concentrations found in the soil solution. In their experiments they tested plants which were mature, after 30 to 70 days of growth. They also found that the proportion of silica in the plants increased progressively with age. They concluded that there is a quantitative relationship between silica in soil water and the amount taken up by the oats and that the uptake was, in fact, passive. In addition, they found that greater transpiration of water led to higher concentrations of silica in plants. On days with higher temperatures, larger amounts of silica were therefore found in the oats since both the transpiration rate and the rate of absorption of monosilicic acid increased. This lends support to the thesis that plants grown in warm climates concentrate silica, especially if more silica is made soluble by addition of irrigation water. Imaizumi and Yoshida (1958) also demonstrated a positive relationship between the silica content of paddies and its uptake by rice plants.

It may be argued that in arid environments increased transpiration alone is enough to concentrate greater amounts of silica in plants. In fact, a positive relationship between greater transpiration and silica deposition has already been established by previous researchers (Hutton and Norrish 1974). This would mean that any plants cultivated in arid environments would contain atypical phytoliths, as has been suggested by Renfrew (1973:17). Greater transpiration cannot, however, be divorced from increased water uptake. It is possible, then, that the degree of silica deposition is much greater in plants grown in a moist soil medium with high percentages of silica. This is also supported by previous laboratory experiments mentioned above.

Finally, it is necessary to investigate the factors which regulate the concentration of monosilicic acid in the soil solution. In order for plants to absorb more silica, there must be more of this substance in the growing medium. Experiments by McKeague and Cline (1963a), Alexander et al. (1954), Siever (1957), and others have shown that the form of silica in the soil solution is monosilicic acid. This acid is un-ionized (Krauskopf 1959) and its solubility is relatively unaffected in a pH range of 5-8, which is normal in most soils (Alexander et al. 1954). In warm wet climates this weathering process increases (Dunne 1978). Although monosilicic acid is formed more rapidly in wet climates, concentrations do not usually build up in the soil solution because greater amounts are leached from the soil profile by rainfall (Dunne 1978). In general, however, tropical soils have much greater concentrations of soluble silica than temperate soils (Siever 1957), especially those which are poorly drained. McKeague and Cline (1963a) likewise found higher concentrations of dissolved silica in mixtures with increasingly higher water-to-soil ratios, but also found that the increase was not infinite and leveled to a slower rate of silica dissolution a day or two after applications of water. Alexander et al. (1954) found the decrease in dissolution to occur after 20 days.

McKeague and Cline (1963a) also discovered that evaporation of soil water did not lead to greater concentrations of soluble silica because silica is adsorbed to the surface of soil particles with drying. In a drier soil, silica is therefore less available for plant absorption. McKeague and Cline concluded from other experiments (1963b) that it is in fact the process of adsorption and desorption which controls the amount of silica in the soil solution rather than the primary formation of monosilicic acid. Other researchers (Beckwith and Reeve 1962) support this conclusion as well. Experiments also showed that aluminum oxides and to a lesser extent iron oxides are active adsorbers of silica (McKeague and Cline 1963b; Okamoto et al. 1957). Individual soils should therefore be tested for these compounds before one can determine availability of soluble silica to plants.

Although monosilicic acid itself is stable in a wide range of soil pH values, the adsorption capacity of soil particles changes with acidity. In very alkaline soils, adsorption increases and therefore leaves less free silica in the soil water. Conversely, acidic soils, such as those which are waterlogged, do not have the same high adsorption rate (McKeague and Cline 1963b; Beckwith and Reeve 1962).

Another variable is evaporation of soil water. This increases the adsorption process so that dry soils do not have high concentrations of monosilicic acid in solution. However, with the addition of water, the silica is once again freed. In addition to freeing silica, irrigation water may also contribute new silica which is carried in solution by the river. Imaizumi and Yoshida (1958) found that irrigation water in Japanese rice paddies contributed about 30% of the silica available to plants. Further support for this is Parry's and Smithson's (1964) discovery of heavy silica deposition in grasses growing in wet habitats. Conversely, grasses grown in dry habitats had fewer types of silicified cells.

In summary, the factors that increase silica in soils are high temperatures (McKeague and Cline 1963a; Okamoto 1957), waterlogged conditions, and to some extent soluble phosphorus and organic acids. Most of these conditions are found in tropical environments with flat topography in which leaching is not an overriding factor. A tropical soil environment may be created on a hot, arid alluvial plain by the addition of irrigation water. Factors that contribute to adsorption and the subsequent decrease of soluble silica in the soil environment are calcareous soils with a high pH, aluminum oxides, the evaporation of soil moisture, or the leaching of soluble minerals. Some of these conditions occur with dry farming on well-drained soils.

These above-mentioned conditions help to explain why silica skeletons commonly form in some farming environments of lowland Central America and the Nile Valley. In Central America, low-relief land with heavy clay soils and impeded drainage leads to the abundant availability of silica. In the Nile Valley, wheat was traditionally cultivated in flood basins after irrigation. Irrigation water remained in these basins approximately 40 days before being released to the main channel (Willcocks and Craig 1913). The initial basin filling began in the middle of August, an extremely hot month. The river brought in abundant soluble silica, saturating the soil water under conditions of high temperatures and standing water. When the water drained out in mid-October or November, temperatures had cooled somewhat and the evaporation rates had lowered, leaving a moist soil ready for wheat cultivation. Silica concentrations should have been high throughout most of the growing season. Shortly before harvest time, hot and parching desert winds again increased plant transpiration, which would have concentrated silica in the plant (Jones and Handreck 1965). This explains why sediments from ancient as well as modern archaeological middens in Egypt contain large quantities of atypical, silicified skeletons of intact epidermal tissue.

Apart from the farming implications of the silica skeletons, they also have significance as microenvironmental indicators. A large number of silica skeletons from noncultigens could indicate the presence of a marshy environment near the site, which was contemporary with the occupation.

Experimental Results

In order to test the use of silica skeletons as a tool for identifying ancient irrigation, experiments were conducted at the Weizmann Institute of Science in Rehovot, Israel (Rosen and Weiner 1994). Here we acquired seeds of domestic emmer (*Triticum turgidum* subsp. *dicoccum*) and cultivated them in two experimental fields at the Gilat Agricultural Research Station in the northern Negev. One of these fields was irrigated and the other dry farmed. The dry farmed crop received 224 mm of effective rainfall during the growing season and the irrigated field received a total of 424 mm. After harvesting we found that the total phytolith yield from the husks of the irrigated wheat was close to twice the weight of phytoliths produced by the nonirrigated emmer.

The silica skeletons from the husks of irrigated emmer were consistently larger and composed of more cells per phytolith than the husk silica skeletons from the dry farmed wheat. These results are shown in histogram form in figure 20.4. In the dry farmed wheat, there are few phytoliths composed of over ten adjacent silicified cells, and over 50% containing only two cells per phytolith. In contrast the irrigated emmer contained over 10% phytoliths with greater than 10 cells each. In addition to this, the irrigated samples contained a number of silica

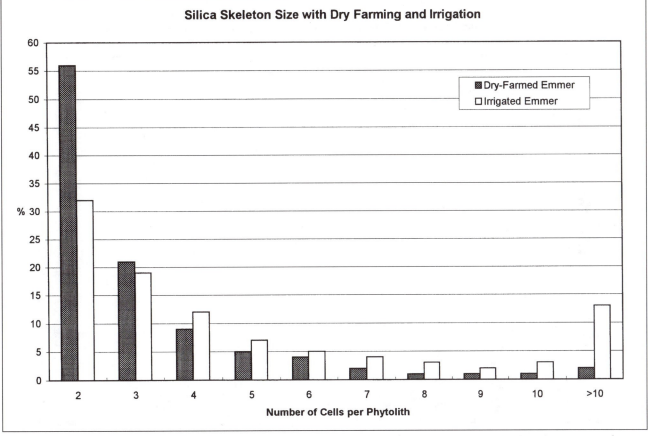

Figure 20.4 Graph showing differences in the size of multicell phytoliths (silica skeletons) from the husks of modern emmer wheat (*Triticum dicoccum*) with dry farming versus irrigation

skeletons that had more than 100 joined cells.

Archaeological Results

This technique was applied to the phytoliths from two Chalcolithic sites in the northern Negev. One was the farming village of Shiqmim located on a low terrace next to the Nahal (Wad) Beer Sheva, and the other was the site of Gilat located near Nahal Patish (Levy 1987; Alon and Levy 1989). The samples were taken from ashy midden and hearth deposits and the wheat phytoliths were identified according to criteria outlined by Rosen (1992). The results for both sites showed cell-number distributions that were very much like those of the modern irrigated wheat (figure 20.5). In the samples from Shiqmim, 29% of the silica skeletons had over 10 cells each, exceeding that of modern irrigated wheat by 16%. The Shiqmim sample also contained a number of phytoliths with hundreds of adjacent silicified cells (Rosen and Weiner 1994).

Given the above results, it is therefore very likely that the emmer wheat from both Gilat and Shiqmim was cultivated in a moist alluvial environment, rather than dry farmed. During the Chalcolithic period the floodplains of the wadis in the northern Negev desert were naturally aggrading (Goldberg and Rosen 1987). The most likely scenario is a situation in which these floodplains were utilized in a system of simple basin irrigation in order to

ensure higher, more predictable crop yields.

This technique can also be applied to sites in other parts of the Levant as well, although the results should be considered tentative since no controlled experimental studies were conducted on modern cereals from higher rainfall areas in the Levant. Greater rainfall, however, should not produce higher numbers of large silica skeletons since, unlike surface irrigation water, rainfall is essentially equivalent to distilled water and will not add additional silica to the soil. To illustrate this, uncontrolled samples of modern bread wheat (*T. aestivum*) were collected from higher rainfall areas in northern Israel (600 mm p.a.) and these yielded only 5.4% and 8.2% silica skeletons with greater than 10 silicified cells each (Rosen and Weiner 1994).

A very limited number of samples were examined from the Pre-Pottery Neolithic sites of Horvat Galil and Nahal Beset I in the Galilee of Israel. These contained emmer wheat phytoliths with relatively low numbers of silicified cells, rarely exceeding 3 cells per phytolith. This could indicate that the wheat cultivated at this site by PPNB peoples was dry farmed on well-drained soils (Rosen 1997). In contrast to this, wheat from Nahal Zehora, a later period Pottery Neolithic site, also located in the Galilee, consistently produced phytoliths with greater than 20 cells per silica skeleton. Although this is suggestive of a farming technique in which water

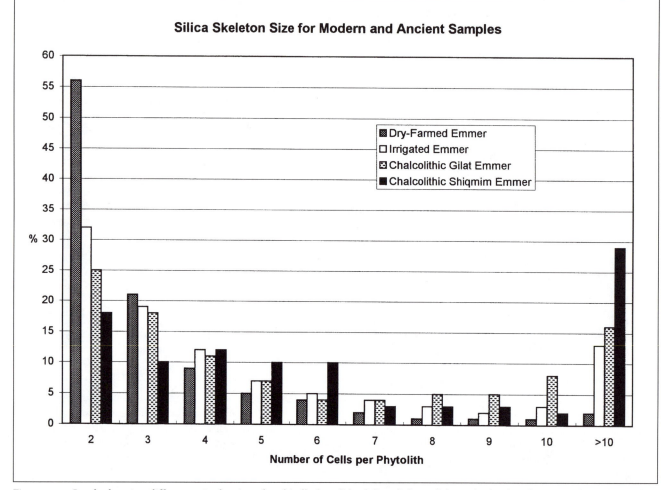

Figure 20.5 Graph showing differences in the size of multicell phytoliths (silica skeletons) from the husks of emmer wheat (*Triticum dicoccum*) in both modern and ancient Chalcolithic samples

manipulation played a major part, statistically valid samples must be counted and compared between sites before a more definitive statement is made about irrigation technologies in the Neolithic.

Silica-skeleton production can be a sensitive indicator of farming environment. It is possible to use these phytoliths to distinguish between cereals cultivated by dry farming on well-drained upland slopes and crops grown in heavy alluvial soils with irrigation or natural floodwater farming. Additionally, large silica skeletons are also indicative of extinct microenvironments. At sites where no marshy areas exist today and the streams are too entrenched for simple irrigation technologies, large silica skeletons suggest that such microenvironments did exist in the past. An example of such a case occurs at the Early Bronze Age I site of Tel Erani in central Israel where both multi-cell silica skeletons and geomorphological investigations attest to the presence of moist floodplains in the third millennium bc which no longer exist today (Rosen 1991). Phytolith analyses have great potential for reconstructing past microenvironments and farming technologies, in addition to their use in plant identification. They therefore not only supplement information obtained from macrobotanical analyses, they also address problems which are sometimes difficult to solve by other paleobotanical techniques.

Acknowledgments. This chapter was partially written while the author was a NEH fellow at the W. F. Albright Institute for Archaeological Research in Jerusalem. It utilizes data accumulated with the help of a Sir Charles Clore research grant administered by the Weizmann Inst. of Science and grants from the (Israel) National Center for Cooperation Between Archaeology and the Natural Sciences, Weizmann Institute, as well as assistance from the Irene Levi Sala CARE Foundation. T. E. Levy and D. Alon kindly provided sediment samples from the Chalcolithic sites of Gilat and Shiqmim, and A. Gopher supplied samples from Neolithic Nahal Beset, Horvat Galil and Nahal Zehora, and Norman Hammond allowed me to sample midden deposits at the Maya site of Cuello, Belize. Y. Amir and I. Mufradi graciously allowed us to utilize experimental fields at the Gilat Agricultural Research Station. I wish to thank K.W. Butzer, P. Goldberg, L. Kaplan, S.A. Rosen, and A.G. Sangster for their comments on an earlier draft of this chapter. All remaining errors and shortcomings are the sole responsibility of the author.

Chapter 21

Evolution of Agricultural Techniques in Eneolithic (Chalcolithic) Bulgaria

Data from use-wear analysis

Natalia N. Skakun

IN THE LAST TEN YEARS, ARCHAEOLOGICAL research has enabled us to reconsider many preconceived ideas about the early agricultural cultures of southeastern Europe. Excavations of several sites and cemeteries from the Danube and Balkans area bear witness to progress made in different areas of the material, social, and religious life of these groups, who display the same level of development as the most advanced cultures of the time (Todorova 1986; Merpert 1995). This progress originated, according to most researchers, in the improvement brought about in one of the key sectors of the economy: agriculture. Such an interpretation, generally founded on a comparison between the levels of development of Neolithic and Eneolithic cultures, requires additional scientific proof. Now, a detailed study of the artifacts produced (over 20,000 items) from Neolithic and Eneolithic villages close to the Black Sea, in Bulgaria, has provided new data concerning techniques that raised Eneolithic agriculture to a higher level (Skakun 1981; 1982; 1985ab; 1986; 1987; 1992; 1993ab; 1996a). This is due to new implements, detected through use-wear analysis: antler ardshares and flint blades of threshing sledges (Skakun 1981a; 1982; 1985a, b; 1986; 1987; 1993a, b; 1996a).

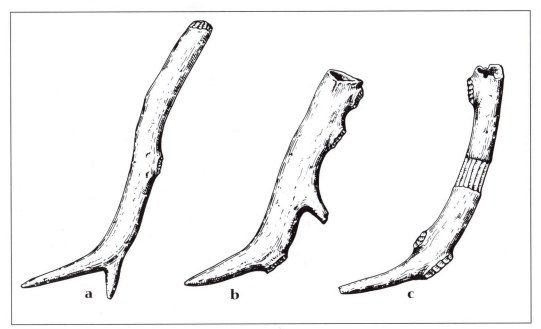

Figure 21.1 Antler ardshares (*ralos*) from Eneolithic settlements, Bulgaria

Ardshares

The literature devoted to agriculture records a few items considered as possible early farming implements (Dumitrescu and Banaetanu 1965; Gaerte 1929; Sach 1961; Krasnov 1970; 1975; 1985), but there is very little or no description of the use-wear traces detected on their working areas. There is only one tool from the site of Novye Rusheshti (Tripolje culture) for which a use-wear analysis is mentioned (Korobkova 1975; 1981a; Chernykh 1982).

Seven peculiar implements were discovered, complete or fragmentary, in the tool assemblage from the Varna Eneolithic culture. The main cultural centers are found in the coastal areas of Bulgaria, near the Black Sea (Todorova 1978), extending to the Danube Valley, over the Ukraine and Moldovian territories (Todorova 1978; 1979; 1986; Skakun 1982; 1986; 1996). All are large elbow-shaped tools made of antler, with evidences of retouch and use. As these findings are unique, I will describe the best preserved objects in detail.

The first tool is 80 cm long and its maximum width is 7 cm. The massive upper part close to the skull (burr) has been removed, and the remaining end reknapped. The section has a regular edge, with a slightly worn notch-shaped area. All lateral branches (tines) have been removed by sawing and the rest reshaped on the central trunk of the antler (beam). In the terminal part (palm), there is a fork remaining, consisting of two branches, one of which (11 cm long and 3 to 3.5 cm across) forms a continuous curve with the beam. The surface of this branch, in particular its extremity, has been heavily polished (figure 21.1a).

On another tool, 37 cm long and 8 cm maximum in width, the base is broken and tines carefully removed. Only one branch remains, which is 17 cm long and 3 to 3.5 cm wide; the surface has a mirror polish and the very end is broken. On the beam, 20 cm from the burr, a 4 cm thick annular band is grooved (figure 21.1b).

The third tool is 63 cm long and 9 cm wide. Its base is broken; two tines and one of the two branches have been cut off. The remaining branch has been retouched, polished. The beam has one tine with a broken end (figure 21.1c).

The fourth tool is about 40 cm long and 5.5 wide; the branch is 15 cm in length and 3.5 cm in diameter. Its upper end is evened using large chop removals in a circle (figure 21.2a). The edges of these chop marks are polished and leveled. The end of the branch is broken, and its surface is visibly polished (figure 21.2b).

These tools, as well as those reconstructed from fragments, have the same shape: a central trunk of antler and a few tines form a continuous curve with the beam. Microscopic analysis showed that these tools had the same type of use-wear in the same locations. Use-wear traces are concentrated on the sharpened end of the branch (figures 21.2b,c), whose entire surface is intensively polished; in some areas, striae and deep grooves run parallel to the longitudinal axis of the antler

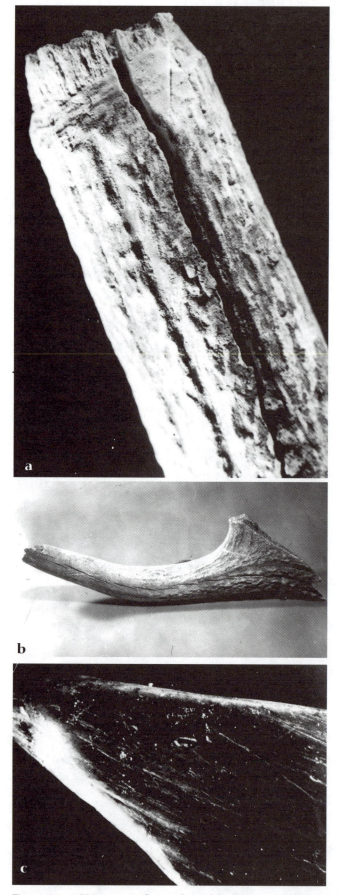

Figure 21.2 *a,* Upper part of an antler ardshare; *b,* working branch; *c,* linear traces of use on the ardshare's working branch (50x)

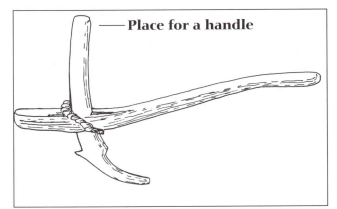

Figure 21.3 Reconstruction of a horn ardshare

Figure 21.5 Half-finished wooden ardshare

Figure 21.4 Work with a wooden ardshare of the nineteenth century, Lithuania, 1972. *Photograph by author*

Figure 21.6 Tillage with a wooden ardshare of the nineteenth century, Bulgaria. *Courtesy of V. Vakarel'ski's archives*

(figure 21.2c). Mirror polish and deformation are observed mainly on the lower surface of the branch. The beam shows use-wear traces on the reknapped parts: the edges of tine stumps appear planed and leveled (figures 21.1a, b, 21.2a).

Observations over many years of experimental studies reveal that this type of use-wear is characteristic of soil-working tools. Such a polish characteristically forms on antler from contact with mounds of earth, and striae result from collision with stones and abrasive particles. The location of polish and deformations, as well as the direction of striae, shows that the terminal branch alone was in the ground, and the greatest load was exerted on its end and lower part. These tools moved with their point facing forward, as though slicing through the earth. These observations indicate the tools were used to work soil, probably as ardshares.

Only two similar tools were found in the area, one from Rumania, at Keschioareli (Dumitrescu and Banaetanu 1965), and one from the Baltic, at Tsodmar (Gaerte 1929). The main similarity between these tools and the Bulgarian ones is that the haft and working area are one unit. There is one difference: the Bulgarian tools do not have holes perforated on the terminal branch. One of them has a sharpened upper end, fitted for insertion in a haft (figure 21.2a, 21.3), and another has a reworked band, meant to facilitate hafting (figure 21.2c). The horn items from Keschioareli and Tsodmar were identified by the authors as early ardshares. Insofar as we can judge from the description given, the observable use-wear (polish) corresponds with that on Varna tools, supporting the idea of the same use for both types: soil working. Keschioareli is close to the Varna sites, from a cultural as well as a chronological standpoint. In contrast to the other tools, one tool found at Novykh Rusesht (Tripolje) has many teeth (Chernykh 1982, 233–234).

The emergence of tilling in the Eneolithic of the eastern areas adjacent to the Black Sea is confirmed by the discovery of bones of traction animals (oxen; Tsalkin 1967; Todorova 1979). The relatively low percentage of horn ardshares preserved may be explained by long use of the same tool by

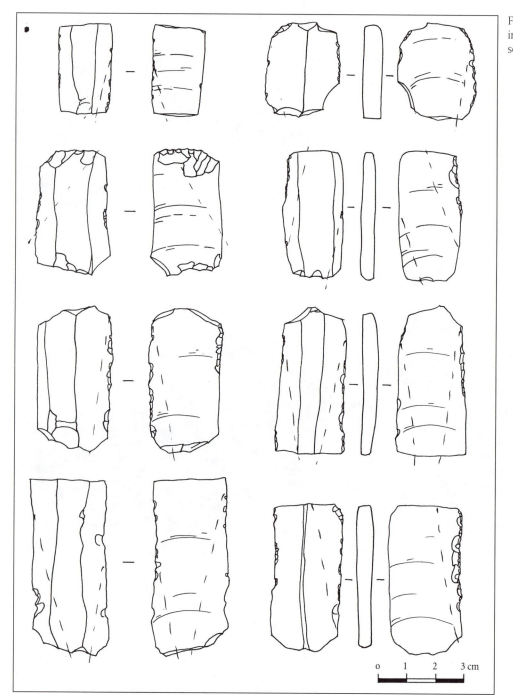

Figure 21.7 Threshing sledge inserts from the Eneolithic settlements of Bulgaria

0   1   2   3 cm

several farm laborers of one Eneolithic village and by probable use of unpreserved wooden implements.

The ethnographic record gives many examples of the use of wooden farming implements (figure 21.4). Bulgarian ethnographer Marinov, a specialist in agricultural tools, informed us that in the Bulgarian countryside at the end of the nineteenth century, wooden tilling tools with no metallic tips were still in use. Prepared from knotty pieces of wood, these tools had a body serving as an ardshare and one branch serving as a hafting device (figure 21.5). One tool was used by several laborers (figure 21.6). After considering the antler implements we found (figure 21.2), Marinov judged, from

their technical characteristics, that they would have been capable of tillage 6 to 8 cm deep. Probably, there were arable implements of another type, where the horn objects traditionally called "hoes" may have been dominant (Krasnov 1985:92, Figure 52.2).

In the literature concerned with the development of agricultural tools, antler tools similar to those from Varna (those from Tsodmar and Keschioareli) are shown with wooden implements of a similar shape from the lake villages of Switzerland; by analogy with Scottish ethnographic tools, they are considered as hand "furrow makers" (Krasnov 1975; 1985). In fact, it is commonly admitted that certain types of

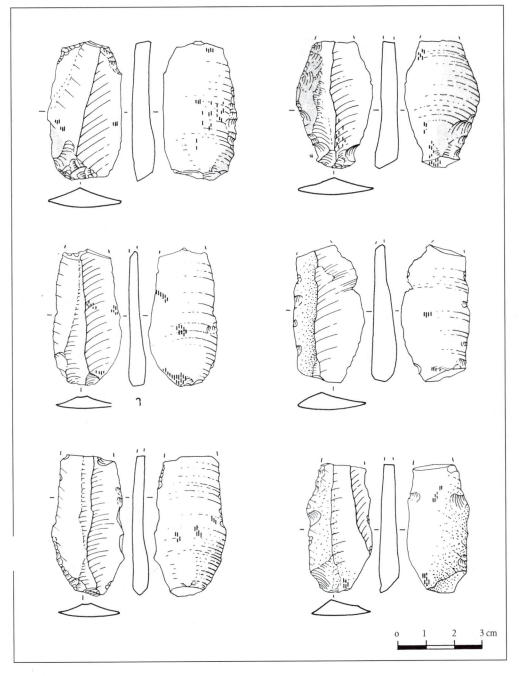

Figure 21.7, *continued*
Threshing sledge inserts
from the Eneolithic
settlements of Bulgaria

0   1   2   3 cm

furrowmakers have (almost) all the structural characteristics of ards. Therefore, it is impossible to define a clear difference between these two categories of tools, in particular for the period when tilling appeared in agriculture.

The essential fact emerging from this discussion is the appearance, in the Eneolithic, of previously unknown tools, used to work soil; they bear witness to the advance in agricultural techniques at that time.

Threshing Sledges

During study of a homogeneous group of the middle part of big and very big blades with traces of utilization (angled mirror polish), usually interpreted as sickle inserts, we noticed a significant difference between them. Some (2–2.5 by 2.5–

3.5), judging by all signs of micro and macro use-wear, including polish, were undoubtedly sickle inserts; another group (2–3.5 by 3.5–4.5) differed in some parameters. As we knew at the time, this group was used as inserts for threshing sledges (figure 21.7). What differences can be seen between the two types?

Threshing sledge inserts have greater use-wear. Their working edges are blunted (rounded in cross section). Experiments show that even after a long period of use, the working parts of sickle inserts are not as worn out and blunted. Besides, it is quite clear that long before such a degree of wear appears, the sickle inserts would not be useful for their main purpose, harvesting cereals, which requires a sharp working edge with a triangular cross section. Some threshing sledge inserts show deformation of their edges by large removals, which is why some of them appear to have been flattened out. As for the use-wear traces on the tools, their polish and linear features are located over rough deformations. The inevitable conclusion is that such destruction of the edges was not a result of use but occurred in tool manufacture, probably during their insertion into grooves. On these tools, linear traces—deep, pitted-appearing, and oriented parallel to one another and to the edge or slightly at an angle to it—are also situated on some areas close to the edge. In fact, they are similar to traces from cutting in one direction. Furthermore, the obliquely oriented polish is common to both kinds of inserts, but it also has some differences (figure 21.8). For the threshing sledge inserts, the limit between the worn and unworn surface is not as marked, and the degree of mirror polish is duller than for the sickles. These combined differences allowed us to distinguish two different functional types of tools among the inserts with a polish situated on one or two angular extremities. One is the well-known group of sickles (figure 21.8a), and another is the threshing sledge inserts (figure 21.8b). Our extensive experimental work and ethnographic data have proven this hypothesis.

The threshing sledge, used in the economy of many regions, even today, attracts the attention of many scientists and travelers by its archaic appearance. Its main areas of diffusion were areas around the Mediterranean: Balkan and Iberian Peninsulas, North Africa, Asia Minor, Syria, and the Caucasus (for example, Pchelina 1932; Lusquet and River 1933). This device is known from ancient Eastern iconography and is cited in Sumerian texts (for example, Kramer 1963; Lurie et al. 1940: 277). The prophet Isaiah tells the people of Israel concerning this tool that "he will do it with a new, toothed threshing sledge" [XLI, 15]. It is described by the name of *tribulum* or *tribula* in the works of some Latin authors, especially Marcus Terentius Varro (1963, p.63, ch.52).

In southeastern Europe (Bulgaria, Moldavia, and the southwest part of Ukraine), it was used till the 1950s and was called *dikanya* (Vakarel'ski 1977). During our excavations of the Eneolithic village Nagornoe II in the Odessa region of the Ukraine (lower Danube Valley; Skakun 1985a, b; 1996a), in the present village of Nagornoe, settled by Bulgarians who immigrated in the nineteenth century (Rossija 1910:197), we discovered several well-preserved threshing sledges (figure 21.9). Older inhabitants said that dikanya were made as follows: First, two or three boards (25 cm wide by 150 cm long), most often of willow, were soaked for several days. Afterward, they were fitted together with horizontal planks and wooden nails, then grooves were made on their underside in a checkerboard pattern (figure 21.9). Bits of flint were driven into them with wooden hammers, so that one oblique

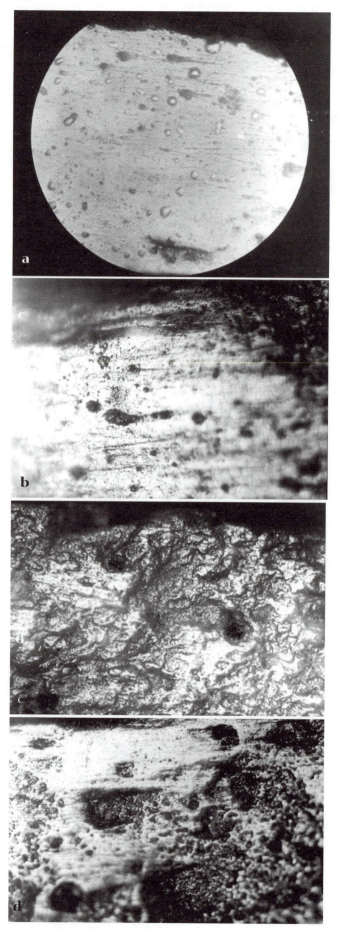

Figure 21.8 Micrographs of the working surfaces (100x): *a,* archaeological sickle insert; *b,* archaeological threshing sledge insert; *c,* ethnographical threshing sledge insert; *d,* experimental threshing sledge insert

Figure 21.9 Threshing sledge of the twentieth century from Nagornoe village

angle and one part of the side protruded. In general, when driving in the flint blades in this manner, large flat flakes came off the working edge (figure 21.10). Analogous deformations of the edges were discovered on some archaeological artifacts. When finished, the implement resembled a sledge; a harness was attached to the raised front end (figure 21.11). This end was bent so that cereal stems would not jam this end and slow the movement during work (figure 21.11, 21.12).

For threshing, a flat surface of 25 to 30 m, called *kharman*, was chosen (a courtyard was often convenient). Two or three days before threshing, the kharman was soaked, then regularly strewn with clean straw, which was tamped down with a stone, the kharman's stone. Once the floor was well dried and hardened, it was carefully swept to become flat, smooth, and durable. The wheat or barley brought from the field was scattered on the whole floor, with ears turned to the center, then conscientiously trodden under foot. Next, oxen or horses (harnessed to the dikanya, on which stones were placed or children seated) were trotted in a circle; the sharp flint edges cut the straw and drove the grain from the seed head. A few women with special forks (*jagby*) shook the stems so that all ears could be husked and grain could fall from them. The work continued until the straw was completely chopped. Once threshing was over, grain and straw were heaped up in the middle of the kharman and separated by winnowing. Chopped straw, dry and softened, served for cattle or for building material.

Figure 21.10 Threshing sledge inserts: *a–c, e,* ethnographic; *d,* experimental. Shaded areas indicate: visible gloss; arrow indicates: burin-like removal

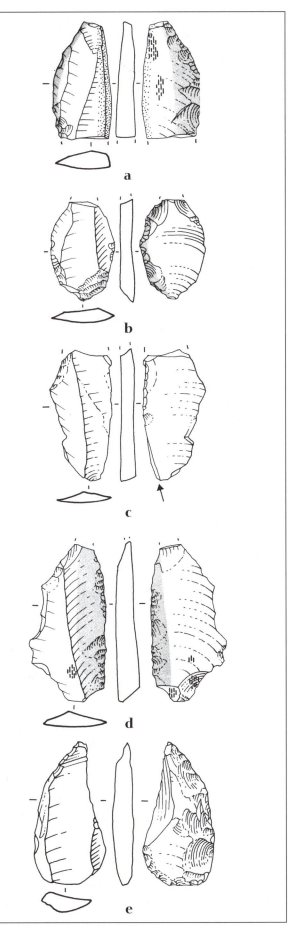

Thus, Nagornoe inhabitants still remember very well how threshing sledges were made, and they allowed us to reproduce the whole process. To check use-wear observations, we borrowed a board from a laborer, which was made around 1930 in the same village, the flint of the blades coming from the Rumanian Dobrudja. In the grooves from which elements had fallen were inserted bits of flint blades from Dobrudja without use-wear traces, found during the excavations of Eneolithic site Nagornoe II (figure 21.10). In the manner described above, a floor was prepared. During the experiment, two *araba* of wheat were threshed and five bags of grain collected (Skakun 1985a,b). The grain was winnowed with an ethnographic winnowing basket.

After the elements of threshing sledges of archaeological, ethnographic, and experimental origin were compared, they presented absolutely identical micro- and macroscopic use-wear traces, which fully confirms the accuracy of the use-wear observations (figures 21.10, 21.13). The greatest difference between them was only in the intensity of wear and deformation of edge on the ethnographic tools. Thus, the greatest alterations are on the ethnographic inserts, because they were hammered into the underside of dikanya with not only wooden but also metallic hammers, and they were used over long periods of time. Also, the archaeological and experimental inserts do not have as high a degree of wear, for all the above-mentioned reasons.

After the experiments, the reasons for general and specific wear traces on sickles and threshing sledges became clearer. The mirror polish on them is related to work with the same material—dry, soil-covered stems of cereals—and the difference in its intensity also depends on contact of the threshing sledge inserts with the earthen floor of the kharman. Its hardness, the weight of the threshing sledge itself, whether it is further weighted (by stones or persons, for example), and the duration of use, were the reasons there is more wear on their edges than on sickle edges, and the difference in the kinetics of their use explains the difference between the kinds of linear traces.

Flint inserts from threshing sledges were found on most sites of the Varna culture (Durankulak, Golyamo Delchevo, Polyanitsa, and Dyadovo). They are all typologically similar and originate in the Eneolithic layers. Some inserts were found in the Neolithic sites of Bulgaria (Skakun 1993c). Unfortunately, their stratigraphical situation is not very certain, and that is why there is no absolute evidence that they belong to the Neolithic. As for archaeological analogies, until recently we could mention only finds of Bronze Age threshing sledges in the Transcaucasus (Piotrovsky 1939; Bunatov 1957).

L. Wooley proposed that this implement had been used frequently in the most ancient settlements of the Near East. Many authors wrote about its modern use in this territory, giving examples of the ethnographic data and the inserts themselves, and they were also surprised at their absence in

Figure 21.11 Threshing in the nineteenth century, Bulgaria

Figure 21.12 Experiment with a threshing sledge, Nagornoe village, 1978

the archaeological material (Wooley 1955; Bordaz 1965; Diamond 1977; Whallon 1978; and chapter 22). Study of all the Bulgarian material showed that this was because of the tradition of interpreting all tools with mirror polish as sickle inserts (Skakun 1981a,b). The most significant is, in our opinion, the discovery of threshing sledge inserts on the settlements of Iraq (Anderson and Inizan 1994). This testifies to its wide distribution, and the hypothesis of its use in the Neolithic of the ancient Near East (Anderson 1994) makes it older and indicates its place of origin.

Consequently, it is necessary to emphasize once more the common features, both in tool structure and frequency, of agricultural implements in the cultures of the Balkans and the Near East. These include earth-working, harvesting, threshing, and grain-grinding tools. The similar features of

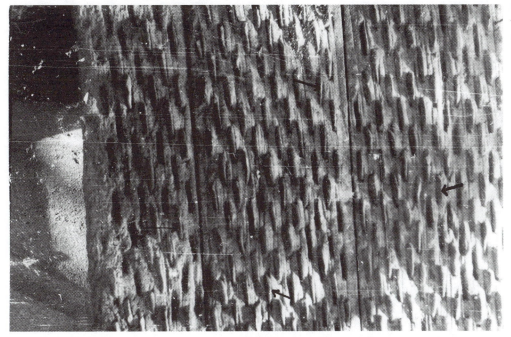

Figure 21.13 Experimental threshing sledge inserts (indicated by arrows)

cultural-economic character shown by southeastern Europe and the Near East explain the common features of the implements (Skakun 1987). The Eneolithic inserts from Bulgaria and from Tell Kutan in Iraq are also similar from the typological viewpoint, because their blanks were middle parts of straight blades known in the Balkans as "Dobrudja blades" (Skakun 1982; 1984; 1996a,b) and in the Near East as "Canaanian blades" (Neuville 1930; Crowfoot 1960; Rosen 1983; Pèlegrin 1996). Their qualitative characteristics depend on the same technique of flint knapping, oriented to producing huge blades, repeatedly described elsewhere (Skakun 1981a; 1984; 1987; 1993a; 1996a, c, d).

Hoes

At the same time as the appearance of new tools (the ardshare and the threshing sledge), the use of implements originating in the prior Neolithic period was also pursued. Nevertheless, these were also subject to transformations, oriented toward perfection or toward the exploitation of a new type of material. Tools such as hoes were made both of horn or stone and of copper, for instance (figure 21.14; Chernykh 1978). Their emergence substantially increased the productivity of digging tools, which play a large part in Mediterranean-type agriculture of southern Europe, because an essential condition of success is to frequently work the soil after tillage so that it can retain some humidity during the summer drought (Clark 1953). Hoes of a similar shape were still used in southern Europe during later historic periods (Semenov 1974).

Among hoes made of a traditional material, antler hoes are the most common (10–25 cm long; figure 21.14c). By the shape of their cutting edge, they are distributed into conical hoes and hoes in the shape of flat axes. Their profile is most often curved and their butt straight or slightly convex. The hafting hole is circular or rectangular. The tools with small holes, which were not convenient for handles, could be fastened to them like ancient Egyptian tools (for example, Lurie 1940:131). The surface of some tools retains a horn film, while the surface of others is completely polished. Their highly worn working edge bears characteristic use-wear striae.

The experiments carried out with horn hoes revealed a difference in efficiency according to blade shape. Hoes with blades in the shape of flat axes are advocated for all types of soils and for terracing; their productivity on loessic soils is between 60 and 100 m². Hoes with conical blades are useful on friable soils (Korobkova 1975; 1980).

Trapezoidal or triangular stone hoes are rarely found on sites. Their working edges are characterized by extremely marked use-wear traces. The facets of large flake scars, which shape the blade, are highly worn and the edge itself is blunted. Two flint axes were used as hoes; apart from the deformation of their working edge, they have a marked polish and deep striae.

Sickles and Harvesting Knives

Harvesting tools are the same as in the Neolithic: sickles of Karanovo type with a curved haft where three or four flint inserts forming a denticulated blade are oriented obliquely (figure 21.15). Despite their similarity to Neolithic sickles, they show a morphological evolution. Their inserts are larger (2–2.5 by 2.5–3 cm), their shape becomes standardized, and their working edge often has denticulate retouch, which is common in the Bronze Age. Highly worn elements bear a mirror-like polish on the angle. Microscopic traces of use-wear include pits with furrowed edges and thin, long striae parallel to one another and to the working edge (figure 21.8a; Semenov 1949).

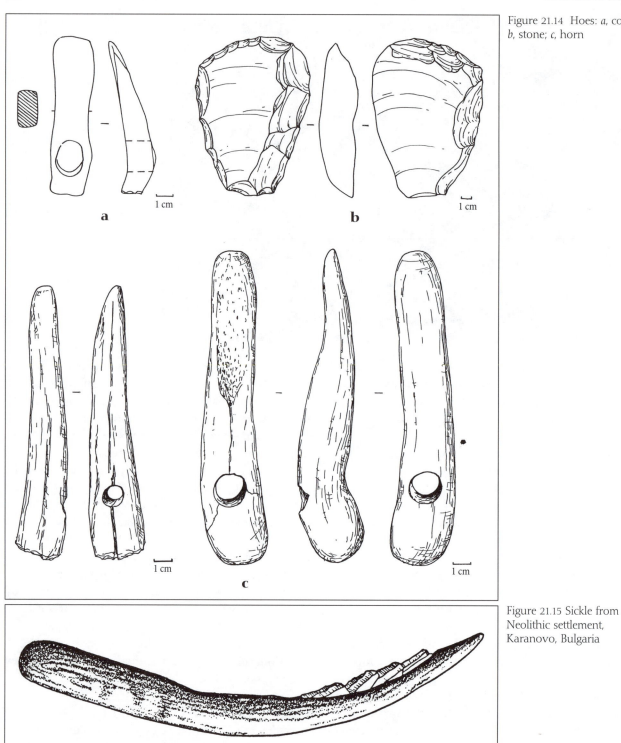

Figure 21.14 Hoes: a, copper; b, stone; c, horn

Figure 21.15 Sickle from Neolithic settlement, Karanovo, Bulgaria

Interestingly, in the Bulgarian material, use-wear analysis shows knives that are used for grass cutting. They differ completely in their structure from tools used for cereal harvesting (figure 21.16). They are large whole blades or long fragments (1.8–2.0 by 2.5–3 cm), with a straight profile and slightly convex distal end (Skakun 1985a,b). Generally, this end is reduced by inverse retouch. On the lateral working edge, the use-wear traces form a thin, bright band, which in places shows microscopic notches arranged into distinct

groups and also thin cobweb striae (figure 21.18). The distal end presents the strongest deformation because it is the area most often in contact with the ground.

Blunted tools were sharpened by retouching. Grass-cutting knives were used either without a haft (in this case, they were rather long and easily held in the hand) or in a straight haft to which they were attached diagonally. Experiments have shown that this form of tool was dictated by its specific use, grass cutting, as grass differs from cereals in physical

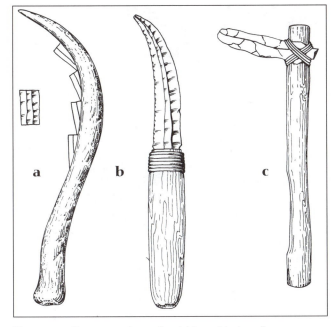

Figure 21.16 Reconstructions of a sickle and knives for grass

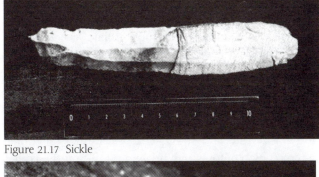

Figure 21.17 Sickle

Figure 21.18 Sickle (40x)

Figure 21.19 Harvesting with a Karanovo-type sickle

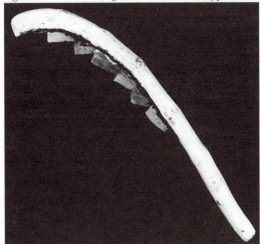

Figure 21.20 Reconstruction of Karanovo-type sickle

properties and mode of growth (figure 21.17, 21.18). We sometimes find large one-bladed knives, which served for cereal harvesting; there are only isolated examples, never a series, suggesting that their use for this function is anecdotal.

It is interesting to observe that sickles serve to cut cereals, which have a relatively dry stem, and knives to reap grass, whose stem contains much humidity which rapidly softens the adhesive on the blades of composite tools such as hooks and puts them out of service. This is why one-blade harvesting knives are more efficient for reaping the different sorts of grass, whether they have a flexible or rigid stem, whether they are short or long. After ten hours' intense work, the blade did not require rehafting or particular repair and remained suitable for use. Grass-cutting tools fitted with a haft resemble, in structure, ethnographic tarpans with a metallic blade and short haft, which served for cutting grass and reeds (Vakarel'ski 1977).

To distinguish correctly which tools were meant for cutting which plants, we can refer to Patricia Anderson's fundamental works on phytoliths (Anderson-Gerfaud 1986). The development of her method is particularly important in solving the complex problems raised by cereal domestication from the appearance and development of agriculture (Lisitsyna and Filipovich 1980; Popova 1985). Thus, thanks to the recent discovery of wild cereals in the Balkans, this territory appears as one possible center of early agriculture (Lisitsyna and Filipovich 1980; Popova 1985). The discovery of ancient agricultural implements confirms this conclusion; however, harvesting tools belonging to the Neolithic have an already elaborate shape (curved sickle of Karanovo type), and it is impossible to trace their evolution from simple to complex shapes: from harvesting knives with blades parallel to the haft up to curved sickles, as observed in the material from central Asia (Korobkova 1978; 1981a,b; 1993; 1994; and chapter 19). On the one hand, this would support the hypothesis of an introduction of agriculture into the Balkans, but on the other, in this area, the period preceding the Neolithic (Mesolithic) is insufficiently studied. As is known from the data given above, the mirror polish is characteristic not only of sickle inserts but also of inserts of threshing sledges and of knives for grass, reed, and straw. That is why the functional interpretation of tools with bright gloss must be based not only on its presence but on all components of the analysis as well: macro-use-wear traces, character and location of polish, linear traces. The few records concerning the presence of plant cutting knives in upper Palaeolithic contexts can only testify, for the moment and in the best of cases, to intensive collecting. Here it seems advisable to bring up the difference between the use-wear traces shown on sickles meant for harvesting cultivated cereals and those on sickles having cut wild cereals. If we understand the process of linear trace formation (Semenov 1974; Korobkova and Yasupov 1977; Korobkova 1994) on these tools, and if we refer to experimental data, we can say that the intensity of such traces depends largely on the abrasive particles contained in the ground, which are fixed to plant stems by natural factors such as wind and rain; that is why the best marked traces are due to cultivated plants, which grow on a worked soil, and not to wild plants, which grow on virgin soil. The problems of diagnosis of sickles for harvesting wild cereals are currently intensely debated (Korobkova 1981a,b; 1994; Korobkova and Yasupov 1977; Anderson-Gerfaud 1983; 1988; Anderson 1991; 1994a,b; and chapters 12 and 13).

Grinding Implements

The last category of agricultural tools in the sites of the Varna culture is grinding implements: querns, handstones, mortars, and pestles (figure 21.21). Compared with their Neolithic counterparts, querns and handstones are appreciably larger, and they are therefore installed permanently in some particular area of the house, on special floors. Two types of clay floors can be identified: trough-shaped (*koryt*), rectangular, surrounded by a small 13 to 15 cm high rim and open on one side (the lower stone of the quern being fixed into the clay, at the bottom of koryt) and horseshoe, with the same placement of the stone. Hand querns, similar to Eneolithic ones, were in use among Bulgarian laborers until the beginning of the twentieth century (Vakarelski 1977). Hand mills, which are no longer used and are kept in a corner of summer kitchens, can still be found in a few houses in the

Figure 21.21 Experimental grain grinding

village of Nagornoe. The lower quern, on a special floor, just as Eneolithic ones were, is sealed into a clay block and surrounded by a small, similarly molded rim which prevents grains and flour from spilling out.

Conclusion

Study of the material belonging to the Eneolithic culture of Varna reveals a highly varied agricultural tool assemblage. The emergence of previously unknown types of tools (ardshares, threshing sledges, and metallic hoes), modification of earlier implements, standardization of sickle blade shapes, increase in quern size, and differentiation and specialization of tools all increased the technological level of agriculture, which in turn seems to reflect the general technical progress made in the Eneolithic overall (Skakun 1987). The level of agricultural production attained with the introduction of tilling contributed to subsequent economic development.

Acknowledgment. This chapter was translated from French by Jacqueline Gaudey, CRA, CNRS, France.

Chapter 22 ❧

Threshing Sledges and Archaeology

Kathryn Ataman

ONE APPROACH TOWARDS THE UNDERSTANDING of past agricultural practices is through the recording and study of the rapidly disappearing technology of traditional agricultural economies. Over the last several decades there has been considerable interest in the continued use of the threshing sledge (figure 22.1) in the eastern Mediterranean region. Archaeological interest in these implements stems from the fact that their undersides are studded with flint flakes (figure 22.2) and that the origin and development of this agricultural practice could possibly be detected through the identification of excavated examples of these flakes. Additional interest derives from the fact that they represent one of the few remaining instances of the production and use of chipped stone tools and their study offers insight into a technology that is for the most part extinct. Two questions arise in this context: Can the use of threshing sledges be recognized archaeologically? Can the earliest use of these implements can be determined? I think the first of these questions can be answered affirmatively, but we cannot yet answer the second.

Previous studies of these implements have concentrated primarily on their manufacture and use (Fox 1985; Pearlman 1984; Hornell 1930; Bordaz 1965, Crawford 1935; Hillman 1984b, 1985; Klaey 1967; Kosay 1951; Dalman 1933) but some researchers have suggested criteria for identifying them in archaeological contexts (Whallon 1978; Fuji 1986; Crawford 1935). Curwen (1937), Adams (1975) and Diamond (1974) have identified what they assume to be archaeological examples of these flakes, but their identifications are not based on the comparison of detailed morphology or wear of archaeological and ethnographic pieces. Additional problems

Figure 22.1 Woman seated on threshing sledge drawn by horses

Figure 22.2 Working face of threshing sledge

with these studies center on the fact that they are based on very small samples which exhibit a narrow range of variation when in fact, the existing ethnographic examples of these artifacts as well as their production, use, and discard practices are extremely diverse.

To evaluate the identifying criteria suggested by previous researchers and to add criteria suggested by the examination of the morphology and wear traces of a large sample of modern sledge elements, in this chapter I would like to review ethnographic and historical data about the manufacture, use, and discard of these sledges.

Modern Manufacture

Modern examples of threshing sledges are still found in Turkey, Cyprus, Syria, and possibly in other areas. Earlier in this century sledges were in use in most of the countries around the Mediterranean. The recent historical distribution of these sledges however may not reflect their distribution in the past. In some parts of mainland Greece and the island of Melos they were introduced in the early twentieth century (Wagstaff 1982). These tools, which are called *düven*, *döven*, or *gem* in Turkey and *doukani* in Cyprus, are now rapidly going out of use as agricultural mechanization spreads even to remote areas.

Although there are slight differences in these sledges from one area to another, there is a great deal of similarity between them. Examination of the modern manufacture, use, and discard of these implements can give us insight into what we might expect from archaeological examples though differences should also be expected. Most of my observations are based on Turkish examples from various regions, but I have also consulted literature from other areas.

Threshing sledges are composed of two or three wooden planks fastened together lengthwise with two or three cross-pieces. One end of the board curves upward to facilitate its smooth travel over the threshing floor. They are approximately 1.5 to 2 m in length and may weigh up to 50 kg, but their size varies in different regions. A rope or chain is attached to the curved end and is fastened to an animal which drags it behind. Donkeys, horses, oxen, water buffaloes, or cows are used to pull the sledges. An adult, an adult and a child, or even several children usually sit or stand on the sledge in order to add weight and steer it around the threshing floor (figures 22.3, 22.4), but the use of stones as weights has also been observed (Forde 1931; Bordaz 1965; White 1967).

The teeth of the threshing sledges are produced from either local raw material which may be flint, basalt, or other flakable stone or may be imported as prepared tool blanks, which are usually made of flint. Bordaz reported in 1965 that the town of Éakmak ("flint" in Turkish) near Bursa in Turkey functioned as a specialist center and produced threshing sledge flakes for most of Turkey. In this area, flint was mined from deep pits and large quantities were produced but there are still other areas which served as such distribution centers in the recent past. Whallon noted (1978) that flakes produced in the Sivas area were sold in Elazig which is a distance of 400 km. Flint sources at Birecik in southeastern Turkey (where the flint erodes from a cliff face) were also utilized by

Figure 22.3 Man using threshing sledge drawn by horses

Figure 22.4 Man and two children using cattle-drawn threshing sledge

Figure 22.5 Flintknapper producing flakes for the repair of threshing sledge, Çankersek village near Bozova in Urfa province

flintknappers from a wide area. A knapper from the city of Urfa, who uses flint from this source told me that both his father and grandfather had been flintknappers and also depended on this source. The range of variation in the raw material of the flints I have collected from several areas in Turkey also supports the idea that many areas near sources functioned as centers for the manufacture and distribution of blanks. Markets in the eastern half of Turkey still offer new sledges as well as replacement flints but very few are sold today.

In Turkey flakes are produced with a specially made double-ended blunt pointed metal hammer or with a double-

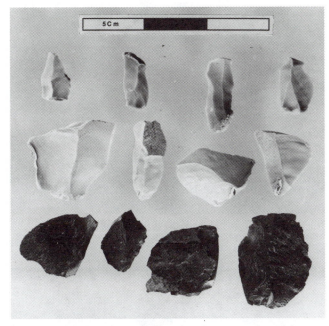

Figure 22.6 Blanks for threshing sledge elements collected from various areas, *Top row*, Çankersek village; *middle row*, city of Urfa; *bottom row*, Beypazari

Table 22.1 Length of unretouched blanks in ethnographic samples (cm)

	SAMPLE 1*	SAMPLE 2**	SAMPLE 3***
1	4.6	5.3	4.7
2	4.3	5.1	6.4
3	3.8	4.9	5.6
4	5.9	4.0	6.9
5			6.2
6			5.7
7			4.8
8			5.8
9			4.0
10			4.6
11			5.8
12			7.9
13			5.8
14			6.4
15			4.9
TOTAL	18.6	19.3	85.5
AVERAGE	4.65	4.825	5.7

*   Çankersek village, Urfa, blades-flint
**   Beypazari, flakes-basalt
*** City of Urfa, flakes and blade-flakes flint

pronged hammer (figure 22.5). A different type of double-ended metal hammer, lighter and more pointed than those seen in Turkey is documented for Cyprus (Pearlman 1984) and is also used in Turkey for retouching the blanks. The blanks produced are blades, flakes, and blade-like flakes whose shape is affected by factors such as raw material availability and knapping skill from one region to another (figure 22.6). The flakes are detached by handheld direct percussion with little platform preparation or core shaping. Three samples of unretouched blanks produced in three different areas were compared (table 22.1). One sample, produced from a fine flint river cobble, consists of true blades with an average length of 4.6 cm. Another sample of basalt flakes had an average length of 4.8 cm. The third sample, made on a fine but not glassy flint which was made into flakes and blade-like flakes, had an average length of 5.7 cm. The blades illustrated by Bordaz made at Çakmak are longer, narrower and more regular than the pieces in these samples.

The flakes are shaped and the edges strengthened with retouch using the same type of hammer, on a stone, a wooden board or sometimes a metal anvil consisting of a large spike driven into a board. In Urfa a sledge maker was observed using one hammer as an anvil and another as a percussor (figure 22.7). The retouching is carried out by the person who inserts the flints and is not usually done in advance as the flakes must be shaped to fit the length of the particular slots.

The boards are nailed together and slots for the flakes put in with a hammer and chisel (figure 22.8). A single flake is fit into each slot. In Cyprus and in Turkey a special chisel used only for threshing sledges which produces a slot designed to tightly hold the flakes is favored (Pearlman 1984). The quantity and arrangement of the slots varies from place to place. Sometimes they are arranged in straight parallel rows and sometimes in a herringbone pattern but they are always aligned with the long axis of the sledge. The orientation of the individual flakes in the slots also varies but often some flakes are angled inwards in order to prevent the threshed material from spreading off the threshing floor. The flakes are pounded into the sledge with a wooden mallet or sometimes with a metal hammer (figure 22.9). Several hundred flakes are included in each sledge.

In some areas liquid bitumen is poured over the bottom of the sledge after the flakes are inserted. This serves both to grip the flakes and to preserve the wood of the sledge. It is interesting to note that the teeth of the threshing sledges mentioned in the Sumerian Farmer's Almanac are described as being fastened with bitumen and leather (Kramer 1963).

The by-products (that is the cores and waste flakes) produced by the manufacture of threshing sledge flints are not very different from the waste produced by the manufacture of most post-Neolithic flint tools. This indicates that manufacturing debris produced by the preparation of flint teeth for threshing sledges in prehistoric contexts could probably not be recognized in the archaeological record and thus cannot be used as an indicator of the presence of of these tools in a prehistoric assemblage.

Use and Discard
Threshing sledges are used for a limited time during the year, only a three- or four-month period during the summer and autumn. Threshing floors are usually located in open areas, sometimes within but usually at the edge or even a bit away from a village, situated so that the wind will not blow the dust

created by this practice into the settlement. During use, some elements may fall out of the sledge and remain on the threshing floor. The entire surface of both faces of these pieces are in contact with the straw and in addition to the gloss which may form on the cutting edge, the highest spots of the flat surfaces may also exhibit gloss. Since sometimes the flints may be replaced in a different orientation in the sledge after being dislocated, the gloss on some pieces may be found on more than one edge. One or more edges may be battered and/or retouched and sometimes one or more edges are heavily rounded.

When sledges lose enough teeth they become less effective and need to be repaired. This may be done with flakes collected from the threshing floor, with pieces purchased at the market for this purpose or with flakes manufactured on the spot. In addition, in the recent past there were specialist itinerant sledge repairers in some villages who repaired the sledges in surrounding villages (Klaey 1967) during several months of the year but few people skilled in this task still remain. The villages where these specialists lived are sometimes identifiable by such names as Çakmakçilar, and Çakmakköy, (Flintknapper's Village, Flint Village).

When finally discarded, sledges may be incorporated into structural features in the village (as doors, for example) or may be left in an outbuilding or courtyard. In much of the area where these sledges are still used today, wood is a scarce and valuable resource and is often reused. Thus flints from threshing sledges could be found in any of a number of contexts which may or may not have had any relation to threshing activities. Bits of straw and grain remaining on threshing floors are also sometimes burned and then collected and spread on fields. I have recovered threshing-sledge flints in the ashes spread on fields as fertilizer.

Therefore, the context in which possible threshing-sledge elements are found may not necessarily help to determine their function. The most useful contexts would be a concentration of these pieces or possibly an association with a threshing floor, if this could be recognized in an archaeological context. Threshing floors are sometimes paved with pebbles or potsherds and their soil is more densely packed than the surrounding area, so it may be possible to recognize these features in an archaeological context. The possibility of discovering such a concentration is not unthinkable since such a large number of threshing-sledge flints are embedded in each sledge.

The use of threshing sledges has changed recently. Today in many areas of Turkey they are more often used to chop straw into small pieces for the production of mudbrick, animal feed, or fuel rather than for threshing grain—although the threshing of pulse crops is still practiced in some areas. The use of chopped straw is also an ancient custom as evidenced by its frequent inclusion in the mudbrick of prehistoric structures. This is another indication that some

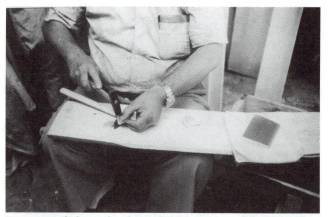

Figure 22.7 Sledge maker (city of Urfa) preparing flint blanks for insertion in sledge, city of Urfa. He is using one hammer as an anvil.

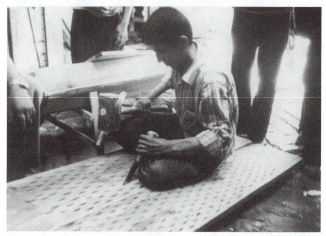

Figure 22.8 Sledge maker making slots in the sledge for the insertion of flints using a special chisel and a wooden mallet

Figure 22.9 Sledge maker inserting flints in slots of sledge underbody, city of Urfa

kind of sledge or harrow may have been used in early periods since straw is difficult to chop in other ways.

The production of flakes for threshing sledges is perhaps one of the last remaining instances of the use of chipped stone technology in present-day agricultural communities. The variation in the production of these pieces as well as the production, distribution and use of the threshing sledges themselves should be properly documented before it disappears completely.

Historical References to the Threshing Sledges

Most of our knowledge of the ancient use of threshing sledges comes from literary evidence. The use of threshing sledges in Roman times is well documented (the Latin name is *tribulum*) and flint as well as iron teeth and the use of both horses and oxen are mentioned (White 1967). There are references to what are probably toothed threshing sledges in the Old Testament (*morag* or *moreg*), probably dating to the eighth or sixth century BC (Isaiah XLI 15), and the teeth of these implements are described with adjectives including "new" and "sharp" but these sledges could have been set with either metal or stone cutting elements. Akkadian references to objects translated as "threshing boards" are also documented but their identification is somewhat problematic. The word for an implement used to thresh in Akkadian is *Dajastu* and in Sumerian *GIS.UR* and there is little doubt about its interpretation as a threshing sledge since clear references to the manufacture and use of such implements exist in the Sumerian Farmer's Almanac (Kramer 1963, Salonen 1968) which dates to the third millennium BC, but again the material the teeth are made of is not specified. How much earlier the threshing sledge could have been employed is not known but it would have been useful as soon as free-threshing cereals were developed and domesticated in the early Neolithic. However it probably was not invented until draft animals were domesticated. In the Near East, the use of animals for carrying burdens and for pulling carts, plows, and other implements may occur as early as the fifth or sixth millennium BC but there is no unambiguous evidence until the fourth millennium (Davis 1987).

There are also many alternative threshing methods which could have been used to process free-threshing grains. These methods include harvesting by hand-stripping (which would negate the need for threshing), animal trampling, flailing, or an archaeologically based reconstruction of a method of stripping using a notched bone tool (Stordeur and Anderson-Gerfaud 1985). Hittite references to threshing are confined to descriptions of animal trampling of grain, and so it is unclear whether sledges were used in Anatolia as early as the Late Bronze Age (Hoffner 1974). Egyptian texts and pictorial representations of grain threshing are also confined to animal-trampling (Wilkinson 1891).

Archaeological Identification of Sledge Elements

Curwen describes a single flint flake recovered from a Roman villa in Sussex and suggests that it may represent one tooth of a Roman threshing sledge (1937). He notes the presence of gloss and heavy wear and compares it to an element extracted from a modern Cypriote sledge. The blade is approximately 4.5 cm in length and 2 cm in width. Most of the surface of the flake is covered in gloss and one edge heavily rounded. It is possible that this does represent a threshing element but the accompanying illustration is not sufficiently detailed to allow evaluation. However it is unlikely that that threshing sledges would have been used in a wet climate like Britain with the exception of large manor farms where very large granaries or barns could have existed and the threshing could have been done under cover (Hillman pers. comm.).

Adams, (1975) suggests that threshing sledges could have been in use at least several hundred years earlier than mentioned in Sumerian texts. He reports on a group of 51 roughly chipped coarse flint flakes found within a 28 m² area from the surface of a site in Iraq probably dating to the late Uruk period. Since the pieces were recovered from the surface, the dating is not definite but as similar modern pieces have not been noted, all the material has been assumed to be contemporary. In this chapter, Adams discusses whether these flakes originally formed part of a prehistoric threshing sledge, a harrow or possibly a group of small hoes. These pieces range in length from approximately 3.5 to 5.5 cm and the two with illustrated sections are about 1.5 cm thick.

These pieces have been chipped into expanding bifacially retouched flakes. The assumed working edge was the expanding edge and is frequently "chipped and battered." The pieces were examined with a x30 hand lens. Grinding or abrasion were not observed, but gloss similar to sickle sheen was observed on the wide edge in at least a few cases.

Experimental replication and microscopic examination of resulting wear traces could suggest whether the identification of these flakes as threshing-sledge elements is a reasonable conclusion. The Uruk pieces are of quite a different shape from modern threshing-sledge elements but they are of a similar size and the described wear traces are roughly similar. The depth to which they must have been embedded in a sledge and whether the protruding flakes allow a stable platform for the sledge must be a critical factor.

In a less specific identification, Pitt-Rivers suggests that one explanation for the presence of unretouched flints in his excavations at two Romano-British sites is that the pieces he recovered could have been elements of threshing sledges (Pitt-Rivers 1888, Vol. II:239–241, Vol. IV:201). In one case from Wicklebury Camp, he describes a group of 445 flakes found within a 4'6" x 2' area. He suggests three possible explanations for their presence: the use of the *tribulum*, the use of flint in historical times for unknown purposes (such as hide scraping), or the possibility that they date to the Neolithic and were excavated from a scatter remaining on an old soil surface. These pieces are not illustrated in General Pitt-Rivers' publication but their examination could suggest whether use as elements of threshing sledges is likely.

I am aware of only one other identification of archaeological pieces as threshing-sledge elements. From the site of Knossos (Diamond 1974), a single obsidian blade

Table 22.2 Attributes of ethnographic threshing-sledge elements

	LENGTH (cm)	WIDTH (cm)	THICKNESS (cm)	BLANK TYPE (B/F/B-F)	BATTERING (# of edges)	HEAVY ROUNDING (# of edges)	GLOSS (# of edges)	EDGE ANGLE (in °)	MICROWEAR TRACES
OBSIDIAN SAMPLES									
Erzerum-Çat									
1	2.8	2.9	0.9	F	4	1	-	106	RLF, abrasion
2	4.1	2.5	1.3	F	2	-	-	54	RLF, heavy parallel
3	3.6	1.8	0.8	F	3	-	-	63	heavy, wide st., abrasion RLF
FLINT SAMPLES (and other occasional material)									
Tunceli-Elaziğ									
4*	3.9	2.7	0.8	F	1	1	1	50	RLF, SG
5	4.4	2.5	0.8	F	2	1	1	57	WG
Cankersek-Urfa									
6	4	2.1	0.8	B-F	1	1	1	83	WG, SG
7	4.1	2.3	0.9	B-F	2	1	1	62	SG
8	3.6	2.1	0.8	B-F	2	1	1	52	WG
9	3.6	1.8	0.6	B-F	1	1	1	59	WG, SG
10	3.9	2.2	0.7	B-F	-	1	1	37	WG, SG
Amasya									
11	4	2.9	0.8	B-F	1	-	1	55	E
12	4.3	2.9	1.1	B-F	1	-	surface	60	SG
13	4	3.6	1.3	F	-	-	-	46	SG
Cümcüme-Urfa									
14	3.7	2.5	0.8	F	2	1	1	54	WG, SG
15	3.9	2.1	0.4	B-F	1	-	-	62	RLF
16	3.8	2.2	0.6	B-F	1	-	1	59	RLF
17	4	2.3	0.8	B-F	2	-	1	84	WG
18	3.4	2.6	1.2	F	2	-	plus surface	80	RLF, SG
19	3.7	2.4	0.6	B-F	1	-	-	55	RLF, SG
20	3.1	1.6	0.9	B	2	-	-	44	SG
21	2.9	1.2	0.5	B	1	-	2	52	WG
22	3	2.3	0.8	F	2	1	2	85	RLF
23	3.8	2.7	0.9	F	2	1	1	57	WG, SG
24	2.9	2.5	0.7	F	2	-	-	40	SG
25	3.7	2.3	0.7	B-F	2	-	1	58	WG, SG
Çorum									
26	3.5	3	3.1	F	1	-	1	56	E, SG
27	3.7	2.6	1	F	1	-	-	61	OBSCURED
28	4.2	2.8	1	F	1	1	1	64	LIGHT1, HEAVY 1
29	4.2	2.9	1.2	F	1	-	1	71	OBSCURED
30	3.3	2.5	1.1	F	1	-	1	65	E, SG
31	4	2.8	1.1	F	2	-	2	49	2 HEAVY, SG
32	3.6	1.9	0.7	F	2	1	1	53	RLF, SG
Beypazari									
33	4	2.8	1.1	F	2	-	2	57	SG
34	3.6	1.9	0.7	F	2	1	1	69	WG, RLF
35	4.6	3.1	0.8	F	1	-	1	82	E, SG
Erzerum									
36	4	2.7	1.4	F	Too coarse to determine wear patterns			92	-
37	4.1	3	1.4	F				89	-
38	3.4	2.5	1.5	F				88	-
39	3	1.3	1	F	-	3	3	90	-
Erzerum-Çat									
40	4.4	2.1	0.7	B	1	1	1	74	WG, RLF, SG
41	4.9	2.1	0.7	B	2	1	1	54	WG, RLF
42	3.2	2.4	0.5	F	1	-	2	63	WG
43	3.6	2.1	0.5	B	1	1	2	61	SG
44	5.2	2.1	0.4	B	1	-	-	56	WG, SG
45	3.4	2.2	0.7	F	2	1	1	73	WG, SG
46	5	2.4	0.8	B	2	1	1	53	WG, RLF, SG

* Bitumen traces present

Notes: WG = Wide grooves, RLF = Random linear features, SG = Surface gloss, E = One edge only

Table 22.2 Attributes of ethnographic threshing sledge elements, *continued*

	LENGTH (cm)	WIDTH (cm)	THICKNESS (cm)	BLANK TYPE (B/F/B-F)	BATTERING (# of edges)	HEAVY ROUNDING (# of edges)	GLOSS (# of edges)	EDGE ANGLE (in °)	MICROWEAR TRACES
FLINT SAMPLES (and other occasional material), *continued*									
Erzerum-Çat, continued									
47	4.7	2.3	0.6	B-F	1	1	1	55	WG, RLF, SG
48	5	2.3	0.6	B	1	-	1	71	WG, RLF
49	5.3	2.1	0.4	B	2	1	surface	57	RLF, SG
50	4.7	2.1	0.5	B-F	1	1	surface	50	WG, RLF
51	4.6	2.3	0.8	B	1	1	1	60	E
52	4.8	2.2	0.6	B	1	1	2	49	WG, SG
53	4.6	2.4	0.7	B	1	1	surface	41	RLF, SG
Cümcüme Sample 2									
54	3.7	2.2	0.8	F	2	1	1	60	WG, RLF, SG
55	3.6	2.4	1	F	1	1	surface	61	RLF
56	4.8	3.1	0.9	B-F	-	-	-	58	RLF, SG
57	3.5	2.7	1	F	2	1	surface	40	SG
58	3.8	3.2	0.8	F	1	-	surface	31	E, SG
59	3.2	2.3	1.1	F	1	1	1	39	RLF, SG
60	4.2	2.1	1.3	F	1	1	surface	72	RLF, SG
61	3	2.2	0.8	F	2	-	-	61	RLF, SG
62	3.6	2	0.6	F	1	-	1	55	RLF, SG
63*	3.6	1.8	0.8	F	2	-	-	57	RLF, SG
64	3.7	2.4	0.9	F	1	1	1	61	RLF, SG
65	3.5	2.7	0.6	F	1	-	-	73	WG
66	2.8	1.8	0.7	F	1	-	1	78	SG
67	3.5	1.9	0.7	F	1	1	-	55	WG, RLF
68	2.7	1.9	0.6	F	1	1	1	73	RLF, SG
69	3.1	1.9	0.7	F	2	-	-	53	E
70	3.2	2.1	0.6	F	3	-	surface	72	SG
71	4.2	2.4	0.8	F	1	-	-	68	SG
72	4	2.6	0.9	F	2	-	-	64	WG, SG
Oxford Museum									
73	4.6	2.1	1	B-F	1	1	1 and surface		
74	4.8	2.2	0.8	B-F	-	1	1		
75	4.5	2.3	0.7	B-F	2	-	1		
76	4.3	2.4	0.9	B-F	1	-	surface		
77	5	2.3	0.7	B-F	2	-	1 and surface		
78	4.3	2.5	1.1	F	1	-	1		
79	5.4	2.5	0.9	B-F	2	1	2		
80	4.4	1.9	0.9	B-F	1	-	1		
81	5.4	2.5	0.7	B-F	-	-	surface		
82	5.1	2.1	0.8	B-F	2	1	2		
83	4.3	2.5	0.8	F	1	1	1		
84	4.8	2.2	0.7	B-F	-	-	2		
Science Museum									
85	5	2.7	0.9	B-F	1	1	1		
86	5	2.5	0.9	B-F	1	-	2		
87	5.4	2.1	1	B	1	1	2		
88	3.5	2.1	0.9	F	2	1	2		
89	4.3	3	0.9	F	1	-	surface		
90	3.6	2.1	0.8	F	1	-	surface		
91	3.5	2.2	0.7	F	1	1	1		
92	4.7	2.2	0.9	B-F	1	1	1 and surface		
93	3.8	2.9	1.1	F	-	-	surface		
94	5.1	2.9	1	B-F	2	-	surface		
95	5.2	2.8	1	B-F	2	1	1		
96	4.8	2.9	1	F	2	-	surface		
97	4.2	3.1	0.9	F	-	-	surface		
98	4.5	3.3	1.1	F	2	-	surface		
99	4.5	3.1	1	F	1	1	1		
100	5.1	2.9	1.1	F	2	-	surface		

* Bitumen traces present
Notes: WG = Wide grooves, RLF = Random linear features, SG = Surface gloss, E = One edge only

was identified as having wear characteristics which might be expected to be present on threshing-sledge elements and several others were mentioned as being possible elements. These pieces were found in an area of the Early Neolithic I occupation area and were associated with an open courtyard area tentatively identified as a threshing floor on the basis of the presence of a scatter of charred grain and ash in an open area within the site.

The examination of the wear traces was made using a stereoscopic microscope and magnifications of up to about 50x. The wear observed consisted of edge rounding and striations parallel to the working edge which Diamond associates with plant-cutting but the consideration of additional edge damage characteristics led him to identify at least one piece as a threshing-sledge element. The piece of obsidian in question is a broken flake measuring approximately 1.5 x 1.0 cm with retouch along two edges. A photograph of the edge of the blade (shown at x48) shows a rounded edge but striations are not visible. This identification must be regarded as speculative as no comparison to ethnographic or experimental threshing elements (whether flint or obsidian) was made although experiments in plant-cutting were undertaken. In my own experiments I have not been able to recognize distinctive plant-cutting traces on obsidian (in particular, sickle gloss), which have been claimed by other researchers (Vaughan 1981; Hurcombe 1986).

In a less specific context, Woolley (1955) suggested that some of the sickle blades recovered from archaeological sites could actually be the flakes from threshing sledges. He notes that any flake that exhibits gloss is usually called a sickle but that the shape and wear on threshing-sledge flints is quite different and could be used to distinguish them from sickles.

The distinction between sickle blades and threshing-sledge elements has also been addressed by Fuji (1986). He lists the frequent or rare occurrence of certain features of prehistoric sickle blades and modern threshing-sledge flints and suggests that these criteria can be used to distinguish between them. These features include details of blank morphology, type of hafting, intensity and distribution of gloss, and edge damage. Although some of Fuji's observations do seem to hold true, such as the edge rounding and battering which is more common on threshing-sledge elements than on sickles, many of the differences which he notes are not paralleled in my own observations of numerous examples of both classes of artifacts. In particular, his observations about the amount and location of retouch (for example the statement that sickles are usually denticulated) and the distribution of polish are probably based on too small a sample.

Clearly the presence of gloss is not exclusively confined either to sickle blades or threshing-sledge flints and cannot be used to distinguish between these two tool classes but there are other characteristics which may be used to separate them. The shape of the blanks are rarely similar and the edge angle on sickles is generally lower than on threshing-sledge elements. The working edge of plant-cutting tools must be relatively sharp and it is unlikely that most threshing sledge flints (which often have a one or more heavily battered edges) could harvest grain efficiently. The use-wear traces found on threshing-sledge elements include the presence of one (or more) battered edge(s), sometimes heavily rounded, and with gloss on the same edge as the rounding and battering. On sickles the edge damage is usually less extensive except when deliberately produced by retouch (in which case the gloss and the edge damage are usually on different edges). In addition, some examples of threshing-sledge flints exhibit gloss over most of the the dorsal and ventral surfaces. Microscopic features can also be used to distinguish them. Sickles with postdepositionally induced edge damage would not usually be confused with sledge elements since the edge damage will be random and not associated with the edge exhibiting gloss. A more important potential instance for confusion is between threshing-sledge flints and battered flakes with postdepositional traces caused by trampling or other factors. The traces on these two types of flakes may be confused but when both microscopic and macrosopic information is combined and larger groups of objects are included in the analysis, most cases of ambiguity can be resolved.

A Sample of Ethnographic Sledge Elements

Examination of modern threshing-sledge flints collected from several areas in Turkey and some museum specimens from Syria and Palestine has shown both similarities and differences between various regions and between individual specimens from a single region. The macroscopic attributes of one hundred of these pieces are noted in table 22.2.

The flakes in this sample are made of a wide variety of material ranging from very fine flint to a very coarse igneous rock found in a sledge near Erzerum. There is also a range in the general morphology of the pieces: a few are blades, many are blade-like flakes but the majority are flakes (figure 22.10). At least one edge is often shaped by retouch. Most of the pieces which are true blades were collected from threshing floors in a single village near Çat in Northeastern Turkey and are the pieces which most resemble archaeologically recovered sickle blades.

The pieces in the sample range from 2.7 to 5.4 cm in length with a mean of 4.1 cm (table 22.3). The thickness of the flakes is extremely variable, reflecting both unstandardized knapping techniques and and unselective choice of flakes for insertion in the sledges. This may be a recent phenomenon resulting from a decline in the practice of flintknapping but regional variation in quality and standardization could also have been a feature of production in the past.

Edge battering may occur on one or more edges (figure 22.11). This battering is seen on the working, not the hafted edge. Although damage may be present on the hafted, edge, it more often takes the form of individual flake scars or snap fractures rather than the more extensive battering which is common on the working edges. If, however, the piece has been reversed in the sledge after being dislodged during use, battering may occur on two edges. The battering is produced by the hammering of the flakes into the sledge as well as by the heavy use it receives.

Traces of bitumen or resin on the hafted edge can be seen on some pieces but evidence of the use of an adhesive visible to the naked eye is not common in this sample.

Severe edge-rounding occurred on slightly less than one-half of the pieces examined. This type of wear seems to be distinctive to this long-term heavy use and does not appear to be produced by other actions except for severe and unusual postdepositional damage. However as this rounding is not produced until after long use, archaeologically recovered threshing-sledge flints (which may be discarded at any time during the life of a sledge) may or may not exhibit this feature.

In addition to this heavy edge damage, many pieces have macroscopic gloss on one or more edges or on the high spots of the flat surfaces. The gloss on the edges is caused by the contact between the flint and the threshed material as the sledge is dragged across the threshing floor. Depending on the angle at which the flints are inserted, the gloss may be confined to one end of the piece resembling the pattern occasionally seen on sickle blades whose hafting has been reconstructed with the blades set at an oblique angle to the handle (Cauvin 1974).

The gloss on flat surfaces may be produced when the pieces fall out of the sledge and are trampled and pushed around in the straw. The amount of gloss is probably related to length of use. Twenty years is not an unusual period of time to retain a sledge especially in dry areas although within this period some flints will be replaced. In the sample examined, the gloss is found most often on a single edge but the presence of gloss on the flat surfaces of the flakes is not uncommon. Occasionally there is gloss on two edges of the flints. The pieces in the museum sample were found in bags of grain imported from Palestine and Syria at the beginning of the century and have a higher incidence of gloss on the flat surfaces than the other pieces in the sample, many of which were extracted directly from threshing sledges. A frequently observed feature is interruption of the gloss by edge damage scars which results in a lower incidence of gloss than is usual on a sickle, the use of which does not often result in heavy edge damage.

The edge angles of 72 of the specimens in the sample were measured (figure 22.12). One measurement, taken from the midpoint of the most heavily used edge, was recorded for each piece. A wide variation in these angles was observed, ranging from 31 to 106 degrees. The median was 59.5 and the

Figure 22.10 Variation in size, shape and raw material of modern threshing-sledge elements can be seen in these samples from various areas of Turkey. The pieces in the top row are made of obsidian.

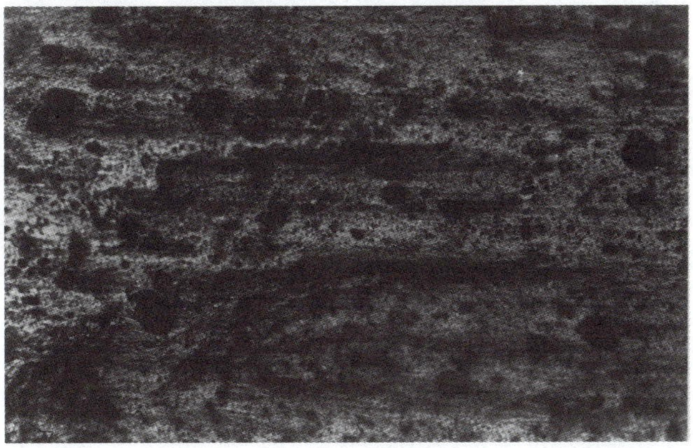

Figure 22.11 Micrograph of polish and comet-like pit on a heavily used ethnographic threshing sledge flint (original magnification x100)

Table 22.3 Summary of data for ethnographic threshing-sledge flints

Number of observations = 100 (measurements in cm)

	MIN	MAX	MED	MEAN	STD DEV
Length	2.7	5.4	4.00	4.06	0.695
Width	1.2	3.6	2.30	2.30	0.417
Thickness	0.3	3.1	0.80	0.88	0.333

Number of observations = 72 (measurements in °)

Edge angles	31	106	59.50	61.78	14.193

mean 61.8. These measurements suggest that edge angle is not a very precise indicator for the identification of threshing-sledge flints. However there are very few pieces with acute angles, only 10% of the pieces measured had angles less than 50 degrees. The use of a flint sickle with such a high angle would not be very efficient.

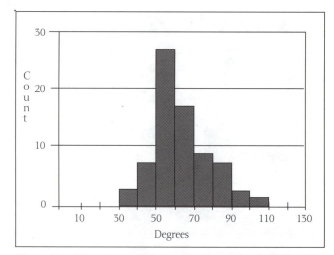

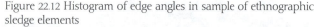

Figure 22.12 Histogram of edge angles in sample of ethnographic sledge elements

Figure 22.13 Micrograph showing polish, rounded edge, and wide striation on a modern threshing–sledge flint (original magnification x100)

Microscopic traces were examined on the same 72 specimens. The appearance of the gloss which the ethnographic pieces exhibit, resembles the gloss found on sickle blades but some differences are also apparent. The pieces with heavy polish and a very flat microtopography bear clear striations as well as so-called comet-shaped pits (Anderson-Gerfaud 1981; Vaughan 1981). On some of these, the striations are very wide (figure 22.13); such striations are not commonly observed on sickle blades. Light polish could be seen on the surfaces of many pieces, especially on ridges and bulbs which form the most exposed areas of their topography. Also, random striations on the surface were seen on many of the pieces. These may be caused by the trampling undergone by the pieces which fall out of sledges onto the threshing floor. Correlations between these features and the flints extracted from sledges as opposed to those collected from threshing floors could not be observed.

When the macroscopic and microscopic features of modern threshing-sledge flints are considered, the co-occurrence of these features could be used to recognize the presence of these pieces in an assemblage, but it must be remembered that there is an extremely wide variation among all of these features. A general size and shape and type of working edge, with any combination of battering, rounding, and the presence of macroscopic polish, along with the presence of microscopic wide striations and random striations and linear features all seem to characterize these pieces. Identification can be more reliable however when large samples are examined.

Although the general morphology of the modern examples of threshing-sledge flints is relevant to our understanding of the morphology of such pieces as used in the past, changes in manufacturing techniques may have influenced the shape of the resulting pieces. The use of metal hammers and chisels could have affected the shape of the flakes; so, perhaps the presence of the wear traces described above may be a more diagnostic feature than flake morphology for the identification of archaeological threshing sledge flints.

There is no doubt that changes in the manufacture and use of these tools have occurred within living memory. Today in Syria, tines of metal table forks or rounded pebbles sometimes replace flints, and in most places in Turkey sledges are no longer used for threshing, having been replaced by machines. In Turkey sheetmetal is used occasionally to reinforce the edges and front of the sledges. The substitution of coarse stones or metal blades for the flint sledge elements which can be seen in some areas may reflect loss of skill in the production of these pieces and the unavailability of flint or sledge blanks, but in my experience replacement flints can still be purchased in many rural market centers, at least in the eastern half of Turkey.

Obsidian Sledge Elements

The possibility of the existence of threshing sledges with obsidian teeth has also been examined in the course of this study. There is a reference to a model of an obsidian threshing sledge from a report of an exhibit in Paris in 1933 (Crawford 1935). I have heard from several individuals who claim to have seen obsidian-studded sledges in use. When I investigated one of these claims in a village south of Erzerum where obsidian is more readily available than flint, I did find two sledges which had a total of four obsidian flakes inserted in them. Many people I spoke to in the villages in that area however, told me that obsidian was never used in threshing sledges; so, its use does not seem to be common. However, as the decline in the use of threshing sledges continues, fewer and fewer people have detailed knowledge of their manufacture and use. It would be interesting to examine sledges in more remote villages in regions where stone other than obsidian must be imported.

The sample of pieces of obsidian threshing-sledge elements available is too small to determine whether distinctive morphological or wear characteristics can be determined, but some features were noted. One of the pieces collected was fragmentary so that only three were examined (figure 22.10). All three pieces had battering on more than one edge and one piece was battered on the entire circumference. This feature is undoubtedly the result of the more brittle nature of obsidian as opposed to flint. Only one example exhibited an edge with macroscopically visible rounding and none exhibited polish as it does not form on obsidian. In terms of microscopic wear, random striations were found on all three pieces but patterned striations oriented parallel to a heavily battered edge were seen on two pieces (figure 22.14). The edge which appeared macroscopically rounded could be seen under the microscope at x100 magnification to be due to severe abrasion not smoothing.

I have also heard reports of obsidian-studded, paddled threshing machines or wains (Turkish *cercer*). I have seen a photo of what is purported to be one of these but could not tell if it was studded only with metal or also with obsidian as claimed by my informant.

With a larger ethnographic or experimental sample, perhaps it would be possible to identify characteristics of obsidian threshing-sledge elements which would allow the recognition of these pieces from archaeological samples but it is not certain that obsidian was ever used for this purpose in the past. The ethnographic examples collected may reflect the decline of the sledge manufacturing industry. Obsidian is not as well suited to this purpose as flint and in areas where flint was readily available, one would not expect to find threshing-sledge elements made of obsidian.

Application

I have been studying the chipped stone industry from the site of Can Hasan III in Central Turkey, which is primarily an Aceramic Neolithic site. Most of this material is made of obsidian but some of the pieces are flint, a number of which have gloss on one or more edges or surfaces.

As I examined this material it was surprising to notice that several specimens resembled threshing-sledge flints (figure 22.15). When these pieces were examined under the microscope, I became convinced that that is indeed what these pieces represent. The stratigraphic context of these pieces suggested that it was not an unreasonable conclusion because all were surface or near-surface contexts and probably derive from historic times. Threshing is known to have been conducted on the site in recent times.

Eight pieces were tentatively identified as threshing-sledge flints. They were made of a variety of flint types, seven were flakes and one was a blade-like flake. The length of these pieces ranged from 2.3 to 3.7 cm. All of the pieces had heavily battered edges and exhibited shiny gloss. The shape and edge angles of all of these pieces, unlike some the ethnographic examples were not suitable for use as sickles, which need a relatively sharp, straight cutting edge. Five showed battering on two edges and three on a single edge. Only two of these

Figure 22.14 Micrograph of wear on a modern obsidian threshing-sledge element collected near Çat in Erzerum province. Heavy abrasion and striations are visible (original magnification x100).

Figure 22.15 Three flakes from the Can Hasan III assemblage (from near surface contexts) interpreted as threshing-sledge elements

pieces showed the heavy rounding which is so distinctive of threshing sledge flints. The macroscopic gloss on six of the pieces was confined to one edge (one of these a distal end) and two showed gloss all over their surfaces. Microscopic examination at x100 showed that all the pieces exhibited a light gloss over all their surfaces as do most of the flint pieces in the assemblage. Five of the pieces showed random striations on their surfaces.

The possibility that obsidian flakes could also have been used at Can Hasan III in this way was considered but the results are less than conclusive. The ethnographic samples of obsidian threshing-sledge elements shows them to be densely covered with random striations, both macroscopic and microscopic. Random striations can also be produced by trampling and other postdepositional factors so this cannot be considered to be a diagnostic feature on its own. Although two of the pieces showed patterned striations, the same pattern may be produced by cutting a number of types of material so this also cannot be used alone as a criterion for recognition of threshing sledge elements. There are a good number of obsidian pieces in the assemblage which could conceivably be pieces from threshing sledges but the ethnographic samples available are just not sufficient to warrant analogies with archaeologically recovered material.

Conclusion

Finally, although I believe that flint elements from threshing sledges can be recognized from archaeological contexts, it has not yet been possible to identify any pieces clearly deriving from prehistoric contexts. It is necessary to carefully examine good samples from a broad geographical and temporal range of well-excavated sites in order to reach the goal of the understanding of the origin and development of this particular agricultural practice. A greater understanding of the variability in the rapidly disappearing ethnographic record could also contribute to this process.

Acknowledgments. I would like to thank G. Hillman, S. Payne and M. Nesbitt for their comments on drafts of this chapter and M. Kislev for his translation of references to threshing sledges in the Old Testament.

Chapter 23

Major Units for the Transformation of Grain

The Grain-grinding Households (e₂-ḪAR.ḪAR) of Southern Mesopotamia at the end of the Third Millennium BCE

Jean-Pierre Grégoire

THE NEAR EAST IS TRADITIONALLY CONSIDERED to have been the birthplace both of the Neolithic revolution[1] and of the urban revolution,[2] which produced one of the earliest great civilizations of the ancient world. Since the Paleolithic period in Southwestern Asia, societies of hunter-gatherers evolved into village communities of producers, and later into stratified urban societies. These developed in the course of the second half of the fourth millennium BCE into State societies, which, from the beginning of the third millennium, gave birth to the first great Empires.[3]

1. Urbanization of Lower Mesopotamia

Large urban centers, surrounded by small settlements, arose in the Near East in the course of the second half of the fourth millennium BCE. These formed aggregates of hierarchically organized sites, reflecting social, political, and economic innovations. The decreasing surface of arable land, brought about by a change in climate at the end of that millennium in the Near East, whose lands had to feed an ever-increasing population, hastened the disintegration of social structures, as illustrated by the appropriation of tillable lands and a marked social stratification. A political and religious élite took hold of the major means of production and developed into a dominating social stratum which controlled the main strategic resources. The Temple played a role of prime importance. In settlements, the community developed around and in relation to this cultic center. It was precisely in large cities that the new State power emerged.

2. Early State

Together with budding urbanization, the main centers underwent the separation and institutionalization of political and economic-religious powers. Until the beginning of the third millennium, the Southern cities were ruled by a political-religious hierarchy that ensured its control over major strategic resources by being in sole charge of cereal production.

The alluvial plain was characterized by enclaves that became separate territorial units forming small sovereign States competing for the control of water resources. These were supplied mainly by the Euphrates, on which almost all Southern States depended. The emergence of a new centralized political power coincided with increasing military activity.

The new State power was equated with a centralized authority based on a specialized administration and on judicial institutions. In Mesopotamia, government was identified with a *Patrimonial State*, administrative and bureaucratic, in which links of subordination were hierarchical and institutionally regulated. The *Patrimonial Sovereign* (lugal) held power by virtue of personal attributes and by divine mandate. In the practice of power, he employed an elaborate hierarchy of officials and scribes to whom he delegated part of his power. Under this political régime, social dividing lines were the outcome of statuses and privileges correlated to the distribution of power and authority.

The State organized production and exchange. This gave rise to a subordination network which was kept under control by military might, a specialized coercive instrument enabling the Sovereign to impose his decisions, both by law and by force.

At the end of the fourth millennium, the Temple played a

political, social, and economic role of prime importance. During the third millennium, it continued to control economic life and to determine its social aspects, but it was subjected to the authority of the State, namely the *Palace* (e₂-gal), seat of central power and administration. The cultural and economic power of the religious stratum was integrated into political power, which it could strengthen through a hierarchy of specialized and highly qualified personnel.

Cuneiform inscriptions describe such major works as the construction of monumental architectural complexes and the creation of a wide network of communication lines and irrigation canals. These were made possible by collective *corvée* labor, which became a permanent institution. The bureaucratization of administration, which originated in the Temple-Household, increased further the tendency towards strong centralization.

3. Patrimonial Economic System

The patrimonial economic system may be considered a *redistributive system*. The production of large estates and economic units, contributions, and tributes were gathered in large collecting centers—*central granaries* (guru₇) and *storehouses* (g̃a₂-nun)—managed by central administration. Once gathered, the goods were partly redistributed in the form of rations, gratifications, or gifts. Products circulated according to a highly complex system of collecting, storing, and redistributing.

The lands, above all those for grain, belonged to the gods, embodied by the *Patrimonial Sovereign*, who administered them, while their exploitation was undertaken by the Temples. This ensured the latter's preeminence in economic and social life. The *Palace* and *Temple-Households* were the true centers of the city. It is around these that the various town units developed, protected by ramparts. The quarters which lay beyond them (*extra muros*) comprised, apart from houses, date-palm groves and gardens, which formed a *green belt*. Beyond it, there lay, as far as the eye could see, crop land, devoid of settlements and forming vast areas, themselves divided into large estates along the watercourses and main canals. Such a threefold division was characteristic of lower Mesopotamia in the third millennium BCE. Thus, each settlement was encompassed by a belt of groves and gardens,[4] and beyond them by a belt of vast expanses of crop land. The Sumerian term for this microcosm was the literary and poetic mùš₃/muš, which also described the aureola, or halo, surrounding a source of light such as a star. In our example, the source is represented by the urban center or town, which shines in the distance and seems surrounded by several aureolas: a dark green one of groves of palm and other trees,[5] which stands out from the second halo of cereal lands of a lighter tint ranging from the delicate green of young shoots to the gold of ripe grain, the third aureola being the ochre and brown, barren land and steppe.

Rural and urban populations were not distinct. There was only a single settlement—city, town, or simple urban center—deriving the main part of its subsistence from the surrounding lands which were exploited by the great *Temple-Households*. Hydro-agriculture led to a tremendous rise in grain production, which changed from an average of 410 kg/ha for dry-farming to 600 to 700 kg/ha for hydro-agriculture. Over-irrigation, however, increased the risk of salinization. To avoid the disastrous effects of this phenomenon, intensive monoculture of barley was practiced, this cereal being characterized by a quicker growth cycle and being better adapted to saline soils. Wheat crops diminished markedly. By the end of the millennium, barley production amounted to 80% of the total production of cereals.

The two closely connected cycles of production and redistribution were managed from the center by a plethora of officials and various categories of specialized staff, to which the considerable amount of cuneiform records currently available bear witness.

The concept most evocative of the socioeconomic system of that time is no doubt that of *Household*, the Mesopotamian *oikos*[6]—a State institution, administered in an authoritarian and bureaucratic manner whose basic function was to cover the needs of the Lord of the *Household*, the *Patrimonial Sovereign*. The *Mesopotamian Household* was the production unit *par excellence*, involving estates, domains, hamlets, centers of administration, residences, manufactures, workshops, granaries and storehouses, cattle pens, groves and gardens, and pastures. It had at its disposal an administrative staff, various productive forces, maintenance and surveillance personnel, all of them hierarchically organized. The most representative and important *Households* were the Temples, which were in charge of exploiting and managing the large estates or domains—in fact of controlling the main economic sector.

A great part of the population formed an integral part of the *Patrimonial Household*, from which it derived its subsistence by receiving rations, allowances, gratifications, or gratuities. Household and army staff were allotted *subsistence lands* (gana₂-šuku-ra).

The absence of advanced technological means compelled central administration to employ a large human labor force. Consequently, those who were not permanently attached to a Household depended, directly or indirectly, upon the Patrimonial Household. These were the numerous *day laborers* (guruš/g̃eme₂-u₄-1;-še₃) and *wage-earning workers* (lu₂-ḫug̃-g̃a₂). They, too, received rations or allowances: *grain rations* (še-ba) and all kinds of *food rations* (sa₂-du₁₁, ša₃-gal), which were distributed on a daily, monthly, yearly, or occasional basis. Therefore, central administration had, on the one hand, to store enormous supplies of grain and produce and, on the other, to manage units of grain transformation in order to ensure the supply of huge quantities of rations.

4. The Great Production Units

During the third millennium BCE, some bodies that were autonomous production units and depended on central administration, that is on the *Sovereign's Palace*, separated from the *Household*, in particular, from the *Temple-Household*. These could reach enormous sizes and had to ensure a large-scale supply of manufactured products, notably textiles and foodstuffs. Their function was to transform raw materials, essentially produced by agriculture and from cattle-breeding. They were structurally associated with the *Patrimonial Households*, such as Temples, which were identically organized. The best-known production units were textile-manufactures or *Weaving-Households* (e$_2$-us-bar), and *Grain-Grinding Households* (e$_2$-HAR.HAR).

5. Weaving-Households or Textile-Manufactures

Cuneiform records from various Southern Mesopotamian urban centers reveal the existence of large production units, notably on the territory of Lagaš. The productive labor forces of these units were mainly female, weaving being traditionally, though not exclusively, women's work. Up to 1,097 women weavers, assisted by 626 youths and children, have been recorded, working daily in a production unit at Ḡir$_2$-su^{ki}.[7] These productive forces were divided into teams of 5 to 12 people each, directed by master-weavers acting as team heads. The productive staff consisted of waged women, of *corvée* laborers, and, in some cases, of prisoners of war, viewed as slaves, as well as of *ordinary prisoners* (dumu-gi$_7$), forced to work in *Textile-Manufactures*. An as-yet-unpublished cuneiform document[8] reports 6,466 women weavers working in *Weaving-Households* at Ḡir$_2$-su^{ki} (1,051), at Ki-nu-nir^{ki}-Ninâ^{ki} (1,143), and at Gu$_2$-ab-ba^{ki} (4,272). They received yearly rations of oil and dates, at the rate of 1 *measure* (sila$_3$), or 1.07 liters, of vegetable oil and 5 *measures* (sila$_3$), or 4.63 liters, of dates per person.[9]

The lexem for "manufacture" used here means, within the historical context of cuneiform records, a specialized unit with an economic dimension—either an architectural unit or a complex of scattered installations—where raw materials were transformed into manufactured products on a large scale. Consequently, it was an establishment whose production exceeded in quantity the production-capacity of a non specialized *Household* such as the *Temple-Household*. The use of modernist terminology such as "industry" or "factory" would be anachronistic and inadequate, since these types of installations, characterized by their size, their technology, the concentration and division of their work process into specialized workshops, as well as their capital, did not exist in Antiquity.

The archaeological excavations undertaken at *Tell Asmar* have uncovered a large building, dubbed the *Northern Palace*, which appears to date from the Akkadian period and could be identified with an e$_2$-uš-bar, a Weaving-Household or Textile-Manufacture.[10]

6. Neo-Sumerian Grain-grinding Households

Another type of production unit, of remarkable size, appeared in the Neo-Sumerian period, in relation with the foundation of the patrimonial empire of the third Ur Dynasty (2113–2006 BCE). These were great *specialized* production units called e$_2$-HAR.HAR or, in other words, *Grain-grinding Households*.

e$_2$-HAR.HAR does not refer to a simple *mill*, *sensu stricto*, but to a far more complex installation, which compels us to use the English term "*Grain-Grinding Household*,"[11] that is, a large installation devoted to the transformation of grain into flour products and also of flour products into various foodstuffs and drinks. Such a definition lies outside the realm of modern dictionaries, which underline the industrial nature of an installation specialized in the transformation of grain into flour. Some specialization of Neo-Sumerian *Grain-Grinding Household* is expressed in the differentiated reading of e$_2$-HAR.HAR, where the lexem HAR/HAR.HAR may be read ar$_3$, ara$_5$, kin$_2$, or kikken, referring to various milling techniques or processes.[12]

The cuneiform records[13] from Ḡir$_2$-su^{ki}-Lagaš^{ki} provide us with most precise and explicit data. The territory of Lagaš^{ki} included several *Grain-Grinding Households*, the largest of which must have been situated at Ḡir$_2$-su^{ki} or in the immediate vicinity of this urban center. Two other main production units—much smaller installations whose importance resulted without doubt from their strategic geographical position—were situated at Sag-da-na^{ki} and Ugnim^{ki}.

Several documents enable us to define the structures and organization of the *New Grain-grinding Household* (e$_2$-HAR.HAR gibil), situated at Ḡir$_2$-su^{ki}, which constituted a two-unit complex: the *Main Grain-grinding Household* (e$_2$-HAR.HAR gu-la) and the *New Grain-grinding Household* (e$_2$-HAR.HAR gibil). It is impossible to decide whether this was a single architectural unit, which was enlarged at some stage, or a complex that incorporated a variety of scattered installations.

6.1. Structures and organization

These installations essentially included the following twelve main departments, each with one or several offices:

1. A *granary* or *silo* (guru$_7$), under the responsibility of a *granary/silo keeper* (ka-guru$_7$), this being an architectural complex where grain—destined to supply the various offices with raw materials—was stored. The granary, or silo, also served as a storehouse for central administration, which drew from it the necessary grain for the rations of various categories of staff, for the functioning of household offices, for feeding cattle as well as for different forms of exchange.

2. Installations allotted to the preparation of grain and its grinding. These buildings housed milling installations and included all the tools necessary for grinding.

3. Structures for the storage of products : storehouses and cellars.

4. *Bakeries* [muḫaldim (e$_2$-muḫaldim(a))] for the production of bread and other flour-based products; for instance, pastry and beer bread (babbir).

5. Malt-Houses, for the preparation of grain in connection with brewing of beer.

6. *Breweries* (e$_2$-babbir) for the production of various sorts of wort and beer.

7. Hand oil presses for the production of vegetable oil, notably linseed oil, as well as unguents and perfumes.

8. *Weaving workshops* (e$_2$-uš-bar).

9. Workshops of craftsmen connected with the complex, notably the cutters of saddle querns and rubbers, which were used for crushing and grinding grain and linseed; potters who supplied specific pottery for various types of products (flour produce and beer); basket weavers who made containers, notably baskets, for storing products such as crushed grain, hulled grain, groats, or coarse semolina (they also made the mats which were used to cover the containers during transport); curriers who supplied leather bags to store and carry flour; joiners-carpenters and masons who erected and repaired the buildings where products were kept; porters who carried raw materials and products inside the *Grain-grinding Household*; and a specialized team of *flour carriers* (zi$_3$-IL$_3$).

10. Buildings for the breeding of hogs[14] and poultry (essentially fattened with grain, and with bran or waste from grinding workshops, Malt-Houses, and Breweries).

11. An *arsenal* (mar-sa), consisting mainly of a building and maintenance site for barges or lighters which carried products; various categories of specialized craftsmen were connected with this arsenal, whose activities were recorded by a *specialized scribe* (dub-sar mar-sa).

12. Finally, palm groves and *gardens* (ĝiš-giri$_{11}$), which employed a permanent and specialized staff.

No precise information is available on the architecture of these complexes and installations, since no production unit of this type has yet been excavated. However, archaeologists and architects believe that it would not have been technologically difficult to erect such complex and impressive architectural units, where hundreds of people (even over a thousand) would have worked in a comparatively restricted space without hindrance to each other, while allowing for a rational production which would have covered the needs and requirements of central administration.

6.2. Management and administration

From an administrative point of view, the *Grain-grinding Household* was controlled in the first place by the *Household Prefect* (šabra-e$_2$), a high official who was in charge of a constituency—the administrative unit of that period—and managed various *Temple-Households*, the central granaries and storehouses, the production units, as well as everything connected with them. He supplied the grain and food necessary for the rations, which were distributed between the various categories of staff and the military personnel. The management of both sections of the *New Grain-grinding Household* was entrusted to two *overseers* (nu-banda$_3$).

The administrative office included, on the one hand, officials, notably specialized scribes of the production unit and chief bookkeepers, scribes for *flour production* (dub-sar-zi$_3$-da) and, perhaps, the *head bookkeeper* (ša$_{13}$-dub-ba), the *granary/silo-keeper* (ka-guru$_7$), the official in charge of weighing *flour products* (KA-la$_2$-a-zi$_3$-da), *scribes* (dub-sar), various *assistants* (šeš-tab-ba), and minor officials, such as *agronomists* (gu-za-la$_2$), and, on the other, the heads of the various departments mentioned above.

6.3. Subjective productive forces

As a whole, the available sources provide us with a precise idea of the different categories of staff or productive forces employed in the *Grain-grinding Household*. Although there is little data concerning the head officials and the members of the administrative bureau, the subjective productive forces of the various departments and offices are comparatively well known.

In Year 48 of the reign of ^{d}Šul-gi, second *Patrimonial Sovereign* of the third Ur Dynasty, the complex of the *Grain-grinding Household* of Ĝir$_2$-su^{ki} employed 1,256 people daily, of whom 1,145 were direct producers, divided into 15 teams directed by *head grinders* (ugula-ḪAR.ḪAR). The production unit was principally managed by two people, one, Lu$_2$-^{d}Nin-šubara, responsible for the *Main Grain-grinding Household* (e$_2$-ḪAR.ḪAR gu-la), and the other, Ur-^{d}En-gal-DU.DU, responsible for the *New Grain-grinding Household* (e$_2$-ḪAR.ḪAR gibil), thus suggesting a complex consisting of two distinct architectural units.

6.3.1. Regular staff. Regular staff (ĝir$_3$-se$_3$-ga), permanently attached to the Household, numbered 134 people in Year 48 of ^{d}Šul-gi's reign, namely:

2 accountant scribes, who were responsible for *flour production* (dub-sar-zi$_3$-da);

1 *arsenal scribe* (dub-sar mar-sa);

1 main *head grinder* (ugula-ḪAR(.ḪAR)), responsible for the various teams directed by the head grinders;

6 supervisors or *gatekeepers* (i$_3$-du$_8$), who held positions of reliability and responsibility. Their number is indicative of a more important architectural complex;

10 *maltsters* (munu$_3$-mu$_2$), thus emphasizing the importance of the brewing department;

6 *basket weavers* (ad-gid), who made baskets and other wood or reed containers for the transport and preservation of products;

1 *joiner-carpenter* (nagar);

2 *curriers* (ašgab);

6 *potters* (baḫar);

1 main *head baker* (muḫaldim), who was responsible for the baking of bread and pastry;

1 *hog breeder* (sibad-šaḫ₂);

Team of 45 *haulers* (lu₂-ma₂-gid₂-da), 18 of whom were eren₂-soldiers, in charge of transporting flour, bread, and beer daily;

2 *masons* (šidim), who specialized in building in *pisé* and in particular were in charge of erecting grain silos;

1 person in charge of the team of *porters* (uĝ₃-IL₂);

Team of 49 arboriculturists who tended the date-palm groves belonging to the *Grain-grinding Household.*

This list may be completed thanks to a text dating from Year 2 of the Third Dynasty, ᵈAmar-ᵈSuena:

8 *boatmen* (ma₂-laḫ₄), in charge of the *Grain-grinding Household*'s flotilla;

5 gu-za-la₂—officials with an ill-defined function, perhaps agronomists;

2 *saddle-quern cutters* (na₄-ḪAR-gul-gul), in charge of the grinding tools;

4 *reed purveyors* (gi-ze₂), who supplied the installation with raw material and fuel, notably for baking ovens;

1 *barber* (šu-i);

1 *official who handled exchanges* (dam-gar₃) and ensured the supply of raw material from outside the *Grain-grinding Household*;

3 men with indeterminate functions.[15]

Other sources mention *musicians* (nar), to whose tunes women ground grain rhythmically.

6.3.2. Waged staff in charge of production. This staff comprised various categories of workers, such as:

- Male and female labor forces, *male grinders* (guruš-ḪAR.ḪAR) and *female grinders* (ĝeme₂-ḪAR.ḪAR), the latter being predominantly assisted by youths and children of both sexes (dumu, dumu-nita₂ and dumu-mi₂), thus 86 men, 669 women, and 103 youths and children, totalling 858 people employed in the two installations of the complex, or 491 people for the *Main Grain-grinding Household* and 367 for the *New Grain-grinding Household*. Eight teams worked in the first unit, and six in the second, under the management of 14 *head grinders* (ugula-ḪAR.ḪAR).

- 6 KA-gaz, apparently specialists in the husking of hulled

grain such as barley and emmer. Their main working tools were the *mortar* (naga₄ (GUM)) and pestle, made of stone or wood.

- Labor forces, notably female, which produced vegetable oil. The hand oil press employed 4 women and 7 youths.

- The *Grain-grinding Household* maintained a weaving workshop where 40 women weavers and 4 youths worked, directed by a *head weaver* (ugula-uš-bar). A team of 21 women and 2 youths were employed in the *Main Grain-grinding Household*, and another of 19 women and 2 youths in the New Grain-grinding Household.

- The arsenal staff numbered 23 men and 2 women, but this installation seems to have been architecturally separate from the complex of the *Grain-grinding Household.*

These subjective productive forces worked throughout the year in the *Grain-grinding Household*'s various departments and received monthly grain rations. Part of this staff were seconded from the departments of other Households, which were therefore responsible for their subsistence. While most of the productive forces worked full time, some were employed on a *half-time* (a₂-1/2) basis. It is notable that these categories did not belong to a regular staff but were waged labor forces.

The latter consisted on the one hand of *waged men* and *women* (lu₂-ḫuĝ-ĝa₂), hired for defined periods of time which are not specified further in the textual sources, and *male* and *female day laborers* (guruš-u₄-1;-še₃, ĝeme₂-u₄-1;-še₃). The former were often specialized workers, but the latter were totally unqualified. The above forces constituted the basic and predominant labor force in all Households and institutions of the Patrimonial system. They were hired in fully fledged groups, in particular the day laborers who were already assembled into teams, each with its own *foreman* (ugula). They were allowed either regular rations of grain and/or of food.

6.3.3. Maintenance and surveillance personnel. The various installations—buildings, workshops, granaries/silos and storehouses, outbuildings and groves—were guarded by a military detachment of men fulfilling their military *corvée* (eren₂), this numbering 57 soldiers under the supervision of the palace guard. Surveillance of the area was also undertaken by *gatekeepers* (i₃-du₈). Cleaning and maintenance were entrusted to a team of specialized employees, who were part of the *regular staff* (ĝir₃-se₃-ga).

6.3.4. Corvée laborers. Lack of elaborate technical means was compensated by the summoning up of the greatest number of available labor forces. Thus, a high (if not the highest) percentage of population was subjected to *corvée* labor. In the daily census lists, *corvée* laborers, waged workers, and day laborers were carefully distinguished. *Corvée* labor was connected above all with the main seasonal agricultural works, notably those related to irrigation, ploughing, and harvesting, great architectural projects, the hauling of boats along the main waterways and canals, as well as all heavy work, which required particular efforts, this being the case in the great production units such as the *Grain-grinding Households*.

Corvée laborers (he$_2$-dab$_5$) were the responsibility of the particular Household or of the institution and received grain and food rations, delivered by the central granaries or by the various Households.

In the case of lack of manpower, and if the situation required it, men or women were seized in the *open street* (sila-a dab$_5$-ba). Naturally, they attempted to avoid labor through *flight* (zah(a)$_3$), and their cases were carefully recorded. It frequently happened that a labor force was levied by the *army* (ĝiš-tugul-e dab$_5$-ba (ĝiš-e dab$_5$-ba)). These were *corvée* laborers who are repeatedly mentioned in the census lists of the *Grain-grinding Households*. A great number of these were levied in the various departments of the Households and institutions of the district.

The *Grain-grinding Household* listed daily its labor forces. Individuals were recorded by name, the category of ration which they deserved being recorded, as well as their origin or provenience, occupation or function, and their administrative or personal dependence. Those most *senior* (libir) were first recorded, that is, those already listed in the registers of the *previous year* (im-e tag$_4$-a), followed by the *newcomers* (gibil). Entire families were thus press-ganged into *corvée* labor. The lists also included members of the *regular staff* (ĝir$_3$-se$_3$-ga) of other Households or Temples, this demonstrating that all *political subjects* were liable to general *corvée* labor. Cases of illness, flight, and death were also scrupulously recorded.

The most explicit census lists are connected with the *Old Grain-grinding Household*, at Saĝ-da-na^{ki}, in the district of Ĝir$_2$-su^{ki}, in which corvée laborers on the one hand and hired specialized labor forces on the other were registered day after day. Comparatively complete sequences are thus available for several months of Year 9 of ^{d}Amar-^{d}Suena's reign and Year 1 of ^{d}Šū-^{d}Suen's reign. These records supply precious information concerning the length of these collective corvées (whole teams being forced into labor for over a year) and indicate the social status, the administrative connection, and the geographical origin of various corvée laborers holding certain positions in various offices of the *Grain-grinding Household*. Since those in charge were also mentioned in these lists, it is possible to reconstruct the organization of most departments in this particular *Grain-grinding Household*. The number of persons listed varied between 31 and 49 individuals, thus implying that each list concerned a single department.

A particular category of *soldiers* (eren$_2$) should be included

in *corvée* labor, notably those performing their military *corvée* and who were levied for the most part in the different departments of the Households and institutions, over the entire territory.[16] These conscripted soldiers were in charge of keeping watch over buildings and installations or of supervising certain categories of *corvée* laborers, but they could also be entrusted with other tasks. Thus, a text informs us that, at harvest time, 21,799 eren$_2$ soldiers had been made to compensate for labor shortage. During this period, the subsistence of this additional manpower was handled by the administration of *Local Sovereigns* (en$_5$-si) and by the *Household Prefects* (šabra-e$_2$) in charge of district administration.[17]

6.3.5. *Dependent staff.*

The *Grain-grinding Household* employed (besides regular staff, waged workers, day laborers and *corvée* laborers) another labor force whose social status was characterized by dependence. This particularly category included:

- All *male* and *female servants* (ir$_{11}$, ĝeme$_2$), who were, however, limited in number. These were obviously people personally subjected to another or others, who had not been enslaved, but frequently had been brought into bondage through debt.

- *Slaves proper* (saĝ-nita$_2$ / saĝ-mi$_2$), whose economic role was insignificant because of their small numbers. Besides, they did not belong to the Household but were attached to single individuals. Some production units employed a greater servile manpower, but these were *prisoners of war* (saĝ-hi-a nam-ra-ag(a)). They were mainly women and children working in specific Temple outbuildings and most often were a personal gift from the *Patrimonial Sovereign* after a victorious military campaign. The death rate of these deportees was extremely high.[18]

- Dependent staff also included those called *vowed* (a-ru-a) in the textual sources.[19] Their status was one of complete subjection to an institution or an individual. These laborers were mainly employed by Temples, since they had often been "vowed" to the god, lord of the *Temple-Household*. They may have been dropouts, underprivileged, handicapped, or socially undesirable beings, to whom the temples had extended hospitality out of charity.

6.4. *Production*

The *Main Grain-grinding Household* employed 8 teams in charge of preparing and transforming cereals, this totalling 420 people led by 8 head grinders. Six teams consisted exclusively of female laborers, one of male laborers, and one of laborers of both sexes. The eighth team seems to have worked for the brewery in the production unit.

The *New Grain-grinding Household* had only 6 teams, one of which consisted exclusively of men, and the other 5 of women, totalling 377 people. Thus, 811 individuals worked daily and exclusively in grinding workshops.

The monthly production of flour products in Year 48 of ^dŠul-gi's reign, amounted to 148,369 liters,[20] thus an average daily production of 4,946 liters, approximately 6 liters (or 3.850 kg) per person. These figures should be treated with caution, for daily production varied according to man, woman, or youth. Moreover, the staff of the *Grain-grinding Households* was often put onto other tasks, notably in agriculture or irrigation, boat hauling, or reed cutting. Female labor was used for weaving fabric in *Weaving-Households*, while female spinners and weavers were seconded to *Grain-grinding Households* for flour production, bakery, or even brewery. Numerous documents supply infinite details as to the work of *head grinders* (ugula-ḪAR.ḪAR).

Thus, a cuneiform tablet[21] from Umma reports on Ur-^dŠara₂, a *head grinder* (ugula-ḪAR.ḪAR), who was responsible for 36 women in charge of grinding grain, one of whom died during this period. His office was supposed to grind 91,878 liters (60,801.638 kg) of cereals into 67,667.35 liters of flour products; for this task, he was allotted 10,304 working days, that is, the number of working days of 36/35 women for 12 months of 30 days each (thus, 12,960 days, once holidays and sick leaves had been deducted). In fact, the office had used 10,715 working days, this implying the temporary hire of additional labor, in order to ensure the production of 51,822.51 liters of barley flour, 15,153.87 liters of semolina, 650.21 liters of emmer groats, and 40.77 liters of first-rate barley groats. The average daily production per woman amounted to about 3.50 liters (2.250 kg) of *flour* (zi₃) and 24.72 liters (16.700 kg) of groats. However, female labor was not used in grain grinding only, but in various tasks in the course of the same year, notably unloading cereals and transferring flour products into baskets which were then loaded onto boats. Judging by this text, the office produced mainly pounded grain, groats, and coarse flour, since these products were transferred into baskets, and not into pottery vessels or leather bags destined for fine flour. These 36 women were also employed variously in agriculture and irrigation. They also handled the transport of straw to a *Temple-Household* and wove fabrics in a *Weaving-Household*.

This evidence is corroborated by another text[22] from Umma, which states that the daily production of a woman was about 9.25 liters (6 kg) of barley flour. Another text,[23] also from Umma and dating from Year 36 of ^dŠul-gi's reign, records a labor force of 141⅓ units per day, in charge of grinding grain for the 13 months of the year, hence, 55,120 working days. Of these, only 45,933 had been used for actual work, since one-sixth of the total corresponded to women's holidays and sick leave. This labor force had produced in toto 203,502 liters of barley flour, the average daily production of

a female labor force amounting to 9.50 liters (6.120 kg).

A balanced account,[24] again from Umma, under the name of Lu₂-diĝir-ra, chief-accountant in a production unit and scribe of *flour products* (dub-sar-zi₃-da), reports that, out of a total of 93,781 working days, 202 women had worked for 86,331 days, of which 27,451⅔ were devoted to the production of 500,498.77 liters of flour and 65,381 liters of bread products. This labor force also fulfilled agricultural and irrigation work, dealt with the subsistence of guards, prepared the pittance of war prisoners, pressed oil, carried the *Grain-grinding Household*'s products to the wharf, and wove textiles.

A tablet[25] from Lagaš^{ki} enumerates the working days accomplished from 05 / 10 / Š 47 to 15 / 06 / Š 48 in the *New Grain-grinding Household*, under the management of Ur-^dEn-gal-DU.DU, totalling 62,134⅚ days of work, of which 50,265 by women and 11,690⅚ by men, and resulting in 386,431 liters of products.

Such examples suffice to establish that the average daily production amounted to about 7 liters (or 4.500 kg) of sundry products from milling. However, daily production varied according to the fineness of the final product. Thus, it did not much exceed 3.50 liters (2.250 kg) of fine flour, whereas a female grinder was able to produce, by the end of the day, up to 9.50 liters of groats. We should remember that these production units provided mainly barley flour, pounded grain, hulled grain and groats, thus relatively coarse maslins, and a small amount of fine flour.

Several texts[26] indicate the global production of a year to have been 1,473,363.10 liters of sundry products, among which 1,421,744.10 liters (912,759.710 kg) of barley flour, 34,323.09 liters of semolina, 7,118.59 liters of fine bolted flour, and 10,177.36 liters of groats. These figures bear witness to the importance of the production units and the rôle they played in feeding the community. It is not easy to imagine precisely the total production of the Lagaš^{ki} territory, since there were small production units beside the large organizations under scrutiny here.[27] We should not forget either that all *Households* (*oikoi*) and institutions had their own teams of female grain grinders. Even teams of porters included one or several women in charge of grinding grain.

7. Techniques of Transformation
7.1. Teams and their work

Male and female grinders worked in teams, led and supervised by one or several head *female grinders* (PA.ĜIŠGAL(!)),[28] and managed by a *foreman* (ugula). Thus, the sixth team of the *Main Grain-grinding Household* was directed by foreman Lu₂-^dUtu, who had a labor force of 52 people under his command: 2 PA.ĜIŠGAL (head female grinders), 43 women working *full time* (ĝeme₂), 3 women working only *half-time* (ĝeme₂ a₂-½), 3 youths or *children* (dumu), and 1 "reformed" *individual* (šu-ge₄).

The administrative office carefully recorded the working

days of the various labor forces in charge of production. For example, in Year 47 of ^{d}Šul-gi's reign, during the twelfh month of Lagaš^{ki} calendar, in the *New Grain-grinding Household*, under the management of Ur-^{d}En-gal-DU.DU, 4,395 working days of female grinders and 1,490^5/$_6$ days of male grinders were allotted to flour production, fulfilled by :

3	PA.ĞIŠGAL for 30 days
120	female grinders for 30 days
30	female grinders for 30 days half-time
17	female grinders for 15 days
13	male grinders for 30 days full time
3	male grinders for 30 days half-time
56	male grinders for 15 days
7	male grinders for 15 days half-time
15	male grinders for 10 days
1	male grinder for 10 days half-time

The above summary shows that the various members of a team did not produce only flour, but that this task was allotted to them solely in order to ensure the production required by central administration. The administrative office of the production unit organized the work and decided apon the number of grinders necessary for daily production. Apart from such grinding work, the same staff performed other tasks, as previously described.

7.2. Transformation work: Grinding

The transformation of grain into flour products and foodstuff involved several stages and was undertaken in various specialized offices. Grain was taken from the *granary* (guru$_7$), which was part of the *Grain-grinding Household*, weighed under the control of the *weighing official* (KA-la$_2$-a) and carried by a team of porters to the workshop in charge of husking.

The cereals of ancient Mesopotamia were essentially hulled cereals, such as barley and emmer. Before grinding, it was advisable to remove hulls, glumes, and glumellas adhering to the grain. To this end, there were several techniques: in one, the grain was slightly roasted, and in another, it was moistened with water before being pounded with pestles in mortars (*roasted grain/barley*, še sa). Cereal roasting was an ancient technique which, in certain circumstances, preceded the storing of grain in silos. After harvesting, the stacks of ears of grain were set up to dry. After being threshed on the threshing floor, they were roasted, this having the advantage of drying out the grain for its preservation in mud silos. Roasting had the additional advantage of converting part of the starch into dextrine, which gives flour a sweet taste. This operation also involved some risks, as some of the grain might be charred and thus unfit for grinding.

The grain was then sent to the grinding workshop, where it was ground by various teams of workers. It was first cleaned of impurities, dust, straw, pebbles, rotten grain, insects, and glumes. In the various installations, naked grain was reduced

to sundry products by pounding, breaking or crushing, and grinding, using a variety of techniques that resulted in different products of greater or lesser coarseness and fineness. These differences are reflected in the Sumerian terminology.

7.2.1. Pounding with a mortar. The quality of the end-product resulted from the grinding techniques that had been applied. *Pounding* (naĝ$_3$ (GAZ)) yielded only a coarse product: either *crushed* or *hulled grain*[29] (ar-za-na; eša), *bruised grain*, or *groats*[30] (ni$_3$-ḪAR-ra), of various sorts (*good*, sig$_5$; *second-rate*, us$_2$-sa; *ordinary*, DU). This was obtained by striking perpendicularly with a pushing gesture or obliquely with beaters, crushing hammers, and *pestles* (naga$_4$ (GUM)). Mortar and pestle were of stone[31] or *wood*[32] (naga$_4$-ĝiš), cylindrical mortars being fashioned from a hollow trunk and wooden pestles reaching 1.50 to 2 m in height. Mortar and pestle were used worldwide and were essential not only in cereal preparation but also in the preparation of all kinds of food, of plants, of minerals, and sometimes even of meat. The mortar was used mainly to separate the glumes and the glumellas from the grain before grinding. It was also used for polishing (as for hulled grain).

Some specialized mortars were used to crush particular ingredients: naga$_4$-gazi (grapes), naga$_4$-ĝešdin (salicornia), naga$_4$-naĝa (onion), naga$_4$-sum, and naga$_4$-sum-bur (spices), naga$_4$-še-lu$_2$ (coriander), and naga$_4$-esir$_2$ (bitumen).

The lexems "ar$_3$" and "kin$_2$" refer to the two main techniques of grain grinding. While the former appears to have provided coarser products, the latter probably resulted in a finer maslin, which is grain reduced to flour proper.

From the Epipaleolithic period onwards, in the entire Near East, cereals were ground[33] on a quern or saddle quern,[34] with a rubber or handstone.

7.2.2. Grinding querns. Maslin was obtained through grinding, by repeatedly striking two tools, one active (percussive), the other passive (repercussive). Therefore, grinding querns consisted of two elements, the lower flat stone, called the saddle quern,[35] and a smaller stone of a different shape, the rubber or the handstone,[36] its length being frequently equal to the width of the saddle quern, in order to avoid edges on the lower stone. These devices are not characteristic of a particular civilization, but belong rather to a particular technological level. By operating the rubber (positioned transversally on the saddle quern) with a pushing movement, the grain was crushed and ground. The person performing the grinding stood behind the tool, in a slight bent forward posture and took his bearing with his knees on the rim of the base supporting the saddle quern or in which it was embedded; the quern was slanted slightly, downwards at the front and upwards at the rear. The worker pushed the rubber forward. His posture allowed him to devote all his energy to this pushing movement. Then, by raising very slightly the handstone, he drove it back to its initial position and propelled it again, whilst rubbing hard on the lower stone and grinding the material between quern and rubber. In a second phase, to obtain a finer product, he modified his technique, by operating the handstone with a continuous circular movement, and no longer with a push.[37] This could lead to the invention of other forms of grain grinding tools and effectively resulted in the *rotary quern*, which seems to have appeared at the end of the second millennium, but only came into general use during the first millennium BCE.[38]

To facilitate this task, the saddle quern was embedded in a lump of clay; it was thus heightened and at a greater slant. An edge at the back of the bench lent support to the grinder's knees, but compelled him to take a posture, torso bent forward, that optimized the power of propelling or pushing. In the Near East and in Asia Minor, clay benches have been found in which rows of querns were embedded. The grinders stood at the rear of the bench, in the usual position, harmonizing their work of grinding according to a common well-marked rhythm, which was sometimes emphasized by musicians whose role was to regulate and punctuate movements as well as to increase productivity. Such an installation was found at Ebla-Tell Mardikh.[39] In a room of the Western Palace (L. 3135), along the three walls facing the entrance, a stone bench had been set at right angles, supporting 16 basalt querns. They were all *in situ* (except one which had been moved to near the door of another room), together with their rubbers. The bench was plastered, and the characteristically convex bases of the querns were partly embedded in the upper surface of the bench. This type of quern was usual in houses and sanctuaries of that period, measuring fairly regularly 70 cm in length, 45 cm in width, and up to 15 cm in thickness. This very simple type of crusher is well known. It resembles the Ḥamā type as well as that prevalent in Northern Syria from the early Bronze IV to the Late Bronze Age.[40] Neo-Sumerian *Grain-grinding Households* included similar, though obviously larger, installations.

Querns were not used only for grinding grain, since in breweries, malt was reduced to flour for the preparation of beer bread. Besides, linseed was crushed on querns in order to extract oil. It is appropriate to recall here that 2 gur (556.14 liters) of linseed produced 2 bariga (129.40 liters) of oil, hence an extraction ratio of about 23%.[41]

These grinding tools would not have changed much since the Epipaleolithic period in the Near East. Saddle querns were simple trays, flat or slightly concave work tables, predominantly in basalt, sandstone, granite, or even limestone. They could be repeatedly pecked: roughening[42] produced a gritty surface which was particularly suited to grinding grain. The rubber could be made of a different material, for instance a stone softer than the one of the saddle quern. The handstone, or crusher, exhibited either one or several abrased face(s) and was regularly (cylindrical, plano-convex and oblong) or irregularly shaped. In great Antiquity,

it was a simple, more or less round pebble, often serving both as pestle and crusher. In the third millennium, querns were mainly of basalt, regular and oblong, the surface of their trays being slightly concave and measuring on average 60 x 35 cm. The handstone was shaped either like a long loaf of bread, with a plane rather than convex lower surface. There is also evidence for the use of wooden rubbers, enabling for instance the husking of hulled grain on saddle querns.[43]

The stone of Mesopotamian rubbers may have come from the *Ǧebel Sinjar*.[44] *Saddle querns* (na$_4$-ḪAR-šu-nu-tug(u)) were frequently cut from basalt, but the *handstone* or *rubber* (na$_4$-ḪAR-šu-se$_3$-ga or na$_4$-ḪAR-šu-gul-gul) could be of a softer stone. Cutting and roughening querns and rubbers[45] were the tasks of a specialized labor force which included a *quern cutter* (na$_4$-ḪAR-gul-gul).

There is less archaeological evidence for the historical periods than for the pre- and proto-historic periods.[46]

7.3. Grinding

Flour production is primarily dependent on the proportion of grain to ground product, for in fact, in Antiquity until the invention of the rotary quern, grain was ground and not milled. This proportion varies according to the quantity of cereal; the weight of a hectoliter is equivalent to the percentage of starchy endosperm, this meaning that barley, for example, weighing 74 kg yields 74% of starchy endosperm and 26% of hulls, glumes, or glumellas.[47]

In general, and until a relatively recent date, it was held that grinding on a quern could supply only a comparatively coarse product. This opinion was notably shared by Lindet, Blümner, Neuberger, Jasny, Curwen, and even Moritz.[48] It was thought that only wholemeal bread could be made with flour from which bran had not been removed[49] and that finer flours from which less than 20% of bran was removed,[50] was obtained through sieving. Besides, it was emphasized that such flour contained stone particles, owing to the wear of the querns and to sand from the crushing of small stones in badly cleaned cereals. These particles become a nuisance only when exceeding 15 to 20g per 100 kg of flour. Even nowadays, flour is considered unfit for consumption if it contains over 20% of impurities.[51] It is thought that ancient flours greatly exceeded this ratio. The above scholars also believed that even if the best sieves possible were used, flours would have contained a high percentage of pulverized bran. Finally, neither the grains from weeds nor ergot—which is admittedly rarer in wheat, emmer, spelt, and barley than in rye—were removed.

Nowadays, these considerations have to be revised, notably as the result of Dr. Max Währen's important research.[52] The results listed below summarize his experiments.

7.3.1. Cereals.
The commonest cereals for making bread were: *Triticum dicoccum Schrank* (emmer wheat), *Triticum monococcum L.* (einkorn); *Triticum aestivum s.l.* (wheat),

and *Hordeum vulgare L.* (barley).

7.3.2. Grinding. The grinding process has been reconstructed in an experiment undertaken with a prehistoric grinding quern, consisting of a saddle quern and rubber, both of stone:

Saddle quern	length	38.5 cm
	rear width	12.5 cm
	front height	6.0 cm
	middle height	4.5 cm
	rear height	8.7 cm
Rubber or handstone	width	10.0 cm
	height	5.5 cm

First experiment. In order to obtain fine flour, it is necessary to grind 15 times the same quantity of grain, producing a flour that contains fine bran elements of 1 to 2 mm (±20.2% = 20.2 g), even finer bran elements mixed with fine flour (7.46% = 7.46 g), and fine flour (72.46 % = 72.46 kg).

Second experiment. In order to obtain fine flour in the course of a timed operation, it is necessary to grind 15 times the same quantity of grain: 102 g in 60 minutes, yielding 73.44 g of fine flour.

The difference between the first experiment and the second was 0.98 g and thus insignificant. We may, however, conclude that the process yields a maslin with an average extraction ratio of 70%, which is a very fine flour. Flours obtained from a 67 to 70% ratio were already mentioned in ancient Mesopotamia.[53]

Third experiment (for comparative purposes). Grinding the same quantity of grain 5 times yields a rather coarse product (234 g ground in 60 minutes), of which fine flour constitutes about 25% and is not fit for baking bread.

Fourth experiment (for comparative purposes). Grinding the same quantity of grain 9 times yields a less coarse product, which contains fewer large particles (150 g ground in 60 minutes) and about 60% fine flour.

All experiments involved two processes of sieving or bolting. The quantity of flour thus obtained is sufficient to make leavened bread. When comparing the product obtained by grinding to modern flour, no difference is visible from a macroscopic point of view, between this product and flour used for modern wholemeal bread.

Währen's experiments and analyses prove that fine flour was produced as early as the European Neolithic period.

More time was needed in order to obtain fine flour. The grinding process had to be repeated several times, while modifying the technique of handling the rubber. To crush and pound grain, an oblong rubber was pushed forward while rubbing the quern, thus grinding the grain between the quern and the rubber. After repeating this operation several times, the same quantity of crushed or pounded grain was ground, but this time by operating the rubber with a rotating

movement. Grinding had to be repeated up to 15 or 16 times to produce ultimately a fine flour with an extraction ratio of about 70%. For coarser ordinary flour, grinding had to be repeated 9 to 10 times, which required, for 3 to 4 small loaves, about 150 g of flour ground in 2½ hours.

Another experiment was carried out by Foxhall,[54] who undertook a number of experiments relating to the transformation of barley and wheat, in order to attempt at defining ancient grinding techniques, particularly those prevalent in Classical Antiquity. Given quantities of naked wheat and hulled barley were ground on a type of grinding quern—characteristic of PPN Jericho—from the collection of the School of Archaeology of Liverpool University.

Results of Foxhall's experiments:

RAW MATERIAL	WEIGHT (in grams)	VOLUME (in liters)
WHEAT		
Before grinding	270	0.345
After grinding	255.65	0.50
Extraction ratio: 94.6%		
BARLEY		
Before grinding	ca. 75	0.10
After grinding	ca. 75	0.15
After sifting and bolting	ca. 45	0.07
Extraction ratio: 60%		

Comparative weights

FLOUR/GRAIN	VOLUME (in liters)	WEIGHT (in grams)
WHEAT		
Whole grain	0.5	391.100
Flour	0.5	255.650

255.65 g (weight of flour) corresponds to 65.4% of 391.10 g (weight of grain)

BARLEY		
Hulled grain	0.5	375
Flour, after grinding	0.5	250
Flour, after sifting and bolting	0.5	321.43

250 g (nonsieved flour) corresponds to 66.6% of 375 g (whole grain)

321.43 g (bolted flour) corresponds to 85.7% of 375 g (grain)

According to this experiment, 1 liter of barley yields 0.643 kg of flour.

In the ancient Near East, barley flour was widespread; it was sometimes mixed with wheat flour. Even though naked barley[55] was known, the peoples of Antiquity essentially used hulled barley, from which glumes and glumellas had to be husked before grinding. Coarse barley flour, without glumes and glumellas, weighs less than hulled grain.

Foxhall had to repeat the experiments, which had been at first unsuccessful, before removing glumellas without damaging the grain. Roasted and nonroasted grain was husked in a mortar with a stone pestle, and then ground on a quern; on another occasion, grain was husked in a pottery mortar, using a pestle also made of pottery. In all these experiments, only some of the glumes and the glumellas were removed. They had been ground together with the grain, so that Foxhall found it impossible to discard particles of glumellas and grain-hull from the flour, without losing a great part of the endosperm. After a few more experiments, Foxhall was able to recreate the process by husking nonroasted barley in a mortar, followed by grinding grain on a quern with a wooden rubber. It was only by using this specific tool that glumes and glumellas could be removed from the grain without crushing the hull, and thus without losing the endosperm. Grinding resulted in a coarse flour, from which part of the bran and other particles could be removed by sieving.

In attempting to remove glumes from einkorn in the course of a similar experiment, Harlan[56] used a wooden pestle to husk grain in a mortar after roasting it. It should be noted that roasted grains easily risk fragmentation.

Another method consists in moistening the cereal before husking, sometimes by heating it over a fire, and then by drying it in the sun. After drying, glumellas and hull may be removed more easily by winnowing the cereal.

Foxhall used English barley, but, since ancient people used above all *alphita* to produce flour, the barley/flour ratio should probably be modified. According to indications given by the FAO,[57] the extraction ratio of hulled barley is 60 to 70%, whereas Foxhall's experiment produced a ratio of 60%. Foxhall's advice is to pursue experiments in the future by relying on the works of Pliny the Elder (*NH* XVIII, 72 ss.).

All these experiments have also shown that it is not easy to determine the weight of grain because the volume of a given quantity of grain increases with grinding—that is, the volume of the product is greater than the volume of the original grain, as confirmed in fact by cuneiform texts—and the weight of a given volume of flour varies according to whether the flour is more or less compressed. Thus, the volume of flour is greater by 50% than the volume of whole grain, but the weight remains constant. Even after sieving and bolting, the volume of the product remains 70% that of the volume of the grain, but its weight is only 60% of the weight of the grain. If the flour is stirred, the volume increases further. If the flour is compressed, the volume decreases. It is generally admitted that flour was not compressed in Antiquity. Consequently, the volume of the product was generally greater than that of the raw material.[58] It is thus very difficult to calculate the weight of flour measured in volume, as was the case in Mesopotamia.

7.3.3. Further experiments. We have conducted experiments in husking and grinding grain which resembled that of ancient Mesopotamia: hulled barley and emmer wheat[59] (figure 23.1). Our grinding experiments largely confirm those of Währen.

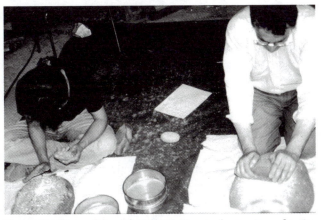

Figure 23.1 The author and H. Procopiou in the process of grain grinding at Jalès

By using querns cut from various types of stone, we have demonstrated that stone-type does have a bearing on the resulting products. Moreover, the various flour products which are mentioned in cuneiform texts necessarily correspond more or less to the various phases of grinding on a quern:

1. Hulled grain
2. Crushed grain
3. Groats
4. Semolina
5. Coarse flour
6. Flour
7. Fine flour

Before grinding, it was necessary to husk hulled grain.[60] One of our aims was to rediscover the ancient techniques leading to effective husking.[61] Our experiments focussed on husking emmer grown at the Jalès Research Center and barley grown by local farmers. Two different techniques were followed. The first method made use of various types of querns of basalt, Cretan sandstone and granite, which had been cut and roughened with a flint core at the Jalès Research Center. The tools used were two rubbers, one in wood, the other of stone. The second method combined a wooden mortar and pestle, which had also been fashioned at the Research Center.

The experiments, which made use of stone saddle querns and of rubbers of wood or stone, were found to be generally satisfactory as regards husking hulled emmer and einkorn but in general to be wanting in the case of husking barley. The percentage of damaged or fragmented barley was far too high for it to be ground. Moreover, when a sandstone quern was used, the rubber tended to produce sandstone powder.

On the other hand, when a basalt quern and rubbers of wood or stone were used, and when the barley was wetted beforehand, the husks fell off easily, thus readily freeing the grain owing to the moistening effect. However, in such a case, it was found necessary to dry the grain in the sunshine, and then to winnow or sieve it. Thus, husking on a quern is feasible, provided the grain is soaked for a few minutes in cold water, and then dried, prior to being husked on a quern.

As regards barley which had been heated at a temperature of 100°C, husking on a quern with a rubber, either of stone or wood, proved unsatisfactory, since too great a percentage of grain was shattered or crushed. This method resembles that which includes the prior roasting of grain.

To sum up, these preliminary experiments show that husking on a stone quern, even with wooden rubbers, is successful only under specific conditions: the grain should first be soaked, although the length and intensity of such a soaking still have to be determined precisely. Roasting grain is not compulsory. Moreover, the risks of shattering or crushing grain increase with roasting. By following the above guidelines, it is possible to husk hulled grain on a quern. However, this technique is not satisfactory in the case of husking great quantities of grain.

To that end, the most effective technique appears to be that making use of a wooden mortar and pestle. Under the action of the pestle and of the power of percussion, the grain is husked little by little, the husk being ultimately reduced to tiny particles and to powder. The cereals rub against each other until the husks slowly break away. The particles and powder fall to the bottom of the mortar. Devoid of their husks, cereals are then winnowed or sieved, so as to collect only the naked grain. Although this technique is both very laborious and extremely lengthy, it is in our opinion the most effective and the most appropriate method for dealing with vast quantities of cereals.

Husking barley in a mortar consisted of four separate experiments: a) husking grain that had been soaked; b) husking roasted barley; c) husking barley that had been both soaked and roasted; and, d) husking barley that had not been previously tampered with. In all cases, the tools used were a mortar and a pestle, both of wood. The above experiments demonstrate that it is possible to husk vast quantities of cereals. The most effective technique seems to be that making use of a wooden mortar and of a wooden pestle. A stone mortar was not available for the above experiments. Husking proved to be laborious and tedious, as attested in the cuneiform texts which describe numerous and various labor forces, notably *corvée* workers, assigned to *husking work* (še-ĝiš-e₃-a).

7.4. Flour and products from flour

Flours are generally defined by their extraction ratio, that is, the weight of flour cleared of impurities by sieving and bolting, compared to 100 kg of cereal due to be ground. The finest products were bolted several times, in order to remove the bran and other impurities as much as possible. Cuneiform records distinguish more than 20 different sorts of flour.

Grain pounding in a mortar with a wooden pestle, for instance, produced *hulled grain* (ar-za-na).[62]

Grinding, repeated 5 times, resulted in *crushed grain* or *groats*,[63] hence a comparatively *coarse product* (ni₃-HAR-ra). The daily production of a groats crusher was 2 ban₃ (18.50 liters) a day, the volume of the product being equal to that of the raw material, *emmer groats* (eša)[64] being distinct from the *flour of emmer groats* (zi₃-eša).

Grinding 9 times yields a finer product, a sort of semolina or coarse flour, otherwise known as *ground corn* (zi₃-šig₁₅)[65], which practically does not lose volume in the course of its transformation, since according to cuneiform texts, the volume of the product was equal to that of the raw material.

By repeating the grinding operation 15 times, a fine flour was obtained, with an average extraction ratio of about 67 to 70%. *Extra fine flour* was called zi₃-gu.

Initial sieving produced coarse flour, containing large chunks, still mixed with bran. Wheat, for instance, yields generally 30% of pure bran.

Once-repeated sieving produced a comparatively pure, medium-fine flour.

A specific bolter corresponded to each type of flour.[66] The fineness of the final product depended upon repeated grinding and sieving, with increasingly finer sieves. Pure wheat flour approximated modern products, even though ancient flour was not blanched.

For all products, there were basically three grades: *good* (sig₅), *second-rate* (us₂-sa), and *ordinary* (DU).

Bran (duḫ) was mainly used for fattening cattle. The staff of the main breeding centers included female grinders, who were in charge of preparing food for large and small livestock.

7.5. Bread

The relation between the weight of bread and the weight of flour is difficult to determine. According to Pliny the Elder (*NH* XVII, 87), *panis militarius* consisted of flour, salt, water, and perhaps a little leaven: the weight of such bread was greater than that of grain by one-third. The weight of flour was only 75% of that of bread.[67]

In modern bread, the weight of flour is 60 to 65% that of bread. Foxhall used 100% of wheat flour, to which only very little salt, leaven, and water were added: the weight of flour was two-thirds (66.66%) of that of bread. Baking and the shape of bread play no role. Flat bread requires baking for a short time at great heat. The quality of flour and appropriateness of cereal type accounts for differences.

Cuneiform texts mention more than twenty different kinds of bread. The lexem, however, which refers to bread, ninda, has a wider meaning and includes any cereal-based food, hence *broth* or *porridge* (tu₇) as well as flat bread and loaves. An Old Babylonian document[68] from Nippur describes food called ninda-i₃-de₂-a, which is most often interpreted as a kind of bread. It is in fact a fine flour–based porridge, to which were added various qualities of dates, clarified butter, dairy produce, raisins, apples, and figs. This food was widespread in Mesopotamia in the third millennium. It was offered to deities in gold cups. Hulled grain, groats, or semolina were used for food similar to modern *burgul* (*bulgur* in Turkish). These products were often mixed with dairy produce (including cheese), various greasy substances (of vegetable or animal origin), fruit, or even meat, enhanced by spices such as cumin or coriander. To chickpea or bean flour were mainly added greasy substances, the resulting dish being reminiscent of modern Near Eastern hummus, which could be savored with vegetables or meat.

Various spices and ingredients were contained in bread. To prepare 6 large *loaves* (ninda-gal), 11.12 liters of coarse barley flour, 0.85 liter of emmer groats, 126 g of samī du spice, 25 g of kamamtum, 37 g of black cumin, 62 g of azupīru, and 126 g of salt were used.[68]

Flat bread constituted the staple diet, but leavened bread had been known since the Neolithic period, as evidenced by cupola ovens, which coexisted in the Near East as early as from the sixth millennium BCE[69] with cylindrical ovens (*tanur*). While the former are suitable for leavened bread, the latter are more appropriate for the baking of flat bread. The great bakeries used mainly cupola ovens.[70]

One burnt loaf of bread dating to the second half of the fourth millennium BCE, was found at Judeideh;[71] this was a leavened loaf, not a flat bread. Loaves dated to the third millennium were made from barley, emmer, or wheat flour and were round, concave, or triangular, or even ball- and ring-shaped.[72]

The kitchens and bakeries of the *Grain-grinding Households* prepared cereal-based food as well as bread, which were brought to and distributed amongst the various categories of staff working for the *Patrimonial Household*.[73]

8. Redistribution

Products—flour, bread, beer, oil, and unguents or scents—were dispatched to distribution centers daily. These were first and foremost such institutions as the Palace, centers of administration, Temples, *Messenger Households*, or various production units to which were granted such deliveries. However, almost all categories of staff in the service of the *Patrimonial Household* received food rations, besides monthly rations of grain, yearly rations of oil and wool, or of textiles, and occasional rations, especially on the occasion of great religious feasts. Part of the production was put aside for cult purposes since Temples were the private *Households* of the gods, whose subsistence had to be ensured and who received their daily food rations, notably meat, flour, bread, and beer, as well as varied dishes, prepared or raw. Part of these rations offerings were in fact redistributed to the Temple staff and other categories of people receiving rations.

The regular staff of the various *Households* had a right to rations of flour products, which were apparently distributed once a year. The size of rations depended on the status of the recipient, who was also entitled to subsistence lands. All categories of *patrimonial* staff were due a share in this system of general redistribution. The same held true for military personnel and people subject to military *corvée*, who had a right to a plot of land and received all sorts of rations, including foodstuffs.[74]

Conclusion

The great complexes for the transformation of grain played a prime role in the social and economic life of the Mesopotamian *Patrimonial* régime, that of ensuring supplies of food and drink within a system of specific redistribution. In view of the period and the available technological means, these large complexes represent a unique phenomenon in the history of Antiquity. This particular phenomenon is remarkable both because of the very size of the complexes themselves and because of the conceptual and organizational genius of those who, at the end of the third millennium BCE, through sheer labor and will, implemented a system of such sophistication that it cannot but compel our admiration. This system, however, was a strategy for survival. Initially, the demographic pressure and the difficulties of the environment raised problems whose solution lay in the development of new means of subsistence and new production techniques likely to intensify productivity and the feeding of an ever-increasing population.

The history of the civilization of Southern Mesopotamia demonstrates clearly that, the more a society is forced into innovation, the more it tends to develop the organization of its socioeconomic, political, and cultural system. The great institutions described above illustrate this rule to perfection.

Acknowledgments. This chapter is dedicated to Professor Dr. Max Währen. The results of this enquiry reflect personal research which shall be discussed separately in a specific publication, *Les Grandes Unités de Transformation des Céréales: Les Minoteries Néo-Sumériennes* (in prep.). The present article in English is based, with additions, on a lecture delivered at the roundtable Conference *La préparation alimentaire des céréales*, at the European University Center for Cultural Goods, Ravello - Villa Rufolo, on April 11–14, 1988. This study is dedicated to Professor Dr. Max Währen, since his researches and suggestions have enabled me to look at cuneiform records in a new light and have clarified for me some technical as well as social and economic aspects mentioned in the texts of ancient Mesopotamia. Special thanks are due to Dr. C. Dauphin for her assistance in preparing the present English text.

Notes

1. To use the expression forged by Gordon V. Childe, *cf. New Light on the Most*

Ancient East, Grove Press, New York, 1928:23.

2. Childe, G. V., The Urban Revolution, *Town Planning Review* 21,1, Liverpool, 1950:179–223.

3. For a global definition of Southern Mesopotamian society in the third millennium BCE, see Grégoire J.-P., L'origine et le développement de la civilisation mésopotamienne du troisième millénaire avant notre ère. *Actes du Colloque "Production, Pouvoir et Parenté dans le Monde Méditerranéen,"* P. Geuthner, Paris, 1981:27–101.

4. In the myth of *Enlil and Ninlil*, the town of Nippur is described as "the town mantled with palm trees;" *cf.* Behrens, H., *Enlil und Ninlil, Ein sumerischer Mythos aus Nippur*, Studia Pohl: Series Maior 8, Rome, 1978:14, l. 3.

5. Comp.: Heimpel, W., *JAOS* 92, 2, 1972:286.

6. In Sumerian, e_2, the "household" consisted both of the buildings, and of the people who were members of such a complex, as well as of all the property belonging to it.

7. Waetzoldt H., *Untersuchungen zur Neusumerischen Textilindustrie*, Studi Economici e Tecnologici-1, Centro per le Antichità e la Storia dell'Arte del Vicino Oriente, Roma, 1972.

8. Kept at the British Museum: BM 20103:95-10-17, 143. This information was provided by R. M. Sigrist, who has kindly allowed me to mention it here, for which I thank him warmly.

9. The yearly rations of a woman-weaver working full time throughout the year included 334 liters (243 kg) of barley, 1.07 liters of vegetable oil, 4 to 5 liters of dates. Besides, occasional rations, notably of dairy produce (cheese), various fruit and vegetables, meat, but especially fish, and other foodstuffs (spices, various ingredients and materials), constituted the yearly food rations of the female labor force.

10. Frankfort, H., Iraq Excavations of the Oriental Institute, 1932/33, *OIC*, 17:23 ss.

11. In French: *"minoterie,"* cf. Grégoire J.-P., *in:* Anderson, P.C., ed., *Préhistoire de l'Agriculture. Nouvelles approches expérimentales et ethnographiques*, Monographie du CRA n° 6, Éditions du CNRS, 1992, 321-339; in German: *"Getreideverarbeitungsanlage."*

12. e_2-ḪAR.ḪAR = e_2-ara_5; (cf.: ḪAR = ar_3: *CST* 627:4; *Or* 20, 82: 130; *AOS* 32, W 30 *sub* a) (e_2-ḪAR-ra = e_2-ar_3-ra); e_2-ḪAR.ḪAR = e_2-kikken(a) (var: e_2-kikken-na; e_2-ḪAR-na = e_2-kin_2-na); cf. ḪAR = kin_2, ḪAR.ḪAR = kikken; comp.: $ĝeme_2$-kin_2-na, $ĝeme_2$-kikken-na (*BIN* 5, 172:2; 173:2; *STA* 5 iii 15–17; *MCS* 8, 91: BM 105711:2).

13. Notably CT 3, pl. 19–20, BM 18344: Š 48 / L. oo / oo; TuT 154 = VAT 2333 : AS 02 / L. oo / oo : documents which enumerate grain-rations distributed among the staff of the Ĝir$_2$-su^{ki} *Grain-grinding Household*.

14. In Pre-Sargonic times, a hog breeder owned 6 female grinders ($ĝeme_2$-ḪAR) to prepare the food for the fattening of hogs.

15. Individuals known solely by their surnames.

16. A document from Umma (Schneider, N., *AnOr* 1, 1931, n° 88), dating from Year 5 of ^{d}Amar-^{d}Suena's reign, records the levying of 913 men (guruš) who had to complete their period of military-*corvée*. These men were mostly members of the regular staff of various departments belonging to several *Temple-Households*. They were divided into units of ten (nam-u), directed by *Heads of Tens* (ugula-u), whereas larger units were led by the nu-banda$_3$(-eren(a)$_2$)-*commanders*.

17. *TCL* 5, pl. 31, AO 6041.

18. *E.g. TCL* 5, pl. 27-28, AO 6039, and Gelb, I. J., Prisoners of War in Early Mesopotamia, *JNES* 32, 1973:70–98.

19. Gelb, I. J., The Arua Institution, *RA* 66, 1972:1–32.

20. 533 gur 2 bariga 5 ban$_3$: *CT* 3, pl. 19–20, BM 18344:07 22: zi$_3$ iti-da-bi 8.53; 2, 5, 0 gur.

21. AO 5670, *TCL* 5, pl. 4, Umma Š 48 / U. 03 / 23 - AS 01 / U. 02 / 07.

22. AO 5668, *TCL* 5, pl. 2, Š 48 / U. 04-12 / 20 (260 days): production: 56,547.48 liters of sundry products.

23. AO 5665, *TCL* 5: Š 36 / U. 01.-13 /-.

24. *STA* 5: AS 02 / U. 01-12 / -.

25. *RA* 47:141-142.

26. For instance, one from Lagaš^{ki}, BM 20012, *CT* 9, pl. 30.

27. Such as the one in Ugnim^{ki}, mentioned in *CT* 10, pl. 44, BM 19065, which employed 14 people only, of whom 4 men, 7 women, and 3 youths.

28. A composite lexem, which has also been read PA.URU, but in fact consists of cuneograms PA+ĜIŠGAL. The duty of such women was to supervise the various members of a team. They thus acted as head workers with, apparently, the added task of recruiting agents. *Cf.* Steinkeller, P., *ZA* 69, 1979:176-187; *idem*, *JCS* 35, 1983:245, citing *MEE* 4, 305:953, 377:0447 : PA.URU = *zu-ḫa-lum/lu-um* = *siḫārum* or *siḫḫarum* and stating that PA.URU seems to be an older spelling of PA.ĜIŠGAL = *saḫḫiru*.

29. In French: "grain concassé, mondé," in German, "Graupen."

30. In French: "gruau," in German, "Grütze."

31. na$_4$-GUM. *Cf.* Stol, M., *On Trees, Mountains and Millstones in the Ancient Near East*, 1979:83-100; *cf.* also: Heimpel, W., *BiOr* 38, 5/6, 1981, col. 632-634 for footnotes concerning previous publication.

32. *Cf.* Thesiger, W., *The Marsh Arabs*. Penguin Travel Library. Penguin Books, repr. 1983: 48: "In front of an another house two girls in long gowns of patterned cloth, one red, the other green, pounded grain in a wooden mortar with long heavy pestles. They struck in turn, bending their bodies forward from the hips and grunted rhythmically with each blow."

33. In French: "broyer," in German, "reiben"; grinding being in French: "broyage," in German: "Vermahlen."

34. In French: "meule," in German, "Reibmühle."

35. In French: "meule dormante," in German: "Reibmühle."

36. In French: "molette," in German: "Reibstein."

37. This second phase of the grinding technique has been identified by Professor Dr. Max Währen. A fine flour product is obtained *only* with this particular technique.

38. There appears to be evidence for a rotary quern at Ras Shamra, *ca.* 1200 BCE. It consisted of two hemispherical stones, the lower one fitted with a tenon which was inserted into the mortice of the upper stone ; the latter was kept in position by the edge of the lower stone ; *cf.* Schaeffer, C., Les fouilles de Minet el-Beida et de Ras Samra, *Syria* 10, 1929:286-287; *Syria* 12, 1931:2; *Syria* 15, 1934:106. At Tell Halaf, circular querns were also discovered with a central tenon in order to maintain in position an upper stone which was fitted with a hole on its side, this enabling the insertion of a wooden handle so that the upper stone could be rotated over the lower one. There are supposedly other examples from Palestine.

39. *Cf.* Matthiae, P., Fouilles de Tell-Mardikh-Ebla, 1980: Le Palais occidental de l'époque amorrhéenne, *Akkadica* 28, 1982:43 ss. and Figures 16, 17. According to P. Matthiae, this installation was located in a fairly well-preserved room in the Western Palace, erected during the Middle Bronze I (2000–1800 BCE). It is thus slightly later than the Neo-Sumerian installations of lower Mesopotamia.

40. Sitting atop querns is still practiced nowadays by villagers of this region, when grinding with almost identical tools. A bent position with knees resting on the bench corresponds better to ancient depictions; *cf.* Matthiae, P., *loc. cit.*

41. After text *Amh.* 50 : Š 47 (a) : i 7-8: 2;0,0,0 še ĝiš-i$_3$ gur / i$_3$-ĝiš-bi 0;2,0,0 /.

42. In French: "bouchardage," in German: "Kröneln."

43. *Cf.* Foxhall, L., Experiments in the Processing of Wheat and Barley. *In:* Foxhall, L., & Forbes, H.A., The Role of Grain as a Staple Food in Classical Antiquity, *Chiron* 12, 1982:41–90, App.: 75–81.

44. Stol, M., *On Trees, Mountains and Millstones in the Ancient Near East*, 1979:83–100; *cf.* also footnotes concerning this publication: Heimpel, W., *BiOr* 38, 5/6, 1981, col. 632–634.

45. Cuneiform document *ITT* 5, 6885, mentions the supply of rubbers (na$_4$-ḪAR-šu-se$_3$-ga) by the quern cutter (na$_4$-ḪAR-gul-gul) for the preparation of the maslin for feeding *corvée* laborers: ša$_3$-gal ḫe$_2$-dab$_5$ ar$_3$-re-de$_3$.

46. *Cf.* Kraybill, N., Pre-Agricultural Tools for the Preparation of Foods in the Old World. *In :* Reed, C. A., ed., *Origins of Agriculture*, Mouton, The Hague, 1977:485-521. Braidwood, L. S., Braidwood, R. J., Howe, B., Reed, C. A. & Watson, P. J., eds, *Prehistoric Archaeology along the Zagros Flanks*, The Oriental Institute of the University of Chicago, Oriental Institute Publications, 105, Chicago, 1987 ; *cf.* notably Hole, F., The Jarmo Chipped Stone: 233–284; Moholy-Nagy, H., Jarmo Artifacts of Pecked and Ground Stone and of Shell: 289–346.

47. Rabute, *Le blé, la farine, le pain - Études pratiques de la meunerie et de la*

boulangerie, Paris, 1909:18.

48. Cf. Lindet, L., Les origines des moulins à grains, Revue archéologique 35, 1899:413, 427; Blümner, H., Technologie und Terminologie der Gewerbe und Künste bei Griechen und Römem, Leipzig, 1912, Bd. I:11–23; Jazny, N., Wheat prices and milling costs in classical Rome. In: Wheat Studies in the Food Research Institute 20, 1944:149 ss.; Curwen, E. C., Antisquity 11:133 ss.; Antiquity 15:15 ss.; Neuberger A., Technik des Altertums, Leipzig, 1919; Moritz, L.-A., Grain-Mills and Flour in Classical Antiquity, Oxford, 1958:144 ss.

49. Blümner, loc. cit., I:71–75.

50. Blümner, loc. cit., I:50.

51. Amman, L., Meunerie, boulangerie, Paris, Baillière, 1914:30.

52. Währen, M., Brote und Getreidebrei von Twann aus dem 3. Jahrautsend vor Christus, Archéologie Suisse 7, 1, 1984:2–6.

53. Währen, M., Brot und Gebäck im Leben und Glauben des Alten Orient, Bern, 1967, 2; Meissner, B., Warenpreise in Babylonien, Abhdlg. D. Preuss. Akad; d. Wiss. Phil-hist. KL Jg. 136, Berlin, 1936:7

54. Foxhall, L., Experiments in the Processing of Wheat and Barley. In: Foxhall, L., & Forbes, H. A. The Role of Grain as a Staple Food in Classical Antiquity, Chiron 12, 1982:41–90, app. 75-81.

55. Renfrew, J., Palaeoethnobotany:70–71.

56. Harlan, J., A Wild Wheat Harvest in Turkey, Archaeology 20, 1967:199–200.

57. Food Composition Tables for International Use, Table 2, item 16.

58. This is confirmed by Moritz, L. A., Grain Mills and Flour: 185–186.

59. These experiments were conducted in April 1994 at the Institut de Préhistoire Orientale in Jalès by the author with the assistance of Hara Procopiou. We attempted several experiments relating, on the one hand, to husking techniques of hulled grain, and on the other, to grinding husked grain. The results of these experiments shall be published ultimately in a specific study focussing on problems of husking hulled grain and of grinding. The grinding experiments were undertaken in close collaboration with Hara Procopiou, using various techniques in order to obtain flour products ranging from crushed grain to fine flour.

60. Grain was most certainly hulled with a mortar.

61. The results of these particular experiments shall be described in a separate publication. Compare H., L'outillage de mouture et de broyage en Crète Minoenne. Ph.D. thesis, Paris 1998.

62. In French: "grain mondé," in German: "Graupen."

63. In French: "gruau," in German: "Grütze."

64. In French: "gruau de blé amidonnier," in German: "Emmergrütze."

65. In French: "grésillon," in German: "Schrot." "Ground corn" refers to barley or emmer.

66. For example, gi-ma-an-sim ni₃-ḪAR-ra: bolter specific to groats; gi-ma-an-sim še-ĝiš-i₃: bolter for linseed; gi-ma-an-sim zi₃-dabin: bolter or sieve for barley flour; gi-ma-an-sim zi₃-gu: bolter or sieve for very fine flour; gi-ma-an-sim zi₃-še₃: bolter or sieve for flour. Cf. Salonen, A., Hausgeräte, I.:67 ss. The frame of such bolters or sieves was made of reed.

67. The weight of bread is very rarely mentioned in cuneiform records. Some information is supplied by ITT 5, 9304. According to this document, bread, of which one ovenful must have consisted of 43 items, weighed 16 mines or 8,080 g, that is 187.90 g per item. These items were in this case flat bread, which had been weighed after baking.

68. Legrain, L., PBS 13, 61.

69. Cf. Währen, M., Brot und Gebäck im Leben und Glauben des Alten Orient, Bern, 1967:11 ss.

70. For fire cooking devices, cf. Barrelet, M.-T., Dispositifs à feu et cuisson des aliments à Ur, Nippur et Uruk, Paléorient 2, 1, 1974:243-300 ; Bromberger, C., Fosses à cuisson dans le Proche-Orient actuel: bilan de quelques observations ethnographiques, loc. cit.: 301–310.

71. Braidwood, R.J. & Braidwood L.S., Excavation in the Plain of Antioch, Chicago, 1960:343. Cf. also Währen, Max., Brot und Gebäck im Leben und Glauben des Alten Orient, Bern, 1967:23 s.

72. Max Währen's research is based mainly on analyses of loaves or of remnants of bread discovered in the course of archaeological excavations. He has published his results in various books and in numerous scientific articles. Max Währen has determined the composition of often minute carbonized remnants of bread dating from Neolithic Period until the Iron Age, as well as the composition of the ingredients, their fineness, the types of flour used, the processes followed in their baking and the problems inherent to their conservation.

Währen, Max, Brot und Gebäck im Leben und Glauben des Alten Orient, Bern, 1967, pp. 23 ss.

Währen, Max, Brot und Gebäck im Leben und Glauben der alten Ägypter, Herausgegeben vom Schweizerischen Archiv für Brot- und Gebäckkunde - Institut zur wissenschaftlichen Bearbeitung und Förderung der Brot- und GeBäckkunde, Bern, 1963.

Währen, Max, Brot und Gebäck im Leben und Glauben des Alten Orient. Schw. Archiv für Brot- und Gebäckkunde, Institut zur wissenschaftlichen Bearbeitung und Förderung der Gebäckkunde Bern. Basel, 1967.

Währen, Max, Gutachten über Ausgrabungsmaterial aus Telgte a.d. Ems. Archäologie und Naturwissenschaften 2, 1981, 254–264.

Währen, Max, 5500 Jahre alter Brotlaib identifiziert. Bulletin der Eidgenössischen Technischen Hochschule Zürich 179 (Mai 1983): S. 7–8.

Währen, Max, Brote und Getreidebrei von Twann aus dem 4. Jahrtausend vor Christus, Archäologie der Schweiz 7 (1984):1–6.

Währen, Max, Die Entwicklungssdtationen vom Korn zum Brot im 5. u. 4. Jahrtausend. Getreide, Mehl und Brot 39 (1985 [Bochum BRD]):373–379.

Währen, Max, Das Brot in der Bronzezeit und älteren Vorrömischen Eisenzeit nördlich der Alpen unter besonderer Berücksichtigung von Brotfunden aus Kreisgrabenfriedhöfen des Münsterlandes, AFWL. Ausgrabungen und Funde in Westfalen-Lippe (Münster) 5 (1987): 23–71, 22 Abb., 6 Tab.

Währen, Max, Brot und Gebäck in der Urgeschichte, mit ausführlicher Berücksichtigung des Weck-Feingebäcks von Ovelgönne und das Haferbrotes von Langenrehm, manuscrit, 04.03.1988.

Währen, Max, Jungsteinzeitlichez Speisereste aus dem Kanton Freiburg, Chronique Archéologique, Archéologie Fribourgeoise, Separatum, 1985,1988, pp. 85–95.

Währen, Max, Brot und Gebäck von der Jungsteinzeit bis zur Römerzeit. Eins Zkizze zum Forschungsstand mit besonderer Berücksichtigung der westschweizerischen Seeufersiedlung, Helvetia Archaeologica 79 (1989): 82–114.

Währen, Max, Identifizierung von gesäuertem Brot in Knochenasche-Kristallen einer Urnenfelderzeitlichen Bestattung in Bellenberg, Ldkr. Neu-Ulm, Kataloge der Prähistorischen Staatssammlung, München 23 (1989): 59–65.

Währen, Max, Die Urgeschichte des Brotes und Gebäckes in der Schweiz, Helvetia Archaeologica 25 (1994-99): 75–89

Währen, Max, & Schneider, Christoph, Die puls. Römischer Getreidebrei. Augster Museumshefte 14, Römermuseum, Augst, 1995.

Währen, Max, Das jungsteinzeitliche Brot von Montmirail, Helvetia archaeologica 28 (1997), 110 (paru en 98), 42–52.

Währen, Max, Des Pains-Gateaux Emballés sous vide, il y a 4400 ans. Brochure: Musée Français du Pain (N.D.).

73. Cuneiform records such as CT 7, 19, BM 12949, a document from Lagaški supply detailed reports on the tasks of bakery superintendents.

74. A great number of cuneiform texts give us a fairly precise idea of these distributions of food, notably a tablet from Ummaki (Ashm. 1912–1142: Š 08/U.00/00), which records the provisions given by central administration to a daughter of the Sovereign who remained for 32 days at Umma, before pursuing her travel by boat to Nippur. See Grégoire, J.-P., Archives Administratives et Inscriptions Cunéiformes de l'Ashmolean Museum et de la Bodleian Collection à Oxford. Contribution à l'Histoire Sociale, Économique, Politique et Culturelle du Proche-Orient Ancien (P. Geuthner: Paris, 1997, Volume I, Les Sources 1, p. 90 et planche 49).

Chapter 24 ✍

Some Aspects and Experiments Concerning the Processing of Glume Wheats

Jutta Meurers–Balke and Jens Lüning

SINCE 1979 THE INSTITUT FÜR UR-UND Frühgeschichte at Cologne University has been carrying out investigations into the early agriculture of Central Europe (Lüning and Meurers-Balke 1980; 1986; Meurers-Balke 1985). The catalyst for these experiments was provided by the extensive archaeological excavations in the Rhenish open-cast lignite mining area (Lüning et al. 1982; Lüning 1983; Schwellnus 1983), which allowed a relatively complete reconstruction of the Linear-Pottery settlement structure in a loess landscape (Lüning 1982). This picture has been supplemented by the examination of carbonized macroscopic botanical remains and through pollen analyses, which provide substantial insights into the economy of the Linear-Pottery period (Knörzer 1986; Kalis 1988).

The most important source of information for the agricultural methods during the Neolithic period in the Rhineland is the carbonized macroscopic botanical remains which found their way into pit-fills as refuse. The extensive palaeoethnobotanical investigations by K.-H. Knörzer have been able to show that cereal production must have held a firm place in the provision of staple foodstuffs (Knörzer 1979). The marked uniformity in the mixture of cereals and weeds leads to the conclusion that the Linear-Pottery farmers must already have sown and cultivated cereals in a routine manner along well-proven lines—and that over several centuries.

In attempting to reconstruct in more detail the most common agricultural methods employed during the Neolithic period, a series of problems arose that could not directly be solved on the basis of the archaeological record but for which a verification by means of experiment seemed to promise

favorable answers. The experiments carried out between 1979 and 1986 concentrated upon sowing, cultivating, harvesting, storing, and processing the cereals (figure 24.1); the experiments, according to the individual problem, were based as far as possible upon the Linear-Pottery find situation.

Several thoughts and experiments are set out below that are concerned with the processing of cereals after harvesting but prior to their being prepared for consumption through grinding, baking, or cooking. The archaeological record provides insufficient clues as to the individual stages in the processing, so that one is forced for this question to look mainly to folklore and to ethnographic observations. Especially important in this respect are the operations whereby the grains can come into contact with heat and thus have the opportunity to become carbonized. Since only carbonized plant remains have survived in aerobic soils, a closer examination of the possibilities of carbonization takes on a greater importance for the interpretation of botanical finds.

The basic material for the investigations was provided by the wheats, *Triticum monococcum* (einkorn), *T. dicoccum* (emmer) and *T. spelta* (spelt), harvested from experimental fields (Lüning and Meurers-Balke 1980). The prehistoric sorts of wheat, einkorn and emmer, which have been cultivated since Linear-Pottery times, as well as spelt, which is known in the Rhineland from Iron Age contexts onwards, are all types of glume wheats, in which the grain is enclosed tightly within a husk.

The first question is to examine whether prehistoric humans tolerated glumes in their diet or whether she prepared their meals from husk-free cereals. A glance at the

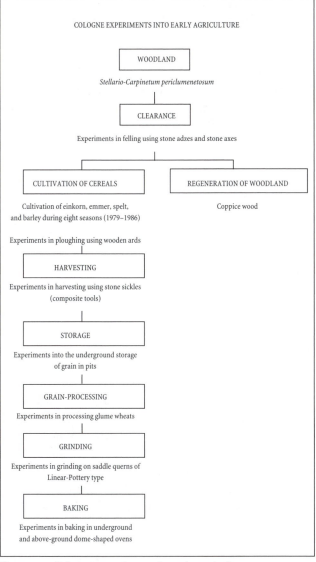

Figure 24.1 Cologne experiments in early agriculture

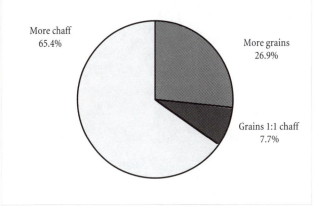

Figure 24.2 Ratio of grains to chaff in Linear-Pottery samples

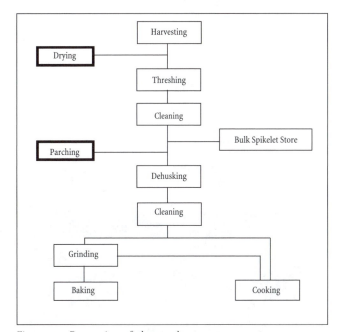

Figure 24.3 Processing of glume wheats

composition of the botanical specimens examined (figure 24.2)[1] shows that only a small proportion (7.7%) displays a grain-to-chaff ratio corresponding to the normal morphological relationship. On the other hand, the proportion of chaff predominates in 65.4% of the samples, in a third of them (q.v. table 24.5) even as much as ten-fold. The assemblage examined proves that dehusking before preparing the meal was a normal working process.[2] Also, K.-H. Knörzer was able to demonstrate in charring experiments on glumed emmer that the husks often remained attached to the grain during charring:

> Da diese Beobachtung bei den subfossilen Funden nie gemacht wurde, möchte ich annehmen, daß sie nicht in ihren Spelzen, sondern als nackte Körner verkohlt sind.

As this observation was never made for subfossil finds, I would like to think that they were not carbonized in their husks but as exposed grains. (Knörzer 1967:10; author's translation)

For the processing of the cereal one therefore arrives at the possible working steps listed in figure 24.3.

Harvesting, Threshing, and Cleaning

The question of whether the cereal after harvesting was dried or not depends upon the method of harvesting, either of the stalk or just the ears. On account of the lack of culm nodes and low-growing weeds in the Linear-Pottery samples, a harvesting of the ears seemed probable (Knörzer 1967:25; Bakels and Rousselle 1985:50). K.-H. Knörzer's experiments on harvesting einkorn and emmer revealed that ripe ears can be easily broken off at their bases without loss of grain, even when several are gripped and snapped off together (Knörzer 1971:103). In order to harvest by picking the ears, it is necessary for the wheat to be fully ripened (Totreife). At this stage the

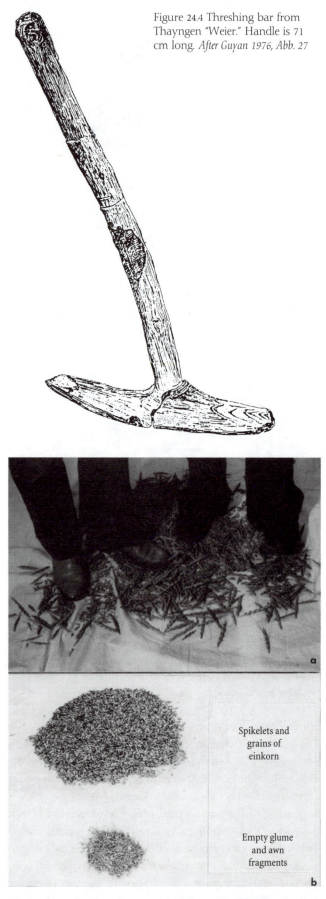

Figure 24.4 Threshing bar from Thayngen "Weier." Handle is 71 cm long. *After Guyan 1976, Abb. 27*

Spikelets and grains of einkorn

Empty glume and awn fragments

Figure 24.5 *a*, threshing by trampling; *b*, result of the threshing process

grains have a water content of between 14 and 16%, so that a drying process for the threshing and storing of the grain is superfluous.

The numerous Linear-Pottery flints with polished edges (sickle blades; Löhr et al. 1977: 223), however make it more probable that the corn was cut with sickles (Frank 1985). The best time for harvesting on the stalk is at the waxy stage (*Gelbreife*), when the grains are ripe in the physiological sense but when the spikelets still sit tight at the rachis and do not fall off during the vibration caused by cutting. The grains at this stage have a water content of 20 to 30%; drying is therefore necessary before additional processing and also before storage. According to folklore parallels, the grain is normally dried in the air, outside or, in unfavorable weather conditions, in the barn or in the house (Neuß 1983:12). In the case of high atmospheric humidity, the use of an oven or kiln might also be necessary during drying.

An interpretation of the archaeological record, on the one hand the lack of culm nodes and of low—growing weeds, on the other the numerous examples of sickleblades—could be that the ears and the stalks were harvested separately: the ears were first collected when fully ripened and then the stalks were cut with sickles. This separation, however, is disadvantageous for the storage of the straw as well as for its use for roofing, as a construction material, and for animal husbandry, since during the first operation of harvesting, the stalks are trampled and thus soiled. The same also applies to another possible mode of harvesting; the pulling out of the whole plant. The damp earth clinging to the roots aids the formation of mould and thereby causes additional problems during storage.

In a further process the dried grain is then threshed, by which either the cut sheaves (stalks with ears) or the ears that have been removed during the harvest or a secondary operation are treated. During threshing the individual spikelets are separated from the rachis.

Trampling and stamping by humans or animals does not require an instrument and is thus not detectable archaeologically. Also, wooden tools from the Linear-Pottery period are unfortunately unrecorded. "Threshing-bars" tools (figure 24.4) from Thayngen "Weier" (Pfyn Culture), as described by W.U. Guyan (1976:110), have an uncanny similarity to Finnish branch flails. In contrast to pieces from Burgäschisee-Süd, which in shape look very similar but which are to be interpreted as tools for cultivation, having as they do a clear base and a tapering point (Müller-Beck 1965:38), the tools from Thayngen "Weier" display a more roundish or rectangular cross-section. On their faces are found traces of wear, as can also be seen on ethnographic threshing flails (Neuß 1983:102). It is also possible to use a simple, unworked wooden stick for threshing.[3]

The threshing of glume wheats results in spikelets with rachis segments and awns (Hillman 1983: Fig. 1). Even during heavy hitting or stamping, the grains are not loosened from their surrounding husks.

The easiest method of cleaning after this operation is winnowing, either in a draught or by casting, whereby the spikelets and the individual, husked grains separate themselves from the barren spikelets and awns owing to their greater weight (figure 24.5). By such a method of cleaning a large part of the lighter weed seeds are discarded (Neuß 1983:58).

Threshing and winnowing, indoors or outdoors, are seasonal activities that can be carried out on a large scale. The grain, once threshed and cleaned, can then be stored. Therefore during the Linear-Pottery period, subterranean silos were probably mainly used for long-term grain storage (Meurers-Balke 1985:16). Two factors support the argument of storing the grain with the husks still on: first, the amount of time necessary for dehusking, allowing only relatively small amounts to be worked (see below), while the dehusking of the whole harvest prior to storage was not possible as a seasonal activity; second, glume wheat without the husks only remains preserved for a short time, because it has only a thin, one-layered epidermis. Free-threshing cereals, which have multilayered epidermis, can be stored without husks (Küster 1985:60).

Dehusking

In contrast to the previous operations, which can be carried out on a large scale following the harvest, the dehusking, cleaning and preparation of the grain for eating belong to the category of daily domestic chores (Hillman 1983).

There are two major questions as far as einkorn, emmer, and spelt are concerned:

- What tools were used for dehusking?
- Was dehusking facilitated by previous kiln drying or parching?

The technical prerequisites for a slow and careful warming of the grain were present during the Neolithic period. Small amounts could be dried over the fire in shallow, dish-like clay vessels. Ovens and dome-shaped kilns, which have been found from the Linear-Pottery period onwards, could have been used for larger amounts (Werner 1986; Petrasch 1986). Neolithic pits with scorched walls have occasionally been interpreted as "drying kilns" (Küster 1985:57; Petrasch 1985:82; *id.* 1986:50).

Dehusking on saddle querns

There are numerous remains of stone saddle querns from the Linear-Pottery Culture and other Neolithic cultures, which are occasionally described as tools used for dehusking (Küster 1985:59f.; Beranová 1987:166). In order to test the suitability of saddle querns for dehusking, a replica was produced that

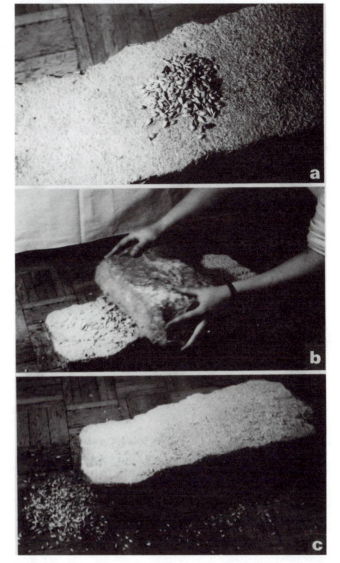

Figure 24.6 Dehusking on a saddle quern: *a,* handful of emmer on the saddle quern; *b,* working action; *c,* result of one working action

corresponded to the Linear-Pottery prototypes in shape and size (Zimmermann 1988).[4] It consisted of a large 56 x 22 cm base stone (*meule, metate*) and a large 35 x 23 cm, upper-stone (*molette, mano*) approximately 9 kg in weight. The working surfaces were carefully roughened by tapping with hammerstones.

Experiment 1: Dehusking untreated emmer on a saddle quern. The first problem was how much grain could practically be placed upon the working surface and whether it ought to be spread out or heaped up. Practice soon showed that too much grain fell from the sides and ends of the base stone when a large initial amount was used and spread out. This naturally reduces the efficiency of the saddle quern, because the fallen grain must then be replaced upon the grinding surface, resulting in further work. These observations led us to restrict the initial amount to a handful (30 g), which was

Table 24.1 Experiment 1: Dehusking untreated emmer on the saddle quern, no previous treatment

AMOUNT	W-A*	% REMAINING ON BASE STONE
30 g	1	97.4
30 g	2	90.4
30 g	3	73.2
30 g	4	63.3
30 g	5	49.2
30 g	6	33.0
30 g	7	30.4
30 g	8	26.1

W-A = working actions
*1 working action = 2 movements

Table 24.2 Experiment 2: Dehusking of emmer on the saddle quern, 4-hour preheating

AMOUNT	W-A	% REMAINING ON BASE STONE			
		50° C	100° C	150° C	200° C
30 g	1	99.3	100.0	97.0	100.0
30 g	2	26.2	93.3	88.5	97.0
30 g	3	64.1	78.0	84.8	88.3
30 g	4	66.2	70.8	61.3	(1)
30 g	5	42.6	56.3	56.4	
30 g	6	33.8	60.6	39.0	
30 g	7	38.4	48.4	39.9	
30 g	8	27.6	39.5	36.1	

W-A = working actions

Table 24.3 Experiment 2: Dehusking of emmer at different degrees of temperature

TREATMENT	W-A	CAT. III	CAT. IV	CAT. V+VI
A) based on the amount left on meule				
None	5	33.5 %	13.5 %	16.0 %
50° C	3	45.0 %	6.5 %	5.0 %
100° C	4	46.0 %	20.5 %	17.0 %
150° C	3	41.5 %	22.5 %	18.0 %
200° C	1	13.0 %	1.5 %	53.5 %
B) based on the whole amount				
None	5	33.0 %	13.0 %	15.5 %
50° C	3	33.5 %	4.0 %	3.0 %
100° C	4	41.0 %	16.2 %	12.0 %
150° C	3	40.5 %	24.0 %	15.3 %
200° C	1	13.0 %	1.5 %	53.5 %

W-A= working action
Notes: Optimum rates of dehusking obtained during the test: (A) based on the amount left on the base stone (meule); (B) based on the whole amount. The values of grain breakage on untreated emmer and emmer dried at 50° C differ greatly, so that one should select a middle value for the analysis, which would probably correspond better to the normal result.

put on the narrow end of the base stone nearest to the proximal working end. The upper stone was placed on it (figure 24.6) and pushed forward without any particular use of pressure towards the distal end and pulled back to the original position (1 working action = 2 movements).

The experiment was repeated eight times, whereby the number of working actions was increased each time in order to ascertain how many movements were necessary to obtain an optimal result for dehusking (table 24.1). For this experiment the quern was operated by the same person.

The material used for this test was spikelets of emmer (with two husked grains each). A first effect of the grinding was the separating of the spikelets, followed by the detaching of the glumes from the grain and, as an undesired side effect, the breaking-up of the grains into several pieces (cracked grain, crushed grain, fine groats, flour).

The specimen for analysis was provided by the residual remains on the grinding surface, that is, that part which had been subjected to complete treatment. Since the aim of dehusking was to obtain as many dehusked but complete grains as possible, the analysis had to judge the proportion of these compared to that of unhusked grains and to that of damaged grains. As a result, six categories are differentiated in the evaluation:

I　　Spikelets (= initial material)
II　　Individual, husked grains
III　　Grains (undamaged, dehusked)
IV　　Cracked grains (greater than half a grain)
V　　Cracked grains (less than half a grain)
VI　　Crushed grain, fine groats, flour (less than 0.5 mm)

The parts of categories I to VI are judged by weight.

As table 24.1 demonstrates, the amount of material remaining on the grinding surface, even with the relatively small amount of original material, is reduced very considerably by increasing the number of working actions. However, the ability and routine of the worker involved may play a part in this. After five working actions about 50% of the grain already lay around the quern; after eight movements, about 75%—comprising different stages of the dehusking and breaking-up processes and thus having a very heterogeneous overall composition.

An examination of the make up of the part that remained on the quern (figure 24.7, untreated emmer) showed that even after four working actions, some 50% of the corn had been dehusked. About a half of this was already cracked or more finely ground. After six actions the proportion of undamaged, dehusked grains had been diminished even more, whereby the ratio of broken grains was so high that the effect of dehusking had been completely supplanted by the effect of grinding.

In this experiment the proportion of dehusked grains (category III) never reached more than about one-third of the original material, whereby the broken grain and the smaller pieces increased dramatically after only four working actions. This method for dehusking has considerable attendant difficulties in separating the grain from the glumes. The categories V and VI (fractions less than half a grain and flour) cannot be isolated from the already partly ground

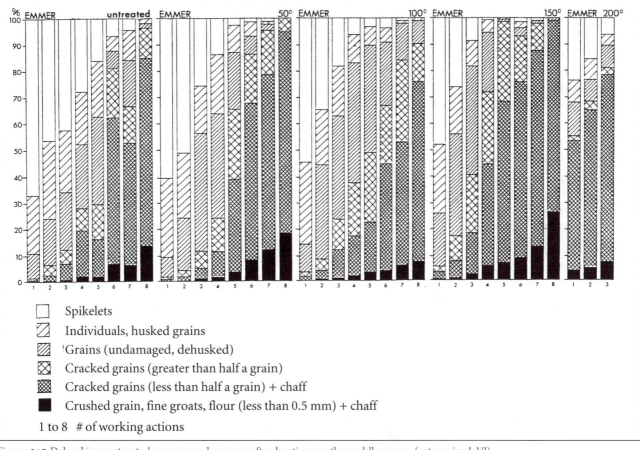

Figure 24.7 Dehusking untreated emmer and emmer after heating on the saddle quern (categories I-VI)

chaff through winnowing and sieving. This part must therefore, be regarded as worthless for human consumption, and can only be used as, for instance, animal fodder.

Experiment 2: Dehusking heated emmer on a saddle quern. A further series of tests had the task of examining how a previous heating of the corn affected the dehusking process. In this case spikelets of emmer were heated in a drying oven for four hours at a time at 50, 100, 150 and 200° C, after which they were worked in the same way as described above in experiment 1. Experiment 2 also demonstrates that the amount of corn remaining on the base stone meule decreased rapidly with the increasing number of working actions (table 24.2). One could have expected the corn to become more brittle with an increase in temperature and, therefore, that it would be ground more quickly and thus be less likely to be pushed off the base stone. Such an effect is perhaps discernible, if one compares the results with table 24.1; for instance, the values of the remains on the grinding surface for the temperatures—cold (untreated), 50° C—were, after 5 working actions, 49.2%, 42.6%, 56.3%, 56.4%—that is, the two cooler temperatures must be contrasted with the two warmer temperatures as regards the hypothesis stated above. Comparing all other tests in this respect, it seems that the individual action plays a far greater role here; in order to define the described effect

more critically, it would be necessary to use a mechanical saddle quern.

On increasing the temperature, the amount of dehusked grains in experiment 2 increased even after the first working action (figure 24.7). Whereas about 10% of the untreated emmer and that dried at 50° C was dehusked after one action (categories III to VI), this proportion rose to 15% at 100° C and to 27% of the initial material at 150° C. After a previous heating to 200° C, as much as 68% was dehusked, but over half of the grain was already broken. This tendency of the ratio of broken grain increasing with the rise in temperature is also made clear by comparing the heavier workload in figure 24.7 (2–8 working actions), even though there are individual variations.

The composition of table 24.3 (A) shows which numbers of working actions in the tests achieved the optimal results for dehusking, that is, the highest possible amount of dehusked grain. With increasing temperature the number of working actions necessary decreases from 5 to 3; the amount of dehusked and unbroken grains reaches a maximum of 46%. At higher temperatures, the proportion with broken grains rises simultaneously to over a third of the original material, not taking into account the extremely brittle grains dried at 200° C.[5] If one accepts that half grains can be effectively separated from the finer pieces through appropriate methods of cleaning, one is still left with a loss of 15 to 20%, made up of fine fractions of husks, cracked grains, crushed grains, and flour. These values refer to the amount of cereal remaining on the base stone.

When compared with the initial material, the grains that had fallen from the quern are lacking (tables 24.1 and 24.2). Were these to be considered too, then we would obtain the results shown in table 24.3 (B).

The conclusion drawn from experiment 2 is that the dehusking of emmer on a saddle quern is aided by previous heating. It was not tested whether a short thermic treatment is sufficient, too, but this is probable. An increase in temperature also tends to lead to a higher ratio of dehusking, affecting some two-thirds of the initial material, if the parts larger than half a grain are included. The loss of grains through crushing into small fragments amounts to some 15%. As only 3 working actions on the quern were sufficient, the necessary expenditure of movement is very little; on the other hand only a small amount of grain (a handful) can be worked at a time.

In conclusion one can establish that glume wheats can be dehusked on Linear-Pottery saddle querns and that a preheating stimulates the process. The proportion of cracked grains always remains high. This should be observable in the palaeoethnobotanical specimens, but, according to K.-H. Knörzer, these include only a few grains that had clearly been broken before carbonization.[6]

In order to reduce the proportion of cracked material during dehusking, that is, to obtain a more effective yield, it is necessary to consider a more careful mechanical influence upon the cereals.

Dehusking in wooden mortars

On the evidence of folkloristic and ethnographic examples for dehusking, wooden mortars must be considered (for example, Maurizio 1927:276; Bielenstein 1907:264; Visted and Stigum 1971:242; Hillman 1983:8; Harlan 1967). Neolithic wooden mortars have also been attested archaeologically; a double-pestle from Thayngen "Weier," for instance, and tub-like wooden vessels of the Pfyn culture with a preserved layer of grain in its base (figure 24.8).

Because nothing is known about the shape and size of such Linear-Pottery tools and original modern mortars were not available, we used normal wooden flower-tubs with walls of staves held together with two iron rings and an inserted flat base (figure 24.9a). Dimensionally these tubs fall into the range of sizes for original recent mortars. It is not clear, however, whether the flat base and the narrow breadth of the walling, which certainly possess a different resonance, are disadvantageous. After the completion of the main experiments in the tub mortars, a shorter control experiment was therefore carried out using a solid mortar that had been produced in the meantime out of a tree trunk (figure 24.9b).

Its cavity was narrower and had a rounded base inside. It was thought that this could increase the rubbing of the grain and accelerate dehusking.

Three round wooden poles with flatly rounded ends were used as pestles:

	LENGTH	DIAMETER	WEIGHT
Pestle A	134 cm	5 cm	1.8 kg
Pestle B	137 cm	7 cm	2.6 kg
Pestle C	143 cm	7 cm	2.9 kg

Experiment 3: Dehusking of einkorn, emmer, and spelt in a tub mortar. The tests were carried out using three types of glume wheat (einkorn, emmer, and spelt). Two kilograms of each cereal were pounded for two hours. At 15-minute intervals the material was well mixed and a sample of 20 g was taken. The results of preheating on the dehusking process were also checked in this experiment. The pattern obtained for all three types of wheat was as follows:

AMOUNT	PREHEATING	TIME OF EXTRACTION	SAMPLE
2 kg	—	after 15 min. pounding	20 G
		after 30 min. pounding	20 g
		after 45 min. pounding	20 g
		after 60 min. pounding	20 g
		after 75 min. pounding	20 g
		after 90 min. pounding	20 g
		after 45 min. pounding	20 g
		after 120 min. pounding	20 g
2 kg	4 hours at 50° C	as above	as above
2 kg	4 hours at 100° C	as above	as above
2 kg	4 hours at 150° C	as above	as above
2 kg	4 hours at 200° C	as above	as above

The analysis of the specimens should show how many grains remained unaffected and how many were dehusked as well as how many were both dehusked and cracked. As a result, the following categories were counted (not weighed):

I   1 spikelet = 2 husked grains (emmer and spelt only)
II   Individual husked grains
III Grains (dehusked, undamaged)
IV   Cracked grain

The values of category I were multiplied by two in order to obtain the number of grains. The values of category IV were divided by two, since the cracked grain was so coarse that each segment on average represented about half a grain. The condition of the initial material was checked before pounding (figure 24.12).

The tests were carried out by students alternating between pounding and documenting (figure 24.10). For the analysis it is therefore necessary to take individual factors into consideration. Random checks were made on how quickly

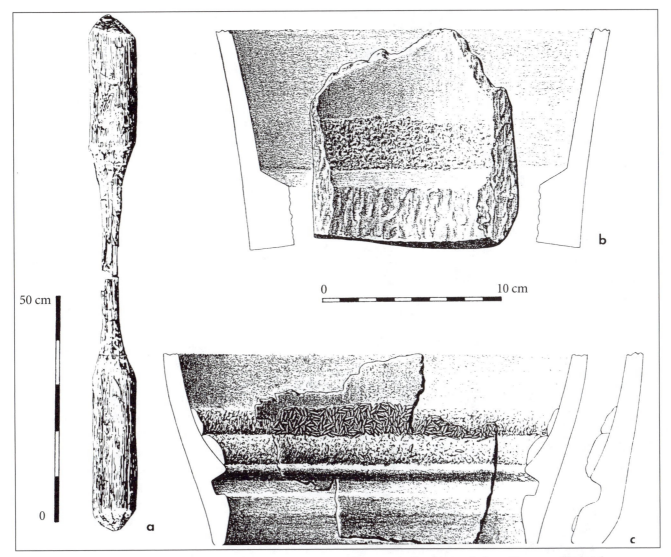

Figure 24.8 *a*, Double-pestle from Thayngen "Weier" from (Guyan 1966, Abb.7); *b*, tub-like wooden vessel worked out of a tree trunk, base broken out (Museum Frauenfeld 628/1); *c*, tub-like wooden vessel with groove to insert the base (Museum Frauenfeld /); *b* and *c*, Niederwil, Egelsee

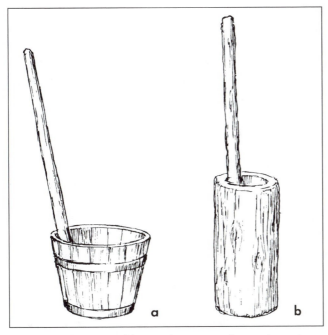

Figure 24.9 Mortars used in experiments 3 and 4: *a*, tub mortar; *b*, solid mortar

the students worked. It was shown that the pestle was moved between 60 and 136 times a minute, that is, an average of some 100 a minute, demonstrating that individual differences occur at this stage. Also, the extraction of 20 g each produced statistical variation.

As the amounts of einkorn in figure 24.12 demonstrate, such divergence does occur. Surprisingly, efficiency is reduced by increased heating to such an extent that different busy hands must have been at work. Random mistakes in the specimens are observable in the emmer (figure 24.12), where successive specimens do not display the increase expected. Unfortunately, the rotation of the workers did not occur systematically, so that these variations cannot be corrected. Tiredness or increased experience further complicate the analysis. A mechanical mortar should probably have been used. Repetition and an increased number of samples could also have led to a better statistical control.

Because of these uncertainties, only a few basic trends of the experiment will be discussed. The most important finding was that glume wheat received very effective treatment in the wooden mortar (figure 24.11), because the proportion of cracked grains, remained constantly below 5% (figure 24.12). The broken grains were mainly larger than half a grain, which can be separated from the lighter chaff through suitable separation and cleaning methods.

The proportion of the category desired, that is, dehusked grains, increased constantly with the length of pounding, although it became apparent even during the operation, that only a very small amount of dehusking took place in the first quarter of an hour, which made the monotonous operation very depressing. The ratio of dehusked grains of emmer increased steadily even after two hours of pounding (figure 24.12), whereas this increase flattened out in most of the series of einkorn and spelt (figure 24.12). In the case of einkorn and emmer about half of the grain was dehusked after an hour, whereas spelt seemed to take longer. Generally, the impression gained during the operation was that einkorn can be dehusked more easily; unfortunately, this is not apparent from the results of the tests given here.

It is difficult to calculate how the preheating affects the results. In the case of spelt, one has the impression that a gradient of temperature does exist. The untreated cereal yields a maximum amount of dehusking of 40%, after heating to 200° C this reaches some 80% (figure 24.12). Whereas emmer displays a relatively small effect of the temperature increase, the special conditions of the einkorn series provide no conclusive evidence (figure 24.12).

The highest rate of dehusking obtained lay between 80 and 90% after preheating to 150 to 200° C. However, this demanded pounding for two hours, without doubt very time-consuming. In the case of emmer and spelt most results show that the efficiency of dehusking fell off after about an hour, so that one should halt the pounding at that stage and insert a cleaning process. It has not yet been tested how the grains which are still husked and then separated out react to a renewed pounding.

Experiment 4: Dehusking of emmer in a solid mortar (hollowed-out tree trunk). Following the experiences gained by using the broad-bottomed tub mortar, use of a narrower mortar was proposed. A narrower cavity would perhaps accelerate the dehusking, since the individual grains would rub against one another more intensively and the glumes would break off more readily.

For experiment 4 a mortar was used which had been prepared from a hollow tree trunk, the cavity measuring some 20 cm in diameter (figure 24.9b). The same pestle (figure 24.9a) was used. The test was carried out using 2 kg of

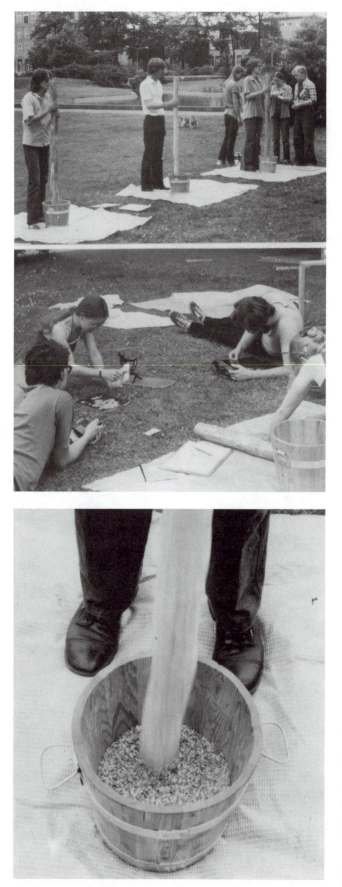

Figure 24.10 Pounding

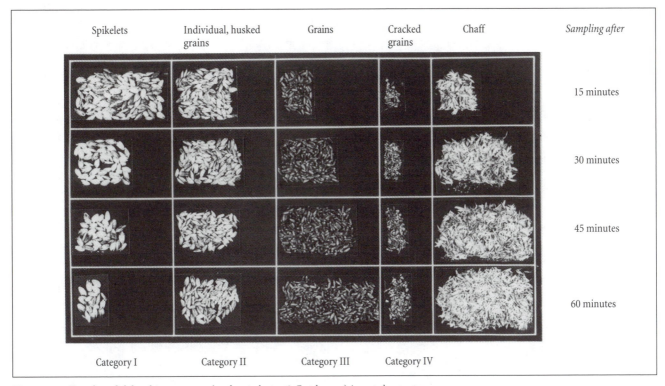

Spikelets	Individual, husked grains	Grains	Cracked grains	Chaff	*Sampling after*
					15 minutes
					30 minutes
					45 minutes
					60 minutes
Category I	Category II	Category III	Category IV		

Figure 24.11 Results of dehusking emmer (preheated at 50° C, 4 hours) in a tub mortar

untreated emmer in the same way already described , that is, the pounding process took two hours with the extraction of 20 g specimens every quarter of an hour. The analysis of the specimens also followed the same method, that is, the grains were counted according to 4 categories.

Figure 24.13 demonstrates that the narrow tree-trunk mortar was clearly much more effective than the improvised tub mortar of experiment 3. Over 70% of the grain was dehusked after only 45 minutes, some 80% after one hour. The proportion of broken grain was a little higher than in the tub mortar. The maximum amount of dehusking was about 95%, achieved after 75 minutes, and even then the grain breakage was only just over 10%.

Comparison Between Quern and Mortar

It is not difficult to decide between the quern and the wooden mortar as a suitable instrument for dehusking glume wheats. The proportion of cracked grain always remained less than 5% in the wooden tub mortar (figure 24.12) and reached a maximum of 10% in the tree-trunk mortar (figure 24.13); on the quern between 20 and 40% of the grains were broken, whereby a quantity was so heavily ground that it could no longer be separated from the chaff.

The working process on the quern is also clumsy and seems less suitable to daily use. Certainly, three to five working actions per handful are executed quickly but the operation has always to be interrupted afterwards. The upper stone (mano) must be taken away, presumably from the nearer (proximal) end of the meule, and lain against the worker's knee, in order to remove the worked grain from the base stone by sweeping or wiping. After that, the next handful of cereal has to be laid upon the base stone and the upper stone placed upon that, before the new process can begin. The small working surface also seems very impractical, as some 25 to 30% of the grain is pushed off the base stone after just three to five working actions. The latter, which has been worked only partly or hardly at all, is then mixed in with the material from the base stone after the optimal three to five actions, thus decreasing the degree of dehusking to below 40% of the initial material (table 24.3:33–41%).

Calculations of time are difficult to reconstruct from the present set of experiments, as no series of tests were carried out on the question of the speed achieved and on routine. Since in the early Neolithic, the hollowed-out tree trunk mortar probably than a tub mortar, it may be assumed that some 75% of the initial amount could be dehusked within an hour. Since 2 kg was found to be a suitable amount for the capacity of the mortar used here, one can obtain some 1.5 kg of dehusked, undamaged grains after one hour's work, that is, 1 kg in 40 minutes. This refers to untreated (non heated) emmer.

After the optimal fifth working action on the quern, one achieves a degree of dehusking of 33% (table 24.3). The processing of a handful of cereal (= 30 g) with five working actions (=10 movements) requires, according to our experience, some 20 seconds. Allowing for small breaks between the individual operations (wiping of the base stone, replacing the grain), one can manage two handfuls (60 g) a minute.

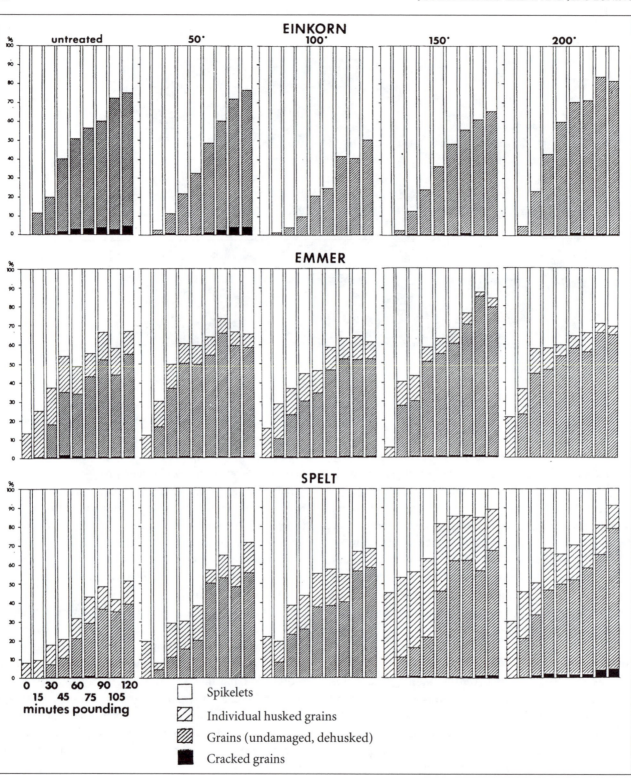

Figure 24.12 Results of dehusking einkorn, emmer and spelt in he tub mortar

In order to compare the efficiency of saddle querns and wooden mortars, one must calculate the time required and the amount of work needed to obtain a kilogram of dehusked, complete grains. For a better comparison the values for untreated emmer given above have been taken. As a correction, it is necessary when considering the results obtained from the experiment with the quern to include the proportion in weight of the glumes and spikelet forks within the husked grains (categories I and II), in order to be able to compare these results with those obtained by counting the grains from the experiment with the mortar. The weight-ratio of chaff was put relatively high in the calculation at 20%

of the spikelet weight.

The comparison in table 24.4 shows that, as far as dehusking is concerned, the wooden mortar is superior to the saddle quern in every respect. It produces the desired dehusked grain in less time (40 as opposed to 50 minutes) and from half of the initial amount (1.3 kg as opposed to 2.8 kg). The effective yield of 94%:53% corresponds to a factor of 1.8 more for the mortar. The degree of yield can be better adjusted by bringing the coarser cracked grain into the calculation. This, however, presupposes thorough cleaning operations, which alters the time taken by the saddle quern to an even more unfavorable extent.

If one accepts that cereal represented a staple food stuff, and the large number of archaeologically observable remains of its production and preparation confirm this, the arguments in favor of the mortar must then weigh all the more— particularly because of the high proportion of loss which is unavoidable using a saddle quern. In preparing one kilogram of dehusked, uncracked grain, a proportion of broken material of only 6% in the wooden mortar stands in contrast to 47% of cracked and already crushed parts from the saddle quern. Even with optimal utilization, that is, including the coarse broken grain, an effective loss of 26% is inevitable on the saddle quern, whereas, theoretically, no loss occurs in the wooden mortar.

Comparing the results of the tests, as concerns effort expended as well as efficiency and the lesser amount of loss, a careful method of dehusking— as in the wooden mortar— is preferable. In the botanical remains, the relatively high ratio of intact rachis segments and spikelet forks, as well as the lack of grains that were clearly broken before carbonization, suggest that such a dehusking method was used during the Linear-Pottery period.

For a normal family of five persons, with a daily need of 5 kg of cereal, even with the most suitable wooden mortar available producing an hourly rate of 1.5 kg, it would still have been necessary for one person to work for 3 hours 20 minutes, not including the cleaning process. Considering this necessary daily expenditure of time, the process of parching as a possible prior treatment would have claimed an inordinate amount of time.

Parching

The above comparison takes into account the results of the experiments obtained with untreated emmer. This decision results from the observation that in the tests a previous thermic treatment displayed only a small effect upon the "readiness to dehusk" of the individual types of glume wheat.

This stands in contrast to the opinion often voiced in archaeological and in palaeoethnobotanical literature that glume wheat must usually be parched before dehusking (Natho 1957:83; Willerding 1970:304; Gall 1975:200; Küster 1985:59). For this reason finds of carbonized grain have

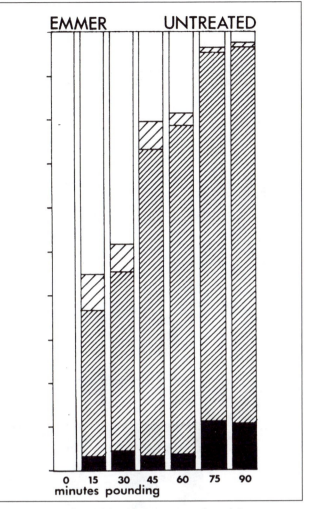

Figure 24.13 Results of dehusking emmer in the solid mortar

Table 24.4 Comparison of efficiency of saddle quern and wooden mortar in dehusking untreated emmer

	SADDLE QUERN		WOODEN MORTAR	
Dehusked grains	36 %	1000 g	75 %	1000 g
Cracked grains	14 %	395 g	5 %	67 g
Fine groats + flour	17 %	485 g		
Husked grains	33 %	920 g	20 %	267 g
Initial amount	100 %	2800 g	100 %	1334 g
Time expended	50 minutes		40 minutes	

Effective yield/loss (initial amount minus husked grains = 100 %)

	YIELD	LOSS	YIELD	LOSS
Grain 1/1	53 %	47 %	94 %	6 %
Grain 1/1 + 1/2	74 %	26 %	100 %	

sometimes been interpreted as "accidents of parching" (Küster 1985:60) and features, such as oven or kilns and burnt pits, seen as "parching-structures" (Petrasch 1986:50; Küster 1985:57).

Decisive for the question of whether the Neolithic farmers routinely parched grain before dehusking is the unit of time needed to work a certain amount and therefore the point in time during which the dehusking process is carried out.

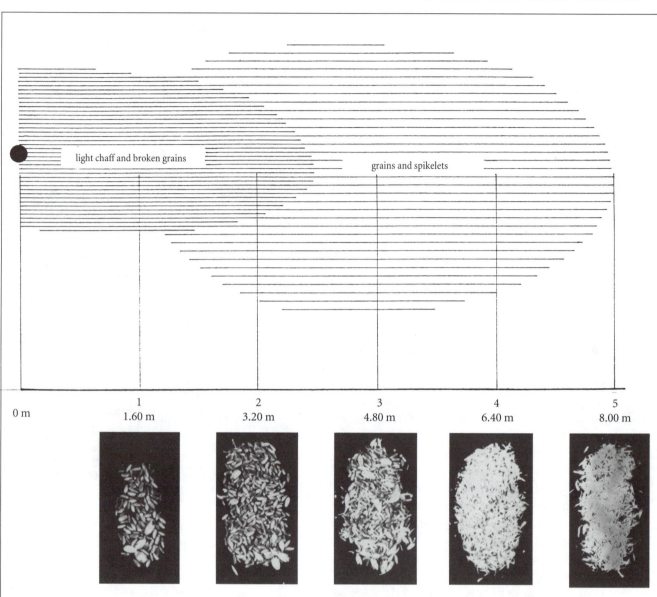

Figure 24.14 Scheme of winnowing cone and composition of the samples from the winnowing cone

Dehusking cannot be regarded as a seasonal task, given that technical methods that could deal with large amounts following the harvest—such as mills with adjustable grinding stones suitable for shelling (Stoll 1902 : 39; Körber-Grohne 1987:69)—were not available then. Rather, it was a part of daily chores connected with preparing meals. This implies the previous storage of the grain (in the husks). Only dry and therefore dehuskable grain is appropriate for storing, irrespective of whether it is kept above ground in domestic or storage buildings or underground in grain silos.[7] The assumption of an additional drying process immediately before dehusking is therefore superfluous.

One could presume an act of drying before storage, (as recorded for Central Europe in historical times in folkloristic literature (for example, Bielenstein 1907-18, 97; Parmentier u.a. 1807:612ff.). This drying with the help of an artificial source of heat served solely to preserve the grain and took

place on a large scale immediately after the harvest (Hinz 1952; *idem* 1954).

During the drying of grain for bread and sowing, one has to make sure that the grain is exposed to only low temperatures, so that its ability to be baked and to germinate is preserved (Neumann-Pelshenke 1954: 235). Proteins are denatured at above 50 to 60° C, numerous enzymes are harmed at temperatures as low as about 40° C. Grain exposed to high temperatures is suitable only for producing porridge. The proof of underground dome-shaped ovens in the Linear-Pottery culture (Petrasch 1986:35) suggests strongly that at least a part of the grain was used for presumably naturally sour and high-rising loaves, which restricts the upper temperature limit for drying to about 60° C.

A look at the composition of the botanical specimens also raises doubts as to whether the drying of grain using an artificial source of heat represented a regular operation during the Linear-Pottery culture in the Rhineland. In the case of accidental overheating between harvest and dehusking possibly leading to carbonization, one would expect a ratio of grains to chaff of 1:1 (table 24.5). However, only 7.7% of the specimens show this.

Cleaning after Dehusking: Winnowing, Sieving, and Casting Up

After dehusking, a cleaning operation must follow in order to separate the mixture of husked and dehusked grains, cracked grains and chaff from one another. The composition of prehistoric botanical samples provides clues to the possible methods of separation used. That a separation was carried out is proven by the ratio of grains to chaff in the specimens of Linear-Pottery grain (figure 24.2; table 24.5), as this does not represent the normal ratio in 92.3% of cases. The amount of grain predominates in 27%, and chaff is preponderant in 65.4% of the samples. The latter is obviously waste from cleaning, which was burnt after separation.

The composition of the samples (proportion of chaff remains and proportion of lighter or heavier, larger or smaller seeds from weeds) allows possible methods of cleaning to be considered (Neuß-Aniol 1987). Possibilities are winnowing in a draught or in an enclosed area, sieving with coarse- or fine-meshed sieves and throwing the grains up on a platter or in a cloth, all methods of cleaning demonstrated in folklore (Hillman 1983).

Experiment 5: Winnowing.
In our experiments the grain dehusked in the wooden mortar separated itself without difficulty from the husked grains and chaff through winnowing and subsequent casting up. Winnowing occurred with a light contrary breeze. The winnowing cone stretched from the casting point approximately 7.5 to 8 m. Five samples were taken at regular intervals (figure 24.14).

Whereas the lighter chaff and a part of the broken grains collected in the forward third of the winnowing cone, the dehusked grains, owing to their weight and the lesser air resistance, flew the furthest (figure 24.14). The central area of the cone contained grains with and without glumes; in this case, it is necessary, by means of an additional operation, for instance by casting up on a flat platter, to isolate the grains with husks in order to subject them to the dehusking process for a second time.

Dehusking and Grinding in One Operation on a Quern

It has been demonstrated that there are good reasons to assume that during the Linear-Pottery culture the glume wheats einkorn and emmer were dehusked in a special operation before meal preparation. For production of flour and cracked grains, grains without glumes were used. For reasons of completeness, a further experiment was carried out in order to see whether a single working step could

Table 24.5 Composition of products obtained during processing of glume wheats compared with samples from the Linear-Pottery period

	GRAINS:CHAFF	% OF SAMPLES	GRAINS:CHAFF	% OF SAMPLES
Harvesting	1:1			
*Drying	1:1			
Threshing	1:1			
Cleaning	1:1	7.7 %		
Storage	1:1			
* Parching	1:1			
Dehusking	1:1			
Cleaning	→ 1:1 ← 10:1 →1:1 → 10:1	26.9 % (13.5 %) (13.5 %)	1:→1 1:←10 1:→1 1:→10	65.4 % (30.8 %) (34.6 %)
* Parching	→1:1			
Grinding				

SUPPLY   WASTE

produce flour suitable for human consumption from husked grains on the saddle quern (Beranová 1981:227). As the results of experiments 1 and 2 show, after only ten working actions on average about 10% of the finest material—that is, flour—was produced (figure 24.7). The question arises as to whether an intensive, continuous grinding of husked grain can produce a useful proportion of flour.

Experiment 6: Grinding of husked grains on a quern

Untreated einkorn from the harvest of 1982 was employed for the test, 500 g of einkorn was subdivided into 10-g portions, which were ground through five grinding operations of five minutes each. The material that had fallen off the base stone was replaced upon the quern several times during each operation. The quern depicted in figure 24.6 was used.

Even while the experiment was being carried out, one gained the impression that a large part of the chaff was ground into the smallest fragments, which were not separable from glume fragments and the flour itself. After 25 minutes of grinding there accrued from the initial amount 42% of fine, relatively white flour (particles less than 0.15 mm) and 12% of coarser flour (0.15-0.4 mm), which is darker owing to the crushed chaff (figure 24.15). Both types are usable for preparing food. All particles over 0.4 mm, comprising after all some 46% of the initial material, do not seem suitable for human consumption because of the high ratio of chaff content (Beranová 1987; 166), even if one presupposes a greater degree of tolerance in prehistoric humans towards the hard chaff rich in silicic acid. Crucial for the question of whether dehusking and grinding in one operation can be assumed for the Linear-Pottery culture is also the presence of fine-meshed sieves able to separate fractions of less than 0.5 mm. The loss of 46% for human consumption is high, as a separation of cracked grain larger than 0.5mm from chaff is only possible with great difficulty.

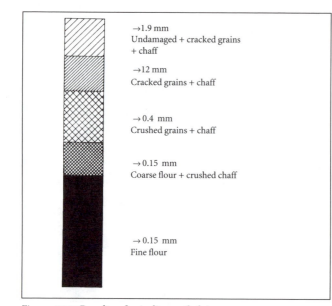

→1.9 mm
Undamaged + cracked grains
+ chaff

→12 mm
Cracked grains + chaff

→0.4 mm
Crushed grains + chaff

→0.15 mm
Coarse flour + crushed chaff

→0.15 mm
Fine flour

Figure 24.15 Results of grinding spikelets

Especially the remains of grain from the Linear-Pottery culture (figure 24.2; table 24.5) argue against the whole process, where, after all, the number of grains outweigh the proportion of chaff in 27% of the samples. During the grinding process described, hardly any whole or half grains remain preserved. Owing to the modest yield and the archaeological evidence in the botanical samples, such a working step can be rejected as far as the Linear-Pottery culture is concerned.

Results

The experiments presented emerged from questions involving possible methods of cereal processing during the Linear-Pottery period in the Rhineland. By comparing preserved plant remains with the products obtained during the experiments, hypotheses can be made as to which working practices are probable for the Linear-Pottery culture, or rather, from which operation the samples examined originate.

In analysing the tests carried out, however, one has to consider that according to the make up of each experiment, they are suitable only for checking the plausibility of a few of the proposed hypotheses concerning these questions. One must, however, sound a note of warning not to translate the results of the experiments uncritically into archaeological reconstructions. In carrying out the tests, we had to subdivide the operations and to be able to reproduce them under well-defined conditions. The absolute values obtained are not directly transferable but interpreted as approximate guides as to relative conditions and tendencies. This refers particularly to measurements of time and efficiency, in which the lack of experience and routine of the experiment's are reflected involuntarily.

The palaeoethnobotanical observation that during the Linear-Pottery period glume wheats were cultivated and that the preserved remains of grain only seldom display the natural, morphological ratio of grains to chaff (figure 24.2) suggests equivalent methods of dehusking and cleaning. From the plethora of methods known from folklore (Neuß 1983) and from ethnographic observations (Hillman 1983), a simple scheme had to be developed that contained only the basic operations necessary for the processing of cereal—with the possible use of fire for drying or for parching being given with particular attention.

The results of the test series have proven that during the Linear-Pottery culture, a parching of the grain before dehusking was neither necessary nor, in view of the botanical remains, probable. Even the use of archaeologically attested saddle querns for dehusking grain is to be rejected, owing to the unavoidable high rate of loss. The comparison between the results of the tests obtained for the saddle quern with those of the wooden mortar proves that the latter was the superior instrument for dehusking in every respect.

The weight of evidence of the results for dehusking obtained in the wooden mortar is limited by the test conditions imposed upon the series of experiments. Thus, the comparison between the results of the narrow solid tree-trunk mortar and the wide-bottomed tub mortar already showed that the amount of time needed could be reduced considerably through use of an instrument wholly adapted to the method. Likewise, the effective proportion of broken grains can certainly be reduced by a daily routine and by long years of experience. One has also, however, to take into account the losses to be expected through the subsequent methods of cleaning.

Flour and crushed grains are wholly unavoidable products of working with saddle querns (see experiments 1, 2, and 6). The large number of stone saddle querns from Neolithic settlements shows that since these were unsuitable for dehusking, at least a part of the meal was prepared from flour and crushed grains, so that one reaches the inevitable conclusion that flat cakes or sour bread were baked. The underground dome-shaped ovens recorded for the Linear-Pottery culture indicate that in fact a part was made using raising agents, most probably leaven.

As shown in table 24.5, two-thirds of the Linear-Pottery samples with remains of grain can be regarded as refuse from the cleaning process after dehusking. In these, the proportion of chaff is preponderant. It is clear that during the Linear-Pottery culture one often burnt the cleaning refuse, because the hard chaff of the glume wheat was not needed in the amounts produced as an admixture for animal fodder or for further uses, such as for the temper of pottery or for wattle-and-daub (Willerding 1970, 313). Perhaps one also tried destroying unwanted weeds by burning the remains of chaff, which are mostly rich in weed seeds (Neuß-Aniol 1987; table 24.10), a sort of active weed killer.

The rubbish accruing from dehusking found its way partly

intentionally, but also partly unintentionally, into the fire, presumably as a rule into the open hearth in the house. In its vicinity the cereal for the daily bread was dehusked in a mortar; afterwards, the grain was ground here as well (Zimmermann 1988). The chaff came directly into the fire or, as far as it was scattered, was collected during cleaning of the house along with lost grains and other rubbish, such as stones and sherds, and occasionally thrown into the hearth too. Thus, after the clearing out of the hearth, these carbonized finds, together with the ashes and charcoal remains, found their way outside and sometimes into pits, where they have remained preserved as "thin, black layers" (Lüning 1977:59).

The product sought in the Linear-Pottery period was dehusked, cleaned, and edible cereal made from whole grains. These could be lost only during grinding and during the preparation of meals, which meant in only small amounts.[8] The possibility of detecting these is, therefore, extremely slight, which corresponds to the archaeological reality.

Acknowledgments. The experiments were carried out with the financial help of the Gerda Henkel Stiftung. We thank Clive Bridger, B.A., Xanten, for translating the text.

Notes

1. The examples cited relate to Bandkeramik samples of at least 50 grains or of the equivalent glume remains. The 52 samples in all formed the basis of a M.A. thesis at Cologne, which dealt with methods of cleaning cereals (Neuß-Aniol 1987).
2. The high amount of glume material in the botanical samples demonstrates that largely the refuse accruing from the working of the grain and unsuitable for human consumption was carbonized and later became mixed in with pit fills as rubbish.
3. Personal communication from Dr. A. Simons on her observations in central Tanzania in 1976.
4. The saddle quern was made by Ferdinand Schmidt, Bernd Langenbrinck, and Jürgen Gaffrey.
5. Since after only 3 working actions the grain previously heated to 200° C had been completely crushed, the series of tests was concluded at this stage.
6. Personal communication from Dr. K.-H. Knörzer.
7. In accordance with these considerations, the untreated grain used in our experiments was from (dry) storage.
8. We forgo an account of the extensive grinding experiments on dehusked grain; these will be described *in extenso* in the detailed report of the Cologne experiments.

Chapter 25

The Interpretation of Sickles
A Cautionary Tale

Annelou van Gijn

ONE OF THE THEMES OF THE CONFERENCE FO-
cuses on the way flint sickles used for harvesting cereals can
be recognized. This constitutes an old problem as is illustrated
by the fact that already in the last century Spurrell tried to
replicate the gloss he observed on Near Eastern blades,
assuming that it was caused by harvesting grain (Spurrell
1892). In the Netherlands, one type of flint tool from the Late
Bronze and Early Iron Age has consistently been classified as
a "sickle." Most of these tools have been found in West-
Friesland, mainly stray finds from somewhat marshy areas
adjacent to levees on which Late Bronze Age settlements are
located. (Near this region one deposit is known [Heiloo].) In
the provinces of Drenthe and Groningen the so-called sickles
derive from Late Bronze Age deposits, while their find location
in Early Iron Age deposits is confined to the terps[1] of northern
Friesland and Groningen (figure 25.1). The raw material from
which these tools are made is found in Denmark and
Schleswig-Holstein; presumably the artifacts were
transported to the west as end-products (van Regteren Altena,
pers. comm.). The presence of deposits with finished products
in the northeastern part of the Netherlands, in strategic
locations for crossing the peat area between Germany and
the Netherlands, supports this idea. Moreover, all implements
interpreted as unused come from deposits (van Gijn
1988:201).[2]

The so-called sickles have a crescent shape, are bifacially
retouched, and vary in length from 10 to 18 cm. Most notable
is a macroscopically visible gloss which covers the greater
part of the surface. One end is not glossy, presumably due to
the former presence of a haft (figure 25.2). Because of their
strong resemblance in shape to traditional sickles they were

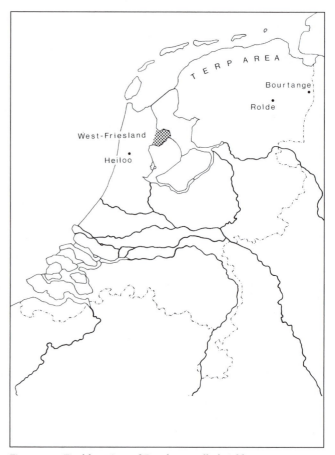

Figure 25.1 Find location of Dutch so-called sickles

referred to as such. This functional attribution seemed to be
corroborated by the high so-called sickle gloss, which is
customarily associated with harvesting cereals.

It must be stressed that postdepositional surface

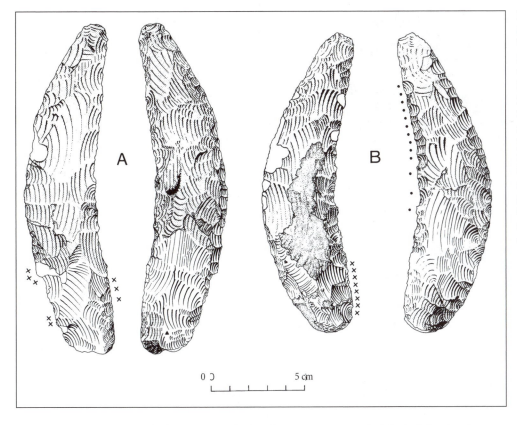

Figure 25.2 Two archaeological sickles from West-Friesland. The shaded area shows where gloss is visible with the naked eye. Dots indicate polish interpreted as being the result of secondary use on siliceous plants. The crosses point out places where rough polish is observed (figure 25.8). The butt end of sickle A displays friction gloss (indicated by a triangle). The latter two types of wear traces are interpreted as being the result of hafting.

0 ☐   5 cm

modifications cannot be held responsible for this intense luster. First, the typical distribution of the gloss across the medial part and distal end of the tool next to a matte butt, is observed on implements from a variety of depositional contexts. Although several sickles displayed discoloration due to the peaty matrix in which they were found, this did not affect the distribution of the polish. Second, some of the sickles found in the deposits of northeastern Netherlands were fresh looking, exhibiting no traces of gloss. They were found adjacent to highly lustered artifacts. Some secondary damage such as edge-removals and scratches were present, but the basic pattern of wear on the archaeological tools appeared to be so consistent that it could only be related to intentional use for a specific task.

Only lately doubts have arisen about the classification of the crescent-shaped tools as sickles used for harvesting agrarian products. First of all, the locations where most implements were unearthed, low-lying marshy areas, are considered to be unsuitable for cultivation. In addition, the edges of the utensils, which in some cases have worn to a trapezoidal shape about 3 to 5 mm wide, seem too blunt for efficient reaping. Finally, the fact that the convex sides also exhibit blunting casts additional doubt on the interpretation of the sickles as harvesting implements.

To examine this problem more objectively it was decided to experiment with harvesting cereals using replicas of the sickles and unretouched blades. Because reeds and horsetails are highly siliceous plants and will cause development of an intense luster, they were also considered as possibly worked material. Soil is also known to produce extensive gloss: experiments involving soil as contact material included hoeing and the cutting of sod. The exact experimental procedures and the rationale behind them have been dealt with in a previous article and will not be further discussed here (van Gijn 1988).

The results of the experiments were compared with the characteristics of twenty-two archaeological sickles, eleven of which came from deposits (Bourtange and Rolde in the northeast, Heiloo near West-Friesland), the remainder from the marshy areas in West-Friesland (van Gijn 1988:201). The Early Iron Age specimens from the terps were excluded from analysis. All experimental tools were subjected to standard chemical cleaning (Keeley 1980). One archaeological implement was submitted to the same procedure but no changes in polish attributes were observed. As HCl can dissolve the surface of more chalky varieties of flint, no risks were taken with the other archaeological artifacts. The latter were therefore only rinsed with water and soap. All implements were studied with a Nikon Optiphot metallographic microscope, with magnifications ranging from 50 to 560x.

A total of twenty-one cereal-harvesting experiments were done involving three replicas of the crescent-shaped sickles and eighteen unretouched blades, eight of which were hafted in various ways. The retouched edges of the sickle replicas were less sharp than the unretouched blades. Cereals included *Triticum dicoccum, Triticum aestivum, Avena sativa, Hordeum vulgare* ssp. *vulgare,* and *Hordeum vulgare* ssp.

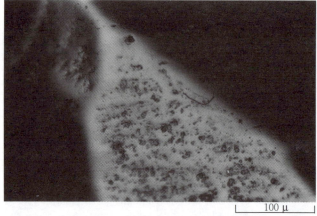

Figure 25.3 Polish resulting from harvesting barley for 90 minutes

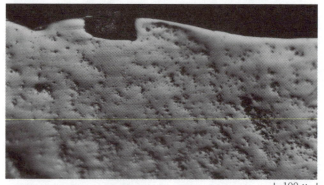

Figure 25.4 Polish resulting from reaping barley for approximately five hours

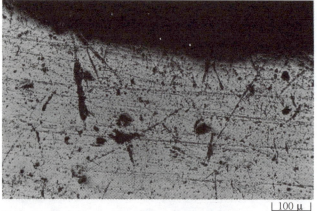

Figure 25.5 Polish on a so-called sickle from Bourtange. Note the predominantly parallel orientation of the striations.

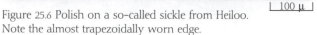

Figure 25.6 Polish on a so-called sickle from Heiloo. Note the almost trapezoidally worn edge.

distichum. Duration of use varied from 30 minutes to 5 hours. All of the experiments produced a maximally 1.5 cm-wide band of highly reflective, very smooth polish which possessed a clear parallel directionality and only few striations (figure 25.3).[3] Where the polish had not linked up, it appeared domed. The edges dulled only very slowly: both tool types hardly decreased in effectiveness, even after 5 hours of harvesting (figure 25.4).

The experimental polish and striations (edge damage was only slight) resembled in no way the wear observed on the archaeological specimens. On the latter, the polish was reflective as well, but more matte and slightly rougher and filled with random striations, although at times there seemed to be a predominant directionality parallel to the edge (figure 25.5).[4] Moreover, as mentioned above, the polish extended across the entire width of the tool instead of being confined to a narrow band. Finally, the experiments made clear that the edges of most of the archaeological sickles must have been too blunt (figure 25.6) for effective harvesting and would have needed resharpening long before the trapezoidal shape displayed by these tools would have been reached. All in all, it therefore seems most unlikely that the Late Bronze Age sickles were employed for the harvesting of cereals.

An alternative use could be the collection of reeds and horsetails; the find location of many of the sickles in less well-drained areas would support this hypothesis. Ten experiments were conducted on *Phragmites* and three on *Equisetum*, all of them with unretouched blades, and working time varied from 7 to 60 minutes. Unfortunately, no crescent-shaped tool was available this time. The experimentally produced gloss again differs markedly from the polish observed on the archaeological specimens: it is extremely smooth and almost wet-looking (figure 25.7), while striations are totally absent. Once more the distribution of the experimental gloss is confined to a band along the edge. To sum up, it is very improbable that the archaeological sickles were used for collecting reeds or horsetails.

We are left with soil as potential contact material. We considered three functional alternatives: coulter in a plow (Bruyn 1986), hoeing implement, and sod-cutting tool. The first possibility had to be rejected because the areas with hafting traces (rough polish [figure 25.8] and friction gloss on the butt end [figure 25.2]) appeared to be too restricted with respect to the amount of leverage exerted on the tool (van Gijn 1988:213–214). One hoeing experiment was executed with a crescent-shaped replica (used for 35 minutes). It proved to be very suitable for this purpose as it easily cut through the weeds just below the surface and was very effective in breaking up clumps of clay. Although the distribution of the polish conforms to that displayed by the archaeological implements, its character is smoother (figure 25.9), and the striations appear oriented in totally random directions, in contrast with the sometimes more parallel orientation of the striae observed on several Late Bronze Age tools. However, we can hardly expect weeding to have been practiced in the low-lying areas, where successful cropping or gardening was barely possible.

The third hypothesis involving soil as contact material, that is, that the sickles were used to cut sod, is not as far-fetched as it may seem, because in the rather treeless environment of much of western and northern Holland sod provided a suitable building material for the construction of houses (Boersma 1988; Therkorn et al. 1986; van Gijn 1984). Moreover both in Drenthe and West-Friesland grave-barrows were erected with sod (van Giffen 1944; 1953). Four sod-cutting experiments were performed; working time amounted to 35 minutes each for two unretouched blades and one hour for the crescent-shaped replica and another large blade. All tools displayed macroscopically visible gloss after only a few minutes of work. The sickle replica penetrated the soil best because of its pointed shape and, as a consequence, the polish extended all the way across the exposed part of the tool instead of being confined to a band along the working edge. The character of the polish strongly resembled the gloss observed on seventeen of the twenty-two archaeological implements (van Gijn 1988): rather rough and flat, very bright but less intense than the experimental wear traces produced by cereals or reeds (figure 25.10). The tool surface was scarred by striations: although many had a random orientation, they predominantly ran parallel to the edge (figure 25.11). Such a distribution can be explained by the presence of small stones and other hard particles in the soil. The edges became blunt very quickly but this did not noticeably decrease their effectiveness. Although more experiments are definitely needed, it would seem at present that the greater part of the Dutch Late Bronze Age sickles were actually used as sod-cutting tools.[5]

An interpretation for sod-cutting does not necessarily mean that the sickles could not have been intended primarily for harvesting. Morphologically similar Neolithic artifacts found in Denmark probably functioned as reaping tools because the gloss is limited to a band of 1.0 to 1.5 cm wide along the concave (inner) edge (Juel Jensen pers. comm.). Moreover, on three of the twenty-two Dutch sickles studied, traces interpreted as the result of contact with plants were observed in resharpening scars on previously blunt (that is, used on soil) edges (figure 25.12). This would indicate that the sickles were considered suitable as plant-cutting implements. It is thus possible that the crescent-shaped utensils were primarily conceived as harvesting tools, only secondarily to be employed for cutting sods, but this assumption cannot be tested, as primary sickle gloss would have become invisible after prolonged secondary contact with soil. However, if sod-cutting was merely a second step in the life-cycle of these sickles, it is strange that this practice was such a widespread phenomenon: evidence for it was found not only on stray

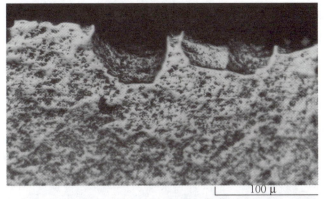

Figure 25.7 Polish on an experimental blade used for cutting reeds for 60 minutes

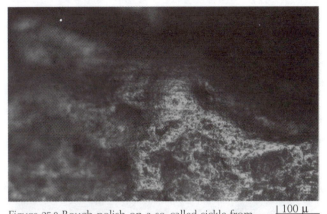

Figure 25.8 Rough polish on a so-called sickle from Heiloo, interpreted as being the result of hafting

Figure 25.9 Polish observed on an experimental hoeing tool used for 35 minutes

Figure 25.10 Polish resulting from cutting sod for 35 minutes

Figure 25.11 Predominantly parallel orientation of the striations on the tool in figure 25.10

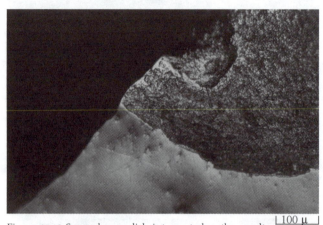

Figure 25.12 Secondary polish interpreted as the result of contact with plants in the resharpening scars of an archaeological "sickle" from West-Friesland

finds from West-Friesland but on implements from deposits in Drenthe and Groningen. In this respect it is useful to remember that sod was necessary both for house construction and for the erection of grave-barrows, activities often surrounded with ceremony. Using the finely manufactured, probably imported sickles for cutting soil might not have been such an inferior application at all.[6] As Anderson-Gerfaud (1983) and Juel Jensen (1988a) have already stressed, we are so preoccupied with the role of flint tools for obtaining food that we tend to overlook the possibility they could also have functioned in craft activities or even in ceremonies.

The purpose of this chapter is to draw attention to the fact that not all sickle gloss is really due to harvesting cereals. Many archaeologists are aware of the possibility that gloss may be the result of postdepositional factors, such as wind-gloss or gloss-patina (Rottlander 1975; Stapert 1976). However, archaeologists not familiar with wear-trace analysis tend to overlook the fact that a high luster can also originate from reaping siliceous plants other than domesticated cereals, such as *Phragmites*, *Equisetum*, or wild grasses (see chapter 12). The example of the Dutch sickles adds yet another contact material, soil, and another activity, cutting sod, to the possible

causatives of so-called sickle gloss. The present case is even more illustrative in that it also demonstrates the danger of simple form-function analogies. This can therefore be considered a cautionary tale, carrying the message to be careful both with the interpretation of "sickle gloss" and with inferring function from shape on the basis of formal analogies.

Postscript: March 1998

Recently nine more sickles were examined for traces of use, all deriving from the northeastern part of the Netherlands. This brief study confirmed the earlier idea (Van Gijn 1988, 1992) that the tools were used to cut sod (or rather turf). The location of the traces and the direction of the striations do not agree with use as a hoe, nor does the tip provide an adequate morphology for such a functional application. It is also quite apparent that the tools were held by hand. The use polish fades out only gradually, something not observed on a hafted tool. Moreover, here and there patches of soil polish are present on the area which was supposedly held. This was most noticeable on the distal end.

As mentioned, it is unlikely that the tools were used to lift the turfs. Most likely this was done with, for example, a shoulder blade of a cow. They are, however, very efficient in loosening the turfs, that is cutting the vegetation layer. Though the cutting of turfs seems to be a rather mundane task, it is obviously a deliberate choice made by these Late Bronze and Early Iron Age communities in the coastal zones of the Netherlands. The pattern is too consistent to be accidental. And, to stress again, turfs constitute a very important building material in these areas, used both for house and for barrow construction.

Several Dutch archeologists still refuse to accept the above explanation, on the basis of purely emotional reasons. This refusal may be attributed to our research focus on subsistence, especially on agriculture. We tend to forget that building activities are frequently surrounded by ceremonial behavior and may require specially valued implements. The sickles may in fact be considered special, as they are imported as finished products. The observation that the depots also contained implements without traces indicates that at least some of the imported tools were probably produced for exchange and were not rejects from northern Germany or southern Denmark.

Notes

1. A terp is an artificial mound, raised to keep the living areas of those inhabiting the salt marshes free of periodic flooding.
2. The interpretation of an archaeological tool as "unused" does not necessarily mean that the implement has never been employed, as diagnostic wear attributes do not always develop. Especially in the case of contact with green plants, meat, and fish, wear traces might be absent (van Gijn 1986; Unrath et al. 1986).
3. Tools used for only a period of 30 to 60 minutes displayed a very narrow band of gloss, that is, 1 to 2 mm wide.

4. The presence of so many striations has also been observed on sickle blades but then the associated polish is generally rougher and more cratered. This kind of rough, heavily striated polish on some Early Neolithic sickle blades has been attributed to the presence of large quantities of weeds on the prehistoric fields (Juel Jensen 1988a). Juel Jensen's own experiments on a weed-infested field in Leyre support this hypothesis, but one experiment by the author under the same conditions produced the smooth variety of sickle gloss. This might be due to the fact that the latter tool was used for a shorter period of time, causing the polish to be less linked; it can be argued that striations only become visible in a well-developed stage of polish formation. Yet another explanation for the presence of many striations in sickle gloss has been proposed by Korobkova (1981b) and Unger-Hamilton (1985a; chapter 13). They propose that the striae are caused by soil particles present especially on the stems of domesticated cereals, because of plowing and weeding. Unger-Hamilton asserts that in this fashion it is possible to differentiate between the polish caused by wild versus domesticated cereals (chapter 13). However, this is not always the case (see van Gijn 1988:205). It seems that the striations so often present in what we call sickle gloss still merit a detailed investigation.

5. Most probably the crescent-shaped tools were not suitable for the actual removal of the sods, once cut loose, because of insufficient leverage. A shoulder blade would be more effective for example, and in fact a heavily polished specimen was found in the Middle Bronze Age site of Bovenkarspel (IJzereef 1981). Obviously the sods can also quite easily be removed by hand by rolling them up.

6. Recently, Stapert examined a sickle from Early Iron Age levels of the terp Middelstum-Boerdamsterweg and arrived at the conclusion that the tool was also probably used on soil, perhaps for cutting sods (Stapert 1988). It is interesting to note that the sickle was found close to small sheds erected with sods (Boersma 1988).

Chapter 26 ✺

Micromorphological Analysis of Soil Structure Modifications Caused by Different Cultivation Implements

Anne Gebhardt

EXPERIMENTAL AGRICULTURE IN ARCHAEOLOGY has recently appeared in Europe in order to understand plant change through domestication, and to this end seed collections have been made and ancient crops have been cultivated and their yields studied. Experimenters have also been interested in the use of reconstructed ancient tools such as sickles, and the microwear traces which form on them. However, in these experiments soils have been largely ignored.

In archaeology, the anthropogenic impact occurring on the agrarian landscape should be studied through the soil, because soil supports cultivation and supplies the plant with its nutrients and it also records the intervention of humans and their cultivation implement. The latter is best studied through micromorphology, because chemical analyses routinely used in pedology (pH, organic matter, cation exchange characterization, base saturation, and so forth) only characterize the present-day state of a soil and provide very little information on its ancient evolution.

Methodology

Micromorphology, a new method of investigation of soils, has been used in archaeology for about ten years, first in England (Romans and Robertson 1983; Macphail 1986), then in France (Courty 1982). Perfected by pedologists, it allows microscopic study of undisturbed loose sediments, sampled in oriented blocks. The samples are then dried, hardened by a polyester resin, sliced into slabs, and machined down to 25 μm to allow observation under the polarizing microscope.

It is then possible to recognize a number of sedimentary, pedological, and anthropogenic features which characterize the natural deposit, its degree of pedological evolution, and the type of anthropogenic disturbances affecting it. This helps give a better understanding of the change induced by humans on their environment at a number of levels (organization of habitat, agricultural exploitation of the surrounding landscape). In the last case, micromorphology can detect features directly related to the agricultural exploitation of a field, on the condition that the soil remains well-protected from modern faunal and agricultural disturbance (buried under an archaeological monument).

Topics

Under many archaeological monuments, we can find well-dated ancient soils preserved from alteration. Unfortunately it is sometimes difficult to interpret certain pedological features because of a lack of reference material. Therefore, in order to make a reference collection of cultivated profiles to compare with those coming from archaeological contexts, different profiles from experimental sites in northwest Europe have been sampled.

Interest is concentrated upon structural modifications caused in the soil by various cultivation implements, with structure and porosity both being important factors in soil suitability for agriculture (Fédoroff 1987). These play an essential part in the migration of water, solid particles, exchangeable bases (Na, K, Ca, Mg), and for iron and aluminum movement. Porosity, which can have a mechanical origin (fissures, cracks), or be biologically formed by animal holes (channels, burrows), encourages plant root growth.

For the present work, the structure of thin-sections was observed through a stereoscopic microscope using the method described by Bullock et al. (1985).

Table 26.1 The different experiments used for structural analysis of cultivated soils

| | CALCAREOUS COLLUVIUM UNDER GRASSLAND | | LOESSIC-LOAM UNDER FOREST | |
	BUTSER	DEHERAIN	GRIGNON	HAMBACHER FORST
TOOL				
Uncultivated	x	x	x	x
Hoe			x	
Ard	x			x
Spade		x		
Cultivator		x		x

Table 26.2 The Deherain plots used for analysis of the influence of manuring on soil structure

	WITHOUT MANURING	STRAW WITHOUT PREHUMIFICATION	STRAW WITH PREHUMIFICATION	STABLE LITTER
Spade	x	x	x	
Cultivator	x			x

The experimental sites

These were all chosen in northwest Europe in order to maintain a pedo-climatic unity and to allow better comparisons between these results and those from the archaeological sites studied. They are:

- Butser Farm (Great Britain), an experimental Iron Age farm where the fields have been ploughed with an ard since 1970. This site is situated on calcareous colluvium, at the bottom of a grassy hill used for pasture (Reynolds 1984).

- Hambacher Forst (Germany), a loessic-loam soil under forest that has been ploughed with an ard for one year by U. Tegmuller (Meurers-Balke 1985).

- The Grignon forest (France, Institut National Agronomique): a loessic-loam that was worked with a wooden hoe of Neolithic type. In order to accelerate the pedological process the experimental plots were intensively watered for one month (about 2000 l in July 1986).

- The Deherain plots (France, Institut National Agronomique), established on calcareous colluvium under grassland to study the influence of different types of manuring on crop yield. Several plots have been worked with a spade or a cultivator since 1929 (Morel et al. 1984).

These four experiments can be divided into two groups (table 26.1); soils on calcareous colluvium under grassland (Butser, Deherain), and soils on loessic-loam under forest (Hambacher Forst, Grignon). Four ways of working the soil are compared: working with a hoe (Grignon); working with an ard (Butser, Hambacher Forst); working with a spade (Deherain): and working with a cultivator (Deherain, Hambacher Forst). All of these sites have an uncultivated soil for reference. On manured Deherain plots, the influence of different organic matter input on soil structure was also studied (table 26.2).

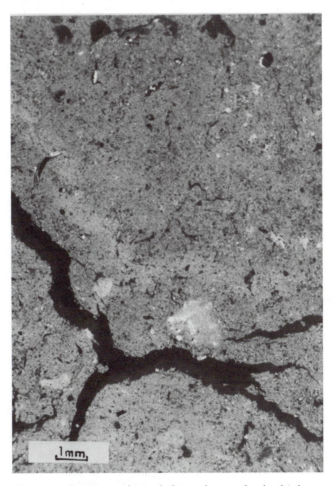

Figure 26.1 Butser, uncultivated plot under grassland: a bird foot-shaped fissure

Results
Tool impact on soil structure

Table 26.3 summarizes the micromorphological observations of the upper horizon structure from the experimental soils studied. For each sort of implement, a number of variables were compared. These are the degree of compaction of the soil and its porosity, ped form and shape, depth of organic matter burial, and the depth of tool impact, which determines

Table 26.3 Comparative structure of soils worked with different tools by site

	SOIL	POROSITY	PEDS	ORGANIC MATTER	COLOR	DEPTH OF IMPACT
UNCULTIVATED						
Butser	Compact	Bird foot-shaped cracks (figure 26.1)	Homogeneous Ø 2 cm	In small quantity chipped	Brown	–
Deherain	Quite compact	Relatively well opened (figure 26.2)	Relatively compacted 0.5 < Ø < 1 cm	Important biological activity (pellets, plant fragments, numerous channels)	Lt brown	–
Grignon	Compact	Bird foot-shaped cracks, channels, chambers (figure 26.3)	Few Ø 0.5 cm	Medium biological activity (intense upwards, some pellets at bottom)	Lt brown	–
Hambacher Forst	Compact	No cracks (figure 26.4)	Coming from B horizon (lighter) disturb the A horizon homogeneity	Intense biological activity (animal burrows, roots, numerous plant remains)	Dk color	–
HOE						
Butser	–	–	–	–	–	–
Deherain	–	–	–	–	–	–
Grignon	Quite compacted	Packing void porosity (chambers with star-shaped concave walls); bird foot-shaped cracks have disappeared (figure 26.5)	–	–	Lt brown	Undefined
Hambacher Forst	–	–	–	–	–	–
ARD						
Butser	Medium compacted, intensive disintegration (without orientation)	Connected chambers and cracks	Quite angular (figure 26.6) (0.25–0.5 cm)	–	–	Undefined
Deherain	–	–	–	–	–	–
Grignon	–	–	–	–	–	–
Hambacher Forst	Compacted	Unfissured	Rounded (0.5 cm), darker than the ground-mass, plough pan (figure 26.7)	Numerous big organic fragments		6 cm
SPADE						
Butser	–	–	–	–	–	–
Deherain	Little compaction	Horizontal cracks everywhere; biggest clods are compacted, with star-shaped cracks (figure 26.8)	Coarse subrounded	–	–	12 cm
Grignon	–	–	–	–	–	–
Hambacher Forst	–	–	–	–	–	–
CULTIVATOR						
Butser	–	–	–	–	–	–
Deherain	Little compaction	Very loose	Numerous peds, bird foot-shaped cracks (figure 26.9)	Little organic matter	–	10–12 cm
Grignon	–	–	–	–	–	–
Hambacher Forst	Little compaction	Crack porosity	Peds broken with clean and straight edges (figure 26.10)	Plant remains buried deeply	–	12 cm

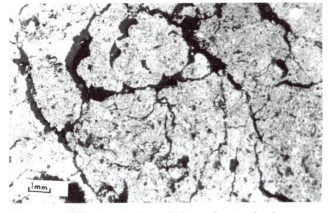

Figure 26.2 Dehérain, uncultivated plot under grassland: compacted peds with an animal burrow

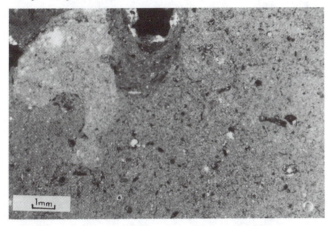

Figure 26.3 Grignon, uncultivated plot under forest: compact soil with little bird foot-shaped fissures and an animal burrow

Figure 26.4 Hambacher Forst, uncultivated plot under forest; compact soil

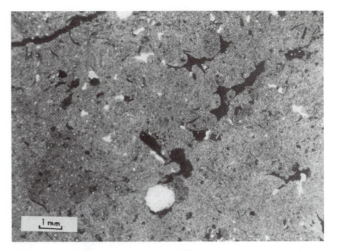

Figure 26.5 Grignon, plot worked with a hoe; quite compact packing of soil with a porosity of star-shaped concave walls

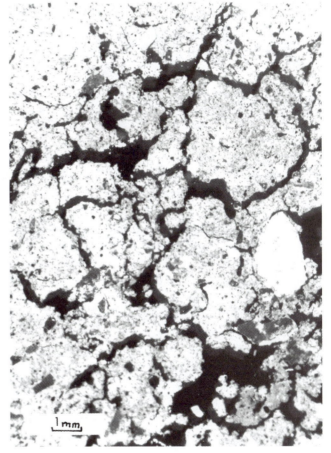

Figure 26.6 Butser, plot ploughed with an ard; medium compacted soil with quite angular peds

the extent of the Ap horizon.

In all cases, the is initially very compacted and well-structured, with characteristic "bird foot-shaped" cracks (with 3 or 4 radiant junctions) isolating soil peds (figures 26.1 and 26.2). Significant biological activity occurred, suggested by animal pellets and root remains and increased porosity, shown by channels and burrows (figures 26.2 and 26.3). The loessic-loam at Hambacher Forst is very compact (figure 26.4), but less porous. The structure collapsed because the original A horizon was badly structured.

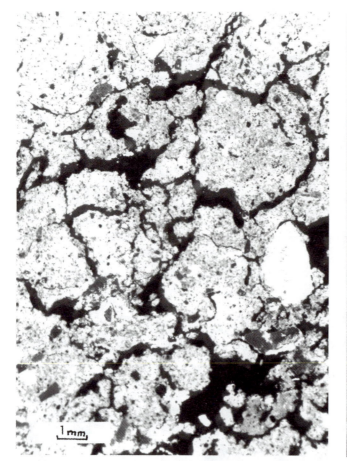

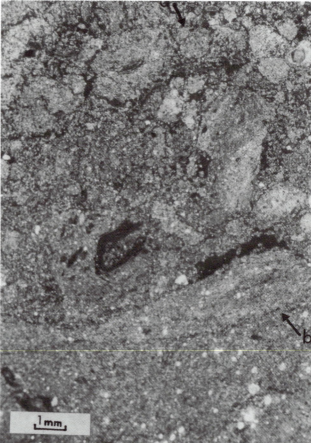

Figure 26.6 Butser, plot ploughed with an ard; medium compacted soil with quite angular peds

Figure 26.7 Hambacher Forst, plot worked with an ard; compact soil with round peds floating in the groundmass, and a plough pan limiting the Ap horizon

After cultivation, the soil becomes looser; the structure is made up of clods of different sizes, according to the tool employed (figures 26.6, 26.7, and 26.9), mixed with smaller angular peds. In the middle of the biggest clods, the original soil structure is still well preserved.

At Hambacher Forst (figure 26.7), clods do not exist because of the badly structured nature of the original horizon, but we can observe numerous rounded peds in the groundmass compacted by the ard. The bottom of the ploughed horizon is compacted into a discontinuous, thin loamy-clay zone (1 cm), is lamellar in structure, and creates a plough pan-like those described in modern ploughed horizons (Jongerius 1970; Collins and Larney 1987). In addition, the cultivator created clods with straight, cleanly broken edges (figure 26.10).

Unfortunately, the hoeing experiment at Grignon did not show real disturbance, with the exception of an increase in star-shaped porosity (figure 26.5); this was certainly caused by excessive watering of the plots over too short a time (Courty and Trichet 1988).

Modifications caused by manuring

Structure. Input of organic matter in the form of pure straw, humidified straw, or stable litter does not affect the structure of any horizon, worked or not. Only the increasing quantity of organic fragments, more or less incorporated into the soil, gives evidence of this input.

Organic activity (table 26.4). Traces of faunal activity seem to be more visible in the uncultivated, unmanured plots than under the ploughed horizons. Whatever the treatment of the plot, microfauna (oribatids, enchytraeids) are more abundant than mesofauna (earthworms). Working the soil hides or destroys traces of organic activity which remain visible deeper in the soil profile.

Discussion

It follows from this work that the type of agricultural exploitation of a soil may be recognized by studying soil structure. Certain quantities of recognizable structural features (little clods, big cleanly broken clods, plough pan) which we found are characteristic of the tool used (hoe, cultivator, ard).

This work also reveals the importance of two experimental factors. The first is the time factor of the experiment, which is very difficult to moderate. As we have seen, in trying to accelerate time, the experimenter only changes the natural pedological processes (Grignon). Second, the soil type, which

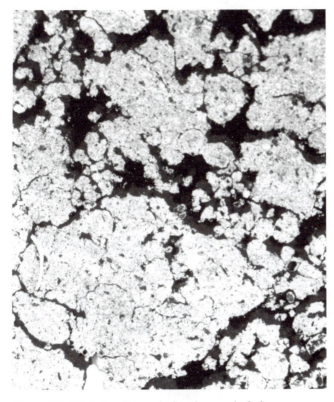

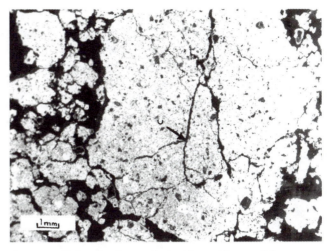

Figure 26.9 Dehérain, plot worked with a cultivator; little compaction with numerous big peds including the original bird foot-shaped cracks

Figure 26.8 Dehérain, plot worked with a spade; little compaction with coarse sub-rounded peds

Table 26.4 Abundance of biological activity in relation to the type of manuring carried out on the Dehérain plots

	MICROFAUNA	MESOFAUNA
UNCULTIVATED		
Surface	++++	++++
At depth	++++	++
SPADE WITHOUT MANURING		
Surface	0	++
At depth	+++	+
SPADE PURE STRAW		
Surface	+	+
At depth	+++	+++
SPADE HUMIDIFIED STRAW		
Surface	+	+
At depth	++	++
CULTIVATOR WITHOUT MANURING		
Surface	+	0
At depth	++	0
CULTIVATOR STABLE LITTER		
Surface	+	0
At depth	++	+++

0 = absent; + = trace; ++ = not very abundant; +++ = abundant; ++++ = very well-developed

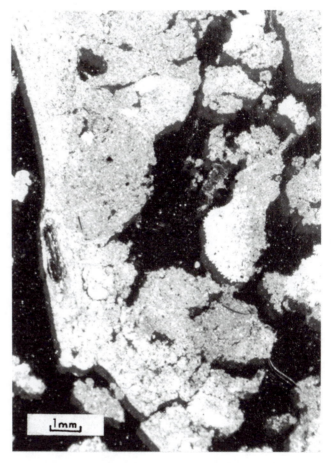

Figure 26.10 Hambacher Forst, plot worked with cultivator; little compaction of peds, broken with clean and straight edges

will behave differently according to the tool used.

At the moment, the experimental sites are all situated in different environments, on soils which are similar but not quite the same. To increase the reliability of these results, we will need to compare a large number of cases. In the future, other sites like the "Ferme Archéologique de Melrand"

(Morbihan, France) or the Lejre experimental center (Denmark) will be investigated.

Unfortunately, as no archaeological experiment has been started on the original Atlantic forest soil, we must be satisfied with extrapolation from more recent soils, with structures which are similar but not identical.

There is another factor which is not very well understood: the behavior of these structures as they age. The weight of sediments, or of any archaeological construction which seals a site, can modify the soil structure. Therefore, when the experimental results are compared to archaeological buried soils protected from modern anthropogenic disturbance, we will have to take such structural modifications into account.

Conclusion

Through this work, we could observe the micromorphological structure of different experimental soils cultivated using different tools and manuring. The small number of soils actually considered, and their great pedological diversity, will lead us to multiply observations in other experiments using different tools. Then we will need to compare them with ancient cultivated soils to be able to recognize ancient techniques used in the past for working a field.

Acknowledgments. I thank R.I. Macphail (Institute of Archaeology, London) and Patricia Anderson (Institut de Préhistoire Orientale, Jalès) for their help with the English version of this article.

Chapter 27 ✎

Crop Yields of the Prehistoric Cereal Types Emmer and Spelt

The Worst Option

Peter J. Reynolds

THE BUTSER ANCIENT FARM PROJECT WAS SET up in 1972 as a unique open-air laboratory dedicated to exploring empirically the archaeological evidence for the agricultural and domestic economy of the latter part of the first millennium BC. In effect the component elements of an Iron Age farm were built as experimental constructs with time utilized as a critical validating factor. The overall program includes investigations into buildings, earthworks, livestock, and crop husbandry. The latter clearly involves field management and fencing as well as grassland maintenance (Reynolds 1979).

Currently Butser Ancient Farm manages four locations, each in a different bioclimatic zone. The original location exploited from 1972 to the present day and the one specifically pertinent to this report is on a spur called Little Butser which juts northwards from Butser Hill, the highest of the chalk downs in Hampshire in southern England (Ordnance Survey Sheet 197, ref. 719208). The history of the spur at 174 m above sea level indicates the hostility of its location. It has only been used as rough pasture within living memory, the grassland remaining unimproved and, therefore, relatively species rich (Tansley 1939). Archaeologically there are several field monuments on the spur. The most recent is a pillow mound, an artificial rabbit warren, probably dating to the eighteenth or nineteenth century (Crawford & Keiller 1928). In addition there is a circular dished depression, which was probably an Iron Age house platform, and a length of unfinished ditch and bank, also of Iron Age date. A number of trackways dating from the Neolithic to the medieval period traverse the site. Archaeological investigation has revealed indications of fairly intensive occupation of the spur from the late Bronze

Age through the Iron Age. There is no evidence of Roman occupation. It would seem that the spur supported a small prehistoric farmstead the fields of which were probably on the eastern slopes of the spur and in the valley to the north. Excavation has shown that the site itself was not cultivated in prehistory. Its abandonment probably occurred during the first century BC. Apart from rough grazing, the wooded slopes of the spur, which support hazel (*Corylus avellana*) and ash (*Fraxinus excelsior*), were clearly used as coppice within the recent past.

The soil cover on Little Butser is a puffy black friable rendzina averaging just 100 mm in depth directly onto middle chalk, the hardest of the three types of chalk of the downlands in southern Britain. In effect the location is extremely hostile. The spur is oriented to the north, being totally exposed to the harsh climatic winter conditions from the northwest round to the east yet shielded from the best summer conditions by the bulk of Butser Hill to the south and southwest. The soil is shallow and relatively poor with an average pH of 8.0. The middle chalk rock allows least transpiration of moisture into the topsoil. These conditions clearly explain why the spur has never been used for arable agriculture in the past, the only benefit being that the site has escaped exploitation by modern agrochemicals. It is without doubt a worst option in the sense that there are extremely narrow margins between success and failure. Any slight variable is likely to be magnified far beyond a more favorable location.

Thus the trials carried out on this site have greater significance in terms of success and failure and that failure is more likely to be total while success does not necessarily reflect a true potential. Notwithstanding, the site was exploited in the Iron Age and, therefore, although there is no evidence for prehistoric cultivation, it provides a valuable experimental area. The core research programs of the Butser Ancient Farm comprising constructs, earthworks, and animal and crop husbandry, which began in 1972, have been subsequently enhanced by parallel programs in less harsh locations, which have allowed valuable comparisons to be drawn. This chapter, however, deals specifically with two elements of the core cropping program on Little Butser and the results are offered as the product of a worst option.

In order to establish a series of constants within the trials, the archaeological evidence for agriculture was examined in some depth. The plough or ard types recovered from waterlogged deposits in Britain (Piggot 1953) and Denmark indicate the presence of three specific implements: the sod buster for initial breaking up of virgin or fallow ground, the tilth maker, and significantly a seed-drill ard (Glob 1951; Reynolds 1981). This last implement is perhaps the most important of all since it indicates more than any other implement the practice of crop management. The greatest enemy of farmers in any area through time are arable weeds evidenced both by carbonized seed deposits recovered from excavations and, indeed, from subsequent Roman writers, notably Virgil who refers to the unremitting struggle against weeds.[1] The clear implication is that cereals were planted in rows allowing hoeing to take place between the rows and thus combat the inevitable weed infestation. Thus an arbitrary decision was made to plant the cereals in the cropping trials in rows set 300 mm apart.

The weeding program is a similar constant in that the cereals are thoroughly hoed on three specific occasions during April, May, and June. The hoeing concentrates upon the spaces between the seed drills with only the larger competitors like docks (*Rumex* sp.) and sow thistle (*Sonchus arvensis*) being carefully pulled out from the drills by hand. A simple proportional analysis is made for each treatment determining the ratio of cereal plants to arable weeds, usually in July.

There is no evidence available either in the writings of the Greek and Roman agriculturalists or from the archaeological evidence for the rate of seed sown. Consequently a second arbitrary decision was made to sow the seed at a rate of 63 kg per hectare (56 pounds per acre). The decision was based upon halving the modern rate of seed sowing as in 1972, which then averaged 125 kilos per hectare (one hundredweight per acre) in Britain. Subsequently this modern rate has increased considerably.

These two constants obtain through all the trials carried out at the Ancient Farm and reported here. Beyond sowing rate and seed drills and their disposition, treatment variables were considered to be extremely important. There is a body of evidence suggesting that the manuring of fields was practiced from as early as the Bronze Age and certainly in the Iron Age. Roman writers refer regularly to the importance and value of manuring. In simple terms the evidence for manuring in northern Europe in the prehistoric period stems from the habit of maintaining livestock indoors during the winter with the consequent build-up of midden material. This is enhanced by the recovery of abraded pottery sherds from prehistoric field systems argued to be the result of their transport with the midden material from the settlement to the fields and subsequently worn smooth by their movement in the soil structure.

The trials reported here, however, do not include the variable of manuring. In parallel trials that examine the effect of manuring, an arbitrary constant was adopted of 50 tonnes per hectare (20 tons per acre). This figure was calculated upon the potential manure yield from an average of six cows of commensurate size to the Celtic Shorthorn per settlement with an average daily output of approximately 25 kilos (56 pounds) per animal. There is abundant evidence that cattle were used as the traction power for the prehistoric ploughs and to maintain a working pair a minimum of six beasts was regarded as essential.

In this way the constants for the trials were established: sowing rate, seed drills, and crop management. The cereals used for the trials were obtained by the Plant Breeding Institute, Cambridge, from Turkey. Effectively the emmer wheat comprises a mix of just two landraces that have proved by chance to be suited to this climate. The types of spelt wheat used were three: bearded black, bearded grey, and beardless grey. Separate trials with these three types have shown virtually no difference in results to the general mix used in the trials.

Because it is impossible to determine exactly which landraces of emmer or spelt were used in Britain from the surviving evidence from excavations of Iron Age sites, the trials are essentially dealing with probability factors. Problems with genetic variations and performance and the extreme difficulty of recognition are explored by Miller (1987A).

Given the above constants, the trials reported below were designed to explore two fundamental questions: the practicability of crop rotation under a spring sowing regime with emmer wheat (*Triticum dicoccum*) following Celtic bean (*Vicia faba minor*) and the performance and comparative qualities of emmer wheat (*Tr. dicoccum*) and spelt (*Tr. spelta*) under an autumn sowing regime.

The abundant presence of Celtic beans amongst the carbonized seed recovered from excavations of Iron Age settlement sites suggests that it was a staple and important crop. It is not unreasonable to suppose that the traditional benefits of exploiting a nitrogen-fixing crop followed by a nitrogen-using crop had been realized by this stage of agricultural development. It may also be hypothesized that the value of other vetches, notably the tufted vetch (*Vicia cracca*) and the narrow-leaved vetch (*Vicia angustifolia*) had been realized not only for the food value (Renfrew 1973) as a wild harvest but also for their symbiotic value within a cereal

Table 27.1 Break crop rotation, wheat (*Triticum dicoccum*) with beans (*Vicia faba minor*), field I, Butser Ancient Farm

YEAR	EAST			CENTRAL			WEST		
	T/H	C/A	RATIO	T/H	C/A	RATIO	T/H	C/A	RATIO
1987	1.90	15.2	1:30	2.22	17.6	1:35	2.80	22.2	1:40
1986	2.22	17.6	1:35	1.89	15.0	1:30	2.02	16.0	1:34
1985	2.12	17.0	1:34	1.93	15.4	1:31	1.96	15.6	1:32
1984	2.11	16.8	1:33	2.47	10.0	1:40	1.61	13.0	1:26
1983	4.40	35.1	1:70	2.83	22.6	1:45	2.10	16.8	1:33
1982	1.87	14.9	1:30	1.90	15.2	1:30	1.82	14.5	1:29
1981	2.02	16.1	1:32	1.83	14.6	1:30	1.27	10.1	1:20
1980	2.90	23.1	1:46	2.46	19.6	1:39	2.42	19.3	1:38
1979	2.46	19.6	1:39	1.31	10.5	1:21	0.80	6.4	1:13
1978	2.68	21.4	1:42	1.79	14.3	1:28	1.31	10.5	1:21
1977	2.58	20.6	1:41	1.59	19.9	1:40	1.37	10.9	1:21
1976	0.78	6.2	1:12	0.82	6.5	1:13	0.73	5.9	1:12
1975	2.49	19.9	1:40	2.00	16.0	1:32	1.27	10.1	1:20
1974	3.70	29.4	1:58	3.00	23.8	1:48	2.40	19.2	1:38
1973	2.90	23.1	1:46	2.40	19.2	1:38	2.00	16.0	1:32

T/H = tonnes per hectare; C/A = hundredweights per acre; RATIO = seed sown to seed yield

crop. The hypothesis explored in these trials is the simple probability that crop rotation was practiced. Because the Celtic bean is susceptible to harsh weather conditions, it is not grown north of the midland region of Britain; for this reason, a spring sowing regime was adopted for both the pulse and cereal crops.

The area of Little Butser exploited for the field trials allows three distinct microclimatic zones to be examined. The natural curve of the spur from east to west gives a zone facing east, a central zone facing south, and a third zone facing west. Consequently although the field is treated as a single managed unit, the data are collected from the three zones of the field, thus giving three distinct sets of results. The zones are indicated on the tables and figures as field I east, central, and west, respectively. The weather pattern on the spur is monitored by a standard meteorological station situated immediately against the central zone of the field area. The station is read daily at 9 hours GMT. Attempts to monitor precisely the three individual microclimates had to be abandoned because of equipment costs and time. Nonetheless the results themselves are sufficiently different to underline the microclimatic variations. In general terms the most favorable zone is the east; the most unfavorable, the west.

In the trials the field area is divided in such a way that after the first year, 1973, when the whole field was originally set up, every succeeding year emmer wheat follows a bean crop. The data are devoted to the wheat crop only. The yield factor is achieved by taking five randomized 1-m squares from each zone, weighing the naked seed weight, averaging the result and converting into tonnes per hectare, hundredweights per acre, and expressing the yield as a ratio to the seed sown. The results from 1973 to 1987 can be seen in table 27.1 and in figures 27.1 to 27.3.

The eastern zone averages 2.48 per ha over the fifteen-year

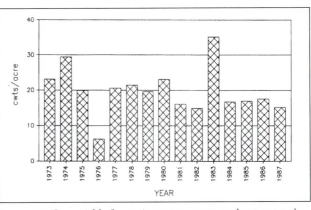

Figure 27.1 Crop yields for spring-sown emmer wheat, rotated with beans, field 1 east, Butser Ancient Farm

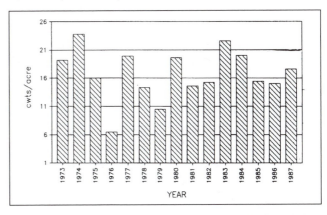

Figure 27.2 Crop yields for spring-sown emmer wheat, rotated with beans, field 1 cental, Butser Ancient Farm

period, the central zone, 2.03, and the western zone, 1.73. The figures are remarkably consistent through time with few exceptions. The most notable variation is in 1976 when drought conditions prevailed in southern England and all crop yields, both ancient and modern, were dramatically reduced. The other variation occurred in 1983 when an

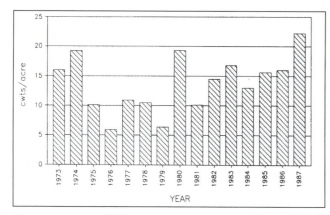

Figure 27.3 Crop yields for spring-sown emmer wheat, rotated with beans, field 1 west, Butser Ancient Farm

Table 27.2 Average annual yield across all microclimatic zones

YEAR	TONS PER HECTARE
1987	2.31
1986	2.04
1985	2.00
1984	2.06
1983	3.11
1982	1.86
1981	1.71
1980	2.59
1979	1.52
1978	1.93
1977	1.85
1976	0.78
1975	1.92
1974	3.03
1973	2.43

Average yield over fifteen seasons: 2.08 tonnes per hectare

exceptional yield was recorded for the eastern sector of 4.4 per ha. In this year frosts in late April and early May initially arrested growth, but subsequently massive tillering gave rise to a heavy crop but with much smaller spikes than normal, averaging approximately 24 seeds per spike against the normal 36 seeds, with as many as eleven to fourteen tillers per plant against the normal three to seven. Normally the western zone is the least successful, with the exception of 1987 when the normal pattern across the field was reversed The particular reason for this reversal is difficult to isolate beyond unusual wind and temperature damage from the east that occurred immediately after germination and the extreme frost damage, which destroyed the autumn-sown cereals in the adjacent field (see table 27.3). The natural contour of the field, in fact, protected the western element of the field.

There are two main observations to be made from this particular long-term trial. The first is the overall consistency of the results; where inconsistencies do arise the vagaries of the weather can be held directly responsible. Although it is virtually impossible to measure and quantify available nitrogen for plant take-up in the soil, the rotation does seem

to have brought about this general state of stability. The second observation is the overall high yield return on what is a poor soil in a hostile location. Although the data are divided into three climatic zones of the field, were they to be averaged across the zones the yields are still adequate and exceed general expectation (table 27.2). The overall average for all zones for the fifteen seasons is a creditable 2.08 per ha.

The second trial is designed to examine the performance and comparative qualities of emmer (*Tr. dicoccum*) and spelt (*Tr. spelta*) under an autumn sowing regime without any manurial input whatsoever. The arguments for setting up this trial, apart from providing comparative figures to the above crop rotation trials and to spring sowing trials not reported here, are relatively straightforward. The most obvious reason is that observations of the natural growth pattern of the cereals after harvest in the wild state show that after a short period of dormancy germination occurs in late September and early October. Given no abnormal conditions, maturation follows in the next summer. Spring sowing therefore would seem to express a deliberate human choice to change the natural order of events. The generally accepted view of prehistoric practice, however, is that spring sowing was the norm especially for emmer wheat. The fact is that there are many landraces of emmer wheat with a wide range of characteristics and some landraces undoubtedly performed better when sown in the spring. Seed morphology, however, does not allow identification of such characteristics, the more so when the seeds in question are carbonized. Yet there is a long held but completely unsubstantiated belief that spelt wheat was introduced into Britain because it was an autumn-sown cereal in contrast to emmer (Applebaum 1954). In fact, the introduction of spelt was regarded as the commencement of a new agricultural age. Therefore, although only two landraces of emmer and three types of spelt were used in the trials to date, the random selection of these lends weight to the program in that the same seed stock is used for all trials whether spring or autumn sown. Given the supposed superiority of spelt as an autumn-sown cereal, a clear result should emerge. The third reason, which has emerged during the trials but can equally be used as a primary cause for them, is the behavior pattern of a particular arable weed, common cleavers (*Galium aparine*). The presence of common cleavers in carbonized seed assemblages from Iron Age sites is relatively well attested.

The plant effectively has two germination periods, a minor one in October, a major one the following March and April. Cultivation during the critical period of germination tends to disrupt germination totally. Consequently in an autumn-sown field, common cleavers tends to be a major pest, while in a spring-sown field it is normally absent. Practical observations over two fields on Little Butser separated by a two m strip of grassland show that the autumn-sown field is regularly pervaded by cleavers while the spring-sown field is

Table 27.3 Yields for continuous cropping, non-manuring regime for autumn-sown spelt wheat, field II, Butser Ancient Farm

	EAST			CENTRAL			WEST		
YEAR	T/H	C/A	RATIO	T/H	C/A	RATIO	T/H	C/A	RATIO
1987	Destroyed by frost	-	-	-	-	-	-	-	-
1986	2.79	22.2	1:44	2.50	19.9	1:40	2.54	20.2	1:40
1985	2.75	21.8	1:43	1.45	19.5	1:39	2.49	19.8	1:39
1984	1.17	9.3	1:18	0.81	6.4	1:13	0.68	5.4	1:11
1983	1.98	15.8	1:31	0.94	7.5	1:15	1.14	9.1	1:18
1982	1.12	9.0	1:18	1.36	10.9	1:21	0.90	7.2	1:14
1981	1.95	15.6	1:31	1.80	14.4	1:29	1.62	12.9	1:26
1980	1.43	11.41	1:23	0.80	6.34	1:13	1.07	8.54	1:18
1979	0.70	6.2	1:12	0.59	4.7	1:10	0.72	5.8	1:12
1978	2.16	17.2	1:34	1.72	13.7	1:27	1.31	10.45	1:21
1977	2.30	18.35	1:37	1.87	14.9	1:30	1.72	13.7	1:27
1976	0.80	7.2	1:14	0.93	7.4	1:15	0.41	3.2	1:7
1975	1.70	13.7	1:28	1.36	10.9	1:21	1.62	12.9	1:26
1974	2.30	18.3	1:37	2.10	16.8	1:34	2.30	18.3	1:36
1973	2.40	19.0	1:38	1.90	15.2	1:30	1.70	13.6	1:27

T/H = tonnes per hectare; C/A = hundredweights per acre; RATIO = seed sown to seed yield

Table 27.4 Yields for continuous cropping, non-manuring regime for autumn-sown emmer wheat, field II, Butser Ancient Farm

	EAST			CENTRAL			WEST		
YEAR	T/H	C/A	RATIO	T/H	C/A	RATIO	T/H	C/A	RATIO
1987		Destroyed by frost	-	-	-	-	-	-	-
1986	2.55	20.3	1:40	2.37	18.9	1:38	2.14	17.0	1:34
1985	2.44	19.4	1:38	2.35	18.6	1:37	2.00	15.9	1:32
1984	1.23	9.78	1:20	1.05	8.4	1:17	0.56	4.5	1:9
1983	3.32	16.5	1:53	2.32	18.5	1:37	2.84	22.7	1:45
1982	0.90	7.2	1:14	1.02	8.1	1:16	0.71	5.7	1:12
1981	2.11	16.8	1:33	1.87	14.9	1:30	2.45	19.6	1:39
1980	1.63	13.01	1:26	1.10	8.8	1:17	0.66	5.3	1:11
1979	0.42	3.4	1:7	0.25	1.9	1:4	0.40	3.2	1:6
1978	2.79	22.30	1:45	1.97	15.72	1:31	1.75	13.96	1:27
1977	2.16	17.20	1:34	1.29	10.3	1:21	1.01	8.10	1:16
1976	0.70	6.4	1:13	1.01	8.1	1:16	0.83	6.6	1:13
1975	1.80	14.1	1:28	2.32	18.5	1:37	2.15	17.0	1:34
1974	3.70	29.8	1:60	2.90	23.4	1:46	2.50	20.3	1:40
1973	2.80	22.8	1:46	2.15	17.2	1:34	1.96	15.6	1:31

T/H = tonnes per hectare; C/A = hundredweights per acre; RATIO = seed sown to seed yield

innocent of the weed. Given the presence of carbonized seeds of cleavers in assemblages of seeds which include cereals, the hypothesis that such assemblages came from a harvest of autumn-sown cereals is not unreasonable. There is a caveat, however, because should the spring sowing be accomplished by the third week in March, the normal spring germination of cleavers proceeds unabated and there is little difference in infestation levels. This was tested by a small three-year control program at the Butser Ancient Farm .

For the autumn sowing trials the field area, designated field II, has exactly the same characteristics of three different microclimatic zones as field I and is treated in exactly the same way. The planting program requires the field to be cultivated in September and early October with the seed being sown in the second week of October. The field is divided into two halves across the zones, one half devoted to emmer and the other half to spelt.

The basic results from the cropping trials can be seen in histograms in figures 27.4 to 27.9 in hundredweights per acre to enhance the differences by utilizing smaller weight units against smaller areas. (19.64 hundredweights per tonne.) The results broadly relate to the crop rotation data from field I in that the major anomalies are directly attributable to the weather—for example, the results for 1976, when drought conditions severely affected the crops. The other anomalies, also brought about by weather conditions, refer specifically to the late autumn and winter. The greatest effect occurred during the early part of 1987 when for the first time the whole autumn-sown cereal crop was totally destroyed by intense and unrelieved frost without any protective snow cover for a period of some fourteen days (Reynolds and Wyman 1988). This complete failure is calculated within the overall yield

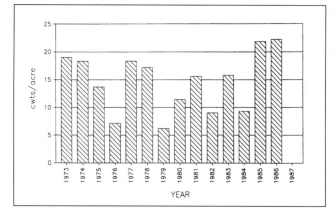

Figure 27.4 Crop yields for autumn-sown spelt wheat, continuous cropping, non-manuring regime, field II east, Butser Ancient Farm

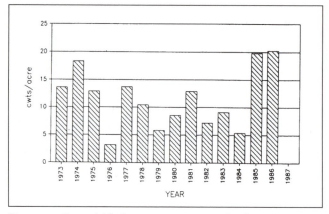

Figure 27.6 Crop yields for autumn-sown spelt wheat, continuous cropping, non-manuring regime, field II west, Butser Ancient Farm

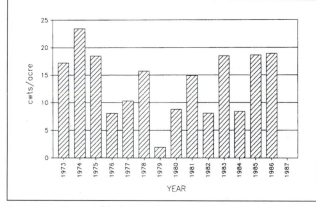

Figure 27.5 Crop yields for autumn-sown spelt wheat, continuous cropping, non-manuring regime, field II central, Butser Ancient Farm

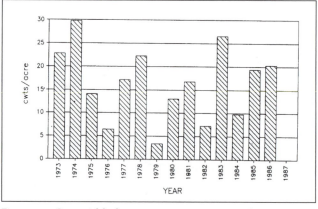

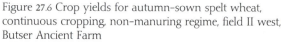

Figure 27.7 Crop yields for autumn-sown emmer wheat, continuous cropping, non-manuring regime, field II east, Butser Ancient Farm

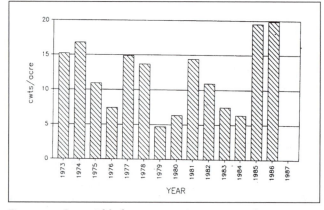

Figure 27.8 Crop yields for autumn-sown emmer wheat, continuous cropping, non-manuring regime, field II central, Butser Ancient Farm

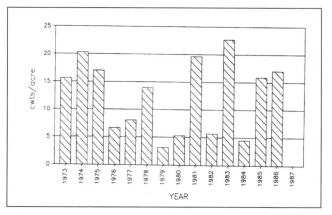

Figure 27.9 Crop yields for autumn-sown emmer wheat, continuous cropping, non-manuring regime, field II west, Butser Ancient Farm

factor results. The 1979 season was characterized by low temperatures but more particularly by low rainfall in the period immediately after sowing which led directly to poor germination and a thin crop. The low figures for 1982 were similarly attributable to poor rainfall and extensive periods of dry but cold weather in the early part of the spring. These anomalies apart, the results are quite consistent and remarkably high bearing in mind the hostility of the location.

There is a correlation between these trials and the ones carried out at Broad Balk at the Rothamstead Experimental Station in Harpenden, Hertfordshire (Rothamstead Experimental Station Report 1969, 1982). There continuous cropping trials have been carried out on the same land area for over one hundred years with viable yields being maintained throughout, with major variations in yield being occasioned by extreme weather conditions. In the case of Little Butser it was initially expected that yield figures would steadily deteriorate to a nil return primarily because of the poor soil. This has obviously not occurred but the variations in crop yield are seemingly directly proportional to the rainfall and ground temperature. The continued fertility of the soil lies in the high organic levels. Initially when the field area was created from the turf cover the organic levels were approximately 24%. Currently, after fifteen years, the level is broadly maintained at 18%. Thus, given adequate rainfall in spring the biodegradation of the fibrous material releases nitrogen and trace elements for plant take-up. Low rainfall leads to less degradation and available nitrogen. The fibre content of the soil is further enhanced by the simple management of inter-row hoeing of the arable weeds which are left in situ. This also had the added effect of inhibiting evaporation of the moisture from the soil.

Data are presented in tonnes per hectare and hundredweights per acre; the yields are also expressed as a ratio of the seed sown to the seed yield (tables 27.3, 27.4). These ratios are significantly higher than any expectation allowed but are nonetheless real. The weights are of the processed and therefore naked seed. Even from the Roman writers yield figures are extremely rare. These range from Varro's estimates of ten to fifteen fold for Italy, Columella fourfold, Cicero eight to ten fold. Other figures recorded for Babylon suggest a hundredfold under good management and fiftyfold under poor management (Theophrastus).

The crux of the matter would seem to lie with the soil, the climate, and good management. However, there is a great probability that technology plays a most important role in understanding the huge difference in these documented yields and also emphasizes the hypothesis concerning the seed drill ard referred to above. From Babylon there is a seal of the second millennium BC depicting an ard with a seed-drill attachment. This is a cup set on a tube fixed to the stilt or handle of the ard through which seed could be dribbled directly into the furrow (Singer et al. 1965). Such seed-drill attachments have survived into the recent historical record in countries like Iran, and it is tempting to see these implements as direct descendants of the Babylonian version bearing in mind that the Persians under Cyrus the Great annexed this area in 538 BC. The theory of technical persistence is well enough attested to allow this to occur. Critically seed delivered into the ard-made furrow at perhaps a depth of 150 to 200 mm is in the ideal position to germinate in this climatic zone. In Europe, on the other hand, this would be too deep. The Hvorslev seed-drill ard, in contrast, draws a shallow furrow approximately 50 to 60 mm deep (Reynolds 1981), which is ideal for the more humid conditions of northwest Europe. The practice evidenced in the countries on the north shore of the Mediterranean is rather the broadcast method. This leaves much to be desired in terms of good husbandry despite the fact that it became the normal practice throughout

Table 27.5 Average yield factors

For each microclimatic zone over fifteen seasons

	EAST	CENTRAL	WEST
Emmer wheat	1.90	1.60	1.46
Spelt wheat	1.70	1.41	1.35

For all microclimatic zones over fifteen seasons

Emmer wheat	1.65
Spelt wheat	1.49

Note: All figures are expressed in tonnes per hectare

Table 27.6 Average annual yield across all microclimatic zones over fifteen seasons

YEAR	EMMER WHEAT	SPELT WHEAT
1987	zero	zero
1986	2.35	2.61
1985	2.26	2.56
1984	0.95	0.89
1983	2.83	1.35
1982	0.88	1.13
1981	2.14	1.79
1980	1.13	1.10
1979	0.36	0.67
1978	2.17	1.73
1977	1.49	1.96
1976	0.84	0.71
1975	2.09	1.56
1974	3.03	2.23
1973	2.30	2.00

Note: All figures are expressed in tonnes per hectare

almost the whole of western Europe until the introduction of the seed drill in the eighteenth and nineteenth centuries. Folklore is filled with commentary on the inefficiency of broadcasting seed, from the biblical parable of the sower to the maxim "One [seed] for God and one for the crow, One to die and one to grow," suggesting in the latter case a 75% seed loss. If this is extended into a yield factor ratio, the simple mathematics are instantly error loaded unless quite fundamental adjustments are made.

The research results should not really be surprising given the nature of the plant with its average of 36 grains per spike. The yield records expressed as ratios from the historic periods in Britain, which refer to returns of seven to ten fold require considerable explanation and presently deserve scepticism if they refer to the actual harvest itself.

To return to the reason for this series of trials, the objective was to examine whether spelt wheat was significantly superior to emmer wheat as an autumn-sown cereal. It can be seen that on an annual basis within specific microclimatic zones (tables 27.3, 27.4) emmer normally outperforms spelt in most particulars. Indeed, the western aspect which is the most hostile of the microclimatic zones is the one area in which, if spelt is a superior autumn-sown cereal, the results should demonstrate the case. In fact, the results are closer for this zone than any other and are uniformly less than the others but still spelt is generally outperformed by emmer. These figures provide the average yields and have been calculated for each zone for each cereal (table 27.5). Given the sample size the results are entirely persuasive that emmer significantly outperforms spelt as an autumn-sown cereal. Similarly if the different microclimatic zones, significant though they are, are ignored and the field is treated as a single entity again the overall averages argue that emmer is the superior autumn-sown cereal (table 27.6). It has been pointed out that were more than two landraces of emmer used in the trials, ideally a mix of landraces with differing characteristics, even the anomalous results would probably be lessened in their impact (Miller 1987a, b). Certainly these results demonstrate that spelt has no particular characteristics indicating its qualities as an autumn-sown cereal and the hypothesis that it was deliberately introduced for this purpose is now in quite serious doubt if not completely invalidated.

To conclude, the overall objective of these and other cropping trials carried out at the Butser Ancient Farm is to explore the agricultural economy of the latter part of the Iron Age period as it may have obtained on this soil type in this bioclimatic zone. The data as they are presented above are the direct result of empirical trials carried out over a fifteen-year period, which means that the averages calculated are significant but only within the confines of the trials. In effect they are representative only of a probability statement given the constants and variables within the design of the trials. Their value as probability statements lies in the rigor by which they were obtained and the overall time span of the trials. Because they are real results and not estimates they can be used more confidently in building a working hypothesis for the agricultural economy but at no time must they be regarded as more than a probability and be converted into a prehistoric fact. As a final caveat, it should be remembered that these results were obtained from a worst option scenario. Any transfer into a better soil in a more favorable bioclimatic zone would require significant enhancement. The long-term objective of supplying validated data that could be employed in computer simulations of agricultural productivity is presently being achieved. In this chapter the data achieved from two specific treatments could be utilized with the necessary restrictions for three different distinct landscape orientations or combinations thereof relating to specific sites and their immediate exploitable land resources. With the future publication of the remaining elements of the cropping programmes at the Butser Ancient Farm these data will be considerably enhanced including different soil types and bioclimatic zones and different treatments.

Note

1. Classical sources consulted included Cato and Varro's *De Agri Cultura,* Columella's *De Re Rustica,* Pliny's *Natural History,* vol. V, Theophrastus's *On Plants,* Virgil's *Georgics, Eclogues* and *The Aeneid.*

Chapter 28 ✍

Yields, Sowing, and Fertility
Analytical Significance of Yields

François Sigaut

IN THIS CHAPTER, I TRY TO GIVE A FEW ELEMENTS to define a problematic of the study of yields. For more than a century, we in Europe have become accustomed to expressing the result of our cereal cultivation in terms of volumes or quantities harvested per unit of surface area (bushels/acre; quintals or tons/ha). Until the eighteenth and nineteenth centuries, our ancestors tended, however, to think in terms of a weight yield for grain sown versus that harvested (5 for 1, 12 for 1). This concept of yield is quite ancient; it is mentioned by Roman agronomists. There are therefore at least two ways of measuring the physical result of a crop. Neither considers the factor of time, which is supposed to be equal to one year in both cases (but is not always so), or the factor of water, even though it is more important than the field surface in irrigated agriculture. There are also factors of scale to take into account; we all feel that a result expressed on a scale of a province or of a country has a different meaning than one obtained from one field only or from an experimental plot of a few m². Considering economic considerations would make the problem still more difficult. Even if I restrict the question to physical aspects, it is clear that no single universal and rational means of measuring the results of a production exists, but rather several, which have different meanings and correspond to different technical and social situations. It is among these different yields (better yet, proportions or ratios) that we must try to make sense so that discussions concerning the quantitative results of ancient agriculture are not biased from the outset.

Volumes or Masses

I begin with an apparently simple question: is it better to count in terms of volume measurements, that is, in bushels or hectolitres, as was commonly done until the end of the nineteenth century, or in terms of mass measurements, that is, in quintals or tons, as is done today?

It is generally believed that the scale is more accurate than the bushel, because the latter's capacity depends on the way in which it is filled, whether grain is compressed or not, and so on. In reality, what is weighed on scales? The envelopes of complete grains, which vary considerably in proportion from one species to the next, and even weight varies from one variety to another, especially between naked and hulled grains, of course; also, grains having different moisture contents, which usually measure between 12 to 13% and 18 to 20% at harvest. As the variation in the humidity ratio alone causes a margin of error of over 5%, it is illusory to think that scales are sufficient for providing an accurate result.

In fact, the use of bushel or hectolitre had the advantage of avoiding a false impression of accuracy. Those using capacity or volume measures in the past knew that a number of bushels or hectolitres was meaningful only in combination with other data, mainly the grain density, which is expressed in pounds per bushel or kilograms per hectolitre (mass volume). Measuring the grain density was not only aimed at converting a volume into a mass; it also happens that grain density is still the best synthetic indication of its quality today: a heavy (that is, dense) grain is always of a better quality, all other things being equal, than a light one; in particular, humidity reduces the grain density and increases the mass of the crop harvested.

In summary, neither mass nor volume alone are sufficient for measuring a crop. A volume measure, added to grain density, is certainly the most efficient method of obtaining the most accurate result for the least effort. I do not believe that mass (weight), when measured alone (which is too often the case), improves accuracy: it only gives a (dangerous) impression of doing so. For a really accurate measurement of mass, one needs to know what is being measured, which means taking into account its degree of humidity and percentage of nonnutritional components This may be complex and expensive and, at any rate, does not guarantee that all nutritional components were actually used by people, given their methods of grinding and flour extraction.

I have no firm conclusion to make, but any textbook of physics begins with the question of errors in measurement. I believe that the same question would be useful in history textbooks and in experimental archaeology texts, if ever these are written.

Yield Per Unit Surface: Questions of Scale

Let us first take a familiar case: an evenly plowed and sown field. We might think that its yield is independent of the field size, but it is not. The border effect and the other reason is well-known: the fact that a small plot is always better kept and protected than a large one, so that results obtained on a small scale are only rarely transposable to a large scale. The literature from the eighteenth and nineteenth century is full of warnings against the misuse of extrapolation of results from small-scale experiments. Such caution remains quite valid today.

The border effect is well-known to experimenters. Inside an evenly sown field, each plant is surrounded by other plants, which limit the space from which it can take water and fertilizers and the quantity of light it receives. The plants that grow on the field borders, can, however, extend their roots further and receive more light, and are therefore usually better developed.

Let us assume that the border effect is felt at 2 m in depth: a square plot of 16 m² will be completely affected and thus able to give a noticeably higher yield (of up to the double, perhaps) than a square plot of 1 ha, in which less than 10% of the surface is affected by the border effect.

Therefore, these are two different scales, of small plots (a few dozen m²) and large plots (about 1 ha), for which the yield per unit surface does not have the same meaning. In addition, we can note that in most nonmechanized agricultural systems, the small plot was the rule, not the large one, whose present form began only in the nineteenth century. Large fields certainly appeared once the ard came into use, in the fourth millennium BC. However, the distribution of the plants was not necessarily uniform, a question for which we have little information available. In Egypt, grain was broadcast sown, whereas in Mesopotamia it was apparently sown within drills, about 60 cm apart (Brun-Cottan 1989). Be that as it may, one conclusion prevails: the significance of a yield per unit surface depends on the size and shape of parcels as well

as the way plants are distributed within it. This means that, from one system to the next (in which these parameters are different), the yields per hectare cannot be compared.

We must not forget that yield/hectare was developed within the context of only one agricultural system, ours, and that it is meant to enable performance comparison within this one system. Outside this specific case, it is applicable or not, depending on the circumstances. At any rate, it is absolutely necessary to justify its use.

Yield Per Unit Surface: Questions of Fertility

The two scales discussed above are not the only ones to take into account in determining the significance of a yield. There is at least one other, which involves soil fertility and the way it is renewed over time, either naturally or through deliberate or unintentional human intervention. Then the relevant scale is no longer that of the small (or large) plot but of the entire territory on which the fertility of the plot depends. Indeed, from Liebig's time (1840), we have known that the fertility of a soil was related to its resources in certain mineral elements, in a form assimilable by plants (for example, N, P, K, and Ca), which we have learnt to extract from the subsoil (essentially P and K) or directly from the atmosphere (N). Therefore, the fertility of a given field now depends only on the industry and trade in manure and chemical fertilizers. Before Liebig, it was the opposite: the fertility of a given plot was detemined mainly by the natural or artificial transfers of fertilizers which occurred.

Natural transfers

First, there exist negative transfers, or losses, because of leaching, which intensifies with humid climate (rainfall/ evaporation relationship), when soils are permeable (sandy) or acid, and when the relief is flat. When there is the slightest slope, runoff increases at the expense of leaching and entails an erosion that may be destructive if too violent, but which is often favourable insofar as it rejuvenates the soils. In many regions with naturally rather acid soils, like Brittany, fields are located more often on moderate slopes than on absolutely flat ground. Leaching is a prime factor in pedogenesis, and so it is fairly easy to evaluate its significance by consulting a soil map.

The opposite of leaching, in hot and dry climates, where the potential for evaporation is higher than that for rainfall, is the rise of mineral elements to the surface. Unfortunately, in all regions where this happens, sodium salts are brought to the surface, making the land almost sterile.

However, leaching and salt rise balance out in some soils, such as the famous black earths (*Tchernozem*) of the Ukraine. Yet it is probable that their reputation for fertility comes not so much from their yields, which would not have been much higher than elsewhere, as from the fact they were obtained without fertilizer. In Hungary and southern Russia, the fact that dung fertilizer was not used surprised travellers such as R. Townson, in the eighteenth century, and L. de Fontenay, in the nineteenth. At the beginning of the twentieth century, the promoters of dry-farming in North America, H. W. Campbell and J. A. Witsoe, believed that arid areas were mankind's future granaries, because their fertility was unlimited (Hargreaves 1977).

In western Europe, it is also the low annual rainfall (maximum of 600 mm) that has always contributed to the fertility of the extensive cereal plains in the Paris Basin and eastern England. It happens that we have a fairly good idea of their very long-term potential fertility. Indeed, between 1852 and 1925, in some plots at Rothamsted (Great-Britain), wheat was cultivated without manure each year, with a mean yield of 10 q/ha/year (Hénin et al. 1969:300). Why did the yield not decrease to nearly nothing over time? Apart from a low level of leaching, there are two sources of natural fertility: nitrogen fixation by soil microorganisms and settling of atmospheric dust (aerosols), either spontaneously or through rain or snow. This dust has diverse origins, including extra-terrestrial ones (earth receives 100,000 tons/year of dust from the cosmos); in France, the Gascony Landes region receives 10 kg/ha/year of potassium, in the form of aerosols from the ocean (Labeyrie 1978).

A third natural source of fertility is alluviation, which concerns the foot of slopes, valleys, and areas of deposit on the seaside. These sites are limited in general, but are historically significant, because people quickly realized their advantages and exploited them to the best of their ability.

A given territory contains a general level of natural fertility, which depends mainly on the relationship between leaching of soils and natural mechanisms that renew their fertility (moderate erosion and aerosols). (For example, this level is 10 q/ha/year of wheat at Rothamsted.) This same territory also contains some privileged areas where fertility accumulates naturally (alluviation) and which may (or may not) be used by humans.

Artificial transfers

It is quite possible that agriculture first colonized such privileged areas, particularly in arid zones, where floodplain agriculture is both the simplest and most productive process imaginable. The main drawback of such areas is their limited size. There are major exceptions, however (the Nile Valley), and it seems that people long derived a major benefit from them, before cultivating more ordinary land; this may hold true even in Europe, according to Sherratt (1980). The problem of ordinary land is its lack of natural renewal of fertility: in dry climates, the crops are variable; in humid climates, leaching and competition with weeds can be a threat. Compensating for these two drawbacks requires a great deal of extra work as well as—of particular interest here—using part of the territory to fertilize others. Here,

transfer of fertility takes on its full meaning. There are two general methods of compensation for leaching:

- Moving the fields, in order to benefit, through grubbing or burn-beating, from the fertility accumulated over several decades. This corresponds to the principle of shifting cultivation, well-known to geographers. Here, no more than 20% of the territory can be used at any one time, often much less. Yields per parcel are high, but they are obtained on only a small area of the territory.

- Fixing the fields, and regularly adding fertilizers collected elsewhere indirectly, through cattle and their excrements, and directly, by gathering plants used as manure.

A few examples

In the Gascony Landes region (very poor sandy land), it was estimated that 40 ha of pastures were required for maintaining the quantity of sheep to produce enough dung for 1 ha of rye and millet (Féret, 1878:519). In all the mountain areas of the southern Midi in France, the practice of clearing of undergrowth meant that, in waste lands and forests, various plant residues, brushwood, weeds, dead leaves and others were collected, then strewn over courtyards and pathways; after a few months, when they had become street dung, they were brought to the fields. In some regions, this was regular practice. In the Béarn, there were true fields of furze (Ulex europeus), devoted exclusively to supplying fertilizer for other lands; in southern Brittany (Morbihan), a metairie normally kept nearly half the land as moors to mattock, for fertilizer. This kind of practice is not solely European and is largely attested to in India and Africa, where the system called citimene was made famous by A. I. Richards' description (1939): branches are trimmed from forest trees and gathered on the site of a future field, where they are burned; sowing is then done in the ashes. Richard gives the figure of 6.25 acres of forest for 1.25 of cultivated land, or a land surface ratio of 5.2/1[1].

What could be the age of this kind of agricultural system? The majority of those revealed by history and ethnography imply significant technical means (iron tools for the gathering of vegetal manure; means of transport) and still greater quantities of labor, which suggests that such systems are recent. However, this is not necessarily always the case: the example from the Landes shows that massive use of animals can replace tools and labor. At any rate, Danish archaeologists believe that this sort of system existed in Europe from the Neolithic (J. Troels-Smith 1984).

Of course, the above examples give only a general idea of the diversity of real practices. Here, the main point is that the whole territory is necessary to produce the crops obtained each year over a small part of this territory, whether this proportion be 2, 5, or 50% of the total. Yield per plot is therefore a partial yield. From an ecological and demographic standpoint, it is the yield of the whole territory that counts, the territory itself being defined by the extent of the transfers of fertility; in a sense, the territory is a fertility watershed.

Seed Yield

The sowing yield (expressed as "for one": 5/1 or 8/1, for instance) was so prevalent in Europe, and doubtless elsewhere, until the nineteenth century that its absence today is surprising. It represents as important an analytical tool as surface yield, and its loss has considerably impoverished analysis. One of its several advantages was that it was not used alone, since it had meaning only when complemented by sowing density, which enabled calculation of surface yield. In the past, everyone was aware that seed yield was only one index among others, which is unfortunately no longer the case for surface yield.

Extraordinary yields

> M. Georges Villers shows us a wheat plant, called "Scottish red wheat," which is a remarkable example of fertility. This plant, produced by a single grain deposited by chance in the Bayeyx cemetery, bore 116 ears having an average of 35 grains, giving a total 4060 grains. (Bull. de la Soc. d'agriculture de Bayeux 1850–1851, 1:296)

Such stories are not unusual. Pliny cites two in his *Natural History* (XVIII, 21). Without special effort, I found ten in my notes on the seventeenth to the twentieth century, in England as well as in France.[2] The record is undoubtedly held by a stalk of barley which, according to Humphry Davy [1820:240], produced 249 stems and over 18,000 grains. Ordinary figures, however, are lower: those found in the literature are 6855, 4060 (example above), about 4000, 1560, 1440, and 1235.

There is no apparent reason to doubt the truth of these anecdotes. They must have occurred with a fairly constant frequency throughout history, but are they of interest to researchers? They have relevance on several levels. First, they illustrate perfectly the effect of scale I described for surface yields. Second, these findings gave rise to comments and technical or selection tests, such as the following: In the 1760s, a Mr. Miller, from Cambridge, tried to find how far one go in multiplying a grain of wheat. Out of one grain sown early in June, and after three transplantings from separation of tufts early in August, in September to October and in March to April, he obtained 21,109 ears containing about 576,840 grains. At the beginning of the twentieth century, quite independently, Russian agronomists, inspired by observations in Manchuria, tried to develop a system of temperate cereal (wheat, rye, and oat) cultivation, based on transplanting and ridging. Diffloth made a cautious analysis: "This system enables rapid multiplication for varieties from which only a small number of seeds are available" (1929:319-348). It was not profitable, however, in the French economic background of his time, even using the various machines developed by Russian agronomists. The same conclusion had been reached by Norman agronomists more than one century before:

> M. de Janville has harvested in his Eterville estate a stalk of wheat which gave 108 ears and 1560 grains. This extraordinary product induced us to try to plant wheat, according to the method practiced in the duchy of Suffolk, in England, and described by Larochefoucault-Liancourt. This first test was unsuccessful. Besides, we observed that planting required too many hands and that manpower was too expensive here for efficiency; it seemed that this method, instead of leading us to perfect the art, would be taking us back to its origins. (Rapport sur les trav. de la Soc. royale d'adg. et de com. de Caen 1806:18)

This latter remark is very important, and I will return to it. First, I wish to give a last example of the consequences of such extraordinary findings in the creation of new varieties. The story is told by W. Marshall, in *The Rural Economy of Yorkshire*:

> Of late, the raising of varieties has perhaps been little attended to […] The only instance in which I have had an opportunity of tracing the variety down to the parent individual has occurred to me in this District.
>
> A man, whose observation is ever on the wing in the field of husbandry, having perceived, in a piece of wheat, a plant of uncommon strength and luxuriance, diffusing its branches on every side, and setting its closely surrounding neighbors at defiance, marked it, and at harvest removed it separately. The produce was fifteen ears, yielding six hundred and four grains, of a strong-bodied liver-colored wheat, different in appearance from every other variety I have seen. The chaff smooth, awnless, and the color of the grain. The straw stout and reedy.
>
> These six hundred grains were planted, singly, nine inches asunder, filling about forty square yards of ground, not in a garden or in a separate piece of ground, but upon a clover stubble; the remainder of which was, at the same time, sown with another wheat, by which means extraordinary trouble and destruction by birds were equally avoided.
>
> The produce of these forty yards was two gallons and a half, weighing twenty pounds and a half, of prime grain, fit for seed; besides some pounds of second. One grain produced thirty-five ears, yielding twelve hundred and thirty-five grains.
>
> The second year's produce being sufficient to plant an acre of ground, the variety was of course sufficiently established.
>
> This, the fifth year, I have seen it grow in quantity; the

season being moist, and the soil good, it was most of it lodged. The crop upon the ground is abundant: seventy full stocks an acre. But the produce of Zealand wheat, in the same piece, is equal to it; and, on examination, I think the grain of this better, its skin is somewhat thinner. [1796, II:5-7 (English)]

This kind of tale must have been repeated thousands upon thousands of times since the emergence of cereal cultivation, but with different frequency for different forms of agriculture. In the eighteenth century Europe, with its wide fields broadcast sown, the events could only have been exceptional, and it was only with the arrival of specialised breeders (for example, Vilmorin in France) that regular production of new varieties became possible. Marshall describes only seven varieties of wheat for Yorkshire, two of which are in the process of disappearing; even though they have not been calculated, we suppose that, in the England of his time, no more than a few dozen varieties existed. Things were quite different for the majority of the tropical countries, for instance India:

> Accustomed as we are to find the plant spoken of merely as rice it is somewhat surprising to learn that there are in Bengal alone 4,000 different sorts, suitable for different soils and climates. And yet the Indian peasant knows the various kinds and the right places in which to grow them. M. C. B. Clarke, an experienced and accurate botanist, speaking of the marvelous intuitive knowledge possessed by the hereditary paddy-cultivators in recognizing the different kinds of rice, says:- "I do not know how, in the young state, the cultivator tells the *ri* (wild rice) from the *aman* (winter rice). I cannot." (J. Kenny, *Intensive farming in India*, 1912:246, English)

Why is there such a difference? The marvelous intuition of peasants in tropical regions evidently plays a much smaller role than a more prosaic factor: the sowing technique and its consequent seed yields.[3]

Ordinary yields and sowing techniques

Undoubtedly for thousands of years, there has been a clear contrast between the sowing techniques of the West (from the Atlantic to Afghanistan) and those of the other parts of the world. In the West, grain is most often broadcast sown, which gives seed yields of 4 to 10 for 1. In the rest of the world, sowing techniques are varied, but broadcast sowing is relatively infrequent. Sowing is generally done either in lines (by hand or with a seed-drill) or by dibbling or by transplanting in seed beds (rice); in many cases, grains are germinated before being sown. Each technique gives a different seed yield, but in general this is between 50 and 150 for 1—that is, 10 to 20 times more than with broadcast sowing. The extraordinary yields above show that there is nothing miraculous about them. Surface yield remains invariable

(except for effects of scale). What changes is the quantity of seed, and it is clear that, if 10 times less is sown for the same harvest, the seed yield will be 10 times higher. The first consequence will be that the selection pressure will be 10 times stronger. It is not merely by chance that corn, the cereal perhaps most transformed by humans, gives the highest seed yields.

Two questions may be asked: can such differences between sowing techniques be explained, and what consequences (other than the evident effect on selection pressure) are attributable to them? The plant's size is certainly one factor: corn and sorgho, among others, are most often dibbled because of their large size. But the reverse can be argued: these plants have acquired their present morphology because they were sown dibbled for thousands of years. Moreover, the same cereals can be sown in different manners in different regions. Wheat and barley were sown with seed-drills in Sumer and broadcast in ancient Egypt; in a region near Quito (Ecuador), in 1735, travellers relate that wheat and barley sown by dibbling, no doubt as for corn, produce 100/1 to 150/1 (Duhamel du Monceau 1765:123-4).

There is not one, but a series of, causes, acting in combination. I lack space here to go into the full complexity of the problem, and also because I do not yet know all the factors. I would like to emphasize one of these factors, which is shown by recent European history and can be analyzed: the relationship between cost of grain and cost of work.

The above anecdote (about M. de Janville) gives us an abridged version of the solution to the problem, but we have to further explain it to make it understandable. This beginning of the nineteenth century in France had been, as for a long time before, a period of Anglophilia, at least for agriculture: everything English was praised, admired, recommended, imitated. Now there had existed for some time an innovation much spoken of in England: the practice of planting—that is, dibbling—wheat, which had begun in a small region situated on the border between Norfolk and Suffolk. It was of recent origin and seemed to have begun as a method applied to peas and beans which was transposed to cereals. Whatever the explanation, it is interesting that this method had become a local tradition, because it enables a comparison, all other things being equal, whose lesson is valuable. What was its result? "A sower of ordinary strength covers an average of four hectares per day with cereals" by broadcast sowing (Moslan:35). Using dibbling, a team composed of a man making holes and three helpers (women or children) planting grains sows one half-acre per day—that is, about 0.2 ha. This means 20 times less area is sown by the team, and 40 to 50 times less per person if the three helpers are considered to be equivalent to one adult worker or a little more. To compensate for this much lower work productivity, there is a single advantage: savings in seed. In Norfolk of 1787, says W. Marshall, the team of dibbling sowers was paid 9 shillings per acre, and the savings in seed were about one half, that is 1.5 bushel or more. Everything comes into play in the cost ratio of grain to labor. It is advisable to save seed when grain is expensive and to sow a maximum amount when labor is costly. Far from being a primitive technique, broadcast sowing is an elaborate one, which can be used only in societies where the price of labour is relatively high.

Therefore, we understand the remark made by the *Société d'agriculture de Caen* in 1806, that planting demanded too many hands and labor was too expensive here that this be efficient: it seemed to them that this method, instead of leading them to perfect the art, would lead them back to its origins. Indeed, grain dibbling was made possible solely because England, in particular Norfolk, had experienced a considerable decrease in real wages from the end of the seventeenth century. N. Riches (1937) spoke of "starvation wages," principally owning to the Act of Settlement of 1662, which reduced the mobility of laborers and placed workers more or less at the mercy of their employer.

In France, at least in Normandy, where exploitation of laborers was not as far advanced, wheat dibbling would appear to be economic regression.

Conclusion

In reality, the only yield of universal value was labor yield, but it is usually very difficult to assess, especially in moneyless economies. Consequently, we are obliged to fall back on other ratios, and this raises for each of them the question of significance and area of validity.

Surface yield is an agronomical concept, applied for barely two centuries. It can be used only in systems with fields, meaning evenly cultivated and sown plots such as those we know today. The very existence of fields is most often related to animal-drawn farming implements. A great number of systems considered as primitive have no such fields and for them a yield per plot means nothing, or at least cannot be compared with its meaning in other systems. The only surface yield to be universally valid is what I have called the territorial yield, which considers the individual plot as well as the entire area supplying, by transfer, the elements necessary to renewing its fertility. Such yield takes the factor of time into consideration as well.

Lastly, we have the seed yield. This yield has fallen into disuse since the second half of the last century, after having been in virtually universal use before. For historical analysis, we would be wrong not to use it, especially as it is rich in significance. Seed yield is meaningful only when the sowing density, hence the sowing technique, is known, but this is just the data required to characterize an agricultural system. Relatively low sowing yields (4 or 5 for 1) do not imply that the system is poor, only that broadcast sowing and thick sowing are used, in other words spared in order to save labor, which is expensive. High yields (100 and more for 1), on the contrary, imply almost certainly cheap labor or only limited technical means available.

Acknowledgements. This chapter was translated from French by Jacqueline Gaudey, Centre de recherches archéologiques, CNRS, France.

Notes

1. About clearing of undergrowth and street dung in, see Sigaut 1975:45-51, 131-133 (France) and Gokhale & Habbu 1927 (India). Since Richards' study, the African system called *citimene* has been the subject of other publications, the latest of which is Stromgaard 1985.
2. On extraordinary yields, my sources are as follow (in chronological order): Tull 1733:61; Turbilly 1761:217,218; Watson 1768; Marshall 1796; Janville 1806 (Davy 1820:240; Villers 1850–1851; Diffloth 1929:322. There surely exist many others. In the 1850s, a M. Mangocé recommended a method consisting in sowing 25 l/ha only and producing 150/1; this was certainly neither the first time nor the last.
3. It is evident that the expression "marvelous intuition" is exaggerated and merely translates its author's surprise. I will not resist citing a few lines from Kenny's preface:

   > To preach dry-farming to men to whom it was a hoary tradition when Englishmen used paint instead of clothing did not appear to me the surest way to gain the confidence of the Kunbi, nor did I consider it wise to suggest seed selection in a land where 4,000 different sorts of paddy are grown in one province alone, and carefully differentiated according to their qualities and the land suitable for them.

   The enthusiasm is effusive, but it perfectly expresses the attitude of anyone who discovers a fact which he had been trained to despise.

Bibliography

Abate Tedla
1993 Personal communication

Adams, M.M., and J.J. Pipoly
1980 Biological structure, classification and distribution of economic legumes. In *Advances in Legume Science,* edited by R.J. Summerfield and A.H. Bunting, 1–16. Kew, Richmond, Surrey: MAFF, Royal Botanic Gardens.

Adams, R. McC.
1975 An ancient Uruk threshing sledge or harrow? *Sumer* 3:17–20.

Agostini, B.B., and D. Khan
1988 Trends, situation and outlook for the world pulse economy. In *World crops: Cool season food legumes,* edited by R.J. Summerfield, 217–228. Dordrecht: Kluwer.

Al-Mouayad Al Azem, A.N.
1991 Crop storage in ancient Syria: A functional analysis using ethnographic modelling. Ph.D. dissertation, University of London.

Aldenderfer, M., L. Kimball, and A. Sievert
1989 Microwear analysis in the Maya lowlands: The use of functional data in a complex society setting. *Journal of Field Archaeology* 15(4).

Alexander, G.B., W.M. Heston, and R.K. Iler
1954 The solubility of amorphous silica in water. *Journal of Physical Chemistry* 58:453–455.

Allen, H.
1974 The Bagundji of the Darling Basin: Cereal gatherers in an uncertain environment. *World Archaeology* 6:309–322.

Allen, J.
1969 Archaeology, and the history of Port Essington. Ph.D. dissertation, Department of Prehistory, Australian National University, Canberra.

Alon, D., and T.E. Levy
1989 The archaeology of cult and the Chalcolithic sanctuary at Gilat. *Journal of Mediterranean Archaeology* 2:163–221.

Amirkhanov, A.A.
1982 Stanovlenie proizvodjaschego khozjaistva na Severnom Kavkaze /po raskopkam Chokhe (Establishing a production economy in N. Caucasus: Chok excavations). *Kul'turnyj progress v epokhu bronzy i rannego zheleza,* 145–147. Erevan.

1985 Tchokhskaya arkheologiya kultura i problema kulturnykh arealov rannego golotsena kurokaspiskoj oblasti (Chokh archaeological culture and problem of the cultural areas of the Early Holocene in the Kourocaspian region). *Drevnie kuliury Severo-Vostochnogo Kavkaza.* Makhachkala.

Amirshahi, M.C.
1979 Food legume production and improvement in Iran. In *Food legume improvement and development,* edited by G.C. Hawtin and G.J. Chancellor, 51–54. Ottawa: ICARDA and IDRC.

Ammerman, A.J., and L.L. Cavalli-Sforza
1984 *The Neolithic transition and the genetics of populations in Europe.* New Jersey: Princeton University Press.

Andersen, H.H,. and H.J. Whitlow
1983 Wear traces and patination on Danish flint artifacts. *Nuclear Instruments and Methods in Physics* 218:468–474.

Andersen, S.T.
1979 Identification of wild grasses and cereal pollen. *Danmarks Geologiske Undersøgelse*, Arbog 1978:69–92.

Anderson, P.C.
1980 A testimony of prehistoric tasks: Diagnostic residues on stone tool working edges. *World Archaeology* 12(2):181–194.

1991 Harvesting of wild cereals during the Natufian as seen from experimental cultivation and harvest of wild einkorn wheat and microwear analysis of stone tools. In *The Natufian Culture of the Levant*, edited by O. Bar-Yosef and F. Valla. Ann Arbor, MI: International Monographs in Prehistory.

1994a Insights into plant harvesting and other activities at Hatoula, as revealed by microscopic functional analysis of selected chipped stone tools. In *Le gisement de Hatoula en Judée occidentale, Israël*, edited by M. Lechevallier and A. Ronen, 277–293. Mémoires et travaux du Centre de Recherche Français de Jérusalem 8. Paris: Association Paléorient.

1994b Interpreting traces of Near Eastern Neolithic craft activities: An ancestor of the threshing sledge for processing domestic crops? In *The use of lithic tools in Neolithic craft activities,* edited by A. van Giln. *Helinium XXIV(2):*306–321.

1994c Reflections on the significance of two PPN typological classes in light of experimentation and microwear analysis: Flint "sickles" and obsidian "Cayonu tools." In *Neolithic chipped stone industries of the fertile crescent. Studies in early Near Eastern Production, subsistence, and environment I*, edited by H.G. Gebel and S. Koslowski. *Ex oriente*, 61–82. Berlin.

1995a   La moisson à Aswad vue à travers des microtraces d'utilisation sur un échantillon d' "outils lustrés." In *Aswad et Ghoriafé: Sites néolithiques en Damascène (Syrie) aux 8e et 7e millénaires avant l'ère chrétienne*, by H. de Conteson et al., 221–231. Beyrouth: IFAPO.

1995b   Technologie agricole et artisanat à El Kowm 2: L'Apport des microtraces d'utilisation sur des outils en silex. In *Une île dans le désert: El Kowm 2: Néolithique précéramique, 8000–7500 BP Syrie*, edited by D. Stordeur. Paris: ERC.

1996   Functional interpretation of obsidian tools from Asikli (pre-pottery Neolithic, Central Anatolia): Microscopic and experimental data. Report.

1998   Phytoliths as a line of evidence of use of the threshing sledge, edited by J.D. Meunier, and L. Faure-Denard. Paper presented at the Second International Meeting on Phytolith Research, August 27-29, 1998, Aix-en Provence. Abstracts, p. 46. Gordon and Breach.

1999   The history of harvesting and threshing techniques for cereals in the prehistoric Near East. In *The origins of agriculture and crop domestication*, edited by A.B. Damania, J. Valkoun, G. Willcox, and C.O. Qualset, 141–155. ICARDA/IPIGRI/GRCP/FAO.

Anderson, P.C., and M.L. Inizan

1994   Utilisation du tribulum au début de IIIe millénaire: Des lames "cananéenes" lustrées à Kutan (Nivive V) dans la region de Mossoul, Iraq. *Paléorient* 20(2): 85–103. Paris.

Anderson, P.C., and F. Valla

1996   "Glossed tools" from Hayonim Terrace: Blank choice and functional tendencies. In *Neolithic chipped stone industries of the fertile crescent, and their contemporaries in adjacent regions*, edited by S.K. Kozlowski and H.G. Gebel, 341–362. Studies in Near Eastern Production, Subsistence and Environment 3. *Ex oriente*. Berlin.

Anderson-Gerfaud, P.

1981   *Contribution méthodologique à l'analyse des microtraces d'utilisation sur les outils préhistoriques*. Thèse de doctorat, Université de Bordeaux I, Talence, France.

1983   A consideration of the uses of certain backed and lustred stone tools from the late Mesolithic and Natufian levels of Abu Hureyra and Mureybet (Syria). In *Traces d'utilisation sur les outils néolithiques du Proche-Orient*, edited by M.C. Cauvin, 77–106. Travaux de la Maison de l'Orient 5. Lyon: Maison de l'Orient.

1985/6   Apports et limites de l'étude des phytolithes. *Nouvelles de l'Archéologie* 18:48–55.

1986   A few comments concerning residue analysis of stone plant-processing tools. In *Technical aspects of microwear studies on stone tools*, edited by L. Owen and G. Unrath, 69–87. *Early Man News* 9–11.

1988   Using prehistoric stone tools to harvest cultivated wild cereals: preliminary observations of traces and impact. In *Industries Lithiques: Tracéologie et Technologie*, edited by S. Beyries, 175–195. BAR International Series 411. Oxford: British Archaeological Reports.

1989   Personal communication

1990   Aspects of behaviour in the Middle Palaeolithic: Functional analysis of stone tools from Southwest France. In *The Emergence of Modern Humans: An archaeological perspective*, edited by P. Mellars, 389–418. Edinburgh: Edinburgh University Press.

Anderson-Gerfaud, P., G. Déraprahamian, and G. Willcox

1991   Les premières cultures de céréales sauvages et domestiques primitives au Proche-Orient néolithique: résultats préliminaires d'expériences à Jalès (Ardèche). *Cahiers de l'Euphrate 5–6* (ADPF): 191–232. Paris.

Anderson-Gerfaud, P., M.L. Inizan, M. Lechevallier, J. Pelegrin, and P. Pernot

1989   Des lames de silex dans un atelier de potier harappéen: interaction des domaines techniques. *Comptes Rendus de l'Académie des Sciences de Paris* 308, Série II: 443–449.

Anderson-Gerfaud, P., E. Moss, and H. Plisson

1987   A quoi ont-ils servi? L'apport de l'analyse fonctionnelle. *Bulletin de la Société Préhistorique Française* 84(8):226–237.

Antoun, A., and A. Quol

1979   Food legume production in the Hashemite Kingdom of Jordan. In *Food legume improvement and development*, edited by G.C. Hawtln and G.J. Chancellor, 47–50. Ottawa: ICARDA and IDRC.

Applebaum, S.

1954   The agriculture of the British Iron Age as exemplified at Figheldean Down, Wiltshire. *Proceedings of the Prehistoric Society* 20:103–114.

Argel, P.J., and L.R. Humphreys

1983   Environmental effects on seed development and hard seededness in *Stylosanthes hamata* cv. *Australian Journal of Agricultural Research* 34:251–287. Verano.

Ataman, K.

1989   The chipped stone assemblage from Can Hasan III: A study in typology, technology and function. Ph.D. dissertation, Institute of Archaeology, University College, London.

Aykroyd, W.R., and J. Doughty

1982   Legumes in human nutrition. *FAO Paper* 20. Rome.

Bakels, C.C.

1982   Der Mohn, die Linearbandkeramik und das westliche Mittelmeergebiet. *Arch. Korrespondenzblatt* 12: 11–13

Bakels, C.C., and R. Rousselle

1985   Restes botaniques et agriculture du Néolithique ancien en Belgique et Pays-Bas. *Helinium* 25:37–57.

Bakhteev

1966   Dalneïshee osushchestvlenie nauchnykh ideï V. I. Vavilova v izuchenii zernovykh (Further development of N. I. Vavilov's scientific ideas on the study of grain). *Voprosy geografii kuliurnykh rasteni i N. I. Vavilov*, Moscow-Leningrad.

Bar-Yosef, O., A. Gopher, and N. Goring-Morris

1980   Netiv Hagdud: a "Sultanian" mound in the Lower Jordan Valley, Israel. *Paléorient*: 201–206.

Bar-Yosef, 0., and N. Goren

1973   Natufian remains in Hayonim Cave. *Paléorient* 1:49–68.

Bar-Yosef, O., and M.E. Kislev

1989   Early farming communities in the Jordan Valley. In *Foraging and farming: The evolution of plant exploitation*, edited by D.R. Harris and G.C. Hillman, 32–642. London: Unwin and Hyman.

Bar-Yosef, 0., and E. Tchernov

1966   Archaeological finds and the fossil faunas of the Natufian and microlithic industries at Hayonim Cave (Western Galilea) Israel. *Israel Journal of Zoology* 15:104–140.

Barber, D.A., and M.G.T. Shone

1966   The absorption of silica from aqueous solutions by plants. *Journal of Experimental Botany* 17:569–78.

Barker, G.

1985   *Prehistoric farming in Europe*. Cambridge: Cambridge University Press.

Barth, H.
1857   *Travels and discoveries in North and Central Africa, being the journal of an expedition under the auspices of Her Britannic Majesty's Government, in the years 1849–1855.* 3 vols. New York: Harper and Bros.

Baruch ,U., and S. Bottema
1991   Palynological evidence for climatic changes in the Levant ca. 17,000–9,000B.P. In *The Natufian Culture in the Levant,* edited by O. Bar-Yosef and F. Valla, 11–20. Ann Arbor: International Monographs in Prehistory.

Basler, F.
1979   Accentuation of weed control problems in the dry areas with relevance to herbicides in food legumes. In *Food legume improvement and development,* edited by G.C. Hawtin and G.J. Chancellor, 136–139.

Bastin, B.
1964   Recherches sur les relations entre la végétation actuelle et le spectre pollinique récent dans la forêt de Soignes (Belgique). *Agricultura* XII(2):344–373, 6 figure, 1 pl.

Beaglehole, E.
1937   Notes on Hopi economic life. *Yale University Publications in Anthropology* 15.

Beaton, J.
1982   Fire and water: Aspects of Australian Aboriginal management of cycads. *Australian Archaeology* 17(1):51–58.

Beck, W., A. Clarke, and L. Head, eds.
1989   Plants in Australian archaeology. *Tempus 1.* St. Lucia: Anthropology Museum, University of Queensland.

Beckwith, R.S., and R. Reeve
1962   Studies on soluble silica in soils: The sorption of silicic acid by soils and minerals. *Australian Journal of Soil Research* 1:157–168.

Behre, K.E.
1981   The interpretation of anthropogenic indicators in pollen diagrams. *Pollen et Spores* XXII(2):225–246, 3 fig.

Bejlzkchi, V.S.
1978   *Rannij eneolit nizovjev Pruta i Dunaja* (Early Chalcolithic in the Prut and Danube Valleys). Kishinev.

Ben-Ze'ev, N., and D. Zohary
1973   Species relationships in the genus *Pisum* L. *Israel Journal of Botany* 22:73–91.

Bender, B.
1978   Gatherer-hunter to farmer: A social perspective. *World Archaeology* 10:361–392.
1985   Prehistoric developments in the American mid-continent and in Brittany, Northwest France. In *Prehistoric hunter-gatherers,* edited by T.D. Price and J. Brown, 21–57.

Beranová, M.
1981   Mahlversuche mit Emmer auf einer latènezeitlichen Hand-Drehmühle. *Varia Archaeologica* 2:227–228.
1987   idem, Zur Frage des Systems der Landwirtschaft im Neolithikum und Äneolithikum in Mitteleuropa. *Archeologické rozhledy* 39:141–198.

Bettinger, R.
1982   Aboriginal exchange and territoriality in Owens Valley, California. In *Contexts for prehistoric exchange,* edited by J. Ericson and T. Earle, 103–127. New York: Academic Press.

Beug, H.J.
1961   *Leitfaden der Pollenbestimmung für Mitlleleuropa und angrenzende Gebeite.* Edited by Gustav Fisher. Verlag: 61. Stuttgart.

Bhalla, P.L., and H.D. Slattery
1984   Callose deposits make clover seeds impermeable to water. *Annals of Botany* 53:125–128.

Bharati, M.P.
1985   Personal communication
1986   Status of *Lathyrus sativus* among grain legumes cultivated in Nepal. In *Lathyrus and Lathyrism,* edited by A.K. Kaul and D. Combes, 142–145. New York: TWMRF.

Bhattarai, A.N., M. P. Bharati, and B.K. Gyawall
1988   Factors which limit the productivity of cool season food legumes in Nepal. In *World Crops: Cool Season Food Legumes,* edited by R.J. Summerfield, 217–228. Dordrecht: Kluwer.

Bielenstein, A.
1907/18 Die Holzbauten der Letten. Ein Beitrag zur Ethnographie, Culturgeschichte und Archäologie der Völker Russlands im Westgebiet. *Erster Teil,* St. Petersburg 1907; *Zweiter Teil,* Petrograd 1918.

Binford, L.R.
1968   Post-pleistocene adaptations. In *New Perspectives in Archaeology,* edited by S.R. Binford and L.R. Binford, 313–341. Chicago: Aldine.

Bintliff, J.L., and A.M. Snodgrass
1985   The Cambridge/Bradford Boeotian expedition: The first four years. *Journal of Field Archaeology* 12(2):123–162.

Blackman, E.
1968   The pattern and sequence of opaline silica deposition in rye (Secale cereale L.). *Annals of Botany* 32:207–218.
1969   Observations on the development of the silica cells of the leaf sheath of wheat (*Triticum aestivum*). *Canadian Journal of Botany* 47:827–838.

Blackman, E., and D.W. Parry
1968   Opaline silica deposition in rye (Secale cereale L.). *Annals of Botany* 32:199–206.

Boersma, J.W.
1988   De datering van een vuurstenen sikkel uit Middelstum-Boerdamsterweg. In *Terpen en wierden in het Fries-Groningse kustgebied,* edited by M. Bierma, A.T. Clason, E. Kramer and G.J. de Langen, 31–35. Groningen: Wolters-Noordhoff/Forsten.

Bohrer, V.l.
1972   On the relation of harvest methods to early agriculture in the Near East. *Economic Botany* 26:145–156.

Bond, D.A., D.A. Lawes, G.C. Hawtin, M.C. Saxena, and J.H. Stephens
1985   Faba bean (*Vicia faba* L.). In *Grain legume crops,* edited by R.J. Summerfield and E. H. Roberts, 199–265. London: Collins.

Bor, N.L.
1968   *Gramineae.* Vol. 9. *Flora of Iraq.* With economic and distributional notes by E. Guest. Baghdad: Ministry of Agriculture Republic of Iraq.

Bordaz, J.
1965   The threshing sledge—ancient Turkish grain separating method still proves efficient. *Natural History* LX-XIV (4):26–29.
1969   Flint flaking in Turkey. *Natural History* LXXVIII (2):73–77.

Borgaonkar, D.S., and J.M.J. de Wet
1960   A cytological study of hybrids between *Dichanthium annulatum* and *Dichanthium fecundum. Phyton* (Argentina) 15:137–144.

Bottema, S.
1975   The interpretation of pollen spectra from prehistoric settlements (with special attention to Liguliflorae). *Palaeohistoria* 17:17–35.
1986   A Late Quaternary pollen diagram from Lake Urmia (northwestern Iran). *Review of Palaeobotany and Palynology* 47:241–261.
1988   The production and distribution of cereal pollen: Experiments on standing and threshed crops. Paper presented at

"Expérimentation en archéologie: bilan et perspectives ," Archéodrome de Beaune, 6–9 April 1988.

Bottema, S., and Y.Barkoudah

1979 Modern pollen precipitation in Syria and Lebanon and its relation to vegetation. *Pollen et Spores* 21:427–480.

Boyeldieu, J.

1980 *Les cultures céréalières.* Coll. Nouvelle Encyclopédie des connaissances agricoles. Paris: Hachette.

Brady, N.C.

1988 Food legume research sponsored by the United States Agency for International Development (AID). In *World Crops: Cool Season Food Legumes,* edited by R.J. Summerfield, 1–16. Dordrecht: Kluwer.

Braidwood, R.J.

1952 *The Near East and the foundation for civilisation.* Oregon.

1960 The agricultural revolution. *Scientific American* 203 (3):131–148.

Bregadze, N.A.

1982a *Ocherki po Agroethnografii Gruzii. (Sketches on the agroethnography of Georgia).* Tiblisi: Akademiya Nauk Gruzinskoi SSR, Institut Istorii, Arkheologii i Ethnografii.

1982b *Études sur l'Agroethnographie géorgienne.* Mecniereba, Tbilisi. (in Russian).

Bronson, B.

1966 Roots and the subsistence of the ancient Maya. *Southwestern Journal of Anthropology* 22:251–279.

Brun-Cottan, M.F.

1989 *Les techniques agricoles en Mésopotamie au chalcolithique et à l'âge du bronze d'après la documentation archéologique.* Thèse, Université de Paris 1.

Brunache, P.

1894 *Le centre de l'Afrique: Autour du Tchad,* 340. Paris: Felix Alcan.

Brunken, J.N., J.M.J. de Wet, and J.R. Harlan

1977 The morphology and domestication of pearl millet. *Economic Botany* 31: 163–174.

Bruyn, A.

1986 Een vuurstenen "sikkel" uit Medemblik. *Jaarverslag* ROB 1984:89–94.

BSTID et al. (Board of Science and Technology for International Development, Commission on Industrial Relations, and National Research Council)

1981 *Postharvest food losses in developing countries.* Washington DC: National Academy of Sciences.

Buddenhagen, I.W., and R.A. Richards,

1988 Breeding cool season food legumes for improved performance in stress environments. In *World crops cool season food legumes,* edited by R.J. Summerfield, 81–95. Dordrecht: Kluwer.

Bukinich, D.D.

1924 Istoria pervobytnogo oroshaemogo zemledeliya v Zakaspiskoï oblasti v sviazi s voprosom o proiskhozhdenii zemledelia i skotovodstva (History of primitive irrigated agriculture in Transcaspian in connection with the question of the origin of agriculture and cattle breeding). *Zhurnal "Khlopkovoe delo",* 3–4, Moscow-Leningrad.

Bullock, P., N. Fedoroff, A. Jongerius, G. Stoops, T. Tursina, and U. Babel

1985 *Handbook for soil thin section description,* 150. Wolverhampton, UK: Waine Research Publication.

Bunatov, T.A.

1957 *Zemeledelie i skotovodstvo v Azerbaidzhane i epokbu bronzy.* Baku.

Butler, A.

1989 Cryptic anatomical characters as evidence of early cultivation in the grain legumes (pulses). In *Foraging and farming: The evolution of plant exploitation,* edited by D.R. Harris and G.C. Hillman, 390–407. London: Unwin and Hyman.

Butler, E.A.

1999 The ethnobotany of *Lathyrus sativus* in Highland Ethiopia. In *Plants and people in Africa: Recent archaeobotanical evidence,* edited by M.van der Veen. New York: Plenum Press.

Buxó i Capdevila, R.

1985 *Dinamica de l'alimentacio vegetal a partir de l'anali de llavors i fruits. interes delseu estudi per la reconstruccio de la dieta vegetal antiga humana.* Mémoire de maître, multigraphié, Université autonome de Barcelone.

Byanya, V.V.

1996 Kavkaz, *Arkheologiya. Neolit Severnoï Evrazii*:73–86. Moscow (Caucase).

Byrne, R.

1987 Climatic change and the origin of agriculture. In *Studies in the Neolithic and Urban Revolutions,* edited by L. Manzanilla, 21–34. BAR International Series 349. Oxford: British Archaeological Reports.

Caillié, R.

1830 *Journal d'un voyage a Témboctou et à Jenné dans l'Afrique centrale, précédé d'observations faites chez les Maures Braknas. les Nalous et d'autres peuples pendant les années 1824, 1825, 1826, 1827, 1828.* 3 vols. Paris: Imprimerie Royale.

Callen, E.O.

1967 The first New World cereal. *American Antiquity* 32:535–538.

Camps, G

1974 *Les civilisations préhistoriques de l'Afrique du Nord et du Sahara.* Paris: Dion

Cane, S.

1989 Australian Aboriginal seed grinding and its archaeological record: A case study from the Western Desert. In *Foraging and farming: The evolution of plant exploitation,* edited by D.R. Harris and G.C. Hillman, 99–120. London: Unwin and Hyman.

Cauvin, J.

1977 Les fouilles de Mureybet (1971–1974) et leur signification pour les origines de la sédentarisation au Proche-orient. *Annals of the American School of Oriental Research* 44:19–48.

1987 L'apparition des premières divinités. *La Recherche* 194:1472–1480.

1989 La néolithisation au Levant et sa première diffusion. In *Néolithisations,* edited by O. Aurenche and J. Cauvin, 3–36. BAR International Series 516. Oxford: British Archaeological Reports

1994 *Naissance des divinités, naissance de l'agriculture.* Paris: CNRS Éditions.

Cauvin, M.C.

1974 Outillage lithique et chronololigie à Tell Aswad (Damascene, Syrie). *Paléorient* 1:103–106.

1983 Les faucilles préhistoriques du Proche-Orient, données morphologiques et fonctionnelles. *Paléorient* 9(1):63–79.

Cauvin, J. and M.C. Cauvin

Personal communication.

Cauvin, J., M-C. Cauvin, D. Helmer, G. Willcox

1998 L'homme et son environnement au Levant Nord entre 30000 et 7500 BP. *Paléorient* 23(2): 51–69. Paris.

Champault, F.D.

1969 *Un oasis Sahara nord-occidental, Tabelbala,* 486. Paris: Editions CNRS.

Chapman, J.C., R.S. Shiel, and S. Batovic

1987 Settlement patterns and land use in Neothermal Dalmatia, Yugoslavia:1983–1984 Seasons. *Journal of Field Archaeology* 14(2):123–146.

Charles, M., and G. Hillman
1992   Vyrashchivanie selskokhoziaïstvennykh kultur v pustynnoj
        zone po rezultatam izuchenia karbonizirovannykh rastitelnykh
        mikroostatkov (Rural cultivation in the desert according to the
        study of carbonized plant microremains). *Novye issledovaniya
        na poselenii Dzheïtun*: 83–94. Ed. Masson V. M., Moscow .

Charles, M.P.
1985   The husbandry of pulses and oil crops in modern Iraq. *Bulletin
        on Sumerian Agriculture* 2:39–62. Cambridge.
1988   Irrigation In Lowland Iraq. *Bulletin on Sumerian Agriculture*
        4:1–39. Cambridge.

Chegin, D.Y.
1979   Novye pamjatniki kul'tury linejno-lentochnoj keramiki na
        Ukraine *SA* No. 2.
1985   Dnepro-donetskaya kulturnaya obshchnost (Community of the
        Dniepr-Donets culture). *Ibidem*:48–58. Moscow.
1996a   Surskaya kultura, *Arkheologiya. Neolit*:40–45. Moscow.

Chernykh, E.K.
1982   *Eneolit Pravoberezhnoj Ukrainy i Moldavii* (Chalcolithic in
        Ukraine and Moldavia). *Eneolit SSSR* 233. Moscow.
1996a   Bugo-dnestrovskaya kultura, *Arkheologii. Neolit*:19–26,
        Moscow.
1996b   Kultura lineïno-lentochnoj keramiki, *Ibidem*:27–33. Moscow.

Chernykh, E.N.
1978   *Gornoe delo i metallurgija v drevnejshej Bolgarii* (Mining and
        metallurgy in ancient Bulgaria). Sofia.

Chevalier, A.
1900a   Une nouvelle plante à sucre de l'Afrique française centrale
        (*Panicum burgou*. Aug. Chev.). *Comptes rendus de l'Assoc. pour
        l'Avance. des Sciences* 1900:642–657.
1900b   *Ressources végétales du Sahara et de ses confines nord et sud*,
        256. Paris: Museum d'Histoire naturelle.

Chikwendu, V.E., and C.E.A. Okezie
1989   Factors responsible for the ennoblement of African yams:
        Inferences from experiments in yam domestication. In
        Foraging and farming: The evolution of plant exploitation,
        edited by D.R. Harris and G.C. Hillman, 344–357. London:
        Unwin and Hyman.

Childe, V.G.
1936   *Man makes himself*. London: Watts.
1942   *What happened in history*. London: Max Parrish.

Chubnishvili, T.N., L.M. Chelidze
1978   K voprosu o nekotorykh opredeliayushchikh priznakakh
        rannezemledelcheskoj kultury VI-IV tysh (Some determinant
        features of the pre-agricultural society in the sixth to
        fourth millennia BC). *Zhurnal Izvestiya Akademii Nauk
        Gruzinskoj SSR. Seria istorii, arkheologii, etnografii i istorii
        iskusstva 1* .

Clark, C., and M. Haswell
1967   *The economics of subsistence agriculture*. London: Macmillan.

Clark, G.
1953   *Doistoricheskaja Evropa* (Prehistoric Europe). Moscow .

Clegg, M.T., A.H.D. Brown, and P.R. Whitfeld
1984   Chloroplast DNA diversity in wild and cultivated barley:
        implication for genetic conservation. *Genetical Research*
        43:339–343.

Cock, J.H.
1985   *Cassava: new potential for a neglected crop*. International
        Agricultural Development Service Development-Oriented
        Literature Series. Boulder, CO: Westview.

Cohen, M.N.
1977   *The food crisis in prehistory*. New Haven: Yale University
        Press.

Colledge, S.
1997   Identifying pre-domestic agriculture using multivariate
        analyses. In *The origins of agriculture and the domestication of
        crop plants in the Near East*, by A. Damania, and J. Valkoun.
        The Harlan Symposium. Aleppo: ICARDA.

Colledge, S.M.
1988   Scanning-electron microscope studies of the pericarp layers of
        some wild wheats and ryes. Methods and problems. In
        Scanning-electron microscopy in archaeology, edited by S.L.
        Olsen, 225–236. BAR International Series 452. Oxford: British
        Archaeological Reports:

Collins J.F., and F.J. Larney
1987   Micromorphological observations of compacted horizons
        (cultivated pans) from various horizons in Irish tillage soils. In
        Soil Micromorphology, edited by N. Fédoroff, L.M. Bresson,
        and M.A. Courty, 451–457. Plaisir, France: AFES.

Coppola, D., and L. Costantini
1987   Le Néolithique ancien littoral et la diffusion des céréales dans
        les Pouilles durant le VIe millénaire: les sites de Fontanelle,
        Torre Cane et Le Machie. In *Les Premières Communautés
        Paysannes en Méditerranée occidentale*, edited by J. Guilaine,
        J. Courtin, J.L. Roudil, and J.L. Vernet, 249–255. Actes du
        colloque de Montpellier, April 1983. Paris: CNRS.

Coqueugniot, E.
1983   Analyse tracéologique d'une série de grattoirs et herminettes
        de Mureybet, Syrie. In *Traces d'utilisation sur les outils
        néolithiques du Proche-Orient*, edited by M.Cl. Cauvin, 163–
        172. Travaux de la Maison de l'Orient 5. Lyon.

Coqueugniot E. and P. Anderson
1996   L'industrie lithique d'El Aoui Safa, un nouveau site khiamien à
        l'est du Jebel el 'Arab (Désert noir, Syrie du sud). In *Neolithic
        Chipped Stone Industries of the Fertile Crescent, and their
        contemporaries in adjacent regions*, edited by S.K. Kozlowski
        and H.G. Gebel *Studies in Near Eastern Production, Subsistence
        and Environment* 3. Ex oriente 421–430. Berlin.

Cortier, M.
1908   *D'une rive à l'autre du Sahara*, 413 Paris: Emile Larose.

Costantini, L.
1981   Semi e carboni del mesolitico e neolitico della Grotta dell' Uzzo,
        Trapani. *Quaternaria* 23:233–246.
1984   The beginning of agriculture in the Kachi plain: The evidence
        of Mehrgarh. In *South Asian Archaeology 1981. Proceedings of
        the 6th International Conference of the Association of South
        Asian Archaeologists in Western Europe*, edited by B. Allchin,
        29–33. Cambridge: Cambridge University Press.

Coursey, D.G.
1967   *Yams: An account of the nature, origins, cultivation and
        utilisation of the useful members of the Dioscoreacae*. London:
        Longmans, Green and Co.
1980   The origins and domestication of yams in Africa. In *West
        African culture dynamics*, edited by B.K. Schwartz, Jr. and R. E.
        Dumett, 67–90. The Hague: Mouton.

Courty, M.A.
1982   Étude géologique de sites archéologiques Holocènes: Définition
        des processus sédimentaires et post-sédimentaires,
        caractérisation de l'impact anthropique. Essais de
        méthodologie. *Thèse de 3e cycle de Géologie du Quaternaire et
        préhistoire (Bordeaux I)*, 310 p.

Courty, M.A., and J. Trichet
1988   Application de la micromorphologie à la caractérisation des
        sols anciens cultivés, *2e colloque Franco-soviétique sur
        l'archéologie de l'Asie Centrale des origines à l'Âge du Fer, Paris
        1985*. Boccard: 237–241.

Cowgill, G.M.
1971   Some comments on *Manihot* subsistence and the ancient
       Maya. *Southwest Journal of Anthropology* 27:51–63.
Crawford, O.G.S.
1935   A primitive threshing machine. *Antiquity* 9:335–339.
Crawford, O.G.S., and A. Keiller
1928   *Wessex from the air.* Oxford.
Crowfoot Payne, J.
1983   The flint industries of Jericho. In *Excavations at Jericho*, edited
       by M. Kenyon and T.A. Holland, vol. 5, 622–759. Oxford:
       Oxford University Press.
Crowfoot, R.J.
1960   Flint implements from Tell al-Judaidah. In *Excavations in the
       plain of Antioch* edited by R.J. Braidwood and L.S. Braidwood,
       525–539. *O.I.P.* 61. Chicago.
Cummings, L.S.
1998   PaleoResearch Labs Technical Report 97–89. Denver.
Curwen, C
1937   A tribulum flint from Sussex. *Antiquity* 11:93–94.
D'Andrea, A.C., Mitiku Haile, E.A. Butler, and D.E.Lyons
1997   Ethnoarchaeological research in the Ethiopian Highlands.
       Nyame Akuma 47:19–26.
N.D.   Ethnoarchaeological studies of traditional agricultural
       practices in the Ethiopian Highlands: Preliminary results. In
       Plants and people in Africa: Recent archaeobotanical evidence,
       edited by M.van der Veen. New York: Plenum Press.
Dalman, G.
1933   *Arbeit und Sitte in Palästina. Zwite Reihe*: 1964 Georg Olms
       Verlagsbuchhandlund Hildesheim. 7 vols.
Damania, A. and J. Valkoun
1997   *The origins of agriculture and the domestication of crop plants
       in the Near East, The Harlan Symposium.* Aleppo: ICARDA .
Damania, A., J. Valkoun, G. Willcox, and C. Qualset
1999   *The origins of agriculture and crop domestication.* Aleppo:
       ICARDA
Danilenko, V.N.
1969   *Neolit Ukrainy*, Kiev.
1985   Sursko-dneprovskaja kul'tura. *Arkheologija Ukrainskoj SSR*,
       tome I:133–139. Kiev.
Darlington, C.D.
1963   *Chromosome botany and the origin of cultivated plants.* 2nd
       edition. London: Allen and Unwin.
1969   *The evolution of man and society.* 1st and 2nd editions.
       London: Allen and Unwin.
Darwin, C.
1859   *On the origin of species by means of natural selection.* London:
       John Murray.
1868/ 1975   *The variation of animals and plants under
       domestication.* 1st and 2nd editions. London: John Murray.
Davies, D.R., G.J. Berry, M.C. Heath, and T.C.K. Dawkins
1985   Pea (*Pisum sativum* L.). In *Grain legume crops*, edited by R.J.
       Summerfield and E.H. Roberts, 147–198. London: Collins.
Davies, M.S. and G.C. Hillman
1992   Domestication of cereals. In *Grass evolution and domestication*,
       edited by G.P.Chapman, 199–224. Cambridge: Cambridge
       University Press.
Davis, D.D.
1975   Patterns of early formative subsistence in southern
       Mesoamerica, 1500–1100 B.C. *Man* (n.s.) 10:41–59.
Davis P.H.
1970   *Flora of Turkey.* Vol. 3. Edinburgh: Edinburgh University
       Press.

Davis, S.J.M.
1987   *The archaeology of animals.* London.
Davy, H. (Sir)
1820   *Éléments de chimie appliquée à l'agriculture, suivis d'un traité
       sur la chimie des terres.* Paris: Audin and Crevot.
De Candolle, A
1886   *Origin of cultivated plants.* English translation of the 2nd
       edition, 1967. New York and London: Hafner.
de Moulins, D.
1994   Agricultural changes at Euphrates and steppe sites in the mid
       eighth to the sixth millennium BC. Ph.D. dissertation. Institute
       of Archaeology, University College, London.
1997   Agricultural changes at Euphrates and steppe sites in the Mid-
       8th to the 6th Millennium B.C. *Bar International Series* 683.
       Oxford: British Archaeological Reports.
De Wet, J.M.J.
1977   Increasing cereals yields: evolution under domestication. In
       Crop resources, edited by D.S. Siegler, 111–118. New York, San
       Francisco and London: Academic Press.
De Wet, J.M.J., and J.R. Harlan
1975   Weeds and domesticates: evolution in the man-made habitat.
       Economic Botany 29:99–107.
DeBoer, W.
1975   The archaeological evidence for manioc cultivation: A
       cautionary note. *American Antiquity* 40:419–433.
Delbiet, D.M.
1857   Paysans en communauté et en polygamie de Bousrah. (Esky
       Cham) dans le pays Haouran (Syrie: Empire Ottoman). In L.F.
       Play, *Les Ouvriers d'Europe.* Tome 11: Les Essaims de la
       Mediterranée. Tours.
Denham, D., H. Clapperton, and W. Oudney
1826   *Narrative of travels and discoveries in northern and central
       Africa in the years 1822, 1823, and 1824.* London: John Murray.
Dennell, R.
1983   *European Economic Prehistory.* Academic Press.
Densmore, F.
1974   *How Indians use wild plants for food, medicine and crafts.* New
       York: Dover.
Dewald, C.L., B.L. Burson, J.M.J. de Wet, and J.R. Harlan
1987   Morphology, inheritance, and evolutionary significance of sex
       reversal in *Tripsacum dactyloides* (Poaceae). *American Journal
       of Botany* 74(4):1055–1059.
Diamond, G.
1977   The nature of so-called polished surfaces on stone artifacts. In
       Lithic use-wear analysis, edited by B. Hayden, 159–166. New
       York.
Diamond, G.P.
1974   *A study of microscopic wear patterns on the chipped stone artifacts
       from the Neolithic and Early Bronze Age levels of Knossos.* Ph.D.
       dissertation, Institute of Archaeology, University of London.
Diamond, J.
1997   Location, location, location: The first farmers. *Science*
       278:1243–1244.
Diekmann, J., and J. Papazian
1985   Mechanisation of production of faba beans, chickpeas, and
       lentils. In *Faba beans, kabuli chickpeas, and lentils in the 1980's*,
       edited by M.C. Saxena and S. Varma, 281–290. Aleppo:
       ICARDA.
Diffloth, P.
1929   *Agriculture générale. Labours et assolement.* Paris: Librairie J.B.
       Baillière and Fils.

Doebley, J.
1990 Molecular evidence and the evolution of maize. In *New perspective on the origin and evolution of New World domesticated plants*, edited by P.K. Bretting, vol. 44. Supplement to Economic Botany.

Dokuchaev, V.V.
1950 *K voprosu o pochvakh Bessarabii* (Question of Bessarabia soil). Kishinev .

Dole, G.
1960 Techniques of preparing manioc flour as a key to culture history in tropical America. In *Men and cultures: Selected papers of the Fifth International Congress of Anthropological and Ethnological Sciences*, edited by A. Wallace, 241–248. Philidelphia: University of Pennsylvania.

Dolukhanov, P.M.
1984 Razvitie prirodnoï sredy i khoziaïstvo pervobytnogo naseleniya Vostochnoï Evropy i Peredneï Azii v pozdnem pleïstotsene (Development of the natural environment and economy of the primitive population of Eastern Europe and Asia Minor in the Late Pleistocene). *Avtoref. dokt. dissertatsii*, Moscow. .

Duhamel du Monceau, H.L.
1765 *Mémoires d'agriculture adressés à M. Duhamel du Monceau par Plusieurs Agriculteurs.* Paris: H.L. Guérin and L.F. Delatour.

Duke, J.A.
1981 *Handbook of legumes of world economic importance.* New York: Plenum Press.

Dumitrescu, V., and T. Banaetanu
1965 A propos d'un soc de charrue primitive en bois de cerf découvert dans la station néolithique de Cascioarele. *Dacia. N. S.* IX: 59–67. Bucuresti.

Dunne, T.
1978 Rates of chemical denudation of silicate rocks in tropical catchments. *Nature* 274:244–246

Duveyrier, H.
1864 *Les Touareg du Nord.* Paris: Challamel Aine, Libraire-Editeur. Reprint Krauss.

Dzhaparidze, O. M.
1976 *K etnicheskoï istorii gruzinskikh plemen po dannym arkheologii* (Ethnic history of Georgian tribes, based on archaeological data). Tbilisi.

Dzhaparidze, O.M., and A.I. Dzhavakhishvili
1971 *Kul'tura drevnejshego zemledel'cheskogo naselenija na territorii Gruzii* (La culture de la plus ancienne population agricole de Géorgie). Tbilisi.

Dzhavakhishvili, A.I.
1973 *Stroitelnoe delo i arkhitektura poseleni Iuzhnogo Kavkaza V-III tysh. do n.e.* (Construction and architecture of South-Caucasian villages in the fifth to third millennium BC). Tbilisi.

Ebeling, W.
1986 *Handbook of Indian foods of arid America,* 971. Berkeley and Los Angeles: University of California Press.

Edwards, P., S. Bourke, S. Colledge, J. Head, and P. Macumber
1988 Late Pleistocene prehistory in the Wadi al Hammeh, Jordan Valley. In *The prehistory of Jordan*, edited by A. Garrard, and H. Gebel. BAR International Series 396:525–565. Oxford: British Archaeological Reports.

El Matt, S.
1979 Food legumes in Syria. In *Food legume improvement and development,* edited by G.C. Hawtin and G.C. Chancellor, 85–87. Ottawa: ICARDA and IDRC.

Elllot, W.A., and G.J. Perlinger
1977 Inheritance of shattering in wild rice. *Crop Science* 17: 851–853.

Engelbrecht, T.H.
1917 Über die Entstehung einiger feldmassig angebauter Kulturpflanzen. *Geographischer Zeitschrift* 22:328–343.

Erroux, J.
1979 L'origine des blés. Historique des théories. *Bull. Soc. Bota. du Centre-Ouest* 10:45–70.

Erskine, W.
1985 Perspectives in lentil breeding. In *Faba beans, kabuli chickpeas, and lentils in the 1980's,* edited by M.C. Saxena and S. Varma, 91–100. Aleppo: ICARDA.

Eser, D.
1979 Grain legume production in Turkey. In *Food legume improvement and development,* edited by G.R. Hawtin and G.C. Chancellor, 71–74. Ottawa: ICARDA and IDRC.

Evans, J.
1897 *The ancient stone implements, weapons and ornaments of Great Britain.* London: Longmers, Green and Co.
1968 The Palace of Knossos. *Annual of the British School at Athens* 63:241–264.

Evans, L.T.
1976 Physiological adaptation to performance as crop plants. *Philosophical Transactions of the Royal Society London* B 275:71–83.

Evenari, M., D. Koller, and Y. Gutterman
1966 Effects of the environment of the mother plant on germination by control of seed-coat permeability to water in *Ononis sicula* Guss. *Australian Journal of Biological Science* 19:1007–1016.

FAO
1985 *Production Yearbook.* Rome: FAO.

Farabee, W.C.
1924 The central Caribs. *University Museum, University of Pennsylvania, Anthropological Publication* 10. Philidelphia: U. of Pennsylvania Museum.

Fédoroff, N.
1987 Sensibilité à l'agriculture intensive des principaux types de sols de l'Europe du nord-ouest. *Actes du Symposium "Fondements scientifiques pour la protection des sols dans la communauté européenne" (Berlin, 6–8 octobre 1986)*, 65–85. Barth et l'Hermile. London and New York: Elsevier Applied Science.

Feldman, M., and E. Sears
1981 Les ressources génétiques naturelles du blé. *Pour la Science* 41:79–89.

Féret, E.
1878 *Statistique générale (...) de la Gironde.* Bordeaux: Féret and Fils.

Firmin, G.
1986 Archéobotanique et archéologie expérimentale au Néolithique. In *Le Néolithique de la France,* edited by J.P. Demoule and J. Guilaine, 53–70.

Flannery, K.V.
1969 Origins and ecological effects of early domestication in Iran and the Near East. In *The domestication and exploitation of plants and animals*, edited by P.J. Ucko and G.W. Dimbleby, 73–100. London: Duckworth.

Follieri, M.
1987 L'agriculture des plus anciennes communautés rurales en Italie. In *Les premières communautés paysannes en Méditerranée occidentale,* edited by J. Guilaine, J. Courtin, J.L. Roudil, and J.L. Vernet, 243–247. Actes du colloque de Montpellier, April 1983. Paris: CNRS.

Fontenay, L. de, s.d.
(1870) *Voyage agricole en Russie.* Paris: A. Goin.

Fotiadis, M.
1985 Economy, ecology, and settlement among subsistence farmers in the Serres Basin, Northeastern Greece, 5000–1000 BC. Ph.D. dissertation, Indiana University.

Fox, W.A.
1985 Dhoukani flake production in Cyprus. *Lithic Technology* 14:62–67.

Foxhall, L.
1982 Experiments in the processing of wheat and barley. In *The role of grain as a staple food in classical antiquity*, edited by L. Foxhall and H.A. Forbes. *Chiron* 12:41–90.

Frank, R.
1964 Dispersal units and rachis breaking in the genera A*egilops, Triticum* and *Hordeum. Teva Wa'arez* 7:2–5. In Hebrew.

Frank, T.
1985 Eine experimentelle Getreideernte mit rekonstruierten bandkeramischen Kompositgeräten. *Arch. Inf.* 8(1):18–21.

Frankel, O.H., and M. Roskams
1975 Stability of floral differentiation in *Triticum*. Procedings of the Royal Society of London B 188:139–162.

Frankel, O.H., Shineberg, and A. Munday
1969 The genetic basis of an invariant character in wheat. *Heredity* 24:571–591.

Fritz, G.J.
1986 Starchy grain crops in the eastern US: Evidence from the desiccated Ozark plant remains. Paper presented at 51st Annual Meeting of the Society for American Archaeology, New Orleans.

Fuji, S.
1986 Criteria for the identification of threshing sledge blade. *Bulletin of the Okayama Orient Museum* 5:1–34.

Fullagar, R.
1988 Microscopic study of artifacts from northern Australia. Report for Dr. B. Meehan, Anthropology Division, Australian Museum, Sydney.

Fullagar, R., and J. Field
1997 Pleistocene seed-grinding implements from the Australian arid zone. *Antiquity* 71:300–307.

Gaerte, W.
1929 *Urgeschichte ostpreussns*. Sig. 34. Konigsberg.

Gall, W.
1975 Rösten und Darren in urgeschichtlicher Zeit. *Alt-Thüringen* 13:196–204.

Garfinkel, Y.
1985 Preliminary report on the excavations of the Neolithic layers at Yiftahel, Area C. *Mitekufat Haeven* 18:45–51.
N.D. Personal communication.

Garfinkel Y., M.E. Kislev, and D. Zohary
1988 Lentil in the pre-pottery Neolithic B Yiftah'el: Additional evidence of its early domestication. *Israel Journal of Botany* 37:49–51.

Garrod, D.
1957 The Natufian culture: The life and economy of a Mesolithic people in the Near East. *Proceedings of the British Academy* 43:211–227.

Garrod, D.A.E., and D.M. Bate
1937 *The Stone Age of Mount Carmel*. Vol. 1. Oxford.

Gast, M.
1968 *Alimentation des populations de l'Ahaggar, etude ethnographique*. Mémoires du Centre de Recherches Anthropologiques. Prehistoires et EthnographIques (Conseil de la Recherche scientiflque en Algérie) VIII, 457. Algier: Publs. CRAPE.

Gentry, H.S.
1942 *Rio Mayo plants: A study of the flora and vegetation of the valley of the Rio Mayo, Sonora*. Publication no. 527. Washington, DC: Carnegie Institution Publications.

Gepts, P., and D.G. Debouck
1991 Origin domestication and evolution of the common bean (*Phaseolus vulgaris* L.). In *Common beans: Research for crop improvement*, edited by A. van Schoonhoven and O. Voysest, 7–53. Wallingford: CAB International.

Ghirshman, R.
1939 *Fouilles de Sialk près de Kashan*. Paris. 1.

Giffen, A.E. van
1944 Grafheuvels te Zwaagdijk, gem. *Westfrieslands Oud en Nieuw* 17:121–143. Wervershoof (N.H.).
1953 Onderzoek van drie bronstijdgrafheuvels bij Grootebroek, gem. Grootebroek. *Westfrieslands Oud en Nieuw* 20:3–32.

Gill, N.T., and K.C. Vear
1980 Monocotyledonous crops. *Agricultural Botany*. Vol. 2. London: Duckworth.

Glob, P.V.
1951 Ard og Plov, Arhus Universistets-forlaget, Jysk Arkaeolegisk, Selskabs Skrifter, l (Arhus).

Gokhale, V.G., and V.S. Habbu
1927 *Trees and shrubs for producing green manure in the Konan and North Kanara*. Bulletin no. 141. Bombay: Department of Agriculture.

Goldberg, P., and A.M. Rosen
1987 Early Holocene palaeoenvironments of Israel. In *Shiqmim I, studies concerning Chalcolithic societies in the northern Negev, Desert, Israel (1982-1984)*, edited by T.E. Levy, 22–33. Oxford: British Archaeological Reports.

Golichaishvili, L.K.
1979 Kizucheniou golotsenovykh landshaftov territorii Kvemo-Kartli (Study of the Holocene landscapes of Kvemo-Kartli). *Materialy po arkheologii Gruzii i Kavkaza, 7* .

Golson, J.
1971 Australian aboriginal food plants: Some ecological and culture-historical implications. In *Aboriginal Man and Environment in Australia*, edited by D.J. Mulvaney and J. Golson, 196–238. Canberra: Australian National University Press.

Gordon-Childe, E.V.
1964 *La naissance de la civilisation*. Paris: Gonthier.

Gott, B.
1982 The ecology of root use by Aborigines in southeastern Australia. *Archaeology in Oceania* 17:59–67.

Greig, J.
1981 The investigation of a medieval barrel latrine from Worcester. *Journal of Archaeological Science* 8: 265–282.
1982 The interpretation of pollen spectra from urban archaeological deposits. In *Environmental archaeology in the urban context*, edited by R.A. Hall and H.K. Kenward, 47–65, fig. Research Report no. 43. London: Council for British Archaeology.

Guest, E.R.
1930 Notes on miscellaneous crops in Iraq. Report quoted, in *Flora of Iraq*, edited by C.C. Townsend and E.R. Guest, vol. 3. Baghdad: Ministry of Agriculture and Agrarian Reform, 1974.

Guilaine et al.
1974 *La Balma de Montbolo et le Néolithique de l'Occident méditerranéen*. Toulouse: Institut pyrénéen d'études anthropologiques.

Guilaine, J.
1976 *Premiers bergers et paysans de l'Occident méditerranéen*. Paris: Mouton.

1985 Les outils des paysans. In *Le grand atlas de l'archéologie.* Encyclopaedia Universalis, 44–45. Paris.

1986 Le Néolithique ancien en Languedoc et Catalogne. In *Le Néolithique de la France, hommage à G. Bailloud,* edited by J.P. Demoule and J. Guilaine, 71–82. Paris: Picard.

Gunther, E.

1927 Klallam ethnography. *University of Washington Publications in Anthropology* 1(5):171–314.

Gurova, Maria

1997-8 Personal communications

Guyan, W.U.

1966 Zur Herstellung und Funktion einiger jungsteinzeitlicher Holzgeräte von Thayngen-Weier. *Helvetia Antiqua* (Festschrift für Emil Vogt): 21–32.

1976 Jungsteinzeitliche Urwald-Wirtschaft am Einzelbeispiel von Thayngen "Weier." *Jahrbuch Schweiz. Ges. Urgesch* 59:93–117.

Hadas,A.

1976 Water uptake and germination of leguminous seeds under changing external water potential in osmotic solutions. *Journal of Experimental Botany* 27:480–489.

Haddad, N.I., A.B. Salkini, P. Jagatheeswaran, and B.A. Snobar

1988 Methods of harvesting pulse crops. In *World crops: Cool season food legumes,* edited by R.J. Summerfield, 342–350. London: Collins.

Haegerlin, H., and E. Gunther

1930 Indians of Puget Sound. *University of Washington Publications In Anthropology* 4(1):1–84.

Halbaek, H.

1959 Die Palaeoethnobotanik des Nahen Ostensund Europas. *Opuscula Ethnologica Memoriae Ludovici Biro Sacra*: 265–289. Budapest.

Hallam, S.

1986 Yams, alluvium and "villages" on the west coastal plains. In *Archaeology at ANZAAS, Canberra,* edited by G.K. Ward, 116-132. Canberra: Canberra Archaeological Society.

Hammer, K.

1984 Das Domestikationssyndrom. *Die Kulturpflanze* 32:11–34.

Hammer, K., E. Skolimowska, and H. Knüpffer

1987 Vorarbeiten zur monografischen Darstellung von Wildpflanzensortimenten: *Secale* L. *Die Kulturpflanze* 35:135–177.

Hammond, N., D. Pring, R. Wilk, S. Donaghey, F. Saul, E. Wing, A. Miller, and L.Feldman

1979 The earliest lowland Maya: Definition of the Swasey phase. *American Antiquity* 44:92–110.

Hansen, J.

1978 The earliest seed remains from Greece: Palaeolithic through Neolithic at Franchthi Cave. *Bericht der Deutsche Botanisches Gesellschaft* 9:39–46.

1980 The Palaeoethnobotany of Franchthi Cave, Greece. Ph.D. dissertation, University of Minnesota.

Hansen, J., and J.M. Renfrew

1978 Palaeolithic-Neolithic seed remains at Franchthi Cave, Greece. *Nature* 271:349–352.

Hargreaves, M.W.M.

1977 The dry-farming movement in retrospect. In Les hommes et leurs sols, numéro spécial du *Journal d'Agriculture traditionnelle et de Botanique appliquée* 24(2/3):213–232.

Harlan, J.R.

1967 A wild wheat harvest in Turkey. *Archaeology* 20:197– 201.

1968 On the origin of barley. In *Barley: Origin, botany, culture, winterhardiness, genetics, utilization,* 9–31. USDA Handbook no. 338.

1975 *Crops and man.* Madison: American Society of Agronomy.

1977 Plant and animal distribution in relation to domestication. In *The early history of agriculture,* edited by H. Hutchinson, J.G.G. Clark, E.M. Jope and R. Riley, 13–26. Oxford: Oxford University Press.

1982 Human interference with grass systematics. In *Grasses and grasslands: Systematics and ecology,* edited by J.R. Estes, R.J. Tyrl and J.N. Brunken, 37–50. Oklahoma: University Press.

1986 Plant domestication: Diffuse origins and diffusions. In *The origin and domestication of cultivated plants,* edited by C. Barigozzi, 21–34. Amsterdam: Elsevier.

1989 Wild-grass seed harvesting in the Sahara and Sub-Sahara of Africa. In *Foraging and farming: The evolution of plant exploitation,* edited by D.R. Harris and G.C. Hillman. London: Unwin and Hyman.

1995 *The living fields. Our agricultural heritage.* Cambridge: Cambridge University Press

Harlan, J.R., R.M. Ahring, and W.R. Kneebone

1956 *Grass seed production under irrigation in Oklahoma.* Bulletin no. B-481. Stillwater: Oklahoma Agricultural Experimental Station.

Harlan, J.R., and J.M.J. de Wet

1974 Sympatric evolution in *Sorghum. Genetics* 78:473–474.

Harlan, J.R., J.M.J. de Wet, and E.G. Price

1973 Comparative evolution in cereals. *Evolution* 27:311–325.

Harlan, J.R., and D. Zohary

1966 The distribution of wild wheats and barley in relation to early domestication. *Science* 153:1074–1080.

Harris, D.

1977 Subsistence strategies across Torres Strait. In *Sunda and Sabul: Prehistoric studies in southeast Asia, Melanesia, and Australia,* edited by J. Allen, J. Golson, and R. Jones, 421–463. London: Academic Press.

Harris, D., S. Limbri

1992 Sovremennoe prirodnoe okruzhenie Dzheituna (Modern natural environment of Djeitun). *Novye issledovaniya na poselenii Dzheitun*:7–13 (Ed. Masson V. M.), Ashkhabad.

Harris, D.R.

1976 Discussion following paper by Pickersgill and Heizer (q.v.). *Philosophical Transactions of the Royal Society* B 275:68–69.

1977 Alternative pathways towards agriculture. In *Origins of agriculture,* edited by C.A. Reed, 197–243. The Hague: Mouton.

1984 Ethnohistorical evidence for the exploitation of wild grasses and forbs: Its scope and archaeological implications. In *Plants and ancient man: Studies in palaeoethnobotany,* edited by W. van Zeist and W.C. Casparie, 63–69. Rotterdam: Balkema.

1989 An evolutionary continuum of people-plant interaction. In *Foraging and farming: The evolution of plant exploitation,* edited by D.R.Harris and G.C.Hillman, 11–26. London: Unwin and Hyman.

1996 The origins and spread of agriculture and pastoralism in Eurasia: An overview. In *The origins and spread of agriculture and pastoralism in Eurasia,* edited by D. Harris, 552–574. London: University College.

Harris, H.

1979 Some aspects of the agroclimatology of West Asia and North Africa. In *Food legume improvement and development,* edited by G.C. Hawtin and G.J. Chancellor, 7–14. Ottawa: ICARDA and IDRC.

Harris, H., and M. Pala

1987 Tillage and stubble management effect on soil conservation, crop establishment and yield, and economics of production. In *Farm resource management program,* 47–50. Aleppo: ICARDA.

Hassan, F.
1981   *Demographic archaeology.* New York: Academic Press.
Hather, J.
1994   The identification of charred root and tuber crops from
       archaeological sites in the Pacific. In *Tropical archaeobotany:
       Applications and new developments,* edited by J. Hather, 51–64.
       New York: Routledge.
Hawkes, J.G.
1969   The ecological background to plant domestication. In
       Domestication and exploitation of plants and animals, edited by
       P.J. Ucko and G.W. Dimbleby, 17–29. London: Duckworth.
1989a *The diversity of crop plants.* Cambridge: Harvard University
       Press.
1989b The domestication of roots and tubers in the American tropics.
       In *Foraging and farming: The evolution of plant exploitation,*
       edited by D.R.Harris and G.C.Hillman, 481–503. London:
       Unwin and Hyman.
Hawtin, G.C. and G.R. Potts
1988   International Development Research Center (IDRC) support
       for research on cool season food legume crops in Asia and
       North Africa. In *World crops: Cool season food legumes,* edited
       by R.J. Summerfield, 17–24. Dordrecht: Kluwer.
Hayden, B.
1990   Nimrods, piscator, pluckers and planters. *Journal of
       Anthropological Archaeology* 9:31–69.
1995   A new overview of domestication. In *Last hunters, first farmers,*
       edited by T.D. Price and A.B. Gebauer. Santa Fe, NM: SAR Press.
Hayward, D.M., and D.W. Parry
1973   Electron-probe microanalysis studies of silica distribution in
       barley (*Hordeum sativum* L.). *Annals of Botany* 37:579–591.
1980   Scanning electron microscopy of silica deposits in the culms,
       floral bracts and awns of barley (*Hordeum sativum* Jess.).
       Annals of Botany 46:541–548.
Head, L.
1987   The Holocene prehistory of a coastal wetland system: Discovery
       Bay, southeastern Australia. *Human Ecology* 15(4): 435–462.
Heim, J.
1970   *Les relations entre les spectres polliniques récents et la végétation
       actuelle en Europe occidentale.* Université de Louvain, Lab. de
       palynologie et de phytosociologie.
Heiser, C.B.
1965   Sunflowers, weeds, and cultivated plants. In *The genetics of
       colonizing species,* edited by H.G. Baker and G.L. Stebbins,
       391–401. New York: Academic Press.
1985   Some botanical considerations of the early domesticated plants
       north of Mexico. In *Prehistoric food production in North
       America,* edited by R.I. Ford, 57–72. Ann Arbor, Michigan:
       Museum of Anthropology, University of Michigan.
1988   Aspects of unconscious selection and the evolution of
       domesticated plants. *Euphytica* 37:77–81.
1989   Domestication of Cucurbitaceae: Cucurbita and Lagenaria. In
       Foraging and farming: The evolution of plant exploitation,
       edited by D.R.Harris and G.C. Hillman, 471–480. London:
       Unwin and Hyman.
Helbaek, H.
1953   Archaeology and agricultural botany. *Annual Report of the
       Institute of Archaeology, University of London* 9:44–59.
1959   Domestication of food plants in the Old World. *Science*
       130:365–372.
1960a The palaeoethnobotany of the Near East and Europe. Chapter
       VIII. In *Prehistoric investigations in Iraqi Kurdistan,* edited by R.J.
       Braidwood and B. Howe, 99–108. Chicago: University Press.
1960b Cereals and weed grasses in phase A. In *Excavations in the

       plain of Antioch I,* edited by R.J. Braidwood and L.J.
       Braidwood, 540–543. Chicago: University of Chicago Press.
1961   Late Bronze Age and Byzantine crops at Beycesultan in
       Anatolia. *Anatolian Studies* 11:77–97.
1963   Palaeothnobotany. In *Science in Archaeology,* edited by D. R.
       Brothwell and E. Higgs, 177–185. London: Thames and
       Hudson.
1964   First impressions of the Atal Hüyük plant husbandry.
       Anatolian Studies 14:121–123.
1966a Pre-Pottery Neolithic farming at Beidha. Appendix to *Five
       seasons at the Pre-Pottery Neolithic Village of Beidha in Jordan,*
       D. Kirkbride. *Palestine Exploration Quaterly* 1:61–66.
1966b Commentary on the phylogenesis of *Triticum* and *Hordeum.*
       Economic Botany 20:350–360.
1969   Plant collecting, dry-farming, and irrigation agriculture in
       prehistoric Deh Luran. In *Prehistory and human ecology of the
       Deh Luran Plain: An early village sequence from Khuzistan,*
       edited by F. Hole, K.V. Flannery and J.A. Neely, 383–426. Ann
       Arbor, Michigan: Memoirs of the Museum of Anthropology of
       the University of Michigan.
1970   The plant husbandry of Hacilar. In *Excavations at Hacilar,*
       edited by J. Mellaart, vol. 1,189–244. Edinburgh: Edinburgh
       University Press.
Helmer, D.
1978   Les rongeurs de Tell Mureybet. Étude préliminaire. In *Tell
       Mureybet: Étude archéozoologique et problèmes d'écologie
       humaine,* edited by P. Ducos, 137–142. Paris: CNRS.
Helmer, D., V. Roitel, M. Sana, and G. Willcox
1998   Interprétations environnementales des données
       archéozoologiques et archéobotaniques en Syrie du nord de
       16000 BP à 7000 BP, et les débuts de la domestication des
       plantes et des animaux. In *Natural space, inhabited space in
       Northern Syria (10th–2nd millennium B.C.),* edited by M.
       Fortin and O. Aurenche. Canadian Society for Mesopotamian
       Studies. *Quebec Bulletin* 33:9–34.
Hénin, S. et al.
1969   *Le profil cultural.* Paris: Masson and Cie.
Henry, D.O., and A. Leroi-Gourhan
1976   The excavation of Hayonim Terrace: An interim report. *Journal
       of Field Archaeology* 3:391–406.
Henry, D.O., A. Leroi-Gourhan, and S. Davis
1981   The excavation of Hayonim Terrace: An examination of the
       terminal Pleistocene climatic and adaptive changes. *Journal of
       Archaeological Sciences* 8:33–58.
Heuglin, M.Th.
1869   *Reise in das Gebiet des weissen Nil und seiner westlichen
       Zuflüsse in den Jahren 1862–1864,* 382. Leipzig: C.F.
       Winter'sche Verlagshandlung.
Heun, M., R. Schäfer-Pregl, D. Klawan, R. Castagna, M. Accerbi, B.
       Borghi, and F. Salamini
1997   Einkorn wheat domestication identified by DNA
       fingerprinting. *Science* 14; 278: 1312–1314.
Hillman, G.C.
1972   Plant remains. In Excavations at Can Hasan III 1969–1970,
       D.H. French et al.. In *Papers in economic prehistory,* edited by
       E.S. Higgs, 181–190. Cambridge: Cambridge University Press.
1973a Crop husbandry and food production: Modern basis for the
       interpretation of plant remains. *Anatolian Studies* 23:241–244.
1973b Agricultural productivity and past population potential at
       Asvan. *Anatolian Studies* 23:225–240.
1973c Agricultural resources and settlement in the Asvan region.
       Anatolian Studies 23:217–224.
1975   The plant remains from Tell Abu Hureyra. In *The excavation of

Tell Abu Hureyra in Syria: A preliminary report, edited by A.M.T. Moore, G.C. Hillman and A.J. Legge. *Proceedings of the Prehistoric Society* 41:70–73.

1978 On the origins of domestic rye-*Secale cereal L.*: Finds from Aceramic Can Hasan III in Turkey. *Anatolian Studies* 28:157–174.

1981 Reconstructing crop husbandry practices from charred remains of crops. In *Farming practice in British prehistory*, edited by R. Mercer, 123–162. Edinburgh: Edinburgh University Press.

1983 Interpretation of archaeological plant remains: The application of ethnographic models from Turkey. In *Plants and Ancient Man. Studies in palaeoethnobotany (Groningen Symposium)*, edited by W. van Zeist and W.A. Casparie, 1–41. Rotterdam.

1984a Interpretation of archaeological plant eemains: The application of ethnographic models from Turkey. In *Plants and Ancient Man,* edited by W. van Zeist and W.A. Casparie, 1–42. Rotterdam: Balkema.

1984b Traditional husbandry and processing of archaic cereals in recent times: The operations, products and equipment which might feature in Sumerian texts. Part I, The glume wheats. *Bulletin on Sumerian Agriculture I*:114–152. Cambridge .

1985 Traditional husbandry and processing of archaic cereals in recent times. Part II, The free-threshing cereals. *Bulletin on Sumerian Agriculture* 2:1–31. Cambridge.

1986 The initial adoption of cereal cultivation in the northern Fertile Crescent: A local model. Paper presented at Conference of Association of Environmental Archaeology, Cardiff, November 1986.

1989a Late Palaeolithic plant foods from Wadi Kubbaniya in Upper Egypt: Dietary diversity, infant weaning, and seasonality in a riverine environment. In *Foraging and farming: Evolution of plant exploitation,* D.R. Harris and G.C. Hillman, 207–239. London: Unwin and Hyman.

1989b The transition to cereal cultivation in the Near Eastern steppe: A new model. In *The beginnings of agriculture*, edited by A. Mills and D. Williams. BAR International Series. Oxford: British Archaeological Reports.

1990 Personal communications

1996 Late Pleistocene changes in wild plant-foods available to hunter-gatherers of the northern Fertile Crescent: Possible preludes to cereal cultivation. In *The origins and spread of agriculture and pastoralism in Eurasia,* edited by D. Harris, 159–203. London: University College.

N.D. Crop husbandry on an alluvial fan in the Konya Basin during the Aceramic Neolithic: The charred remains from Can Hasan III in central Anatolia.

Hillman, G.C., S.M. Colledge, and D.R. Harris

1989 Plant food economy during the Epipalaeolithic period at Tell Abu Hureyra, Syria: Dietary diversity, seasonality and modes of exploitation. In *Foraging and farming: Evolution of plant exploitation*, edited by D.R. Harris and G.C. Hillman, 240–268. London: Unwin and Hyman.

Hillman, G.C., and M.S. Davies

1990a Measured domestication rates in wild wheats and barley under primitive cultivation, and their archaeological implications. *Journal of World Prehistory* 4, 2:157–219.

1990b Domestication rates in populations of wild einkorn wheat under primitive systems of cultivation. *Botanical Journal of the Linnaean Society* 39:39–78. London.

Hillman, G.C., E. Madeyska, and J.G. Hather

1989 Wild plant foods and diet at Late Palaeolithic Wadi Kubbaniya: evidence from the charred remains. In *The Prehistory of Wadi Kubbaniya*: Palaeoeconomy, environment and stratigraphy, compiled by F. Wendorf and R. Schild, and edited by A. Close. Vol. 2, 162–242; vol. 3:830–854). Dallas: Southern Methodist University Press.

Hillman, G.C., and F.McLaren

N.D. Early finds of grains of domestic-type rye from Abu Hureyra in Syria.

Hillman, G.C., G.V. Robins, C.E.R. Jones, and C.S. Gutteridge

N.D. Testing the limits of the taxonomic resolution of pyrolysis mass spectrometry in ancient wheat grain: Preliminary results.

Hilu, K.W., and J.M.J. de Wet

1976 Domestication of *Eleusine coracana* (L.) Gaertner. *Economic Botany* 30:199–208.

Hinz, H.

1952 Über Erntebergung in der Urzeit. *Die Heimat* 232–234.

1954 Zur Entwicklung des Darrenwesens. *Zeitschrift für Volkskunde* 51:88–105.

HNAI (Handbook of North American Indians)

1986 *Great Basin.* Vol. 11. Washington, DC: Smithsonian Institution.

Ho, P.T.

1969 The loess and the origin of Chinese agriculture. *American Historical Review* 75:1–36.

Hodson, M.J., and A.G. Sangster

1988 Silica deposition in the inflorescence bracts of wheat (*Triticum aestivum*). I. Scanning electron microscopy and light microscopy. *Canadian Journal of Botany* 66:829–838.

Hoffner, H.A. Jr.

1974 *Alimenta Hethaeorum: Food production in Asia Minor.* New Haven: American Oriental Society,

Hopf, M.

1962 Bericht über die Untersuchung von Samen und Holzkohlenresten von der Argissa Magoula aus den Präkeramischen bis Mittel Bronzeitlichen Schichten. In *Die Deutschen Ausgrabungen auf der Argissa Maghoula in Thessalien I. Das Präkeramische Neolithicum sowie die Tier- und pflanzenreste*, edited by V. Milojcic, J. Boessneck, and M. Hopf, 101–102. Bonn.

1966 *Triticum monococcum* L. y *Triticum dicoccum* Schübl, en el Neolitico antigo espanol. *Archivo de Prehistoria Levantina* 11:53–81.

1983 Jericho plant remains. In *Excavations at Jericho,* edited by K.M. Keynion and T.A. Holland, vol. 5, 576–621. London: British School of Archaeology in Jerusalem.

Hopf, M., and O. Bar-Yosef

1987 Plant remains from Hayonim Cave, Western Galilee. *Paléorient* 13(1):117–120.

Hornell, J.

1930 The Cypriote threshing sledge. *Man XXX*:135–139.

Hurcombe, L

1986 Paper presented at Microwear Symposium, Tübingen.

Hutton, J.T., and K. Norrish

1974 Silicon content of wheat husks in relation to water transpired. *Australian Journal of Agricultural Research* 25:203–212.

ICARDA (International Center for Agricultural Research in Dry Areas)

1980 Post-harvest processing of winter crops in NW Syria. Aleppo.

IJzereef, G.F.

1981 Bronze Age animal bones from Bovenkarspel. The excavation at Het Valkje. *Nederlandse Oudheden* 10.

Iler, R.K.

1955 *The colloid chemistry of silica and silicates.* Ithaca, NY: Cornell University Press.

Imaizumi, K., and S. Yoshida

1958 Edaphological studies on silicon-supplying power of paddy fields. *Bulletin of the National Institute of Agricultural Science (Japan)* B 8:261–304.

Irvine, F.R.
1957   Wild and emergency foods of Australian and Tasmanian aborigines. *Oceania* 28:113–142.

Islammagomedov, A.I.
1967   *Poselenia. Zhilishcha. Materialnaiya kultura avartsev* (Villages. Houses. Material culture of Avares). Makhachkala.

Islamov, O.I.
1975   *Peschera Machaj.* Tashkent.
1980   *Obishirskaya kultura,* Tachkent.

Ismail, A.M.A.
1988   The ecological and agronomic role of seed polymorphism in Simmondsia chinensis. *Journal of Arid Environments* 14:35–42.

Iversen, J.
1973   The development of Danmark's nature since the Last Glacial. *Geology of Denmark III* (Danmarks Geologiske Undersogelse V, Raekke 7^e), 126 p.

Jacomet, S., and H. Schlichtherle
1984   Der kleine Pfahlbauweizen Oswald Herr's - Neue Untersuchungen zur Morphologie neolithischer Nacktweizen-Ahren. In *Plants and Ancient Man*, edited by W. van Zeist and W.A. Casparie, 153–176. Rotterdam/Boston: Balkema.

Jardin, C.
1967   *List of foods used in Africa,* 320. Rome: FAO.

Jarman, H.N.
1972   The origins of wheat and barley cultivation. In *Papers in economic prehistory*, edited by E.S. Higgs, 15–26. Cambridge: Cambridge University Press.

Johns, T.
1989   A chemical ecological model of root and tuber domestication in the Andes. In *Foraging and farming: The evolution of plant exploitation*, edited by D.R. Harris and G.C. Hillman, 504–519. London: Unwin and Hyman.

Johnson, B.L., and H.S. Dhaliwal
1976   Reproductive isolation of *Triticum boeoticum* and *Triticum urartu* and the origins of the tetraploid wheats. *American Journal of Botany* 63:1088–1094.

Jones, G.E.M.
1983   *The Use of Ethnographic and Ecological Models In the Interpretation of Archaeological Plant Remains.* Ph.D. dissertation, University of Cambridge.
1984   Interpretation of archaeological plant remains: Ethnographic models from Greece. In *Plants and Ancient Man*, edited by W. van Zeist and W.A. Casparie, 43–61. Rotterdam: Balkema.
1992   Ancient and modern cultivation of *Lathyrus ochrus* (L.) DC in the Greek Islands. *The Annual of the British School of Archaeology in Athens* 87:211–217.

Jones, L.H.P., and A.A. Milne
1963   Studies of silica in the oat plant: I. Chemical and physical properties of the silica. *Plant and Soil* 28:207–20.

Jones, L.H.P., and K.A. Handreck
1965   Studies of silica in the oat plant: III. Uptake of silica from soils by the plant. *Plant and Soil* 32:79–96.

Jones, R.
1969   Fire-stick farming. *Australian Natural History* 16:224–228.
1980   Hunters in the Australian savanna. In *Human ecology in savanna environments,* edited by D. Harris, 107–146. London: Academic Press.

Jones, R., and B. Meehan
1977   Floating bark and hollow trunks. *Hemisphere* 21(4):16–21.

Jones, R., and N. White
1988   Point blank: Stone tool manufacture at the Ngilipitji Quarry, northeastern Arnhem Land, 1981. In *Archaeology with ethnography: An Australian perspective,* edited by B. Meehan and R. Jones, 51–87. Canberra: Department of Prehistory, Research School of Pacific Studies, Australian National University.

Jongerius, A.
1970   Some morphological aspects of regrouping phenomena in Dutch soils. *Geoderma* 4:311–331.

Jorgensen, J.
1980   *Western Indians.* San Francisco: W.H. Freeman.

Juan-Tresseras, J.
1997   Processado y preparacion de alimentos vegetales para consumo humano. Ph.D. dissertation, University of Barcelona, Spain.

Juel Jensen, H.
1986   Unretouched blades in the Late Mesolithic of Southern Scandinavia. A functional study. *Oxford Journal of Archaeology* 5(1):19–33.
1988a   Microdenticulates in the Danish Stone Age: A functional puzzle. In *Industries lithiques: Tracéologie et technologie,* edited by S. Beyries, 231–252. BAR International Series 411(1). Oxford: British Archaeological Reports.
1988b   Functional analysis of prehistoric flint tools by high-power microscopy: A review of West European research. *Journal of World Prehistory* 2(1):53–88.
1994   *Flint tools and plant working. Hidden traces of stone age technology.* Aarhus: Aarhus University Press.

Kalis, A.J.
1988   Zur Umwelt des frühneolithischen Menschen, ein Beitrag der Pollenanalyse. In *Der prähistorische Mensch und seine Umwelt* (Festschrift für U. Körber-Grohne), Forschungen u. Berichte zur Vor- und Frühgeschichte in Baden-Württemberg Bd. 31:125–137.

Kamminga, J.
1979   The nature of use-polish and abrasive smoothing on stone tools. In *Lithic use-wear analysis,* edited by B. Hayden, 143–158. New York: Academic Press.

Kardulius, P.N. and Yerkes, R.W.
1996   Microwear and metric analysis of threshing sledge flints from Greece and Cyprus. *Journal of Archaeological Sciences* 23:657–666.

Keeley, L.H.
1980   *Experimental determinations of stone tool uses: A microwear analysis.* Chicago: University of Chicago.
1988   Hunter-gatherer economic complexity and "population pressure": A cross-cultural analysis. *Journal of Anthropological Archaeology* 7.
1995   Protoagricultural practices among hunter-gatherers. In *Last hunters, first farmers,* edited by T.D. Price and A.B. Gebauer. Santa Fe, NM: SAR Press.

Keeley, L.H., and M.H. Newcomer
1977   Microwear analysis of experimental flint tools: A test case. *Journal of Archaeological Science* 4:29–62.

Keeley, L.H., and N. Toth
1981   Microwear polishes on early stone tools from Koobi-Fora, Kenya. *Nature* 293:464–465.

Kelly, R.
1985   Hunter-gatherer mobility strategies. *Journal of Anthropological Research* 39:277–306.

Kempe S., and E.T. Degens
1978   Lake Van varve record: The last 10,420 years. In *The Geology of*

Lake Van, edited by E.T. Degens and F. Kurtman, vol. 169, 56–
  65. Ankara Report: MTA Press.

Kenny, J.
1912   *Intensive farming in India.* Madras: Higginbotham and Co and
        London: Luzac and Co.

Kenyon, K.
1981   *Excavations at Jericho.* British School of Archaeology in
        Jerusalem.

Khayrallah, W.A.
1981   The Mechanisation of lentil harvesting. In *Lentils,* edited by C.
        Webb and G. Hawtin, 131–141. Slough: ICARDA and CAB.

Kiguradze, T.
1976   *Periodizatsiya rannezemledeltsheskoï kultury Vostochnogo
        Zakavkazya* (Periodisation of the pre-agricultural culture of
        Eastern Transcaucasia). Tbilisi

Kishk, F.
1979   The role of the IDRC in food legume improvement research. In
        Food legume improvement and development, edited by G.C.
        Hawtin and G.J. Chancellor, 192–193. Ottawa: ICARDA and
        IDRC.

Kislev, M. E.
1980a   Contenu d'un silo à blé de l'époque du fer ancien. In *Tell
        Keisan,* edited by J. Briend and J.B. Humbert, 361–378. With
        summary in English. Fribourg: Éditions Universitaires.
1980b   *Triticum parvicoccum* sp. nov., the oldest naked wheat. *Israel
        Journal of Botany* 28:95–107.
1984a   Botanical evidence for ancient naked wheats in the Near
        East. In *Plants and Ancient Man,* edited by W. van Zeist and
        W.A. Casparie, 141–152. Balkema, Rotterdam/Boston.
1984b   Emergence of wheat agriculture. *Paleorient* 10 (2):61–70.
1985   Early Neolithic horsebean from Yiftah'el, Israel. *Science*
        228:319–320.
1986   Archaeobotanical findings on the origins of *Lathyrus sativus*
        and *L. cicera.* In *Lathyrus and lathyrism,* edited by A.K. Kaul
        and D. Combes, 46–51. New York: Third World Medical
        Research Foundation.
1987   Could humans have selected better fruit trees before
        domestication of cereals? *XIV International Botanical Congress,
        Berlin* (Abstracts): 289.
1988a   Nahal Hemar cave, desiccated plant remains: An interim
        report. *Atiqot* 18:76–81.
1989a   Origin and cultivation of *Lathyrus sativus* and *L. cicera*
        (Fabaceae). *Economic Botany* 43:262–270.
1989b   Pre-domesticated cereals in the pre-pottery Neolithic A period.
        In *Man and culture in change,* edited by I. Hershkovitz, 147–
        151. British Archaeological Reports International Series 508(i).
        Oxford: British Archaeological Reports.
1997   Early agriculture and palaeoecology of Netiv Hagdud. In *An
        early Neolithic village in the Jordan Valley, part 1: The
        Archaeology of Netiv Hagdud,* edited by O. Bar-Yosef and A.
        Gopher, 201–235. Cambridge, MA: Peabody Museum of
        Archaeology and Ethnology, Harvard University.

Kislev, M.E., and O. Bar–Yosef
1988   The legumes: The earliest domesticated plants in the Near
        East? *Current Anthropology* 29:175–179.

Kislev, M.E., O. Bar Yosef, and A. Gopher
1986   Early Neolithic domesticated and wild barley from the Netiv
        Hagdud region in the Jordan Valley. *Israel Journal of Botany*
        35:197–201.

Klaey, E.J.
1967-68 Alaca Höyük: Etnographische Skizzen eines anatolischen
        Dorfes Struktur des Landwirtshaft und die materielle Kultur.
        Jahrbuch des bernischen historischen Museums in Bern, 47/

48:233–375.

Klingen, I.I.
1960   *Sredi patriarkhov zemeledelia narodov Blizhnego i Dalnego
        Vostoka.* Moscow.

Knörzer, K.H.
1967   Untesuchungen subfossiler pflanzlicher Grossreste im
        Rheinland. *Archaeo-Physika* 2.
1971   Urgeschichtliche Unkräuter im Rheinland, ein Beitrag zur
        Entstehung der Segetalgesellschaften. *Vegetatio* 23:89–111.
1974   Bandkeramisch Pflanzenfunde von Bedburg-Garsdorff Kreis
        Bergheim Erfr. *Rheinische Ausgrabungen* 15:173–192.
1979   Über den Wandel der angebauten Körnerfrüchte und ihrer
        Unkrautvegetation auf einer niederrheinischen Lößfläche seit
        dem Frühneolithikum. *Archaeo-Physika* 8, (Festschrift für M.
        Hopf), 147–163.
1986   Vom neolithischen Ackerbau im Rheinland. *Archäologie in
        Deutschland* 1:32–37.

Körber-Grohne, U.
1957   Die Bedeutung des Phasenkontrastverfahrens für die
        Pollenanalyse, dargelegt am Beispiel der Gramineenpollen vom
        Getreidetyp. *Photographie und Forschung* 7:237–248.
1981   Distinguishing prehistoric grains of *Triticum* and *Secale* on the
        basis of their surface patterns using scanning electron
        microscopy. *Journal of Archaeological Science* 8:197–204.
1987   *Nutzpflanzen in Deutschland. Kulturgeschichte und Biologie.*
        Stuttgart.

Körnicke, F.
1885   *Die Arten und Varietaten des Getreides. Hundbuch des
        Getreidebaues.* Vol. 1. Berlin: Paul Parey.

Korobkova, G.F.
1969   *Orudija truda i khozjajstvo neoliticheskikh plemen Srednej Azii.*
        MIA no. 158.
1972a   *Trasologicheskoe issledovanie kamennogo inventarja
        Samarkandskoj stojanki.* MIA no. 185:157–168.
1972b   Lokalnye razlichia v ekonomike rannikh zemledelchesko-
        skotovodcheskikh obshchestv (k postanovke problemy) (Local
        differences in the economy of early agriculturo-pastoral
        societies [formulation of the problem]). *Uspekhi
        Sredneaziatskoï arkheologii,* 1:16–22. Leningrad.
1974   Trudnyj khleb pervykh gorozhdan. *Pamjatniki Turkmenistana*
        2(18):17–19. Ashkhabad.
1975   Tripol'skie motygi i problema tripol'skogo zemledelija (Hoes
        from Tripoli and the question of agriculture).*150 let
        Odesskomu arkheologicheskomu muzeyu AN USSR.* Kiev.
1978   The most ancient harvesting implements and their
        productivity: An experimental-traceological study. (In
        Russian). *Sovyetskaya Archeologia* 4:37–53.
1979a   Drevnejshie zemlekopnye orudija iz Arukhlo I. *Materialy po
        arkheologii i Gruzii i Kavkaza,* VII:97–100. Tbilisi.
1979b   Drevnejshie zhatvennye orudija i ikh proizvoditel'nost (The
        oldest harvesting tools and their production. *Sovetskaya
        arkheologia* 4: 36–52. Moscow.
1980   Paleoekonomicheskie razrabotki v arkheologii i
        eksperimental'no-trasologicheskie issledovanija. *Pervobytnaja
        arkheologija poiski i nakhodki* 212–225. Kiev.
1981a   *Khozjajstvennye kompleksy rannikh zemledel'hesko-
        skotovodcheskikh obshestv juga SSSR* (Agricultural complexes
        from ancient farming-breeding societies of southern Europe).
        Avtoref. kand. diss. Moscow.
1981b   Ancient reaping tools and their productivity in the light of
        experimental tracewear analysis. In *The Bronze Age Civilisation
        of Central Asia,* edited by P.L. Kohl, 325–349. New York: M.E.
        Sharpe.

1987   *Khoziaïstvennye kompleksy rannikh zemledelchesko-skotovodcheskikh obshchestv iuga SSSR* (Economic complexes of the early agriculturo-pastoral societies in the Southern USSR). Leningrad.

1989   Predposylki slozhenia proizvodyashchego khoziaïstva v Severo-Zapadnom Prichernomorie (Beginnings of the formation of husbandry in the North-Western Black Sea area). *Pervobytny chelovek i prirodnaya sreda*: 63–76. Kiev.

1993   La différenciation des outils de moisson d'après les données archéologiques, l'étude des traces et l'expérimentation, *Traces et fonction: les gestes retrouvés*, 2(50):369–382. Liège.

1994   Orudiya truda i nachalo zemledelia na Blizhnem Vostoke (Tool use and the beginning of agriculture in the Near East). *Zhurnal "Arkheologicheskie vesti"*, 3:166–180, + 4 tabl. (Ed. Masson V. M.), St. Petersburg.

1996a   Djeitunskaya kultura, *Arkheologiya. Neolit Severnoï Evrazii*: 87–98 (Ed. Oshibkina S. V.), Moscow.

1996b   Gissarskaya kultura, *Ibidem*:110–116, Moscow.

1996c   Kelteminarskaya kultura, *Ibidem*:98–110, Moscow.

Korobkova, G.F., G.V. Sapozhnikov, I.V. Sapozhnikov

1995   *Khoziaïstvo i kultura naseleniya iuzhnogo Pobuzhiya v pozdnem paleolite i mesolite* (Economy and culture of the population of the Southern Bug area in the Late Palaeolithic and Mesolithic). Odessa-St. Petersburg.

Korobkova, G.F., and K.Y Yusupov

1977   Khozjajstvo neoliticheskikh plemen Verkhnego Uzboja. (L'économie des populations néolithiques du haut Uzboj). *Izvestija AN Turkm. SSR, serija obschestv. nauk*, Ashkhabad, 5:82–86.

Kosay, H.Z.

1951   *Anadolunun Ethnografya ve Folklorina Dair Malzeme I: Alaca Höyük*. Ankara: Türk Tarih Kurumu Basimevi.

Kotovich, V.

1964   *Kamenny vek Dagestana* (The Stone Age in Daghestan). Makhachkala.

Kramer, S.N.

1963   *The Sumarians: Their history, culture and character*. Chicago.

Krasnov, Ju. A.

1970   Ob odnoj gruppe rogovykh i derevjannykh orudij epokhi neolita i bronzy (Concerning a tool type in antler and wood from the Neolithic and Bronze Age). *Kratkie soobshchenia Instituta arkheologii . AN SSSR* 123: 42–47. Moscow.

1975   *Drevnejshie uprjazhnye pakhotnye orudija* (The oldest attested soil-working instruments). 153–176. Moscow.

1985   *Drevnie i srednevekovye pakhotnye orudia Vostochnoy Evropy*. Moscow.

Krauskopf, K.B.

1959   The geochemistry of silica in sedimentary environments. In *Silica in sediments*, Special Publ. 7, edited by M.A. Ireland, 44–19. Oklahoma: Society of Economic Paleontology and Mineralogy.

Kremenetski, K.V.

1987   *Prigodnye uslovija neoliticheskikh poselenij Prichernomor'ja*. Avtoref. kand. dissertatsii, Moscow.

Krizhevskaya, L.Y.

1974   K voprosu o formakh khoziaïstva neoliticheskogo naseleniya v Severo-Vostochnom Priazove (Question of the forms of economy in the Neolithic population from the North-Eastern Azov Sea area). *Pervobytny chelovek i prirodnaya sreda*: 263–268, Moscow.

Kroll, H.

1981   Thessalische Kulturpflanzen. *Archaeo-Physika* 8:173–189.

Krupennikov, P.R., R. I. Luneva, L.N. Rjabinina, and I.I. Shilikhina

1960   Osnovnye polozhenija bonifirovki pochv Moldavii. *Voprosy issledovanija i ispol'zovanija pochv Moldavii*, 128–141. Kishinev.

1993   *Iuzhny Kavkaz v IX-II m. do n.e. Etapy kulturnogo i sotsialnogo-ekonomicheskogo razvitiya (Ed.* Masson V. M.), St. Peterburg (Southern Caucasus from the ninth to second millennia BC. Stages of the cultural and socioeconomic development).

Kuckuck, H.

1964   Experimentelle Untersuchung zur Entstehung der Kulturweizen. I: Die Variation der iranischen Spelzweizens and seine genetischen Beziehungen.... *Zeitschrift für Pflanzenzuchtung* 51:97–140.

1979   On the origins of *Triticum carthlicum* NEVSKI (*Triticum persicum* VAV.). *Wheat Information Service* 50:1–5.

Kukula, S., A. Haddad, and H. Masri

1985   Weed control in lentils, faba beans and chickpeas. In *Faba beans, kabuli chickpeas, and lentils in the 1980's*, edited by M.C. Saxena and S. Varma, 169–177. Aleppo: ICARDA.

Kuper, R., H. Löhr, J. Lüning, P. Stehli, and A. Zimmermann

1977   Der bandkeramische Siedlungsplatz Langweiler 9, Gemeinde Aldenhoven, Kreis Düren. *Rheinische Ausgrabungen* 18. Bonn.

Kushnareva, K.KH.

1986   *Juzhnyj Kavkaz v VI-II tys. do n.e. /Etapy kul'turnogo i sotsial'no-ekonomicheskogo razvitija/* Avtoref. doktorskoj dissertatsii, Erevan.

Küster, H.

1985   Neolithische Pflanzenreste aus Hochdorf, Gemeinde Eberdingen (Kreis Ludwigsburg). In *Hochdorf I. Forschungen und Berichte zur Vor-und Frühgeschichte in Baden-Württemberg*, edited by H. Küster and U. Körber- Grohne, vol. 19, 15–83.

Labeyrie, J.

1978   Les aérosols. *La Recherche* 87:209–218.

Ladizinsky, G.

1975   A new cicer from Turkey. *Notes from the Royal Botanic Garden Edinburgh* 34: 201–202.

1979   Seed dispersal in relation to the domestication of Middle East legumes. *Economic Botany* 73:284–289.

1985a   The genetics of hard seed coat in the genus *Lens*. *Euphytica* 34:539–543.

1985b   Founder effects in crop evolution. *Economic Botany* 39:191–199.

1987a   Seed dispersal in relation to the domestication of middle eastern legumes. *Economic Botany* 41:60–65.

1987b   Pulse domestication before cultivation. *Economic Botany* 41:60–65.

1989a   Origin and domestication of the southwest Asian grain legumes. In *Foraging and farming: The evolution of plant exploitation*, edited by D.R. Harris and G.C. Hillman, 374–389. London: Unwin and Hyman.

1989b   Pulse domestication: fact or fiction? *Economic Botany* 43:131–132.

Ladizinsky, G., D. Braun, D. Goshen, and F.J. Muehlbauer

1984   The biological species in the genus *Lens* L. *Botanical Gazette* 145:253–261.

Lahoud, R., M. Mustafa, and M. Shehadeh,

1979   Food production and improvement in Lebanon. In *Food legume improvement and development*, edited by G.C. Hawtin and G.J. Chancellor, 69–70. Ottawa: ICARDA and IDRC.

Lal, S.

1985   Lentil, an ideal pulse crop for dryland farming. *Indian Farming*

35:23–24.

Larina, O.V.
1988 *Kultura lineïno-lentochnoj keramiki iugo-zapada SSSR (Moldavskaya gruppa)* (LBK culture in southwestern USSR [Moldavian group]). Leningrad

Lathrap, D.W.
1973 The antiquity and importance of long-distance trade relationships in the moist tropics of Pre-Columbian South America. *World Archaeology* 5(2):170–186.

Lee, R.
1968 What hunters do for a living, or how to make out on scarce resources. In *Man, the hunter,* edited by R. Lee and I. DeVore, 30–48.
1979 *The !Kung San: Men, women and work in a foraging society.* Cambridge: Cambridge University Press.

Lee, R., and I. DeVore, eds.
1968 *Man, the hunter.* Chicago: Aldine.

Legge, A.J.
1989 Milking the evidence: A reply to Entwhistle and Grant. In *The beginnings of agriculture,* edited by A. Milles, D. Williams and N. Gardner, 217–242. BAR International Series. Oxford: British Archaeological Reports.

Léon, J.
1977 Origin, evolution and dispersal of root and tuber crops. In *Proceedings of the Fourth Symposium of the International Society for Tropical Root Crops Held at CIAT, Cali, Colombia, 1–7 August 1976,* edited by J. Cock, R. Macintyre and M. Graham, 20–36. Ottawa: International Development Research Centre.

Leontev, O.K., G.N. Rychagov
1982 Kharakter i prichiny kolebanya urovnia Kaspiya v poslelednikovoe vremya (Nature and causes of the oscillation of the Caspian Sea level in the post-Glacial). *Tezisy doklada XI kongressa INKVA,* 3:11,12, Moscow .

Leroi-Gourhan, A.
1974 Étude palynologique des derniers 11,000 ans de Syrie semi-désertique. *Paléorient* 2(2):443–451.

Leser, P.
1970 *Entstehung und Verbreitung des Pfluges.* Munster: Anthropos Bibliothek.

Levi-Sala, A.
1988 Processes of polish formation on flint tool surfaces. In *Industries lithiques: tracéologie et technologie,* edited by S. Beyries, 83–98. BAR International Series 411. Oxford: British Archaeological Reports.

Levy, T.E., ed.
1987 *Shiqmim 1: Studies concerning Chalcolithic societies in the northern Negev Desert, Israel (1982-1984).* BAR International Series 356. Oxford: British Archaeological Reports.

Lewenstein S.
1987 *Stone tool use at Cerros.* Austin: University of Texas Press.

Lewenstein, S., and J. Walker
1984 The obsidian chip/manioc grating hypothesis and the Mesoamericanpreclassic. *Journal of New World Archaeology* 6(2):25–38.

Lewthwaite, J.
1986 The transition to food production: A Mediterranean perspective. In *Hunters in transition,* edited by M. Zvelebil, 5–16. Cambridge: Cambridge University Press.

Lichardus-Itten, M.
1986 Premières influences méditerranéennes dans le Néolithique du Bassin parisien. In *Le Néolithique de la France, hommage à G. Bailloud,* edited by J.P. Demoule and J. Guilaine, 147–160. Paris: Picard.

Lisitsyna, G.N.
1978 *Stanovlenie i razvitie oroshaemogo zemledelija v Juzhnoj Turkmenii: opyt istoricheskogo analiza materialov kompleksnogo issledovanija na juge SSSR i Blizhnem Vostoke.* Moscow.
1984 The Caucasus: A center of ancient farming in Russia. *Plants and Ancient Man.* Rotterdam-Boston.

Lisitsyna, G.F., and G.I. Filipovich
1980 Paleobotanicheskie nakhodki na Balkanskom poluostrove (Archaeobotanical discoveries in the Balkan peninsula). *Studia Praehistorica* 4. Sofia.

Lisitsyna, G.N., and V.P. Kostiouchenko
1973 *Nekotorye zakonomernosti istoricheskogo razvitija irrigatsionnogo zemledelija v aridnykh rajonakh.* Moscow.

Lisitsyna, G.N., and L.V. Prishchepenko
1977 *Paleobotanicheskie nakhodki Kavkaza i Blizhnego Vostoka,* Moscow.

Löhr, H., A. Zimmermann, and J. Hahn
1977 Feuersteinartefakte. In *Der bandkeramische Siedlungsplatz Langweiler 9, Gemeinde Aldenhoven, Kreis Düren,* edited by R. Kuper et al., 131–266.

Lourandos, H.
1985 Intensification and Australian prehistory. In *Prehistoric hunter-gatherers: The emergence of cultural complexity,* edited by T.D. Price and J.A. Brown, 385–426. London: Academic Press.

Love, H.H., and W.T. Craig
1924 The genetic relation between *Triticum dicoccum dicoccoides* and a similar morphological type produced synthetically. *Journal of Agriculture Research* 8:515–519.

Loy, T.
1994 Methods in the analysis of starch residues on prehistoric stone tools. In *Tropical archaeobotany: Applications and new developments,* edited by J. Hather, 86–114. New York: Routledge.

Loy, T.H.
1983 Prehistoric blood residues: Detection on tool surfaces and identification of species of origin. *Science* 220:1269–1271.
1987 Residues and microscopic remains. Recent advances in blood residue analysis. In *Archaeometry: Further Australian studies,* edited by W.R. Ambrose and J.M.J. Mummery, 57-65. Canberra: The Australian National University.

Lüning, J.
1977 Gruben. In *Der bandkeramische Siedlungsplatz Langweiler 9, Gemeinde Aldenhoven, Kreis Düren,* edited by R. Kuper et al. 1977:41–81.
1982 Siedlung und Siedlungslandschaft in bandkeramischer und Rössener Zeit. *Offa* 39:9–33.
1983 Stand und Aufgaben der siedlungsarchäologischen Erforschung des Neolithikums im Rheinischen Braunkohlenrevier. *Rhein. Ausgr.* 24:33–46.

Lüning J., (Redaktion) et al.
1982 Untersuchungen zur neolithischen Besiedlung der Aldenhovener Platte XII. *Bonner Jahrbücher* 182:307–324.

Lüning, J., and J. Meurers-Balke
1980 Experimenteller Getreideanbau im Hambacher Forst, Gemeinde Elsdorf, Kr. Bergheim/Rheinland. *Bonner Jahrbücher* 180:305–344.
1986 Archäologie im Experiment. *Archäologie in Deutschland* 1:4–7.

Lurie, I., K. Lyapunova, M. Matie, B. Piotrovsky, and N. Flittner
1940 *Ocherki po istorii tekhniki drevnego Vostoka.* Moscow.

Lusquet, G.H., and J.H. River
1933 *Sur le tribulum.* Melanges. N.Y.O.K.G.A., 613–638.

Macphail, R.I.
1986   Paleosols in archeology: Their role in understanding Flandrian pedogenesis. In *Paleosols: Their recognition and interpretation,* edited by V. Paul Wright, 263–290. Oxford: Blackwell Scientific.

Malik, B.A., M.M. Verma, M.M. Rahmann, and A.N. Bhattarai
1988   Production of chickpea, lentil, pea and faba bean in southeast Asia. In *World crops: Cool season food legumes,* edited by R.J. Summerfield, 1095–1111. Dordrecht: Kluwer.

Marbach, I., and A.M. Mayer
1975   Changes in catechol oxidase and a permeability to water in seed coats of *Pisum elatius* during seed development and maturation. *Plant Physiology* 56:93–96.

Marcus, J.
1982   The plant world of the sixteenth and seventeenth century Lowland Maya. In *Maya Subsistence: Studies in Memory of Dennis E. Puleston,* edited by K. Flannery, 239–273. New York: Academic Press.

Mardaleshivili, R.K., and C.P. Dzhanelidze
1984   *Sravnitel'nyj analiz diagnosticheskikh pokazatelej sovremennykh i golotsenovykh pogrebennykh pochv Marneul'skoj ravniny,* 89–91. Tbilisi.

Marinval, P.
1988   *Cueillette, Agriculture et Alimentation végétale de l'Épipaléolithique jusqu'au 2ᵉ Âge du Fer en France méridionale. Apports palethnographiques de la carpologie.* Paris: Multicopié, EHESS.

Markevich, V.I.
1974   *Bugo-Dnestrovskaja kul'tura na territorii Moldavii.* Kishinev.

Markov, G.E.
1966   Grot Dam-Dam-Cheshme II v Vostochnom Prikaspii. *Zhurnal Sovetskaja Arkheologija* 2 :104–125.

Marshall, W.
1796   *The rural economy of Yorkshire.* London: G. Nicol.

Marsi, L.R.
1979   The food legume improvement and development program of the field crops section at ACSAD. In *Food legume improvement and development,* edited by G.C. Hawtin and G.J. Chancellor, 190–191. Ottawa: ICARDA and IDRC.

Masson, V.M.
1966   Gissarskaya kultura v Zapadnom Tadzhikistane, *Sredniaya Aziya v epokhu kamnia i bronzy.* Moscow-Leningrad.
1970   Problema neoliticheskoj revoliutsii v svete novykh dannykh arkheologii (Problem of the Neolithic revolution in light of new archaeological data). V*estnik istorii* 6.
1971   *Poselenie Dzheitun.* MIA no. 180. Leningrad.
1976   *Ekonomika i sotsial'nyj stroj drevnikh obschestv /v svete dannykh arkheologii/.* Leningrad.

Mathon, C.C.
1985   La recherche du patrimoine: sur quelques blés traditionnels du sud-est de la France. Supplement du *Bulletin Mensuel de la Societé Linnéenne de Lyon* 4: VII–XXXIV .

Maurizio, A.
1927   *Die Geschichte unserer Pflanzennahrung von den Urzeiten bis zur Gegenwart.* Berlin: Parey.

Mayouf, M.A.
1979   Food Legumes in Iraq. In *Food legume improvement and development,* edited by G.C. Hawtin and G.J. Chancellor, 55–57. Ottawa: ICARDA and IDRC.

McCann, J.C.
1995   *People of the plow.* Madison, WI: U. of Wisconsin Press

McCreery, D.
1985   The plant remains. In *'Ain Ghazal,* edited by G.O. Rollefson et al., 96–104. Mitteilungen der deutschen Orient Gesellschaft 117.

McGrath, A.
1987   *Born in the cattle.* Sydney: Allen and Unwin.

McKeague, J.A., and M.C. Clink
1963a   Silica in soil solutions: I. The form and concentration of dissolved silica in aqueous extracts of some soils. *Canadian Journal of Soil Science* 43:70–82.
1963b   Silica in soil solutions: II. The adsorption of monosilicic acid by soil and other substances. *Canadian Journal of Soil Science* 43:83–96.

McLaren, F.S., J. Evans, and G.C. Hillman
1990   Identification of charred seeds from SW Asia. In *Archaeometry 190: Proceedings of the 26ᵗʰ International Symposium on Archaeometry, Heidelberg 1990,* edited by E. Pernicka and G.A. Wagner, 797–806. Basel: Birkhäuser Verlag.
N.D.   The potential of infrared spectroscopy for identifying charred remains of wheats and ryes from archaeological sites.

Meehan, B.
1981   The context of collecting: Its effect upon our concept of a society. *COMA Bulletin* 8:2–5.
1982   *Shell bed to shell midden.* Canberra: Australian Institute of Aboriginal Studies.

Meehan, B., P. Gaffey, and R. Jones
1979   Fire to steel: Aboriginal exploitation of pandanus and some wider implications. *Occasional Papers in Anthropology* 9: 73-96. University of Queensland.

Meggars, B.
1971   *Amazonia: Man and culture in a counterfeit paradise.* Chicago: Aldine.

Merpert, N.Ya.
1995   Bolgarskie zemli v VI-IV tys. do n.e. i nekotorye voprosy drevneyshey istorii Evropy. *Peterburgsky arkheologichesky vestnik* 9. St. Petersburg.

Meurers-Balke, J.
1985,   Experimente zum Anbau und zur Verarbeitung prähistorischer Getreidearten. *Archäologische Informationen* 8 (1):8–17.

Micsicek, C.H.
1987   Formation processes in the archaeological record. *Advances in Archaeological Method and Theory* 10:211–247.

Miller, N.F.
1991   The Near East. In *Progress in Old World palaeoethnobotany,* edited by W. van Zeist, K. Wasylikowa, and K.E. Behre, 133–160. Rotterdam: Balkema.

Miller, T.E.
1987a   Systematics and evolution. In *Wheat breeding: Its scientific basis,* edited by F.G.H. Lupton, 1–30. London: Chapman and Hall.
1987b   Personal communication

Minashina, N.G.
1974   *Oroshaemye pochvy pustyni i ikh melioratsija.* Moscow.

Mirchandani, T.J., and D.K. Misra
1957   Associated growth of cereal and legumes. *Indian Journal of Agronomy* 1:237–243.

Moore, A.M.T.
1979   A pre-Neolithic farmers' village on the Euphrates. *Scientific American* 241:50–58.
1982   Agricultural origins in the Near East : A model for the 1980's. *World Archaeology* 14/2:224–236.
1985   The development of Neolithic societies in the Near East. *Advances in World Archaeology* 4:1–69.
1989   The transition from foraging to farming in Southwest Asia: Present problems and future directions. In *Foraging and*

farming: The evolution of plant exploitation, edited by D.R. Harris and G.C. Hillman, 620–631. London: Unwin and Hyman.

1991   Abu Hureyra 1 and the Middle Euphrates. *Natufian Culture in Levant*:277–294.

Moore, A.M.T., and G.C. Hillman

1992   The Pleistocene to Holocene transition and human economy in southwest Asia: The impact of the younger Dryas. *American Antiquity* 57:482–494.

Moore, A.M.T., G.C. Hillman, and A.J. Legge

1975   The excavation of Tell Abu Hureyra in Syria: A preliminary report. *Proceedings of the Prehistoric Society* 41:50–77.

1999   *Excavations at Abu Hureyra.* Oxford: Oxford University Press. In press.

Morel, R., T. Lasnier, and S. Bourgeois

1984   Les essais de fertilisation de longue durée de la station agronomique de Grignon. Dispositif Dehérain et des 36 parcelles. Résultats expérimentaux (période 1938–1982). Publication *INRA Paris-Grignon.*

Morris, R., and E.R. Sears

1967   In *Wheat and wheat improvement,* edited by K.S. Quisenbury and L.P. Reitz, 19–87. American Society of Agronomy.

Moslan s.d.

1880-90   *Les semailles à la main.* Paris: Le Bailly.

Moss, E.H.

1983a   *The functional analysis of flint implements: Pincivent and Pont d'Ambon: Two case studies from the French Final Palaeolithic.* BAR International Series 177. Oxford: British Archaeological Reports.

1983b   Microwear analysis of burins and points from Tell Abu Hureyra, Syria. In *Traces d'Utilisation sur les outils néolithiques du Proche-Orient,* edited by M.Cl. Cauvin, 143–161. Travaux de la Maison de l'Orient 5. Lyon.

Muehlbauer, F.J., J.I. Cubero, and R.J. Summerfield

1985   Lentil (*Lens culinaris* Medic.). In *Grain legume crops,* edited by R.J. Summerfield and E.H.Roberts, 266–311. London: Collins.

Müller-Beck, H.

1965   Holzgeräte und Holzbearbeitung. Seeberg, Burgäschisee-Süd 5. *Acta Bernensia* 2.

Munchaev, R.M.

1982   Pamiatniki kultury eneolita Kavkaza (Sites of the Eneolithic culture in the Caucasus). *Arkheologiya SSSR. Eneolit SSSR*: 100–164 (Ed. Masson V. M. and Merpert N. Ia.), Moscow.

Muramatsu, M.

1986   The vulgare supergene, Q: Its universality in durum wheat and its phenotypic effects in tetraploid and hexaploid wheats. *Canadian Journal of Genetics and Cytology* 28:30–41.

Murdock, G.

1967   *Ethnographic atlas.* Pittsburgh: U. of Pittsburgh Press.

1981   *Atlas of world cultures.* Pittsburgh: U. of Pittsburgh Press.

Murinda, M.V., and M.C. Saxena

1985   Agronomy of faba beans, lentils and chickpeas. In *Faba beans, kabuli chickpeas, and lens in the 1980's,* edited by M.C. Saxena and S. Varma, 229–244. Aleppo: ICARDA.

Nachtigal, G.

1881   *Sahara und Sudan. Kawar, Bomu, Kanem, Borku, Ennedi.* Vol. 2. Berlin: Paul Parey.

Narimanov, I.G.

1966   Drevnejshaja zemledel'cheskaja kul'tura Zakavkaz'ja. In *VII Mezhdunarodnyj kongress doistorikov i protoistorikov.* Moscow.

1987   *Kultura drevneïshego zemledeliheskogo-skotovodcheskogo naseleniya Azerbaïdzhana* (Culture of the ancient agricolturo-pastoral population of Azerbaijan). Baku.

Nassib, A.M., D. Sakar, M. Solh, and F. Salik

1988   Production of cool season food legumes in West Asia and North Africa. In *World crops: Cool season food legumes,* edited by R.J.Summerfield, 1081–1094. Dordrecht: Kluwer

Natho, I.

1957   Die neolithischen Pflanzenreste aus Burgliebenau bei Merseburg. *Beitr. Frühgeschichte Landwirtschaft* 3:99–138.

Neale D.B., M.A. Saghai-Maroof, R.W. Allard, Q. Zhang, and R.A. Jorgensen

1988   Chloroplast DNA diversity in populations of wild and cultivated barley. *Genetics* 120: 1105–1110.

Nebieridze, L.D.

1972   *Neolit zapadnogo Zakavkazja,* Avtoref. kand. dissertatsii, Tbilisi.

1978   *Darkvetskij mnogoslojnyj naves.* Tbilisi.

1986   *Rannie stupeni razvitiya zapadno-zakavkazskoj zemledelcheskoï kultury* (in Georgian, abstract in Russian) (First stages in the development of the West-Transcaucasian agricultural society). Tbilisi.

Nesbitt, M.

1995   Clues to agricultural origins in the northern Fertile Crescent. *Diversity: A news journal for the international genetic resources community* 11(1/2): 142–143.

Nesbitt, M., and D. Samuel

1996   From staple crop to extinction? The archaeology and history of the hulled wheats. In *Hulled wheats,* edited by S. Padulosi, K. Hammer, and J. Heller, 41–100. Rome: International Plant Genetic Resources Institute.

Neumann-Pelshenke, P.F.

1954   *Brotgetreide und Brot. Handbuch über die Theorie und Praxis der Brotgetreideverarbeitung 5. Auflage* (neubearbeitet von P.F. Pelshenke), Berlin-Hamburg.

Neuß, H.

1983   *Anbau und Verarbeitung von Getreide in der bandkeramischen und Rössener Kultur des Rheinlandes unter Berücksichtigung volkskundlicher Quellen.* Magisterarbeit Köln (J. Lüning).

Neuß-Aniol, H.

1987   Rekonstruktion von Methoden der Getreidereinigung anhand bandkeramischer Pflanzenreste des Rheinlandes unter Berücksichtigung volkskundlicher Quellen. *Praehistorische Zeitschrift* 62(1):22–51.

Neuville, R.

1930   *Notes de Prehistoire palestinienne.* J.P.O.S. X. P. 193–221.

Newcomer, M.H., R.Grace, and R. Unger-Hamilton

1986   Investigating microwear analysis with blind tests. *Journal of Archaeological Science* 13:203–217.

Nicolaisen, J.

1963   *Ecology and culture of the pastoral Tuareg,* 548. Copenhagen: Copenhagen Nat. Mus.

Nierlé, M.C.

1982   Mureybet et Cheikh Hassan (Syrie): Outillage de mouture et de broyage (9ᵉ et 8ᵉ millénaires). *Cahiers de l'Euphrate* 3:177–216.

Nilan, R.A.

1964   The cytology and genetics of barley, 1951–1962. Wa*shington State Research Studies* 32:1–278. Pullman, WA.

Noy, T., J. Schuldenrein, and E. Tchernov

1980   Gilgal, a Pre-Pottery Neolithic A site in the Lower Jordan Valley. *Exploration* 30:63–82.

Noy, T., A.J. Legge, and E.S. Higgs

1973   Recent excavations at Nahal Oren, Israel. *Proceedings of the Prehistoric Society* 39:75–99.

Nozzolillo, C., and M. de Bezada

1984   Browning of lentil seeds, a concomitant loss of viability and the possible role of soluble tannins in both phenomena. *Canadian Journal of Plant Science* 66:241–246.

O'Connell, J.F., P.K. Latz, and P. Barnett
1983   Traditional and modern plant use among the Alyawara of Central Australia. *Economic Botany* 37:80–109.

Oka, H.I.
1988   *Origin of cultivated rice*. Tokyo: Japan Scientific Societies Press and Amsterdam: Elsevier.

Oka, H.I., and H. Morishima
1971   The dynamics of plant domestication: Cultivation experiments with *Oryza perennis* and its hybrid with *O. sativa*. *Evolution* 25:356–364.

Okamoto, G., T. Okura, and K. Goto
1957   Properties of silica in water. *Geochimica et Cosmochimica Acta* 12:123–132.

Okladnikov, A.P.
1958   Issledovanya pamyatnikov kamennogo veka Tadzhikistana (Research on the sites from the Stone Age in Tadjikistan). *MIA* no. 66:11–71

Olson, R.
1936   The Quinault Indians. *University of Washington Publications in Anthropology* 6(1):1–190.

Onwueme, I.C.
1978   *The tropical tuber crops: Yams, cassava, sweet potato, and cocoyams*. New York: John Wiley and Sons.

Osgood, C.
1936   Contributions to the ethnography of the Kutchin. *Yale University Publications in Anthropology* 14.
1937   The ethnography of the Tanaina. *Yale University Publications in Anthropology* 16.

Osman, A.E., M. Pagnotta, L. Russi, P.S. Cocks, and M. Falcinelli
1990   The role of legumes in improving marginal lands. In *The role of legumes in the farming systems of the Mediterranean areas*, edited by A.E.Osman, M.H.Ibrahim and M.A. Jones, 205–216. Dordrecht: Kluwer.

Özdogan, M.
1979   A surface survey for prehistoric and early historic sites in Northwestern Turkey. *National Geographic Research Reports, 1979 Projects*:517–541.

Pala, M., and T. Nordblom
1987   Improved production practices for chickpea in farm assessments. In *Farm resource management program*, 69–84. Aleppo: ICARDA.

Palmer, J.D., R.A. Jorgensen, and W.F. Thompson
1985   Chloroplast DNA variation and evolution in Pisum: Patterns of change and phylogenetic analysis. *Genetics* 109:195–213.

Papendick, R.I., S.L.Chowdhury, and C. Johansen
1988   Managing systems for increasing productivity of pulses in dryland agriculture. In *World crops: Cool season food legumes*, edited by R.J. Summerfield, 237–255. Dordrecht: Kluwer.

Parmentier, Rozier, Lasteyrie, and Delalause
1807   *Theoretische und practische Abhandlung über die Cultur des Getreides, und die Kunst Brot zu machen*. Wien.

Parry, D.W., and F. Smithson
1964   Types of opaline silica depositions in the leaves of British grasses. *Annals of Botany, N.S.* 28:169–85.

Pashkevich, G.A.
1982   Paleobotanicheskaja kharakteristika poselenija Mirnoe. In STANKO V.N., *Mirnoe - Problema mezolita stepej Severnogo Prichernomorja*, 132–138. Kiev.

Passek, T.S., and E.K. Chernysh
1970   *Neolit severnogo Prichernomorja*, MIA no. 166.

Pasternak, R.
1995   Die botanischen Funfe aus Nevali Cori, Türkei (Akeramisches Neolithikum) -Ein Vorbericht. In *Res archaeobotanicae: International Workgroup for Palaeoethnobotany Proceedings of the ninth Symposium Kiel 1992*, edited by H. Kroll and R. Pasternak. Kiel: Verlag.

Pchelina, E.
1932   Po kurdistanskomu uyezdu Azerbaidzhana. *Sovetskaya etnographia* 4: 108–121. Moscow.

Pearlman, D.A.
1984   *Threshing sledges in the east Mediterranean: Ethnoarchaeology with chert knappers and Dhoukanes in Cyprus*. M.A. thesis, University of Minnesota.

Pearsall, D.M.
1982   Phytolith analysis: Applications of a new paleobotanical technique in archaeology. *American Anthropologist* 84:862–871.

Pelegrin, J.
1994   Lithic technology in Harappan times. *South Asia Archaeology* 1993, vol. 2/II: 285–298. Helsinki.

Peña Chocarro, L.
1995   *Prehistoric agriculture in southern Spain: The application of ethnographic models*. Ph.D. dissertation, University of London.

Pendlebury, J.D.S.
1965   *The Archaeology of Crete*. The Norton Library.

Percival, J.
1921   *The wheat plant, a monograph*. London: Duckworth and Co.

Perlès, C.
1987   *Les Industries Lithiques Taillées de Franchthi: Tome I, Présentation Générale et Industries Paléolithique*. Indiana: Indiana University Press.
1991   *Les Industries Lithique Taillées de Franchthi: Tome II: Mesolithique et Néolithic "précéramique."* Indiana: Indiana University Press.

Pernès, J.
1984   *Gestion des ressources génétiques des plantes*. Tome 1: Monographies. Technique et Documentation. Paris: Lavoisier.

Perrot, J.
1966   Le gisement natoufien de Mallaha (Eynan), Israël. *L'Anthropologie* 70, 5–6:437–483.

Perry, C.C., S. Mann, R.J.P. Williams, F. Watt , G.W. Grime, and J. Takacs
1984   A scanning proton microprobe study of macrohairs from the lemma of the grass *Phalaris canariensis* L. *Proceedings of the Royal Society* 222:439–445

Pesson, P., and J. Louveaux
1984   *Pollinisation et productions végétales*. Éd. INRA.

Peterson, R.F.
1965   *Wheat*. New York.

Petrasch, J.
1985   Typologie und Funktion neolithischer Öfen in Mittel- und Südosteuropa. *Arch. Inf.* 8(1):82–84.
1986   Typologie und Funktion neolithischer Öfen in Mittel- und Südosteuropa. *Acta Praehistorica et Archaeologica* 18:33–83.

Pétrequin, P.
1974   Interprétation d'un habitat néolithique en grotte: Le niveau XI de Gonvillars, Haute-Saône. *Bulletin Soc. Préhist. Française* 2:489–534.

Pickersgill, B.
1971   Relationships between some weedy and cultivated forms in some species of chilli peppers (genus *Capsicum*). *Evolution* 25:683–691.
1989   Cytological and genetical evidence for the domestication and

diffusion of crops within the Americas. In *Foraging and farming: The evolution of plant exploitation,* edited by D.R. Harris and G.C. Hillman, 426–439. London: Unwin and Hyman.

Pickersgill, B., and C.B. Heiser
1976   Cytogenetics and evolutionary change under domestication. *Philosophical transactions of the Royal Society* B 275:55–69.

Pickersgill, B., C.B. Heiser, and J. McNeill
1979   Numerical taxonomic studies on variation and domestication in some species of *Capsicum*. In *The biology and taxonomy of the Solonaceae,* edited by J.G. Hawkes, R.N. Lester and A.D. Skelding, 679–700. London: Academic Press.

Piggot, C.M.
1953   Milton Loch Crannog I: A native house of the second century A.D. in Kirkcudbrightshire'. *Proc. Prehist. Antiq.* 87:134–51. Scotland.

Piotrovsky, B.B.
1939   *Urartu - drevneysheye gosudarstvo Zakavkazya.* Leningrad.

Piperno, D.R.
1988   *Phytolith analysis: An archaeological and geological perspective.* New York: Academic Press.

Pitt-Rivers, A.
1888   Excavations in Wicklebury Camp. In *Excavations in Cranborne Chase,* vol. II, 239–240. Excavation on Martin Down. In *Excavations in Cranborne Chase,* vol. IV, 201.

Plisson, H.
1985   *Étude fonctionnelle des outillages lithiques préhistoriques par l'analyse des microtraces d'usure: recherche méthodologique et archéologique.* Ph.D. dissertation, Université de Paris I.

Plisson, H., and M. Mauger
1988   Chemical and mechanical alteration of microwear polishes: An experimental approach. *Helinium* 38(1):3–16.

Polhill, R.M., and I.J.G.van der Maesen
1985   Taxonomy of grain legumes. In *Grain legume crops,* edited by R.J. Summerfield and E.H. Roberts, 1–36. London: Collins.

Pope, K.O., and Tj.H. van Andel
1984   Late Quaternary alluviation and soil formation in the southern Argolid: Its history, causes and archaeological implications. *Journal of Archaeological Science* II:281–306.

Popova, Ts.
1985   *Kulturnye rastenja na rannjkh poselenijakh Bolgarii po paleobotanicheskim dannym* (Cultivated plants in ancient Bulgaria villages, according to archeobotanical data). Avtoref. kand. diss. Kishinev.

Potushnyak, M.F.
1985   Neolit Zakarpat'ja: Kul'tury Krish i raspisnoj keramiki. In *Arkheologija Ukrainskoj SSR,* t. I:139–150. Kiev.
1996   Neolit Zakarpatya (The Neolithic in Transkarpathia). *Arkheologiya. Neolit Severnoj Evrazii*:33–36 (Ed. Oshibkina S. V.), Moscow.

Price, T.D., and J. Brown
1985   *Prehistoric hunter-gatherers: The emergence of cultural complexity.* New York: Academic Press.

Pringle, H.
1998   The slow birth of agriculture. *Science* 20(282): 1446.

Ranov, V.A.
1985   Gissarskaya kultura - neolit gornykh oblastej Srednej Azii (Hissar culture- Neolithic in the mountain areas of Central Asia). *Kamenny vek Severnoïj Srednei i Vostochnoj Azii*:10–35. Novosibirsk.

Ranov, V.A., and G.F. Korobkova
1971   Tutkaul - mnogoslojnoe poselenie gissarskoj kul'tury v Juzhnom Tadzhikistane. *SA* 2:133–147.

Rassam, A., and D. Tully
1986   Aspects of agricultural labor in northwestern Syria. In *Farming systems program,*133–141. Aleppo: ICARDA.

Ray, V.
1930   The Sanpoil and Nespelem. *University of Washington Publications in Anthropology* 5.

Rechinger, K.H.
1943   *Flora Aegaea; Flora der Inseln und Halbinseln des Ägäischen Meers.* Vienna.

Reddy, M.V., and K.B. Singh
1985   Exploitation of host plant resistance in the management of ascochyta blight and other diseases of chickpeas. In *Faba beans, kabuli chickpeas, and lentils in the 1980's,* edited by M.C.Saxena and S. Varma, 139–151. Aleppo: ICARDA.

Redman, C.L.
1978   *The rise of civilization: Early farmers to urban society in the Near East.* San Francisco: Freeman.

Regteren Altena, J.F. van
N.D.   Personal communications

Reinert, H.
1922   *Pfahlbauten am Badensee Ausburg*: tabl. 13. Stuttgart.

Renfrew, J.M.
1966   A report on recent finds of carbonized cereal grains and seeds from prehistoric Thessaly. *Thessaliká* 5:21–36.
1973   *Palaeoethnobotany: The prehistoric food plants of the Near East and Europe.* New York: Columbia University Press.
1979   The first farmers in south east Europe. *Archaeo-Physika* 8:243–265.

Report
1969   *Rothamsted Experimental Station Report for 1968. Part 2.* Harpenden.
1982   *Rothamsted Experimental Station Report for 1982. Part 2, 5–44.* Harpenden.

Reynolds, P.J.
1979   *Iron age farm: The Butser experiment.* London: British Museum Publications.
1981   Deadstock and livestock. In *Farming practice in British Prehistory,* edited by R. Mercer, 97–122. Edinburgh: Edinburgh University Press.

Reynolds, P.J., and A.R.W. Wyman
1988   *Meteorological data 1987.* Horndean: Butser Ancient Farm.

Richard, H.
1985   Un exemple de pollution anthropique dans les analyses polliniques: les habitats néolithiques du Grand Lac de Clairvaux (Jura). Actes des Journées *Palynologie archéologique,* Valbonne 25–27 janvier 1984, Notes et monographies techniques du CRA 17:279–297, 5 fig.

Richards, A.I.
1939   *Land, labour and diet in Northern Rhodesia.* London: International African Institute.

Riches, N.
1937   *The agricultural revolution in Norfolk.* London: Frank Cass.

Riley, R.
1965   Cytogenetics and the evolution of wheat. In *Crop plant evolution,* edited by J. Hutchinson, 103–122. Cambridge: Cambridge University Press.

Rindos, D.
1984   *The origins of agriculture: An evolutionary perspective.* New York: Academic Press.
1989   Darwinism and its role in the explanation of domestication. In *Foraging and farming: The evolution of plant exploitation,* edited by D.R. Harris and G.C. Hillman, 27–41. London: Unwin and Hyman.

Robert-Chaleix, D.
  1985   Une production millénaire: La céramique d'Afrique. In *Le Grand Atlas de l'Archéologie*, 318–319. Paris: Encyclopaedia Universalis.
Robinson, M., and R.N.L.B. Hubbard
  1977   The transport of pollen in the bracts of hulled cereals. *Journal of Archaeological Science* 4:197–199.
Rohlfs, G.
  1872   *Gerhard Rohlfs' Reise duren Nord-Afrika vom Mittelandischen Meere bis zum Büsen von Guinea 1865 bis 1867. 2. Halfte: von Kuka nach Lagos (Bomu, Bautschi, Saria, Nupe, Yoruba).* Erganzungsheft no.34 zu Petermann's "Geographischen Mittheilungen." Gotha: Justus Perthes.
Roitel, V., and G. Willcox
  1999   Analyses of Charcoal from Epipalaeolithic levels at Abu Hureyra. In *Excavations at Abu Hureyra 1*, edited by A. Moore, G. Hillman, and A. Legge. Oxford: Oxford University Press.
Rollefson, G.O., A.H. Simmons, M.L. Donaldson, W. Gillespie, Z. Kafafi, I.U. Kohler-Rollefson, E. McAdam, S.L. Ralston, and M.K. Tubb
  1985   Excavation at the Pre-Pottery Neolithic B village of 'Ain Ghazal (Jordan), 1983. *Mitteilungen der Deutschen Orient-Geselischaft zu Berlin* 117:69–116.
Romans, J.C.C., and L. Robertson
  1983   *The general effect of early agriculture on the soil profile*. BAR International Series 49. Oxford: British Archaeological Reports.
Rona Tas, A.
  1959   Some data on the agriculture of the Mongols. In *Opuscula Ethnologica Memoriae Ludovici Biro' Sacra*, 443–469. Budapest: Academiae Kiado.
Roosevelt, A.
  1980   *Parmana: Prehistoric maize and manioc subsistence along the Amazon and Orinoco*. New York: Academic Press.
Rosen, A.M.
  1983   Phytoliths and marginal land agriculture in the Chalcolithic period of the Negev Desert, Israel. Paper presented at the 48th annual meeting, Society for American Archaeology, Pittsburgh, April, 1983.
  1987   Phytolith studies at Shiqmim. In *Shiqmim 1*, edited by T.E. Levy, 243–249. BAR International Series 356. Oxford: British Archaeological Reports.
  1991   Early Bronze Age Tel Erani: An environmental perspective. *Tel Aviv* 18:192–204.
  1992   Preliminary identification of silica skeletons from Near Eastern archaeological sites: An anatomical approach. In *Phytolith systematics: Emerging issues*, edited by G.J. Rapp and S.C. Mulholland, 129–147. New York: Plenum.
  1997   Phytolith evidence for cereal cultivation at Horvat Galil and Nahal Beset. *Tel Aviv* 24: 229–236.
Rosen, A.M., and S. Weiner
  1994   Identifying ancient irrigation: A new method using opaline phytoliths from emmer wheat. *Journal of Archaeological Science* 21:132–135.
Rosen, S.A.
  1983   The Canananean blade and Early Bronze Age. Archaeological Survey of Israel. *Israel Exploration Journal* 33: 15–29.
Rosenzweig, M.
  1968   Net primary productivity of terrestrial communities: Prediction, from climatological data. *American Naturalist* 102:67–74.
Rossija
  1910   *Polnoe geograficheskoe oipisanie nashego Otechestva* (A complete description of our nation). Vol. 14. Novrossia i Krym. St. Petersburg.

Roth, W. E.
  1924   An introductory study of the arts, crafts, and customs of the Guiana Indians. *Annual Report of the Bureau of American Ethnology 1916–1917*. Vol 38. Washington DC: Smithsonian Institution.
Rottlander, R.
  1975   The formation of patina on flint. *Archaeometry* 17:106–110.
Roudil, J.L., and M. Soulier
  1984   Le gisement néolithique ancien de Peiro Signado Portiragnes, Hérault. Étude préliminaire. In *Cong. Préhist. de France*, 21e session, Montauban, Cahors, September 1979, vol. 2: 258–279.
Rovner, I.
  1971   Potential of opal phytoliths for use in paleoecological reconstruction. *Quaternary Research* 1:343–359.
  1983   Plant opal phytolith analysis: Major advances in archaeobotanical research. In *Advances in archaeological method and theory* 6, edited by M. Schiffer. New York: Academic Press.
Rowley-Conwy, P.
  1986   Between cave painters and crop planters: Aspects of the temperate European Mesolithic. In *Hunters in transition: Mesolithic societies of temperate Eurasia and their transition to farming*, edited by M. Zvelebil, 17–32. Cambridge: Cambridge University Press.
Runnels, C.N.
  1988   The earlier prehistory of Thessaly and the transition from the Middle to Upper Palaeolithic in Greece. *Journal of Field Archaeology* 15:3.
Runnels, C.N., and Tj.H. van Andel
  1987   The evolution of settlement in the southern Argolid, Greece: An economic explanation. *Hesperia* 56:303–334.
  1988   Trade and the origins of agriculture in the Near East and southeastern Europe. *Journal of Mediterranean Archaeology* 1:83–109.
Russell, K.W.
  1988   *After Eden: The behavioural ecology of early food production in the Near East and North Africa*. BAR International Series 391. Oxford: British Archaeological Reports
Sach, F.
  1961   Radlo a pluh na uzeni Ceskoslovenska. *Vedecke prace Zemedelskeho Musea* 5: 348–349. Praha.
Sakamoto, S.
  1982   The Middle East as a cradle for crops and weeds. In *Biology and ecology of weeds*, edited by W. Holzner and N. Numata, 97–109. The Hague: W. Junk Publishers.
Sakar, D., N. Durutan, and K. Meyreci
  1988   Factors which limit the productivity of cool season food legumes in Turkey. In *World crops: Cool season food legumes*, edited by R.J. Summerfield, 137–145. Dordrecht: Kluwer.
Salaman, R.
  1985   *The history and social influence of the potato*. Cambridge: Cambridge University Press.
Salonen, A.
  1968   *Agricultura Mesopotamica*. Helsinki.
Sanderson, F.H., and S. Roy
  1979   *Food trends and prospects in India*. Washington, DC: The Brookings Institution.
Sangster, A.G.
  1970   The intracellular silica deposition in mature and senescent leaves of Sieglingia decumbens L. *Annals of Botany* 34:557–70.
Sarpaki, A., and G.E.M. Jones
  1990   Ancient and modern cultivation of *Lathyrus clymenum* L. in

the Greek Islands. *Proceedings of the British School of Archaeology in Athens* 85:363–369.

Sauer, C.O.
1958   Jericho and composite sickles. *Antiquity* 32:187–189.

Saxena, M.C.
1979   Some agronomic and physiological aspects of the important food legume crops in West Asia. In *Food legume improvement and development,* edited by G.C. Hawtin and G.J. Chancellor, 155–165. Ottawa: ICARDA and IDRC.
1981   Agronomy of lentils. In *Lentils,* edited by C. Webb and G. Hawtin, 111–129. Slough: ICARDA and CAB.

Saxena, M.C., and G.C. Hawtin
1981   Morphology and growth patterns. In *Lentils,* edited by C. Webb and G.C. Hawtin, 39–52. London: Collins.

Schalk, R.
1982   Landuse and organizational complexity among foragers of northwestern North America. In *Affluent foragers,* edited by S. Koyama and D. Thomas, 53–76.

Schelienskii, V.E.
1983   Towards the study of techniques of technology, manufacture and function of tools from the Mouterian period (in Russian). In *Techniques of production in the Paleolithic epoch,* edited by A. N. Rogachev, 72–133. Leningrad:Nauka.

Schellenberg, H.C.
1908   The remains of plants from the North Kurgan, Anau. In *Explorations in Turkestan,* edited by R. Pumpelly, vol. 2, 471–471. Washington DC: Carnegie Institute.

Schick, T.
1988   Nahal Hemar cave: Cordage, basketry and fabrics. *'Atiqot* 38:31–48. Dept. Antiquities and Museums, Jerusalem.

Schiemann, E.
1932   *Entstehung der Kulturpflanzen.* Berlin: Borntraeger.
1948   *Weizen, Roggen, Gerste: Systematik, Geschichte und Verwendung.* Jena: Gustav Fischer.

Schire, C.
1982   The Alligator Rivers: Prehistory and ecology in western Arnhem Land. *Terra Australis* 7. Canberra: Department of Prehistory, Research School of Pacific Studies, Australian National University.

Schwanitz, F.
1937   *The origin of cultivated plants.* 1966 translation from the German original. Cambridge: Harvard University Press.

Schweinfurth, G.
1874   *The heart of Africa.* Translated by E.E. Frewer. New York: Harper and Bros.

Schwellnus, W.
1983   Archäologische Untersuchungen im Rheinischen Braunkohlengebiet 1977–1981. *Rhein. Augsgr.* 24:1–31.

Scudder, T.
1971   Gathering among African savannah cultivators. *Zambian Papers* no. 5. Lusaka (Zambia) and Manchester (U.K.):Institute for African Studies of the University of Zambia.

Semenov, S.
1964   *Prehistoric technology.* Bradford on Avon: Moonraker.

Semenov, S.A.
1949   Zhztvennye nozhi iz pozdneneoliticheskogo poselenia Luka-Vrublevetskaya na Dnestre. *Sovetskaya arkheologia* XI: 151–154. Moscow.
1954   Drevnjshie kamennye serpy (The oldest stone sickles). *Sovetskaya arkheologia* XXI: 366. Moscow.
1974   *Proiskhozhdenie zemledelia* (Origins of agriculture). Leningrad.

Sencer, H.Â., and J.G. Hawkes
1980   On the origin of cultivated rye. *Biological Journal of the Linnean Society* 13:299–313.

Shao, Q.Q.
1980   Semi-wild wheat from Xizang (Tibet). *Acta Genetica Sinica* 7:149–156.

Sharma, H.C., and J.G. Waines
1980   Inheritance of tough rachis in crosses of *Triticum monococcum* and *T. boeoticum. The Journal of Heredity* 71:214–216.
1981   The relationships between male and female fertility and amongst taxa in diploid wheats. *American Journal of Botany* 68:449–451.

Sherratt, A.
1980   Water, soil, and seasonality in early cereal cultivation. *World Archeology* 11(3):313–330.

Siever, R.
1957   The silica budget in the sedimentary cycle. *American Mineralogist* 42:821–841.

Sigaut, F.
1975   *L'agriculture et le feu.* Paris: Mouton.
1978   Identification des techniques de récolte des graines alimentaires. *Journal d'Agriculture Traditionnelle et de Botanique Appliquée* 24(3):145–161.
1984   Personal communication
1988   L'évolution technique des agricultures européennes avant l'époque industrielle. *Revue archéologique du centre de la France* 27(1):7–41.

Sillen, A.
1984   Dietary change in the Epi-Palaeolithic and Neolithic of the Levant: The Sr/Ca evidence. *Paléorient* 10:149–155.

Singer, C., E.J. Molmyard, and A.R. Hall
1965   *A history of technology.* Vol. I. Oxford: Clarendon Press.

Sinskaia, E.N.
1969   *Istoricheskaja geografija kul'turnoj flory.* Leningrad.

Skakun, N.N.
1981a   Cho takoe trasologja v arkheologii? (What is traceology in archaeology?). *Interdistsiplinarni issledovanija* 7: 33–40. Sofia.
1981b   Eksperimenty v ekspeditsii "Dobrudzha 1979" (Experiments in the Dobrudzha 1979 expedition). *Interdistsiplinarni issledovanija* 7: 59–64. Sofia.
1982   Progressivnje javlenija v ekonomike rannezemledel'cheskikh kul'tur Bolgarii (Successive developments in economy of ancient agricultural societies of Bulgaria). *Kul'turny progress v epokhu bronzy i rannego zheleza*: 94–97. Erevan.
1984   Kremneabrabatyvayushcheye proizvodstvo v epokhu paleometalla v Bolgarii. IIId Seminar on petroarchaeology. *Reports,* 83–92. Plovdiv.
1985a   Novye dannye o razvitii proizvodstva v epokhu eneolita na territorii Bolgarii (New data on evolution of production on Bulgarian Territory). *Arkheologija* 52: 33–42. Kiev.
1985b   Raskopki poselenija Nagornoe II v 1983 (1983 excavations of the Nagornoe II village). *Arkheologicheskie otkrytija 1983 goda*: 354–355. Moscow.
1986   Orudija truda i khozjajstva bol'garskoj Aldeni II eneoliticheskoj kul'tury (Working and economic instruments in the Bulgarian Chalcolithic culture Aldeni II). *Studia Prehistorica,* 91–107. Sofia.
1987   *Opyt rekonstruktsii khozjajstva drevnezemledel'cheskikh obschestv epokhi eneolita Prichernomorskogo rajona Severo-Vostochnoj Bolgarii v svete eksperimental'no- trasologicheskikh dannykh* (Attempts at reconstruction of ancient agricultural societies during the Chalcolithic, in the coastal region of the Black Sea in NW Bulgaria, in the light of experimental and use-wear data). Avtoref. kand. diss. Leningrad.
1993a   Agricultural implements in the Neolithic and Eneolithic cultures of Bulgaria. Traces et fonction: Les gestes retrouves.

edited by P. Anderson, S. Beyries, M. Otte and H. Plisson
Colloque international de Liege. Ed. ERAUL. Vol. 50:361–368.

1993b   Tehniska framsteg inom jordbruhskulturerna i sydostra
Europa under kopparstenaldern. *Forntida Tehnik,* 4–24.
Frosen, Sweden.

1993c   Results of traceological examination of flint implements from
Neolithic settlements in Western Bulgaria. Gatsov I. *Neolithic
chipped stone industry in Western Bulgaria,* 52–54. Krakow.

1996a   Razvitie proizvodstv v epokhu paleometalla v Bolgarii.
Pulpudeva 6: 152–164. Seminares Philippopolitaines de
l'histoire et de la culture trace.

1996b   New excavations of Eneolithic settlements in the Lower
Danube region. Cucuteni ajourd'hui. Bibliotheca memoriae
antiquitatis II, 142–158. Peatra Neamt.

1996c   Le role et l'importance du silex dans le Chalcolithique du sud-
est de l' Europe. *La prehistoire au quotidien,* edited by Marc
Groenen, 223–235. Grenoble.

Smith, B.D.
1987   The independent domestication of indigenous seed-bearing
plants in eastern North America. In *Emergent horticultural
economies of the Eastern Woodlands,* edited by W.F. Keegan.
Center for Archaeological Investigations, Occasional Paper no.
7, 3–47. Carbondale: Southern Illinois University.

Smith, L.
1936   Cytogenetic studies in *Triticum monococcum* L. and *T.
aegilopoides* Bal. *Montana Agricultural Experimental Station
Research Bulletin* 248:1–38.

1939   Mutants and linkage studies in *T. moncoccum* and *T.
aegilopoides. Montana Agricultural Experimental Station
Research Bulletin* 298:1–26.

Smith, M.A.
1988   Central Australian seed grinding implements and Pleistocene
grindstones. In *Archaeology with ethnography: An Australian
perspective,* edited by B. Meehan and R. Jones, 94–108.
Canberra: Department of Prehistory, Research School of Pacific
Studies, Australian National University.

Smith, P.E.L.
1970   Ganjdareh Tepe. *Iran* 8:78–80.

Smith, P.E.L., and T.C. Young Jr.
1983   The force of numbers: Population pressure in the central
western Zagros 12,000–4,500 B.C. In *The hilly flanks and
beyond: Essays on the prehistory of SW Asia. (Braidwood
Festschrift),* edited by T.C. Young Jr., P.E.L. Smith and P.
Mortensen, 141–161. Studies in Ancient Oriental Civilization
36. Chicago: University of Chicago Press.

Smithson, J.B., J.A. Thompson, and R.J. Summerfield
1985   Chickpea (*Cicer arietinum* L.). In *Grain legume crops,* edited by
R.J. Summerfield and E.H. Roberts, 312–390. London: Collins.

Snobar, B.A., D.E. Wilkins, A. Hadjichiistodoloum, and N.I. Haddad
1988   Stand Establishment in Pulse Crops. In *World Crops: Cool
season food legumes,* edited by R.J.Summerfield, 257–269.
London: Collins.

Spencer, P.S., D.N. Roy , V.S. Palmer, and M.P. Dwivedi
1986   *Lathyrus sativus* L. The need for a strain lacking human and
animal neurotoxic properties. In *Lathyrus and lathyrism,*
edited by A.K. Kaul and D. Combes, 297–305. New York: Third
World Medical Research Foundation.

Spier, L., and E. Sapir
1932   Wishram ethnography. *University of Washington Publications
in Anthropology* 3(3):151–300.

Spurrell, F.
1892   Notes on early sickles. *Archaeological Journal* 49:53–59.

Srinivas, T.
1969   Genetic and anatomical analysis of rachis disarticulation in
wheat. *Indian Journal of Genetics and Plant Breeding* 29:73–78.

Stapert, D.
1976   Some natural modifications on flint in the Netherlands.
Palaeohistoria 18:7–41.

1988   Een sikkel en een halffabrikaat uit Middelstum-
Boerdamsterweg. In *Terpen en wierden in het Fries-Groningse
kustgebied,* edited by M. Bierma, A.T. Clason, E. Kramer and
G.J. de Langen, 36–49. Groningen: Wolters-Noordhoff/Forsten.

Steensberg, A.
1986   *Man, the manipulator. An ethno-archaeological study for
reconstructing the past.* The Royal Danish Academy of Sciences
and Letters' Commission for Research on the History of
Agricultural Implements and Field Structures Publications 5,
199. Copenhagen: The National Museum of Denmark.

Stern, T.
1965   The Klamath tribe. In *American Ethnological Society
Monograph* 41, edited by J. Helm. University of Washington.

Steward, J.
1933   The Owens Valley Paiute. *University of California Publications
in American Archaeology and Ethnology* 33:233–350.

1938   Basin-Plateau aboriginal sociopolitical groups. *Smithsonian
Institution, Bureau of American Ethnology Bulletin* 120.

1941   Culture element distributions. XIII: Nevada Shoshoni.
Anthropological Records of University of California 4:209–359.

Stirling, M.W.
1938   Historical and ethnographical material on the Jivaro Indians.
Bureau of American Ethnology Bulletin 117. Washington DC:
Smithsonian Institution.

Stoll, H.
1902   *Der Spelz, seine Geschichte, Kultur und Züchtung.* Berlin.

Stordeur, D., and P.C. Anderson-Gerfaud
1985   Les omoplates encochées néolithiques de Ganj Dareh (Iran).
Étude morphologique et fonctionnelle. *Cahiers de l'Euphrate*
4:289–313.

Stromgaard, P.
1985   Subsistence society under pressure: The Bemba of Rhodesia.
Africa 55(1):39–59.

Sturtevant, W.C.
1969   History and ethnography of some West Indian starches. In
Domestication and exploitation of plants and animals, edited by P.
J. Ucko and G. W. Dimbleby, 177–199. London: Duckworth.

Subbotin, L.V.
1983   *Pamjatniki kul'tury Gumel'nitsa Jugo-Zapadnoj Ukrainy* (Sites
of the Gumelnitsa culture int he SW Ukraine). Kiev.

Summerfield, R.J., and E.H. Roberts, eds.
1985   *Grain legume crops.* London: Collins.

Suttles, W.
1968   Coping with abundance: Subsistence on the Northwest Coast.
In *Man, the hunter,* edited by R. Lee and I. DeVore, 56–68.

Swaminathan, M.S., and M.V.P. Rao
1961   Macro-mutations and sub-specific differentiations in *Triticum.
Wheat Information Service* 13:9–11.

Szafer, W.
1966   *The vegetation of Poland.* New York: Pergamon Press.

Takahashi, R.
1964   Further studies on the phylogenetic differentiation of
cultivated barley. Proceedings of the 1st international barley
genetics symposium, Wageningen. *Barley genetics,* 19–26.

1972   Non-brittle rachis 1 and Non-brittle rachis 2. *Barley genetics
Newsletter* 2:181–2.

Talkowski, J.
1931   *Narzedia rolinicze type rilkowego.* Lwow.

Tansley, A.G.
1939   *The British Islands and their vegetation.* 2 vols. Cambridge: Cambridge University Press.

Taylor, D.
1938   The Caribs of Dominica. *Smithsonian Institution, Bureau of American Ethnology Bulletin* 119(3):103–204.

Telaye, A.
1979   Broad beans (*Vicia faba*) and dry peas (*Pisum sativum*) in Ethiopia. In *Food legume improvement and development,* edited by G.C. Hawtin and G.J. Chancellor, 80–84. Ottawa: ICARDA and IDRC.

Theochares, D.R.
1973   *Neolithic Greece.* National Bank of Greece.

Therkorn, L.L, P. Van Rijn, and M. Verhagen
1986   Uitgeesterbroekpolder. In Kroniek van Noord-Holland over 1985, edited by P. Woltering, 84–88. *Holland* 18.

Thomas, D.H.
1972   A computer simulation model of Great Basin Shoshonean subsistence, and settlement patterns. In *Models in archaeology,* edited by D. Clarke, 671–704. London: Methuen.

Thomas, K.D.
1983   Agriculture and Subsistence Systems of the 3rd Millenium BC in Northwest Pakistan: A Speculative Outline. In *Integrating the Subsistence Economy,* edited by M. Jones, 279–314. BAR International Series 181. Oxford: British Archaeological Reports.

Thulin, M.
1983   Leguminosae of Ethiopia. *Opera Botanica* 69:1–223.

Tiwari, A.S.
1979   Food legumes in India. In *Food legume improvement and development,* edited by G.C. Hawtin and G.J. Chancellor, 94–97. Ottawa: ICARDA and IDRC.

Todorova, A.
1978   Die Stätäneolitikum an der Westlichen Schwatzmeer küste. *Studia Prehistorica* 1–2: 136–145. Sofia.
1979   *Eneolit Bolgarii* (The Eneolithic of Bulgaria). Sofia.
1986   *Kamennomednata epokha v Bulgarii* (The stone and copper ages in Bulgaria). Sofia.

Townsend, C.C., and E.R. Guest
1974   *Flora of Iraq.* Vol. 3. Baghdad: Ministry of Agriculture and Agrarian Reform of the Republic of Iraq.

Townson, R.
1797   *Travels in Hungary.* London: G.G. and J. Robinson.

Trewartha, G., and L. Horn
1980   *An introduction to climate.* 5th edition. New York: McGraw-Hill.

Triat-Laval, H.
1985   Pollen analyse des sédiments du comblement de la corne du port antique de Marseille. *Documents d'Archéologie Méridionale* 8:111–183.

Trigger, D.
1981   Blackfellows, whitefellows and head lice. *Australian Institute of Aboriginal Studies Newsletter* 15:63–72.

Troels-Smith, J.
1984   Stall-feeding and field-manuring in Switzerland about 6000 years ago. *Tools and Tillage* 5(1):13–25.

Tsalkin, V.I.
1967   Fauna iz raskopok poselenij kul'tury Gumel'nitsa v SSSR (The fauna from excavations of villages from the Gumelnitsa culture in the USSR). *Kratkie soobshchenia Instituta arkheologii AN SSSR* 111: 147–153. Moscow.

Tsereteli, L.D., N.B. Klopotovskaya, and G.M. Maîsuradze
1978   Peshchernaia stoyanka Apiancha (Ki Bogaz), *Arkheologiya i paleogeografiya rannego paleolita Kryma i Kavkaza.* Moscow.

Tull, J.
1733   *The horse-hoeing husbandry, or an essay on the principles of tillage and vegetation.* London.

Turbilly Marquis de
1761   *Mémoire sur les défrichements.* Paris: Vve Houry.

Turville-Petre, F.
1932   Excavations in the Mugharet elkebara. *Journal of the Royal Anthropological Institute* 62:271–276.

Ugent, D.
1994   Chemostystematics in archaeology: A preliminary study of the use of chromatography and spectrophotometry in the identification of four prehistoric root crop species from the desert coast of Peru. In *Tropical Archaeobotany: Applications and New Developments,* edited by J. Hather, 215–226. New York: Routledge.

Ugent, D., S. Pozorski, and T. Pozorski
1981   Prehistoric remains of the sweet potato in from the Casma Valley of Peru. *Phytologia* 49:401–15.
1982   Archaeological tuber remains from the Casma Valley of Peru. *Economic Botany* 36:182–92.
1984   New evidence for ancient cultivation of *Canna edulis* in Peru. *Economic Botany* 38:417–32.
1986   Archaeological manioc (*Manihot*) from coastal Peru. *Economic Botany* 40:78–102..

Unger-Hamilton, R.
1983   An investigation into the variables affecting the development and the appearance of plant polish on flint blades. In *Traces d'utilisation sur les outils néolithiques du Proche-Orient,* edited by M.C. Cauvin, 243–250. Travaux de la Maison de l'Orient 5. Lyon: Maison de l'Orient.
1985   Microscopic striations on flint sickle-blades as an indication of plant cultivation: Preliminary results. *World Archaeology* 17(1):121–126.
1988a   *Method in microwear analysis: Prehistoric sickles and other stone tools from Arjoune, Syria.* BAR International Series 435. Oxford: British Archaeological Reports.
1988b   Personal communication
1989   Epipalaeolithic Palestine and the beginnings of plant cultivation: The evidence from harvesting experiments and microwear studies. *Current Anthropology* 30:88–103.

Unger-Hamilton, R., R. Grace, R. Miller, and C. Bergman
1987   Drill bits from Abu Salabikh. In *La Main et l'Outil,* edited by D. Stordeur, 269–285. Travaux de la Maison de l'Orient 15. Lyon: Maison de l'Orient.

Unrath, G., L. Owen, A. Van Gijn, E. Moss, H. Plisson, and P. Vaughn
1986   An evaluation of use-wear studies: A multi-analyst approach. In *Technical aspects of microwear studies on stone tools,* edited by L. Owen and G. Unrath, 117–176. *Early Man News* 9–11. Tübingen.

Vaillancourt, P., A. E. Slinkard, and R. D. Reichart
1986   The inheritance of condensed tannin concentration in *Lens. Canadian Journal of Plant Science* 66:241–246.

Vakarel'ski, V.
1977   *Etnografija na B'lgaria* (Bulgarian ethnography). Sofia.

Valkoun, J.
1992   Exploration mission for wild cereals in Syria. *Genetic resources unit Annual report for 1991,* 16-18. Aleppo: ICARDA.

Valkoun, J., J. Waines, and J. Konopka
1997   Current geographical distribution and habitat of wild wheats

and barley. In *The Origins of agriculture and the domestication of crop plants in the Near East, The Harlan Symposium*, edited by A. Damania and J. Valkoun. Aleppo: ICARDA.

Valla, F.R.

1984   Les Industries de silex de Mallaha (Eynan) et du Natufien dans le Levant. *Mémoires et Travaux du Centre de Recherche Francaise de Jérusalem* 3. Paris: Association Paléorient.

1987   Chronologie absolue et chronologie relative dans le Natoufien. In *Chronologies du Proche-Orient*, edited by O. Aurenche, J. Evin, and F. Hours, 267–291. BAR International Series 379. Oxford: British Archaeological Reports.

1988   Les premiers sédentaires de Palestine. *La Recherche* 199:576–584.

1989   A propos du Kébarien géométrique de la Terrasse d'Hayonim (fouilles D. Henry, 1974–1975). In *Contribution à l'étude de l'homme au sud Levant: Anthropologie, Préhistoire, Paleo-environnement*, edited by B. Vandermeersch, and 0. Bar-Yosef, 255–274. BAR International Series 497. Oxford: British Arcaeological Reports.

Valla, F.R., H. Plisson, and R. Buxó

1989   Notes préliminaires sur les fouilles en cours sur la Terrasse d'Hayonim. *Paléorient*. 15(1):245–257.

Valkoun, J.

1992   Exploration mission for wild cereals in Syria. *Genetic resources unit annual report for 1991*, 16–18. Aleppo: ICARDA.

Valkoun, J., J. Waines, and J. Konopka

1997   Current geographical distribution and habitat of wild wheats and barley. In *The Origins of agriculture and the domestication of crop plants in the Near East, The Harlan Symposium*, edited by A. Damania and J. Valkoun. Aleppo: ICARDA.

van Andel, Tj.H., T.W. Jacobsen, J.B. Jolly, and N.Lianos

1980   Late Quaternary history of the coastal zone near Franchthi Cave, southern Argolid, Greece. *Journal of Field Archaeology* 7:389–402.

van Andel, Tj.H., and C.N. Runnels

1987   *Beyond the Acropolis: A rural Greek past*. Stanford: Stanford University Press.

van Andel, Tj.H., C.N. Runnels , and K.O. Pope

1986   Five thousand years of land use and abuse in the southern Argolid, Greece. *Hesperia* 55:103–128.

van Andel, Tj.H., and J.C. Shackleton

1982   Late Paleolithic and Mesolithic coastlines of Greece and the Aegean. *Journal of Field Archaeology* 9:445–454.

van der Maesen, L.J.G.

1972   *Cicer* L., a monograph of the genus, with special reference to the chickpea (*Cicer arietinum* L.), its ecology and cultivation. Communication No. 72/10. Wageningen, The Netherlands: Agricultural University.

1987   Origin, history and taxonomy of chickpea. In *The chickpea*, edited by M.C. Saxsana and K.B. Singh, 11–34. Cambridge: CAB International.

van Gijn, A.L.

1984   Uitgeest 2. In *Archeologische Kroniek van Holland over 1983*, edited by P.J. Woltering. I: Noord Holland. *Holland* 16:217–218.

1986   Fish polish, fact and fiction. In *Technical aspects of microwear studies on stone tools*, edited by L.R. Owen and G. Unrath, 13–28. *Early Man News* 9/10/11, Tubingen.

1988   The use of Bronze Age flint sickles in the Netherlands: A preliminary report. In *Industries lithiques, tracéologie et technologie*, edited by S. Beyries, 197–218. BAR International Series 411(1). Oxford: British Archaeological Reports.

1996   Personal communication.

van Zeist, W.

1970a   The Oriental Institute excavations at Mureybit, Syria: Preliminary report on the 1965 campaign, Part II: The Paleobotany. *Journal of Near Eastern Studies* 29:171–199.

1970b   The Oriental Institute excavations at Mureybit, Syria: Preliminary report on the 1965 campaign. Part III: Paleobotany. *Journal of Near Eastern Studies* 29:167–176.

1972   Palaeobotanical results of the 1970 season at Cayonu, Turkey. *Helinium* 12:3–19.

1980   Aperçu sur la diffusion des végétaux cultivés dans la région méditerranéenne. In *Colloque de la Fondation L. Emberger. "La mise en place, l'évaluation et la caractérisation de la flore et de la végétation circum-méditerranéenne."* Naturalia Monspeliensia, no hors série: 129–145.

1986   Plant remains from Neolithic El Kowm, central Syria. In *A Neolithic village at Tell El Kowm in the Syrian Desert*, edited by R.H. Dornemann, 65–68. Chicago: The Oriental Institute.

van Zeist W., and J.A.H. Bakker-Heeres

1979   Some economic and ecological aspects of the plant husbandry at Tell Aswad. *Paléorient* 5:161–169.

1982   Archaeobotanical studies in the Levant. I. Neolithic sites in the Damascus Basin: Aswad, Ghoraifé, Ramad. *Palaeohistoria* 24:165–256.

1984   Archaeobotanical studies in the Levant, 3. Late paleolithic Mureybit. *Palaeohistoria* 26:171–199.

van Zeist, W., and S. Bottema

1971   Plant husbandry in Early Neolithic Nea Nikomedeia, Greece. *Acta Botanica Neerlandica* 20(5):524–538.

1977   Palynological investigations in western Iran. *Palaeohistoria* 19:19–95.

1982   Vegetational history of the eastern Mediterranean and the Near East during the last 20,000 years. In *Palaeoclimates, palaeoenvironments and human communities in the Eastern Mediterranean region in later prehistory*, edited by J.L. Bintliff and W. van Zeist, 277–321. BAR International Series 133. Oxford: British Archaeological Reports.

1983   Palaeobotanical studies of Carthage. A comparison of microscopic and macroscopic plant remains. *CEDAC Carthage Bulletin* 5:18–22.

van Zeist W., and W. Casparie

1968   Wild einkorn wheat and barley from Tell Mureybit in northern Syria. *Acta Botanica Neerlandica* 17:44–53.

van Zeist, W., and G.J. de Roller

1994   The plant husbandry of Aceramic Çayönü, SE Turkey. *Palaeohistoria* 33/34:65–96.

1995   Plant remains from Asikli Höyük, a Pre-Pottery Neolithic site in central Anatolia. *Vegetation History and Archaeobotany* 4:179–185.

van Zeist, W., P.E.L. Smith, R.M. Palfenier-Vegter, M. Suwijn, and W.A. Casparie

1984   An archaeobotanical study of Ganj Dareh Tepe, Iran. *Palaeohistoria* 26:201–224.

van Zeist, W., R.W. Timmers, and S. Bottema

1968 (1970)   Studies of modern and Holocene pollen precipitation in southeastern Turkey. *Palaeohistoria* 14:19–39.

van Zeist, W., K. Wasylikowa, and K.H. Behre, eds.

1991   *Progress in Old World palaeoethnobotany*. Rotterdam: Balkema.

van Zeist, W., and Waterbolk-van Rooyen

1983   A preliminary note on the palaeobotany. In *Bouqras revisited: Preliminary report on a project in eastern Syria*, edited by P.A. Akkermans et al., 335–372. Proceedings of the Prehistoric Society 49.

van Zeist, W., and H. Woldring
  1980 Holocene vegetation and climate of northwestern Syria. *Palaeohistoria* 22:111–125.
van Zeist, W., H. Woldring, and D. Stapert
  1975 Late Quaternary vegetation and climate of southwestern Turkey. *Palaeohistoria* 17:53–143.
Vaughan, P.
  1981 *Lithic microwear experimentation and the functional analysis of a lower Magdalenian stone tool assemblage.* Ann Arbor: University Microfilms.
  1985 *Use wear analysis of flaked stone tools.* Tucson: University of Arizona Press.
Vaughan, P., C. Jarrige, and P. Anderson-Gerfaud
  1987 Sickles and harvesting motions in Baluchistan (Pakistan). In *La main et l'outil: Manches et emmanchements préhistoriques.* TMO 15:311–318.
Vavilov, N.I.
  1917 On the origin of cultivated rye (In Russian with an English summary). *Bulletin of Applied Botany and Plant Breeding* 10:561–590.
  1926 *Studies on the origin of cultivated plants.* Leningrad: Institute of Applied Botany and Plant Breeding.
  1951 The origin, variation, immunity and breeding of cultivated plants. *Chronica Botanica.* New York.
  1957 *Opyt agroekologicheskogo obozrenia vazhneïshikh polevykh kultur* (Attempt at agro-ecological comments on the main field crops). Moscow-Leningrad.
  1960 *Botanico-geograficheskie osnovy Selektsii.* Moscow, tome 2.
  1965 *Mirovoï opyt zemledelcheskogo osvoenia vysokogori* (World experiment of agricultural exploitation of high-mountain areas). *Izb. trudy* 5.
Vayson de Pradennes, A.
  1919 Faucille préhistorique de Solférino (étude comparative). *L'Anthropologie* 29:393–422.
Villaret-Von Rochow, M.
  1974 Détermination des céréales du niveau XI. Annexe II. In Interprétation d'un habitat néolithique en grotte: Le niveau XI de Gonvillars, Haute-Saône, edited by P. Pétrequin, 495–497.
Vinogradov, A.V.
  1981 *Drevnie okhotniki i rybolovtsy Sredneaziatskogo Mezhdurechja.* Moscow.
Visted, K., and. H. Stigum
  1971 Vaar gamle Bondekultur. *Trdje utgave.* Bind 1. Oslo.
Vita-Finzi, C., and E.S. Higgs
  1970 Prehistoric economy in the Mount Carmel area of Palestine: Site catchment analysis. *Proceedings of the Prehistoric Society* 36(1):1–37.
Wagstaff, M
  1982 Post-Classical exchange. In *An island polity: The archaeology of exploitation in Melos,* edited by C. Renfrew and M. Wagstaff, 236–243.
Währen, M.
  1984 Brote und Getreidebrei von Twann aus dem. Jahrtausend vor Christus. *Archéologie Suisse* 7(1):2–6.
Waines, J.G.
  1996 Molecular characterization of einkorn wheat. In *Hulled wheats,* edited by S. Padulosi, K. Hammer, and J. Heller, 193–197. Rome: International Plant Genetic Resources Institute.
Waines, J.G., and D. Barnhart
  1992 Biosystematic research in Aegilops and Triticum. *Hereditas* 116: 207–212.
Walker, J.B.
  1980 Analysis and replication of the lithic artifacts from the Sugar Factory Pier Site, St. Kitts, West Indies. Master's thesis. Department of Anthropology, Washington State University.
Wassimi, N.
  1979 Status of food legume production in Afghanistan. In *Food legume improvement and development,* edited by G.C.Hawtin and G.J. Chancellor, 91–93. Ottawa: ICARDA and IDRC.
Watson, W.
  1768 An account of some experiments by Mr. Miller of Cambridge, on the sowing of wheat. *Philosophical Transactions* 58:203–206.
Weinberg, S.
  1970 The Stone Age in the Aegean. In *The Cambridge ancient history,* edited by I.E.S. Edwards, C.J. Gadd, and N.G.L. Hammond, vol. 1, no. 1, 557–618.
Weinstein, J.M.
  1984 Radiocarbon dating in the southern Levant. *Radiocarbon* 26(3):297–366.
Werker, E., I. Marbach, and A.M. Mayer
  1979 Relation between the anatomy of the testa, water permeability and presence of phenolics in the genus Pisum. *Annals of Botany* 43:765–771.
Werner, A.
  1986 Experimentelle Untersuchungen zur Rekonstruktion neolithischer Kuppelbacköfen. *Arch. Inf.* 9(2):155–157.
Westphal, E.
  1974 *Pulses in Ethiopia: Their taxonomy and agricultural significance.* Wageningen: Centre for Agricultural Publishing and Documentation.
Whallon, R.J.
  1978 Threshing sledge flints: A distinctive pattern of wear. *Paléorient* 4:319–321.
White, K.D
  1967 *Agricultural implements of the Roman World.* Cambridge: Cambridge University Press.
Wilbert, J.
  1972 *Survivors of El Dorado: Four Indian cultures of South America.* , New York: Praeger.
Wilke, P.J., R. Bettinger , T.F. King, and J.F. O'Connell
  1972 Harvest selection and domestication in seed plants. *Antiquity* 46:203–209.
Wilkes, G.
  1986 Personal communication
  1989 Maize: Domestication, racial evolution and spread. In *Foraging and farming: the evolution of plant exploitation,* edited by D.R. Harris and G.C. Hillman, 440–455. London: Unwin & Hyman.
Wilkinson, J.G.
  1891 *A second series of the manners and customs of the ancient Egyptians.* Vol.1:88–95.
Willcocks,W., and J.I. Craig
  1913 *Egyptian irrigation.* Vol. 1. 3rd edition. New York: Spon and Chamberlain.
Willcox, G.
  1995 Wild and domestic cereal cultivation: new evidence from early Neolithic sites in the northern Levant and south-eastern Anatolia. *ARX World Journal of Prehistoric and Ancient Studies.* 1(1):9–16.
  1996 Evidence for plant exploitation and vegetation history from three early Neolithic pre-pottery sites on the Euphrates (Syria) *Vegetation History and Archaeobotany* 5(1/2):143–152.
  1997 Archaeobotanical evidence for the beginnings of agriculture in southwest Asia. In *The Origins of agriculture and the domestication of crop plants in the Near East, The Harlan Symposium,* edited by A. Damania and J. Valkoun, 35. Aleppo: ICARDA.

N.D.   Agrarian change and the beginnings of cultivation in the Near East: Evidence from wild progenitors, experimental cultivation and archaeobotanical data. In *Prehistory of Food*, edited by C. Gosden and J. Hather. London: Routledge. In press.

Willcox, G., and P.C. Anderson

1991   Una aproximacio experimental als inicis de agricultura al sud-oest d'Asia. Resultats del conreu d'espelta petita silvestra a l'Institut de Prehistoria Oriental del CNRS a Jalès, França (in Catalonian). *Cota Zero* 7:47–57.

Willcox, G., and S. Fornite

N.D.   Impressions of wild cereal chaff in pisé from the tenth millennium at Jerf el Ahmar and Mureybet: Northern Syria. *Vegetation History and Archaeobotany.* In press.

Willcox, G.H.

1988   Personal communication.

Willerding, U.

1970   Vor- und frühgeschichtliche Kulturpflanzenfunde in Mitteleuropa. *Neue Ausgrabungen u. Forschungen in Niedersachsen* 5:287–375.

Willerding, V.

1980   Zum Ackerbau der Bandkeramiker. *Materialhelfe zur Ur-und-Frühgeschichte Niederschsens,* 16:421–456.

Wilson, H.D., and C.B. Heiser

1979   The origin and evolutionary relationship of huauzontle (*Chenopodium nuttalliae* Safford), domestic chenopod of Mexico. *American Journal of Botany* 66:198–206.

Woodburn, J

1968   An introduction to Hadza ecology. In *Man, the hunter*, edited by R. Lee and 1. DeVore, 49–55.

Wooley, L.

1955   *Ur Excavations IV. The early periods.* London and Philadelphia.

1961   *Ur khaldoyev.* Moscow.

Wright Jr., H.E., J.H. McAndrews, and W. van Zeist

1967   Modern pollen rain in western Iran, and its relation to plant geography and Quaternary vegetational history. *Journal of Ecology* 55:415–443.

Wright, G.M.

1972   Fertile glumes in primitive cultivated wheats. *Evolution* 26:415–426.

Yanovsky, E.

1936   *Food plants of the North American Indians.* Miscellaneous Publication no. 237. Washington, DC: USDA.

Yanushevich, Z.V.

1976   *Kulturnye rasteniya Iugo-Zapada SSSR po paleobotanicheskim dannym* (Cultivated plants in southwestern USSR according to palaeobotanical data). Kishinev.

1986a   *Kulturnye rasteniya Severnogo Prichernomorya. Paleobotanicheskie issledovania* (Cultivated plants in the Northern Black Sea area. Palaeobotanical research). Kishinev.

1986b   Recent advances in the understanding of plant domestication and early agriculture. World Archaeological Congress 1–7, September 1986, Southampton and London.

Yellen, J., and R.B. Lee

1976   The Dobe-/Du/da environment: Background to a hunting and gathering way of life. In *Kalahari hunter-gatherers: Studies of the !Kung San and their neighbors,* edited by R. B. Lee and I. DeVore, 27–46. Cambridge: Harvard University Press.

Yerkes, R., and P. N. Kardulias

1993   Recent developments in the analysis of lithic artifacts. *Journal of Archaeological Research* 1:89–119.

Yoshida, S., Y. Ohnishi, and K. Kitagishi

1959a   The chemical nature of silicon in the rice plant. *Soil and Plant Food* 5:23–27.

1959b   Role of silicon in rice nutrition. *Soil and Plant Food* 5:127–33.

Yukovski, P.M.

1971   *Kulturnye rastenia i ikh sorodichi* (Cultivated plants and their relatives). Moscow.

Zhukovsky, P.M.

1924   Investigation of peasants' seed materials in East Georgia (with English summary). *Isvestia Tiflisskogo Gosudasrstvennogo Politekhnicheskogo Instituta,*44–46. Tiflis.

Zigman, M.L.

1941   Ethnobotanical studies amongst California and Great Basin Shoshoneans. Ph.D. dissertation, Department of Anthropology, Yale University, New Haven, Connecticut.

Zimmermann, J.G.

1934   Anatomische und morphologische Untersuchungen uber die Bruchigkeit der Ahrenspindel in der Gattung *Triticum. Zeitschrift fur Pflanzenzuchtung* 19:164–182.

1988   Steinmaterial. In U. Boelicke, D. von Brandt, J. Lüning, P. Stehli and A. Zimmermann, Der bandkeramische Siedlungsplatz Langweiler 8, Gemeinde Aldenhoven, Kreis Düren. *Rheinische Ausgrabungen* 28. Bonn.

Zohary, D.

1960   Studies on the origin of cultivated barley. *Israel Journal of Botany* 9:21–42.

1963   Spontaneous brittle six-row barleys, their nature and origin. *Barley Genetics I: Proceedings of the First International Barley Genetics Symposium,* 27–31. Wageningen.

1969   The progenitors of wheat and barley in relation to domestication and agricultural dispersal in the Old World. In *The domestication and exploitation of plants and animals,* edited by J. Ucko and G.W. Dimbleby, 35–66. London: Duckworth.

1971   Origin of southwest Asiatic cereals: Wheats, barley, oats, and rye. In *Plant life of southwest Asia,* edited by P.H. Davis, 235–263. Edinburgh: Edinburgh University Press.

1973   The origin of cultivated cereals and pulses in the Near East. *Chromosomes Today* 4:265–263.

1981   Personal communication.

1984   Modes of evolution in plants under domestication. In *Plant biosystematics,* edited by W. Grant, 579–596. Toronto: Academic Press Canada.

1988   Personal communication.

1989a   Domestication of the southwest Asian Neolithic crop assemblages of cereals, pulses, and flax: The evidence from the living plants. In *Foraging and farming: The evolution of plant exploitation,* edited by D.R. Harris and G.C. Hillman, 359–373. London: Unwin and Hyman.

1989b   Pulse domestication and cereal domestication: How different are they? *Economic Botany* 43:31–34.

1989c   Personal communication.

1990   Personal communication.

1996   The mode of domestication of the founder crops of southwest Asian agriculture. In *The origins and spread of agriculture and pastoralism in Eurasia,* edited by D.R. Harris, 142–158. London: University College Press.

Zohary, D., and M. Hopf

1973   Domestication of pulses in the Old World. *Science* 182:867–894.

1988   *Domestication of plants in the Old World.* Oxford:Clarendon Press.

1993   *Domestication of plants in the Old World.* 2nd edition. Oxford: Oxford University Press.

Zvelebil, M.

1986   Introduction: The scope of the present volume. In *Hunters in transition: Mesolithic societies of temperate Eurasia and their transition to farming,* edited by M. Zvelebil, 1–4. Cambridge: Cambridge University Press.

Contributors

Jack R. Harlan
Professor Emeritus, Plant Genetics
University of Illinois
Died in August 1998

Lawrence H. Keeley
University of Illinois at Chicago
Department of Anthropology (M/C 027)
1007 W. Harrison Street
Chicago, IL 60607

Richard Fullager
Australian Museum
Sydney, NSW 2000, Australia
BM: currently National Museum of Australia
GPO Box 1901
Canberra, ACT 2601, Australia

Betty Meehan
Australian Museum
Sydney, NSW 2000, Australia
BM: currently National Museum of Australia
GPO Box 1901
Canberra, ACT 2601, Australia

Rhys Jones
RMB 148
The Plains Road
Via Bungendore, NSW 2621, Australia

April K. Sievert
Department of Anthropology
Indiana University
Bloomington, IN 47405

Ann Butler
Department of Human Environment
Institute of Archaeology, University College
31–34 Gordon Square, London, WC1 HOPY

Daniel Zohary
Department of Genetics
The Hebrew University
Jerusalem 91904, Israel

Mordechai E. Kislev
Department of Life Sciences
Bar–Ilan University
Ramat–Gan 52900, Israel

Sytze Bottema
The Groningen Institute of Archaeology
Poststraat 6, 9712 ER
Groningen, The Netherlands.

Marie–Françoise Diot
Ministère de la Culture
Centre National de Préhistoire
UMR 5808 du CNRS, 38 rue du 26e R.I.,
24000 Périgueux, France

Gordon C. Hillman
Department of Human Environment
Institute of Archaeology, University College
31–34 Gordon Square
London, WC1 HOPY, United Kingdom

M. Stuart Davies
School of Pure and Applied Biology
University of Wales, College of Cardiff
Wales, United Kingdom

George H. Willcox
Institut de Préhistoire Orientale
UPR 7537, CNRS
Jalès, 07460 Berrias, France

Patricia C. Anderson
Centre de Recherches Archéologiques
USR 708, CNRS
250 rue A.Einstein, Sophia Antipolis
06560, Valbonne, France

Romana Unger–Hamilton
1 Wendover Court
Chilton Street
London E2 6DZ, United Kingdom

Ramon Buxó i Capdevila
Centre de Recherches Archeologiques
Gaspar Casal S/N, 17001 Gerona, Spain

Julie Hansen
Department of Archaeology
Boston University
675 Commonwealth Avenue
Boston, Massachusetts 02215

Terry E. Miller
John Innes Centre
Colney Lane
Norwich, NR4 7UJ, United Kingdom

Philippe Marinval
UPR 289 of CNRS
Centre d'anthropologie des sociétés rurales, 56 rue du
Taur, 31000 Toulouse, France.

Jacques Cauvin
Institut de Préhistoire Orientale
UPR 7537, CRA, CNRS
Jalès, 07460 Berrias, France

Galina F. Korobkova
Traceology Laboratory, Institute of Archaeology
Dvortzovaja nab., 18, 191025
St. Petersburg, Russia

Arlene Miller Rosen
Department of Archaeology, Ben Gurion University
P.O.Box 653
Beer Sheva, 84105, Israel

Natalia N. Skakun
Traceology Laboratory, Institute of Archaeology
Dvortzovaja nad., 18
191025 St. Petersburg, Russia

Kathryn Ataman
Intermountain Research, Drawer A
Silver City, Nevada 89428
USA

Jean–Pierre Grégoire
CNRS, UMR 7571–Protasi
BP15709
75422, Paris Cedex 09, France

Jutta Meurers–Balke
Institut für Ur–und Frühgeschichte
Weyertal 125
5000 Köln 4, Germany

Jens Lüning
Seminar für Vor–und Frühgeschichte
Frankfurt/Main, Germany

Annelou van Gijn
Faculty of Archaeology, PB 9515
2300 RA Leiden, The Netherlands.

Anne Gebhardt
Laboratoire de Géographie physique, URA 141
CNRS, Bat. Y, 1, pl. A. Briand
92195 Mendon, France

Peter J. Reynolds
Butser Ancient Farm
3 St. James Close, Clanfield, Waterlooville
Hants PO8 8JY, United Kingdom

François Sigaut
Centre de Recherches Historiques
UMR 19, CNRS, Histoire des Techniques
54 Boulevard Raspail
75270 Paris Cedex 06, France.